MATRONA DOCTA

MATRONA DOCTA

Educated women in the Roman élite from
Cornelia to Julia Domna

Emily A. Hemelrijk

Routledge
Taylor & Francis Group

LONDON AND NEW YORK

First published 1999
by Routledge
2 Park Square, Milton Park, Abingdon, Oxon OX14 4RN

Simultaneously published in the USA and Canada
by Routledge
711 Third Avenue, New York NY 10017

Paperback edition first published 2004

Routledge is an imprint of the Taylor & Francis Group

Typeset in Baskerville by RefineCatch Limited, Bungay, Suffolk

British Library Cataloguing in Publication Data
A catalogue record for this book is available from the British Library

Library of Congress Cataloging in Publication Data
A catalog record has been requested

ISBN 978–0–415–19693-2 (hbk)
ISBN 978–0–415–34127-1 (pbk)

TO SJOERD
TO MY CHILDREN RUBEN, ESTHER
AND DANIËL

CONTENTS

CONTENTS

PLATES

ACKNOWLEDGEMENTS

This book owes much to many. Prof. L. de Blois and Prof. H. S. Versnel, who acted as my supervisors when I worked on it as a thesis, have encouraged me throughout the period of writing with advice and inspiring criticism. Friends and colleagues have generously devoted their time to reading (parts of) the text in earlier drafts. Prof. M.-Th. Raepsaet-Charlier of the Université Libre de Bruxelles was involved almost from the start, reading earlier versions of all chapters as the work grew. Her critical and stimulating comments have been very helpful and her prosopographical study of senatorial women under the empire was essential in providing the biographical details of most women discussed in this work. Dr J.-J. Flinterman, Dr M. Grever and Dr V. Hunink read (parts of) chapters 4 and 5, and Dr L. de Ligt chapter 1, in earlier versions; I am very grateful for their comments. Prof. P. H. Schrijvers and Prof. B. Rawson (University of Canberra, Australia) read the entire typescript after it was completed and made a number of helpful suggestions.

This work could not have been written without the financial support of the Foundation for History, Archaeology and Art History, which is subsidized by the Netherlands Organization for Scientific Research (NWO). Thanks to a grant from this organization I also had the pleasure of two weeks of undisturbed work in the excellent library of the Fondation Hardt at Genève-Vandœuvres. For permission to use translations from Greek and Latin texts grateful acknowledgement is made to Harvard University Press (Loeb Classical Library), Cambridge University Press, the University of Pennsylvania Press and the British Museum Press. There is a list of the translations used before the bibliography. I wish to thank the German Archaeological Institute (DAI) in Rome, the Soprintendenza Archeologica of Naples and Carla van Battum for providing the photographs for plates 1–5.

My father went through the entire text more than once and with remarkable patience corrected my English, insisting on a simple style of writing. My mother has read the final version with painstaking care, signalling even the smallest inconsistencies in spelling and grammar. Of course, all faults remain my own.

Finally, I wish to thank my husband Sjoerd and my children Ruben, Esther and Daniël for their loving support throughout the years of writing. The book is dedicated to them.

Emily Hemelrijk
Haarlem, October 1998

ABBREVIATIONS

The names of ancient authors and their works are abbreviated according to the standard practice used in Liddell–Scott–Jones' *A Greek–English Lexicon* and Lewis and Short's *A Latin Dictionary*. Abbreviations of periodicals are those of *L'Année philologique* with the following additions:

AE   *L'Année épigraphique*, Paris 1888 – .

ANRW Temporini, H. and Haase, W. (eds) (1972–) *Aufstieg und Niedergang der römischen Welt: Geschichte und Kultur Roms im Spiegel der neueren Forschung*, Berlin and New York: De Gruyter.

AP   *Anthologia Palatina.*

A. Pl.   *Anthologia Planudea.*

BE   *Bulletin épigraphique* in *Revue des études grecques.*

CIG   *Corpus Inscriptionum Graecarum*, Berlin 1825–77.

CIL   *Corpus Inscriptionum Latinarum*, Berlin 1863– .

CLE   Bücheler, F. *Carmina Latina Epigraphica* vols 1, 2 and 3 (*Supplementum* by E. Lommatzsch), Leipzig: Teubner, 1894–1926 (repr. Amsterdam, 1972).

Dig.   *Digesta Iustiniani.*

F. Gr. H. Jacoby, F. (1923–) *Die Fragmente der griechischen Historiker*, Berlin and Leiden.

FOS   Raepsaet-Charlier, M.-Th. (1987) *Prosopographie des femmes de l'ordre sénatorial (Ier–IIe siècles)* (2 vols), Louvain: Peeters.

IG   *Inscriptiones Graecae*, Berlin 1873– .

IGR   *Inscriptiones Graecae ad res Romanas pertinentes*, Paris 1906–27.

ILLRP *Inscriptiones Latinae Liberae Rei Publicae*, ed. A. Degrassi (Florence 1957– 63).

ILS   *Inscriptiones Latinae Selectae* (3 vols), ed. H. Dessau (Berlin 1892–1916).

MSG   Jan, C. von (1962) *Musici Scriptores Graeci*, Hildesheim: Olms (1st edition, Leipzig 1895).

PIR[1], *PIR*[2] *Prosopographia Imperii Romani*, Berlin 1897–8; 2nd edition, Berlin and Leipzig 1933– .

RE	Pauly–Wissowa–Kroll, *Real-Encyclopädie der classischen Altertumswissenschaft*, Stuttgart 1894– .
SEG	*Supplementum Epigraphicum Graecum*, Leiden 1923– .
SHA	*Scriptores Historiae Augustae.*
*Syll*³	Dittenberger, W. *Sylloge Inscriptionum Graecarum*, Leipzig 1915–24 (3rd edition).
Tituli 4, 5	*Atti del Colloquio Internationale AIEGL su Epigrafia e ordine senatorio* (2 vols), Roma 1982 (Edizioni di Storia e Letteratura).
TLL	*Thesaurus Linguae Latinae*, Leipzig 1900– .

SOME USEFUL DATES

The start of the late republic is usually dated 133 BC with the tribunate of Tiberius Gracchus (the eldest son of Cornelia). The imperial period starts in 27 BC, when Octavian adopted the title Augustus. Most of the following dates are necessarily approximate; in some cases only the year of marriage (m.) or death (d.) is known. Names of emperors are printed in small capitals with the dates of their reign.

Aemilia Pudentilla (Apuleius' wife)	2nd century AD
Agrippina Maior	14 BC–AD 33
Agrippina Minor	AD 15–59
Antonia Minor (daughter of Octavia)	36 BC–AD 37
Argentaria Polla	c. AD 45–after 98
Attica (daughter of Atticus)	51 BC–?
AUGUSTUS	27 BC–AD 14
Caerellia (Cicero's friend)	1st century BC
CALIGULA	AD 37–41
Calpurnia (wife of Pliny the Younger)	m. AD 104
CARACALLA	AD 211–17
Catullus	84–54 BC
Cicero	106–43 BC
Clodia Metelli	c. 95–after 45 BC
Cornelia (mother of the Gracchi)	2nd century BC
Cornelia (wife of Pompey)	m. 55 and 52 BC
Cornificia	1st century BC
Dio Cassius	c. AD 164–after 229
Domitia Longina (wife of DOMITIAN)	d. between AD 127 and 140
Domitia Lucilla (MARCUS AURELIUS' mother)	2nd century AD
DOMITIAN	AD 81–96
ELEGABALUS	AD 218–22
Fronto	c. AD 95–166
Fundania (Varro's wife)	1st century BC
HADRIAN	AD 117–38

Helvia (mother of the younger Seneca)	c. 25 BC–after AD 41
Hortensia	1st century BC
Jerome	c. AD 347–420
Julia (daughter of AUGUSTUS)	39 BC–AD 14
Julia Balbilla	d. after AD 130
Julia Domna (SEPTIMIUS SEVERUS' wife)	m. AD 187, d. AD 217
Julia Mamaea	d. AD 235
Julia Soaemias (mother of ELEGABALUS)	c. AD 180–222
Juvenal	c. AD 60–after 130
Laelia	c. 150–after 90 BC
Livia (wife of AUGUSTUS)	58 BC–AD 29
Livy	59 BC–AD 17
Lucan	AD 39–65
Lucian	2nd century AD
Marcia (daughter of Cremutius Cordus)	c. 25 BC–after AD 41
MARCUS AURELIUS	AD 161–80
Martial	c. AD 40–104
Matidia the Younger	c. AD 85–after 160
Minicia Marcella	AD 93–105/6
Musonius Rufus	c. AD 30–101/2
Nepos	c. 110–24 BC
NERO	AD 54–68
Nicomachus of Gerasa	between AD 50 and 150
Octavia (sister of AUGUSTUS)	m. 54 BC, d. 11 BC
Ovid	43 BC–AD 17
'Perilla' (Ovid's stepdaughter?)	m. AD 12, d. before AD 58
Plautus	c. 205–184 BC
Pliny the Elder	AD 23/4–79
Pliny the Younger	c. AD 61–112
Plotina (wife of TRAJAN)	d. AD 123
Plutarch	c. AD 50–after 120
Pompeia (daughter of Pompey)	m. 54/3 BC
Pompey	106–48 BC
Poppaea (NERO's wife)	c. AD 32–65
Propertius	c. 50 BC–?
Quintilian	c. AD 35–before 100
Sabina (HADRIAN's wife)	c. AD 84–137
Sallust	86–35 BC
Sempronia	1st century BC
Seneca the Elder	c. 50 BC–AD 40
Seneca the Younger	before AD 1–65
SEPTIMIUS SEVERUS	AD 193–211
Statius	AD 45–before 96
Suetonius	c. AD 70–130

Sulpicia the elegist	late 1st century BC
Sulpicia Caleni	d. between AD 95 and 98
Tacitus	*c.* AD 56–after 120
TIBERIUS	AD 14–37
Tibullus	*c.* 50–19 BC
TRAJAN	AD 98–117
Tullia (Cicero's daughter)	79–45 BC
Ulpian	d. AD 223
Ummidia Quadratilla	AD 27–107
VESPASIAN	AD 69–79
Vibia Perpetua	AD 182–203

INTRODUCTION

The education of Roman women is veiled in obscurity. Ancient sources do not pay much attention to it and modern historians, when addressing the problem at all, usually restrict themselves to vague generalizations, such as that Roman women of the late republic were 'inconspicuous in intellectual life', that 'upper-class women could be well-educated', or that 'the majority of women within the aristocracy must have been, in the cultural sphere, as highly educated as their brothers'.[1] These general and, sometimes, contradictory statements are not founded on any systematic investigation; rather, they are imprecise impressions, usually based on one or two well-known examples of educated women which are repeated again and again in modern studies and are quoted as if representing Roman upper-class women in general. In spite of the continuous interest in the study of ancient women during the last twenty-five years and the earlier wave of interest in this subject around the beginning of this century, no modern study is devoted to the education of Roman (upper-class) women, its aims, impediments and controversies, and to the place of women in the educated society of their days.[2] The present study is an attempt to remedy this omission.

Its aim is twofold: first of all, I wish to present and discuss the main evidence for the education of upper-class women and their activities in the world of literature and learning in order to provide a useful survey for future study. Second, I have tried to explain and evaluate the obscure and, as it seemed, insignificant role of women in the field of learning and the disparity between the education of a few individual women named in our sources and the majority of women of the same class whose education is left unmentioned. In order to avoid the danger of distortion as a consequence of studying only a small number of, perhaps exceptional, upper-class women, I have examined Roman opinions regarding educated women in general and other factors that may have influenced the opportunities of upper-class women to receive an education; such factors are, for example, the period they lived in, their domicile, class and wealth, the circumstances and disposition of their families, their age at marriage and their marital state. The assessment of the relative importance of these aspects and their interaction with gender plays a considerable part in this study. The way in which the results are represented is mainly synchronic since I seek to describe the extent

1

and limitations of women's participation in the various fields of education and the complex relations between gender and the various social factors that were responsible for the nature and scope of their education and for the obscurity of Roman women in the field of learning. Less attention is, therefore, paid to the chronological development; the more so since the scarcity and unevenness of the evidence make it almost impossible to trace any such development with confidence.

In treating 'educated women' I limit my attention to women of the upper classes in Rome and Italy during the central period of Roman history (second century BC–AD 235). Upper-class women of the Latin-speaking western provinces are occasionally discussed as they are affected by Roman culture; because of the difference in cultural tradition, women of the Greek-speaking eastern provinces and Christian women are excluded. The restriction in this study to women of the upper classes (the senatorial, equestrian and decurial orders), which formed only a tiny fraction of the Roman population, needs some justification. Despite considerable diversity in birth, wealth and social prestige among members of the governing classes and the gradations of status that existed in each of these orders, the upper classes can be regarded as more or less homogeneous in respect of culture and moral values.[3] Moreover, any education women of the lower classes might receive was usually meant to prepare them for a profession.[4] Needless to say, our sources, especially the literary ones, are relatively rich in references to women of the élite in comparison to women of the lower classes. It should be noted that, as regards the former, most of our evidence relates to women of the leading senatorial families and the female relatives of the emperors; much less is known of the life and education of women of equestrian and decurial families.[5]

In order to reconstruct the opportunities upper-class women had to get an education and their activities in the field of learning I have systematically searched the literary sources for information. Besides, epigraphical and archaeological evidence has been used whenever relevant testimonies could be found, but in this respect I do not claim that my research has been exhaustive. In examining the ancient sources the following questions were taken as a point of departure. What were the scope and nature of the education of Roman upper-class women, and why do we hear so little of it? How did upper-class women acquire their education? In what fields and to what level were they educated before they married and what opportunities did they have to add to their education in adult life? Was their education somehow different from that of men of their class and if so, how and why? What aims did their education serve and what obstacles and impediments did they meet? What feelings did educated women provoke? Did they arouse praise or contempt, or were they judged more soberly? How are we to relate the very few upper-class women whose excellent education is mentioned in the literary sources to the majority of women of the same class about whose education we know so little? Were they the proverbial 'exception to the rule' that women usually lacked an education, or do they represent, so to speak, the 'tip of an iceberg', implying that there were many more educated women who are unknown to us? What role did upper-class women play as patronesses of literature and learning, and how do their activities in this field compare to those of male patrons? What did women write and why is so little of their writing left? Was it somehow lost, or did Roman women actually write so very little?

In the following chapters these and other questions concerning the education of upper-class women are discussed. Chapter 1 surveys their social position as a background to their educational opportunities and their place in educated society. This short chapter deals with modifications in the role and position of an upper-class woman during the course of her life from an unmarried daughter to a wife, mother and, eventually, a widow. Further, it discusses the women's uncertain and indirect relation to the leading *ordines* (that is, as depending on their male relatives) and the norms and rules prescribing the behaviour of the upper-class *matrona*.

The second chapter examines the opportunities upper-class women had to acquire an education. Starting with the education of unmarried girls, the influence of the period they lived in, their domicile, class and wealth, family background and age at marriage are discussed. It is argued that the education of upper-class girls depended to a greater degree on such circumstances than that of boys of their class; consequently, it was bound to be more haphazard and to vary more widely. As regards the opportunities of adult women to add to their education, several are examined, such as: tuition by a husband or father or by a private teacher, participation in social life (by attending cultured dinner parties or recitations and by visiting the theatre), self-study and the use of (private) libraries. The irregularity of such studies, access to which depended on factors similar to those for the education of girls, confirms the haphazard nature of the education of women.

The third chapter falls into two parts. The first discusses the aims and ideals underlying the education of upper-class girls, in other words, the question: why did Roman upper-class families give their daughters a literary education? Four possible reasons are surveyed and their relative importance estimated. It is concluded that motives connected with the social position and duties of the upper-class *matrona* and with the prestige resulting from a literary education formed the main consideration, and that ideals of moral education and 'educated motherhood' as propagated by moralistic authors served to justify the education of women rather than forming the actual reasons for it. The second part is devoted to ancient opinions on educated women. As will be shown, such women provoked contradictory feelings in Roman society ranging from admiration to disgust. In this part an attempt is made to unravel the conflicting feelings and controversies regarding women's education and to trace possible developments and changes in fashion in the course of the roughly four hundred years between the second century BC and the early third century AD.

The fourth chapter deals with patronage of literature and learning. It is asked what role upper-class women played in this field as compared to male patrons. In studying patronesses of literature and learning, both within the imperial family and outside it, attention is paid to the motives these women had to exercise patronage, the conditions that favoured it and the impediments they met, the services they exchanged with their protégés and the terms in which they were praised. The relatively rich evidence for certain individual patronesses allows us not only to outline more clearly the limitations of women's patronage, but also to discover the tactics women adopted to cope with the restrictions imposed upon them and how they used notions of traditional female behaviour to their own advantage.

The fifth and sixth chapters are concerned with the writings of women, with poetry and prose respectively, and with their place in Roman literary life.[6] Apart from the discussion of the female authors whose names are known to us and the few remains of their work, they address the problem of the meagre amount of women's writings and the possible causes of if. It is argued that explanations that have been proposed so far ('because women wrote so very little' or 'because their work was somehow suppressed') are unsatisfactory. Instead of choosing between these views we shall investigate a wider range of social factors which led not only to the relative rarity of women's writing, but also to the nearly total loss of their work. The concluding chapter comprises a summary of the main arguments of each chapter.

At the end of this introduction some words are needed about the ancient sources which form the basis of this study. First, the limitations of the literary sources have to be noted. Since they contain mostly fragmentary and anecdotal information on women and may be biassed towards the exceptional, they cannot always be regarded as representative of (the education of) upper-class women in general. This makes it risky to generalize and does not allow firm conclusions on, for instance, the numbers of educated women within the élite families or the precise level of their education. In interpreting any particular passage the rules of the genre, the bias and purpose of the author, and the intended audience must be kept in mind, the more so since much evidence consists in biassed comments in favour of, or against, women's education and praising or criticizing educated women. Fortunately, the argument based on the literary texts can, in some instances, be checked by epigraphical or archaeological evidence; nevertheless, we often cannot go beyond formulating probabilities, and much of what follows is, therefore, conjectural in nature.

Because of their close association with family life and female values most women probably lived quiet lives ignored by our sources. This, however, calls for caution as regards the relative 'silence' of our sources on their activities in the field of education: it should not simply be assumed that this 'silence' is a direct reflection of a dearth, or even absence, of educated women in actual life. As in the case of other non-dominant groups in Roman society, women, even those of the upper classes, are largely omitted from the historical narrative and, if mentioned at all, they are often described according to certain fixed characteristics, such as the devoted mother, the evil stepmother, the domineering, or the self-effacing, wife, etc. Education is only rarely part of such standard portrayals and, therefore, it is apt to be ignored. Consequently, other explanations seem possible to account for the relative 'silence' of our sources on the education of upper-class women: for example, a lack of interest in the male-authored sources concerning the education of women, their preference for the salacious and the spectacular, a tendency to describe women in traditional female terms disregarding activities outside the female preserve (except for scoffing at them), and, perhaps, uneasy feelings as regards educated women in general. In the following I have tried to fit the scattered evidence into a meaningful whole, taking into account the various possible interpretations of the relative 'silence' of our sources. Though in the individual chapters the evidence may seem meagre, the total sum of the evidence presented all through the book will, to my mind, make it sufficiently clear that the education of women was a matter of serious concern in Roman upper-class circles and that, unlike the education of men, it brought its recipients not only prestige but also problems.

1

THE SOCIAL POSITION OF
UPPER-CLASS WOMEN

When studying educated women in Roman society one is struck by the scarcity of women of learning mentioned in our sources. Not even the term *matrona docta*, used in the title of this study, is found in Roman literature. It is a concoction of *matrona*, the married Roman woman of rank, and *puella docta*, the 'learned girl' whose praises were sung in love poetry.[1] Both terms are loaded with moral values. The *matrona* is closely associated with traditional female values such as chastity, modesty, austerity, domesticity and devotion to husband and children. In contrast, the *puella docta* of Augustan love poetry was praised for her cultural accomplishments (in poetry, music and dance), but in traditional Roman eyes her morals raised suspicion; moreover, the typical *puella docta* does not seem to have belonged to the élite. Of course, words and social practice do not always coincide, but the lack of a term for a respectable 'learned' woman to counterbalance the doubtful reputation of the *puella docta* indicates how ambivalent Roman feelings were as regards women's education.

Since in the Roman society of our period there were no Christian convents in which girls could be taught and to which women could retreat to devote their life to study and prayer (as almost all women who were famous for learning in the Middle Ages did), and as no other institutions, customs or opportunities existed which offered women an alternative to marriage and motherhood,[2] it is perhaps understandable that we hardly hear of any famous learned women in Roman society. Yet, as we shall see, some upper-class women were highly educated. So, what may have caused their obscurity in the world of education?

We should keep in mind that in Roman society education and learning were typically male pursuits; knowledge of literary culture and the liberal arts was the mark of the upper-class 'gentleman'. For upper-class men education, apart from its practical value for a political career, was a field of competition and an instrument of class differentation: the enjoyment and display of education distinguished members of the élite from members of other classes. Yet, though learning conferred prestige and though education was essential for one's social status, intellectual pursuits, insofar as they did not contribute to serious aristocratic activities such as politics and the practice of law, belonged to leisure (*otium*) and were therefore, according to the old republican notion, of secondary importance.

During the principate there was a shift in the attitude towards education: with the peace and prosperity of the principate and the decline of political power of the senatorial class intellectual activities gained esteem. This gave more scope for pursuits that had little practical value or had been considered frivolous before (such as the writing of light poetry), but members of the senatorial class always remained amateurs in literary and other intellectual pursuits – or so they pretended – being 'good without seeming to try'.[3] The pretence of amateurism as regards intellectual activities was of great importance for the attitude of the upper classes towards education, and a life entirely devoted to study was uncommon, as it was among the members of the equestrian and decurial class (though less so).

This amateur ethos also affected the women of the upper classes; on the one hand, it may have facilitated their participation, and on the other, it prohibited a life devoted to study, since this ran contrary to the traditions of their class (and gender). Of course, women's 'leisure' differed fundamentally from that of the men of their class: being barred from politics, public office-holding and military matters, upper-class women, whose lives passed, or were expected to pass, in the privacy of their homes and families, were condemned to a life of *otium* (which is not to say that they had nothing to do).[4] Did this allow them to devote their leisure hours to study which was comparable to the *otium honestum* of their male peers? Needless to say, it did not. There is no female counterpart of the respectful qualification *vir doctus*, which denotes a man of culture, trained in the liberal arts and civilized in conduct; *docta* is sometimes used for a woman, but it is not always meant as a compliment.[5] This does not imply that education was considered unsuitable for all women and that distinctions of class were of no consequence. As we shall see, matters were more complicated: class, wealth, family background and other factors connected with the social position of upper-class women interacted with gender in determining the nature of their education.

Therefore, in the present chapter, before we start our inquiry into their education, some words are needed about the social position of upper-class women. Fortunately, in recent years a number of excellent studies have appeared on the life of women, their juridical, financial and social position in Roman society and their place within the Roman family; therefore, a brief survey with some references to further reading may suffice here.[6] This survey focusses on the last decennia of the republic and the first two centuries of the empire, and sketches in a synchronic way aspects of the social position of upper-class women in so far as these are relevant to our study. Three issues are of importance: the changing position of upper-class women within the family at the different stages of their life (daughter, wife, mother and widow), their relation to the three leading *ordines*, and, third, the norms and rules prescribing the behaviour of the upper-class *matrona*. It is argued that the social position of upper-class women was marked by ambiguity and by contradictory demands of class and gender. Besides, their life was closely circumscribed by their family background and by the various roles they fulfilled within the family in the successive stages of their life.

As regards the position of daughters, not much can be said. Emotionally, according to J. P. Hallett, a daughter was highly valued, even more highly than a son, at least in upper-class families, and her 'structurally central' position in the élite family paved her way to prominence as an adult.[7] This view seems too positive: examples of high emotional valuation of daughters (such as the extraordinary devotion of Cicero to Tullia) are counterbalanced by the frequent unfavourable treatment of daughters in wills,[8] and the cold-blooded use of daughters as marriage-partners to negotiate political alliances.

For Roman girls childhood was brief: upper-class girls married young, somewhere between the age of 12 (the legal minimum age fixed by Augustan legislation) and their late teens; this in contrast with girls outside the élite, who married somewhat later (in their late teens or early twenties). Marriage was a major transition in the life of an upper-class girl, changing her, rather abruptly, from a girl into a *matrona*; as a symbol of this transition she dedicated her dolls and other toys to Venus or to the household gods on the eve of her marriage.[9] Since in Rome virtually all women married, upper-class girls invariably became *matronae*. A girl's marriage was arranged by her parents, sometimes in conjunction with other relatives. Though the formal consent of the bride was needed, a 15-year-old girl was in no position to resist the wishes of her family and in most cases she must have submitted to their choice. In a first marriage her husband might be about ten years older, upper-class men marrying around their mid-twenties, unless, of course, she married a man entering upon his second, third or subsequent marriage, in which case the difference in age (and probably the inequality in power) would be considerably greater. On the other hand, the second or third marriage of a woman might lead to a greater equality in age between the partners and, in some cases, a greater influence of the woman on the choice of a husband; we may also assume that an adult woman in her second or third marriage would be less compliant and submissive than a young girl in her first.[10]

The arrangement of her marriage and the choice of a husband was a matter of serious concern to the family, for a marriage was, in the first place, a deal between families. Though harmony and affection between the partners was desirable – during the empire the ideal of matrimonial *concordia* was fashionable – the most important thing was that the match was suitable, and to this end it was of great importance that the partners were equal in birth, wealth and social standing, though shortcomings in one of these might be compensated by a high position in the others.[11]

As a wife and a (potential) mother an upper-class woman occupied a position of authority in the house and participated in all its social activities. Though in a large town-house or villa she might have her own private apartments, she was not confined to them, nor were there rooms from which she was excluded; as the mistress of the household she moved freely through the entire house. The *atrium*, the central and most public area of the house where her husband received his morning callers, was the place from where she – probably at different hours – directed and supervised the work of the household slaves. Marriage brought full participation in social life: wives were expected to entertain their husbands' guests and to accompany their husbands on social visits and to dinner parties. Behind the scenes a wife might be involved in her husband's business, the management of his estates and his political career. Though debarred from active political life, she was expected, for instance, to maintain his political connections and inform him of the situation in Rome during his absences abroad for military duties, governorship of a province, or in the turmoils of civil war. From the reign of Tiberius onwards wives were allowed to accompany their husbands when they went as magistrates to the provinces, and so, it seems, many of them did.[12]

The integration of women in the house and the social life of the family went hand in hand with a marked division along gender lines of tasks and social activities and a segregation of husband and wife for part or most of their daily activities. For instance, when guests were invited, the wife was to issue invitations to the ladies while her husband invited the male guests. When receiving guests the wife (or if she was absent, the mother, daughter or sister of the host) acted as a hostess to the female guests; for a man to receive guests of both sexes on his own was considered inappropriate. Similarly, at official celebrations the emperor might feast the senate (or the people) of Rome, while the empress was expected to invite the leading ladies.[13] Some of the social activities were fulfilled separately by husband and wife, though we are less well informed of the activities of the wife. Like men (and sometimes together with them) women attended birthday parties, weddings, funerals or religious gatherings and visited the games and the theatre; they travelled freely and exchanged invitations with their female friends for visits or a short holiday. They had their own personal attendants and, often, their own staff of slaves. Like their husbands, they received visitors and callers (relatives, friends, clients, servants, bailiffs, etc.) at home, where they conducted their private business and administered their possessions and estates. Further, time was spent on their toilet, the supervision of domestic work, the upbringing of their children, their husbands' needs, the care of their relatives during illness and other traditionally 'female' tasks, whereas men engaged in a public career and in political and intellectual discussions with male friends in which wives, though they were sometimes present, are usually not mentioned as participating.

A woman's status and her authority in the family grew when she became a mother, especially of sons. As has been shown by S. Dixon, a Roman upper-class mother had an authoritarian and disciplinary role in the upbringing of her children, which did not differ much from that of the father.[14] Her authority increased when she was widowed: thanks to her wealth and the respect due to her as a parent, an upper-class widow could exercise great power over her sons, despite her lack of legal *potestas* over them. It was through sons, more than through husbands, that some high-born women exercised political power (Agrippina Minor being a notorious example), and it was as widows, especially as wealthy elderly widows, that women could come into the limelight managing their own affairs, supervising the education of their sons, occupying a position of respect in their families and, in some cases, in their cities in general because of their wealth and the public use they made of it.[15]

To summarize, a woman's life and social position were far from static: in the course of her life things changed according to the circumstances of her family and the successive stages of her life, which usually brought her a position of increasing authority. Generally speaking, the position of a woman within her house and family was ambiguous: it was marked by both integration in the social life of the family and segregation as regards most tasks and daily activities. As women were debarred from active political and military life, their lives centred on the house and family. Yet, as we have seen, they were not confined to the house or to domestic concerns; because of their wealth, their elevated position as daughters, sisters, wives and mothers of upper-class men and the blurring of the social and political spheres in Rome they could expand their influence well outside the house and engage in various social, financial and even (in an indirect way) political activities.

This brings us to the second issue to be dealt with: their relation to the three leading *ordines*. As regards the relation between class and gender, upper-class women were in an uncertain position: as members of the ruling class but of the subordinate sex they shared some of the prestige and distinctions of their class, but at the same time they were regarded as socially inferior to the men of their class or were ranked with minors.[16] This contradictory position was due to the ambiguous way in which upper-class women were connected with the three leading orders. Whereas men belonged to the senatorial, equestrian or decurial order by virtue of their birth, wealth and public career, women were bound to these orders only indirectly: their claim to social rank depended on that of their fathers or husbands, since they received their fathers' rank at birth and adopted that of their husbands at marriage.

As regards a woman's rank, marriage superseded birth: when marrying, a woman received the rank of her husband, whatever her rank at birth (though in practice the social gap between the marriage-partners was seldom wide). Thus, marriage could bring social change. This social 'mobility' could be upwards or downwards: a woman gained senatorial rank by marriage to a senator, if she herself was of a family of inferior (in most cases equestrian) class, and she kept this rank when widowed or divorced. But, as can be attested from about the middle of the second century AD onwards, a woman of senatorial rank (whether she inherited it from her father or acquired it through marriage) lost her senatorial dignity when she (re-)married a man of inferior status. Thus, for such a woman a marriage beneath her station meant lowering her status.[17] Yet, as her family remained of consequence, her high birth might facilitate the social rise of her male descendants.

As women were only indirectly bound to the upper classes, their connection with the élite orders was uncertain. With the exception of senatorial rank, which from the Augustan period onwards became a hereditary rank extending also to daughters, the élite orders strictly speaking were all male; girls born in equestrian and decurial families did not formally belong to these orders. However, in practice, equestrian and decurial dignity extended also to close female relatives of members of these orders, especially their wives and daughters, and during the empire a semi-hereditary status, analogous to that of women of senatorial rank, seems to have been established also for women from equestrian families.[18] Thus, it seems justified to speak of women of equestrian or decurial rank when denoting wives and daughters of equestrians or decurials who, though strictly speaking they did not inherit this rank, were included in its dignity and liable to its constraints.

As upper-class women had no independent claim to rank, their social status was somewhat ambiguous.[19] This is reflected in the comment of the early third-century jurist Ulpian on the question of precedence of class or gender in determining social hierarchy:

> That a man of consular rank always takes precedence over a lady of consular rank is a point no one doubts. But whether a man of prefectorial rank takes precedence over a lady of consular rank remains to be seen. I should think he does, because greater dignity inheres in the male sex.
>
> (*Dig.* 1.9.1 *pr.*)[20]

Admittedly, Ulpian lived at a time when senatorial power was in decline and was giving way to the increasing power and prestige of the leading equestrians; yet, to allow a man of high equestrian rank to take precedence over a woman married to a consul (or ex-consul) shows how uncertain and subordinate the position of women was within the upper classes.

The uncertainty of the relation of upper-class women to the élite orders is somewhat compensated by the puzzling *ordo matronarum*. This 'order of matrons' seems to have come into being in analogy with, and in imitation of, the élite orders of men, but since it was not a formal order, it is not clearly defined. Its origins perhaps go back to the early republic, but as an organization of women it comes to the fore mainly during the empire. The term *ordo matronarum* is used loosely in our sources to denote married upper-class women when acting as a group in public, as distinguished from women of the lower 'orders'. Thus, for example, the *matronae* of the plebeian nobility gathering for the cult of Pudicitia Plebeia in the early third century BC were marked off by Livy from the '*feminae* of all (other) orders', and Plautus has two freedwomen of the 'order' of courtesans jealously complaining about the closely knit group of high-born matrons. Closer inspection of these and other examples tells us that the term *ordo matronarum* is nearly always used to denote women of senatorial rank when acting in concert in a public role.[21]

In some respects the *ordo matronarum* duplicated the senatorial order. The criteria for membership of the *ordo matronarum* (high birth, wealth and marriage) were similar to those of the senatorial order and, as was the case with men, their privileged station in life was justified by their supposed moral excellence – women's virtues being regarded as different from, but complementary to, those of men.[22] Also their insignia of rank were comparable to those of the male senatorial order; they comprised the distinctive dress of the *matrona* (*stola, vittae* and the use of purple) – the equivalent of the *toga* and the *latus clavus* (the broad purple band) of male senatorial dress – and the use of certain carriages within the city: the two-wheeled covered carriage, the *carpentum*, and its four-wheeled luxury version, the *pilentum*; during the empire the use of the *carpentum* within the city of Rome was a special mark of distinction permitted only to very few matrons, mainly of the imperial family. As the *ordo matronarum* was not a formal order and therefore lacked a formal grant of insignia, these symbols of status were alleged to have originated in legendary times when upper-class women were said to have received them by senatorial decree as marks of honour awarded for courageous actions or in gratitude for contributions of money or gold to the state in periods of crisis.[23]

The marks of distinction symbolizing the high status of the *matronae* emphasized the social distance between them and women of inferior rank. But there was also an internal hierarchy within the *ordo matronarum*, which was probably shown by subtle gradations in these outward marks. Birth, wealth and the career and social standing of her husband determined a woman's position within the privileged group of women who formed the *ordo matronarum* and the scant evidence of the puzzling *conventus matronarum*, the assembly of matrons of Rome attested during the empire, points to an intense competition for status among them.[24] Their preoccupation with status and hierarchy is ridiculed in the disputed, and probably at least partly fictitious, account of the *Historia Augusta* of the so-called 'women's senate' established by the emperor Elegabalus and presided over by his mother Julia Soaemias. This senate is said to have issued:

> absurd decrees concerning rules to be applied to matrons, namely, what kind of clothing each might wear in public, who was to yield precedence and to whom, who was to advance to kiss another, who might ride in a chariot (*pilentum*), on a horse, on a pack-animal, or on an ass, who might drive in a carriage (*carpentum*) drawn by mules or in one drawn by oxen, who might be carried in a litter, and whether the litter might be made of leather, or of bone, or covered with ivory or with silver, and lastly, who might wear gold or jewels on her shoes.
>
> (*SHA Elegab.* 4.4; Loeb trans.)[25]

Though much of this account is mockery, ridiculing both Elegabalus and women's preoccupation with status by presenting their petty discussions in terms of senatorial decrees, it is not impossible that it refers to actual rules of precedence negotiated in the assembly of women of senatorial class. In any case, the *ordo* and *conventus matronarum*, meeting for religious and other purposes on certain festal days and on special occasions and discussing matters of importance to them, point to an organization of senatorial women in imitation of that of the male senatorial order, by which they established their place in Roman society vis-à-vis that of upper-class men and that of women of other classes and in which in a finely graded hierarchy they competed for status among themselves.

Thus, women of senatorial class were marked off from women of lower rank by this pseudo 'order' and the assembly of matrons formed on the model of the male senatorial order. At the same time, however, there existed another division of society which, disregarding distinctions of class and status, threw women together. 'Women' are sometimes mentioned as a group or an 'order' as distinct from other groups of society (such as the people, equestrians and senators);[26] this may point to a division in society on the basis of political privilege which excluded women of all ranks. Such a division is found in the seating arrangements in the theatre and amphitheatre, where women were relegated to the top rows at the back of the theatre (in between the sections for the slaves, the non-citizens and the urban poor), whereas men were seated according to class and to other divisions of status, senators occupying the front rows, equestrians the 'fourteen rows' behind them and the people, subdivided according to age, marital state and other criteria, being seated in separate sections in the middle rows of the auditorium. Only very few women were excepted from this segregation according to gender: the Vestal Virgins and the women of the imperial family had privileged seats near the front.[27]

To summarize, upper-class women's connection with class was indirect (*viz.* dependent on their fathers or husbands, through whom they gained their rank) and contradictory: on the one hand, they were distinguished from women of the lower classes by the symbols of their rank and their organization in the *ordo matronarum*, but on the other, women of all ranks were seen as an undifferentiated mass and segregated from men without regard for their social distinctions.

A similar ambiguity of rank and gender is found in the third and last problem to be discussed in this chapter: the norms and rules prescribing the behaviour of the upper-class *matrona*. Besides her role as a wife and mother in the private sphere of the house, an upper-class woman was known as a *matrona* in relation to the outside world. This term not only indicated her married state and her (potential) motherhood, but was also closely bound up with the traditional female virtues of chastity, modesty, simplicity, frugality, reticence and domesticity. *Matronae* were expected to live a retired life, to be chaste and devoted wives and mothers and to marry only once, remaining faithful widows after their husbands' death (*univirae*).[28] To distinguish them from unmarried girls, non-citizens and women who were disreputable (*infames*) such as adulteresses, prostitutes, actresses, entertainers and women occupied in catering, *matronae*, when in public, wore a special dress as a mark of their respectability: they were allowed to wear the *stola*, a long overgarment covering the ankles, which is also indicated with the word *instita* (a disputed term probably referring to the seam or the shoulder-straps of the *stola*). In her hair she wore *vittae* (woollen fillets or bands).

Though by the Augustan period or perhaps even earlier both *stola* and *vittae* had gone out of fashion and may have been worn only on formal occasions, these terms continued to be used as indicators of the respectability of the *matrona*, whose moral behaviour was the object of Augustus' legislation on marriage and adultery. So Ovid, when pretending to warn the respectable married women against reading his *Ars Amatoria*, writes: 'Keep far away, slender fillets, symbol of modesty, and the long skirt that hides half the feet in its folds.'[29] Thus, *stola*, *instita*, *vittae* and *matrona* were used to denote the respectability of the legally married Roman citizen-woman. Apart from a shift from the concrete to the morally charged, there seems to have been a narrowing of the range of women to whom these terms could be applied, but this development is not altogether clear. The following is, therefore, somewhat speculative, and the usage of these terms may, in fact, have been vaguer and less strict than here described.

During the republic *matrona* seems to have been used for any respectable married woman, her social rank perhaps being shown by stripes woven into her *stola*, just as broad and narrow stripes respectively marked senatorial and equestrian male dress. However, during the first two centuries of the empire the terms *matrona* and *stola* (with their connotation of respectability) were used increasingly, and from the Flavian period onwards perhaps even exclusively, for women of senatorial rank (though towards the end of our period they appear also to have been used for women of equestrian rank). A remark by the elder Pliny reflects this change. When complaining of the excessive use of gold by wealthy women he exclaims: 'are even their feet to be shod with gold, and shall gold create this female order of knighthood, intermediate between the *stola* and the common people?'[30] Distinguishing women of senatorial rank from women of the other classes by the *stola*, he sketches a mock-official hierarchy of women analogous to that of men, with a female equestrian order (distinguished by gold ornaments, comparable to the gold ring of the *equites*) in between. Thus, as we have seen above, the terms *matrona* and *stola* not only signified respectability, but during the empire came to be used as marks of senatorial (or perhaps more generally, upper-class) status as well.

In contrast with the various social obligations of upper-class women, and the financial and political activities that followed from their eminent station in life and their family background, the norms and rules prescribing the behaviour of the upper-class *matrona* were highly restrictive and remained so during our entire period. The tension between these restrictive norms and the manifold demands made on upper-class women in daily life is apparent in many aspects of their life, but here attention is only paid to its effects on their activities in the field of education. In the following chapters the ambiguity in the social position of upper-class women and the contradictory demands of class and gender must be constantly borne in mind. Women's dependence on the circumstances of their families and their changing familial roles, their indirect and uncertain relation to the élite orders and the traditional values prescribing the behaviour of the upper-class *matrona* will recur again and again. Together, these three aspects constitute a framework which enables us better to understand both the educational opportunities of upper-class women and the limitations imposed upon them.

2

THE EDUCATION OF UPPER-CLASS WOMEN

Opportunities and impediments

The young woman had many charms apart from her youthful beauty. She was well versed in literature, in playing the lyre, and in geometry, and had been accustomed to listen to philosophical discourses with profit. In addition to this, she had a nature which was free from that unpleasant meddlesomeness which such accomplishments are apt to impart to young women.

(Plut. *Pomp.* 55; Loeb trans., modified)

In birth and beauty, in her husband also and children, she was abundantly favoured by fortune; she was well read in Greek and Latin literature, able to play the lyre and dance more skilfully than a respectable woman need, and had many other accomplishments which minister to voluptuousness.

(Sall. *Cat.* 25; Loeb trans., modified)

These texts, Plutarch's portrait of Cornelia (Pompey's last wife) and Sallust's portrait of Sempronia, show us two women of leading senatorial families during the late republic who had a similar education but were judged quite differently.[1] Whatever the historical truth of these portraits, literary education, supplemented with music and, in the case of Cornelia, with geometry and philosophy, seems to have been a regular element in it. Are we allowed to conclude from such examples that upper-class girls, as a rule, received a thorough education in Greek and Roman literature, and perhaps in music, mathematics and philosophy, or were such women exceptional and was that the reason why they attracted the attention of our sources?

So far the education of Roman girls and women has not been treated as a separate subject of study. Since the ancient sources usually do not speak of the education of girls or are prejudiced when the education of women comes up for discussion, even the most basic facts are hard to establish. Childhood as such did not much interest Roman authors and, whereas boys were cherished for their promise of a future career, girls did not figure prominently in public life and were simply omitted from record.[2] Since our sources hardly speak of the education of

17

girls, we have to gather our information from what is implied, comparing it with what we know of the education of boys.

In the present chapter an attempt is made to reconstruct the education of upper-class girls and women on the basis of those sources that deal directly with their opportunities to receive an education; the next chapter is devoted to the objectives of women's education and to ancient opinions on educated women. Though the educated women discussed in the following chapters bear witness to the level and content of their education, they are, as a rule, not discussed here in order to avoid repetition. Three questions will guide us: did upper-class girls, as a rule, receive some education, and, if so, during how long a period and to what level? Second, what opportunities did they have to continue their studies after their wedding-day? Third, did the nature and scope of their education during girlhood influence their possible studies in adult life? Before starting the discussion a few words should be said about the organization of Roman education in general.

Roman education

Roman education is usually divided into three stages.[3] The first stage, primary or elementary education, comprised reading, writing and some arithmetic and was taught by a *magister ludi* or a *litterator*. This stage is usually thought to have started at the age of 7 and to have ended at about 11. After this stage some of the boys (both ancient and modern discussions speak almost exclusively of boys) came under the tuition of a *grammaticus*, who taught literature, especially poetry, which was read, explained and evaluated; this formed the basis for further study of grammar, orthography, metrics, and other subjects, such as mythology or geography. Near the end of the 'grammar' course there were some preliminary exercises in prose-composition, but, strictly speaking, this was the field of the rhetorician.[4]

At about 15 or 16, the age at which boys exchanged the *toga praetexta* for the *toga virilis*, the third and most important stage of education was reached: rhetorical training, which prepared upper-class boys for a public career. For most of them the study of rhetoric was the final stage of their education and as such it was the main formative influence on adult life. However, since the toga of manhood now allowed them some freedom of choice, some of them chose to study philosophy together with rhetoric, or after they had finished their course in rhetoric; and to complete their education upper-class young men might tour the Greek-speaking world and visit Athens, or another Greek city, to study with a Greek rhetorician or philosopher.[5]

This traditional division of Roman education into three clear-cut stages is, of course, too rigid: in practice, the distinction between the successive stages was vaguer, especially in the case of home tuition; also, the age at which the boys were taught by a *magister*, a *grammaticus* or a *rhetor* could vary widely.[6] Moreover, this three-stage division dates from the last decennia of the republic and especially from the imperial period. In earlier days education was much more informal and, according to sources of later date which idealized old times, it was kept within the family under the strict guidance and personal tuition of the father; practical training and moral precepts formed an important part.[7] In those days, an upper-class boy when reaching the age of 16 (when the man's toga was assumed) was entrusted to a distinguished man of politics to learn the ways of the forum and to study under his guidance, instead of entering a school of rhetoric.

The greatest change in Roman education took place in the second and first centuries BC, when the Greek ideal of a general education (*enkuklios paideia*) was taken over by members of the Roman aristocracy. The *artes liberales*, disciplines appropriate to a freeborn man (or rather, a gentleman), as they called the subjects of this Greek-inspired education, consisted of grammar, rhetoric, dialectic, geometry, arithmetic, astronomy and musical theory. However, in practice, the study of 'grammar' (language and literature, chiefly poetry) and rhetoric were the most important subjects of Roman education and the mathematical sciences tended to be neglected or were only superficially taught as a preliminary to the study of philosophy.[8]

The introduction of Greek education in Roman upper-class circles and the influx of teachers and scholars from the Greek-speaking world caused grammatical and rhetorical education to be mainly taught by Greeks and in Greek, especially in the earlier days when there was no Latin literature to speak of. In those days, *grammatici* taught chiefly Greek poetry (foremost Homer, the tragedians and Menander) and some older Latin poetry, such as Ennius, Naevius, Plautus and Terence. Thus, for the Roman upper classes a liberal education and bilingualism went hand in hand. However, as time went on, the curriculum changed. In the first century BC schools of Latin rhetoric appeared next to the Greek ones and despite initial resistance they attracted many pupils; moreover, during the reign of Augustus the new Latin poetry (Virgil, Horace and the elegiac poets) was introduced into the curriculum of the *grammaticus* and partly replaced the older Latin writers.[9] As the new Latin poetry could challenge Greek poetry, it posed a threat to Greek education. During the early principate the increase of Latin education resulted in a separation of the *grammaticus Graecus* and the *grammaticus Latinus* – as it had led to separate teachers of Greek and Latin rhetoric before – possibly to the detriment of the knowledge of Greek language and literature among all but the wealthy upper classes.[10] Thus, fluency in both languages and knowledge of Greek and Latin literature were marks of distinction among the upper classes as they required an expensive literary education.[11]

During the principate educational facilities, such as schools and libraries, steadily increased. From Vespasian onwards emperors subsidized higher education in Rome by appointing a Latin and a Greek rhetorician at a regular salary and in some Italian towns a *grammaticus* was hired 'publicly' or a school founded by a wealthy benefactor, for example, by the younger Pliny in his home-town.[12] Schools, which probably were mainly, but not exclusively, attended by children of the sub-élite,[13] are attested at various places in Roman Italy (though most evidence, as is to be expected, comes from Rome). As a consequence, literary education seems not entirely to have been restricted to the upper classes during the empire, though, apart from a small group of professionals, it remained on the whole the privilege of well-to-do families in Rome and other major urban centres.

The increasing number of schools has led to the view that education, at least at the elementary level, was fairly widespread in Rome and Italy during the late republic and the first two centuries AD. This optimistic view of Roman literacy has been criticized by, among others, W. V. Harris, who argues that even during the late republic and the principate only a small proportion of the Roman male population and an even smaller percentage of the female population were fully literate, though he believes in the probability of complete literacy among the upper classes, both male and female.[14] Harris is perhaps somewhat pessimistic in his estimate of Roman literacy, but the lack of a state-supported school system and the fact that the responsibility for the education of children was left to their parents caused Roman education to be far from homogeneous and seriously diminished opportunities for the less wealthy boys, especially those living in the countryside. It also restricted opportunities for girls, even those of the upper classes. To them we may turn now.

The education of upper-class girls and women

In ancient societies women were less favoured than men in respect of literacy and education: in the schools female pupils, if present, were vastly outnumbered by male ones and, as a consequence, fewer women than men were literate. More-over, since men studied longer, they reached a higher level. This general condition also obtained in Rome, but we cannot tell exactly what proportion of women were literate and how far their education lagged behind that of men.[15] The scant evidence for female education has given rise to widely different opinions ranging from a somewhat naive belief in equal opportunities for Roman boys and girls (at least at the elementary level) to the assumption that only a very small proportion of girls received any education at all.[16] Even when we restrict our inquiry to women of the upper classes, some of whom, as we shall see, were highly edu-cated, it is impossible to estimate the proportion of educated women among the upper classes or the extent of their education – though it seems likely that among them illiteracy was rare, at least from the late republic onwards.[17]

Before discussing the evidence two points should be mentioned which dis-tinguished the education of upper-class girls and women from that of their male peers. First, the education of upper-class girls lacked the main objective of that of boys: to produce good public speakers. As we have seen, upper-class boys were, as a rule, trained for a public career which required a thorough education in oratory (and sometimes law) following on the study of 'grammar' and some general education in the liberal arts. This common purpose gave a certain unity and coherence to their education. For upper-class girls, however, there was no such fixed aim: unlike boys (of all classes) and girls of the lower (mostly servile) classes – some of whom were trained for a profession (for instance, as a hair-dresser, midwife, secretary, musician or even bookkeeper) or worked in bars and shops –[18] women of the upper classes had no profession or career open to them.

Second, upper-class girls did not enjoy a period of adolescence which in the case of boys of their class was devoted to study and preparation for their future career and went on until the age of 19 or 20, or even beyond. A Roman upper-class girl usually married in her early or mid teens.[19] Marriage meant a decisive change also in respect of her education, as it put an end to her life (and educa-tion) as an unmarried daughter under the care of her parents. Though, as we shall see, some women went on studying during marriage, or were able to resume study when widowed, the much shorter period before their marriages reduced their education.

As upper-class girls were not trained to become public speakers and married early, the usual three-stage division of education (elementary, grammatical, rhe-torical) cannot be applied to them: since marriage was the main transition in their life, a division into a pre-marital and a married stage of education is to be preferred.

Pre-marital education

There is not much information on the way upper-class girls learned to read and write and only slightly more on their more advanced education, in what is usually called the 'grammar' phase. In order to provide a tentative reconstruction of their education, and to find out how common such an education may have been among upper-class girls, the evidence for girls going to school or being taught at home will be discussed first; after this we shall look in some detail at the possible factors influencing their opportunities (such as the period they lived in, their domicile, class, wealth, family background and age at marriage).

Sources speaking of girls going to school or being taught at home begin in the late republic. There is some evidence suggesting that from this period onwards girls (of unspecified class) attended school together with boys, both in the elemen-tary and in the grammar phase.[20] Apparently, some schools were mixed, not only at the elementary level but also at the grammar stage. The matter-of-fact tone of the sources, most of them stemming from Rome in the late republic and the principate, seems to imply that in Rome during this period it was not felt to be exceptional for girls to go to school. However, we are totally ignorant of the number of girls in question, and it seems reasonable to assume that they formed only a minority among the pupils. Generally speaking, schoolgirls belonged to well-to-do urban families who had a school in their home-town and could afford to send both their sons and daughters to it.

Most upper-class families hired (or bought) private tutors to teach their chil-dren at home, at least for the elementary and grammar stages of their education.

Since in families with sons and daughters usually only the sons are mentioned, we are at a loss as to the extent to which the daughters were taught. We do hear, however, of families without sons which employed teachers for the education of their daughters: Cicero's friend Atticus kept a slave *paedagogus* for the elementary education of his only daughter Caecilia Attica and a freedman *grammaticus*, the famous Q. Caecilius Epirota, for her education in grammar. During the principate Minicia Marcella and her sister, the daughters of one of the friends of the younger Pliny, had their own *paedagogi* for their elementary education and *praeceptores* for grammatical education and the liberal arts; and inscriptions mentioning *paedagogi* of girls show that these examples were not the only ones.[21]

Considering the dearth of information on home-tuition of upper-class girls, it is not clear whether in families with children of both sexes the girls profited from the presence of private tutors and if they were perhaps actually educated together with their brothers. It should be noted that remarks about private teachers employed for the education of children (in the masculine plural) do not necessarily refer exclusively to sons; girls may have been included, though concealed by the masculine form. For instance, when Strabo reports that Aristodemus of Nyssa, a well-known grammarian and rhetorician, was a tutor of the children of Pompey the Great, we should perhaps not accept (as is usually done) that Gnaeus and Sextus were his only pupils, but conjecture that Pompey's daughter, Pompeia, was taught by him as well.[22] From an anecdote in Plutarch's section on inopportune quotations it appears that she received a thorough education in both Greek and Roman literature from a private tutor: at Pompey's homecoming from his great campaigns in the East 'the tutor of his daughter arranged a demonstration of her progress: after a book was brought, he gave the child the following line to start from: "You came back from the war; I wish you had died there." '[23] The quotation from the *Iliad*, a line spoken by Helen to Paris, was obviously a most unhappy choice for Pompeia to read to her father at his return from his eastern campaigns (which had kept him away from home for several years). However, if historical, it shows that, like her brothers, Pompeia received the bilingual education that was a distinctive mark of her class and that, at the early age of about 8 or 9 she had already progressed so far as to read Homer, an author usually associated with the beginning of the 'grammar' phase in Roman education.[24]

Similarly, when we are told that Augustus appointed the grammarian M. Verrius Flaccus,[25] a very successful teacher, as tutor of his grandsons and made him move his school to the palace, paying him a salary of a hundred thousand sesterces a year, it seems likely that Verrius was also employed for the instruction of Augustus' granddaughters, Julia and Agrippina. At first sight, this is contradicted by Suetonius, who relates that 'in bringing up his daughter and his granddaughters he [i.e. Augustus] even had them taught spinning and weaving, and he forbade them to say or do anything except openly and such as might be recorded in the household diary'.[26] Augustus tried to revive within his own household the ideals of traditional Roman education, which laid great stress on the moral virtues and domestic accomplishments of daughters. This agrees with his legal policy of reviving traditional morality, in which he prided himself on having set an example.[27] But we should not misunderstand Suetonius' words: they do not imply that Augustus' daughter and granddaughters were exclusively taught domestic duties and nothing else, like the girls of the good old days. On the contrary, they appear to have received a thorough literary education. In a section on the sayings of Augustus' daughter Julia, Macrobius mentions her 'love of letters and great erudition, not hard to come by in her house' and in a letter, quoted by Suetonius, Augustus praises the rhetorical talent of his granddaughter Agrippina (Maior) but exhorts her 'to take care not to write and talk affectedly'.[28] Augustus, who according to Suetonius preferred a simple and unaffected style of speaking and writing, probably urged her not to use far-fetched words or an ornate style. Apparently, Agrippina had followed a full course in 'grammar' including the preliminary exercises in prose-composition which some grammarians taught as a preparation for the study of rhetoric.[29]

Thus, Suetonius' account of the traditional education which Augustus prescribed for his female offspring is somewhat misleading and should not be taken at face value. By having his daughter and granddaughters taught spinning and weaving Augustus kept up an appearance of conforming to traditional ideals of female education, but this did not prevent him from providing his female relatives with the extensive literary education of their class and from taking great interest in their progress. This discrepancy between norms and practice partly accounts for the reticence of our sources.

To return to our initial question, *viz.* whether in families with both sons and daughters the girls also profited from the presence of private teachers, the answer should, in my opinion, be tentatively positive, although we cannot tell how many upper-class girls were educated in this way, or whether they took their lessons together with their brothers. As to the level and content of their education, the evidence, meagre though it is, is consistent in showing that elementary education and a 'grammar' course formed its core, while some even progressed as far as the exercises in prose-composition which formed the transition to the study of rhetoric. As is to be expected, there is no indication that girls were given a formal rhetorical training, but the way in which they were taught at both the primary and the 'grammar' stage seems not to have differed from that of boys: we find girls reading the same school authors as boys, such as Homer and Menander, and in late antiquity little Paula, daughter of a high-born Roman family turned Christian, still learned her alphabet in the way prescribed by Quintilian.[30]

However, the evidence is, of course, far too meagre for definitive conclusions. Rather than attempting to generalize on the basis of insufficient evidence it seems useful to study the differences in the education of girls according to the period and place they lived in, their wealth and class, family background, age at marriage and the like. In the following sections it will be asked how these factors influenced the educational chances of upper-class girls, the substance of their studies and the level they might reach before marrying.

The period in question

Roman society underwent great changes during our period, and so did its literary culture and education. In the second century BC Cornelia, the mother of the Gracchi, must have been taught by a Greek grammarian since she was fluent in Greek and able to entertain, and patronize, Greek scholars and men of letters in her villa in Misenum. Moreover, she had received enough training in Latin rhetoric to be noted for her excellent style of speaking and writing, and her letters were published and admired for their style.[31] So comprehensive an education of a girl at so early a date may seem surprising; as tradition has it, early Roman education of girls was confined to spinning and weaving and other domestic tasks. Of course, because of the growth of Greek cultural influence, education was changing rapidly in Cornelia's days, but she must have been among the very first girls of her class to benefit from the higher education which Greek scholars and tutors provided.[32] Leaving aside, for the moment, the influence of her family, to which I shall return, I shall first examine what effect the period in which she lived had upon her education.

Cornelia's proficiency in Greek literature and in Latin rhetoric was remarkable – in the eyes of ancient authors too. Her proficiency in Greek is perhaps to be expected in the light of what was taught by the grammarians of the time,[33] but her competence in rhetoric was uncommon for a woman. It may be explained by the fact that in Cornelia's days rhetorical training had not yet been institutionalized: no schools of Latin rhetoric existed as yet and prospective politicians learned the art of public speaking during their *tirocinium fori* (from which, needless to say, women were excluded). Such rhetorical courses as there were were taught by grammarians in combination with a course in grammar and thus, we may conjecture, they were more easily accessible to upper-class women than they were in later days.[34] Though Cornelia may have possessed a natural gift for rhetoric, we may suspect that her style of speaking and writing was cultivated by the rhetorical training she received from a grammarian.

From the first century BC onwards schools and other educational facilities, such as libraries, steadily increased. With the spread of education in the first two centuries of the empire we hear of more well-educated women. Not only in the upper classes but probably also among well-to-do urban sub-élite families, daughters were now sent to school or taught at home at the elementary stage and (part of) the grammar stage. Yet, we are ignorant of what percentage of girls had access to such teaching; the increase from the middle republic seems considerable, but we should keep in mind that it may be partly due to the increase in the number and variety of our sources.[35]

As compared to Cornelia's training there were innovations also in the curriculum, the most conspicuous being music-lessons (mainly singing and playing the lyre), which now became popular with some élite families – though they were still disapproved of by the more traditional-minded among the upper classes.[36] The introduction of music in Roman education led to the combined literary and musical education of Cornelia (Pompey's wife) and Sempronia, the two women with whom we started this chapter. Their education seems representative of a (small) group of daughters of 'progressive' upper-class families during the late republic and the early empire, which were open to this rather controversial aspect of Greek education.

The growth of interest in philosophy, apparent from the late republic onwards, led certain women to study philosophy in adult life,[37] but we have no indication that it formed a regular part of the education of girls, nor were they formally taught rhetoric. The institution of schools of Latin rhetoric in the first century BC curtailed the little rhetorical training that some women may previously have had under the tuition of a grammarian and, with the exception of Hortensia, the daughter of the famous orator Q. Hortensius Hortalus, hardly any Roman woman was known for rhetorical proficiency. Yet, at the very end of our period, when rhetoric had developed from public speaking in the political and juridical arena into the show-oratory of the sophists, we find the empress Julia Domna studying rhetoric; as far as we know, she was the first woman to do so since Cornelia, the mother of the Gracchi.[38]

Domicile

Our sources, especially the literary ones, mainly deal with Rome and leave the Italian municipalities in the dark. It is doubtful whether we may apply our knowledge of the situation in Rome to Italian municipalities. Are we to assume that there was a degree of cultural uniformity in the cities of Italy after the social war, or at least from the start of the principate onwards, so that the education of girls in the Italian municipalities was more or less like that in Rome?[39] Though the larger cities provided good educational facilities, more remote and smaller towns seem to have lagged behind, which induced ambitious families to send their sons to a neighbouring town, or even to Rome, for the completion of their education.[40] But what happened to their daughters?

A letter of the younger Pliny may throw some light on local customs. Pliny's home-town Comum had no school for grammar education.[41] Therefore, some fathers sent their sons to Mediolanum (Milan). Girls are not mentioned and it seems unlikely that they should have gone to Milan to attend school, since they would have had to stay with relatives or in lodgings, or perhaps in a sort of boarding-school, like the boys. We do not know for certain whether the boys in Pliny's letter were from upper-class families,[42] but their families were at least sufficiently well-to-do to be able to send their sons to Milan for an education. Apparently these families were not in a position to engage private teachers. This does not necessarily mean that they did not belong to the municipal élite. There was plenty of variation in wealth between the *decuriones* of different towns, mainly dependent on the size of the town. In a small town, like Comum, the local élite was of modest means: the census qualification for decurions was 100,000 sesterces, a sum that the freedman-tutor Verrius Flaccus earned in a year by teaching Augustus' grandchildren – but his salary was, of course, uncommonly high for a mere grammarian.[43] However, these families apparently possessed enough money between them to establish a 'grammar' school in their home-town and to pay the fees of the teachers; in addition, Pliny promised to contribute one-third of what they collected and wished them to appoint teachers of such repute that they would attract pupils from the neighbouring towns and villages as well.

No word about the education of girls in this story. Presumably they were sitting at home or had married at the age their brothers went to Milan to study. Apparently, it was not for them that Pliny's educational foundation was created, though we may suspect that, once the 'grammar' school had been established, not only boys, but also some girls benefited from it. Most of the wealthier girls are likely to have had private teachers, but we hear only of the moral training they received, such as Pliny's wife Calpurnia had been given by her aunt in Comum. Calpurnia Hispulla closely supervised her orphaned niece's education, giving her moral precepts and her own good example, an old-fashioned education that may have remained customary in small municipalities. This does not, of course, preclude the possibility that Calpurnia had teachers at home for the grammar stage of her education (she probably had in view of her proficiency in adult life), but we are not told so. On the whole, the Italian municipalities were more conservative than Rome in questions of family life and moral values, and this must have influenced the education of girls.[44] Unlike boys, girls were not sent for study to Rome, or to a town in the neighbourhood. Thus, with the exception of the wealthiest among them, who probably employed private teachers, their education depended wholly on the presence of local schools. As most upper-class girls lived in urban centres, or in Rome, for the greater part of their lives, they had, of course, much better opportunities than girls (or even boys) of the lower classes living in the countryside,[45] but it surely made a difference whether a girl was the daughter of a decurion of a little town (like Comum) or the daughter of a senator at Rome.

Wealth and class

The Roman upper classes were far from homogeneous. Apart from the traditional distinctions between the three leading orders, senators, *equites* and the municipal élite, the *decuriones*, there was a great variation in wealth and social status among the members of each of these orders. Though, theoretically, members of the upper classes shared the same literary culture and education, we should not assume that they all educated their daughters to the same extent.[46] Most women discussed in this study stemmed from senatorial families, and it seems reasonable to assume that because of their wealth and their residence in Rome women of the senatorial class stood the best chance of a good education. However, our evidence is distributed very unequally over the three élite orders: the women of the highest rank (those of the imperial household and of the leading senatorial families) enjoyed disproportionately greater attention than the much more numerous women of equestrian and decurial families. Therefore, the reticence of our sources about the education of women of equestrian and decurial families should not make us believe without due consideration that women of these classes were, as a rule, less educated. Rather, we should try to find out how their chances of an education compared to those of women of senatorial rank.

Though the evidence is limited, it seems that the education of daughters of the wealthier equestrian families closely followed that of girls of senatorial rank. Among the wealthy and prominent *equites* in Rome who tried to emulate the senatorial way of life, education in the 'liberal arts' was in high esteem as one of the ways to enhance their status. When among the leading senatorial families the education of girls came into fashion, the less distinguished families probably followed suit. A good example is that of Attica, the daughter of Cicero's wealthy and cultured friend Atticus, who, as we have seen, had private teachers both for the elementary and the grammar phase of her education. The wealth and learning of her father (and perhaps her own education) procured a great rise in status for her family: in spite of her equestrian birth Attica married the senator M. Vipsanius Agrippa (Octavian's friend) and her daughter Vipsania Agrippina was to become the first wife of the later emperor Tiberius.[47]

Anecdotes offer us further glimpses of the practice of female education among people of non-senatorial status, such as the case of the *eques* Pontius Aufidianus, who killed both his daughter and her *paedagogus* Fannius Saturninus because of their suspected love-affair, thus displaying, according to Valerius Maximus, a remarkable strength of character.[48] The matter-of-fact tone in which Valerius Maximus tells this story suggests that he does not find it out of the ordinary that a girl of equestrian family received an education. From outside the capital (indirect) evidence may be added: in view of her literary interests and accomplishments as an adult Calpurnia, the wife of the younger Pliny, must have been taught by private teachers in her native town of Comum during the elementary stage of her education and (part of) the grammar course; and a surprisingly outstanding education (considering her domicile) is evident in the case of Aemilia Pudentilla, a wealthy widow of equestrian family in the city of Oea in the Roman province of Africa, who was fluent in Latin and Greek both in reading and in writing.[49]

It seems likely that equestrian families, at least the wealthier among them, followed senatorial example, but families of the municipal upper classes may also have done so in due course, though here we have very little to go on. The wealthier among them may have had private teachers for their sons, and perhaps also for their daughters, but many others must have relied on schools in their home-town, or have sent their sons, but not their daughters, to a larger town nearby. In these less wealthy groups the education of girls must have depended to a much greater extent than that of boys on the presence of schools in their home-town.

Family background

Though a good education was, as a rule, held in high esteem among the upper classes, families and individuals varied in their interest in literature and learning. As the education of upper-class girls lacked the main objective of that of the boys of their class, *viz.* a career as a public speaker, it depended on the choice and inclination of a family whether, and to what extent, daughters were educated. The discussion of the motives and objectives of families in giving their daughters a literary education will be left to the next chapter, but as (private) education was expensive and, in the earlier period, uncommon for girls, wealth and a tradition of learning running in a family were very important factors, as were the presence of teachers and books. It seems likely that apart from their more formal training by private tutors, girls in wealthy and well-educated families might improve their education by daily association with, and by imitating the example of, their fathers and brothers, and by reading books from the family library. As we shall see, such informal ways of learning were also characteristic of the education of adult women. We may assume, for instance, that the excellent education of Cornelia, the mother of the Gracchi, depended on the great wealth, high standing and intellectual interests of her family, which was among the first of Roman senatorial families to embrace Greek culture and education. She probably received home-tuition, perhaps together with her brothers and sister, but the great learning of the male members of her family and their Greek tutors and famous Greek library (shipped home by her uncle, Aemilius Paullus, from his campaign in Greece) must have furthered her education.[50]

In the following chapters the influence of the family will return again and again. Especially important are the father and, during marriage, the husband. The father's influence and his example (apart from hereditary talent) were held responsible for the uncommon proficiency some women displayed in the field of oratory, and we sometimes find education and eloquence running in a family through several generations, displayed and transmitted not only by the male but also by its female members.[51] Here education by private tutors and by daily association with the male members of the family went hand in hand. By contrast, very little is said about the part mothers may have had in the intellectual education of their daughters. Though mothers and other female relatives played an important role by supervising not only the education of their sons, but also, and perhaps more frequently, that of their daughters, we hear only of moral guidance where the education of daughters is concerned – this in contrast with the attention paid to mothers supervising their sons' studies.[52]

Age at marriage

As has been said above (p. 21), upper-class girls usually married in their early or mid teens, that is, at an age when most boys were only halfway through the second stage of their education (the tuition by a *grammaticus*). Consequently, girls lacked the time to complete their education before marriage: on their wedding-day they were, as a rule, only half educated as compared to their much older husbands. However, though upper-class girls were allowed to marry from the age of 12 onwards and though many of them actually married before the age of 15, not all were destined to marry at so early an age and so we hear of certain upper-class girls who, for some reason or other, married only in their late teens or early twenties.[53]

This variation of age at first marriage must have entailed differences in education, and we may suspect that a girl who married at the age of about 18, had completed her 'grammar' course – if she had been given such a course – whereas a girl who married at the age of about 13 had not. The level of education of those who married early cannot be ascertained – because of the variations found in private teaching it may have varied widely[54] – but in view of the time boys needed for their grammatical education most of these girls must have been no more than half educated at the time of their marriage (i.e. about halfway through their grammatical curriculum). Girls marrying late stood a better chance of completing their grammar course. Though this is, of course, hard to prove, it may be illustrated by two examples of upper-class women who are set widely apart in respect of wealth, rank, domicile and period: first, as we have seen, Agrippina Maior, who married at the age of about 18, seems to have been given a full course in 'grammar' including the preliminary exercises in prose-composition that belonged to the field of the rhetorician; and second, we may infer from the 'prison-diary' of the early third-century North African martyr Vibia Perpetua, who married at the age of 18 or 19, that she was educated to the same high level.[55]

To summarize, we may draw the following conclusions. First, it seems likely that from the late republic onwards – when education had spread to include girls of the sub-élite – most, if not all, upper-class girls were educated at least to the level of basic literacy. Beyond this, matters become less simple. Evidently some girls (also of urban sub-élite families) went on to the next stage, instruction by a grammarian, perhaps continuing to attend school until puberty. Girls of the upper classes, at least the wealthier ones, mostly received home-tuition instead of going to school, and they may have continued their studies until the day of their marriage. There are no indications that the education of girls differed in substance from that of boys, or was tailored to their future condition as wives and mothers (but many of them were probably taught spinning and weaving, and other domestic skills, as well); rather, in the first and second stage of Roman education they followed the education of boys, while the third stage (rhetorical training) was, as a rule, denied them.

Further, as we have seen, beyond the elementary stage the education of an upper-class girl depended to a greater extent on personal circumstances, such as the period and town she lived in, her wealth and class, the disposition of her family and her age at marriage. Moreover, differences in the capacity and interest of individual girls and the uncertainties of private teaching must have produced considerable variation in the level of education they reached before marriage. Some of these factors also affected the educational opportunities of boys, but usually less so or in a different way: for instance, the establishment of schools of Latin rhetoric in the first century BC increased the opportunity of boys to study rhetoric, whereas it diminished that of girls, who were excluded from such schools. Similarly, residence in a small town with few or no educational facilities proved an impediment for girls from less wealthy upper-class families, but not to the same degree for boys of the same class since they might be sent to school in a larger town in the neighbourhood.

In short, we cannot speak of *the* education of *the* upper-class girls in Rome and Italy, as if they formed a homogeneous and unchanging group, nor may we assume that the changes in Roman education that occurred in the course of time affected girls in the same way as boys of their class. Therefore, to our initial question whether the education of women like Sempronia and Pompey's wife Cornelia was representative of that of upper-class women in general, no clear-cut answer can be given. Obviously, what we know of their education cannot be applied to all, or even the majority, of upper-class women during the whole of our period, but their education may well have been representative of that of the daughters of a group of leading senatorial families in the late republic, which were open to the Greek-style education of their days. Their numbers cannot be estimated. In the second and early first centuries BC there were only very few of them, or so it seems, but when, by the end of the first century BC, the Greek style of education became fashionable among the urban élite, the number of well-educated girls steadily increased. Because of the wealth and social standing of their families and their residence in the capital girls of senatorial families had, as a rule, the best chances of receiving a good literary education, but even in their case an early marriage might be the end of their studies, leaving them about halfway through their course in grammar. Thus, to become fully educated, a girl had to continue her education beyond her wedding-day.

The education of adult women

Generally speaking, married women of the upper classes have received more attention from ancient authors than unmarried girls. Because of their wealth and economic activities, their religious duties, their social prominence and their (indirect) political influence upper-class *matronae* were much less hidden from the public eye than the girls of their class. As a consequence we know more about them, as we do of their achievements in the field of education, though the evidence is, as usual, very limited and complicated by the fact that most texts speaking of the education of women are biassed (either against or in favour of it). In the second part of this chapter, about the education of adult women, the opportunities upper-class women had to continue their studies after their wedding-day will be examined, and it will be asked whether the scope and content of their education during girlhood were of influence on the nature of their studies (if any) in adult life. The following modes of (self-) education are discussed: husbands teaching their wives, private teachers, opportunities to add to their education by taking part in social life (by attending dinner parties, recitations, or the theatre), reading habits and access to books and libraries. In the next chapter, the motives and prejudices that come to light in the sources form the basis for the study of the aims of education of upper-class women and of ancient opinions on educated women.

The husband as a teacher of his wife

As we have seen, most upper-class women were mere girls when they first married. Even those who had received the best possible education must have been ignorant compared to their much older husbands. The discrepancy in age and education gave the husband the dominant role right from the outset. It also made him the 'natural' teacher of his wife, in accordance with contemporary ideas (and ideals) of male superiority. When a husband undertook his wife's education, the first thing he presumably had to do was to finish her course in grammar. However, this is not what we find: as far as we can see, learned husbands initiated their youthful wives in their own intellectual pursuits, be it philosophy, prose-composition or the study of poetry, earning applause for their teaching from moralists like the younger Pliny and Plutarch.

Our evidence does not begin until the end of the first century AD, *viz.* with the letters of the younger Pliny. In a letter to the scholarly Erucius Clarus Pliny praises the eloquence and erudition of their mutual friend, Pompeius Saturninus. During one of their literary conversations Saturninus read him certain letters

> which he said were written by his wife, but sounded to me like Plautus or Terence in prose. Whether they are really his wife's (as he positively affirms) or his own (which he denies), he deserves equal applause; whether for writing them himself, or for having so cultivated and refined the talent of his wife, who was but a girl when he married her.
>
> (Plin. *Ep.* 1.16.6)[56]

From this it may be inferred that Saturninus had taught his wife to write polished letters in the archaizing style in which there was a growing interest in his days. If we may believe Pliny's praise he was very successful at it, and Pliny flatters him by expressing his doubts that the letters were indeed written by his wife and not by himself.

In this letter Pliny calls his friend's wife, whose name is not mentioned, a *virgo* when he married her; apparently, Saturninus was her first husband, which means that she was in her teens when she married him. In view of the Roman habit of keeping to one's class when marrying, she probably was, like her husband, of equestrian birth. Since her name is unknown we are ignorant of the financial

31

means, residence and disposition of her family, but in the light of the evidence for the education of girls of equestrian family discussed above we may suspect that she received home-tuition at the elementary and probably also (part of) the grammar level. Her education in 'grammar' perhaps included reading Plautus and Terence, but it does not mean that she was trained in prose-composition, since, apart from a few preliminary exercises which might be taught at the end of the grammar course, this belonged to the field of the rhetorician. Her proficiency in writing archaizing letters must therefore be due to the teaching of her husband. Perhaps he had her study his own writings or gave her books to read from his library, but in doing so he could build on the basic training she had received as a girl in her parents' home. This is not mentioned by Pliny; on the contrary, he falsely represents her as a *tabula rasa* at the time of her marriage, thus overstating her husband's merit in educating her.

Pliny's own marriage offers another example of a married woman taught by her husband, and here too the inequality of this relationship shows clearly. In his forties, Pliny married Calpurnia,[57] a girl in her early or mid teens, who was born and bred in his home-town, Comum in northern Italy. She stemmed from a wealthy equestrian family and was the daughter of a deceased friend of Pliny's. As she was an orphan, she was brought up by her (paternal) aunt, Calpurnia Hispulla, who lived with her aged father, Calpurnius Fabatus, in Comum.[58] Thus, Calpurnia grew up in a small town with few educational facilities (as we have seen above, pp. 25f., Comum had no grammar school as yet) and her education may be taken as an example of the way the daughters of the wealthier families in such small towns were educated in her days. In view of her wealth and her equestrian birth she was probably taught at home by private teachers during the elementary and, perhaps, part of the grammar stage – but in his letter Pliny mentions only the moral training she had received from her aunt. Like his friend Saturninus he seems to have taken the completion of her education upon himself, though he wanted it to appear as if she herself had taken the initiative, out of love for him:

> Her affection for me has given her an interest in literature. My writings are continually in her hands; she reads them again and again and even learns them by heart. How full of solicitude she is when I am entering upon a cause! How happy she is when it is over! She stations messengers to inform her what reception, what applauses I receive, and what verdict I win in the case. When I recite my works, she sits nearby, concealed behind a curtain, and greedily drinks in my praises. She sings my verses and sets them to her lyre, with no other teacher but love, who is the best instructor.
>
> (Plin. *Ep.* 4.19)[59]

Elsewhere he praises the charm of her letters and reports that she clung to his works to find consolation for his absence when she was in Campania to recover from an illness.[60]

In this rather rose-coloured portrait of Calpurnia as his devoted and self-effacing wife the intellectual education she had received at her aunt's house is ignored. Yet, obviously she could not have read her husband's works, or put his verses to music or written charming letters, if she had not at least been taught to read and write, and to play the lyre. Besides, her appreciation of literature implies some understanding of it, which she had probably acquired from the teaching of a grammarian when she was a girl. Thus, like other girls of her class and days, she must have received elementary and grammar education, supplemented by the music-lessons fashionable at the time. Pliny probably completed her education by giving her some training in prose-composition, thus polishing the style of her letters. He also took care of her literary education, but in this respect, if we may believe his letter, his teaching was rather limited: it was only his own work Calpurnia was reading and setting to music – or so he says – and with relish he describes how she read and reread his work (even learning it by heart) and sang his verses, and how she listened, modestly concealed behind a curtain, to the praise bestowed on his recitations.

When trying to assess the veracity of Pliny's portrait of his marriage we should keep in mind that these letters were selected (and perhaps reworked) for publication. Therefore, their value as a description of Calpurnia's feelings and education is limited, but they do show Pliny's idea of a good marriage, an opinion which, he assumed, his social peers approved of. In all his letters to and about Calpurnia she is represented as the ideal wife: affectionate, chaste, thrifty, cheerful, modest, intelligent, docile and devoted to her husband's interests. Pliny stresses the harmony of their marriage, a marriage in which he, conscious of being the superior in experience, education and age, carefully moulded his young wife to accommodate herself to his way of life and his literary taste.[61] Though Pliny portrays himself in his letters as liberal-minded, his ideas form a striking confirmation of the submissiveness expected from women. In order to contribute to the harmony of their marriage Calpurnia had to devote herself to his interests and to adapt to his taste. Besides, by describing both Calpurnia and the wife of Pompeius Saturninus as *tabulae rasae* at the time of their marriage Pliny laid their literary accomplishments wholly to the credit of their husbands.

In the two marriages here discussed the roles of husband and teacher and those of wife and pupil merge. This may be partly due to the youthfulness and inexperience of the wife, for both Calpurnia and Saturninus' wife were in their first marriage, in which the difference in age and experience between husband and wife was at its greatest.[62] Yet, it may also be due to a change in the ideals of marriage: under the empire emphasis is laid on harmony and companionship in marriage, and the open expression of mutual love and devotion, which under the republic was considered undignified in upper-class marriages, now became acceptable and even desirable among the upper classes.[63] The ideal of an affectionate and harmonious marriage did not entail equality of the sexes; on the contrary, for all their intelligence and education both Pliny's wife and Saturninus' wife were expected to fulfil the conventional role of the submissive and respectful housewife. In educating his young and allegedly ignorant wife according to his own intellectual taste the husband adopted a patronizing attitude, which shows clearly also in Plutarch's essay on 'marital advice': taking the subordination of the wife for granted he urges the husband to become her philosophical mentor, arguing that by his guidance a husband was to prevent his wife from forming untoward ideas of her own.[64]

We meet the ideal of a husband teaching his wife for the first time in the works of the younger Pliny and Plutarch, that is, in the world of well-educated upper-class Romans and Greeks of the first two centuries of the principate. This does not necessarily mean that husbands did not teach their wives before this time,[65] but shows that from then onwards it was regarded as a particularly desirable habit which was in agreement with the ideal of a harmonious marriage. We can trace the development of this ideal only sporadically in the literary sources;[66] fortunately, however, archaeology provides further evidence.

On Roman sarcophagi of a slightly later date a husband teaching his wife is a frequent subject; this probably indicates that this conception of the ideal marriage had in the mean time spread to wider circles (those who could afford a sarcophagus) than appears from the literary sources. With minor variations these reliefs show a seated man reading from a book-roll or commenting on a text to a woman who is standing before him and listens attentively to his reading, her head modestly veiled by her *palla* (Plate 1). Sometimes the woman holds a closed *volumen* in her hand and often she is accompanied by other women. From their central position on the sarcophagi these figures are usually believed to represent the deceased couple. This is confirmed by the fact that their heads are mostly worked into portraits, but in some cases it is difficult to decide whether the woman is meant to represent the wife or a Muse (symbolizing the deceased man's learning). However, as Muses are usually identified by special attributes (masks, musical instruments, or feathers on their heads),[67] a listening woman without any such attribute should represent the wife, especially when her head is veiled by her *palla*. The lack of a clear distinction between wife and Muse may have been intentional: the portrayal of a woman as a Muse signifies her education and perhaps shows her in the role of a 'Muse' inspiring her husband. This explains why women are often portrayed in the so-called 'Polyhymnia' pose, a pose of attentive listening characteristic of the Muse Polyhymnia, and why they are often accompanied by eight Muses as if they were one of the *doctae sorores* themselves.[68]

This motif of a husband reading to his wife was popular in funerary art from the late second and early third century AD onwards. Though it allows women a place in intellectual life, it confirms their subordination as pupils to their husband-masters. In its emphasis on the sharing of intellectual interest within marriage, with the husband as the undisputed superior, the theme is similar to the ideals expressed in Pliny's letters. Though still very patriarchal as regards the male–female relationship, these ideals seem new inasmuch as they advertise harmony and partnership in marriage represented by a couple studying together. Such ideals may have had some impact on actual practice, but they do not, of

Plate 1 Sarcophagus of the *eques* L. Pullius Peregrinus and his wife, around the middle of the third century AD (Rome, Museo Torlonia: inv. no. 424). The seated husband is reading to his wife, who is standing before him and listening attentively. They are surrounded by six philosophers and eight Muses, which suggests that they are to be regarded as the seventh Wise Man and the ninth Muse. Photo courtesy of the German Archaeological Institute in Rome.

course, reflect everyday reality, which in many cases may have been very differ-ent. For one thing, not all women will have accommodated themselves to the submissiveness expected from them as willingly as Pliny's wife Calpurnia is reported to have done. As will be discussed in the next chapter, traditionalists feared that intellectual education might incite women to follow their own incli-nations regardless of the wishes of their husbands. If so, the matrimonial ideals found in Pliny and Plutarch and depicted on numerous sarcophagi may well have aimed at restricting the possible self-assertiveness of educated women by allowing them a place, but only a subordinate one, in the world of education.

Education by a private teacher

For a young woman in her first marriage instruction by her husband was regarded as the appropriate way to polish her education – at least, it was during the empire, when it was closely connected with notions about marital harmony and with traditional gender roles. But there were also other ways in which a married woman could continue her education: for instance, she might employ private teachers, as she had done (or rather, as her parents had done for her) as a girl, or she might continue to attend the lessons of the grammarian who had taught her before her marriage.

An example of this is the case of Attica, the daughter of Cicero's friend Atticus. During her marriage to M. Vipsanius Agrippa she was taught by the famous grammarian Q. Caecilius Epirota, a freedman of her father's, who is known as the first grammarian to introduce Virgil and other recent poets into the curriculum. Though, strictly speaking, we are not told that he had been teaching her before her marriage, this is suggested by the fact that he was her father's freedman (perhaps, at that time, still his slave). As Attica married young, at the age of about 14, she may have wished to complete her education with the same teacher. We owe our information on Epirota's lessons during her marriage to a scandal: in his description of the life of Epirota Suetonius remarks that 'while he was teaching his patron's daughter, who was married to Marcus Agrippa, he was suspected of improper conduct towards her and dismissed'.[69] Whatever the truth of this story, it shows that the relation of a teacher with his female pupil easily came under suspicion – as is confirmed by certain stories of adultery in which grammarians were involved in one way or another. Tutors were expected not only to teach their pupils, both male and female, but also to guide their morals; yet, because of the influence they were thought to have on their pupils they were easily suspected of having corrupted them when things went wrong.[70]

Wealthy women could hire, or buy, their own teachers – though we have little evidence for this;[71] they could also consult *grammatici*, and other scholars, employed by the men of the house. Thus, Livia sought the support of the Greek philosopher Areius, who was the personal adviser of her husband Augustus, when at the death of her son Drusus she was in need of consolation.[72] When under the empire Greek learning became fashionable in Roman upper-class society, many Greek scholars were employed by wealthy Roman families as tutors and (moral) advisers. Women living in such educated households might easily pick up bits of learning by regular contact with the scholars employed by their husbands or sons.

The custom of engaging learned men, most of them Greeks, was ridiculed by Lucian, who mocks both the servile flattery of the Greeks and the ignorance and boorishness of the wealthy Romans employing them, who – in Lucian's eyes – wanted to appear educated by having a man of learning about them rather than be troubled with his learning.[73] In Lucian's parody wealthy women even beat men when it came to arrogance, pretentiousness and stupidity:

> After all, one could perhaps put up with the conduct of the men. But the women –! That is another thing women are keen about – to have edu-cated men living in their households on a salary and following their litters. They count it as an embellishment if they are said to be cultured, to have an interest in philosophy and to write songs that are hardly inferior to Sappho's. To that end they too trail hired rhetoricians and grammarians and philosophers along, and listen to their lectures – when? it is ludicrous! – either while their toilet is being made and their hair dressed, or at dinner; at other times they are too busy! And often while the philosopher is delivering a discourse, the maid comes in and hands her a note from her lover, so that the lecture on chastity is kept waiting until she has written a reply to the lover and hurries back to hear it.
>
> (Lucian *Merc. Cond.* 36; Loeb trans., modified)[74]

Lucian's mockery would make no sense if it did not reflect to some degree actual practice among the upper-class women of his time. Two things may be inferred: first, in Lucian's days a Greek-style education had become fashionable not only among Roman upper-class men, but also among women. Second, in order to become educated – or to appear so – these women engaged Greek scholars, thus emulating men. In the light of what we know about the education of girls we would expect them to employ chiefly grammarians, but, if we may believe Lucian, they also hired the more prestigious – and perhaps more exciting – rhetoricians and philosophers. To assume from this satirical essay alone that in Lucian's days there was a fashion for studying rhetoric among upper-class women would stretch the evidence too far, but, as we shall see, under the empire certain upper-class women did show a marked interest in philosophy.

In Lucian's eyes these women hired men of learning only for showing off. Because of their alleged ignorance and conceit they treated men of learning with contempt: an interruption of a discourse on chastity for the exchange of notes with a lover is but one of the many humiliations a philosopher in their service had to endure. In a humorous description of the trials of a Stoic philosopher in the service of a wealthy and distinguished woman he relates the indignities the stern old philosopher was subjected to when escorting his mistress to one of her estates in the country: during the journey he had to put up with her effeminate favourite, whose depilated legs and rouged cheeks disgusted him, and with her pregnant Maltese lapdog, who licked his beard, wet his clothes and finally gave birth to puppies in his cloak.[75]

By an unusual stroke of fortune Lucian's harsh description of the humiliating treatment of a Greek scholar by his Roman mistress can be contrasted with a roughly contemporary letter written by such a Greek scholar to his absent mistress. It is the *Enchiridion Harmonicon*, a manual of harmonics, written in the second century AD by the Neopythagorean philosopher and mathematician Nicomachus of Gerasa.[76] The treatise is written in the form of a letter to a high-born Roman woman, who is not known to us by name. There is no reason to regard her as fictional; her name must originally have been mentioned in the heading of the letter, but was probably suppressed when the treatise was published. From the humble way in which Nicomachus repeatedly addresses her, we may conclude that she was an upper-class woman, who at the time of the composition of the treatise had embarked upon a long journey, probably in the eastern provinces of the empire. We may guess that she was the wife of a provincial governor or some other high imperial official and that she accompanied her husband to his province.[77]

As Nicomachus remarks, the *Enchiridion* was written at the request of this high-born lady who had formerly been studying with him, but seems to have interrupted her lessons because of this journey. Nicomachus himself was also travelling – though in a far less leisurely fashion – when his pupil's request reached him in which she asked him a brief exposition of harmonics in order to continue her studies during his (and her) absence.[78] Nicomachus hastily complied with this request, 'taking it for an order', and in spite of the difficult circumstances of his uncomfortable journey he composed the *Enchiridion* in the form of a long letter containing a synopsis of the subject, while promising a fuller treatment later:

> nevertheless, best and noblest of women, I must summon my greatest efforts, since it is you who have bidden me at least to set out the major propositions for you in a simple form, without elaboration or complex demonstrations, and to do so at once, so that by having these propositions collected in a single synopsis, and by using these brief notes as a manual, you may remind yourself of what is stated and taught there in rough outline under each heading. If the gods are willing, as soon as I have some leisure and a break from my travels, I will put together for you a longer and more accurate introduction to these matters, articulated with full reasoning, as the saying goes: it will be in several books, and I shall send it to you at the first opportunity, wherever I am told that you are living.
>
> (Nicomachus *Ench.* 1; trans. Barker (1989) 248, modified)[79]

At the end of his treatise he again apologizes for his cursory treatment of the subject:

> Forgive the hasty nature of this essay: as you are aware, you set me this task just as I was poised to go off on my journey: and with your accustomed great kindness and thoughtfulness for your friends, accept it as a beginning and a friendly offering. You can expect, if the gods are favourable, a most thorough and altogether a most complete technical treatise on these matters, which I will send you as soon as the first opportunity arises.
>
> (Nicomachus *Ench.* 12; trans. Barker (1989) 269)[80]

The speed with which Nicomachus obeys, his elaborate apology for the hasty treatment of the subject, his promise to write a definitive account as soon as he has leisure and the respectful way in which he addresses the unknown lady show that he was her subordinate. The unknown woman had, it seems, previously employed Nicomachus as her teacher. Nicomachus directly refers to his teaching at the close of his introductory chapter immediately before entering upon his actual subject: 'But now, to make my exposition easier to follow, I shall begin from the same place where I began my instruction when I was expounding these things to you in person.'[81] She seems to have been an eager student since she urgently asked Nicomachus to send her a summary of his teachings with all possible speed in order to continue her studies even while travelling.[82] With his apologies for the simplicity and brevity of his manual Nicomachus pays credit to her learning and intelligence (as it suggests that it would be too simple for her), and he frequently refers to his promised thorough and systematic account (now lost) for a more satisfactory treatment.

However, we can only judge the level of her education from the contents of the extant *Enchiridion*. This brief, elementary introduction to the Pythagorean theory of harmonics shows two peculiar traits: first, it lays great emphasis on the heroic figure of Pythagoras by falsely attributing all musico-theoretical discoveries (such as the discovery of the octave) to him, and, second, though giving an exposition of the theory of harmonics from the Pythagorean point of view it draws heavily on the terminology – and on some of the ideas – of the rival school of musical theory, that of the followers of Aristoxenus.[83] As a result the argumentation is sometimes confused. Because of this, it has been assumed that the *Enchiridion* was not meant to offer a systematic treatise on harmonics, but that its first aim was to impress the addressee with the eminence of Pythagoras and his teachings in order to convert her to Pythagorean thought.[84] But another interpretation is, to my mind, more convincing. According to A. Barker, Nicomachus' short treatise bridged the gap between the two competing schools of harmonics that flourished during the first two or three centuries AD: that of the followers of Aristoxenus and the 'Pythagorean' or 'Platonist' school. By drawing on the musicological terminology of the Aristoxenian tradition of harmonics, with which the educated reader of his days was familiar through school texts, Nicomachus could more easily expound the ideas of the mathematically more sophisticated Pythagorean school of musical theory, whose writings were normally designed for a public of specialists only. Thus, by using the terminology the educated public of his days was familiar with and by giving a rather straightforward exposition of the musical aspects of Pythagorean philosophy without the usual mathematical complexities Nicomachus popularized Pythagorean thought for the non-specialist.[85]

If so, the *Enchiridion*, beside its immediate addressee, was meant for the generally educated readers of the time, who had a basic knowledge of arithmetic and geometry and were familiar with the terminology of the Aristoxenian tradition of harmonics. We may suppose that, if she was to understand the treatise addressed to her, the unknown lady had received a similar training, whether from Nicomachus himself or from some other teacher.[86] Moreover, she must have had a good mastery of Greek to be able to understand Nicomachus' long and complicated sentences. Her education, therefore, had gone beyond the grammar stage to include the mathematical sciences, if not further. This incidental glimpse of the relation between a philosopher and his female pupil of rank[87] may be contrasted with Lucian's caricature of the Greek scholar fawning upon his wealthy, ignorant, upper-class female employer. Though Nicomachus adopts a respectful attitude to his addressee, he does not flatter her unduly. Moreover, far from being ignorant his student seems a woman of more than average studiousness and erudition.

We should not overestimate the liberty wealthy, upper-class women enjoyed in following their desire for learning and in hiring (or buying) their private teachers. In more old-fashioned families, especially those of municipal or provincial extraction, the opinion of the husband or father seems to have been decisive and they did not always appreciate female learning. Seneca's mother Helvia provides an interesting example. She was born and bred in Spain and was given a strict education by her stepmother (her own mother had died at her birth), which reportedly made her into a paragon of old-fashioned virtue, but no intellectual education is mentioned.[88] She was married at an early age to L. Annaeus Seneca, about thirty years senior, who belonged to a wealthy equestrian family of Italian stock at Corduba. She bore him three sons, the middle one of whom, L. Annaeus Seneca, was the well-known philosopher and teacher of Nero. Both her husband and her sons spent the greater part of their lives in Rome, but we do not know whether she joined them or remained at her husband's estate in Spain for most of the time.[89] After her husband's death in AD 39 or 40 she probably lived with her father on the family estates in Spain and occasionally visited her sons and grandchildren in Rome.[90]

In our main source about her life, Seneca's 'consolation to his mother Helvia' – written because of his exile – she is depicted as an intelligent and studious woman. However, her husband's opposition had kept her from studying to her heart's content. In his *consolatio*, the younger Seneca deplores this:

but, so far as the old-fashioned strictness of my father permitted you, though you have not indeed fully grasped all the liberal arts, still you have had some dealings with them. Would that my father, truly the best of men, had surrendered less to the practice of his forefathers, and had been willing to have you acquire a thorough knowledge of the teachings of philosophy instead of a mere smattering!

(Sen. *Cons. Helv.* 17.3–4; Loeb trans. modified)[91]

Seneca's complaint concerns her advanced education, the study of the liberal arts and of philosophy; apparently, her education at the elementary level and that in grammar were taken for granted. We may assume that after having received this basic training as a girl, she was drawn to the study of philosophy – and perhaps to that of the mathematical sciences, which were taught as a preparation to the study of philosophy – in adult life. Her husband's opposition, for reasons of female propriety, had hampered her studies, but had not totally prevented them; if we may believe her son, she had been able, because of her quick intelligence, to acquire at least a basic knowledge of philosophy and the liberal arts.[92]

How did she acquire this knowledge, elementary though it may have been? Surely not by the instruction of her husband, who was opposed to it, or by engaging a private teacher. She may, of course, have had recourse to self-study by reading books from the family library, but it seems more likely that she profited from the studies of her son, the younger Seneca. Seneca refers to their companionship in studying when summing up the reasons for her grief at his banishment: 'Where are the talks, of which I [i.e. Helvia] could never have enough? Where are the studies, which I attended with more than a woman's pleasure, more than a mother's intimacy?'[93] As Seneca has it, she shared his studies (in philosophy and the liberal arts, presumably) with unusual keenness, and these are the studies he advises her to take up again as a consolation for his exile. Seneca warns her that to shield her against the blows of fortune philosophy and liberal studies are more effective than travelling or visiting the games, which offer only temporary relief. He does not specify how she should take up her studies now that he has been exiled, but as, in his opinion, 'the foundations of all disciplines' had been laid,[94] he probably believed her to be able to study by herself from books. By that time a widow, she was, in any case, no longer hampered by her husband's opposition.

Taking part in social life

Could women add to their education in other ways than those mentioned so far? We saw in chapter 1 that upper-class women fully participated in the social life of their families; did this offer an opportunity to further their education? To answer this question we have to examine the place of women in those events in Roman social life in which culture played a part: refined dinner parties, recitations and performances in the theatre.

Dinner parties

One of the fundamental differences between the classical Greek, or rather Athenian, way of life and the Roman is that in Roman houses there was no segregation according to gender: Roman women were fully integrated in the house and social life of the family. This contrast between Greek and Roman custom obtained also in dinners and *symposia* (or, in Latin, *convivia*): as has been observed by Nepos, the family-minded Romans took their wives to dinner parties, while Greeks, or rather Athenians of the classical period, did not:

> For instance, what Roman would blush to take his wife to a dinner party? What matron does not occupy the main place in her house and does not show herself in public? This is very different in Greece; for there a woman is not admitted to a dinner party, unless only relatives are present, and she keeps to the more retired part of the house called 'the women's quarters', to which no man has access who is not near of kin.
>
> (Nepos *Vir. Ill. praef.* 6–8; Loeb trans., modified)[95]

Whereas in the classical Greek world women attending a *symposium* were *hetairai*, professional dancers and musicians or other persons of low repute, in Rome respectable *matronae* reclined with their husbands amidst the guests. However, Roman tradition has it that in earlier days women did not recline, but were seated on chairs or on low benches at the feet of the couches, as was also expected from children. This ancestral habit was still propagated by some traditionalists during the empire, but from the late republic onwards, if not earlier, upper-class women enjoyed the privilege of reclining at dinner – normally sharing a couch with their husbands.[96]

Dinner parties held by wealthy Romans were not merely meant for eating and conversation, but were social events providing all kinds of amusement, during which the host could regale his guests with his wealth or culture. Entertainment during, or after, the meal played an important role: mimes, pantomimes, performances of clowns, jugglers, acrobats, male dancers, Spanish dancing-girls, story-tellers, dwarfs or magicians. Extraordinary stories of gladiator fights or executions of criminals during dinner fascinated Roman authors, but must have been extremely rare, if not wholly fictitious.[97] Among the educated, entertainment during dinner would be sober: it might consist of recitations, music, the performance of a play or the discussion of grammatical, rhetorical or philosophical issues.[98] According to Nepos 'dinner was never served at Atticus' house without a reading of some kind' and during the dinners of the younger Pliny a comedy was performed, a book read or music played. In a discussion of the most appropriate kind of entertainment during dinner Plutarch surveys a whole range of possibilities: a performance of a dialogue of Plato, tragedy, (panto)mime or comedy, the singing of poems by Anacreon and Sappho, or music and dance. Among these entertainments tragedy, mime and certain kinds of dance were rejected, but new comedy, especially Menander, was highly appreciated (in contrast to old comedy), as was music, especially as an accompaniment to poetry. However, in Plutarch's eyes the best kind of entertainment was guests amusing each other with philosophical discussions.[99]

Upper-class women are only rarely mentioned as taking part in (after-) dinner entertainment, but from their regular presence at dinner parties we may infer that they often watched the entertainment and listened to the discussions. We have Pliny's evidence for the presence of his wife Calpurnia during his meals: 'At supper, if I have only my wife or a few friends with me, a book is read to us; after supper we are entertained either with a comedy or with music.' Similarly, the wife of the emperor Pertinax was present when her husband discussed literature with a friend during dinner, as he was reported to do when there were no other guests. These were private occasions, but other testimonies suggest that the presence of wives was taken for granted at all kinds of dinner entertainment, sometimes to the regret of moralistic authors.[100] Moreover, female presence was not restricted to wives; single women (widowed or divorced) might organize the entertainment themselves, as the aged Ummidia Quadratilla did, who kept a troupe of pantomime players for the purpose – sending her grandson away when they performed.[101]

Clearly, women were allowed to attend dinner entertainment, but whether they actively took part in the (literary) discussions is another matter. In spite of the Roman practice of mixed dinners the guests mentioned in our sources which deal with learned table-talk are all male. Of course, some dinner parties were exclusively male (or with courtesans as the only women present); besides, it is likely that at mixed dinner parties men outnumbered women, since it was common for a man to attend a dinner party on his own, but not for a woman – though this was not impossible.[102] However, there is another reason why women attending dinner parties receive so little note in our sources: in mixed company, whatever the proportion of men and women present, men probably dominated the conversation. The reticence of our sources about female guests indicates that modesty at dinner and refraining from participation in the discussion was expected of them: just like men of lower status, women were supposed only to be seen, not heard.[103] This, of course, does not mean that women actually kept silent during dinner, but that their words were not likely to be recorded by the (male) authors – except for criticism.

That women who actually took part in the discussion were felt to trespass on a male preserve is shown by Juvenal's caricature of a woman dominating the conversation during dinner:

> But most intolerable of all is the woman who as soon as she has reclined
> for dinner recommends Virgil, pardons the dying Dido, and pits the
> poets against each other, putting Virgil in the one scale and Homer in the
> other. The grammarians give way to her; the rhetoricians give in, all fall
> silent [. . .] if she is so determined to prove herself both learned and

eloquent, she ought to tuck up her tunica knee-high, sacrifice a pig to
Silvanus, and take a penny-bath.

(Juv. 6.434–9 and 445–7; Loeb trans., modified)[104]

In this passage traditional gender roles are reversed: a woman does most of the
talking at dinner, silencing the rest of the company. Moreover, the subjects in
which she excels, grammar and oratory, are the fields of learning of upper-class
men. She is depicted as a caricature of a professional grammarian who compares
the literary merits of Homer and Virgil, or as a rhetorician who overpowers the
audience with a torrent of arguments. In the end she is advised to turn into a
man: if she wants to appear learned and eloquent she should wear a *tunica*,
instead of a woman's dress, worship Silvanus and bathe in the men's baths.[105]

As the relation between satire and life is highly complicated, we are not to infer
from Juvenal's caricature that women usually dominated the discussion at dinner
in his days – though it is clear that such behaviour was not inconceivable. Rather,
his satire seems to confirm the view that women, when present, were normally
expected to refrain from taking part in the discussions and that, as a rule, participation was considered as a breach of custom.[106] Therefore, the reticence of our
sources should not lead us to conclude that women never attended dinner parties,
or, for that matter, that they were totally silent at such occasions, but only that
they were expected to behave modestly and unobtrusively.

Recitations

Recitations, mainly of poetry, but also of history, oratory and philosophy, were
fashionable in Rome from the late republic onwards. Both professional and amateur poets and authors sought publicity or useful criticism by reading their work
to an audience. Such a reading could take place in the forum, a theatre or some
other public place (a colonnade or the baths) or at home before an audience of
friends; if in a public locality, the author would aim at publicity through a smooth
performance of his finished work; if at home, he allegedly did so to improve his
'work in progress' by the literary criticism of a carefully selected and well-
educated audience.[107] We may suspect that women were present at public recitations held in a theatre (but not in the forum or at the baths), but this is difficult to
prove;[108] even the attendance of women at private recitations in a domestic
setting is hardly confirmed by ancient evidence – and perhaps we should
conclude that it was rather unusual.

It is again to the letters of the younger Pliny that we owe our main information. Pliny repeatedly speaks of recitations in his letters and was himself
in the habit of reading his poetry at home during dinner or in his *cubiculum*
(private room, bedroom) in front of a small group of *intimi*.[109] As regards
women he only mentions the presence of the nearest female relatives of the
performer: at a reading of a learned poem on astronomy by Calpurnius Piso the
poet-reciter's mother was present, and, as we have seen above (pp. 32ff.), Pliny's

wife Calpurnia was present whenever her husband recited, though hidden behind a curtain.[110]

That Calpurnia should hide at such occasions seems surprising, especially since Pliny's recitations took place in his own house. In fact, we know of only one other woman concealing herself behind a curtain from an all-male company, but this was in totally different circumstances: at a meeting of the senate in the imperial palace Agrippina Minor, Nero's mother, was seated at the senators' back behind a curtain, in order to listen to the discussions without being seen.[111] Because of his professed aim in reciting (to elicit literary criticism and thereby improve his work) Pliny used to invite a carefully selected and probably exclusively male audience consisting of intimate friends and literary connoisseurs, and this perhaps made the presence of his wife slightly awkward: yet, her behaviour is surprising. If it is not to be ascribed to her singular modesty, praised by Pliny in his letters, it may perhaps be taken as an indication that the presence of women at private literary recitations was felt to be unusual.[112]

The few examples our sources provide of the presence of women at recitations (such as Octavia attending Virgil's reading of his *Aeneid* to Augustus) seem to confirm this; like Calpurnia, they were female relatives of the poet-performer or of the host who put his house at the disposal of a friend or a protégé to give a recitation of his work.[113] Unless the presence of women at private recitations was habitually overlooked in our sources, we may conclude that it was restricted to an occasional female relative. Like literary coteries private recitations were presumably, as a rule, all-male affairs.[114]

Theatre

In contrast to the scantiness of the evidence for women attending literary recitations there is ample proof that they visited the theatre, the amphitheatre and the circus. With most of this we are not concerned here, since we are dealing with women's literary and intellectual interests, not with their (alleged) love of gladiatorial shows or chariot-races.[115] In the theatres women could attend all kinds of cultural entertainment, from performances of plays (mostly during the republic), mime or pantomime (especially popular during the principate), to recitations of poetry and declamations.[116] If they were lower class, they might be involved in the theatre as actresses, and some wealthy upper-class women acted as benefactresses to their cities by financing the repair of a theatre or some public entertainment.[117] As spectators women seem to have frequented the theatre just like men, but from the start of the empire onwards, if not earlier, their place in the theatre (and amphitheatre) was very different.

During most of the republic men and women sat together at plays and gladiatorial shows, but in the theatre some form of *de facto* segregation of upper-class women seems to have been introduced when, for the first time in 194 BC, the front rows were reserved for senators and, by the *Lex Roscia* of 67 BC, the first 'fourteen rows' behind the senators for *equites*; this special seating of the two leading orders did not include their female relatives.[118] The segregation by social rank and gender was expanded by the reforms of Augustus. In an attempt to restore social order after the civil wars Augustus tightened the rules of the theatre and extended them to the amphitheatre, where mixed seating was allowed before his time. Not only did he appoint separate places for different social groups in both theatre and amphitheatre, seating them in a hierarchical fashion distinguished by seat and dress, but he also segregated women from men by relegating them to the highest rows of seats at the rear of the *cavea*, while forbidding them to attend athletics contests altogether. The only women to receive special seats at the front were the Vestal Virgins and women of the imperial family, who sat with the emperor or with the Vestal Virgins.[119]

We do not know whether Augustus' arrangement was always strictly applied; it may have taken some time before it was generally observed and a series of laws of subsequent emperors reinforcing the segregation by social rank suggests that the rules were often broken.[120] Moreover, the ancient evidence is vague when it comes to the details of the seats for women, who are treated in our sources as an undifferentiated mass. They probably sat in separate sections (*cunei*) at the rear of the *cavea*, in between the *cunei* allotted to the *pullati*, the togaless free poor, the slaves and the non-citizens, but it is not clear whether Augustus, or later emperors, separated women according to rank and status within these sections. Judging from the segregation by social rank among male spectators and from Augustus' regulation that separate rows of seats were assigned to married men (though, strictly speaking, Suetonius speaks only of plebeian married men), one would expect separate rows of seats for upper-class *matronae*, who were possibly also distinguished by their ceremonial dress, the *stola* – but for this there is no evidence.[121]

Thus, though the presence of women at plays and games was taken for granted, their treatment was different from that of men: banned to the top rows of the (amphi)theatre, they had to watch the plays and spectacles from afar.[122] Their relegation to the *summa cavea*, together with the urban poor, non-citizens and slaves, gave women much less room than men (who, besides occupying part of the *summa cavea*, also occupied the entire *cavea ima* and *media*), so that women can only have formed a minority among the audience as a whole.[123] One wonders whether there was sufficient room for all women who wished to attend, and we may suspect that their sections were often overcrowded. Besides, their relegation to the top rows, among slaves and the urban poor, must have been humiliating, especially to the high-ranking among them, who from their seats at the rear would have seen their male relatives in seats of honour in the orchestra and the 'fourteen rows'.[124] Thus, though the presence of women in the theatre was taken for granted, their position in it was literally a marginal one.

Summarizing we may say that women's participation in social life afforded them a chance to improve their education; however, we should not overestimate its importance. Their best opportunity seems to have been attending dinners where a book was read or another cultural entertainment provided, the enjoyment of which, incidentally, required a certain amount of education. Therefore, it only increased the learning of those who were already well edu-cated. Women could attend the theatre and watch the plays or mimes, but during the empire they were banned to the top rows with less room and a less satisfactory view of the stage than that enjoyed by men. Even less advantageous than their place at the theatre, was, it seems, their place at private recitations which were popular during the empire: apart from an occasional female relative the presence of women at such recitations is not attested.

Reading habits

What did women read? Did their taste and literary preference differ noticeably from those of men, or is no difference to be found between the reading habits of men and women? A cursory survey of the literary sources tells us that the great writers of love poetry and epigram believed that they were much read by women: Catullus, Tibullus, Propertius, Ovid and Martial frequently mention or address women as their readers, not only their own (possibly fictitious) mistresses, but also other women of various ages and situations, both unmarried girls and *matronae*. The frequency with which they speak of women as their readers may be taken as an indication of the importance they attached to a female public.[125]

Apart from love poetry and epigrams, other genres of literature hardly ever contain any reference to women as readers. Though some are addressed in philo-sophical treatises and though women are occasionally mentioned as readers of 'school' authors such as Homer, Virgil and Menander, their reading seems to have been remarkably one-sided: no history, no orators or rhetorical treatises, no didactic poetry (except on love), no biography, little epic and only once a work on agriculture.[126] Are we to conclude from this that, apart from some (moral) philosophy, women read nothing but love poetry and epigrams?

Here caution is needed. Since we have no lists of books owned by women, we have no knowledge of their literary preferences apart from what the ancient authors tell us. This may easily lead to circular reasoning, especially since those authors who mention female readers nearly always refer to women reading their own poetry: Propertius speaks of women reading Propertius, Ovid of women reading Ovid and Martial of women reading Martial.[127] How can we know if such statements are correct and, if so, what else women read? Though it is clear that Martial and the love poets *wanted*, and perhaps *expected*, to be read by women, this by itself does not constitute sufficient grounds for concluding that women preferred love poetry and epigram to all other genres of literature.

Yet, this is what these poets want us to believe: *viz.* that women valued love poetry, or even obscene verses, above epic and other serious writings.[128] Obviously, such a preference clashed with the chastity and modesty expected of upper-class girls and *matronae*, and this conflict became especially acute after Augustus had passed his laws on marriage and adultery. To clear himself of accusations of corrupting respectable *matronae* Ovid vigorously (but unsuccessfully) disclaimed that his *Ars Amatoria* was written for upper-class *matronae*, pretending that it aimed at the instruction of freedwomen and courtesans, who were free from the moral constraints imposed on *matronae*: 'Keep far away, slender fillets, symbol of modesty, and the long skirt that hides the feet in its folds. Of safe love-making do I sing, and permitted secrecy, and in my verse shall be no wrong-doing', but he implicitly acknowledges that his poetry on love was read by upper-class matrons as well.[129] Again, Martial feigns to try and deter *matronae* from reading his indecent verses – only to find that they read them more avidly.[130] Both imply that upper-class girls and women were expected to read poetry – but only of a decent and morally uplifting kind – and both want it to appear that women preferred their exciting verses to the dull stuff of more serious poets. What are we to believe?

The reconstruction of the ancient reading public, both male and female, is a difficult problem. Most ancient authors do not speak of the audience they address and even if they had, it would have been uncertain whether their intended readers were the same as their actual public. Whenever a book was dedicated to a certain individual – usually an upper-class man – we may accept that it was written for him and his social equals, but we cannot tell who (else) actually read it. It seems reasonable to assume that upper-class men writing about history, political biography, oratory, law or agriculture composed their work for men like themselves, public speakers, politicians and property-holders interested in such work, and perhaps they were actually read mainly by them. But what about poetry, philosophical treatises, drama or novels, to mention only a few other genres? May we assume that these genres appealed to a wider public, not only to men of the upper classes but perhaps also to educated men from the middle classes, literate freedmen (or even slaves), and, possibly, women?[131]

All this is hard to decide; because of the almost total lack of evidence the ancient reading public is mostly beyond our reach. Besides, what seems likely to us now is not necessarily true of Roman society. This may be illustrated by the question of the readership of the ancient novel. According to a theory of long standing the readers of the ancient novel consisted chiefly of women, juveniles and 'the poor-in-spirit'.[132] This assumption was based on the depreciation of the novel as trivial reading matter, which was thought to be fit for the semi-educated only, *in casu* women, young people and the newly literate of the middle classes. Since women play a major role in the novel – the heroine often being the most impressive character – and since the theme of love and marriage is central to the plot, it was thought that women could easily identify themselves with these characters and that the sentimentality of the main theme heightened the appeal for them. Besides, the fact that from the eighteenth century onwards women were in the habit of reading novels has led some to believe that the same was the case in Roman times. Therefore, it was thought that women were the principal readers of the ancient novel.[133]

Though it is, of course, not impossible, or unlikely, that ancient women actually read novels, and though women may have been attracted by the heroines and the theme of love and marriage, this is no proof that women were the main readers of the ancient novel. If this were so, what would we say of tragedy with its great female characters, and what would we conclude from epic heroines such as Helena, Penelope and Dido? Should we suppose that these works were mainly read by women too? Besides, it is clear that prejudices against women come into play when it is said that it was because of its triviality that the ancient novel found its main support among women. Last but not least, the assumption of a mainly female public is not supported by the evidence: with one exception, ancient references to readers of novels speak of upper-class men, not women.[134]

Lately, the belief in a popular, female or juvenile readership has declined and, instead, recent studies draw attention to the great number of literary allusions in ancient novels and to the influence of rhetoric; the argument is that the authors of novels expected their readers to be the same sort of persons as the readers of other literary work. The consistently male perspective adopted in the novel, and the literary and rhetorical education required to appreciate it, point to a reader-ship consisting mainly of educated upper-class men – though members of other groups may occasionally have read novels as well.[135] Though women may have been among them,[136] it seems clear that the theory that women formed the main audience of the ancient novel is untenable.

In view of the fallacy of traditional assumptions about the supposed literary preference of women, what are we to believe in respect of the reading habits of Roman upper-class women? Let us return to love poetry and epigram. What arguments do we have that women were among the readers of these genres, and how important were they? As we have seen in the case of the novel, the argument that women played a major role in love poetry does not indicate that its readers were mainly female, nor does the submissive pose of the poet-lover to his beloved (*servitium amoris*),[137] though both elements may have appealed to them. Against such arguments it should be pointed out that appreciation of the Augustan ele-gists required a good literary and some rhetorical education, and that the love poets were mainly concerned with their own (masculine) feelings of love and anger, therefore writing for a mainly male upper-class public.

Yet, we have more evidence for women reading love poetry and epigram than novels. Above I mentioned the frequent references to women as readers of these genres, which deserve consideration. They imply that women were known to read poetry and that writers such as Ovid, Propertius and Martial expected them to prefer their kind of poetry to other works. Indirect evidence points in the same direction: whereas many upper-class women had at least a basic familiarity with reading and interpreting poetry through the teachings of the grammarian, they had none whatsoever with the prose-genres, which were the field of the rhetori-cian.[138] Moreover, epigrams figure prominently among the gifts offered by poets to female patrons, and short personal poetry, chiefly elegiac epigram, was the genre women chose when writing themselves.[139] But there is another indication which should be briefly discussed: in the third book of his *Ars Amatoria* Ovid gives a list of authors with whom, in his view, women should be acquainted. Though the list reflects Ovid's ideal rather than the actual reading-programme of Roman women, it shows what literature Ovid wished sophisticated women to be acquainted with. Like the entire *Ars Amatoria* his reading-list is professedly aimed at freedwomen and courtesans, not at upper-class *matronae*. It is wedged in between an exposition about women making music and one on dancing; together these passages provide a picture of Ovid's view of the accomplishments of an attractive, cultured girl. His reading-list is impressive: in an elaborate way, to be understood by an erudite public only, he alludes to the poetry of Callimachus, Philetas, Anacreon, Sappho, Menander, Propertius, Gallus, Tibullus, the *Argonautica* of Varro of Atax, Virgil's *Aeneid* and, finally, his own poetry (the *Ars Amatoria*, the *Amores* and the *Heroides*).[140]

Two things stand out in this list: all recommended authors are poets, and most of them wrote lyric or elegiac poetry dealing with personal themes, mainly that of love. Apart from this, Ovid's list is also remarkable because of the literary education it presupposes. The authors listed are writers of learned and highly finished poetry which, because of style and literary-mythological allusions, could only be appreciated by a public of good education and sophisticated taste – not to mention the intimate knowledge of Greek needed to read such poets as Sappho or Callimachus. Are we to assume that Ovid's professed female readers, freedwomen and courtesans, had received an education that enabled them to appreciate these poets? Perhaps some, being professional actresses or entertainers, had, and others, being of Greek origin, may have had no difficulty in reading Greek (though Sappho's obsolete Lesbian dialect must have been very difficult also for them). We should, of course, keep in mind that much of this poetry was recited, sung at banquets, or staged in the theatre accompanied by song and dance and that women of various classes might be familiar with it through such media. Yet, we may take it that only a few women from the lower classes actually lived up to Ovid's ideal.[141] Upper-class women stood a far better chance: those who had received a full grammar course must have possessed sufficient knowledge of Greek and of poetic techniques to be able to read and appreciate the works recommended by Ovid. We know from an epigram by Crinagoras that he presented Antonia Minor with the complete works of Anacreon as a birthday-present, and we may guess that, for instance, Sulpicia the elegist (to be discussed in chapter 5) had read several of the works prescribed by Ovid; at least she must have been familiar with Latin elegiac poetry of her days in order to be able to play with poetic conventions in the way she did.[142]

When we compare Ovid's list with the range of authors Quintilian recommends for boys in the grammar and rhetoric phases of their education we find a remarkable contrast: the two lists supplement each other like two halves of a jig-saw puzzle: apart from Virgil, who is approved by both of them, authors recommended by Quintilian are lacking in Ovid's list and *vice versa*. For boys in the grammar phase Quintilian recommends Homer and Virgil, both to be read more than once because of the sublimity of their verses and their lofty theme. Further, tragedy is useful, but lyric poetry should be carefully selected so as to avoid licentious verses; elegy, especially erotic elegy, is to be banned entirely, and comedy (Menander) should be left to an age at which the fear of contaminating the pupil's morals had disappeared. Finally, the old Latin poets are thought valuable.[143] The poetry forbidden or postponed to a more mature age by Quintilian is exactly that recommended by Ovid, *viz.* licentious lyric verses, erotic elegy and Menander. For adult students of oratory Quintilian is less stringent: almost all authors have their value for the future orator. The reading-list he prescribes for students in rhetoric is huge and, starting with Homer, comprises a wide range of authors of Greek and Latin literature, both ancient and contemporary ones: orators, poets, historians and philosophers. However, even in this impressive, but far from realistic, list some authors recommended by Ovid are omitted: apart from epigram, which is not considered a serious genre, the Greek elegiac poets, notably Callimachus and Philetas, are left for a later stage, while the Augustan elegiac poets (Tibullus, Propertius, Ovid and Gallus) are only mentioned in passing and Sappho and Anacreon not at all.[144]

Both Ovid and Quintilian sketch what they regard as the ideal reading-list, Ovid for (professedly lower-class) girls and women, Quintilian for upper-class boys and men. The lists reflect the difference in aims and outlook between Quintilian, who represents the old-fashioned, moralizing part of upper-class society, and the more frivolous Ovid; obviously, they do not represent the actual reading habits of the sexes. Yet, the fact that they are nearly mutually exclusive indicates that distinctions of class and gender were felt to be of importance: women (and perhaps men of the less wealthy classes)[145] reading poetry on love and other personal themes and conservative upper-class men keeping to the respectable and time-honoured authors of the past. Though it cannot be doubted that men formed the main public of both the serious authors and the poets,[146] women were important enough as readers of the latter to be mentioned often. We may speculate that from the late republic onwards the increase in their wealth and education, and the leisure they enjoyed, made upper-class women into a new and interesting public for young, unconventional poets such as Catullus, Tibullus, Propertius and Ovid, who perhaps catered to their (supposed) taste for subjects such as love and other personal themes.

Distinctions according to age and family might modify women's reading habits. The love poets and Martial welcomed women as readers, but in elderly women interest in love and sexuality was thought despicable.[147] As love was considered a privilege of the young, respectable upper-class girls and young matrons were permitted to read love poetry though it conflicted with traditional notions of female chastity, but elderly women had to turn to other genres to avoid being ridiculed. For them a respectable field was moral philosophy. We meet dignified, elderly *matronae*, most of them widows, reading philosophical treatises: upper-class women such as Marcia, Helvia and the empress Livia turned to moral philosophy to cope with the blows of fortune and were applauded for it.[148] For young women, however, the study of philosophy was regarded with suspicion: it was feared that it might lead to arrogance, or that studying philosophy might prevent them from fulfilling their traditional female duties such as the management of their households.[149] Thus, age cut across the division according to gender: whereas a preference for love poetry was accepted in youthful women, philosophy was considered suitable for more mature women.

Beside this distinction there was the influence of the family: women are addressed in literary works written by male relatives, usually their husbands, or are reported to have acted as first critics, and this brought a wider range of literature under their eyes than is usually suggested by our sources: poetry, about other than personal themes, agriculture, speeches, biography and even history. Of course, such works were meant for a wider public, and we cannot always be sure that the women who were addressed actually read them. We may assume that Ovid's wife read his verse-epistles sent to her from exile and that Statius' wife read his poem, addressed to her, about his planned return to his native Naples,[150] but what about Varro's wife Fundania: did she really read the entire *Res Rusticae*, which her husband dedicated to her, and, what is more, the fifty-odd Greek treatises on agriculture he advises her to consult? Though Varro's remarks presuppose that she was able to do so, we may doubt whether she actually did – or even whether he himself had read all the works he prescribes for his wife. Varro claims that he dedicated the work to her because she had bought an estate which she wanted to make profitable by good cultivation, but his work shows signs of being a hasty compilation and he actually dedicated only the first book to her; the other two were addressed to other people.[151]

Apart from having a work dedicated to them, wives are frequently mentioned as the first to hear, and judge, the literary work of their husbands. Though this is usually meant to emphasize the harmony of the marriage, it is not necessarily untrue: as we have seen, wives might be well educated, and so their literary judgement and support may well have mattered to their husbands. Here again, involvement in their husbands' work extended the boundaries of their reading – or rather, hearing; the work was usually read to them by their husbands. In his *ecloga ad uxorem*, in which he praises his wife Claudia as his loyal and life-long comrade, Statius claims that she had been the first to listen to his epos, the *Thebaid*: 'Your wakeful ears caught the first notes of the songs I ventured and whole nights of murmered sound; you alone knew of my long labour and my Thebaid grew with the years of your companionship.'[152] His picture of the harmony of their marriage, in which his wife acted as a sounding-board for his compositions, brings to mind the ideal of the studious couple, which we have met in the section about the husband as a teacher of his wife. Even his wife's daughter participated in this harmonious family life: as Pliny's wife Calpurnia did with her husband's poetry, she put her stepfather's poems to music and sang them.[153]

According to the kind of literary occupation her husband pursued, a woman might read, or hear, poetry, a play or speeches;[154] but she could also play a more active role in her husband's, or father's, work by rescuing it if it was threatened by imperial damnation and thus preserving it for posterity. Marcia, the daughter of

Cremutius Cordus, rescued her father's history of the civil wars when under Tiberius he was prosecuted for treason because of it (he starved himself to death).[155] By decree of the senate copies of his *Annals* were tracked down and publicly burnt. Marcia, however, secretly kept a copy, and as soon as the new emperor, Caligula, gave permission, she had the work republished after cautiously removing the most dangerous passages. The 'expurgated' edition of her father's work survived to the time of Quintilian.[156] Similarly, Fannia tried to keep the memory and ideas of her deceased husband Helvidius Priscus alive by asking one of his partisans to write his biography, and to this end she supplied him with her husband's private notes.[157] When tried and banished by Domitian for her assistance in writing the biography she managed to preserve a copy of it, although the senate had ordered it to be burnt; she took it with her into exile, possibly with an eye to eventual republication.[158] After Domitian's death she returned to Rome, but we hear no more of her husband's biography.

These women reading, or listening to, such uncommon works as an epos, an agricultural treatise, speeches, history or political biography, and those who were involved in rescuing them, show that the literary interests of the family influenced the reading habits of individual women. However, in general, the evidence indicates that women usually read, or were expected to read, personal poetry and perhaps, at a later stage of their lives, some (moral) philosophy. Yet, we should not overestimate their importance as a reading public; the number of upper-class men reading personal poetry and philosophy must always have been far greater. The difference between male and female readers seems rather to consist in the fact that, unlike men, women were largely confined to a narrow range of works – except when the influence of other members of the family widened their reading.

Books and libraries

For education, books and libraries were essential; not only did professional scholars need a good library, but the *poeta doctus* had need of a collection of Greek and Latin texts. So did his educated readers if they were to understand his learned poetry. When relegated to Tomis Ovid sorely felt the want of his library, and Martial, after his return to his native Spain, longed for the libraries of Rome.[159] However, even in Rome good texts were rare and expensive. Many texts were of doubtful quality as the copyists were often forced to work hastily and were apt to make numerous errors in copying. Complaints about the defects of texts and about plagiarism abound in Roman literature.[160] Bookshops were scarce, at least during the republic, and the best way to acquire a good copy was to borrow a text from a friend of the author's, or directly from the author himself, and then to make a copy before returning it. However, such private channels were accessible to few people, mainly members of the educated upper classes.[161]

Women are almost totally ignored both by the ancient sources dealing with books and libraries and by modern studies on ancient book collecting.[162] Yet, as we shall see, they were not wholly absent from this field. In the following, two questions are to be answered: did upper-class women have access to books and libraries, and why are they so rarely mentioned in connection with libraries in the ancient sources?

Private libraries

The first great libraries in Rome came from the Greek East. They were brought to Rome by conquering Roman generals as part of their booty. L. Aemilius Paullus was the first to acquire such a library, that of the Macedonian king Perseus, and, after him, Lucullus and Sulla transported complete libraries from Greece and Pontus. Greek scholars, many of them slaves or freedmen, were engaged to organize these libraries and to classify the books. Others came to study; a good private library attracted scholars, some of whom befriended the owner and lived in his house as a protégé for a considerable time: the possession of a good private library was one of the channels of patronage of literature and learning.[163] Educated upper-class men like Atticus and Cicero collected their libraries by buying books or copying them from friends. Cicero took much trouble over the libraries he had in his house in Rome and in his villas at Tusculum and Antium (and probably in his other villas); in this he was greatly helped by Atticus. From the late republic onwards more and more houses of the wealthy contained collections of books in both Greek and Latin.[164] During the first two centuries AD a library came to be regarded as an essential asset of the household of any high-ranking Roman family. It became a status-symbol for wealthy upstarts who wanted to be accepted among the political élite but were not of aristocratic descent and lacked education. Their 'bibliomania' was ridiculed by Seneca, Juvenal and Lucian who mocked the ignorant owners of these ostentatious libraries.[165]

Although private libraries are frequently mentioned, we have hardly any information on the possession of books or the use of libraries by women. Yet, there is no reason to believe that wealthy women did not own books – Horace's cruel derision of a wealthy elderly lady displaying Stoic booklets between her silk pillows shows us perhaps a glimpse of it[166] – and we may assume that private libraries were used for the education of both sons and daughters. Like men, adult women who wanted to continue their studies depended on the family library, or on their own collection of books. Thus, we may suspect that Cornelia, the mother of the Gracchi, benefited from the great Greek library of her uncle Aemilius Paullus. After his death in 160 BC the library was inherited by his son Scipio Aemilianus, Cornelia's cousin and son-in-law, who may have shared it with his brother, but we cannot tell what happened to it after the sudden death of the childless Scipio Aemilianus in 129 BC. It seems possible that Cornelia acquired (some of) the books, and her patronage of Greek scholars and men of letters in her later years may perhaps be partly due to the presence of a fine library in her villa at Misenum.[167] Other examples point in the same direction:

Varro's wife Fundania must have used her husband's great library if she was actually to read some of the treatises on agriculture he advised her to consult, and we may assume that Pliny's wife Calpurnia did the same for her literary studies.[168] Caecilia Attica, the studious daughter of Cicero's friend Atticus, probably profited from the extensive library of her father, which she may have inherited after his death.[169] Ovid's addressee Perilla is described as regularly absorbed in books (her own?), Antonia Minor seems to have had her own female librarian, and Seneca's widowed mother Helvia must have possessed books in order to take up her philosophical studies during her son's exile.[170]

To acquire libraries women had to borrow and copy books from relatives and friends, just as men did; they preferred to copy from the author himself since the best copies were taken directly from the author's own text. This is recorded of Caerellia, a wealthy old lady, probably a widow, who was on friendly terms with Cicero. Caerellia frequently figures in his letters of the last years of his life: she exchanged letters with him, lent him money and tried to reconcile him, unasked, with his divorced second wife Publilia.[171] Her interest in books is mentioned only incidentally: wanting to get hold of Cicero's philosophical treatise *De Finibus* she had it copied without Cicero's permission from Atticus' copyists (or copies) before it was released to the public, and even before the first copy was presented to its dedicatee, Brutus. As he was still working on it, Cicero was rather annoyed: in a letter he reproached Atticus that he had been careless in keeping track of the copies, but he excused Caerellia because of her 'great love of philosophy'.[172] From her eagerness to be the first to secure a copy of Cicero's new work we may infer that she owned a private collection of books to which she wanted to add new books in a way common to educated persons of her class, by copying directly from the manuscript of the author.

In most cases mentioned so far the possession or use of a private library by upper-class women is implied rather than explicitly stated; explicit confirmation that women used the family library dates from a much later time: it is found in one of the letters of the fifth-century Christian writer Sidonius Apollinaris, who gives an elaborate description of the estate of Tonantius Ferreolus, a relative of his wife's, near Nîmes in southern Gaul. When speaking of the richly equipped library of the villa he tells us that 'the manuscripts near the ladies' seats were of a devotional type, while those among the gentlemen's benches were works distinguished by the grandeur of Latin eloquence'.[173] This does not mean that there was a strict division according to gender between Christian and pagan literature: the next lines of Sidonius' letter show that men read both the more highly literary Christian authors (like Augustine and Prudentius) and pagan authors. Yet, light, morally edifying Christian literature was thought more suitable for women (who were not trained in rhetoric). For reading such devotional works women had their own seats[174] and books in the family library. Though we cannot be certain that this was true also of upper-class Roman women of the pagan era, the examples given above suggest that their presence in private libraries was as much a matter of course as it was for the female relatives of Tonantius Ferreolus.

Public libraries

From the end of the republic onwards public libraries were founded in Rome, probably in imitation of the great libraries of Alexandria and Pergamum. Caesar planned a public library of Greek and Latin authors and commissioned Varro to collect the books for it, but his plans remained unfulfilled. The first public library was created by C. Asinius Pollio in 39 BC in the Atrium Libertatis; it was financed with the spoils from his Illyrian victory.[175] Augustus founded a public library adjacent to the temple of Apollo on the Palatine and his sister Octavia one in the Porticus Octaviae, which she dedicated to the memory of her son Marcellus; both libraries had two departments, a Greek and a Latin one. Other emperors followed: Tiberius, Vespasian, Domitian and Trajan founded or restored public libraries in Rome, and Matidia the Younger, the great-niece of the emperor Trajan, built one in the Campanian municipality Suessa Aurunca.[176]

Though upper-class women could be patronesses of public libraries, founding them or obtaining an appointment in them for a protégé,[177] we do not know if they were in a position to use them. Though, to my knowledge, no law or formal rule prohibited women from entering a public library, we are not told that they ever did. Ancient authors who speak of reading or conversing in public libraries never mention any woman as studying there or taking part in the discussion. Of course, their presence in public libraries may have been ignored by male authors as uninteresting, or women may have used public libraries at special hours only, as they did public baths – though this would probably have been recorded. Yet, the complete silence about women in public libraries is puzzling. Do we have to understand that women were not expected to go there and that they did not noticeably break this rule? Or was their presence regarded as so much a matter of course that it was left unmentioned?

The former assumption seems more plausible. Unlike private libraries public libraries were part of the public domain and served various purposes. Apart from being a repository of books a library served as a record-office. It had an important social function as a centre of studies and as a meeting-place for literary men: discussions and public readings were held in the reading-room or in the *schola*, if present. Sometimes even a meeting of the senate took place in one of the libraries and the emperor could exert an indirect form of censorship through public libraries by removing certain works he disapproved of.[178] These social and political functions suggest that public libraries were regarded as a public domain from which women were mostly excluded – if not by law, then by custom. This seems to be confirmed by Ovid, who, when giving a list of the favourite meeting-places for men and women in Rome, mentions porticoes, temples, public spectacles and even law-courts, but does not mention public libraries, though they often bordered on porticoes and temples. Apparently, they were not a place where the sexes met.[179]

The answer to the question why women collecting books or using libraries are so rarely mentioned is not the same for private libraries and for public ones. As we have seen, upper-class women using the family library or owning books were accepted, and the fact that they are hardly mentioned in our sources is probably due to the feeling that their use of private libraries was a matter of course. Yet, whereas men were often actively engaged in building up a private library, it seems that women mostly depended on its presence in the family home; it is probably no coincidence that those women whom we find collecting or owning books themselves were all widows (Caerellia, Antonia Minor, Helvia). As regards public libraries the lack of evidence for women using them seems to point to their exclusion. Though it cannot be ruled out that the occasional presence of women in public libraries was ignored by male authors, the public function of these libraries makes their presence unlikely.

Conclusions

Though the evidence is scanty and does not permit quantification, some conclusions may be drawn here. In respect of education women were less favoured than men: fewer women than men received an education, and their education was of a shorter duration. Though it seems likely that most, if not all, upper-class girls received an elementary education and quite a few of them also took (part of) the grammar course, the most important stage of Roman education, rhetorical training, was usually denied them. As a consequence, the main formative influence on their adult life differed from that of upper-class men: whereas men were moulded by rhetorical training, educated women were formed by the tuition of a grammarian. In adult life they very seldom progressed beyond this stage; thus, we find adult women reading, and writing, poetry, mostly short personal poetry, more than anything else, with the possible exception of the study of moral philosophy, which was considered suitable for respectable, elderly women to help them cope with the blows of fortune.

From the late republic onwards opportunities for girls to acquire an education increased; in the first centuries AD it spread beyond the upper classes to include girls of well-to-do families of the sub-élite. Some schools were coeducational, both at the elementary and at the grammar stage, but the number of girls receiving an education must at all times have been far lower than that of boys. As regards the scope and level of their education, we should be wary of generalizations. Though illiteracy was probably uncommon among upper-class women, the number of those who received an education in grammar, or in the liberal arts and philosophy, cannot be estimated, nor can we be sure of the level they reached. The most conspicuous trait of women's education seems to have been that it varied so much. As upper-class girls depended on private tuition and as their studies, unlike those of boys of their class, lacked the unity and coherence provided by a common aim, their education depended to a great extent on individual circumstances, such as the period and town they lived in, the class they belonged to, the wealth and inclination of their families, their age at marriage and, of course, their own interests and capacities. Wealth, high rank and interest in learning within a family usually favoured their education, but even for girls who had the best opportunities early marriage must have interrupted their education about halfway through the grammar stage. Thus, to complete it they had to continue their studies beyond their wedding-day.

As regards the opportunities of upper-class women to continue their studies during adult life, various ways were open to them: they might be taught by their husbands, or by private teachers; and they could add to their education by reading books from the family library, by attending cultured dinner parties or by visiting the theatre for a play or a recital of poetry. Of course, not all these possibilities were actually open to all; much depended on personal circumstances such as the inclination of the husband and the presence of teachers and a private library. Also, contemporary fashion may have come into play: for instance, during the principate the popularity of the theme of the husband teaching his wife reflects contemporary ideals of harmony and partnership in marriage and education. As a consequence, the scope and level of the education of upper-class women probably varied widely and the few known examples of highly educated women cannot be taken as representative of upper-class women in general. Rather, we should conclude that this was the level an upper-class woman might reach when the wealth and disposition of her family, and her own inclination, favoured education.

One final remark should be made in respect of the scarcity of the evidence. It has been repeatedly argued in this chapter that we should be cautious in interpreting the relative silence of our sources and not immediately assume that when nothing is said, there was nothing to tell. There may have been other reasons: the education of girls was probably thought of little interest, and the presence of women in private libraries, at learned discussions and perhaps at recitations may have been habitually overlooked. Further, male authors tended to ignore the intellectual accomplishments of girls and women they respected, preferring to stress their traditional female virtues instead. But here we are entering upon ancient value judgements, which are discussed in the next chapter.

3

THE EDUCATION OF
UPPER-CLASS WOMEN
Aims and opinions

In the preceding chapter we saw that the education of upper-class girls lacked a fixed goal. Since they were excluded from a public career, these girls had only one prospect: marriage and motherhood. Yet, though they were expected to be able to spin and weave, their education was not tailored to the domestic tasks of wife and mother. From the late republic onwards upper-class girls, as a rule, received an elementary education and quite a number of them followed (part of) the course in grammar on a level with the boys of their class, during which they were instructed in the same subjects and read the same 'school' authors. In addition to this, some of them were instructed in the liberal arts, especially mathematics and philosophy. What purpose did this education of upper-class girls serve? Why were they – up to a certain level – educated in the same way as boys although they were excluded from a public career? These questions are discussed in the first part of the present chapter, which deals with 'objectives and ideals'.

Though quite a few upper-class girls were taught 'grammar', their education usually stopped short at the study of rhetoric. As a consequence their knowledge of prose and oratory was usually meagre, whereas their familiarity with poetry and – for the more widely educated – with the liberal arts could be considerable. In adult life some upper-class women returned to the subjects which they had been taught during their youth and continued their study of poetry, mathematics or philosophy. Such educated women were not universally admired in Roman society, where opinion on them varied from idealization of the *docta puella* to contempt for the 'intolerable' bluestocking. How are these contradictory feelings to be explained? Is there any development in the judgement made of educated women in Roman society? These questions are dealt with in the second section of this chapter ('Conflicting views').

Objectives and ideals

In the following, four objectives of the education of upper-class women will be surveyed. The first two sub-sections, those on 'moral education' and on 'the ideal of educated motherhood', deal with the ideals of education of women as expressed by the literary sources, mainly the writings of moral philosophers and conservative senators of the imperial period. These sources stress the beneficial effects of education on women's morals and the fulfilment of their traditional role as wives and mothers. After this, in the sub-sections on 'the social role of the upper-class *matrona*' and 'education as a mark of social status', I shall turn to other possible reasons Roman families may have had for educating their daughters. It will be argued that social motives and, more particularly, reasons of social prestige underlie the custom of giving upper-class girls a literary education, and that the ideals of women's education as expressed in the moralizing sources, rather than giving the initial reasons for it, served to defend this education in the face of criticism.

Moral education

The *locus classicus* of the ideals of education of an upper-class girl is a letter of the younger Pliny concerning the death of Minicia Marcella, the younger daughter of his friend Minicius Fundanus, who died at the age of (nearly) 13.[1] She died shortly before her marriage: the wedding-day was fixed, the guests (including Pliny) had been invited and money had been set aside for clothes, pearls and jewels for the wedding – money which was now used for incense, ointment and spices for her funeral. The letter shows us a girl at the close of her pre-marital education. What was her education believed to have given her?

From her age and from the fact that she was taught by *praeceptores* (i.e. teachers in a specialized field) we may infer that she had finished her elementary education and was being taught 'grammar' and the liberal arts, but Pliny does not speak of the content of her education. Instead, he praises her moral qualities: she was amiable and affectionate, she loved her father dearly, and behaved modestly and lovingly towards his friends. She was kind to her nurses and teachers, industrious and intelligent in her studies and restrained while playing.[2] When she was in her last illness, she bore her illness with great patience and courage and even tried to cheer her father and sister (her mother had died before her). Her mental powers remained unbroken till the end. In short, in spite of her youth she possessed the virtues of the Roman *matrona*: modesty, *pietas* and self-restraint – and this made her premature death the more grievous.

The emphasis on moral qualities is found in many ancient texts dealing with education. Moral instruction played an important part in Roman education both of boys and girls: by precepts, by reading and copying elevating lines of poetry, the pupils were taught virtues such as self-control, love and respect for parents, unselfishness, industry, prudence and veracity.[3] In particular, 'adult' qualities were recommended, as appears from the frequent occurrence of the theme of the *puer senex* in laudatory inscriptions. Children, especially those who died prematurely, are praised for their mature intellectual qualities and behaviour.[4] They are portrayed as the persons they would have become, had they lived, and this made their loss the more distressing. In the same vein, Pliny praises Minicia's character and summarizes: 'she already possessed the wisdom of old age and the dignity of a *matrona* without losing her girlish sweetness and the modesty of a virgin'.[5]

Pliny's letter reflects the ideals of education of a girl of an erudite upper-class family of his days. Minicia's father, Fundanus, who himself was devoted to philosophy and the liberal arts, brought his daughters up – he had no sons – in his own image: Pliny praises Minicia as a true copy of her father, not only in outer appearance, but also in manners and character.[6] Both she and her elder sister seem to have received an all-round education comprising not only the grammatical *curriculum* but possibly also philosophy and the mathematical subjects.[7] Fundanus engaged private tutors for them: *paedagogi* for their elementary education and *praeceptores* for their advanced studies; they must have had access to books – probably in their father's library – and they may have been present at the conversations between Fundanus and his learned friends, such as Pliny, whom, as appears from his letter, they knew well.

So broad an education may seem surprising in a girl whose only prospect was marriage and motherhood, but, as we may infer from Pliny's letter, Fundanus hoped to breed high moral virtues in his daughter by educating her: she was to become a dignified *matrona*, a modest and agreeable wife, a prudent mother and a wise grandmother. If we may believe Pliny's letter, this is what Minicia Marcella would have been had she lived, for it showed in her behaviour as a little girl and in her courage, endurance and cheerfulness during her last illness. Minicia's father was not alone in believing that such virtues were to be acquired through study, especially of philosophy. Apart from the fact that his view was shared by his friend, the younger Pliny, similar notions have come down to us of two influential moral philosophers of the time, Fundanus' teacher Musonius Rufus and his friend Plutarch.[8] Their words shed further light on the ideals of education of upper-class girls like Minicia Marcella.

A well-known fragment of a discourse by C. Musonius Rufus, a Stoic philosopher who enjoyed great fame in Rome and who had many distinguished men among his pupils, is called: 'should daughters be educated in roughly the same way as sons?'[9] This treatise, which together with most of the longer fragments of Musonius has been preserved by Stobaeus, was published some time after Musonius' death by one of his pupils, who had taken notes during his lectures.[10] It is composed in the form of a moral *diatribe*, a lecture in answer to a fictitious question put by a listener; in it Musonius argues that boys and girls should receive a similar education. His main point is that, as women are capable of the same virtues as men, both should arrive at these virtues through the same teaching, i.e. philosophy. His argument centres on the four main virtues of the Stoics: *phronēsis* (insight or understanding), which he defines as the ability to distinguish between good and evil; *dikaiosunē* (justice), which is thought to consist of impartiality, the avoidance of greed, a desire to help and an unwillingness to do harm; *sōphrosunē* (self-control and temperance), which is described as the opposite of adultery, gluttony, drunkenness and other related vices, and *andreia* (courage), here described as endurance of toil and hardship, as fearlessness in the face of death and the ability to defend oneself, if necessary.[11] As men and women possess the same natural aptitude for these virtues, they should receive the same education to acquire them: equal virtues require equal training.

Because of this opinion Musonius has been called a 'feminist',[12] but, in fact, he is no advocate of equality of the sexes or of an identical education; he argues only for moral equality between men and women. It does not matter whether men and women differ in knowledge of technical details, provided that they receive the same training as regards the most important thing: virtue.[13] He is against what he regards as useless theoretical knowledge: 'I do not mean to say, that women should possess technical skill and acuteness in argument, which would be rather superfluous, since they will philosophize as women.'[14] The great benefit to be derived from philosophy, in his eyes, is the attainment of moral excellence. Though allowing for circumstances in which male and female duties are interchangeable, he accepts the traditional division of tasks: as each sex has its own tasks for which it is better equipped, men for a life outdoors and a public career and women for a life at home, their schooling in virtue is meant to make men into good citizens and women into good housewives.[15]

Thus, the education of girls served a moral end and would make them into good housewives and mothers. Apparently, Musonius' ideas are not as revolutionary as is sometimes believed. Similarly, in his treatise 'that women too should study philosophy' the purpose of educating women is wholly in keeping with traditional female virtues and in this respect he may even be called conservative.[16] Contradicting habitual objections to women who study philosophy, *viz.* that they talk like sophists, neglect their household in order to discuss philosophical issues and grow arrogant and presumptuous by it, Musonius argues that this study is to make them into good wives, mothers and housekeepers capable of controlling their emotions and showing unselfishness and loving care of husband and children; thus, he reaffirms the traditional female role.[17]

A similar emphasis on the moral purpose of education is found in the work of another friend of Minicius Fundanus, Plutarch. In his essay on 'marital advice', the *Praecepta Coniugalia*, dedicated to the newly wed Pollianus and Eurydice, he instructs husband and wife how to live harmoniously together. In the last paragraph, devoted to the rejection of luxury and extravagance and to the study of philosophy of the couple,[18] Pollianus is advised to be 'guide, philosopher, and teacher' of his young wife. Left to themselves – Plutarch contends – women, especially young women, conceive harmful ideas, which he compares to uterine growths that develop spontaneously. The mind of a woman needs guidance, preferably by her husband's teaching: 'for if they do not receive the seed of good doctrines and share intellectual advancement with their husbands, but are left to themselves, they conceive many untoward ideas and low designs and emotions'.[19] Therefore, Pollianus is advised to choose suitable philosophical doctrines and discuss them with his wife as her mentor. Apart from this, Plutarch encourages

Eurydice to follow the example of virtuous women of the past, such as Cornelia, the mother of the Gracchi, and to adorn herself with their spiritual qualities instead of jewelry and silk.[20]

Plutarch gives several reasons why the study of philosophy (and that of the preliminary, mathematical, subjects) was suitable for women, all of which reaffirm traditional female virtues:

> Studies of this sort, in the first place, divert women from all untoward conduct; for a woman studying geometry will be ashamed to be a dancer, and she will not swallow any beliefs in magic charms while she is under the charm of Plato's or Xenophon's words. And if anybody professes power to pull down the moon from the sky, she will laugh at the ignorance and stupidity of women who believe these things, in as much as she herself is not unschooled in astronomy.
>
> (Plut. *Mor.* 145C; Loeb trans.)[21]

Since women educated in philosophy and the related sciences, geometry and astronomy, were to be free from the vices and superstition commonly associated with women,[22] these studies, in Plutarch's eyes, contributed to the happiness of marriage.

The most detailed description, or rather prescription, of how and with what purpose an upper-class girl should be educated dates from a much later period. In a letter to a high-born Roman lady, Laeta, dealing with the education of her daughter Paula, Jerome instructs Laeta to prepare little Paula for a life in the service of God: apart from learning to read and write both Greek and Latin, Paula was to study the scriptures, to pray and to learn working in wool. Besides, she was to lead a life of chastity and asceticism: she had to abstain from luxurious food and dress, despise pleasure, be deaf to all musical instruments and keep far from the world and all worldly affairs; for a companion she was to be given a girl 'grave and pale, carelessly dressed and inclined to melancholy', and her mother was to be present incessantly to supervise her morals. This severe education, which in our eyes borders on maltreatment, was successful: Paula eventually succeeded her aunt Eustochium as head of the nunnery in Bethlehem.[23] Jerome's letter is comparable to that of Pliny about Minicia Marcella in that it shows a keen interest in the moral effect of a girl's studies, but the Christian context and the explicit aim of Paula's education, a life of asceticism in the service of God, sets her education apart from that of pagan Roman girls of earlier times.

To summarize, we have found that among moral philosophers of the first two centuries AD, such as Musonius Rufus and Plutarch, and their followers among cultured upper-class Roman families, a thorough education for girls was recommended, comprising literature, philosophy and, possibly, some mathematics. This extensive education was not meant to make a girl into a public speaker or a professional philosopher, but served a more conventional aim: to make her a chaste wife, a prudent manager of the household and a good mother, who would guide her children and grandchildren by her example. Moreover, the study of philosophy fortified her against the blows of fortune and taught her courage in the face of death.

Musonius Rufus and Plutarch were not the only or, for that matter, the earliest, philosophers to express such views on the education of girls and women.[24] Seneca's advice to his mother Helvia for the education of her granddaughter Novatilla, who had recently lost her own mother, is couched in similar moral terms:

> Now is the time to form her character, now is the time to shape it; instruction that is stamped upon the malleable years leaves a deeper mark. Let her become accustomed to your conversation, let her be moulded to your pleasure; you will give her much even if you give her nothing but your example.
>
> (Sen. *Cons. Helv.* 18.8; Loeb trans., modified)[25]

In his view, the undisciplined nature of women could be countered only by (philosophical) education:

> What does it matter [. . .] how many lackeys she has for her litter, how heavily weighted her ears, how roomy her sedan? She is just the same unthinking creature – wild and unrestrained in her passions – unless she has gained knowledge and much erudition.
>
> (Sen. *Const. Sap.* 14.1; Loeb trans., modified)[26]

Such remarks confirm that, in the eyes of philosophers and moralists of the first two centuries AD, the education of women was to serve a conventional moral end.

The ideal of educated motherhood

The second ideal of women's education expressed in the ancient sources should be discussed in connection with a well-known woman whom we have met several times before: Cornelia, the mother of the Gracchi. She is not only the earliest highly educated woman we know of, but because of the virtues attributed to her and because of the exemplary education of her sons, she was also held up as a model to upper-class women of later generations. Though controversial in her own time, because of the political activities of her sons and her own interference in politics,[27] she was more and more idealized from the late republic onwards; she was represented as a model of traditional Roman virtues: a loving wife and an *univira*, who, though widowed comparatively early, remained faithful to the memory of her late husband,[28] a mother devoted to her twelve children, simple and unassuming in spite of her immense wealth, and a dignified and self-controlled widow.[29] Modern studies have taken an interest in her exemplary role as Roman *matrona* and her political prominence;[30] less attention has been paid to her education and her role as a patroness. Yet, as we shall see, it is her excellent education which, together with her idealized role as the model of Roman motherhood, left an indelible mark on Roman women of later generations.

Cornelia was the younger daughter[31] of P. Cornelius Scipio Africanus Maior, the famous conqueror of Hannibal and one of the most wealthy and powerful men of his time. He was among the first Roman nobles to show a keen interest in Greek culture.[32] Her mother Aemilia sprang from the distinguished family of the Aemilii Paulli. Aemilia was known mainly for her wealth and her ostentatious display of it, but her brother, Cornelia's uncle L. Aemilius Paullus Macedonicus, the victor at Pydna, was noted for his philhellenism. As far as we know, he was the first Roman to ship a complete library from Greece, which he used for the education of his sons, but it seems likely that other relatives also profited by this rich collection.[33] His son Scipio Aemilianus, who was Cornelia's cousin – and later became her nephew by adoption and her son-in-law (because of his marriage to her daughter Sempronia) – was renowned not only for his interest in Greek literature and philosophy, but also for his close friendship with the historian Polybius and for a (perhaps unhistoric) patronage of writers and philosophers such as Terence, Lucilius and Panaetius.[34] Her elder brother P. Cornelius Scipio – the adoptive father of her cousin Scipio Aemilianus – was also a man of considerable learning and eloquence and is said to have written a historical work in Greek.[35]

In view of the philhellenism and learning of the male members of her family and the presence of a large Greek library, education must have been easy to come by in her home. As a grown-up Cornelia seems to have spoken Greek fluently; she chose Greek tutors for her sons, closely supervised their education in Greek literature and, in her later years, received Greek scholars in her villa in Misenum. Moreover, she was noted for the purity of her diction and her good style of writing in Latin. As far as we know, she was the first Roman woman who was knowledgeable in Greek and Latin literature and learning, and who patronized Greek scholars in her later years.[36]

Cornelia's thorough education did not hinder her from carrying out her traditional female tasks: marriage and motherhood. Somewhere around 175 BC she married Tiberius Sempronius Gracchus, who was many years her senior.[37] They had twelve children, most of whom probably died at an early age. We know next to nothing of their married life, which lasted till Gracchus' death around 154 BC. Consequently, we do not know if Cornelia continued studying during her marriage. In fact, she came to the fore only as a widow. In the ancient sources she is praised as the exemplary widow, who chose not to remarry but dedicated her life to the memory of her husband and the education of her children.[38] Three of her children grew up to maturity: her daughter Sempronia, whose education was almost completed at the time of her father's death and who married soon after,[39] and her two famous sons, Tiberius and Gaius, the one 9 years old at the time, the other a baby or about to be born.

It is in her role of a widow who brought up her sons without any noticeable intervention of a *tutor*[40] that her intellectual qualities become notable. The education she gave her sons was highly idealized by the authors of late republican and imperial times; she was portrayed as bringing her sons up 'at her breast' and 'on her lap' in the old traditional way instead of leaving them to the care of attendants.[41] But she not only gave them her loving care, but also formed their minds by her excellent style of speaking and writing: 'we have read the letters of Cornelia, mother of the Gracchi; they make it plain that her sons were nursed not less by their mother's speech than at her breast'.[42] Because of her good education she was able to choose the best Greek teachers for her sons:

> Gracchus, thanks to the affectionate pains of his mother Cornelia, had been trained from boyhood and was thoroughly grounded in Greek letters. He had always enjoyed the instruction of Greek teachers carefully chosen, among whom, when he was still in his early manhood, Diophanes of Mytilene, who was considered to be the ablest speaker of Greece in those days.
>
> (Cic. *Brut.* 104; Loeb trans., modified)[43]

Her decisive influence on the eloquence of her sons was generally admired, and when Roman authors needed an example of a well-educated woman who contributed much to the eloquence of her sons, Cornelia usually came to mind first.[44]

In the idealized portrait of Cornelia in the later sources her excellent education was subordinated to her dedication as a mother. This idealization was not restricted to the literary sources; it also appeared in the bronze statue which was erected in her honour in the Augustan age (now lost). The elder Pliny saw the statue himself:

> there is the statue of Cornelia the mother of the Gracchi and daughter of the elder Scipio Africanus. It represents her in a sitting position and is remarkable because of the strapless sandals; it stood in the public colonnade of Metellus, but is now in Octavia's buildings.
>
> (Plin. *NH* 34.31; Loeb trans., modified)[45]

The question when this statue was erected has been much debated; because of Pliny's remark that it originally stood in the Porticus Metelli, it has been suggested that it dated from the end of the second century BC. However, the existence of such a statue before the Augustan period does not seem likely, since life-size honorific statues of women erected in a public place are not attested in Rome at so early a date.[46] The only thing we know for certain is that it was placed in the Porticus Octaviae, built by Augustus in honour of his sister Octavia on the site of what was once the Porticus Metelli some time after 27 BC, and that Pliny saw it there. By an exceptional stroke of luck its marble base was found *in situ* in the Porticus Octaviae in 1878. It bears an inscription of Augustan date reading 'Cornelia Africani f. / Gracchorum'. In this surprisingly concise inscription

Cornelia is identified as the daughter and mother of famous men, but the fact that such a concise inscription was understood bears witness to her own fame in the Augustan age.[47] The unusual dedication of a honorary statue to a noble-woman of the middle republic erected in a public building that was dedicated to Octavia probably served some propagandistic aim. It may be compared to Augustus' erection of statues of the great Roman leaders of the past in the colonnades of his own forum which reflected his political principles and served as examples for himself and for future rulers. Thus, a statue of a great lady of the past placed in the portico of his sister must have been meant as an example for the female aristocracy.[48] The Porticus Octaviae was an appropriate place since Octavia also was held in high esteem because of her exemplary motherhood: not only was she the mother of Augustus' intended successor Marcellus and of four other children by her husbands Marcellus and Antonius, but she also dutifully brought up the children of Antonius' former marriages, thus rearing at least ten children all told.[49] Cornelia's fecundity and the exemplary virtues ascribed to her had made her into a symbol that Augustus could use for his moral reform: she became a model for the aristocratic women of his days.[50] In this connection Pliny's remark about her sandals (*soleae*) is telling: sandals were worn mostly at home and strapless ones probably indicated domesticity and simplicity.[51]

The nature of the evidence makes it impossible to discover the historical Cornelia: the Cornelia we know is to a high degree a creation of later times. In the idealizing sources of a later period (both literary and in art) she is no longer the controversial person she had been in her own days when the policy of her sons provoked not only applause but also great hostility: now she had become exemplary, almost legendary. Her prominent political role and her almost regal style of living in her villa in Misenum[52] were all but ignored, but her excellent education was highly admired – though mainly because it was believed to have furthered the education of her sons. It seems unlikely that she had been given such an education for this purpose only; rather, in the later sources her devotion as a mother served as a justification of her extraordinary education. Yet, in the course of time cause and effect may have been reversed and girls may have been given a good education in view of the favourable effect this was believed to have on their children.[53] Thus, the idealization of Cornelia and the role her education played in it influenced the appreciation of the education of upper-class women in later days.

The ideal of well-educated motherhood as personified in Cornelia was emulated by Augustus' sister Octavia and her daughter Antonia Minor. Like Cornelia both were high-born, wealthy and well-educated widows who carefully reared a great number of children – not only their own but also those of relatives and of foreign royal families – and the praise of their virtues and maternal devotion masked their less conventional activities in politics and patronage.[54] These idealized imperial women were themselves regarded as models for the aristocratic women of their time and thus, by following the example of Cornelia, they kept it alive.

Directly or indirectly, 'Cornelia' served as a model for quite a few upper-class women, most of them widows, who were praised in similar terms for the devotion to and education of their distinguished sons. These idealized portraits do not necessarily reflect reality. However, the standard of behaviour they exemplify is significant of Roman ideals of motherhood and as such it may have influenced daily life.

As has been pointed out by Dixon,[55] Roman upper-class women were not the loving and tender mothers appreciated in our own time; on the contrary, their task was a disciplinary one: they were supposed to supervise the moral and intellectual education of their children and grandchildren and to interfere whenever undesirable interests or inclinations arose. Apart from this, 'exemplary' mothers were praised for handling personally the domestic and menial tasks involved in taking care of them – instead of employing slaves or hired servants as nurses and attendants, which was the custom among the wealthy from the late republic onwards. In his *Dialogus de Oratoribus* Tacitus idealizes the role of mothers in ancient Rome:

> In the good old days, every man's son, born in wedlock, was brought up not in the chamber of some hireling nurse, but in his mother's lap, and at her knee. And that mother could have no higher praise than that she managed the house and gave herself to her children. Again, some elderly relative would be selected in order that to her as a person who had been tried and never found wanting, might be entrusted the care of all the youthful scions of the same house; in her presence no base word could be uttered without grave offence, and no wrong deed done. Religiously and with the utmost delicacy she regulated not only the serious tasks of her youthful charges, but also their recreations and their games. It was in this spirit, we are told, that Cornelia, the mother of the Gracchi, directed their upbringing, Aurelia that of Caesar, Atia of Augustus: thus it was that these mothers trained their princely children.
>
> (Tac. *Dial.* 28; Loeb trans.)[56]

Again, Cornelia serves as the model of motherhood, but Tacitus attributes a similar devotion and strictness to Caesar's mother Aurelia and Augustus' mother Atia, both widows with young children. In the *Agricola* he praises the widowed mother of Julius Agricola (Tacitus' father-in-law) for the education of her son.[57] She curbed a passion for philosophy in her son because too profound an interest in philosophy was considered incompatible with the dignity of a senator:

> His mother was Julia Procilla, a woman of rare virtue. He was educated under her loving care: his boyhood and youth he passed in the pursuit of all liberal accomplishments; [. . .] I remember how he used himself to tell that in early life he was inclined to drink more deeply of philosophy

than is permitted to a Roman senator, had not his mother's discretion imposed a check upon his enkindled and glowing spirit.

(Tac. *Agr.* 4.2–3; Loeb trans., modified)[58]

In this interference with her son's studies Julia Procilla was no exception: other (mostly widowed) mothers too were praised for keeping their sons from an undesirable intellectual pursuit, such as a passion for philosophy, which was considered a hindrance to an active political life, or a wish to write about a dangerous subject in history. Thus, Agrippina Minor was said to have checked Nero's ardour for philosophy and Domitia Lucilla, the mother of the future emperor Marcus Aurelius, stopped her son from sleeping on the ground like a philosopher. Similarly, the future emperor Claudius was dissuaded from writing a history of the civil wars by the critical remarks of his mother Antonia and his grandmother Livia.[59]

It has recently been doubted that women needed to be well-educated in order to be able to supervise the education of their sons. This doubt seems unjustified:[60] not only because most of the women mentioned above had received a good education, but also because the importance of the mother's education is explicitly acknowledged by both Cicero and Quintilian in connection with the training of future orators. Cicero mentions the mother among those who by their speech shape the proficiency of the young boy as a speaker, and Quintilian stresses the importance of a thorough education of both parents for the oratorical training of their sons; moreover, widely different persons like Vitruvius and Martial profess to owe their education to both their parents.[61] Since the choice of teachers was normally the task of the father, the education of the mother and her ability to choose good teachers for her son(s) came to the fore only when she had become a widow; thus, it seems no coincidence that most of our examples are widows with young children. The praise of upper-class widows who, after the loss of their husbands, successfully educated their sons and supervised their studies by themselves reveals both the advantages of 'educated motherhood' and the vulnerability of (upper-class) family life: once the father had died, the education of the son, so important for his future career, depended on the mother's education, which, as we have seen, varied greatly.[62]

Though well-educated mothers can be attested from the days of Cornelia onwards, the ideal of educated motherhood does not appear until the late republic. This seems to be in keeping with the development of the time which showed an increasing number of educated women, a greater *de facto* independence of married women in financial matters and greater responsibilities for the welfare of their children.[63] Obviously, the ideal reaffirmed traditional female virtues. However, the women who are praised in our sources for their devotion as mothers were not those who quietly and submissively dedicated themselves exclusively to the care of their children: such women usually remain unnoticed. On the contrary, they were publicly prominent because of their distinguished sons and because their own activities were not confined to their maternal duties. Thus, as we shall see again and again, the virtues women were praised for were not necessarily the actual or only reason for their praise, and a reputation for dedicated motherhood formed a mask for well-educated and socially eminent women.[64]

The two ideals of education of upper-class women discussed so far can only partially account for the literary education given to upper-class girls. In the first place, they are found only in a small group of upper-class men with philosophical interests and in moral philosophers, such as the younger Pliny, Musonius Rufus and Plutarch, and some conservative senators – who, however, because of their social eminence, may have influenced greater groups of society. Second, and more importantly, these ideals were expressed at a time when the education of girls and women was already fairly widespread among the upper classes. To my knowledge, outspoken approval of women's education on moral grounds is not found in Roman society until the first century AD. This may be due to the uneven preservation of the sources, but, as it agrees with contemporary matrimonial ideals, it seems more likely that it reflects a change in view as regards male–female relationships in the early principate.[65] If so, it can have had no bearing on the motives of Romans of earlier times to educate their daughters. It does not explain, for instance, why Scipio educated Cornelia the way he did, or Cicero Tullia, Pompcius Pompeia or Augustus Julia. Moreover, the emphasis both Musonius and Plutarch put on the traditional female virtues to be derived from the study of philosophy suggests that they were on the defensive against opponents of female education. We have seen that Musonius rejects suggestions that women studying philosophy become arrogant and that they abandon their domestic tasks for philosophical discussions with men. Plutarch stresses the importance of philosophy as a safeguard against immodest behaviour and other 'female' vices such as credulity and lack of self-control. By emphasizing the traditional female virtues to be derived from studying, they contradicted the supposed bad effects of the education of girls. Thus, rather than revealing the initial purpose of the education of women, these texts served to defend the custom of educating one's daughters against criticism by stressing its beneficial effects on women's morals.

The same holds for the ideal of educated motherhood, which follows on, rather than precedes, the custom of educating upper-class girls. To make it respected, virtuous and well-educated women of the past were cited as examples, women who, because of their noble lineage and the fact that they had lived in the good old days, could easily be idealized: the great education of Cornelia is justified in later days by her dedication as a mother and her excellent education of her sons. Thus, we are not to conclude that the acquisition of virtue and the ideal of educated motherhood were the original, or the actual, reasons for the education of girls – though, of course, such justifications may have influenced public opinion and thus, eventually, they may have furthered the opportunities for girls to get an education. Rather, they seem to be secondary motives, formulated at a time when the education of upper-class girls was common enough to attract the attention of the literary sources and defining the rules or conditions under which such an education was to be approved of. Not surprisingly, both ideals reaffirm traditional female virtues.

If the ideals of female education as expressed in the literary sources served to justify an established practice and to circumscribe the conditions under which this was to be accepted, they do not help us in answering our initial question why upper-class girls were educated in the first place – up to a certain level – in the same way as boys of their class though they were denied a public career. We may guess that upper-class families had various motives for educating their daughters, such as family prestige, a genuine interest in learning, the wish to educate all their children according to their own ideals (not only the boys) and to prepare their daughters for the social and semi-public role of the upper-class *matrona*, or a desire to give them a useful occupation during the years before marriage; or perhaps sometimes the reason was a marked intelligence and a strong literary interest on the part of the girl. Such reasons are usually not mentioned in our sources and must have depended on individual circumstances. Two reasons allow closer inspection: the social role of the upper-class *matrona* and education as a mark of high social status. It will be argued that social reasons such as these account for much of the education of upper-class girls.

The social role of the upper-class matrona

As we saw in chapter 1, upper-class women were fully integrated in the social life of the family; they received guests and accompanied their husbands to dinner parties, and other social events, as a matter of course. Apart from this, they ran large households and, when *sui iuris*, they administered their own property, and sometimes looked after that of their male relatives when these were abroad – all this without noticeable intervention by a guardian. Though it was perhaps not absolutely vital to be able to read and write for these tasks – in theory, this could be left to literate servants, the secretaries and readers who usually formed part of a wealthy household – literacy must have been extremely useful. This holds even more for the political support a woman of the leading classes was expected to give to her husband (and sometimes to other male relatives): during his absence abroad she had to maintain his political connections, support his cause in the case of exile, and inform him by letter of what happened in Rome and should be known to him.[66]

For these reasons an elementary education for upper-class girls was highly advisable. Knowledge of Greek and Latin literature was, of course, not required for administering property or running a household, but had its importance for social reasons. In entertaining guests, visiting friends, attending dinner parties or the theatre, in short in participating in social life and maintaining the social, and political, relations between upper-class families, women preferably had to be conversant in the literary culture of their days, which was so important for the life and social status of their husbands. Though this did not require great learning, a general literary education must have eased their social contacts with the men of their class. The reason for their education should, therefore, partly be sought in the social role of the upper-class *matrona* which required basic literacy, and preferably some knowledge of literature as well. Girls like Minicia Marcella (see pp. 60ff.) were brought up to stand their ground in the complicated and sophisticated social life of the capital. This brings us to the last motive for educating girls to be discussed here: social prestige.

Education as a mark of social status

As we have seen, already in the second century BC some women of the most distinguished families were highly educated. In fact, the education of upper-class girls seems to have started as soon as ideals of a general education (*enkuklios paideia*) were introduced in Rome by Greek scholars. During the republic well-educated women were exceptional, and, as far as we know, they were at first found only in the most distinguished senatorial families: in those days education was the privilege of the highest circles, since it required wealth, leisure, the employment of private teachers and the possession of books. We may assume that the thorough bilingual education of Cornelia, the mother of the Gracchi – or, for that matter, that of Laelia, the daughter of C. Laelius[67] – was due to the wealth and learning in her family, in which a great family pride may have over-ruled the usual restrictions imposed upon her sex; in other words, members of her family, whatever their sex, were expected to be well educated, because this was considered of importance for the family. Since the literary education of a daughter did not serve a clear practical purpose, it may have increased the prestige of the family even more, since to spend time and money on something so unproductive as the education of a daughter was definitive proof of wealth and cultural eminence; in Rome, as elsewhere, wealth and high social status 'are displayed in the superfluities rather than in the necessities of life'.[68]

From the beginning the women of leading senatorial families and, during the empire, those of the imperial house had the best opportunities for education.[69] Because of their prominence and high social status they served as a model for other women. With the peace and prosperity of the principate and the increase in educational facilities a literary education came within reach of a wider range of people – not only those from the upper classes, but also those from well-to-do families of the sub-élite; it became an object of pride among those who could afford it. For upper-class women it was regarded as a mark of their rank – Martial mocks the ideal (but in his opinion unbearable) wife as being 'rich, noble, erudite and chaste'[70] – but it also spread downwards, since persons lower down the social scale copied the life-style of the élite. Inscriptions praising the intellectual accomplishments of girls and women of various social standing, representations of girls of unknown status receiving reading- and writing-lessons and of women reading or holding book-rolls on funerary reliefs indicate that a well-educated daughter or wife was felt to lend distinction to her family and that pride in the education of girls and women was not restricted to the upper classes.[71]

This must also be the meaning of the well-known Pompeian paintings of young women holding a pen and writing-tablets, though they have sometimes been explained in quite a different way. The two most famous portraits of this kind are: a thoughtful young woman holding a pen (stylus) to her lips as if pondering what to write on her writing-tablets (a four-tablet codex), and the double portrait of a man and woman, the latter holding a pen to her lips and her writing-tablets (a diptych) opened, as it seems, towards the onlooker, while the man holds a closed papyrus roll (plates 2 and 3). The former picture has been misinterpreted as a portrait of Sappho or some other, unidentified poetess, and the second as a wedding picture in which the husband holds the marriage-contract and his wife is calculating her household expenses.[72] In this romantic interpretation, now generally abandoned, it was not taken into account that both women are portrayed in the same pose and that in its original setting the so-called Sappho was probably also balanced by a portrait of a young man holding a papyrus roll; thus, like the portrait of the couple, 'Sappho' and its supposed companion piece represented contemporary Pompeians.[73]

Also the assumption that the portrait of the couple was a wedding picture is untenable.[74] Though it is clear that the man and woman are a married couple, the roll and the writing utensils are not necessarily connected with their marriage. Papyrus rolls were used for many purposes, not only for marriage-contracts and other legal documents but also for letters and literature. Moreover, the roll carries a little red label or *titulus*. Such *tituli* were regularly attached to literary and scientific works in both private and public libraries and indicated their contents. Unfortunately, nothing is written on this *titulus*, but on two other Pompeian paintings of young men holding book-rolls the labels indicate works of Homer and Plato, thus referring to the erudition of the portrayed.[75] Further, writing-tablets were used for all kinds of purposes: not only for legal and financial documents, but also, and more commonly, for letters, drafts of poetry, school-exercises, rough notes and other casual purposes; therefore, they are not to be connected with the woman's marriage. Rather, they symbolize her literacy, and since a diptych and a book-roll are also attributes of the Muses Calliope and Clio, they indicate the literary interests of the couple: by holding a book-roll and writing-tablets both man and woman show that they were knowledgeable in the literary culture of the upper classes.[76]

Most portraits of this type were found in atriums of Pompeian houses or in the adjoining rooms such as an *exedra* opening off the atrium or a *triclinium*, i.e. in reception areas which were decorated so as to reflect (and enhance) the social status of their owners. The women are usually finely dressed and wear gold ornaments or pearls in their hair and ears suggesting wealth and refinement; but judging from the size of some of the houses in which the portraits were found, they probably did not belong to the élite.[77] Their dress, jewelry and elegance

Plate 2 Portrait of a young Pompeian woman holding a pen and writing-tablets (Naples, National Museum: inv. no. 9084). Photo courtesy of the German Archaeological Institute in Rome.

Plate 3 Portrait of a Pompeian couple: the man holds a papyrus roll and the woman a pen and writing-tablets (Naples, National Museum: inv. no. 9058). Photo courtesy of the Soprintendenza Archeologica di Napoli.

show that the pictures are (idealized) representations of young Roman women of some standing, probably the mistresses of the house, who wanted to be portrayed not only as young and prosperous, but also as well educated by means of their pencil and writing-tablets. This is more interesting if they are what they seem: well-to-do Pompeians belonging to the sub-élite. It would show their assimilation to the values and literary culture of the upper classes and the emphasis on education as a mark of status among those who lacked high birth.[78]

By emphasizing their prosperity and education these women imitated the women of the highest circles of Roman society. As appears from the elegance of their dress and youthful beauty they did not model themselves upon the elderly, well-educated upper-class women of earlier days, such as Cornelia, the mother of the Gracchi; rather they seem to have imitated contemporary young aristocratic women such as Augustus' daughter Julia or Nero's wife Poppaea: young, beautiful and wealthy women of noble birth, whose excellent education reflected their high social status. Yet, as we shall see,[79] the moral reputation of these high-ranking and well-educated women was doubtful and an excellent education was not wholeheartedly appreciated for women in Roman society: though marking a high social status, it aroused not only praise. This brings us to the second part of this chapter.

Conflicting views

When reading the remarks of ancient authors about educated women one is struck by their ambiguity: in Roman society the education of women was the object of both admiration and criticism. These differing opinions cannot simply be explained by attributing them to different periods or to different groups of persons: conflicting views coexisted in one and the same period and sometimes even in one and the same person. Though a sign of wealth and high social status, and emulated for that reason by women of less elevated birth, education was not an infallible source of prestige for upper-class women, as it was for the men of their class. Throughout our period it was a matter of controversy. In the following, various aspects of this ambivalence are examined, first without considerations of chronology; after this I shall tentatively sketch a possible development in the opinion on educated women in a brief chronological survey.

The education of women and traditional morality

The Romans idealized past ages, when – it was said – men and women of all classes lived a simple and frugal life, loyal to their country and families and carrying out their distinct tasks: the men farmed their own land, defended their country and fathered families, the women bore legal children, kept house and took care of their families. In spite of the rapid changes in the society of the late republic and, with it, in the life-style of the élite, these ideals kept a powerful hold on the minds of the Romans.[80] Therefore, the influence of Greek culture and the steadily increasing sophistication of the élite, though it led to a high regard for literature and education among the upper classes, provoked mixed feelings among the more conservative Romans of the republic,[81] especially as regards the women of their class. As we shall see, educated women were felt to break with traditional ideals in two respects: their sophisticated way of life and their Hellenized education formed a sharp contrast with the simple life of women in the idealized past, and by their learning they usurped a male privilege, thus transgressing the limits of the traditional role of the Roman *matrona*. Both these forms of transgression are criticized in the ancient sources. Thus, Roman response to educated women was at least partly shaped by the idealization of the past.

During the late republic and the early principate traditionalists among the élite seem to have kept to the old Roman principles as regards female education, which stressed domestic duties (symbolized by spinning and weaving); they were disinclined openly to accept the 'modern' fashion of educating girls in Greek and Latin literature, though in the privacy of their homes they may have followed it. Cicero, for instance, does not speak in his letters about the education of his beloved daughter Tullia, though he shows a keen interest in the education and intellectual progress of his son Marcus and his nephew Quintus.[82] Yet, he mentions Tullia's resemblance to himself both in appearance and in speech and mind, a compliment which refers to her intelligence and education.[83] It seems that as a topic of correspondence he regarded Tullia's education as uninteresting, or inappropriate, though he may have bestowed much care on it privately. Cicero's reticence about the education of his female relatives and acquaintances may be explained by his compliance with traditional upper-class *mores* as regards the proper place of women. As a 'new man' in the Roman senate he had to conform to the traditional rules much more strictly than members of the old senatorial families: having to compete with the highest circles he could not afford to deviate from social conventions, as members of the old great houses might do.

Cicero's reticence may seem at variance with his outspoken approval of the thoroughly educated women of the past such as Cornelia, the mother of the Gracchi, and Laelia; speaking of the oratorical talent running in the family of the latter, he writes:

> It was my good fortune more than once to hear Laelia, the daughter of Gaius, speak, and it was apparent that her careful usage was coloured by her father's elegance of speaking, and the same was true of her two daughters Muciae, with both of whom I have talked, and of her granddaughters the Liciniae, both of whom I have heard; one, the wife of Scipio, I imagine that you too, Brutus, have sometimes heard speak. 'Yes', said Brutus, 'and with great pleasure; the more so because she was the daughter of Lucius Crassus.'
>
> (Cic. *Brut.* 211; Loeb trans., modified)[84]

Thus, we see that Cicero appreciated the education and the purity of diction of

Laelia, that of her daughters and granddaughters, all of whom he had known personally, and he greatly admired the rhetorical talent and juridical expertise of their fathers, C. Laelius, Q. Mucius Scaevola and L. Licinius Crassus. In fact, by praising the women he indirectly honoured these men. In particular Laelia's manner of expressing herself was of interest to Cicero, as, according to him, it reproduced that of her famous father who had died before Cicero's days:

> For my own part [the speaker is the orator L. Licinius Crassus] when I hear my wife's mother Laelia – since it is easier for women to keep the old pronunciation unspoiled, as they do not converse with great numbers of people and so always retain the accents they heard first – well, I listen to her with the feeling that I am listening to Plautus or Naevius: the actual sound of her voice is so unaffected and natural that she seems to introduce no trace of display or affectation; and I consequently infer that that was how her father and her ancestors used to speak – not harshly, like the person I mentioned, nor with a broad or countrified or jerky pronunciation, but neatly and evenly and smoothly.
>
> (Cic. *De Or.* 3.45; Loeb trans.)[85]

These women are praised by Cicero as transmitters of the speech of their fathers and as moulding that of their children; their education is presented in terms of their traditional female role. Moreover, since they were members of Rome's leading senatorial families and themselves of unblemished reputation (Laelia's retired way of life showing itself in her old-fashioned accent), their education was beyond criticism. Cicero's praise of these women of the past shows that his approval of the education of women was conditional and, therefore, there is no real contrast with his reticence about the education of the women of his own family. Similarly, Augustus was prompted by tradition when he insisted that his daughter and granddaughters should learn to spin and weave – but, as we have seen (chapter 2, pp. 22f.), he gave them a good literary education privately.

There are also cases in which old-fashioned ideas about the education of women can be shown to have actually hampered their studies; for instance, those of Seneca's mother Helvia.[86] The opposition of her husband had thwarted her interest in philosophy and as a consequence her knowledge of it had remained superficial, much to the regret of her son, who considers his father to have been overmuch 'given to ancestral convention' in this respect. The reason of the elder Seneca for checking his wife's studies was the usual prejudice against educated women in imperial Rome: in the words of the younger Seneca, his father 'did not suffer you to pursue your studies because of those women who do not employ learning as a means to wisdom, but equip themselves with it for the purpose of display'.[87]

In their judgement of the education of women, upper-class men like Cicero and the elder Seneca were highly ambivalent: though they valued education in itself, they feared the negative effect it might have on women. Education of

77

women was, as we have seen, appreciated only when it served their traditional female role; in itself it was not considered a reason to praise a woman. Thus, when a traditional-minded author praises a woman's erudition, he usually takes care to mention it as part of, or in the service of, the conventional female virtues. As we have seen, well-educated girls and women are praised first and foremost as modest daughters (such as Minicia Marcella), devoted mothers (such as Cornelia, the mother of the Gracchi), and virtuous wives (such as Pliny's wife Calpurnia). This betrays a certain uneasiness in the way the education of women was regarded in Roman society.

A striking example of this ambivalence is provided by Plutarch. In his portrait of Cornelia, the daughter of Q. Metellus Scipio and the fifth wife of Pompey the Great, he writes about her education:

> The young woman had many charms apart from her youthful beauty. She was well versed in literature, in playing the lyre, and in geometry, and had been accustomed to listen to philosophical discourses with profit. In addition to this, she had a nature which was free from that unpleasant meddlesomeness which such accomplishments are apt to impart to young women.
>
> (Plut. *Pomp.* 55)[88]

Cornelia's circumstances had favoured her education: not only did she stem from a highly aristocratic family with a marked tradition of learning, but her family was also noted for the education of its women at a time when this was still rare in Rome: her father's mother Licinia, his grandmother Mucia and his great-grandmother Laelia were praised for the purity of their Latin (see above pp. 76f.). Her own extensive education comprised literature, geometry, music and philosophy.[89] As she married young (when marrying Pompey she was already widowed by the death of her first husband P. Licinius Crassus, son of the triumvir), she must have continued her studies during marriage, when she probably also attended the lectures of philosophers.

Yet, unlike certain other young women who had received a similar extensive education, she had not been made insufferable by her studies – an unexpected observation for Plutarch, who propagated the education of women in an essay on 'marital advice' discussed in the first part of this chapter. Here, Plutarch's contradictory feelings as regards the education of women come to the fore; though, on the one hand, he defends the education of women in his *Praecepta Coniugalia* because of its beneficial effect on their morals, on the other, he is anxious to show that Cornelia was not affected by the bad effects such an extensive education was generally supposed to have on young women. She is described as a faithful and loving wife and a mournful young widow, who lost her two successive husbands in war and who, though innocent of their defeat and death, reproached herself for their ill fortune.[90] Thus she is made to meet traditional standards.

Roman traditionalists resemble the moral philosophers discussed in the first part of this chapter in putting traditional female virtues first. But whereas moral philosophers such as Plutarch and Musonius Rufus publicly defended the education of women because this was to teach them modesty, industry and self-restraint, while keeping superstition and other allegedly female vices in check, traditionalists mostly kept silent about the education of women they respected – unless it was excused by their descent (as daughters of famous fathers) or by their role as educators of their sons.

The 'docta puella': a counter-ideal

In stark contrast with these old-fashioned views held by conservative upper-class men and with the moral teaching of the philosophers are the wholly unconventional ideas of the Roman love poets of the late republic and the Augustan age. Catullus, Tibullus, Propertius, Ovid and others express opinions about women, female behaviour and male–female relationships which in many respects are a reversal of the traditional values: in their poetry the (probably fictional) beloved is the domineering party and her poet-lover the humble servant who puts his love-affair above the traditional Roman pursuit of a military or political career.[91] Part of this role-reversal and the unconventional attitude towards women found expression in the poets' admiration of the *docta puella*. With this rather vague term the poets denoted any attractive young woman skilled in the Greek educational triad of poetry, music and dance.[92] In the poets' eyes the charms of her accomplishments, her taste for poetry, gift for music, skill in dancing and witty conversation, rank above birth and wealth, and compensate for her supposed lack of traditional virtues.

Cynthia, the beloved of Propertius, is a good example. Apart from her beauty she is praised as a skilful musician, who put her lover's verses to music and sang them to the accompaniment of her lyre, as an elegant dancer, a witty conversationalist and – last but not least – a woman with a good taste for poetry, in fact, a poetess herself, able to judge and appreciate her lover's poetry as his most discerning critic.[93] However, these accomplishments, which she shares with other *doctae puellae* such as Ovid's Corinna,[94] more closely resemble the charms of the educated courtesan than the erudition of the respectable upper-class women discussed so far; the more so as her literary and musical accomplishments are depicted as part of her erotic attraction. Sexually she seems independent: though in some cases a husband is mentioned, the *puella* is portrayed as free to entertain conversation and even a (secret) love-affair with her poet-lover and – much to his chagrin – with other lovers. Her sexual freedom, free behaviour and accomplishments have given rise to the assumption that the women of Roman love poetry are of the 'demi-monde', possibly Greek women of freed status, but the social status of the love poets' mistresses is unclear and their possible relation to identifiable women remains doubtful.[95]

What concerns us here is the existence of the *ideal* of the *docta puella* in Roman love poetry of the late republic and Augustan period, which, because of its strong

79

sexual implications, runs counter to traditional morality. Because of these implications the accomplishments typical of the *docta puella* were regarded with suspicion in Roman society: in the conservative Roman view the Greek combination of poetry, music and dance was associated with *meretrices* and, therefore, utterly unsuitable for *matronae* of the upper classes. Thus, to call an upper-class woman a *docta puella* or to attribute to her the accomplishments associated with it damaged her reputation. For instance, presenting the skills of Clodia Metelli and Sempronia, women of senatorial family, as similar to those of Catullus' Lesbia and Propertius' Cynthia, throws doubt upon their morals.[96] Well-educated upper-class women, especially when they were young, easily came under suspicion whenever their musical interest and literary taste deviated from the austerity of Cornelia, the mother of the Gracchi, or could not be excused by their usefulness for the education of their sons. Even the love poets themselves seem to have been aware of the discredit the compliment *docta* might bring: when applied to known individuals they avoided its sexual connotation by stressing the chastity of the *puella*.[97]

As an ideal the *docta puella* contrasted with the traditional Roman *matrona casta*, but in practice the relation between poetry and life was more complicated. The interaction between literature and life, as discussed by J. Griffin,[98] suggests that the *docta puella* of love poetry was at least partly based on reality, *viz.* on the accomplishments and life of (possibly lower-class) women of the time, but also that love poetry itself, by its popularity, influenced the behaviour of women and the relation between men and women, at least among the educated. Thus, the type of the *docta puella* adored in love poetry may have inspired some upper-class women to follow their example in certain respects, in spite of the risk of a conflict with traditional standards.

One of them may have been Augustus' daughter Julia. In the ancient sources she is described as a smart young woman: lively, gay, attractive, wealthy, cultured and conscious of her high birth, but she is also accused of licentiousness and promiscuity, which results in a highly ambiguous portrait; accusations of adultery eventually led to her downfall.[99] A positive judgement on her is preserved in the fifth-century author Macrobius, who devotes a section of his *Saturnalia* to her witticisms and who describes her good education as one of her charms. After mildly criticizing her for 'youthful' behaviour, which, in his opinion, conflicted with her age (she was in her thirty-eighth year, which Macrobius regards as bordering on old age), he continues: 'nevertheless, she had a love of literature and great learning (not surprising in such a home) and besides a gentle humanity and a kind character free from all rudeness, all of which made her immensely popular'.[100] Julia represents a type of educated woman very different from the dignified upper-class women discussed above. Though she was a mother of five children and twice widowed, her portrait resembles the type of the *docta puella* of contemporary love poetry. The liveliness, wit, education and sociability ascribed to her seem to have made her popular with the Roman people, but – as we saw above – such qualities gave rise to mixed feelings in conservative upper-class men and her candid acknowledgement of her promiscuity (according to the jokes attributed to her) must have strengthened their prejudices.

In the course of the empire the ideal of the *puella docta* was stripped of its connotation of sexual licence and incorporated into the ideals of married life. In the younger Pliny's letters to and about his wife, the influence of Augustan love poetry is seen: apart from praising her traditional virtues Pliny publicly confesses his love and even his passion for his wife in a manner unusual (and perhaps even unthinkable) among men of his class before the empire. In his letters to Calpurnia he adopts the literary conventions and imagery of love poetry: he is tormented by anxiety when she is away from him in Campania to recover from an illness, he lies awake at night longing for her, and her letters to him both delight and torture him.[101] Pliny's letters demonstrate the eventual 'domestication' of the ideal of the *docta puella* by its incorporation into married life. Without using the term he describes his young wife as a *docta puella*, who reads his works, sings his verses and sets them to the lyre, but unlike the *doctae puellae* of love poetry she does so for her lawful husband, not for a lover.[102] Thus, the sophisticated and exciting *puella docta* of love poetry had turned into the well-educated, devoted wife.

Music and dance: a vice or a social grace?

Music and dance as part of the education of upper-class women gave rise to similar conflicting feelings: praised by some as a social grace, they were severely censured by others as morally corrupting and leading to sexual licentiousness.[103] In traditional Roman education music and dance played only a minor part. In his *Life of Epaminondas* Nepos contrasts Greek and Roman tradition in this respect; comparing fourth-century Greece (Epaminondas) with the Rome of his own days (the first century BC) he warns his readers:

> not to judge the customs of other nations by their own, and not to consider conduct which in their opinion is undignified as regarded in the same way by other people. We know, for example, that according to our ideas music is unsuited to a personage of importance, while dancing is even numbered among the vices; but with the Greeks all such accomplishments are regarded as becoming and even praiseworthy.
> (Nep. *Epam.* 1; Loeb trans., modified)[104]

Nepos omits to mention that even in Greece music and dance were not unconditionally appreciated and that, on the other hand, on certain occasions music and dance were thought respectable also in Rome, for example, when hymns were sung by men and women of the élite at religious ceremonies, or when songs and dances were performed on festal days, or at a funeral – and, in the seclusion of the home, even for pleasure. On such occasions respectability was said to be strictly observed: boys and girls solemnly sang in choruses, men danced in a manly way and matrons, when asked to sing or dance, did so with modesty and restraint.[105]

In contrast with the appreciation of this dignified kind of music and dance of earlier days, contemporary music and dance were severely criticized for their lasciviousness by Roman authors of the late republic and early principate.[106] For this Greek influence was blamed. In the second century BC Greek music and dance had been introduced in Rome and had gained great popularity among the upper classes too, causing dismay among the traditional-minded. According to a, possibly fictitious, anecdote in a speech of Scipio Aemilianus, as reported by the fifth-century author Macrobius, Scipio was shocked to find that boys and girls from the upper classes were taught to sing, dance and play instruments in music and dancing schools:

> They are instructed in dishonourable tricks; together with shameless companions and carrying cither and lute they frequent schools of actors, they learn singing songs that our ancestors wanted to be regarded as unfit for young people of free birth; yes, I tell you, girls and boys of free birth go to schools of dancing amidst disreputable people. When I was told as much, I could not bring myself to believe that men of noble birth allowed their children to be taught such things, but when I was introduced in a dancing school, I saw in it, I swear, over fifty boys and girls, and among them – and for this I utterly pitied the Roman state – a boy with his youthful *bulla* [amulet] on his neck, the son of a candidate for public office, less than twelve years old; I saw, I say, how he danced with castanets in a way which would have been disreputable even for a shameless little slave.
>
> (Macr. *Sat.* 3.14.7)[107]

Macrobius himself is particularly dismayed at the behaviour of upper-class women during the days of the republic, who instead of demonstrating the dignified behaviour expected of them 'did not find dancing dishonourable, but even among the most respectable of them there was a real passion for dancing, with the only provision that it was not taken so seriously as to produce professional perfection' and 'the sons and – what is worse – also the unmarried daughters of noble families counted training in dancing among the subjects of serious study'.[108]

Here Macrobius echoes criticism from authors of the late republic and early principate; for instance, Seneca was shocked by the contemporary craze for dancing of both men and women: 'the acting-stage resounds in private homes throughout the entire city. On it both men and women dance. Husbands and wives contend over which of the two is more delicate in the movements of the body.'[109] In its anxiety about the corrupting influence of music and dance Roman prejudice against Greek influence coincided with upper-class contempt for the pursuits of the lower classes. In Roman eyes 'Greece' was associated not only with learning and sophistication but also with luxury and effeminacy; 'effeminate' Greek music and dance were thought to corrupt the sturdy and morally superior Roman élite.[110] Professional dancers and musicians, who in growing numbers performed at dinners, festivities and funerals of wealthy Romans from the late republic onwards, were mostly slaves or freedmen (and -women); because of their low status and the erotic nature of their performances female musicians and dancing-girls were regarded as little better than prostitutes.[111] Thus, association with loose morals made Greek-influenced music and dance highly dubious activities for members of the Roman élite and too great a skill in playing the lyre and dancing was criticized as a sign of licentiousness in an upper-class woman.[112]

In contrast with this disapproval the love poets of the Augustan age, foremost Ovid and Propertius, praised musical accomplishments and dancing in women (Ovid pretends to speak only of freedwomen). In their opinion, such skill added to the charms of the sophisticated *docta puella* who was the object of their love and idealization: 'at the revel's close she dances wondrously, even as Ariadne led the Maenad dance and when she essays to sing to the Aeolian lyre she rivals the harp of Aganippe in her skill in playing'.[113] As we have seen, this is a kind of counter-ideal, formed in opposition to traditional values, and its strong erotic overtones made it incompatible with the chaste behaviour expected of a *matrona*.

Yet, the popularity of Latin love poetry and its ideal of the *docta puella* eventually had, as we have seen (p. 81), some influence on Roman attitudes, and with the gradual acceptance of the Greek educational curriculum during the principate there came a conditional, hesitating approval of music and dance as part of the education of upper-class women.[114] Women of more modest descent followed their example: epitaphs praising their musical accomplishments and numerous sarcophagi depicting women with musical instruments witness to the prestige conveyed by such skills also to women of the sub-élite classes.[115] An example of this is Statius' praise of his stepdaughter, a child from an earlier marriage of his wife Claudia. In his *ecloga ad uxorem* he writes about her:

> So assuredly does she deserve [*scil.* marriage] for her sweet appearance and virtuous mind; whether she clasps and strikes the lute, or with a voice as tuneful as her father's sings melodies worthy to be learned by the Muses, or sets my poems to music, or whether with subtle movement she spreads her snow-white arms: her innocence and modesty surpass her talent and her skill.
>
> (Stat. *Silv.* 3.5.63–7; Loeb trans., modified)[116]

Here we again meet the dubious *docta puella* in a 'domesticated' form: as Statius was aware that such accomplishments might easily lead to a suspicion of promiscuity, he stressed the old-fashioned virtues of his stepdaughter; her modesty and innocence are said to surpass her musical accomplishments. In a similar vein, Pliny praises his wife Calpurnia, who, as he claims, sang his verses and set them to the lyre without ever having received musical training.[117] By belittling her education (while stressing her chastity and modesty) he marks the difference between his wife and a professional musician.

Though in the course of the principate musical training came to be accepted in Roman society and could be regarded as a sign of high social status also for women,[118] the stigma of debauchery did not completely disappear. Disapproval is found not only in Roman authors; Plutarch also objects to dancing, and in his portrait of Pompey's wife Cornelia he mentions her skill in playing the lyre as one of her charms, but qualifies his approval by stressing her virtues as a faithful and lovable wife *in spite of* her accomplishments (which comprised not only music but also literature, geometry and philosophy).[119] Thus, approval remained conditional: upper-class dignity and morality had to come first.

Prejudice against educated women

As we have seen, educated women caused mixed feelings varying from admiration to aversion; in this sub-section we shall concentrate on the negative feelings. Three kinds of charges can be distinguished: educated women were accused of moral depravity, in particular of sexual licentiousness, education was thought to lead to ostentatious display and pretentiousness and, third, it made women meddlesome and priggish, and therefore insufferable – especially to their husbands. Of course, the stereotypes, invectives and satirical descriptions of educated women cannot be used as evidence of how these women really were, but they may be used as a source for the male author's opinion, and perhaps for that of part of his public, of educated women.

Sexual licentiousness

A well-known example of an invective in which the education of an upper-class woman plays a role is Sallust's portrait of Sempronia, a well-educated woman from a high-ranking family and the wife of a consul; she is extensively described by Sallust as one of the female associates of Catiline, but her actual role in the conspiracy is unclear and seems negligible.[120] Sallust's elaborate portrayal of her is preceded by a description of the female adherents of Catiline generally:

> At that time Catiline is said to have gained the support of many men of all conditions and even of some women, who in their earlier days had met their enormous expenses by prostitution, but later, when their time of life had set a limit to their traffic but not to their extravagance, had contracted a huge debt.
>
> (Sall. *Cat.* 24.3; Loeb trans., modified)[121]

Thus, accusations of promiscuity, extravagance and debts prepare for the character sketch of Sempronia:

Now among these women was Sempronia, who had often committed many crimes of masculine daring. In birth and beauty, in her husband also and children, she was abundantly favoured by fortune; she was well read in Greek and Latin literature, able to play the lyre and dance more skilfully than a respectable woman need, and had many other accomplishments which minister to voluptuousness. But there was nothing that she held so cheap as modesty and chastity; you could not easily say whether she was less sparing of her money or of her reputation; her desires were so ardent that she sought men more often than she was sought by them. Even before the time of the conspiracy she had frequently broken her word, repudiated her debts, been privy to murder; extravagance and impecuniousness combined had driven her headlong. Nevertheless, she was a woman of no mean endowments; she could write verses, tell jokes, and use language which was modest, or tender, or wanton; in fine, she possessed a high degree of wit and charm.

(Sall. *Cat.* 25; Loeb trans., modified)[122]

It has been noted that Sallust's portrayal of Sempronia serves as the female counterpart to his character sketch of Catiline, with which he illustrates the political corruption and moral depravity among aristocratic men.[123] Like his characterization of Catiline, this invective is of a complicated nature. It comprises both praise and blame: Sempronia's 'masculine' daring, extravagance and promiscuity are contrasted with the excellence of her birth, marriage, children, beauty, education and intellect.[124] However, these positive qualities are judged ambiguously: on the one hand, her education is presented as a sign of her high birth and social standing and as an addition to her charm and prestige, but, on the other, by associating it with moral laxity, Sallust puts Sempronia's upper-class education in a dubious light. Being better at music, dance and witty conversation than a woman of her class should be, she is made to resemble lower-class courtesans, or the *puella docta* of love poetry, with, of course, a damning effect on her reputation.[125]

Sallust's portrait of Sempronia, with which he exemplifies aristocratic female perversion, obscures her actual personality and behaviour. We shall never know whether or not Sempronia's morals were truly loose. That she was of high birth and noble family made her alleged deviation from the traditional norms only the more despicable. Since upper-class women (and men) were expected to set an example in moral behaviour, their 'corruption' caused particular anxiety. This combination of upper-class birth, beauty, and education with moral depravity, especially sexual licentiousness, is a recurring theme in Roman literature. In the late republic and the early principate we meet several examples of this stereotype: women like Clodia Metelli, Augustus' daughter Julia and Nero's wife Poppaea Sabina, well-educated and socially prominent women, are all abused for loose morals, which are presented as in some way connected with their sophistication and accomplishments.[126]

Modern studies of the portrayal of such upper-class women concentrate on their intrusion into the male world of politics in order to explain the attacks on them. As women's intrusion into the public realm was felt to endanger the established order, it was criticized by means of sexual stereotypes or, as T. Hillard puns: a woman who 'went public' risked being branded a 'public woman'.[127] Invective, especially sexual invective, was common in Roman rhetoric and literature and could be directed against both men and women, usually political adversaries. However, as *pudicitia* was one of the central virtues of the Roman *matrona*, criticism of licentiousness was more devastating for a woman's reputation than for a man's. Since a woman's transgression of the norms reflected on the reputation of the men with whom she was associated (and who were apparently unable, or unwilling, to check her), a male opponent could be effectively attacked by blackening the reputation of his female relatives or associates.[128] Thus, by portraying Sempronia as a morally degenerate aristocratic woman Sallust both condemns the moral decline among the aristocracy of his days and throws a dubious light on the conspiracy of Catiline.

In this line of thought no attention is paid to the role education played in these stereotypes. As we have seen, too great a skill in poetry, music and dance could damage a woman's reputation as it reminded one of the accomplished courtesan or the type of the *puella docta*. As a consequence, educated women were especially open to the charge of wantonness. Moreover, learning was the field of men, and the display of education which was not excused by traditional or moral aims (such as the education of children or the interest of husband or family) was regarded as an intrusion into the male domain, in a way comparable to women's intrusion into the world of politics. As we shall see, criticism of such transgression of gender boundaries might take various forms; however, all are directly or indirectly connected with a woman's sexual reputation.

Ostentation and pretension

As we have seen, education was a source of prestige for women, but not unconditionally so: women who paraded their education (or who perhaps did not succeed in hiding it behind traditional behaviour) came into conflict with traditional morality, which expected modesty and a retired way of life from them. For the elder Seneca the ostentation of education and the extravagance of some educated women of his days were a ground for cutting short his wife's philosophical study.[129] Lucian satirizes the pretentiousness of Roman upper-class women who, in order to appear learned, engaged grammarians, rhetoricians and philosophers, whom they trailed all over the place without finding time to listen to them. According to him these women hired scholars only to show off.[130]

Both the elder Seneca and Lucian objected to what they saw as a tendency among upper-class women of their days to desire an education for the sake of impressing others; in Lucian's eyes, the (fake) learning of these women was a cover for their real interests: prestige and promiscuity. In a similar vein, Juvenal and Martial ridicule Roman upper-class women for speaking Greek. This is attacked not only as pretentious, but also as connected with lasciviousness since the Greek they are said to be speaking is the bedroom language of Greek courtesans.[131] Thus, ostentatious learning and sexual licentiousness are maliciously linked.

Meddlesomeness and priggishness

The third prejudice strikes a different note: education was believed to make a woman meddlesome and priggish, to turn her into a desexualized bluestocking, who was regarded as unbearable for all men, but especially for her husband. In his description of Pompey's wife Cornelia, Plutarch suggests that young women were especially prone to this vice, and Musonius Rufus defends women studying philosophy against the charge:

> that women who associate with philosophers are bound to be arrogant for the most part and presumptuous, in that abandoning their own households and turning to the company of men they practice speeches, talk like sophists, and analyze syllogisms, when they ought to be sitting at home spinning.
>
> (Mus. Ruf. fr. III.54–8; trans. Lutz (1947) 43)[132]

This cliché is also found in satirical poetry. In his famous caricature of a woman dominating the conversation during dinner Juvenal ridicules her learning and her priggishness in correcting her poor husband. Her torrent of words silences everybody and is likely even to ward off an eclipse of the moon. In her desire to appear learned and eloquent she usurps the male role; in short, as a wife she is unbearable:

> Let the wife, who reclines with you at dinner, not possess a rhetorical style of her own, let her not hurl at you in whirling speech the well-rounded syllogism. Let her not know all history. Let there be some things in her reading which she does not understand. I hate a woman who is always consulting and poring over the grammatical treatise of Palaemon, who observes all the rules and laws of correct speech, who with antiquarian zeal quotes verses that I have never heard of, and corrects her ignorant female friend for slips of speech that no man need trouble about: let a husband at least be allowed to make his solecisms [slips in syntax] in peace.
>
> (Juv. 6. 448–56; Loeb trans., modified)[133]

Juvenal does not question the woman's learning – though he describes it as both excessive and trivial, the typical learning of the pedant grammarian; he questions her femininity. This stereotype is also behind Martial's abhorrence of a learned wife. Three of his epigrams hint at the unsuitability of an educated woman for matters of love and marriage. In an idealizing vision of the simple life as opposed to the ambitions of men striving for glory and wealth, Martial muses: 'let me have a plump home-born slave, have a wife not too learned, have my nights with sleep, have my days without a lawsuit'. A learned wife, as is suggested in this epigram, adds to the prestige, but not to the enjoyments, of life. Her overbearing nature produces impotence in a man: 'Do you ask why I don't want to marry you, Galla? You are eloquent. My prick often commits a solecism'; or it drives him to the company of boys.[134]

In the three ways in which educated women were ridiculed, there is one recurring theme: all women are judged in terms of their sexual reputation; in the first two, women are, directly or indirectly, charged with licentiousness, and in the third, they are depicted as masculine and desexualized. Moreover, women are defined in terms of their family relationships, in particular their relation to their husbands. The speaker in satire and invective takes a conservative male point of view: women ought to be loyal and devoted wives who care for their husbands and families, and women who transgress these limits are attacked by means of stereotypes depicting them as promiscuous adulteresses, wanton old hags, overbearing wives or priggish, desexualized bluestockings. By scoffing at the unconventional behaviour of women satire supports the traditional norms.[135]

It is perhaps no coincidence that the most vicious invectives against Roman women (Sallust's portrait of Sempronia, Cicero's *Pro Caelio* and Juvenal's sixth satire) date from the late republic and the early empire, a time of transformation and shifting of values, when, among other things, we find a greater prominence, and an unprecedented power, of some women, especially the well-educated and politically active women of the upper classes and the imperial family.[136] Satire and invective against the unconventional behaviour of women may be regarded as a defence against this shift of values, reflecting the tension between the social and political prominence of educated, upper-class women and the traditional image of the modest and submissive Roman *matrona*. As the charges against educated women, especially the accusation of sexual licentiousness, closely resemble the criticism of women involved in political matters and as upper-class women who were politically active were, as a rule, also well educated, it may be assumed that the abuse was directed at their usurpation of political power, rather than at their education. However, when their education is mentioned, this is usually done in order to discredit them. By scolding educated women as promiscuous, or (the opposite) as desexualized, male authors perhaps hoped to discourage women from following their example, but the main purpose of this type of literature seems to have been to strengthen conservative (male) opinion as regards the proper place of women and, thus, to keep them in their traditional role.[137]

A male mind in a female body

A peculiar kind of prejudice against the education of women is shown whenever an educated woman is compared to a man or is said to have a 'male' mind. The designation of 'masculinity' was not only used for educated women: women who were distinguished in other male fields were also sometimes called masculine. Unlike what might be expected, 'masculinity' is an ambiguous notion when used for women, implying both approval and disapproval. Approval of 'masculinity' in women is connected with the Roman tendency to 'gender' virtues, i.e. to associate separate virtues with either men or women: thus, courage was regarded as a male virtue, chastity as the main female virtue. When remarkable courage was manifested by a woman, this did not alter the belief that courage was a male virtue; on the contrary, a woman acting courageously was said to 'display courage like a man'. By showing courage she surpassed what was expected from her sex, thus rising to male standards of behaviour;[138] but if such 'masculine' virtues were to be desirable qualities in a woman, she had to exhibit the main female virtues also.

Examples of women being admired for 'masculine' qualities are the legendary heroines Lucretia and Cloelia. Lucretia's exemplary courage in defending her chastity made Valerius Maximus remark: 'by a malicious mistake of fortune her masculine mind is incorporated in a female body', and Cloelia's 'male' *virtus* (manliness, courage) in war was honoured, according to legend, with a typically male token of honour: the erection of an equestrian statue in a public place.[139] As both women also exemplified 'female' modesty and chastity – and as their courage was displayed for the public good – they could be held up as models for upper-class women of later times. Porcia, the wife of Brutus and the daughter of Cato Minor, provides another example: her constancy in bearing pain and her brave suicide, in which she followed and even surpassed her father's example, are praised in masculine terms. Yet, her 'masculine' attitude was balanced by her 'feminine' virtues, such as chastity, loyalty and affability, which made her 'male' qualities the more praiseworthy.[140]

In a kind of inverted praise a woman could be admired for showing a lack of 'female' weakness, which, implicitly, raised her to the level of men. For example, the younger Seneca when exhorting his mother Helvia not to give in to excessive mourning, writes: 'the excuse of being a woman can be of no avail to one who has always lacked all the weaknesses of a woman'. By this he means – judging from the list he gives – unchastity, love of luxury, shame at being pregnant, abortions and excessive care of the body, cosmetics and dress. By transcending 'female weaknesses' (but keeping to the female virtues) Helvia was considered to display the 'male' virtue of self-control.[141]

Yet, 'masculinity' in women was not always the object of praise. Women whose masculinity was not balanced by female virtues, who publicly trespassed into a male field for their own good, or who adopted what were considered to be men's bad habits, were regarded quite differently. In one of his letters Seneca imputes the illnesses of women suffering from 'male' diseases (such as baldness and gout) to their 'unnatural' imitation of male behaviour:

> The great founder of the science and profession of medicine observed that women never lost their hair or suffered from pain in the feet. But in our own day their hair falls out and they are afflicted with gout. This does not mean that women's anatomy has changed, but that it has been subverted; by competing with men in their indulgences, they have also sought to outdo men in their illnesses. They stay up just as late and drink just as much alcohol; they challenge men in wrestling and revelling; they are no less given to vomiting from swollen stomachs and thus throwing up all their wine again; nor are they behind men in gnawing at ice to relieve their disturbed digestions. And they even (may the gods and goddesses confound them!) match men in their sexual desires, although they were created to feel love passively. They think up the most impossible varieties of immoral sexual practices, and when they are with men they play the man's part. It is no great surprise then that our observations confound the statement of the greatest and most expert doctor, when so many women are gout-ridden and bald! By their vices, women have forfeited the privileges of their sex; they have spurned their womanly natures and are therefore condemned to suffer the diseases of men.
>
> (Sen. *Ep.* 95.20–1)[142]

Here Seneca connects the undesirable 'male' behaviour of women with a susceptibility to male complaints. This reasoning by analogy seems influenced by the Roman tendency to connect different fields of behaviour which, in our opinion, may seem totally distinct.[143] Similarly, undesirable 'male' behaviour by a woman in politics might be maliciously associated with alleged 'male' behaviour in, for instance, sexual matters, as we have seen in Sallust's portrait of Sempronia. Sempronia is portrayed as adopting an inappropriate gender role: she allegedly committed 'crimes of masculine daring', repudiated her debts and took the initiative in sexual matters, without any regard for the 'female' virtues of modesty, chastity and frugality.[144] A similar mixture of 'masculine' behaviour and sexual misconduct is found in Cicero's portrait of Clodia Metelli, though, again, the accusation seems rather to be due to Cicero's personal enmity towards her brother, the radical tribune P. Clodius Pulcher, and to his wish to magnify Clodia's role in his *Pro Caelio* in order to distract the attention from his defendant.[145]

Another cliché describes women who intrude into the male field of politics as domineering, desexualized, and 'masculine'. Because of their social and political eminence and greater access to political influence, women of the élite were readily accused of such faults. To mention only two: Antony's wife Fulvia and Nero's mother Agrippina Minor were criticized for their 'masculine' characters. Fulvia is described as a domineering and headstrong woman 'who never gave a thought to spinning or housekeeping' and who 'had nothing womanly about her apart from her body' and Agrippina Minor as a fierce-tempered, power-hungry woman who imposed 'a tight-drawn, almost masculine tyranny' upon Rome.[146] Their abhorred masculinity may be partly explained by the fact that these women were either the wife or the mother of detested men and that they showed no regard for the traditional female virtues. Similar masculine traits in the elder Agrippina, wife of the venerated Germanicus, led to a much more balanced appraisal: in spite of her undesirable 'masculine' traits (her fierce temper and headstrong, domineering character) she is praised for her incorruptible chastity, her loyalty and devotion to her husband and her exemplary fecundity.[147]

Not only were virtues and vices tied to gender, but women's minds were thought to differ from those of men: women were believed to be irrational and lacking in judgement as contrasted with 'male' rationality and good judgement.[148] Here gender interacts with social standing, since 'male rationality' was associated with the good judgement of a well-educated man of the upper classes. As rationality and good judgement were believed to be acquired through education, women were sometimes put on a level with men of the lower classes because of their (supposed) lack of education.[149] Women who did show a rational judgement were regarded as surpassing the expectations of their sex and were consequently praised for their 'male mind'; thus, a change in the concept of 'male' rationality was avoided. Just like women who were noted for their 'manly' courage or self-control, they became, so to speak, honorary men. For example, Philo, who had no high opinion of the intellect of women – in his work 'woman' symbolizes the world of the senses and 'man' the realm of the mind – judged that the empress Livia rose above her sex, since her excellent education 'gave virility to her reasoning power'.[150] Similarly, Martial praises the good judgement of the learned Theophila by calling it 'unwomanly' and Sappho is called 'masculine' by Horace in admiration of her extraordinary poetic talent.[151]

The Roman habit of complimenting a woman for resembling her father in mind or character is also based on the appreciation of 'male' intellectual qualities in women. For example, Hortensia, the daughter of the famous orator Q. Hortensius Hortalus, was praised for displaying her father's rhetorical gifts when speaking in public to the triumvirs in 42 BC, causing her father to 'come to life again in his daughter's words'. Similarly, daughters of other talented upper-class men, such as Cicero's daughter Tullia, Laelius' daughter Laelia and Fundanus' daughter Minicia Marcella, were praised for possessing their fathers' intellectual gifts.[152] The ability of women to inherit (and transmit) 'male' intellectual qualities was regarded as a credit to their male relatives, especially their fathers. The fact that most of these women had no brothers to follow in their fathers' footsteps or had brothers who disappointed expectations may, of course, have helped to bring their qualities to the fore.

By contrast, educated women might also be criticized for their intrusion into the male domain: instead of being praised as 'honorary men' they were scorned as 'failed men', or as persons of an intermediate sex. Two examples may illustrate this. In his much-quoted caricature of an educated woman, who dominated the conversation at dinner and excelled in such male fields as grammar, oratory and philosophy, Juvenal advised her to assume masculine dress, attend male religious customs and visit the men's bath.[153] She is ridiculed as of an intermediate sex: though a woman, she behaves like a man trying to equal men in erudition and eloquence. Valerius Maximus relates that a certain Maesia of Sentinum defended herself successfully against a criminal charge before the praetor and was consequently nicknamed 'Man-woman': 'because, under her female appearance, she bore a male spirit, they called her "Androgyne"'.[154] Though less clearly negative, this judgement puts her in an intermediate category, halfway between 'man' and 'woman'.

Both examples depict educated women as if their sex were doubtful: they are neither male nor wholly female. As Roman traditionalism demanded that everyone stuck to his or her role, women who displayed 'male' behaviour disturbed the 'natural' order and were therefore regarded with misgivings. Praise is misleading in this respect: women praised for their masculine minds were not accepted for what they were, educated women, but were praised as 'honorary men'. In becoming learned they ceased to be women. The notion of the sexual ambiguity of educated women is also found in other periods of history: they were viewed as male in intellect but female in body, and therefore their sexual identity was considered ambiguous.[155] This caused learned women, beings of compound and indefinite sexuality, to be excluded from the natural order of things and confirmed the notion that learning (or courage or politics) was the field of men. The treatment of women who intruded into this field as if they were 'male' in mind and, therefore, not wholly feminine, maintains the *status quo* and, in a sense, even confirms it, since the exceptions are incorporated into the norm. For the women in question this mechanism reduced them to sexual ambiguity and banished them to the fringes of society; it probably formed an impediment to full participation by women in intellectual life.

Educated women: a chronological survey

So far the aims of and the opinions on women's education have been discussed thematically, without much attention to chronology, almost as if, during the roughly four hundred years between the second century BC and the early third century AD, they were hardly subject to change. This, of course, is not the case. But, though changes took place, it is not easy to find out exactly when and how. What follows, therefore, is no more than an attempt to make sense of the evidence by putting it in chronological order.

Before tracing a chronological development three points should be made. First, the increased evidence of educated women, and their more diverse social status, in the first and second centuries AD (as compared to the much smaller number of educated women, all of them belonging to the highest nobility, in the second century BC) may be partly due to the fact that our sources are richer and more varied in the first two centuries AD. Thus, we should beware of overestimating the (undeniable) differences between these two periods. Second, changes in mentality, such as notions about women's education, are a matter of long-term development which cannot be pinpointed. They are only partially and indirectly affected by political and institutional change: I have found no direct link between changes in the assessment of educated women and the transition from the republic to imperial government – although in the long run ideals and notions in this field were affected by the political and social changes produced by the imperial regime. Therefore, there is no reason to draw a sharp line between the (late) republic and the principate[156] as regards the assessment of women's education; rather, the most conspicuous change seems to have taken place during the principate, in the course of the first century AD, when together with the greater appreciation of a Greek-style education we meet a growing number of educated women and a greater openness as regards their learning – though satirists and champions of traditional morality remain highly critical, as is to be expected.[157] Third, we should not suppose that the development necessarily followed a straight course from the second century BC (when there were few educated women) to the first and second centuries AD, when learning seems to have been the fashion also among women and when education – with certain limitations – was regarded as a source of prestige for them. The development seems uneven and halting: women's education aroused conflicting feelings which might coexist; and themes hotly disputed in one period (such as the *puella docta*) were accepted in a modified form in the next.

The Hellenization of Roman society and the status attached to a (Greek) education in the Roman upper classes are of great influence on the assessment of the education of women. As is to be expected, the first Roman woman famous for her education, Cornelia, the mother of the Gracchi, stemmed from a family steeped in Greek culture. Though opposed by some, Greek learning brought prestige at the time provided it was kept within the bounds of aristocratic dignity and subordinated to obligations to the state.[158] It was quite unusual for a woman of her time to receive such an extensive education, but members of the leading families of Rome probably had more freedom to deviate from social convention and to start new fashions than persons of less elevated birth. We may suspect that in Cornelia's case considerations of social standing overruled the conventional restrictions imposed upon women: as a member of a family of the highest nobility she had to maintain the family prestige, and her education probably served this end.[159] In later times opinion on Cornelia underwent remarkable changes. The 'Hellenizing' aspects of her life (her patronage of Greek scholars, her familiarity with Hellenistic kings and her grand style of living) are mentioned only by Plutarch, whereas Roman authors of the late republic and early principate stress the purity of her Latin and her sober and dignified way of living. In the process of idealization her education was made subservient to that of her sons: she was idealized as a model of motherhood and a paragon of Roman virtue.

Roman ambivalence in the late republic and early principate as regards educated women runs parallel to their attitude towards the Hellenization of Roman society, which varied from appreciation to disgust.[160] On the one hand, Greek culture was depreciated as luxurious and effeminate, a source of corruption for the morally superior Roman élite, or despised as a form of useless verbosity; on the other hand, it was greatly admired: to be familiar with Greek culture was a sign of sophistication. Members of the Roman upper class vied with each other in their knowledge of Greek literature and learning, but to be too deeply engrossed in Greek culture provoked criticism because it distracted attention from one's duties to the state and was felt to clash with Roman *dignitas*. In the late republic and early principate criticism seems to have been stronger than before; perhaps the increasing Hellenization of Roman society and the influx of Greeks from the Hellenistic East inspired a greater aversion to Greek influence, as it was felt to threaten Roman cultural identity. Against the superiority of Greek culture upper-class Romans set Roman moral superiority, which was believed to be especially proper to the upper classes and was partly attributed to Rome's 'good old days'. It is here that the idealization of Cornelia comes in; her high birth, the great number of her children and her long and dignified widowhood made her an object of reverence: as a model of motherhood and of traditional Roman virtues she became an example of Roman moral superiority.

From the late republic onwards the number of educated women increased, causing mixed feelings in Roman society. Conservative senators, such as Cicero and Sallust, championed dignity and traditional virtues for the women of their class, and this clashed with the life of luxury and pleasure associated with Greek culture. Therefore, they ignored Greek learning in women they respected, speaking of the education of women and, especially, their skill in music and dance only when they wanted to vilify female opponents. This does not mean that they were opposed to women's education in private life, but in their writings they put traditional morality first. In opposition to the ideal of the chaste upper-class *matrona* the love poets of the late republic and Augustan period, such as Propertius and Ovid, idealized the *docta puella*, a young woman of indefinite social status and loose sexual morals who was skilled in the Greek educational triad of poetry, music and dance. Thus, we see that opposite views coexisted, though in different groups of society: the love poets were young equestrians who opposed the strict moral standards prescribed for members of the élite as revived in the moral legislation of Augustus.

In the course of the first century AD Greek culture, despite attempts to curb its influence and the life of luxury and leisure that was associated with it, spread throughout Roman society and became a status symbol for members of the sub-élite too. Educational facilities, such as libraries, increased in number and numerous Greek scholars were serving in the households of the wealthy. The peace and prosperity of the principate showed a growing appreciation of education and of literary activities among the upper classes. Greek culture was also cultivated by a growing number of upper-class women, the well-educated women of the imperial family, from Augustus' sister Octavia and her daughter Antonia onwards, perhaps serving as models. Since education was regarded as a mark of high social status, it was imitated also by well-to-do women of more modest descent. Yet, authors of the first and second centuries AD showed various prejudices against educated women: they ridiculed their affectation or priggishness, doubted their morals or even their sex, and objected to their ostentation. On the other hand, moral philosophers, such as Musonius Rufus and Plutarch, and the younger Pliny defended the education of women for moral reasons and traditionalists excused it, under certain conditions, by pointing to their role as educators of sons. Thus, a studious girl might be praised for her dignified and modest behaviour displayed in her love of learning as well as in her restraint at play, or a wife for following the guidance of her husband in their common studies, and elderly widows were applauded for finding a dignified refuge from sorrow in the study of moral philosophy.

Because of the scarcity of the literary sources only a few examples of educated women of the period of the later second and early third centuries AD are known to us, most of them belonging to the imperial family. The matter-of-fact way in which their learning is mentioned shows that it was considered natural in members of the upper classes and proper to their elevated social status. To mention only the most famous: for Julia Domna the study of philosophy provided a dignified refuge from the complications of life at court. Also outside the aristocracy education was a mark of prestige: in this period sarcophagi appear that portray learned couples, thus testifying to pride in the education of both husband and wife among those who could afford a sarcophagus, i.e. well-to-do persons who did not necessarily belong to the upper classes.

As appears from this chronological sketch, the development and changes in the judgement on educated women and the vicissitudes of the assimilation of Greek culture in Roman society run more or less parallel: both show a similar development from an initial acceptance as a status symbol among a small group of families of the highest nobility in the early second century BC through a period of intense dispute and ambivalence in the late republic and the early principate to a *de facto* acceptance and appreciation (despite occasional criticism) among the highest circles in the course of the empire. But the Hellenization of Roman society and the assessment of the education of women are also connected in another way: just as Greek culture had to be subordinated to Roman national values in order to be accepted, so women's education had to be subordinated to the ideals of the Roman *matrona*. Though marking a high social rank, education remained a dubious achievement in an upper-class woman since she shared some of her accomplishments with Greek freedwomen, actresses, courtesans and the like. Besides, learning and erudition were considered the preserve of men; women who distinguished themselves in the male field of grammar, oratory and philosophy were likely to be accused of meddlesomeness and arrogance or of masculine behaviour. To avoid accusations of luxuriousness and depravity on the one hand, and meddlesomeness or 'masculinity' on the other, they must have felt as if they were steering between Scylla and Charybdis with only traditional morality as a guide and haven. Only the conventional role of devoted and chaste daughter, wife and mother made it possible for their education to lose its risky aspects and be praised as contributing to the well-being and reputation of the whole family.

4

PATRONESSES OF LITERATURE AND LEARNING

> Cornelia is reported to have borne her misfortunes in a noble and magnanimous spirit, and to have said of the sacred places where her sons had been murdered that they were tombs worthy of the dead who occupied them. She herself resided near the promontory called Misenum without the slightest change in her customary way of life. She had many friends and kept a good table which was always thronged with guests; there were always Greeks and literary men around her, and all the reigning kings exchanged gifts with her.
>
> (Plut. *CG* 19; Loeb trans., modified)[1]

We have met Cornelia, the mother of the Gracchi, several times before in this study, invariably as the model of Roman womanhood: the devoted wife and mother, who lived soberly despite her wealth and who put her excellent education at the service of her sons. Here we have a somewhat different account of her, no less laudatory, but showing that she lived in an almost regal style in her villa at the bay of Naples (a favourite place for the villas of wealthy Romans) and that she used her wide learning for other purposes than the upbringing of her children alone. In contrast with her much-praised sobriety her way of life at Misenum as described by Plutarch resembles that of a Hellenistic queen, living in a grand style, patronizing Greek scholars and dealing with Hellenistic kings on an equal footing.[2] This unexpected side of her personality concerns us here.

It seems that Cornelia had moved to her villa at the promontory of Misenum after the death of her son Tiberius, or perhaps even earlier, at a time when the first luxurious Roman villas appeared along the coast of Campania. In the course of time these great Campanian villas became famous for the civilized leisure and intellectual activities of their owners, and for their patronage of Greek scholars. Cornelia may have provided one of the first examples of this villa-based patronage in Campania and she herself is, as far as we know, the earliest example of a Roman woman who acted as a patroness of literature and learning.[3]

Though this seems unusual for a Roman woman of her time, there are several factors that may explain it. As we saw above (chapter 3), patronage of scholars and men of letters was nothing out of the ordinary in her family; in fact, as a patroness of Greek scholars and in dealing on an equal footing with foreign kings she continued what may be called a family tradition. Her acting as a patroness can therefore, at least partly, be explained by the status and tradition of her family, whose fame and dignity she carried on by her grand reception of friends and men of learning. This may have been the more acceptable in Roman eyes (despite the fact that she was a woman), as in her later days she was the only surviving member of the family who could do so.[4] The fact that she had grown up in an extraordinarily wealthy and cultured family with many contacts with men of learning may explain her ease in dealing with Greek scholars, whom she knew well enough to pick and choose good teachers for her sons. Moreover, as a widow whose nearest male relatives had all died she must have had *de facto* control of her own resources and apart from her pleasant conversation and her good table, both reported by Plutarch, she presumably kept a good Greek library in her villa which would have attracted Greek scholars who may have stayed for some time, as was common in her days when fine libraries were scarce.[5]

The precise nature of her dealings with Greek scholars cannot be established from the brief description given by Plutarch. Unfortunately, he is our only witness.[6] Therefore, her acting as a patron is perhaps not beyond all doubt, but, to my mind, it is highly probable. Certain conditions were essential to it: her wealth, which, as a widow with no close male relatives living, she could manage independently (without noticeable intervention by her guardian), her excellent education, the tradition of patronage in her family and her authority as an elderly widow of a leading family. We may perhaps assume that, after her political influence had ceased because of the death of her sons, she devoted her energy and attention to scholarly pursuits, which, as befitted a member of her family and standing, she served best by receiving and supporting men of learning. In the following these and other aspects of female patronage of literature and learning will be examined with the help of other examples of Roman women who acted as patronesses. But first a few remarks about Roman patronage in general are needed.

Roman patronage

Patronage is one of the characteristic features of Roman life. Its importance as an instrument of social and political control has been discussed elsewhere and need not be reconsidered here. However, an adequate description of female cultural patronage should be set against the background of the better-known patronage by men. The following brief summary covers both the republic and the principate: though patronage was sometimes regarded as a typical republican phenomenon, R. Saller has shown that it continued to be important during the empire.[7]

Two forms of patronage may be distinguished. First, there is the patronage by a rich and powerful individual of a community or a collectivity. The *patronus* of a community may offer legal protection or his money for, say, public buildings (such as a public bath, an amphitheatre or a *porticus*) and may then be honoured by the grateful community with a statue or an inscription, in which he may be called *patronus* in the sense of 'protector' or 'benefactor'.[8] This type of 'collective' or 'civic' patronage is mainly attested in inscriptions. Save one or two exceptions it does not concern us here.

Second, there is the patronage by an individual of another individual. This type entails a relationship between two persons of unequal status and is usually called personal patronage. It is defined by Saller as a personal, reciprocal, and asymmetrical relationship of some duration in which services are exchanged.[9] In literary texts the relationship is not sharply defined; the exchange of services varies and the Latin terminology is unclear and often intentionally ambiguous, avoiding direct references to patronage.[10] As it is a voluntary association between freeborn persons, it resembles friendship in its personal character and the reciprocal exchange of goods or services. However, the participants are of unequal status (though both may be aristocrats[11]) and offer each other different kinds of goods and services; in contrast to friendship between equals, their roles are not reversible. The patron may use his superior power, status or wealth to further his client's career by means of his political influence and advice, to offer legal assistance and protection or to support him financially. To repay the *beneficium* the client gives his *gratia* in return. This gratitude is generally expressed by a deferential attitude towards his patron and, depending on the status of the client, may be shown by publicizing the patron's *beneficia* and thereby enhancing his reputation, by following his advice, by loyalty to him (in the republican period often expressed by voting for him), by attendance at the morning *salutatio* or even by being at his disposal the whole day.

Personal patronage is usually studied in a political or economic context. In this study, however, we shall deal with a special type of personal patronage, *viz.* 'literary' and 'intellectual' patronage, i.e. patronage of poets, writers and men of learning. For the sake of brevity I shall speak only of the patronage of poets, but where I speak of 'poets', prose-writers and men of learning are meant as well.

Recent discussions of literary patronage distinguish two kinds of support on the part of the patron: one consisted in material support and the other in encouragement. The first kind involved gifts of money or property to one's 'poet-friend' or his appointment to a sinecure providing for his livelihood.[12] The second consisted in preparing a favourable audience for the poet's work with the help of one's friends and connections, in circulating his books, in talking literature with him and sponsoring and attending his recitations, in protecting him against bad publicity and plagiarism, in short, in publicizing his work and giving him all sorts of literary backing.[13] Of course, ideal patrons did both and provided permanent support,[14] but most patrons acted according to circumstances and their own inclinations and possibilities, so that no patron–poet relationship was like any other. In return, the poet, or man of learning, might perform the same sort of services as other dependants of great houses did, such as the *salutatio*, escort to the forum or attendance at household ceremonies, but – and this distinguishes him from the more humble client – he was also expected to provide his greater friend with educated company and to offer his verses as his part of the exchange, thus rendering the exceptional service of 'immortalizing' his patron in his work. By this immaterial, or symbolic, exchange inherent in literary patronage the patron and the poet conferred status on each other: the patron by connecting his name with that of the poet and the poet by honouring the patron in his poetry.[15]

Since in the relationship of personal patronage the language of *amicitia* was generally used, and the outright mentioning of payment was considered bad manners, it is sometimes difficult to distinguish a patron from a friend. However, whereas the relationship between friends is based on equality, that between a patron and his lesser friend is not. Therefore, the use of certain key words (such as *dominus, rex, beneficium, officium* and *gratia*)[16] indicating the inequality of the two may be regarded as a mark of patronage.

Women as patrons of literature and learning

Discussions of patronage are mainly concerned with men. When we turn to the much sparser evidence for female patronage,[17] several questions arise. When women acted as patrons of literature and learning – as, for instance, Cornelia is said to have done – what enabled them to do so, what services did they exchange with their learned or literary *amici* and in what terms were they praised for their benefactions? What differences were there between male and female patrons apart from their numbers? For instance, did female patrons act in their own right, paying the expenses themselves (which implies independent control of their finances), or were they only mediators between the poet or scholar on the one hand and their husband, father or son on the other? And why is the number of patronesses known to us so small?

As Roman patronage of letters was *domus*-based,[18] we should expect Roman upper-class women to be able to play some part in it. Yet, in comparison to the number of male patrons of literature and learning only very few women seem to have acted as such and none of them attained the renown of a Maecenas. We may suspect that, since wealth, education, a high social status and a public career or position were important conditions for male literary patronage, women's social position limited their possibilities. Apart from their ambiguous social status (chapter 1) and their more haphazard education (chapter 2) they faced three disadvantages: the retired way of life expected of women, which clashed with the public role of a patron, their lack of a public career or position, which limited the support they could offer, and the restrictions that existed for some of them in respect of their independent control of their wealth. These three points must be touched upon before the evidence for female patronage of literature and learning is discussed.

First, we may ask whether the retired way of life expected of (upper-class) women was, perhaps partly, responsible for the scarcity of female patrons, and whether and to what extent it affected the terms in which a female patron was usually praised in the works addressed to her, that is, as a modest girl (or bride), faithful wife (or widow) or devoted mother, and not, as might be expected, for her generosity or for more personal traits. As we shall see, the uniformity of women's praise often makes it hard to decide whether a certain woman acted as a patroness or not, and impairs our understanding of her dealings with her protégés. But it may also have affected the women themselves, and we shall see below that all women who acted as patrons had to come to terms with the conflict between the public role of the patron and traditional female values. In the following I hope to show that the risk of criticism and of loss of reputation caused by their intrusion into a male domain could be countered successfully by a strict observance – at least outwardly – of the traditional rules of female behaviour.

As regards the second point, the lack of a public career or position probably impaired the scope and effect of women's patronage. Since they were themselves unable to give legal or political support, their patronage was of a limited kind, restricted to material rewards and literary encouragement. However, this restriction does not hold for women of the imperial family, or, at least, it does so to a lesser degree. Their closeness to the emperor and their public status (for instance, as the empress, or the emperor's mother or sister) gave them, *de facto* though not *de iure*, an unprecedented power, and by mediating with the emperor they could secure great rewards (such as privileges, appointments or immunities) for their protégés. Because of their exceptional position women of the imperial family will be discussed separately.

The third point, the question whether or not women could exercise independent control over their finances, allows of no simple answer: much depended on time and circumstances. Let us take, for example, Cornelia, the mother of the Gracchi: as she lived in the second century BC we may assume that she married with *manus*, as was customary in her days. This brought her, and her property, into the *potestas* of her husband (or into that of his father if alive). Thus, during her marriage she could not possess property in her own right, but upon her husband's death (which, in her case, occurred when she was still fairly young) she became *sui iuris* and juridically capable of owning and administering property, though requiring the consent of a *tutor* (guardian) for certain legal transactions. As she had been married with *manus* she had the same rights of intestate succession from her husband as her children. Moreover, her dowry, which consisted of the enormous sum of fifty talents, was returned to her at widowhood. As her sons died before her, she may also have inherited part of their fortunes. Thus, in the later stage of her life she had control of great riches. Like all women who were *sui iuris* she needed the authorization of a guardian for certain legal and financial transactions which might diminish the property, such as selling or alienating land, manumitting slaves or making a will, but his interference was not required for other financial activities or for the administration of her possessions. Unlike a guardian of minors, a guardian of a woman did not administer a woman's property; he was only required to give, or withhold, his consent to certain transactions. The fact that Cornelia's nearest male relatives (husband, father, brothers, sons and son-in-law) had all died probably increased her independence. Moreover, as she had married with *manus*, her husband in his will could give her the right to choose her own guardian (though we do not know if Tiberius Gracchus did so).[19] In short, widowhood and perhaps the death of her sons (her daughter Sempronia was the only one to survive her) brought Cornelia great wealth, which she could mainly spend at will. Therefore, it is far from surprising that she lived in a grand style in her luxury villa at Misenum and patronized Greek scholars in her later years.

Unlike Cornelia, most other women discussed in this chapter probably married without *manus*, *manus* marriages falling into disuse from about the first century BC onwards. Thus, though married, they remained in the *potestas* of their fathers and kept their rights at intestate succession in their family of birth. As a *filiafamilias* in the power of her father an adult woman could not acquire or possess property, but at his death she became *sui iuris*, needing the authorization of a guardian, as mentioned above, only for certain transactions. Because of the strict separation of property between husband and wife in non-*manus* marriages, a woman married without *manus* whose father had died could acquire, administer and control property in her own right, save for those transactions for which the authorization of a guardian was required. Cicero's wife Terentia provides a striking example of the great independence a woman enjoyed under such circumstances.[20]

By contrast, a woman married without *manus* whose father was still alive could not possess property in her own right. Thus, Cicero's daughter Tullia, though an adult woman in her third marriage, was still dependent on the financial support of her father and her plight caused by Cicero's difficulties in paying up painfully reveals the financial dependence of women who were *alieni iuris* (subject to another's control).[21] Compared to a woman like Tullia, who died before her father and therefore remained under his control all her life, women *sui iuris* could manage their possessions with considerable independence. During the first two centuries AD successive modifications in the *tutela* of women, starting with Augustus' *ius liberorum* (which freed women from *tutela* when they had borne three or more children and were *sui iuris*), reduced the power of the guardian and changed the guardianship of women from an effective control of their property in the interest of the family into a burdensome task for the guardian and only a slight inconvenience to the woman concerned.[22]

However, this should not lead us to assume that all women *sui iuris* actually controlled their possessions without male interference. Speaking of upper-class women in the Greek East in the Hellenistic and Roman periods H. C. van Bremen points out that legal control by a guardian was not the only possible male control over a woman's finances; she emphasizes the effect of social control by male relatives and of 'family strategies' on the way in which a woman might spend her wealth.[23] As this kind of male control varied for each individual woman and also changed during her lifetime depending on the death of male relatives, there are no general rules to judge the restrictions that could follow from it: in most cases, the precise effect of family strategies and of informal male control over a woman's finances are beyond our grasp. The only thing we can say is that the fewer living male relatives a woman had, the greater the chance that she managed her finances independently.

These three points must be taken into account in discussing the evidence of patronage of literature and learning among upper-class women. The discussion falls into two parts: first, the evidence pertaining to women of the imperial family will be discussed in chronological order. They will be considered in four groups: the female relatives of Augustus, those of Nero and Domitian, those of Trajan and Hadrian, and, fourth, the women of the Severi. After this, we shall turn to upper-class women outside the imperial family who, with the exception of Cornelia (who will not be discussed again), all belong to the principate. Because of the scarcity of the evidence the questions posed above (p. 100) can only be answered tentatively and, though there may have been some sort of a chrono-logical development, this is mostly beyond our reach. Nevertheless, some patterns can be traced which shed light on the motives, opportunities and disadvantages of upper-class women who patronized men of literature and learning, and on the nature and scope of their patronage.

Women of the imperial family

Above I gave a sketch of Roman patronage without paying attention to changes due to the establishment of the principate. However, with the creation of monarchic rule the channels of patronage changed: though aristocratic patron-age continued to be of importance, the emperor became the universal patron and connections with him were vital for political (and literary) success. This gave prominence also to the female members of the imperial family: because of their direct access to the emperor they could wield great power.[24] However, it is difficult to assess how far their relation with poets and men of learning can be described as patronage: for instance, if a literary or learned work is dedicated to a woman of the imperial family, it does not always follow that she acted as a patron to its author; it may have been presented to her merely to attract the attention of the emperor. A poet or scholar in need of support usually dedicated his work to a person of wealth and high status in the hope of receiving some sort of recom-pense. If he happened to be a Greek living at the imperial court, his dependence on the imperial family was, of course, even greater. Therefore, he was apt to court not only the emperor himself but also those members of the imperial family who might appreciate his poetry or treatises. As a consequence, the dedi-cation of a scholarly or literary work to female relatives of the emperor may not always be understood as an indication of patronage.

Also, it is hard to make out whether in supporting scholars or men of letters the women of the imperial family acted in their own right, or whether they should rather be compared to male senatorial 'brokers' of patronage mediating between the emperor and their protégés.[25] The evidence is often dubious, allow-ing both for a role as patronesses in their own right and for an intermediary one occasioned by their closeness to the emperor; in any case, it seems likely that nearly all patronage of imperial women was to some extent bound up with their close relationship with the emperor.

This brings us to the role of the emperor himself. Of course, not all emperors were cultural enthusiasts: apart from Augustus, Nero, Domitian and Hadrian, who actively encouraged literature and learning, many emperors were largely uninterested in such things.[26] Yet, as favour with the emperor could yield great profits, poets, philosophers and scholars flocked to court in the hope of gaining the emperor's sympathy. They recited or dedicated their work to him and presented treatises or poetry on events in the life of members of his family, hoping to receive a handsome reward. An amusing anecdote in Macrobius may be cited to illustrate the mercenary way in which poets – and other intellectuals – might approach the emperor. A Greek poet who had tried for days to present an epigram to Augustus eventually succeeded in handing it to him and hoped to receive a handsome sum of money in return. To his surprise and disappointment Augustus responded to his present with an extempore poem of his own. The poet read and praised the poem and giving a few coins to Augustus added: 'I would have given more, if I could.' Augustus, it is said, rewarded this witty reply with a hundred thousand sesterces. Though this anecdote is probably fictitious, substantial sums could indeed be earned by a favourable reception by the emperor; and not only money, but also gifts in kind, appointments, privileges and immunities were the rewards of those who were successful in gaining his favour.[27]

All members of the imperial house, both male and female, must have grown accustomed to men of letters and learning flocking around them. Some of these, mostly Greeks, actually lived in the imperial palace for long periods, as they used to do in the houses of the wealthy and educated upper class; they were employed as court poets, moral advisers and teachers, or appointed as imperial secretaries (*ab epistulis*), and accompanied the emperor on his journeys. As teachers in particular they stood in close contact with the women of the imperial family, who supervised the education of their own children and sometimes also that of many other children of the imperial family. Against this background we may assess the fragmentary evidence of our earliest imperial patronesses: Augustus' sister Octavia and her youngest daughter by Antony, Antonia Minor.

Patronage and motherhood: Octavia and Antonia

Augustus' beloved sister Octavia is mainly known as the faithful, but tragic, wife of Antony – her humiliating treatment by her husband was exploited by Octavian in his propaganda during the civil war – and as the mother of the celebrated Marcellus whose early death left her inconsolable.[28] The picture of this virtuous wife and ever-mourning mother has hidden from view other aspects of her life, such as her education and patronage. These concern us here.

As a patron of literature and learning Octavia has left some, admittedly vague, traces in our sources. The most straightforward piece of evidence is found in the work of the architect Vitruvius. In the preface to his *De Architectura*, dedicated to

Augustus, he tells us that, after being appointed by Octavian as a surveyor of the construction and repair of war engines,

> I received rewards, together with my colleagues, and after first granting me this recognition, you continued them by the recommendation of your sister. Therefore, since I was indebted to you for such benefits that, to the end of my life, I had no fear of poverty, I set about the composition of this work for you.
>
> (Vitr. *Arch.* 1 *praef.* 2–3)[29]

Apparently, it was thanks to Octavia's recommendation that the rewards, which he had received from Octavian for his past services, were continued. Thus, Vitruvius was guaranteed an income for the rest of his life, which allowed him the leisure to write his *magnum opus* on architecture, which he gratefully dedicated to Augustus. The passage shows that Octavia's patronage of Vitruvius did not consist in financial support but in her successful mediation with her brother; she played the part of a patron-broker obtaining a *beneficium* from the emperor for her protégé. Of course, as Augustus' beloved sister she was in an excellent position to do so.[30]

Evidence of a different kind of cultural patronage exercised by Octavia is found in Plutarch's 'life of Marcellus'. According to his account she dedicated a library to the memory of her son Marcellus, who had died as a young man in 23 BC, only two years after his marriage to Augustus' daughter Julia which had marked him out as Augustus' prospective heir. The library, which had separate Greek and Latin sections, was built within the enclosure of the Porticus Octaviae, which itself had been constructed shortly before by Augustus in honour of his sister.[31] This, and Augustus' restoration of another *porticus* with a very similar name, the Porticus Octavia, in 33 BC, seems to have led to confusion: Dio mistakenly believes that both the library and the Porticus Octaviae were built by Augustus in honour of his sister and were financed with the spoils of war of his Dalmatian campaign in 33 BC.[32] The contradiction between the two accounts has left its traces in modern studies, some assuming that the library was founded by Octavia and others that Augustus built it. An attempt has been made to reconcile these views by arguing that Augustus started building the *porticus* and the library in 33 BC and that when the work was finished, Octavia dedicated the library to the memory of her son.[33] However, this assumption seems unnecessary, and in support of Plutarch's account a more or less contemporary source may be adduced, which has been overlooked so far: in his first book of the *Ars Amatoria* Ovid advises young men who were in search of an attractive girl to take a walk in one of the many porticoes of Rome where they could be sure to find one, referring to the Porticus Octaviae with the words 'where the mother has added her own gifts to her son's'. This may refer to the donation of the library by Octavia, but what Marcellus' gifts may have consisted of is unclear: should we assume that Marcellus' private library formed the nucleus of this newly built library?[34]

Another, somewhat dubious, indication of literary patronage is also connected with the death of Marcellus. As he was much loved and regarded as Augustus' prospective successor, his death was felt to be a national calamity and many poets and artists commemorated him in poems and portraits, hoping, of course, to receive a substantial reward. Octavia, however, rejected all poetry in commemoration of Marcellus and did not want to be presented with his portrait; she even forbade his name to be mentioned in her presence. When, not long after Marcellus' death, Virgil recited the second, fourth and sixth books of the *Aeneid* to Augustus in her presence, she is reported to have fainted when unexpectedly he mentioned Marcellus. Yet, she could neither prevent Virgil's verses nor Propertius' poem that lamented his death and, according to certain (admittedly dubious) evidence, she actually rewarded Virgil for his verses.[35]

Our last reference to patronage by Octavia is again usually associated with the death of Marcellus. In his 'life of Publicola' Plutarch tells us that Athenodorus of Tarsus, a Stoic philosopher who lived at the court as a tutor and adviser of Augustus, dedicated a book to her. Unfortunately, Plutarch gives no information on its contents. At the end of his story about Mucius Scaevola he writes: 'All other writers agree in giving this Mucius the surname of Scaevola, but Athenodorus, the son of Sandon, in his book addressed to Octavia, the sister of the emperor Augustus, says that his surname was Postumus.'[36] From this incidental remark it has been inferred that the book dedicated to her was a *consolatio* for the death of her son Marcellus in 23 BC,[37] but are we to accept this?

Consolationes for women mourning the death of a son are a well-known genre in the Greek and Roman world, and Octavia was considered to be in dire need of such a consolation as she mourned excessively for her only son. Yet, two objections can be proffered to the assumption that Athenodorus' work was a *consolatio*. First there is the date. If the book was a *consolatio* for Marcellus' death, it must have been written after 23 BC. This does not agree with the date of Athenodorus' position as a court philosopher, since he seems to have resided in Rome only till shortly after 30 BC, when Augustus sent him to his native city of Tarsus to reorganize its constitution.[38] Yet, this does not disprove that the book was a *consolatio*, since it may have been sent to her from Tarsus.

Second, there is the problem of its contents. How does Plutarch's remark that Mucius Scaevola was also called Postumus by Athenodorus fit into a *consolatio* for Octavia? Since Athenodorus was a Stoic philosopher, we may assume that his book was a philosophical treatise of some kind. He may have used the exemplary endurance of Mucius Scaevola[39] to encourage Octavia amidst the numerous sorrows of her life: the death of her first husband, the humiliating treatment by her second husband, the civil war fought between her second husband and her brother, and, finally, the death of her son Marcellus. However, as we have seen, she is said to have closed her ears to all attempts to console her after his death,[40] and this may well have deterred Athenodorus from addressing a *consolatio* to her. Therefore, we cannot exclude the possibility that Athenodorus' philosophical treatise bore no relation to her life whatsoever; it may have been dedicated to her during his stay in Rome as a mark of esteem or because of her possible interest in (Stoic) philosophy.

To summarize the evidence, we have seen that Octavia's patronage of literature and learning was of different kinds. On the one hand, she acted as a broker of patronage, obtaining a privilege for Vitruvius by mediating with Augustus. On the other, she may have acted as a patroness herself in her relationship with Athenodorus. Because of Athenodorus' position as a court philosopher he was dependent on gifts and favours from Augustus and other members of the imperial family. Octavia may have given him money or some gift in kind in return for his book addressed to her, or perhaps his work was dedicated to her to repay some past *beneficium*. The dedication of a library of Greek and Latin literature, the most expensive of her cultural benefactions, was probably paid for out of her own resources. As Augustus had granted her the right to dispense with a guardian in control of her finances, she was able to spend her money at will – though one wonders if Augustus would have tolerated a less suitable use of it.[41]

As regards the quality of her education, which next to wealth, and the independent use of it, was (as we have seen in the case of Cornelia) essential to cultural patronage by women, all sources suggest that she was very well educated. She must have received the grammatical education typical of her class and time (see chapter 2), and her lengthy stay in Greece during her marriage with Antony must have improved her knowledge of the Greek language and culture. In any case, her Greek was good enough for Athenodorus to dedicate a philosophical treatise to her. Besides, the fact that she supported Vitruvius and dedicated a public library of Greek and Latin literature indicates her interest in literature and learning.[42]

As regards her social position, her patronage was closely bound up with her status as the emperor's sister. As she was on very good terms with Augustus and lived in his palace after her divorce from Antony, she must have been well acquainted with the poets, philosophers and men of letters who flocked around her brother. Also Athenodorus, a house-philosopher and teacher of Augustus, came into contact with her in this way and the dedication of his work to her must have been due, at least partly, to the fact that she was the sister of his imperial patron. Similarly, the poetry and works of art presented to her at the death of her son were proffered because she was the sister of the emperor and the mother of his deceased heir presumptive. The same holds for a work addressed to her by Augustus' friend Maecenas, which from the one line that is left of it (quoted by a sixth-century grammarian) seems to have been an encomium: 'you have combed your hair, which is comely by the gifts of nature'.[43] Maecenas, of course, was a gentleman poet like Augustus himself and not in search of patronage; his dedication of a poem (if such it is) to Octavia should be regarded as a mark of esteem prompted, at least partly, by his friendship with Augustus. Possibly Augustus' patronage of literature and learning had inspired his sister: the dedication of a public library by her was a form of public munificence heartily approved of by

Augustus, who himself had founded a public library on the Palatine in 28 BC. Further, as we have seen, she attended Virgil's recitation of the *Aeneid* in the retinue of Augustus, and her position as the emperor's sister enabled her to act as a successful broker.[44]

In contrast with her activities as a patron the judgement of Octavia found in our sources emphasizes her traditional virtues: she is extolled for her beauty, wifely devotion and excellent motherhood. The careful way in which she educated the ten or more children under her care – only five of whom were her own – and her life-long allegiance to the traditional female role won her much sympathy: she is described as a blameless woman and a model of womanhood, beautiful, virtuous, intelligent, dignified, an excellent mother and a loyal wife, even when seriously wronged.[45]

In this exemplary life her activity as a patron of literature and learning was neither entirely ignored nor much spoken of: it is mentioned only briefly and in a matter-of-fact way – by which, incidentally, it gains credit. It may be assumed that she exercised patronage in so modest a way that it was acceptable even to the most traditional-minded. Only the dedication of the public library must have been widely known. But here again, her role was that of a mother, a grieving mother at that, seeking fame not for herself but for her son. Despite the fact that, strictly speaking, she intruded into a male field by acting as a patroness, it is never even suggested that she overstepped the boundary between the male and female worlds. She never tried to gain a public position of power; on the contrary, she dutifully did what was expected of her as a woman of the imperial family: she strengthened her brother's political alliance by her marriage to Antony (although she had only just been widowed), and bore and reared children who were related to Augustus in order to provide him with a successor from his own family. Her tragedy was that she failed in both, and this may explain her excessive sorrow during the last twelve years of her life: in spite of her mediation, undertaken with so much zeal and at first successfully, her husband Antony and her brother in the end engaged in civil war, and her promising son Marcellus, marked out by Augustus as his successor, died at the age of 19.[46] Because of her strict observance of traditional rules of female behaviour her patronage of literature and learning was socially acceptable; it must have been one of the few ways open to a woman of her position to exert power without incurring blame.

Octavia's youngest daughter, Antonia Minor, though a strong-minded and influential woman, displayed a similar modesty in public, and this may have made her activities as a patroness (supposing she actually acted as such) acceptable in the eyes of her contemporaries. We are only very vaguely informed of possible instances of patronage of poetry on her part. She is addressed in three poems by Augustus' court-poet and companion, the epigrammatist Crinagoras of Mytilene. The most interesting of these poems accompanied five books of lyric verses (consisting of convivial and amatory poetry by Anacreon) which he presented to her as a gift. It runs:

> The sweet quintet of lyric books in this box brings works of inimitable charm – the works of Anacreon, which that merry old man from Teos wrote with the help of wine or desire. We come on her festal day as a gift for Antonia who wins the highest prize in beauty and mind.
>
> $(AP\,9.239)^{47}$

The gift of books of poetry introduced by a poem praising the recipient points to an existing, or perhaps only desired, relationship of patronage between Crinagoras and the Antonia mentioned.[48] As her name is not accompanied by a title of deference or some other addition, we cannot be absolutely certain that Antonia Minor is meant, but the following shows this to be likely.

Crinagoras of Mytilene lived in Rome as a court-poet from 26 BC onwards and was familiar with many members of the imperial family. He accompanied Augustus on his voyages and he commemorated events in the lives of members of the imperial family in his epigrams.[49] Therefore, the Antonia addressed in his poetry is likely to be one of the two daughters of Octavia and Antony, who were both called Antonia. Not much is known of the elder Antonia, but her younger sister, Antonia Minor, was a prominent woman both as a personality and because of her station in life. The daughter of Octavia and thus Augustus' niece, she married Tiberius' brother Drusus and by this marriage became the mother of Germanicus, Claudius and Livilla, the grandmother of Gaius Caligula and eventually the great-grandmother of Nero. Widowed at the age of 27, she lived with her mother-in-law Livia in the imperial palace and was alone among the young widows in Augustus' family in maintaining her decision not to remarry.[50] Plutarch tells us that she was famous for prudence and beauty, a statement resembling the last line of the poem by Crinagoras quoted above.[51]

Another poem by Crinagoras mentions an Antonia who is about to give birth. The poem is a prayer to Hera and Zeus to grant her an easy delivery:

> Hera, mother of the goddesses of childbirth, Hera of marriage-rites, and Zeus, common father to all that are born, be gracious and grant that labour may come to Antonia gently with the soft hands of Epione, so that her husband, her mother and her mother-in-law may rejoice. Truly her womb bears the blood of princely houses.
>
> $(AP\,6.244;$ trans. Gow and Page (1968) I: 205, modified$)^{52}$

Again, this Antonia is not explicitly identified, but the last line shows her to be a member of the imperial family and supports an identification with Antonia Minor. If this is right, the poem must have been written before 11 BC, the year of Octavia's death, since in the fifth line of the poem three members of Antonia's family are mentioned as rejoicing at the birth of one of her children: her mother (Octavia), her husband (Drusus) and her mother-in-law (Livia). As the child in question must therefore have been born before 11 BC it was probably her eldest son, Germanicus, who was born in 15 BC, or his sister Livilla, born about 13 BC (that is, if it was one of her surviving children).

The third poem accompanied a birthday present of winter-roses:

> Roses once bloomed in spring; now in mid-winter we have opened our purple buds, glad and smiling on your birthday, so near to your bridal-bed. Better to be wreathed on the temples of the loveliest of women than to wait for the sun of spring.
>
> (*AP* 6.345; trans. Gow and Page (1968) I: 201–3, modified)[53]

No clue is given to the name or identity of this lady who is soon to be married. Therefore, the identification is a matter of speculation, but considering Crinagoras' position as a court-poet, his other poems dedicated to Antonia and her birthday in mid-winter, an identification with Antonia Minor seems a reasonable guess.[54]

The relation between Antonia and Crinagoras resembles a relationship of patronage between a Greek court-poet and a respected member of the imperial family. Crinagoras honoured Antonia with his poetry, commenting upon events in her life and occasionally presenting her with delicate gifts as witnesses to her sophistication. Antonia may have offered him money or some other kind of support in return, though, as usual, we have no information on this. The intimacy speaking from the poems and their spread over time indicate a relationship of some duration; during the more than forty years that Crinagoras stayed in Rome, nearly always employed at the imperial court, they must have become closely acquainted.[55]

Crinagoras of Mytilene was possibly not the only poet supported by Antonia. Thallus and Honestus, two other Greek poets of the 'Garland of Philip', are also sometimes regarded as her poet-clients – though in both cases the evidence is slight. Of the obscure Thallus of Milete we have only five epigrams, preserved in the Garland of Philip. Because of his *gentilicium* Antonius, which, however, is attested only once, C. Cichorius rather boldly infers that he had obtained Roman citizenship through the patronage of Antonia Minor.[56] Though Roman citizenship is one of the rewards an imperial woman like Antonia might have procured for an educated protégé by mediation with the emperor and though Thallus possibly did write a poem in honour of her son Germanicus,[57] we have no secure evidence pointing to a relationship of patronage between them.

Slightly more is known of Honestus of Corinth. He was active as a poet during the reign of Tiberius and probably sought, or enjoyed, patronage at the imperial court. He was the author of ten epigrams in the Garland of Philip and of another twelve that were inscribed on the statue-bases of the monument of the Muses found near Thespiae in Boeotia and on the bases of some other statues nearby.[58] One of the epigrams was inscribed on the statue-base of an Augusta. It reads: 'Augusta, who can boast of two divine sceptred Caesars, set light to twin torches of Peace; fit company for the learned Heliconian Muses, a choir-mate of wise counsel, her wisdom was the whole world's saviour.'[59] Who was this Augusta?

As the statue is lost we have no information apart from the poem. It provides several clues, which, however, leave room for various explanations. In an influential study Cichorius identified the Augusta with Antonia Minor, arguing that the 'two divine sceptred Caesars' mentioned in the poem are her grandsons Caius Caligula and Tiberius Gemellus, both of whom were nominated by Tiberius for his succession.[60] In his view her wisdom that saved the world (line 4) refers to her alleged exposure of the plot of Sejanus in AD 31, and he connects the remark about her wise counsel and her fitting companionship of the Muses with her literary interests and her patronage of men of letters such as Crinagoras.

However, Cichorius' ingenious interpretation has not remained unchallenged and indeed contains some weak points. First, Antonia is said to have declined the title of Augusta, which was conferred on her by her grandson, the emperor Caligula, in AD 37 only shortly before her death; in Rome she is called Augusta only posthumously.[61] This does not necessarily disprove the identification, as Greek provincial inscriptions honouring members of the imperial family were often more liberal with honorific titles.[62] The identification of the two Caesars as Caligula and Tiberius Gemellus raises more serious problems. Their title as 'divine sceptred Caesars' strictly speaking rules out Tiberius Gemellus, who, though proclaimed joint heir with his cousin Caligula by Tiberius and adopted by Caligula shortly after his accession in AD 37 as his prospective successor, never actually reigned but was killed by Caligula within a year of his adoption. Even if we take the 'divine sceptred Caesars' to mean designated successors only, assuming they were given these honorific titles before their due, it is difficult to imagine that Tiberius Gemellus and Caligula were honoured on an equal footing. Especially after the latter's accession the difference between the two must have been manifest – unless we should assume that from a provincial point of view, as grandsons and heirs of Tiberius, both were equally regarded as Caesars.[63] Consequently the identification of the Augusta as Antonia Minor, though attractive, cannot be proved and her patronage of Honestus should be rejected for lack of proof.[64]

All in all, the evidence for Antonia's literary patronage is weak. Her possible activities in this field must have been rather inconspicuous. Nevertheless, she was a prominent woman in her days. As a niece of Augustus and closely related to all the other emperors of the Julio-Claudian dynasty she held an important position at the imperial court. She was influential with Augustus, to whom she demonstrated a distinct self-assertiveness in her successful refusal to remarry, and with her brother-in-law Tiberius, who had a high regard for her; all this made her a potentially powerful patroness in political matters. After the death of Livia in AD 29 she must have been the most eminent woman of the court: as the emperor Tiberius was a widower, there was no empress to rival her.[65]

The conditions of her life were also favourable to literary patronage. Like her mother, she was a woman of great wealth, which she probably controlled independently: as a mother of three children she was allowed to dispense with a guardian according to the *ius liberorum*. Moreover, she is reported to have been intelligent and, like the other women of Augustus' family, she was probably well educated in both Latin and Greek. As she lived at the imperial palace for most of her life she must have been well acquainted with the poets and scholars of Augustus' entourage. Thus, her wealth, her education, the tradition of patronage in her family and her eminent position must have made her attractive as a patroness; we may assume that Greek poets who offered her verses or small gifts tried to gain or maintain her patronage or, through her mediation, that of the emperor.

In spite of her prominence at the court and her public status Antonia Minor is described in our sources in traditional terms. The modesty of her public behaviour is emphasized and she is mainly praised for traditional female qualities: beauty, chastity, loyalty and fidelity to her (deceased) husband, strictness in educating her children and a traditional way of living. Though the actual reason for not remarrying may, of course, have been totally different, she lived up to the traditional ideal of the *univira*. During her long and self-imposed widowhood (from the age of 27 till her death at the age of 72) she lived in the palace – at first with her mother-in-law, Livia – and supervised the education of a great number of children: her own three children, the children of her son Germanicus and several children of eastern royal houses, who were held as hostages in Rome.[66] We may assume that, as in the case of her mother, her allegiance to traditional rules of female behaviour made her occasional intrusion into the male world of patronage generally acceptable.

Though their personalities seem to have been very different, there are distinct similarities between the lives and circumstances of Antonia Minor and her mother Octavia. Both were well educated and possessed great wealth, which they were allowed to control without a guardian. Both were widows during much of their lives and as respected members of the emperor's family they enjoyed an eminent position. As educators of a great number of children they stood in close contact with Greek scholars, who were employed as their teachers.[67] These circumstances favoured the exercise of patronage and made them powerful both as 'brokers' and as patronesses in their own right.

Bearing this in mind, the way in which our sources praise them extolling their traditional virtues seems to be rather one-sided. Two explanations may be proposed, which, though contradictory at first sight, seem to enforce each other. First, it seems likely that Octavia and Antonia actually were the loyal wives, devoted mothers and faithful widows they were said to be. Yet, this would not have prevented them from interfering – though in an unobtrusive way – in traditional male fields, such as patronage and politics. Second, women were customarily praised in traditional terms: on epitaphs and in the literary sources there is not always a direct relation between the reason a woman was praised for (for example, financial generosity) and the terms in which her praise was expressed (traditional virtues).[68] Thus, less conventional activities of women may be concealed behind praise of traditional virtues. But since we may assume that the actual reason for a woman's praise was usually well known, at least to the people concerned and in her surroundings, these activities were implicitly approved of.

To illustrate this, part of an incomplete funerary inscription from the Augustan period may be cited, which speaks in an unusually frank way of the complexity of women's praise. It was set up for a woman called Murdia, who married twice, by the eldest son from her first marriage in gratitude to the fairness of her financial dealings as established in her will: mindful of the wishes of his deceased father she had not only made him and his half-brothers equal heirs to her estate (her daughter received a legacy), but had also given him a prior legacy from his father's patrimony. Though she was, in fact, praised because of the good administration of her estate and because of her tact and justice in drawing up her will, the terms in which she is praised are fashioned according to traditional notions. But before entering upon the conventional list of female virtues her son explains:

> For these reasons, since the praise of all good women is by custom simple and similar, because their natural qualities over which they keep guard themselves do not require a variegated language, and since it is enough that all of them have done the same to gain a good reputation and since it is hard for a woman to earn new forms of praise, as their life undergoes a smaller variety of fortunes, it is necessary to honour the virtues they hold in common in order not to lose anything from fair precepts and thereby debase what remains. In this sense my dearest mother earned the greatest praise of all, because in modesty, decency, chastity, obedience, woolworking, industry and loyalty she was equal to other good women and she was second to none in the excellence of her work and her wisdom in the face of dangers.
>
> (*CIL* VI 10230)[69]

These words show that the uniformity of women's praise can easily be misleading; though their lives may have been less varied than those of men, women were not wholly confined to a life of domestic virtue, and the standard catalogue of female virtues, both here and elsewhere, may hide the fact that a woman was actually admired for quite different qualities. This should be kept in mind when other examples of female patronage are discussed.

'Wicked' women: Agrippina, Poppaea and Domitia Longina

Apart from Octavia and Antonia there is little evidence for literary patronage on the part of the women of the Julio-Claudian dynasty. For instance, Livia, who because of her great wealth and her eminent position as the wife and mother of reigning emperors was a powerful patroness in political matters, and who, besides, was known for public building and for her philanthropic activities, was never, as far as we know, active as a patron of literature and learning.[70] Only Augustus' great-granddaughter Agrippina Minor, the last wife of Claudius and the mother of Nero, and Poppaea, Nero's second wife, may occasionally have acted as such, but the evidence is scarce and ambiguous. Of the female relatives of the succeeding dynasty, that of the Flavian emperors, we know only very little,[71] but Domitia Longina, the wife of Domitian, seems to have acted as a literary patroness at least once. In contrast to the blameless reputation of Octavia and Antonia, discussed above, the reputation of these three imperial women was bad. The cause of this was not only their own behaviour, but perhaps also that they were associated with two emperors who were much hated by the senate: Nero and Domitian.

In support of Agrippina's possible patronage of literature and learning there are only two pieces of evidence. First, Tacitus relates that in AD 49 Agrippina Minor:

> secured the recall of Annaeus Seneca from exile, and a praetorship for him, since she believed that because of his literary fame her intervention would be applauded by the public; she also desired that Domitius [i.e. Nero] would grow up under the guidance of so excellent a tutor, and hoped that they would profit from his advice in connection with their designs upon the throne.
>
> (Tac. *Ann.* 12.8)[72]

Apparently, Agrippina Minor acted as a patron-broker by mediating with her husband, the emperor Claudius. However, she did so not out of interest in philosophy (which she even banned from her son's curriculum) or in rhetoric, but to ingratiate herself with the people and for other (chiefly political) reasons: her undoubted patronage of Seneca seems to have been of a political nature.

The second piece of evidence is a poem addressed to her by Leonidas of Alexandria, a Greek poet attached to Nero's court. Leonidas had turned from astronomy (or astrology) to poetry, and when in Rome, he enjoyed the patronage of Nero and possibly of other members of the imperial family. He was famous for his *isopsephia*, ingenious epigrams in which the sum of the letters taken as numerical signs is identical in each distich.[73] The epigram addressed to Nero's mother Agrippina, one of these *isopsephia*, was sent to her as a birthday-present. It reads: 'One will send crystal, another silver, a third topazes, rich birthday gifts. But I, look, having merely made two "isopsephon" distichs for Agrippina, am content with this my gift that envy shall not damage.'[74] Contrasting his small gift of two distichs to the rich gifts of other people he alludes to the *topos* of the poor poet who has only his poetry to offer. By giving a poem as a birthday-present he draws attention to Agrippina's understanding of sophisticated poetry, but she is not personally praised in it either for intellectual or for traditional female virtues and therefore the poem is insufficient evidence for a conclusion that Agrippina was Leonidas' patron. Rather, it seems to be an obligatory birthday-poem on a stock theme sent to Agrippina because she was the mother of his patron, the emperor Nero.

Nero's second wife Poppaea Sabina was the addressee of another isopsephic poem written by Leonidas. It accompanied a celestial globe, which the ex-astronomer, or astrologer, sent to her for her birthday. It reads: 'Poppaea Augusta, spouse of Zeus, receive from the Egyptian Leonidas this map of the heavens on your natal day; for you take pleasure in gifts worthy of your marriage and your learning.'[75] This is a well-balanced poem: as Nero is equated with Zeus, the celestial god, a celestial globe is a worthy gift to his wife. The reference to her learning in the last line agrees with Tacitus' grudging remark that she possessed a lively intelligence. However, as suggested by this poem, her learning may have consisted especially in knowledge of astrology.[76] Tacitus tells us that Poppaea surrounded herself with *mathematici*, astrologers, as her counsellors, and con-temptuously describes them as an untrustworthy and deceitful lot, but in the higher Roman society of the time such men were very fashionable and even the emperors often resorted to astrologers for advice.[77]

For Poppaea's relation to Leonidas this poem is our only evidence. Its deferen-tial tone, the sophisticated gift and the reference to her learning indicate that he may have sought, or gained, her patronage. Her eminent position as Nero's wife, her wealth and her education made her attractive as a patron, and we know that she successfully supported her favourites in political matters.[78] Yet, this poem is insufficient ground for a definite conclusion that she was a patron of poets.

For literary patronage by Domitia Longina, the wife of Domitian, we have only one indication. At the end of his *Vita* Flavius Josephus mentions his cordial relationship to the Flavian emperors, who had supported and honoured him in various ways. One woman is included in his list of imperial benefactors, Domitian's wife Domitia Longina, who 'accomplished much for me by being my benefactress'.[79] Josephus does not specify the nature of her benefactions, which may have consisted in financial support or in mediation on his behalf with her husband, the emperor. Though Josephus' remark seems trustworthy enough, we have no further information about any patronage of men of literature or learning on Domitia Longina's part;[80] our sources devote more attention to her alleged adulteries.

Agrippina Minor, Poppaea and Domitia Longina were women of very bad repute. Though the first two, Agrippina Minor and Poppaea, differed in social status and personality, and were arch-enemies during their lifetimes, competing with each other for influence with Nero, they have in common that they are both portrayed as utterly ambitious and eager for power. Moreover, both were wealthy, well educated and well connected (though, of course, Agrippina was greatly superior to Poppaea in birth and social status), and through Nero both wielded power in political matters. Though political and cultural patronage were not mutually exclusive (we have seen that Octavia and Antonia probably exercised both), Agrippina and, perhaps less, Poppaea seem to have concentrated on political ambitions, seeking power for themselves through their son or husband.

Devoting most of her attention to political power and prestige Agrippina Minor seems to have avoided the more sheltered life and the less conspicuous prestige that patronage of culture might have offered. In contrast to Octavia and Antonia, she transgressed the boundaries imposed upon her gender by openly interfering in politics: she went so far as to receive embassies and to attend a meeting of the senate (though hidden behind a curtain). This led to sharp criticism for 'male' behaviour by most ancient authors, most notably Tacitus, who describes her as an overbearing and cruel personality prone to political intrigue and exercising power like a man.

Like Poppaea, Domitia Longina is depicted as an adulterous and promiscuous woman. Her complicated relation to her husband, the emperor Domitian (it is said that they divorced and remarried), her alleged love-affair with Paris, the famous actor of pantomime, and with many other men, and her supposed complicity in the murder of Domitian receive much attention in our sources, but for most of these accusations there is little ground.[81] Because of their breach of rules in overstepping the boundary of respectable female behaviour and perhaps also because of their association with notoriously 'bad' emperors, all three of them were portrayed in the ancient sources as stereotypes of wicked women: Agrippina as the fierce, cruel and dominant 'masculine' woman, Poppaea as the seductive, scheming and murderous adulteress and Domitia Longina as the arrogant adulteress who took pride in her promiscuity. As such, they formed the negative counterpart of the traditional 'good' women, modest wives and devoted mothers, like Octavia and Antonia, who, though also active in 'male' undertakings, were so in a socially acceptable way complying with traditional rules of female behaviour.

Modest and self-effacing: Plotina, Sabina and the younger Matidia

During the reigns of Trajan and Hadrian the women of the imperial family are only rarely mentioned: our literary sources praise them according to Roman ideology as modest, unassuming and self-effacing. In comparison to the prominent women of the Julio-Claudian dynasty they remain in the background.[82] The little information we have about their patronage of literature and learning mainly stems from inscriptions.

A bilingual inscription of AD 121 found in Athens contains the correspondence of Plotina and Hadrian on the succession of the head of the Epicurean school at Athens.[83] Apparently, Plotina (then widow of Trajan and the empress-mother of his adopted son and successor Hadrian) acted as a patron, or rather as a broker of patronage, for the Athenian Epicureans, obtaining a favour for them by her mediation with the emperor. In her first letter, in Latin, she asks Hadrian to grant the school freedom from restrictions in the choice of a successor. It reads:

How much I am interested in the School of Epicurus, you know very well, *domine*. Your help is needed in the matter of the succession; for in view of the ineligibility of all but Roman citizens, the range of choice is narrow. I ask therefore in the name of Popillius Theotimus, the present successor at Athens, to allow him to write in Greek that part of his disposition which deals with regulating the succession and grant him the power of filling his place by a successor of peregrine status, should personal considerations make it advisable; and let the future successors of the School of Epicurus henceforth enjoy the same right as you grant to Theotimus; all the more since the practice is that each time the testator has made a mistake in the choice of his successor, the disciples of the above School after a general deliberation put in his place the best man, a result that will be more easily attained if he is selected from a larger group.

(ILS 7784)[84]

Apparently, a restriction existed as regards the choice of a successor: the head of the Epicurean school was obliged to appoint his successor by a will made up in Latin choosing from among Roman citizens only.[85] In her letter Plotina requests Hadrian on behalf of Popillius Theotimus, the head of the school, to abolish it both for himself and for his successors and to make it possible to appoint the best person available, whether a Roman citizen or a *peregrinus*.

Plotina's letter to Hadrian is a rather formal request, lacking a formula of address and farewell; it resembles a *libellus*, a written petition of a private person to the emperor. Hadrian answered favourably. His brief reply in Latin takes the form of a *subscriptio*, an imperial rescript, addressed to Popillius Theotimus[86] and is inscribed immediately below Plotina's request. Then follows Plotina's long Greek letter, addressed to the Epicureans in Athens, in which she communicates the imperial decision. Unlike her petition to Hadrian and Hadrian's reply, this letter is written in a personal and cordial style. She jubilantly announces that their request has been granted and then summarizes the favours that have been bestowed, emphasizing the gratitude due to Hadrian and the responsibility that now rests on each head of the school to choose a successor impartially on the basis of excellence only. Then the letter becomes fragmentary and finally it breaks off.

The inscription proves that Plotina acted as a patron to Popillius Theotimus and the Epicurean school in Athens; moreover, it sheds light on certain details of her patronage. Towards her Epicurean protégés she uses the language of *amicitia*, and the cordial tone of her letter, which contains much advice for the succession of the school, betrays a personal relationship of some duration. Her petition to Hadrian, on the other hand, is written in a modest, almost submissive tone, carefully avoiding asking too much and providing good grounds for her request. She shows her respect for Hadrian by formally addressing him as *dominus*, and in her letter to the Epicureans she gives him all the credit, calling him 'truly the benefactor and overseer of all education'.[87] However, at the same time she stresses her closeness to the emperor: in her Greek letter she praises him as the 'most august emperor, who is most dear to me in every way both as an excellent lord and as my good son',[88] and in her Latin petition she refers to the fact that her sentiments towards the Epicurean school are well known to him.

Hadrian's favourable reply may be regarded as a token of his respect for Plotina and, as such, it boosted her prestige. Her closeness to the emperor as well as her modesty in asking favours contributed to her success. As a broker she had to act carefully, balancing between her desire to further the interests of her protégés and her fear of asking too much and being rejected (which would have been a blow to her prestige). Thus, she was successful; in his funeral speech for Plotina Hadrian is reported to have said: 'though she asked much of me, she was never refused anything', which according to Dio should be understood as: 'her requests were of such a character that they neither burdened me nor gave me any justification for opposing them', which is another sign of the care with which she formulated her requests.[89]

Modesty seems to have been her abiding trait throughout her life, and Dio characterizes her subtly by quoting her when she first entered the palace: 'I enter here as the kind of woman I wish to be when I depart.'[90] Though her education and her high station as the wife of Trajan and the adoptive mother of his successor might have allowed her a greater influence in cultural matters, this inscription is our only evidence of Plotina's patronage of learning.[91] Also in political matters we have little information on such influence; compared to powerful women like Livia and Agrippina Minor her political involvement seems to have been slight.[92] Almost all literary sources speak of her allegiance to traditional female values: a faithful wife, a widow of old-fashioned virtue, a woman who was unassuming despite her high station and who lived a retired, domestic life in harmony with her husband and his female relatives, that is the rather one-sided portrait emerging of her; but for this single inscription we would never have known of the other side of her personality: her lively interest in philosophy and her patronage of the Epicurean school.[93]

Not much is known about Sabina, the great-niece of Trajan and the wife of Hadrian; most of our evidence deals with the rumours of her unhappy marriage. However, numerous statues of her have been found all over the empire, and from her portraiture and the few remarks to her in the ancient sources it has been inferred that she was an educated lady with an interest in literature and learning.[94] She was with Hadrian on several of his imperial journeys, and on their tour to Egypt in AD 130 she was accompanied by the poetess Julia Balbilla, who left a record of their visit to the 'singing' Colossus of Memnon in Thebes in four epigrams carefully inscribed on the left leg and foot of the statue (see chapter 5). Sabina herself added a short inscription in prose reporting her experience of hearing Memnon sing.[95]

Julia Balbilla was a woman of about the same age as Sabina or slightly older; since no husband is mentioned, she was probably a widow. Modern scholars usually call her a friend or a lady-in-waiting of the empress, but her social status seems too high for the latter and not high enough for the former. Therefore, another possible relationship may be considered: that of a female poet-friend of the empress (or of the imperial couple). Sabina's relation with Balbilla suits our definition of literary patronage: Balbilla's affectionate tone when writing about the empress and her exuberant praise of both emperor and empress suggest a personal and unequal relationship and, as court-poets usually did, she accompanied her patroness on her tour of Egypt, providing educated company and commemorating in verses her visit to the Colossus of Memnon. In return, Balbilla's social status was enhanced by her 'friendship' with the empress and the imperial recognition of her poetic ambition. No further privileges, favours or benefits are known, but, of course, such things are often ignored in poetry. As a court-poetess, if such she was, she probably belonged to the personal retinue of the empress – like men of their class, high-born women were usually surrounded by an entourage of friends and dependants[96] – which explains her presence in Egypt; yet, certainty about their relationship cannot be gained and other possibilities, such as her being a friend or *comes* (companion) of the empress, cannot be excluded.

There is one more, rather obscure, reference that points to Sabina's contacts with men of learning and perhaps to her patronage of them: in the *Historia Augusta* Hadrian is reported to have dismissed Septicius Clarus, Suetonius Tranquillus and many others 'because without his consent they had behaved in the presence of his wife, Sabina, in a more informal fashion than the etiquette of the court required'.[97] These eminent men of learning, the praetorian prefect Septicius Clarus, who was the dedicatee of Pliny's letters (or at least of the first instalment of them) and of Suetonius' 'Lives of the Caesars', and the scholar and author Suetonius, Hadrian's *ab epistulis*, probably accompanied Hadrian and Sabina during their visit to Britain in AD 122 when they, and many others, were dismissed because of what was seen as unacceptable familiarity with Sabina.[98] The actual reason for their dismissal is not clear. A possible guess, but no more, is that Sabina communicated with them in a rather informal way, perhaps gathering men of learning around her in the way Julia Domna did at a later date (see below, pp. 122ff.). Because of his suspicious nature and his loathing of his wife Hadrian may have mistrusted their gatherings, believing them to be of a political nature, perhaps even a conspiracy, and this may have been the reason why he dismissed them.

This is all the evidence we have of any possible cultural patronage of Sabina's. As has been said, she has left few traces in the literary sources. Only Julia Balbilla praises her in her poetry, and she does so for the standard female virtues: her beauty and moral integrity. Perhaps the unhappiness of her marriage and the fact that she died before her husband were the reason why her influence, both in political and in cultural matters, remained slight.

Sabina's sister, or half-sister, Matidia the Younger has also left few traces in our literary record, but inscriptions are more kind to her, showing her as a wealthy and generous benefactress. An inscription set up by the decurions of the Campanian municipality Suessa Aurunca at the end of the second century AD shows that the decurions met in the Bybliotheca Matidiana. The name suggests that the library was donated by one of the two Matidiae, Matidia the Elder, Trajan's niece, or her daughter Matidia the Younger. Four more inscriptions found on statue-bases in Suessa Aurunca and dating from the reign of Antoninus Pius pay honour to the younger Matidia, identifying her as the granddaughter of Trajan's sister Marciana, the daughter of the elder Matidia, the sister of Sabina and the maternal aunt of Antoninus Pius. As at least one of these inscriptions was set up by a procurator of hers, she probably possessed estates in the neighbourhood. Apparently Matidia the Younger had ties with Suessa Aurunca: therefore, it seems likely that she was also the one who founded the library.[99] Unfortunately, we have no further information on this, but other evidence may throw some light on her benefactions.

First, her birth and family.[100] Matidia was related to the imperial house through the female line: her grandmother Marciana was Trajan's sister, her mother Matidia the Elder his niece and her younger sister, or half-sister, Sabina became Hadrian's wife. Thus, she herself was Trajan's great-niece and Hadrian's sister-in-law and, though she was not related by blood to his successor Antoninus Pius, his adoption by Hadrian caused her to be identified as his maternal aunt. By the same process she was the adoptive great-aunt of his successor Marcus Aurelius and as such she figures in some of his letters to Fronto. Though rather remote, her connection with the imperial family was important: her grandmother Marciana, a widow, lived with her brother Trajan and her sister-in-law Plotina until her death, and from early in Trajan's reign onwards also her mother, Matidia the Elder, who was widowed at an early age, had moved to the imperial palace taking Matidia and her younger sister, or half-sister, Sabina with her. Thus, together with her mother, (half-)sister and grandmother, she must have spent part of her youth in the imperial palace. In most honorary inscriptions erected for Matidia her connections with the imperial family are duly emphasized, but, curiously enough, we do not even know the name of her father.[101] Nor do we hear of a husband. Because of our total ignorance in this respect it has been assumed that she never married, but this seems unlikely: women remaining single all their lives are very rare in Rome before Christian times.[102] It seems more likely that, like her mother and grandmother, she was widowed early and preferred not to remarry, and that her deceased husband, being less eminent than her imperial relations, was omitted from record, like her father.

Second, her wealth. Inscriptions show that she was a very rich woman possessing estates and houses in various parts of Italy, North Africa and Asia Minor. Childless and without close male relatives, she probably had *de facto* independent control over her possessions. She made a generous use of her wealth as a benefactress and spent money on various kinds of public munificence, such as an alimentary foundation for boys and girls (perhaps in Capua), a public library and a road built at Suessa Aurunca, and a fund for statues for the imperial cult in Vicetia.[103] Because of her benefactions to several Italian municipalities, for example, the foundation of the library at Suessa Aurunca, Matidia's generosity is more like that of a private benefactor such as the younger Pliny than that of a member of the imperial family (who had the privilege of public building in Rome).[104] Her foundation of the library was, of course, a sign of great wealth, but it may also be taken as an indication of her education and cultural interest.

This impression of Matidia as a woman of great wealth and prestige is confirmed by the correspondence of Fronto and Marcus Aurelius, in which she figures as a wealthy and childless old lady who was on intimate terms with, and highly respected by, the emperor Marcus Aurelius and his family. She does not seem to have used her close relationship with the emperor to gain political influence, or to ask favours for herself or her protégés. The correspondence shows her in a retired, domestic role, for instance, looking after the little daughters of Marcus Aurelius. It also describes a legal dispute about her will: she had dutifully appointed the empress Faustina as her heir, leaving legacies to her daughters and annuities to certain protégés, but some unscrupulous legacy hunters had tried to steal their way into the inheritance by sealing up certain codicils which she had annulled long before and by trying to pass them off as valid.[105] In a letter to Marcus Aurelius Fronto urges him to uphold her will, describing Matidia as 'a most noble lady of the highest lineage and the greatest wealth, who has deserved the best of you'.[106]

Summarizing the foregoing, we may conclude that, with the exception of Sabina, the imperial women of the Trajanic and Hadrianic period are portrayed as exemplary women. Apart from their more conventional female virtues their lack of pretence and the harmony with which they lived together are extolled. Also their restraint in political matters is noted: in his *Panegyricus* of Trajan the younger Pliny praises Plotina for not trying to gain anything from Trajan's eminent position except the natural pleasure it gave her; and in his funeral speech for his mother-in-law, Matidia the Elder, Hadrian praises her for her exceptional modesty, which among other things was shown by the fact that she never asked him a favour, though he would have liked to grant it.[107] Though their close relationship with the emperors made these much-respected women important brokers of patronage, their modesty seems to have kept them back.

In contrast to the reserved attitude speaking from the literary sources, the rich epigraphical and archaeological evidence shows that they received great public honour: Plotina, Trajan's sister Marciana, Matidia the Elder and Sabina were all granted the title Augusta, coins were struck with their portraits and numerous statues and inscriptions were erected for them, they were deified at their death and praised in funeral orations, and temples and other buildings were dedicated to their memory.[108] However, the younger Matidia was only granted a public funeral, which may be explained by the fact that she was less closely connected to the imperial house and had no place in the pseudo-dynasty of Trajan and Hadrian, which linked Hadrian to Trajan via Hadrian's wife Sabina, who was the granddaughter of Trajan's sister Marciana. Perhaps Matidia's more distant relation to the throne also explains why she enjoyed greater freedom in the choice of public munificence, and it may have been responsible for the fact that she could make herself known more widely by her generosity in financial matters; but, as regards reticence and allegiance to traditional female virtues she seems to have been equal to the other women of her family.[109]

The difference between the literary record and the epigraphical and archaeo-logical evidence is striking: whereas the scanty literary sources stress their old-fashioned virtues, or gossip about Plotina's political intervention in favour of Hadrian or about Sabina's unhappy marriage, the countless statues, coins, build-ings and inscriptions speak of the wealth, public position, patronage and esteem of these women. These sources supplement the rather one-sided portrait in the literary sources; though their allegiance to traditional female virtues seems too consistent to be ascribed solely to imperial propaganda, the epigraphic evidence shows that their lives were far more varied.

A refuge from the hazards of politics? The patronage of Julia Domna

We now turn to the, rather controversial, 'circle' of sophists and philosophers around Julia Domna, the wife of the emperor Septimius Severus, which beyond reasonable doubt shows that she acted as a patroness of literature and learning. The word 'circle' is used by Philostratus in his introduction to his life of the wonder-worker and Neopythagorean philosopher Apollonius of Tyana, a work he wrote at the request of Julia Domna:

> As I belonged to the circle of the empress – for she was a devoted admirer of all rhetorical exercises – she commanded me to rewrite and edit these essays [i.e. the biography of Apollonius supposedly written by a disciple of his, a certain Damis of Nineveh] and to pay special atten-tion to its style and diction; for the man of Nineveh had told his story clearly enough, but not very skilfully.
>
> (Philostr. *VA* 1.3; Loeb trans., modified)[110]

Thus, the existence of the 'circle' of Julia Domna is certain, as well as the name of one of its members, the sophist Philostratus, but its character and the identity of the other members are under debate. Earlier scholars have tended to overrate it, claiming (without any evidence) that almost all known intellectuals of the time were members. Rejecting these suggestions as mere fantasy G. Bowersock plays down the importance of the circle, arguing that membership can only be attested for the sophists Philostratus and Philiscus the Thessalian, and perhaps for

Gordian, the dedicatee of Philostratus' *Vitae Sophistarum*, who is to be identified with the later emperor Gordian I.[111]

The evidence concerning her circle, though meagre, allows us to have a closer look at Julia Domna's possible motives in gathering men of learning around her and at her dealings with her learned protégés. Her motives are indicated by Dio. In his treatment of the events of AD 200 he describes the increasing arrogance and power of the praetorian prefect C. Fulvius Plautianus, whose influence on Septimius Severus became excessive; an example of his abuse of power concerns Julia Domna:

> So greatly did Plautianus have the mastery in every way over the emperor, that he often treated even Julia Augusta in an outrageous manner; for he cordially detested her and always slandered her violently to Severus. He used to conduct investigations into her conduct as well as to gather evidence against her by torturing women of the nobility. For this reason she began to study philosophy and passed her days in the company of sophists.
>
> (Dio 75.15.6–7; Loeb trans., modified)[112]

From Dio's remark it is usually inferred that Julia Domna's 'circle' came into being around AD 200 when she turned to the study of philosophy to escape from the attacks of Plautianus, who could not bear a rival in his influence on Severus. If so, her studies formed a refuge from, and probably a dignified alternative to, the political influence she was supposed to exercise. Though we have no evidence of any political power wielded by Julia Domna before the reign of her son Caracalla, the fact that she was the emperor's wife and continually accompanied him on her journeys and military expeditions must have given Plautianus ample reason to fear her influence.[113] However this may be, her interest in philosophy and rhetoric outlived its immediate cause and seems to have been genuine, as her dealings with sophists and other intellectuals continued beyond Plautianus' fall and death in AD 205.

What we know of the members of her circle throws some light on the relationship between the empress and her scholarly friends. Philostratus, himself a member of her circle for over a decade, provides most of the evidence. His introduction to Julia Domna and his admittance to her circle probably took place when he practised as a sophist in Rome, most likely at some date between the return of the imperial family from their visit to Africa in AD 203 and the expedition to Britain in AD 208. He seems to have continued in Julia Domna's entourage until her suicide in AD 217, accompanying the imperial family on their voyages and expeditions.[114] During all these years Philostratus probably taught the empress and offered her his scholarly company; besides, at her request, he started writing a biography of Apollonius of Tyana. As the work is not dedicated to her, it is usually assumed that she did not live to see it finished.[115] We do not know of any reward given by Julia Domna, but she may have presented him with cash or property. Besides, his close relation to the empress and to the imperial court enhanced his social status, and so did the imperial recognition of his rhetorical gifts.[116]

The only other undoubted member of Julia Domna's circle, the sophist Philiscus of Thessaly, received, thanks to Julia Domna's patronage, one of the chief rewards for a successful sophist: the imperial chair of rhetoric in Athens. In AD 212, during Caracalla's sole reign, this sophist travelled to Rome to defend himself in a suit before the emperor and, according to Philostratus' account, 'there he attached himself closely to Julia's circle of geometricians and philosophers, and obtained from her with the Emperor's consent the chair of rhetoric at Athens'.[117] Here, we see Julia successfully acting as a broker of patronage, securing a favour for her protégé from her son, the emperor Caracalla.

Apart from these two sophists no other member of her circle is attested, though it comprised not only sophists (probably more than only these two) but, according to Philostratus, also geometricians and philosophers.[118] There is some ground for speculation about a possible membership of Diogenes Laertius, who wrote his 'Lives of the Eminent Philosophers' for an unknown woman interested in (Platonic) philosophy.[119] Also the 'iatrosophist' Galen, who was the court-physician of Septimius Severus, had some dealings with her: in a work written during the reign of Septimius Severus he remarks that his digression on embellishment (dealing with, among other things, recipes for hair-dye) was written 'at the request of the imperial women or the emperors themselves', which includes Julia Domna and perhaps her sister Julia Maesa.[120] Yet, it stretches the evidence too far to claim that he was a member of her circle.

It seems useless to indulge in further speculation about possible members of her circle. Instead, I shall discuss one last piece of evidence which permits a view from the inside, so to speak, of the relationship of the empress with a protégé of long standing, the sophist Philostratus. In Philostratus' extant letter to Julia Domna, once discredited but now generally accepted as genuine,[121] he defends the sophists, especially Gorgias, from criticism uttered by Plutarch (in a lost work) by arguing that even the venerated Plato admired the sophists and imitated Gorgias' rhetorical style. The letter is apparently a continuation of a discussion between himself and Julia Domna (and perhaps other members of her circle) about the relative merits of rhetoric and philosophy, in which he defends the adorned rhetorical style of the sophists, especially Gorgias, against the simpler style of, for instance, Aeschines Socraticus, which seems to have been preferred by Julia Domna. It is a learned letter, full of references and allusions to literary and philosophical works and persons; yet, the tone is light and playful. Philostratus even allows himself a rather bold compliment by implicitly comparing the empress to Pericles' concubine Aspasia, famous for her rhetorical gifts as well as for her looks,[122] and he closes his letter with a polite joke (unfortunately not completely intelligible now) in which in a deliberate anachronism he urges the empress to deal summarily with Plutarch if he refuses to be convinced of the eminence of Gorgias:

So, my empress, persuade Plutarch, who is more forward than any other Greek, not to be annoyed at the sophists, nor to resort to slandering Gorgias. If you cannot persuade him, then you in your wisdom and knowledge know what epithet must be bestowed on such a person. I myself can say what that epithet is – and yet cannot do so.

(Philostr. *Ep.* 73; trans. Penella (1979) 163)[123]

What does all this mean for Julia Domna's cultural patronage? First of all, she appears to have been a patroness of note, assembling around her a circle of men of learning and continuing to do so for many years, from about AD 200, when she was robbed of her influence by Plautianus, until her suicide in AD 217. Second, she seems to have been an inquisitive and discriminating patroness entering upon lively discussions with the members of her circle on the relative merits of sophistry and philosophy, and stimulating the intellectual life of her time by commissioning men of learning to write on themes that interested her: a biography of Apollonius of Tyana by Philostratus, an exposition on beautification by Galen, and perhaps the compendium of the lives and doctrines of important philosophers by Diogenes Laertius.

Because of her wealth, education and high social status as the emperor's wife or mother, she must have been an important patroness. This has been denied by Bowersock[124] in his somewhat too sobering account of her circle. He argues that only lesser sophists and philosophers would have been interested in membership of Julia Domna's circle, great and ambitious men considering it a waste of time to 'edify an empress'. For the duration of Plautianus' power Bowersock may be right – allegiance to Julia Domna may even then have been risky – but during the reign of Caracalla the situation had changed totally. Dio reports that during his reign Julia Domna acted as a kind of adviser giving much excellent advice (often unheeded by Caracalla) and that, when he left for the East for his campaign against the Parthians, Caracalla appointed her to receive petitions and to be in charge of the imperial correspondence in both languages, except in very important cases. She resided in Nicomedia and Antioch and received signals of dignity (among other things a royal retinue and a guard of praetorians) almost as if she herself was a reigning empress; her name was included in Caracalla's official correspondence with the senate and she held public receptions for 'all the most prominent men', just as the emperor did. But whereas he indulged in cruelty and greed, and sought the company of freedmen and magicians despising the senators, she 'devoted herself more and more to the study of philosophy with these [i.e. the most prominent] men'. With these words Dio testifies to the importance of the men she surrounded herself with and suggests that her studies intensified in her later years.[125] Her power being real both because of her closeness to the emperor and because of the routine administration he delegated to her, she must have had ample means of rewarding her protégés; this is confirmed by the fact that she caused the Athenian chair of rhetoric to be awarded to one of them, the sophist Philiscus of Thessaly, a favour only bestowed by an emperor.[126]

Thus, it seems wrong to assume that only minor students of philosophy and rhetoric would have belonged to her circle.

On the other hand, the character of her circle may have been much more informal than is usually assumed. Nothing in the ancient sources suggests strictly regulated group meetings or a fixed membership. Instead, it seems more likely that it was a loosely formed circle with a fluctuating number of sophists, philosophers and other intellectuals discussing philosophical and rhetorical topics with the empress, writing essays at her request and deriving prestige, and some of them more tangible rewards, from their attendance. Her dealings with some of these intellectuals may not have been unlike those of her niece, Julia Mamaea, the mother of the emperor Alexander Severus, who, according to Eusebius, when she heard of the fame of the Christian writer Origen, summoned him to Antioch with a military escort and had him stay with her for some time to demonstrate his learning and his understanding of divine things – after which he hastened back to his normal duties.[127] Thus, rather than belittling the prominence of its members, I am inclined to regard the circle as an informal and fluctuating group of men of learning.

In summarizing the evidence regarding imperial patronesses some conclusions may be drawn. To begin with, women of the imperial family were in a favourable position for the exercise of cultural patronage: because of their wealth, which many, if not most, of them were allowed to control without the intervention of a guardian,[128] their education and their eminent social status as the emperor's wife, mother or sister, they could be important patronesses both in their own right and as 'brokers' between the emperor and their protégés. Yet, as far as we know, few women of the imperial family acted as such, and most of them were not very prominent in doing so. This may, at least partly, be due to the scarcity of evidence, but other factors may have been responsible as well, such as the retired way of life that was expected of women, including imperial ones, their comparative lack of power compared to their male relatives and, of course, their personal inclination.

As we have seen, the patronage of imperial women was to a large extent bound up with their proximity to the emperor, and it is probably no coincidence that most patronesses are found among the female relatives of those emperors who themselves acted as patrons of literature and learning (Augustus, Nero, Domitian and Hadrian). Their position at the court brought them into contact with men of literature and learning who had gained the favour of the emperor and, on the other hand, those who wanted to come into contact with him might court his female relatives for their recommendation.[129] Thus, patronage and brokerage were closely interconnected for women of the imperial family. Whether or not their position allowed them to follow their personal inclinations in the choice of their protégés is another question. The evidence is contradictory: Octavia and Antonia, for instance, seem to have followed Augustus, but Plotina and Julia Domna acted more independently, supporting men of their own choice.

As regards the conditions of their patronage some rules may be briefly sketched. Cornelia, the mother of the Gracchi, who resembles the imperial women of later date in the exceptional status of her family, may serve as a model: the conditions which favoured her patronage (her wealth and education, the tradition of patronage in her family and her authority as an elderly widow of a leading family) and the conventional terms in which she is praised (her exemplary motherhood and widowhood, and other female virtues) reappear in the case of Octavia and Antonia Minor. Both were highly born, wealthy and well educated; the tradition of patronage in their family, exercised by Augustus, facilitated contact with men of learning, as did their supervision of the education of their children. Despite their activities in the male field of patronage both strictly observed the traditional rules of female behaviour and were praised for it in our sources. As in the case of Cornelia, praise of their conventional virtues overshadowed their activities as patrons of literature and learning and made their intrusion into the male domain of patronage socially acceptable.

A sharp contrast to these exemplary women (followed by Plotina, the younger Matidia, and, less clearly, Sabina) is formed by the 'wicked' women, such as Agrippina Minor and, to a lesser extent, Poppaea and Domitia Longina, who transgressed the male–female dividing-line by striving after political power or by showing a 'male' predilection for promiscuity. Cultural patronage seems to have occupied only a minor place in their lives, if at all, and their intrusion into the male world of politics earned them severe criticism. From these examples it might seem as if there were an inverse relation between political power and patronage of culture: on the one hand, 'virtuous' women who, in a modest way, exercised cultural patronage, and, on the other, 'wicked women' who were chiefly involved in politics. However, the example of Julia Domna shows that the relation between the two is more complicated than it may seem at first sight.

As we have seen, Julia Domna's cultural patronage perhaps began when she was ousted from her position of influence with Septimius Severus by Plautianus. Her reaction, as described by Dio, resembles that of male senators who, when retreating from politics after defeat or humiliation, filled their leisure time with liberal studies. Her retreat into a life of studies and cultural patronage was a dignified one, which moreover allowed her to keep a prominent position and to show her commitment to the intellectual culture of the upper classes without the dangers ensuing from political emnity with Plautianus. After Plautianus' death she regained her position of influence and during the reign of her son Caracalla she wielded considerable power. Yet, she did not end her patronage of men of learning but continued her studies with them, combining political power and administration with the study of philosophy and rhetoric. Her life as described by Dio resembles that of a reigning emperor; Dio even suggests that she considered usurping sole power after the death of Caracalla. Since women wielding political power, like Livia and Agrippina Minor, are usually vilified in the ancient sources, the mainly positive judgement on Julia Domna found in the ancient sources is remarkable.[130] Of course, the acceptance of imperial rule in her days, as opposed to the lingering republican feelings of the days of Livia and Agrippina, eased her prominent position as a leading woman of the imperial family. Yet, it also shows that, at least in her days, political power and cultural patronage were by no means mutually exclusive for women of the imperial family.

A closer look at the women discussed above confirms this: as we have seen, 'virtuous' women such as Octavia, Antonia and Plotina also exercised political patronage, mediating with the emperor on behalf of their protégés, and 'wicked' women such as Agrippina Minor and Poppaea, though chiefly concentrating on political power, may still have paid some attention to cultural patronage. Also Cornelia, the mother of the Gracchi, who, it seems, turned more fully to the patronage of men of learning after her political influence had ceased, continued to maintain contact with foreign kings. Thus, most of the women discussed above show a mixture of both activities with varying emphasis on the one or the other – though patronage of culture did fit in more easily with a life of traditional virtue. Since a public position and political power were essential for a patron in the full sense, political influence with the emperor was one of the conditions favouring their patronage of culture. In this respect women of the imperial family were exceedingly well placed for cultural patronage.

Non-imperial women

As we have seen, women of the imperial family whose patronage of men of literature and learning is known to us were few in number, but our knowledge of patronesses outside the imperial family is even less. Apart from Cornelia (discussed at the beginning of this chapter) and two anonymous women who will not be discussed here since their patronage is uncertain,[131] only four patronesses may be identified with anything like certainty; all four are known from the poems of Statius and Martial. As a background to the discussion of these patronesses a brief introduction to the literary patronage of their period (the reign of Domitian) is called for.

Unlike the republican and Augustan periods, when only a few great men (such as Maecenas) acted as literary patrons on a grand scale, poets and scholars of the first century AD attached themselves to several wealthy persons at a time; over and above these patrons the emperor dominated literary patronage by his superior wealth and power. Most of these (major and minor) patrons were men of letters and amateur poets themselves.[132] Statius addresses eighteen friends and patrons apart from the emperor, and Martial actually names more than a hundred. Among them only four women may be singled out as Martial's patronesses, one of them being a patroness of Statius as well.[133] What dealings did they have with their literary protégés, and how can we distinguish a patroness from a woman who is praised or addressed in poetry for other reasons?

As there is hardly any record of them apart from the poems in which they appear, their activities as patrons have to be inferred from these poems alone. In an influential article P. White[134] has pointed out that there were three ways of presenting a poem to a patron before it was published in a book: impromptu performance, recitation and a private brochure (*libellus*). The first two ways consisted in oral performance and will not be discussed here,[135] but the third has a bearing on our discussion. According to White, a *libellus* was a selection of still unpublished epigrams (or one longer poem) sent privately to a patron and introduced by a dedicatory poem asking for benevolent reading, or literary criticism and advice, protection against slander or plagiarism, recommendation of the poems to other people or simply a kind reception. The poet could choose a different selection of his poems for each patron with a view to his or her taste and circumstances and could offer a more or less luxurious copy of his poems as a gift. Sometimes a single epigram might be sent as a solitary missive such as a poem of congratulation or condolence or a poem accompanying a (birthday) present. The dedicatory poems of the *libelli* and the single epigrams could eventually be incorporated in the published book, which in its turn might be dedicated to another patron.[136] To be named and praised in poetry written for private circulation was regarded as an honour, but eventual publication considerably increased the value of such verses for a patron, because of the lasting fame it was expected to bestow. Important friends and patrons might receive more than one epigram, which, published in different books, gave them the much-valued 'serial publicity'[137] which was so important for their social prestige. Moreover, as a special honour a patron could be the dedicatee of the book as a whole.

How do our four patronesses fit in with all this? Let me first admit that it is not always easy to make out whether some person praised or addressed in poetry is a patron or a friend; this holds for men as well as for women. In singling out these four women from among the greater number of women mentioned, praised or addressed in Martial's poetry I have used the following criteria. First, I have asked whether they (and not their husbands or a third party) were the addressees of one or more published poems commemorating some event in their life or the recipients of a *libellus* of recent poetry. Second, I have taken into account the way in which they were praised – regarding references to their wealth and sophistication as possible hints of patronage – and whether or not certain titles of respect or other words belonging to the vocabulary of patronage were to be found in the poem. Finally, the most reliable indication is a poem containing an expression of gratitude for a past benefaction received from the woman in question. Four women, Argentaria Polla, Mummia Nigrina, Sabina and Marcella meet one or more of these conditions.[138] In the following I shall discuss them in some detail, keeping in mind the questions posed in the first part of this chapter as regards the motives, conditions and scope of women's patronage, the services they exchanged with their literary *amici* and the terms in which they were praised.

Argentaria Polla

In the preface to the second book of his *Silvae*, published in AD 93, Statius writes: 'The volume closes with "Lucan's Birthday Ode", for which Polla Argentaria, rarest of wives, desired to be held accountable, when we happened to be considering the celebration of the day.'[139] The verb *imputare* (here used in the passive tense 'to be charged to someone's account') belongs to the language of bookkeeping and may be a pun on the name of the commissioner 'Argentaria'.[140] As it implies reciprocity, it is a rather straightforward indication that Statius expected some (financial) recompense in return for his services, i.e. his poem. The relationship between Statius and Polla Argentaria is therefore generally regarded as one of literary patronage.

From Statius' preface, quoted above, it does not appear that Lucan had died nearly twenty-five years before.[141] The celebration organized by Polla may have been in honour of what would have been his fiftieth anniversary and, if so, it may be dated in November AD 89. The elevated tone of the poem and especially its closing lines suggest that the celebration was a special one, not to be repeated every year.[142] To enhance the ceremony Polla commissioned poems commemorating the birthday (perhaps to be recited during the ceremony), a request that was complied with not only by Statius, but also by Martial.[143] The greater part of the poem which Statius wrote for the occasion is taken up by his *encomium* of Lucan – put into the mouth of the Muse Calliope – in which his poetry is extolled and Nero is condemned for his death. However, Statius did not forget Polla, the dedicatee of his poem. In the preface to his second book he makes it clear that he has written the *Genethliacon Lucani* at her instigation, and in the poem itself she is much praised, becoming more and more prominent towards the end.[144] In about the middle of the poem, in a passage extolling their marriage, Polla is praised for her 'beauty, simplicity, friendliness, wealth, lineage, charm and grace'; besides, she is called 'learned and suited to your [i.e. Lucan's] genius'. Earlier in the poem she is called 'chaste' and in the preface she is named 'the rarest of wives'.[145] Some of these are conventional epithets, but Statius' emphasis on her social and literary qualities shows her in her role most important to him, that of a wealthy and well-educated lady who was his literary patroness.

At Polla's request also Martial commemorated the occasion. He composed three epigrams of the same length (four lines) and the same metre which together form a cycle.[146] In the first and the last poem (7.21 and 23) he addresses Polla, in the central one, Lucan. Together the poems constitute an *encomium* of Lucan: his poetry is exalted and Nero is denounced as the cause of his death. Further, they include some of the topics of Roman birthday-poems (somewhat modified to suit the occasion): the day is named, the gods are invoked and a birthday wish expressed.[147] The shortness of the poems leaves no room for praise of Polla apart from her being mentioned as Lucan's loving and reverential wife and widow, but the fact that she is addressed twice at a prominent place, in the beginning and at the end of the triad, shows that she commissioned the poems and was their dedicatee.[148]

Despite their difference in length, the poems by Statius and Martial share the themes of Lucan's origin, his work and significance as a poet (both compare him to Virgil),[149] Nero's villainy in causing his death, and praise of Polla as his faithful wife and devoted widow, while omitting any references to, for instance, Lucan's senatorial career and his involvement in the conspiracy against Nero. According to Hardie[150] such similarities are due to 'patron-guidance', the direction of the patron as regards the themes and contents of the poems to be written. If so, not only did Polla commission the poems, but she was also involved in planning them. This agrees with what is suggested about her education and her interest in poetry. Statius represents Polla as a well-educated woman with a good taste for poetry, who was, therefore, well matched to the intellectual and creative spirit of Lucan, and remarks that also Lucan himself had publicly acknowledged her literary taste by addressing her in an elegant *adlocutio*.[151] According to Sidonius Apollinaris she had even helped Lucan with the composition of his verses, but as Sidonius wrote at a much later date and is notoriously unreliable when giving historical examples, he cannot be used as a witness.[152]

There is a marked difference in tone between the poems of the two poets. Apart from praising Polla exuberantly Statius pictures her in lively detail; he even describes her spiritual contact with her deceased husband and his golden portrait hanging over her bed.[153] In contrast with Statius' affectionate tone no epithet betrays what Martial thought of Polla. He seems to have been much less intimate with her than Statius: his acquaintance with Polla may have been vague, probably originating from his connection with Lucan, who was a fellow-Spaniard and a member of the house of the Annaei, his patrons in his first days in Rome.[154] At any rate, these three epigrams cannot serve as a proof that there was a relationship of patronage between them beyond the occasion of Lucan's anniversary.

Fortunately, another epigram by Martial addressed to Polla throws light on their connection at a later date. In 10.64, an epigram of six lines published in AD 98, he humbly addresses her as his *regina* (queen). The epigram reads:

> If you, Polla, my queen, will handle my little volumes, accept my poetic jests with no frowning look. He, your own bard, the glory of our Helicon, although on his Pierian trumpet he resoundingly sang of wild wars, yet he did not blush to write in playful verse: 'If I am not being buggered, Cotta, what am I doing here?'
>
> (Mart. *Ep*. 10.64; Loeb trans., modified)[155]

The poem introduces one or more little books (*libelli*) of his poetry, which he sends to her as a present. In his wish to get a sympathetic hearing for his poems he apologizes for his sometimes indecent jests – as he should do when addressing a respectable lady of senatorial rank. In his defence, however, he quotes an obscene verse of homo-erotic content written by her late husband, arguing that, if even the revered Lucan did not blush to write lascivious verses, Polla should not frown when reading Martial's verses.[156] The quotation from one of Lucan's scurrilous verses, probably taken from a lost mime, may seem somewhat crude to us when his widow was being addressed. Yet, it was probably a compliment to Polla, as it showed her to be an educated lady who was well acquainted with poetry and knew the rules of the genre. Again, no personal epithet is used for Polla, but the word *regina* is telling. Like its male counterpart, *rex*, it is a term of great deference:[157] in calling Polla his *regina* Martial humbly declares her to be his patroness, ranking high above him. Perhaps the quotation from Lucan's obscene verses is meant to redress the balance.

On account of the poems by Statius and Martial, Polla Argentaria is generally thought to have been a patroness of poets.[158] To judge the conditions and scope of her patronage we should know more about her background, wealth and social position. Unfortunately, there is no such evidence apart from the poems in which she appears, so we have to judge by this rather meagre information.

There is the problem of her name and lineage. Statius calls her Polla Argentaria in the preface to the second book of the *Silvae* and simply Polla in the *Genethliacon Lucani*. Martialis calls her Polla and Sidonius Apollinaris, Argentaria. Because of her *gentilicium* Argentaria, which is rare, she is usually assumed to have been the daughter, or granddaughter, of Marcus Argentarius, a rhetorician and epigrammatist of, it seems, Greek descent living in Rome, but there is no firm evidence to support this connection and it remains, at best, an attractive hypothesis.[159] Yet, her name may well point to provincial (Greek or Spanish) extraction and is generally undistinguished; thus, it is highly unlikely that she belonged to the Roman senatorial élite by birth.[160]

In view of her inconspicuous background her marriage into the distinguished family of the Annaei seems surprising, but it may perhaps be explained by a possible Spanish origin, which would make her Lucan's compatriot, or by the fact that her supposed (grand)father Marcus Argentarius, the declaimer, was acquainted with the elder Seneca, the grandfather of Lucan. As to the difference in rank between Lucan and his bride we should keep in mind that Lucan, for all his wealth and fame as a poet, was a new man in the senate and of provincial (Spanish) birth. Moreover, he may have married Argentaria Polla before he was adlected into the senate.[161] When Lucan was compelled to commit suicide at the age of 25 because of his involvement in the conspiracy of Piso in AD 65, she was left a widow. At the time, she probably was in her late teens or early twenties, if we may judge by the early age at which women in the Roman world usually married.[162] Lucan had been very wealthy and may have wished to leave some of his wealth to his wife. However, as his father Annaeus Mela still lived he was *in patria potestate*, and after his death his possessions reverted automatically to his father. It has been suggested that Argentaria Polla eventually inherited part of the family fortunes of the Annaei when in AD 65 and 66 this distinguished house was destroyed by Nero and she was virtually the only one left.[163] This is highly hypothetical – though, of course, not impossible. In fact, we have no information whatsoever about the wealth she may have inherited from Lucan's family or, for that matter, about that of her own family.

As a young and, it seems, childless widow Argentaria Polla was expected to remarry in accordance with the Augustan laws and contemporary practice.[164] Unfortunately, our only evidence for a second marriage is the usually not very trustworthy Sidonius Apollinaris, who calls her 'twice yoked in wedlock' and in the same couplet alludes to her patronage of poets. The identity of the second husband has been the subject of much speculation, a problem that is complicated by the assumption that the poets referred to by Sidonius Apollinaris should also be her husbands. This has even led to the absurd idea that her second husband was Statius.[165] In a much-quoted article R. G. M. Nisbet argues that there is no sufficient reason to accept the identification of the poets and husbands, the poets being, as is generally accepted, Lucan and Statius, and the husbands, so he contends, Lucan and Pollius Felix.[166] Nisbet is not the first to defend the theory of Argentaria Polla's second marriage to the wealthy poet and patron of literature Pollius Felix, but he does so with great vigour. As his opinion has found wide acceptance and has some bearing on her patronage of poets, it has to be discussed here.

The main point is the identification of Argentaria Polla with Polla, the wife of Statius' patron Pollius Felix.[167] Polla, the wife of Pollius, figures in three poems by Statius, two of them dedicated to Pollius himself and one to his son-in-law Julius Menecrates. In Statius' *Silvae* 2.2, an elaborate description of Pollius' sumptuous Surrentine villa, Polla is treated as the equal of her erudite husband, the couple being described as living together harmoniously in Epicurean serenity. In Statius' poems Pollius is represented as a man of wide literary and philosophical interests, a writer of poetry himself and an adherent of Epicureanism; Polla is praised for her tranquillity, her youthful charm, her elegance, her bright serenity, her loving care and, possibly, her education and taste for poetry.[168] Moreover, her wealth is praised in such a way as to suggest a generous use of it for the patronage of poets: 'Your wealth is not hidden away and stifled in a sterile coffer, nor is your mind racked by the loss of usurious interest. Your capital is placed on view, and you have learned how to employ it with discretion.'[169] This passage provides Nisbet's main argument for the identification: drawing attention to the use of banking terms which are unusual in connection with a woman, he suggests that they are a pun on the name Argentaria.

There is something to say for the identification of the two Pollas. Like Argentaria Polla Pollius' wife figures prominently in Statius' poetry,[170] and like her she is depicted as a wealthy and charming lady, devoted to her husband but not inferior to him, sharing his interests and enjoying serenity and peace of mind. Moreover, both Pollas are patronesses of poets. However, there are some inconsistencies in the way they are portrayed. In the *Genethliacon Lucani* Polla's social and intellectual qualities are praised (apart from her devoted widowhood), whereas Polla, the wife of Pollius, mainly appears in a domestic role: middle-aged, enjoying a harmonious marriage and minding the grandchildren. In my opinion these inconsistencies are not necessarily incompatible with the identification of the two Pollas, as they may show once again that praise depended on circumstances and on the position of the person praised. In commissioning the *Genethliacon* Polla Lucani acts as a patroness herself and she is the actual addressee of the poem, whereas in the poems in which Polla Pollii is mentioned, it is Pollius (or in 4.8 his son-in-law

Iulius Menecrates) who is the dedicatee and Polla is merely portrayed as the wife of one of Statius' most important patrons (though by coincidence she is also a patroness herself). In these poems her personality is, therefore, pushed a little into the background, but in such a way that it does not disprove that she was a patroness of Statius in the *Genethliacon*. Similarly, Argentaria Polla's celebration of her deceased husband's birthday as described in Statius' *Genethliacon Lucani* does not necessarily contradict the identification with Polla, happily married to Pollius Felix. As pointed out above, second marriages were not objectionable at the time – for widowed or divorced women of childbearing age they were even the norm – and for a widow a second marriage did not mean that there was no loyalty and devotion to her first husband. On the contrary, this was regarded as laudable fidelity, as can be learned from the example of Statius himself, who in a poem praises his wife Claudia for her devotion to her deceased first husband.[171]

However, there is no direct evidence for the identification, and it seems odd that Statius should not have mentioned it. If we may pass over some minor points,[172] there is one major objection that should be mentioned. This is the difference in social status between Pollius Felix and Argentaria Polla. Though a man of great wealth and wide-ranging literary and philosophical education, who enjoyed respect and privileges as a local benefactor and magistrate in Naples and Puteoli, Pollius Felix may have been of humble origin, even a freedman's son.[173] Thus, his status was (far) beneath that of Argentaria Polla, who by her marriage to Lucan had acquired senatorial rank. Would she be prepared to marry a man beneath her station and in doing so perhaps even lose her rank? Though, of course, such a marriage is not unprecedented, especially not in the case of men who were social climbers, we do not have many examples of senatorial women marrying beneath their station in the first century AD.[174] For Pollius the benefits of such a marriage are obvious: since he was, at best, a member of the local élite, a marriage to a woman of senatorial rank greatly raised his prestige and furthered the chances of social advance for his descendants.[175] However, for Argentaria Polla the advantages are less clear, unless, perhaps, she found herself in financial difficulties after Lucan's death and unable to maintain the life-style expected of a woman of her class.[176] Thus, the marriage, though highly hypothetical, is not altogether out of the question: for Argentaria Polla, Pollius' wealth, education and personality may have outweighed the social drawback of marrying a man beneath her standing.

All in all we have to admit, I think, that because of the scarcity of information the question cannot be decided. On the whole, the odds seem to be slightly against a marriage with Pollius Felix. Martial does not mention Pollius. Perhaps he did not know him personally; as we have seen, his acquaintance with Argentaria Polla was due to his connection with Lucan. But Statius knew both Pollius and Polla well; yet, in his poem dedicated to Argentaria Polla he does not refer to Pollius (or, incidentally, to any other second husband); besides, he does not hint at an earlier marriage of Polla Pollii in his poems mentioning her.

For our purpose the possible second marriage of Argentaria Polla to Pollius

Felix is of importance only in so far as it may have affected her patronage of poets. What difference may it have made? If Argentaria Polla was the same person as Polla, the wife of Pollius, it can be demonstrated that she was acquainted with Statius for a period of several years at least, the connection between them possibly originating from Pollius, who was one of Statius' main patrons. Such a long personal acquaintance between them may explain the warmth and intimacy with which she is portrayed by Statius and is, as we have seen above, one of the distinguishing characteristics of patronage. The fact that she was the wife of one of Statius' most important patrons does not conflict with a role as a patroness in her own right. As has been said above,[177] there was a strict separation of property between husband and wife in non-*manus* marriages (which were the rule from the late republic onwards), and though Pollius' wealth may have allowed her to live a life of affluence beyond her own resources, the money she spent on her poet-friends must have been her own. This is also suggested by Statius' allusion to her generosity in *Silvae* 2.2.151–4 quoted above (p. 133), and by his presentation of her as his sole addressee in the *Genethliacon*, who, moreover, 'desired to be held accountable' for the poem. However, unlike Statius, Martial had no connection with Pollius, and Polla's patronage of him was not in any way bound up with her possible remarriage. This brings us to the second possibility.

If Argentaria Polla did not marry again after Lucan's death, we have to do with two different patronesses of poets bearing the same *cognomen* and sharing at least one poet-friend, Statius. About Polla Pollii not much can be said, as she is not mentioned outside the poems of Statius.[178] As Argentaria Polla, however, is addressed in only one poem by Statius, it seems uncertain whether their relationship was a personal and continuing one which allows her to be regarded as Statius' patroness. Yet, there are two arguments in favour of this. First, most of Statius' patrons receive only one poem in the published collection. Second, the poem itself shows them to have been well acquainted, thus proving that their relationship was a personal one of some duration. If Argentaria Polla acted as a patroness of poets while remaining a widow, we have to assume that by birth or inheritance she was wealthy enough to afford a standard of living in keeping with her senatorial rank and sufficient to give material support to poets.[179]

Thus, both possibilities allow for a role as a patroness of poets. Of course, there is a third possibility, *viz.* that she did remarry, though the new husband was not Pollius, but someone else unknown to us. We would expect this second husband to be of senatorial, or perhaps equestrian, rank, but in the absence of any evidence such speculation is useless. Being unable to decide the matter I shall ignore her possible second marriage in the discussion of her patronage of poets. The following questions will be dealt with: what can we say about the scope and importance of her patronage and about the services she exchanged with her poet-friends, and what can we infer from the way she was portrayed in their poetry?

As regards the scope of her patronage opinions are divided. Whereas no one doubts that she was a patron of Statius, White minimizes the importance of her patronage of Martial, assuming that they were only superficially acquainted. By contrast, J. P. Sullivan calls her one of Martial's 'most generous patrons' and assumes that after the death of Lucan and Seneca Argentaria Polla took up their patronage of Martial, continuing her activities as a patron throughout his stay in Rome.[180] The latter opinion is perhaps too confident: though Argentaria Polla's acquaintance with Martial is likely to have been brought about through her husband Lucan, there is no evidence of such generosity in supporting him as assumed by Sullivan, nor is there any indication of the contact between them in the years between AD 65 (the death of Lucan) and 89 (the celebration of his fiftieth anniversary).[181] White, on the other hand, seems too cautious: though the tone of some of Martial's poems addressed to her is admittedly rather reserved, his daring quotation from Lucan's work suggests that they were on easy terms and perhaps implies that literary discussions had gone on between them. His use of *regina* in addressing her, which emphasizes her superior wealth and social status, is not in conflict with some degree of familiarity existing between them, as appears from Martial's poems to other eminent patrons. Rather, it stresses her importance as a patron.[182] Thus, it seems reasonable to assume that there was a relationship of patronage between them for almost ten years at least: from the celebration of Lucan's anniversary in AD 89 until the publication of Martial's tenth book shortly before he left Rome to return to his native town in Spain in AD 98.

As for the services Argentaria Polla exchanged with her literary protégés: Statius' praise of her wealth and his allusion to financial recompense suggest that she gave material support in return for their poems. But it seems likely that she also offered non-material support. Being, as was implied by both Statius and Martial, a well-educated woman with good literary tastes, who was married to, and possibly descended from, poets, she must have been well acquainted with poets and poetry and able to provide various kinds of literary encouragement to the poets of her choice: literary discussions,[183] and perhaps opening her house for recitations of their poetry or giving publicity to their work by circulating it among her friends and connections. In any case, she appears to have been a judicious patroness both in commissioning poems for a specific occasion and in appreciating poetry sent to her unasked.

Yet, the way in which she is praised in these poems is rather one-sided, and remarkably uniform; this, as was mentioned earlier, may be due to 'patron-guidance'.[184] Lucan's fame as a poet and his untimely death are the main subjects of the poems presented to her; Polla herself is portrayed chiefly as a chaste and loving wife and a faithful widow devoted to the memory of her husband. In the third place, her education and her refined taste for poetry are mentioned, though in somewhat guarded terms, which together with the praise of her social qualities, lineage and wealth represents her as a rich and high-ranking patroness.[185] If Martial's and Statius' portrait of her was to her liking – and it probably was since even if she did not actually direct their writing they must have known her preferences just as they knew those of their other patrons – this must have been the way she actually wanted to be known to the world.

There is a remarkable difference between this portrait of Argentaria Polla and that of male patrons in the poems of Statius and Martial: whereas the latter could be praised for all sorts of things, Argentaria Polla is chiefly praised for the traditional virtues of a devoted wife and widow, which overshadow her activities as a patron.[186] Her example shows once more that women might be praised for traditional virtues and could nevertheless act independently in a male domain. As has been shown above (p. 112f), women (and men) were honoured according to contemporary standards of behaviour, so that the virtues they were praised for (for example, being a devoted wife or widow) were not necessarily the actual reason for their being praised (which may have been generosity and encouragement as a patroness).

However, our discussion of Argentaria Polla has, I hope, also made clear that there is more to this: not only did men habitually praise women according to traditional notions even when they were in fact honouring them for totally different reasons, but women themselves expected to be praised in such terms and, if we may take Argentaria Polla as their representative, they could use these notions to their own advantage. Though her motives for acting as a patroness were probably the same as those of most patrons – i.e. apart from a genuine interest in poets and poetry the desire to gain prestige and perhaps even 'immortality' by being named and praised in poetry – Argentaria Polla professed to seek this glory only for her dead husband and had herself included first and foremost as a widow devoted to the memory of her husband. The reason for her doing so should be sought not only in women's (probable) acceptance of traditional standards of behaviour, but also, I think, in the risk of criticism and of loss of reputation which women ran when they encroached on a traditionally male domain, such as literary patronage. To counterbalance their unconventional behaviour traditional virtues had to be stressed.

When we consider the poems from the point of view of the ancient reading public, it may be asked whether ancient readers took the praise of Argentaria Polla as a loyal wife and widow at face value and believed that she was just that, and not also an educated and wealthy woman actively involved with poets and poetry (and perhaps happily remarried). To my mind, they did not. Not only do the poems themselves indicate her role as a patroness, but the mere fact that poetry is addressed to her in which she is named and praised is a sure sign that she did not just live the quiet and inconspicuous life of the traditional grieving widow. This must have been obvious to the ancient reader, and it seems likely that Polla also wanted it to be known, in an unobtrusive way, that apart from being a devoted widow she was also a wealthy, well-educated woman and a high-ranking friend of poets.

Here, her deceased husband Lucan comes in. He figures prominently in all poems addressed to her, and also in the poem which Martial sent to her unasked. White[187] regards this as a sign that Martial and Polla were only vaguely

137

acquainted: according to his view her marriage to Lucan was the only thing Martial knew of her (even though Lucan had died almost thirty-three years before at that time). This is hardly convincing. It seems more likely that Martial knew that Lucan, and his fame as a poet, were favourite topics of hers and that this was the reason why he mentioned him (quoting, typically for Martial, an obscene verse from his work). This emphasis on her marriage to Lucan confirmed her reputation as a devoted wife and widow. But it was also socially profitable in another respect: her prestige may have been greatly enhanced by Lucan's fame as a poet, as had been the case in earlier days with his father Mela,[188] and her marriage to him had brought her senatorial rank. Thus, by keeping her connection with Lucan alive in the eyes of the public she maintained her social status. Though it is not improbable that Argentaria Polla (even when remarried) actually was the devoted widow she was portrayed to be by Martial and Statius, she may have had other, more self-interested reasons to have Lucan and her marriage to him celebrated in the poetry of two fashionable poets. By means of her patronage of poets she not only honoured her deceased husband, but also supported her own prestige.

Mummia Nigrina

Compared to the discussion of Argentaria Polla little can be said about Mummia Nigrina. Martial presented two poems to her: one commemorating her generosity during her marriage and the other her mourning at the death of her husband. As was usual when addressing someone in a poem or letter, he only mentions her *cognomen*, Nigrina. In epigram 4.75, published in AD 89, he jubilantly praises her marriage and her self-effacing love for her husband, comparing her to the mythological heroines Euadne and Alcestis, who sacrificed themselves for their husbands. Nigrina did better: instead of dying to prove her love, she gave proof of it during her lifetime by generously sharing her paternal wealth with her husband – an act of unusual generosity in view of the strict legal separation of property in Roman non-*manus* marriages.[189] Epigram 9.30, published in AD 95, speaks of the death of her husband, Antistius Rusticus, in Cappadocia. It describes how Nigrina brought his ashes back to Rome – as a widow was expected to do – mourning him and 'envying his tomb' for containing his urn. The poem resembles the cycle of epigrams written for Argentaria Polla (7.21–3) in its denunciation of the place (or the person) held responsible for the husband's death and in its emphasis on the devotion of his wife.

In the epigrams Martial praises Nigrina as a wealthy woman and a loving wife, but gives no details of her social status or her possible literary patronage. Fortunately, the name and career of her husband, the senator L. Antistius Rusticus, provide some information. From an epitaph of one of their slaves, we know her full name to have been Mummia Nigrina, a woman who belonged, as her name shows, to a wealthy and distinguished family of the Spanish province from Baetica.[190] In AD 87, or somewhat earlier, she married L. Antistius Rusticus, a member of the local aristocracy of Corduba in the province of Baetica who had entered upon a senatorial career under the Flavii. After being adlected *inter praetorios* in AD 73/4 he was a proconsul of Baetica in the eighties and *consul suffectus* in AD 90. After this, he went to Cappadocia-Galatia as a governor.[191] As appears from Martial's epigram he died in Cappadocia-Galatia in AD 93 or 94 during his term as a governor. Mummia Nigrina, who had accompanied him to his province, returned to Rome with his ashes. After this, we hear no more of her.

From this it seems that Mummia Nigrina was a wealthy woman of Spanish birth, who had acquired senatorial rank by marriage. Martial may have known both her and her husband through his Spanish connections, but his poems are centred on her; she is the addressee of 4.75 and the subject and the supposed addressee of 9.30, whereas her husband is only mentioned by name once (9.30.1–2), when his death is announced. Thus, she herself, and not her husband, must have acted as a patron to Martial. The epigrams, written with an interval of about six years, were probably sent to her unaccompanied by other poems and were afterwards incorporated by Martial into his published books. Though they do not show great intimacy, they probably reflect a relationship of several years of which they are the only signs left. There are no hints at patronage, but Martial's praise of her wealth and of the fact that she had successfully adapted herself to Roman culture may perhaps count as such.[192] However, he praises her first and foremost as a devoted wife and widow, virtues which we have met earlier in Argentaria Polla, and which should not lead us to believe that this was her only aim in life. In accepting, or perhaps commissioning, poems on private events of her life she showed herself to be an educated woman who appreciated poetry. We may assume that she also knew how to show gratitude for Martial's verses.

Sabina

Apart from Argentaria Polla the unknown Sabina of Ateste (a town in Gallia Cisalpina) is the only woman in Martial's poetry to be presented with a *libellus* of his recent verses. In epigram 10.93, which serves as its dedication, a man called Clemens is asked to deliver the copy to her when travelling north:

> If before me, Clemens, you shall see Helicaon's Venetian shores, and the fields covered with vine-clad trellises, carry to Sabina of Ateste poems unpublished as yet and newly arrayed in a purple wrapper. As the rose delights us that is just picked by the finger, so a papyrus roll pleases us when it is new and unsoiled by the chin.
>
> (Mart. *Ep.* 10.93; Loeb trans., modified)[193]

The poem does not tell us anything about the recipient except her name and residence. As it seems, Martial did not know her personally and desired to make her acquaintance through an intermediary. This indirect approach to an unknown or high-placed recipient was one of the ways open to a poet when trying to win a new patron.[194] The care with which the copy was produced, written on a new papyrus roll and wrapped in a purple cover, shows that Martial was anxious to make a good impression. Thus, though the possibility cannot be excluded that a relationship of patronage already existed, it seems more likely that he hoped to win her over by presenting her with this attractive copy of his recent poetry.

As we have no independent evidence concerning Sabina we can only guess at her social status. She must have been a wealthy woman, perhaps belonging to the municipal élite. Apparently Martial expected, or knew, that she was well educated and well read in poetry (or else she would not have been able to appreciate his work), and that she liked her name to be included in the poetry of a fashionable author. Living in northern Italy she may have been useful to him in spreading his work among new readers and potential patrons in the area, but whether his attempt at securing her patronage was successful, we cannot tell.

Marcella

In AD 98 Martial returned to his native Bilbilis in Spain. Pliny gave him his travelling money out of gratitude for the verses Martial had written about him.[195] In Spain Martial enjoyed the support of two native patrons, Terentius Priscus, who had already been his patron in Rome, and his countrywoman Marcella. Though Terentius Priscus appears to have been the more important patron, as he was Martial's literary friend for many years, giving him generous material support and a critical reading of his poetry,[196] Marcella undoubtedly acted as his patron as well. When he returned to Spain, she gave him a house and an estate in his native Bilbilis, which, together with the support he received from Terentius Priscus, provided him with the leisure he had long sought in vain in Rome. In 12.31 he calls her his *domina*, a title of respect used for a patroness,[197] and describes in loving detail his little estate in Spain. According to his description it included, apart from the house, a forest, springs, a water conduit, meadows, a green-house, rose beds, a vineyard, tanks of eels and a dove-cote full of white doves.

Unfortunately, nothing is known of Marcella apart from what may be inferred from the two epigrams in which she is mentioned.[198] Apparently she was wealthy enough to provide him with a small but comfortable estate, and we may infer that she belonged to the local élite. She was also well educated, or so Martial says. In 12.21, which is addressed to her, he praises her as a young woman whose sophistication belies her provincial background and who can easily compete with the most refined women of Rome:

> Who would think, Marcella, that you were a citizen of iron-tempering Salo, who, that you were born in my native land? So rare, so sweet is your

wisdom. The Palatine will declare, should it but hear you once, that you are its own; nor will a daughter of mid Subura, nor a nursling of the Capitoline hill, vie with you: nor soon shall the most glorious of foreign birth laugh at one whom it would befit to be a Roman bride. You ask me to mitigate my longing for the Queen city: you by yourself make a Rome for me!

(Mart. *Ep*. 12.21; Loeb trans. modified)[199]

Martial's compliment that Marcella makes up for his longing for Rome and that to him she even is Rome is, of course, not quite truthful. In the letter to Terentius Priscus, which forms the preface to book 12, he appears to miss Rome for reasons weightier than any single person, however cultured, might compensate for: its appreciative audience, its refined critical judgement, its libraries and theatres, all things that stand in sharp contrast to the solitude and rusticity of a provincial town in Spain.[200] Yet, he wants it to be known that Marcella was an erudite woman whose education could meet Roman standards and who, apart from giving him an estate, enlivened his tedious life in Spain with her company. Thus, the two poems written for Marcella represent her as the patroness Martial had always longed for: one who gave him both literary encouragement and an estate that permitted him to live a life of leisure.

As we have seen, Polla Argentaria, Mummia Nigrina, Sabina and Marcella were addressed in poems commemorating some private event, or received a *libellus* of Martial's recent work as a present, and they were praised and immortalized in Martial's (and Statius') published books. Praise of their wealth or education, the use of certain titles of respect or gratitude for a past benefaction show that they acted as patronesses. Of course, they were not the only patrons of Martial and Statius, nor did they support them during their entire careers, but this holds also for most male patrons. According to our definition of literary patronage as a personal, reciprocal and asymmetrical relationship of some duration in which services (partly consisting of poetry) are exchanged, they may be called literary patronesses, though there may be some doubt as regards Sabina, who is addressed only once in Martial's extant poetry.

In return for the honour of being named and praised in poetry some recompense was expected of patrons, and we may assume that our patronesses rewarded their poet-friends with money or gifts in kind. As is to be expected, the poems do not speak of this, with the notable exception of Statius' preface to his second book of *Silvae* (about Argentaria Polla) and Martial's poem expressing gratitude for the estate he had received from Marcella.

In patronizing poets these four women encroached upon a male domain, but they were honoured in a way different from men. Though they were occasionally praised for their erudition, they were mainly honoured for traditional female virtues and in the epigrams they commissioned they figured first and foremost as devoted wives and widows. This emphasis on traditional virtues was, as we have seen, a standard formula in the praise of women, but it may also have been expected, and perhaps even desired, by the women themselves. Marcella forms an exception to this rule: she is praised for her generosity and education more straightforwardly than is usual. Perhaps Marcella's residence in a provincial backwater required emphasis on her erudition.[201]

As regards their motives in patronizing poets, those usually assumed for male patrons may be accepted also for them: *viz.* an interest in poetry, pleasure in the company of poets, and a desire to be celebrated in verse. Yet, an additional motive may be suggested for at least two (Argentaria Polla and Mummia Nigrina) and possibly for all four women discussed above: the wish to gain prestige in upper-class circles by displaying their advanced education and their commitment to Roman literary culture. This may have been especially desirable as they were all from a municipal or provincial background and from non-senatorial families: Sabina and Marcella seem to have belonged to the municipal and provincial élite respectively; Argentaria Polla and Mummia Nigrina, though living in Rome, were of provincial descent. Though the latter two acquired senatorial rank through marriage, their husbands, who were also of provincial (Spanish) birth, were newcomers in the senate; neither of them had a brilliant senatorial career.[202] Therefore, their wives may not have been easily accepted in Roman upper-class circles. In spite of her wealth and high standing within the provincial status system and her marriage to a senator, Mummia Nigrina may have lacked the prestige in Roman social life which she thought her due. Also Argentaria Polla, despite her (brief) marriage to the senator and renowned poet Lucan, may have felt socially hampered by her non-aristocratic birth and her provincial back-ground (her possible second marriage to Pollius Felix can only have worsened her social position). However, as regards their education all four could compete with the most refined women of the capital – or so it was claimed by the poets who praised them. The modern concept of 'status inconsistency'[203] may therefore be applied to them: by virtue of their wealth, education and marriages to senators they felt entitled to a higher status and prestige than they were credited with in Rome.

To reduce this inconsistency and to compensate for their provincial extraction and their non-senatorial birth these wealthy and well-educated women may have sought to heighten their prestige by patronizing poets. This may have been the more important to them as prejudice against provincial and municipal men (and women) was mainly of a cultural kind. The Roman élite judged them to be rustics and lacking in urbanity.[204] Patronage of poets enabled these women to display their erudition, thus countering the prejudice of rusticity and demon-strating their commitment to the literary culture of the Roman upper classes. Moreover, the way in which they are praised in the poems refutes all suspicion of un-Roman behaviour: they are presented as models of traditional Roman wifehood and widowhood, from whom upper-class women of Rome could learn a thing or two and whose education and conversation were equal to the highest standards of the capital.

Conclusions

In this chapter I have discussed the meagre and widely scattered evidence of patronesses of literature and learning. As literary patronage in Roman society was *domus*-based, it was to be expected that upper-class women could play some part in it. This is indeed what we find, but the number of upper-class women acting as patrons is far smaller than that of men and, besides, they exercised patronage on a more modest scale. Compared to male patronage that of women suffered from a serious drawback: since they were excluded from political office women could not, themselves, bestow the rewards of a powerful public position such as legal protection or a sinecure. Besides, the retired way of life expected of them, their more haphazard education (chapter 2), the restricted control of their wealth (especially in the earlier period), and their ambiguous social status (chapter 1) hampered their patronage. The predominance of widows among our patronesses, such as Cornelia, Octavia, Plotina, Matidia, Julia Domna, Argentaria Polla and Mummia Nigrina, is probably to be explained by a greater *de facto* financial autonomy of wealthy widows, who by the deaths of their male relatives were freed of the informal family control of their finances. Wealth, age and widowhood seem to have brought at least some of them into a position of autonomy, respect and authority. The precise proportion of male and female patrons cannot be established because of the scarcity of the evidence. The only sources which allow quantification, Martial's epigrams and the *Silvae* of Statius, inform us of four women as opposed to about sixty male patrons (Martial) or one as opposed to seventeen (Statius), which may perhaps be taken as a rough indication of the actual proportions.[205]

This brings us to the spread of the evidence in the course of time, the unevenness of which makes it impossible to trace a chronological development: we know of one probable patroness (Cornelia) in the republican period, of eight or nine women of the imperial family who, with varying degrees of certainty, may be called patronesses of literature or learning, and of four non-imperial patronesses. That we hear of so many more cases under the principate than in the republican period may be partly misleading: women of the imperial family left more traces in the literary sources than those of other classes and, besides, our knowledge of non-imperial patronesses of the principate is entirely dependent on the works of Martial and Statius.

Yet, changes in the nature of literary patronage caused by the establishment of the empire seem to have favoured women's participation. We may suspect that the predominance of the 'great aristocratic patron' of the republican period left little room for women, whose retired way of life seems incompatible with the public stature of the great patron and with the grand scale of his generosity. Moreover, *manus* marriages, still common in the second century BC, excluded all married women (but not widows) from possessing property in their own right. Cornelia, therefore, must have been rather exceptional for her time in patronizing men of letters in her villa in Misenum. Apart from her widowhood, wealth and excellent education, the prominence of her family and its tradition of patronage seem to have been essential to her role as a patron.

Under the principate, however, conditions changed: apart from the emperor, who dominated literary patronage, there were a large number of literary patrons of more varied social status – many of them wealthy but undistinguished in public life. This change allowed for the participation, on the one hand, of female relatives of the emperor, and on the other, of a more varied group of wealthy women, who patronized one or more poets on a more modest scale. We cannot tell whether in patronizing men of letters upper-class women were inspired by women of the imperial family. Though empresses, and other imperial women, served as models for women of the upper classes in fashion, hairstyle and other such things, and though some emperors propagated ideals of female and marital behaviour by means of the legends on coins bearing their portraits,[206] there is no firm evidence that women of the imperial family set a fashion of patronizing men of letters. Yet, imperial precedence may, of course, have heightened the attraction and prestige of such activities.

In exercising patronage the women of the imperial family were in a favourable position: because of their close relation to the emperor they were regarded as public figures, whose birthdays and marriages as well as the births of whose children were commemorated in verse, at least by Greek epigrammatic poets. They also attracted men of learning, if only because of the prestige derived from such an illustrious connection. Moreover, their public status made them potentially powerful as patronesses, both in their own right and as 'brokers', able to secure great rewards for their protégés. In comparison to political interference, patronage of a cultural kind seems to have been unobjectionable – perhaps even a respected activity – for women of the imperial family. Yet, it should be kept in mind that in comparison with their male relatives, especially the emperor, their patronage was of limited scope: apart from Julia Domna and, to a lesser extent, Plotina, they did not make much use of their privileged position in this respect.

The patronage of non-imperial women was of a more restricted kind. Since they could not bestow rewards deriving from a powerful public position, they could only repay the poems addressed to them with gifts of money or property, and perhaps with literary encouragement. As regards the latter the evidence is meagre: for instance, there is nothing to show that women organized public recitations of poetry (though they may have done so at home for invited guests); yet some of them (Argentaria Polla, Marcella) seem to have engaged in literary conversation and all may have recommended the work of their poet-friend(s) to their friends and acquaintances, thus performing much the same services as male patrons of their time, many of whom were men of leisure and not actively involved in politics. Like other patrons of their days (and unlike Cornelia, our only republican patroness) the four patronesses of Martial and Statius did not stem from great political families, but belonged to the fringes of the élite. Their motives for acting as patronesses may have been partly bound up with this marginal status.

As far as we know, wealthy and cultured women of the upper classes played only a minor role in Roman literary patronage. It is impossible to tell whether the four patronesses of Martial and Statius were representative of non-imperial patronesses of letters during the principate. We may suspect that they were not the only ones: the wider spread of education among upper-class women during the empire, their increased social prominence, their greater financial independence in non-*manus* marriages caused by the decline of the power of the *tutor*, and a marked tendency in contemporary poetry to focus on private and social concerns suggest that other women of wealth and standing may also have patronized poets. Thus, K. Hopkins (see n. 203) may be right in assuming that high-ranking women of the time lived in a 'competitive salon-culture' (though evidence is sadly lacking), and perhaps we may suspect that Argentaria Polla made capital of Lucan's anniversary in this kind of 'competition'.

Changed circumstances favoured women's patronage during the principate, both that of women of the imperial family and that of other upper-class women. Though there is no proof that the former group directly influenced the latter, there is one point in which they closely resembled each other: the terms in which they were praised. There is a marked tendency in our sources to praise women according to traditional notions of womanhood, extolling them as loving wives, faithful widows, or devoted mothers. Despite the greater variation in the way they might arrange their lives, such traditional virtues remained essential for their social repute from Cornelia to Julia Domna (whose coinage and honorific titles stress her role as wife and mother despite her large role in politics[207]), and it has been argued above that women expected – and perhaps even desired – to be praised in such terms. Praise of traditional virtues countered possible criticism of unconventional behaviour aroused by their intrusion into the public domain of patronage. Moreover, it confirmed their commitment to traditional Roman values without detracting from the prestige derived from their patronage of letters. Though the uniformity of women's praise obscures for us their individual traits and activities, for Roman women it seems to have been a welcome disguise for entering upon a more varied way of living.

5

WOMEN AND WRITING: POETRY

Women writing poetry or prose have left very few traces in Roman literary history: only a small number of names have been transmitted, and very little of their work has reached us. The virtual absence of women from literary history was taken for granted in the past, so much so that even the poems that have come down to us under the name of Sulpicia were ascribed by some to a male pseudonymous author; others judged them amateurish.[1] Both judgements imply that literature was regarded as a purely male field from which women were excluded. Recent feminist scholarship of the seventies and eighties has attempted to redress the balance and to restore the 'lost voices' of women to literary tradition. This went hand in hand with a, sometimes implicit, assumption that women had a distinct literary 'voice' and tradition which was marginalized or suppressed by a dominant male literary tradition. Though this approach went too far in looking for a 'lost tradition' of female writers and, as a consequence, has gone out of fashion in the nineties, it has the merit of questioning the lack of importance of female writers and of posing the problem of their virtual absence from literary history.[2]

In a recent article on the North African martyr Vibia Perpetua, B. D. Shaw attacks the notion that there must have been a great tradition of female writers but that it was lost and forgotten afterwards.[3] In his opinion, there are no signs that there was a 'lost tradition' of female authors in antiquity; rather, it is the absence of any such tradition that needs to be explained. Incidentally, his own article on Perpetua provides a clear example of a male attempt to suppress a woman's style of writing: he describes how the editor and subsequent interpreters of Perpetua's autobiographical account of her martyrdom tried to rewrite her narrative so that it would suit the male-dominated church. Yet, it seems clear that, instead of positing a 'lost tradition' (for which there is no evidence), we have to try and explain why so little work by women has reached us and what may have hindered them from writing and publishing.

In this, and the following, chapter I shall make a tentative reconstruction of the role of upper-class women in the literary life of Roman society and of the circumstances under which they wrote, dealing with their endeavours in poetry in this chapter and with prose in the next. In studying the problem of the dearth of women's writings, we shall look both at the question why female authors were so rare in Roman society and at the possible reasons why their work was almost totally lost. The discussion of the evidence is not arranged in chronological order: the evidence is too scarce and too unevenly spread over time for any definite chronological development to be established. Instead, it is discussed with an eye to a number of themes belonging to the central problem: the place of upper-class women in Roman literary life. As a result of the thematical arrangement of the evidence we shall occasionally meet one and the same author under different headings. This may seem a little confusing, and therefore a brief chronological survey of women's activities in the field of writing is found at the end of chapter 6.

As has been said, in Latin literature female authors seem all but non-existent; with the exception of the poetess Sulpicia they are at best mentioned in footnotes in works on literary history. Therefore, in the exposition of the evidence I shall not only deal with their literary work but also pay attention to their private and sub-literary writings.[4] In other words, both the published and the unpublished work of women has to be considered: since women, as we shall see, did not have easy access to Roman literary life and to the channels of publication, it would be misleading to restrict this survey to their published work only.[5]

Three questions will be considered in the three main sections of this chapter: what place did women occupy in Roman literary circles and production? Did female poets differ significantly from male ones in style, genre, subject-matter or in respect of their audience (and was this the reason why they were excluded from the mainstream of literary tradition)? Third, what was the Roman attitude towards women who wrote poetry? Though the evidence is insufficient to deal fully with all these matters individually (some of them can be broached more satisfactorily than others), taken together they present, as I hope to show, a plausible picture of the place women poets occupied in Roman literary life and throw some light on the reasons why so little of their poetry is preserved.[6]

As the chronological order of the women discussed in the present chapter may not be generally known, approximate dates may be mentioned here: Sempronia, Clodia Metelli and Cornificia were probably born in the first decennia of the first century BC; Sulpicia and 'Perilla' wrote their poetry in the Augustan period, and the (probably fictitious) mistresses of the love poets date from the same period. In the first century AD we have Sulpicia Caleni and in the second century AD (the Hadrianic period) Julia Balbilla and Terentia; anonymous or otherwise unknown poetesses who have been compared to Sappho range from the first century BC to the late second century AD.

Literary coteries and the publication of poetry: the place of women

Latin literature was a matter of groups of friends or 'coteries': friends played an important role in the process of writing, revising and 'publishing' a literary work.[7]

Once a work was conceived and drafted it passed through several stages before it was released to the public. Though these could, of course, vary greatly, roughly three stages can be distinguished. First, a copy was sent to a close friend who was asked for critical comment. Then, after the work was revised, it would be read to a small group of friends to test its reception, or copies could be sent to them for criticism. If, after one or more revisions, the author felt sufficiently certain that this was his final version, presentation copies were sent to a wider group of friends, first of all the dedicatee – if there was one. It was at this stage that the work was made public, or to use an anachronistic term, 'published', as further copying and circulation of the work were now out of the author's control: people unknown to the author could copy from the text of a friend, buy a copy in a bookshop or copy from a volume deposited in a public library – but the last two were relatively late developments. Friends (and patrons) played an important role also at this stage of 'publication', as they could help to make the book known to a wider public by recommending it to their friends and acquaintances or by organizing a public recitation.[8]

Literary friendship seems to have been virtually an all-male affair: as far as we know, women had hardly any place in it. Though quite a few upper-class women were well read in poetry and some even acted as patrons to poets, there is only one case that perhaps justifies the assumption that a woman – under certain conditions – could join a literary coterie: Sulpicia the elegist. Theoretically it is, of course, possible that women had literary coteries of their own in which their work circulated, but for this there is no evidence. Women's rare access to, or total absence from, male literary friendship must have been a hindrance to their literary work: even if they had the necessary education, leisure and talent to write poetry, they lacked the encouragement of literary friends who would read and criticize their work and further its publication. Yet, all women known to have written poetry must have circulated their work in some way or other among educated men, or we would not have known of its existence. How did they manage this? The most likely answer seems to be that, like female writers in other periods of history,[9] they found the necessary contacts for the production and circulation of their work through their male relatives. This will be elucidated by a discussion of the literary connections of three female poets of the late republic and the Augustan period, Cornificia, Ovid's 'Perilla' and Sulpicia the elegist, all of whom seem to have been encouraged by male relatives who were poets or literary patrons themselves. I shall start with the less famous ones, Cornificia and 'Perilla', and then deal with the only example of a woman who may have joined a literary coterie, Sulpicia the elegist, the survival of whose poems demonstrates the importance of such contacts. The discussion of the poems themselves will be postponed to the next section.

Cornificia, a woman of senatorial rank, lived in Rome around the middle of the first century BC.[10] Of her life and personality we know next to nothing, nor do we have even the slightest scrap of her work. Yet, she enjoyed an unusual renown on account of her poetry, which must have circulated widely since it was still known, and perhaps even available, more than four centuries after her death. This appears from the 'Chronicle' of Jerome, in which he speaks of her 'remarkable epigrams' in the context of the death of her brother: 'The poet Cornificius died abandoned by his soldiers whom when they fled he had repeatedly scolded as hares in helmets. His sister was Cornificia, whose remarkable epigrams are still extant.'[11] It is usually assumed that Jerome has this information from Suetonius' lost life of her brother, the Neoteric poet and orator Q. Cornificius, which would have been included in his 'lives of the poets' (de poetis).[12] Yet, it is not certain that any such life ever existed, and even if Jerome actually drew on Suetonius for his story about Cornificius, his remark about Cornificia's poetry may have been based on personal knowledge. Thus, it seems likely, or at least possible, that copies of her poems still circulated in the fourth century AD.

Despite the fame of her epigrams, we are much better informed about her brother. Probably, it was he who formed Cornificia's main connection with the literary coteries of her days, particularly that of Catullus. He was a very wealthy and cultured man who, apart from his military career, was known as an orator and a poet and was a friend of both Cicero's and Catullus'. His own poetry, of which only tiny scraps remain, conformed to the fashion of the new poetry of the time, the main representative of which was Catullus, and in this he seems to have been relatively successful.[13] We may conjecture that his friendship with Catullus paved the way for his talented sister, and his library and copyists may have helped her to acquire the necessary books and to circulate copies of her work. That she was closely acquainted with friends of Catullus' appears from a now lost inscription which mentions her as the wife of a certain Camerius, another friend of Catullus'.[14] Thus, both through her brother and through her husband she was connected with the literary coterie of Catullus. These ramifications into the coterie of Catullus may have helped her in circulating and publishing her poetry in such a way that copies of it probably still existed in the days of Jerome. How precisely her male relatives contributed to this, remains obscure. This aspect can be observed in some detail in the second example to be discussed now: Ovid's 'Perilla'.

Of Ovid's 'Perilla' we know even less than of Cornificia; not even her actual name has been preserved. She was the addressee of one of Ovid's *Tristia* (3.7), a poetic 'letter' sent to her from Tomis. The name 'Perilla' must be a pseudonym: in the *Tristia* Ovid does not mention the names of his addressees for fear of embarrassing them. This pseudonym was a well-known one: the love poet Ticida, or Ticidas, a contemporary of Catullus, had used it, according to Apuleius, to conceal his beloved Metella, and Ovid himself mentions a Perilla as the pseudonym of a Metella who was celebrated by some poets whom he does not mention by name.[15] He may have chosen it as a poetic tribute to these poets, who belonged to the generation before him.

In his poem Ovid addresses 'Perilla' as a young unmarried woman living with her mother: his letter, personified as a messenger, will find her, so he imagines, sitting with her mother (a *topos* of female chastity) or among her books and her beloved Muses.[16] Judging from the way he writes about her 'modest fortune' and her personal library she may have belonged to the same (equestrian) class as Ovid himself. He frequently refers to the intimate and cordial relationship between them which dated from her 'tender years of girlhood' and in which he was to her 'like a father to his daughter'. From these remarks it has been assumed that Perilla was his stepdaughter, the daughter of his third wife from an earlier marriage.[17] There is much to say for this view: their long and cordial relationship from her early youth onwards, the similarity in the way he describes his relationship to 'Perilla' ('like a father to his daughter') and that to his anonymous stepdaughter (whom, in a poem of later date addressed to her husband, he calls 'almost my daughter') and perhaps also the fact that he portrays 'Perilla' as a *docta puella*, but emphatically as a chaste one. If the name of Ovid's stepdaughter was Nerulla – which in view of the *cognomen* of her son (Nerullinus) certainly seems possible – this would provide an additional argument for her identification with 'Perilla' because of the metrical equivalence of the name.[18] Yet, certainty cannot be reached; Ovid's paternal attitude towards 'Perilla' may have been meant metaphorically and some other relationship, though presumably a family relationship, cannot be ruled out.[19]

From Ovid's poem 'Perilla' emerges as a young, talented woman, whose poetic gifts he stimulated himself. The most interesting part of the poem is that in which he deals with their poetic collaboration before his relegation to Tomis. Through the mouth of his personified letter he asks her whether she has remained true to their common pursuit of composing learned verse and reminds her of his help in guiding her talent from her earliest youth onwards. Here we see a young woman working on her poetry just as male poets used to do when starting upon a poetic career: she is assiduously advised and encouraged by a senior friend. Ovid acknowledges her poetic talent, which, as he proudly remarks, he had been the first to discover: 'I was the first to discern this in the tender years of your girlhood when, as a father to his daughter, I was your guide and comrade [*duxque comesque*].'[20] The military terminology used for their poetic collaboration is a common one, and shows that she was accepted into the male world of literary friendship, in which an older, more experienced, poet as 'a leader and a fellow soldier' used to guide younger ones.[21] According to Ovid's description, he and 'Perilla' read and criticized each other's poetry, a cooperation in which, being the senior poet, he firmly took the lead:

> Whenever I could, I often used to read your verse to myself and mine to you; often I was your critic, often your teacher, now lending my ear to the verses you had recently composed, now causing you to blush when you had been idle.
>
> (Ovid *Trist.* 3.7.23–6; Loeb trans., modified)[22]

150

He probably also set her the example of his own poetry, though hers may have been of a different kind.[23] Publication had been their common aim at the time they collaborated in Rome and by means of this verse-epistle Ovid urges her from far-distant Tomis to forget her fear and to publish her verses: the immortality he predicts both for his own poetry and for that of 'Perilla' – if only she continues writing – is to be esteemed the highest aim of all and should be set above all transitory possessions of life.[24]

In this poem we find a young woman participating, as a junior partner, in the male world of literary friendship. As outside this poem nothing is known of her, she remains shadowy. If she is to be identified with Ovid's stepdaughter, she lived, in adult life, the anonymous life of most Roman women: getting married and having children.[25] But as an unmarried girl she was a promising poetess of learned verse, who, stimulated by a senior poet, composed poetry with an eye to publication. Whether she continued writing during her married life and whether her poems were eventually published, we cannot tell; there is no further mention of it in our sources, nor is there even the slightest scrap left of her work. For more information about the publication of a woman's poetry, we have to turn to our third, and last, example: Sulpicia, the elegist.

Sulpicia is unique in that she is the only female writer of Latin poetry whose work is, at least partly, preserved; six short elegies of hers have come down to us in the *corpus* of Tibullus.[26] In the present section I shall only deal with her literary connections and with the 'publication' of her poems; the poems themselves will be discussed in the next section.

Sulpicia was a young noblewoman who lived in Rome during the Augustan period and probably wrote poetry in the last decennia BC. From one of her poems, in which she calls herself 'Servius' daughter Sulpicia', she has been identified with a daughter of Servius Sulpicius Rufus, son of the well-known jurist of that name, and Valeria, a sister of M. Valerius Messalla Corvinus. Consensus on this identification has been reached in the course of the past centuries and it is now generally accepted (though occasionally some doubt is expressed): we may take it that the poet of the six short love elegies in the *Corpus Tibullianum* was a young, probably still unmarried, woman of a very distinguished and highly educated senatorial family.[27] Her father was a man of culture and an accomplished orator who wrote love poetry in his leisure time, and her maternal uncle Messalla, who, after the early death of her father, may have been her guardian, was a well-known literary patron and himself an amateur poet who wrote erotic and bucolic poetry.[28]

Sulpicia's six elegies, totalling a mere forty lines and singing her love for a man she calls Cerinthus, have come down to us in the *Corpus Tibullianum*, a miscellaneous collection of poetry which was added as a third book to the two books of Tibullus (one of the poets patronized by her uncle Messalla). The survival of six of her poems, so exceptional for the poetry of a Roman woman, is usually explained by her supposed membership of Messalla's literary coterie. How should we assess such a membership, uncommon as it is for a woman? Does it mean that she read and revised her poetry in collaboration with other members of the coterie as male poets did and that she actually wrote poetry for publication?

Until recently, most scholars believed that Sulpicia did not compose her poetry with an eye to publication. According to the traditional view publication took place only after her death, together with that of the other poems of the *Corpus Tibullianum* with the help of the 'archives' of Messalla at a time when there was still some interest in the poetry of Messalla's coterie.[29] Her poems were considered to be of a private nature, 'billets doux' intended for none other than the addressee, and publication during her lifetime was thought to have been too embarrassing for a woman of her standing. M. Santirocco is the first to have noticed that this view is contradicted by the introductory poem (3.13), which is all about making her love-affair known to the world and in which she expresses her belief in the power of poetry to make her feelings publicly known just as it had brought her lover into her arms.[30] She refuses – or so she professes – to entrust her feelings to 'sealed tablets' to hide them from the eyes of the public (the behaviour expected of a woman of her standing), but proudly flaunts them in the face of the world:

> At last love has come, Rumour, of such a kind that it would shame me more to keep it hidden than to disclose it to anyone. Won over by my Muses [i.e. poems] the Goddess of Love has brought and placed him in my arms. [. . .] I would not wish to entrust anything to sealed tablets, so that no one might read my feelings before my beloved, but I love to have sinned and I hate to wear a mask for the sake of reputation: let it be told that we have been together, a worthy woman with a worthy man.
>
> ([Tib.] 3.13.1–4 and 7–10)[31]

Thus announced as a public statement of her love the poem expresses her intention to give publicity to her verses.

That Sulpicia wrote for publication is now generally accepted, but whether she succeeded in publishing her verses during her lifetime cannot be decided. The possibility that poems of a later date are included in the *Corpus Tibullianum* seems to point to posthumous publication.[32] Nevertheless we may suppose that, to be included in the published collection, her poetry must, at least, have circulated among Messalla's literary friends and acquaintances. It is here that her uncle Messalla comes in. He forms the most likely link between his niece and his literary friends. From one of Sulpicia's poems, in which she addresses him, we may infer that he took a strong personal interest in her, and though it is uncertain whether he was her guardian, he clearly looked after his fatherless niece; he must have been aware of her talent.[33] Perhaps we may reason from analogy: above we have seen how Ovid encouraged 'Perilla' to compose and to publish, and how he had collaborated with her in Rome by listening to her verses and by criticizing them. We know that Messalla did the same for the young poets of his coterie, such as Tibullus and Ovid. May we assume that he collaborated with his niece in a similar way encouraging her to write and publish her verses, and that, as a consequence, her poems circulated among his literary friends? The fact that the only poetry of a Roman woman that has survived in a manuscript tradition was written by the niece of one of the greatest patrons of poetry of the time cannot be mere coincidence. If this is right, Sulpicia owed the publication and the eventual preservation of her verses not so much to her remarkable talent as to the fact that she was a niece, and perhaps even a ward, of a prominent literary patron.

The examples of Cornificia, Perilla and Sulpicia show three successive stages in the process of composing and publishing a literary work: literary connections (Cornificia), poetic collaboration ('Perilla') and 'publication' (Sulpicia). Yet, women's participation in the world of literary friendship must have been rare. As far as we know, Roman literary coteries normally consisted exclusively of men; no female poet is mentioned among the literary protégés of Maecenas or of any other literary patron. The military metaphor (*duxque comesque*) used for the poetic cooperation between a senior poet and a younger one – in this case applied to that between Ovid and 'Perilla' – clearly reflects the fact that the world of literary production was all-male. Yet, as we have seen, women of talent could occasionally gain access to literary coteries and to the channels of publication; at least, when they had the support of male relatives who were poets or literary patrons themselves.

Of course, three female poets, all writing in about the same period (from the middle of the first century BC to the beginning of the first century AD), do not prove that talented women could not join a literary coterie or publish their poetry unless they were encouraged by male relatives. It is perhaps possible that in the late first and second centuries AD, when writing poetry was the fashion among both men and, it seems, women of the upper classes, access to literary coteries became more open to women. Yet, the other female poets discussed in this chapter (in so far as we know anything about their male relatives) confirm the view that support by male relatives was essential.[34] Therefore, it seems reasonable to assume that the all-male nature of literary coteries deterred all women, except for a few well-connected ones, from trying to gain admittance.

As literary contacts and encouragement were essential, the limited access of women to literary coteries severely restricted the number of women who were in a position to circulate and publish their work. Though this does not preclude endeavours in poetry in the privacy of their homes, their relative isolation from literary life made it almost impossible for them to make their poetry known to their contemporaries, and thus, eventually, to us. The few cases that form an exception have to be considered now.

Women's literary 'voices'

The present section of this chapter is devoted to four female poets of whom a poem, or at least some lines, have been preserved: they are, in chronological order, Sulpicia the elegist, whom we met in the previous section, Sulpicia Caleni, Julia Balbilla and Terentia. Three of them are Roman women and one of them, Julia Balbilla, is a woman of Greek descent but born and bred in Rome, who wrote poems for a Roman emperor.[35] Their poetry has come down to us in several ways: six elegies of Sulpicia's are, as we have seen, transmitted in a larger *corpus* of miscellaneous verse through manuscript tradition. Of the work of her namesake, Sulpicia Caleni, only two lines are preserved, quoted in a scholion of Juvenal; and four poems by Julia Balbilla and one by Terentia are inscribed on the Colossus of Memnon and one of the pyramids at Gizeh respectively. So few poems from a period covering three centuries (first century BC to second century AD) cannot be regarded as representative of the poetry of Roman upper-class women in general, but, as here we have at least some remains of their writings, we should study them in some detail and try to answer the second of our three questions, which was: did female poets differ significantly from male ones in style, genre, subject-matter or in respect of their audience?

Sulpicia, the elegist

Since the six elegies of Sulpicia are the earliest, and the only substantial, example left to us of Latin poetry written by a woman, we shall start with her. In discussing her poetry in connection with that of contemporary male poets working in the same genre we have to consider three points, which are treated in the three sub-sections that follow: first, the way in which she portrays herself in her poetry, second, her poetic play with the theme of reputation, and third, the inversion of elegiac gender roles. But first we have to say a few words about the poems themselves and about the shift in the appreciation of them in recent literature.

As Sulpicia's poems are well known I shall not give a full translation, but only summarize their contents. In the opening poem of ten lines (3.13) Sulpicia announces her love-affair to the world, thus deliberately defying public opinion. The second and third poems (3.14 and 15), respectively eight and four lines long, deal with her imminent birthday: in 3.14, addressed to her uncle Messalla, the birthday is called 'hated', as Messalla is planning a visit to the country for her (which meant a separation from her beloved Cerinthus); but in 3.15, addressed to Cerinthus, the visit appears to have been cancelled and Sulpicia proclaims her happiness at being able to stay in the city. In the next poem (3.16), consisting of six lines, addressed to Cerinthus with biting sarcasm,[36] she scolds him for infidelity. Poem 3.17, of six lines, is again addressed to Cerinthus; in it she speaks of an illness that has befallen her and of her anxiety that Cerinthus may not care. The last poem (3.18 of six lines) consists of one long sentence and is an apology to

Cerinthus for her abrupt departure the evening before, which was caused by her desire to conceal her passion.

Incidentally, two more poems have been attributed to Sulpicia: in a recent article H. Parker argues that poems 3.9 and 11, which are traditionally assigned to the puzzling *auctor de Sulpicia*, or *amicus Sulpiciae*, an anonymous author who wrote about Sulpicia's love-affair, are in fact by Sulpicia herself.[37] Both poems are written in the feminine first person, as if Sulpicia herself were speaking; they deal with Sulpicia's anxiety for Cerinthus when hunting (3.9) and with his birthday (3.11). As these poems are much longer than the six whose authorship seems certain, they would more than double the volume of poetry left of her. Though Parker's suggestion is attractive and accounts for some peculiarities of the poems, I am not convinced that they are from her hand, for several reasons but mainly because of their greater length, their smoother and more conventional style and their more reserved wording. Therefore, as long as Sulpicia's authorship of these two poems has not been established beyond doubt, I prefer to omit them from this discussion.

At first, Sulpicia's poems were attributed to male pseudonymous poets, especially to Tibullus and Ovid; however, since O. Gruppe in 1838 divided the poems into two groups (one assigned to the *auctor de Sulpicia* and the other to Sulpicia herself), they have mostly been regarded as the work of a woman. This influenced their interpretation and appreciation. Because of the absence of any mythological adornment, because of certain oddities and obscurities in language and syntax, and because of her use of colloquialisms Sulpicia's elegies were in all but the most recent studies regarded as amateurish, lacking in poetic technique and typically 'feminine' (i.e. artless and emotional) in style and thought. They were only praised for what was seen as their straightforward simplicity and spontaneous outpouring of emotion, which in the rather patronizing appraisal of the time was considered part of their 'feminine' charm.[38] As they were regarded as documentary love-letters instead of works of art, the preserved sequence of the poems was changed to make them fit the supposed chronology of the affair and a happy ending was supplied by identifying Cerinthus with M. Caecilius Cornutus, a man of senatorial rank and a writer, who in a poem of his friend Tibullus was portrayed as newly and happily married.[39] After her marriage Sulpicia was assumed never to have written another line.

Though the small size of the surviving *corpus* does not permit a detailed analysis of her language, syntax and metre as is usual in the study of the male love poets of her time, her elegies have recently been studied from the point of view of their poetic merit and are assessed very differently. Instead of their supposed amateurish spontaneity and autobiographical simplicity, the emphasis is at present on their sophistication and accomplished technique. This shift in appreciation has also influenced opinion as regards the sequence of the poems: in the traditional view, which regarded her poetry as the private love-letters of 'a charming Roman girl', the opening poem (3.13) was seen as depicting the culmination of the love-affair and therefore it was usually put last in the series. However, as

Santirocco[40] has pointed out, there is no good reason to change the order of the poems. In the arrangement of the manuscripts, the opening poem, which is the only one without addressee, serves as a preface to the reader and as a programmatic heading to the other poems. Its theme, the public announcement of her love-affair, may be contrasted with that of the last poem of the series (3.18), which describes her (regretted) attempt to conceal her feelings. Thus the first and the last poem frame the series, forming a poetic cycle characterized by the conflict between openness and concealment and that between regard and disregard of her reputation as the main themes. Besides, Sulpicia is shown to have used many of the stylistic devices found in the work of her male colleagues, such as Catullus, Tibullus and Ovid; and her neologisms and her colloquialisms now appear to be deliberate, effectively creating an *impression* of spontaneity.[41] In their brevity and deceptive simplicity Sulpicia's short elegies come close to the epigrams of Catullus; her subject-matter (love and separation, a birthday, an illness, a trip to the countryside, the supposed infidelity of the beloved), her amatory vocabulary and her defiant attitude are common to the genre of love elegy. Thus, her brief 'elegiac epigrams' are indebted to both Neoteric and elegiac love poetry. Instead of an artless amateur, she is now generally regarded as an accomplished poet who was well aware of the literary tradition of the genre she worked in; however, she handled its conventional themes in a novel way, as we shall see.

A poetic self-portrait

Following the convention of Roman 'subjective' love poetry, Sulpicia composed her poems in an autobiographical style. However, the apparent simplicity and immediacy of her poetic self-portrait is deceptive. Instead of a straightforward picture of an upper-class girl writing love-letters to her beloved (which these poems were taken to be in the past), the poetic portrait Sulpicia creates of herself is complicated and contradictory. Three aspects or positions may be distinguished: her social position, her poetic position and, third, her 'generic' position, by which I mean her place within the genre of love poetry.

As regards her social position, Sulpicia portrays herself as a young woman of the high aristocracy of Rome, proud of her class and family. This is reflected in the repetition of 'digno digna' (expressing the equality in moral and social rank between herself and her beloved) in the closing line of her first poem;[42] but it is even more apparent in her bitter poem about Cerinthus' supposed unfaithfulness: 'let care for a toga and a whore loaded down with her wool-basket be more to you than Sulpicia, the daughter of Servius'. In this poem, in which she emphatically calls herself *Sulpicia Servi filia*, expressing her high birth, her rank is contrasted with the low birth of her rival, a spinning-girl (probably of slave status) and a 'whore' loaded down with her wool-basket and dressed in a toga, which marks her infamy.[43] The difference in rank returns in a less marked way in the difficult last couplet of the poem, which reads: 'There are persons concerned about me, to whom this is the greatest cause of distress, that I may yield my place to an obscure bed [*i.e* an ignoble rival].'[44] Sulpicia is, indeed, as has been remarked by N. J. Lowe, remarkably forthcoming with autobiographical information, since her uncle Messalla, addressed informally in 3.14.5 – 'Take a break, Messalla, don't be over-concerned with me' – is explicitly called 'my dear relative' in the next line, which emphasizes their family relationship.[45] However, rather than finding this a reason for suspicion, I take it that Sulpicia wanted to make it perfectly clear that she belonged to a distinguished aristocratic family.

Unlike her social status her poetic position is highly ambiguous. Next to the role of a chaste and sheltered upper-class young woman Sulpicia adopts the role of the elegiac *puella*, a sophisticated young woman of the city going through the various stages of love-and-separation of an elegiac love-affair in an attitude of defiance of traditional morality.[46] The tension between these two conflicting female roles gives her poetry a great intensity of feeling as regards the openness (or concealment) of her love-affair and the regard (or disregard) for her reputation. This theme will be discussed in greater detail in the following sub-section, entitled 'The politics of reputation'.

As regards the third point, her position within the genre of elegiac love poetry is a unique one. In writing love poetry according to the conventions of the genre Sulpicia assumes the (male) role of the poet-lover who celebrates the beloved (usually a woman) under a Greek pseudonym, thus reversing elegiac gender expectations. Since inversion of gender roles is a characteristic trait of the genre itself (the male poet-lover portraying himself as subservient to his dominant beloved), Sulpicia's poems are, in a sense, an inversion of an inversion, but this does not mean that they come full circle to the conventional situation of the dominant male and the muted female. The implications of the 'inversion of elegiac gender roles' that follow from her unique position as a woman working in a male genre will be dealt with in the third section of the discussion of her poetry.

Taken together these three contradictory positions account for the complicated poetic *persona* of Sulpicia. The conflict between the requirements of her first and her second position, that of the young woman of senatorial class and the *puella* of love elegy, is responsible for the way in which she plays with the theme of her reputation, which lends a distinctly female perspective to her poetry. The third position, that of a woman writing in a male genre, entails her idiosyncratic inversion of elegiac gender roles. Taken together, Sulpicia's complex 'subject-position',[47] complicated because of its unusual combination of a male and two conflicting female roles, gives her poetry a unique place in the elegiac tradition.

The politics of reputation

Sulpicia seems well aware of the doubts with which upper-class women who wrote poetry, and love poetry at that, were regarded in traditional Roman opinion and of the secrecy expected of an upper-class woman as regards her erotic feelings. Right at the beginning, in the opening poem, she introduces the theme of her moral reputation. As has been pointed out by Santirocco,[48] this poem deals not only with her love but also with her *fama*, which is a keyword in both its opening couplet and in its closing one. *Fama* has a double meaning here, denoting both her fame as a poet and her moral reputation. She is aware of the modesty (*pudor*, line 1) and the discretion expected of a young unmarried woman of the upper classes in matters of love and sexual desire. It was essential to the reputation of a woman of her class to hide her feelings and to keep up appearances: if she was not actually as chaste as was expected of a woman of her standing, she had to pretend to be chaste, or, in Sulpicia's words, 'to wear a mask for the sake of reputation'.[49]

In defiance of these traditional values Sulpicia's poem publicly announces her love-affair, stating that in her eyes it is more shameful to conceal it than to 'lay it bare' even if that means gossip and a bad reputation: she refuses to hide her feelings, but proudly exhibits her affair, taking pleasure in her 'sin'.[50] Just as Catullus in his famous poem waved away the gossip of disapproving old men, she dismisses the talk of the strait-laced scandalmonger: 'Let him [or her?] tell of my joys, whosoever will be said to have lacked joys of his [her?] own.'[51] Her defiant attitude as regards her reputation is underlined by the use of the subjunctive of verbs of speaking: she loves 'being talked about' (line 5: 'narret' and 10: 'ferar'), which is precisely what a respectable woman should avoid most. Moreover, her use of sexual terms and word-play intensifies the tone of defiance.[52] In this poem her two female roles come into conflict: as a woman of the upper class she was expected to hide her erotic feelings, but as an elegiac *puella* she deliberately defies such traditional codes.

Also in the final poem (3.18) she plays upon the theme of female modesty, but again she defies traditional expectation. In this poem, which is cleverly composed in a single sentence conveying the impression of a breathless outpouring, Sulpicia apologizes for having left Cerinthus the previous evening. The reason she gives for her unexpected departure is that she wanted to conceal the heat of her passion.[53] This is exactly how a young upper-class Roman woman was expected to behave: chaste, modest and hiding her erotic desires. However, Sulpicia shows no satisfaction in her modest behaviour. On the contrary, with some exaggeration she calls it the most stupid thing she has ever done and deeply regrets it. Her defiance of traditional values is reflected in the blatantly erotic terms used in the poem which clash with the coyness described.[54] Thus, the first and the last poems of the series show complementary emotions as regards conventional morality: in the first poem she takes pleasure in her 'sin' and in the publicity she gives to it, and in the last she repents her modesty and the concealment of her feelings.

With this defiance Sulpicia follows contemporary elegiac conventions, but it differs from that of her male colleagues. Whereas male love poets turned the traditional hierarchy of male values upside down, describing their love-affairs with metaphors drawn from a military or political career,[55] Sulpicia attacked the highest female values: flaunting her affair in the face of the world, she publicized her erotic feelings. Instead of the military and legal terminology of the male love poets (the absence of which contributed to the verdict of amateurism of her work), Sulpicia uses the 'female' terms of reputation, rumour and gossip.

Inversion of elegiac gender roles

Sulpicia's defiance of traditional morality is closely bound up with the inversion of gender roles so prominent in her poetry. Here her third role, that of the poet-lover, comes in. As a rule, Latin love poets celebrated their beloved under a Greek pseudonym, but kept their own name themselves. In following this tradition Sulpicia inverts the usual gender roles of love poetry: keeping her own name she assumes the (male) role of the poet-lover and woos a young man under a Greek pseudonym, whereas Cerinthus is given the (usually female) role of the silent beloved. Her own name, family and status are clearly indicated, but she is vague about Cerinthus.[56] Like his female counterparts, the *puellae* of love elegy, he is a puzzling figure, and it seems useless to try and find out his 'real' name or social rank. In fact, we do not even know whether the pseudonym actually conceals a real person or not.[57] Compared with elegiac *puellae* such as Cynthia, whose marked personality gives colour to Propertius' poems, Cerinthus is a much more shadowy figure who remains silent throughout Sulpicia's poetry. This silence, unusual for a man, stands in sharp contrast with the way Sulpicia publicizes her erotic feelings.[58]

Not only gender roles, but also conventional elegiac themes are more or less inverted in her poems. Here the ambiguity of her role as both the elegiac *puella* and the poet-lover adds to the peculiarity of the way in which she handles elegiac themes. Instead of a joyful occasion her birthday is called 'hated' because it would separate her from Cerinthus; and the countryside, idealized by some other love poets such as Tibullus, she describes as unfit for an urbane *puella* like herself. Also the theme of illness is inverted showing the female poet-lover ill and the male beloved indifferent to her illness; further, the conventional *servitium amoris* is absent from her poetry; it is replaced by a more equal relation between herself and her beloved.[59]

Though the reversal of elegiac gender roles may seem natural for a female love poet who wants to conform to the conventions of the genre, the particular way in which she inverts conventional themes and elegiac roles adds to the novelty and artistry of her poetry and was, no doubt, adopted deliberately.[60]

Sulpicia's poems are unique among Latin love elegies because of their consistently female standpoint. Though working within the elegiac tradition and employing the same themes and emotions as male love poets, she also deviates from this tradition by the inversion of elegiac gender roles and by her use of the 'female' notions of gossip and reputation instead of the usual male terminology of a military or political career. The three roles Sulpicia adopts (that of the upper-class girl, that of the elegiac *puella* and that of the poet-lover) partly account for the complexity and originality of her poetry. In it she plays with the tension between her social position as an upper-class woman and her combined role of the poet-lover and the elegiac *puella*: her claim to independence of feeling conflicts with the anxious concern of her relatives, and her desire for publicity with the apprehension for her reputation.

To some extent, her language and style also differ from those of the male love poets, though a mere forty lines do not allow a detailed comparison. Her difficult syntax and compressed thought on the one hand and her use of colloquialisms and word-repetition and the absence of mythological allusions and of military and legal terminology on the other have in the past been ascribed to poetic inexperience as a consequence of her seclusion as a woman of rank, but recent studies have shown them to be deliberate features of poetic technique.[61] Perhaps, with her short and seemingly simple poems and the female perspective adopted in them, she intended to reach a wider public, of women as well as men.[62] There is no evidence whether she succeeded in this or not. That her poetry was read and appreciated by men seems certain, since her six poems were included in the published collection and survived, but also because of the five poems of the mysterious *amicus Sulpiciae*.[63] These are generally regarded as a poetic tribute to the poems of Sulpicia, for the unknown poet takes her love-affair as the subject of his poetry and plays with her themes and even with her inversion of elegiac gender roles. Thus, despite (or, perhaps, because of) the difference in language and style and her consistent female standpoint Sulpicia's poetry appealed to male readers, who perhaps cherished her poetry for its ingenious play with poetic gender roles.[64] If the unknown *amicus Sulpiciae* is indeed, as he seems to be, a poet of later date who took Sulpicia's poems as a source of inspiration, it is remarkable that he imitated and even elaborated Sulpicia's inversion of elegiac gender roles: he emphasizes the mutedness of Cerinthus and Sulpicia's role as the speaking person by introducing her as the poet-lover in two of his own poems.[65]

A well-educated young woman of aristocratic family who composes love poetry speaking of female erotic feelings and reaching the level of a professional poet; an unmarried upper-class girl, who defies traditional morality, inverts elegiac gender roles and the conventional themes of elegy and consistently adopts a female point of view within the male genre of elegy: such a woman seems almost 'too good to be true'.[66] It is a pity that, lacking other substantial examples of love poetry written by women of her time, we are unable to tell whether she was in any way typical of upper-class women writing love poetry or not.

Sulpicia Caleni

'Let all young women, who wish to please one man alone, read Sulpicia; let all husbands, who wish to please one bride alone, read Sulpicia':[67] thus Martial recommends the poetry of his female contemporary Sulpicia, the only other Roman woman poet of whose poetry anything has been preserved (a mere two lines only) and who, curiously enough, was also called Sulpicia. We know very little of her. Sulpicia Caleni, as she is usually called to distinguish her from

Sulpicia the elegist, lived in Rome during the reign of Domitian and wrote remarkably frank verses about her own married life and her erotic feelings for her husband Calenus. Martial, who was a friend or a protégé of her husband's, praises her work and marriage in two epigrams (10.35 and 38): he extols her love for and faithfulness to her husband and their mutual happiness in marriage, comparing her to Egeria, the Muse and exemplary wife of the mythical king Numa.[68] From Martial's epigram addressed to Calenus (10.38), which seems to be a *consolatio* for Sulpicia's death commemorating the happiness of their marriage, we may infer that she had died between AD 95 and 98, after fifteen years of marriage.[69] The aristocratic ring of her name and the probability that her husband, the unknown Calenus, was a patron of Martial's suggest that she belonged to the upper classes.

By a stroke of luck we can compare Martial's judgement of Sulpicia's poetry with two lines of her work (iambic trimeters) that seem to have been preserved: they were quoted by a fourth-century scholiast of Juvenal to explain the then obsolete word *cadurcum* (linen, especially used for bedlinen and mattresses).[70] Unfortunately, the text is corrupt and though various emendations have been proposed, the interpretation remains uncertain. To show how little we know, even of these two surviving lines, the main difficulties may be indicated here. As transmitted by the fifteenth-century scholar Giorgio Valla the text reads: 'Unde ait Sulpicius[!]: "ne cadurcis restitutis fasciis / nudum Calaeno concubentem proferat"', which is both unintelligible and metrically incorrect. Because of the reference to Calenus all editors, following the sixteenth-century scholar Pierre Pithou, have changed 'Sulpicius' to 'Sulpicia' and have identified her with the poetess praised by Martial. Bücheler's ingenious emendation 'Sulpicia si me' for 'Sulpicius ne', which corrects both the gender of the speaker and the metre of the verse, is adopted in most recent editions. Skipping some minor questions this eventually leads to the now accepted reading: 'Unde ait Sulpicia: "si me cadurci restitutis fasciis / nudam Caleno concubantem proferat"'. This may be translated as: 'Whence Sulpicia says: "If [something] reveals me lying naked with Calenus when the linen bed-girth has been restored"'.[71]

This is puzzling: not only does the fragment lack a subject to explain 'proferat', but it is also hard to make sense of the obscure first line. For this reason A. Baehrens in his edition of 1886 preferred a different reading, which may be easier to understand but contains some very bold emendations. Suggesting 'lux' for 'si' and accepting Bücheler's emendation 'dissolutis' for Valla's 'restitutis' his text reads: 'Unde ait Sulpicia: "lux me cadurci dissolutis fasciis / nudam Caleno concubantem proferat"', which may be translated as: 'Whence Sulpicia says: "Let the light reveal me lying naked with Calenus when the linen bed-girth has been loosened"'.[72] However, the previous reading, cited above, is usually preferred as it is closer to the transmitted text. W. Morel in his edition of 1927 takes *cadurcum* (in its meaning of 'mattress') metaphorically to mean 'marriage bed' and thus 'marriage', and comments that Sulpicia hopes that her marriage, which is disturbed for some unknown reason, will be restored to her. He is followed in this by A. Richlin, who believes that the fragment refers to a quarrel between Sulpicia

and Calenus, or a divorce.[73] Parker has recently suggested a more literal interpretation: assuming that *cadurcum* means a mattress or a duvet of a bed and that
the *fasciae* are the straps of the bed supporting the mattress, he translates: 'So
Sulpicia says: "If, when the straps for the mattress have been restored, (it) might
reveal me naked sleeping with Calenus"', suggesting that the bed was broken 'by
the intensity of her and her husband's lovemaking'.[74] On account of the corruption of the text and the loss of its context none of these interpretations is wholly
convincing. In fact, even the notion that the author is female is an emendation.
Yet, if we accept this emendation, which is plausible, there can hardly be any
doubt about the setting of the poem: the lines must stem from one of Sulpicia's
erotic poems, mentioned by Martial, which describe her nights spent with her
husband Calenus.[75] The second line of the fragment seems very outspoken in its
emphasis on her being naked and her 'sleeping with' her husband, which is
indicated with striking candour.

Erotic poetry of a chaste univira

The outspokenness of the fragment is in accordance with Martial's description
of Sulpicia's poetry. According to him she avoided mythical themes, but wrote
about her love for her husband, frankly describing their erotic intimacies. Yet, he
hastens to stress her chastity: Sulpicia is a faithful and loving *univira* teaching
decent marital love and her poetry can be recommended to all respectable young
women (and men): 'she teaches chaste and honest loves, games, delights and
playful jests'.[76] In his epigram addressing her husband Calenus (10.38) he
describes the happiness of the fifteen years of their wedded life in erotic terms
reminiscent of the imagery of love poetry and perhaps echoing Sulpicia's own
poems. In particular, his lines describing the couch and the lamp witnessing their
embraces: 'Oh, what battles, what fights on both sides did the happy little bed
and lamp witness', though of course a variation on a well-known theme in Latin
love poetry, are vaguely reminiscent of Sulpicia's surviving fragment.[77]

In spite of Martial's vigorous defence of her moral reputation her straightforward expression of sexual pleasure is astonishing for a married Roman
woman, especially if she was, as she seems to have been, of upper-class rank.
Like her namesake Sulpicia the elegist, she seems to have adopted two conflicting
female roles in her poetry (apart from that of the, usually male, poet-lover): the
role of the respectable *matrona* and that of the *puella* of love poetry. The conflict
between these two is noticeable in the epigrams of Martial, in which he takes
pains to show that in spite of the wantonness of her poetry she was a chaste wife
who succeeded in combining the life of the devoted *univira* with the language and
imagery of passionate love poetry: 'One who judges her songs rightly, will say no
woman is naughtier, will say no woman is holier.'[78]

Whether her poetry about marital love described from the female point of
view earned her a female public, as was recommended by Martial, cannot be
made out, but that her poetry was read by men seems certain. Not only did an

unknown *grammaticus* or scholiast remember her verses when commenting on Juvenal's use of the word *cadurcum*, but in the fourth and fifth centuries AD a number of references to Sulpicia's poetry indicate the fame it still enjoyed at the time. The sexual frankness of her poetry seems to have been its most conspicuous feature in the eyes of these later authors. Some of them refer to its (apparently widely known) wantonness when they apologize for the frivolity of their own work. The fourth-century author Ausonius includes Sulpicia in his list of eminent literary predecessors whose personal lives were beyond reproach though their verses were lascivious: 'Sulpicia's little work is wanton, her outlook prim' (compare the well-known *topos* 'my page is wanton, my life chaste'), and the fifth-century author Sidonius Apollinaris mentions Sulpicia in a long list of poets he will *not* imitate: 'not the winsome jest of Sulpicia's Muse which she wrote to her Calenus'.[79] Though we cannot be sure that these authors had, all of them, actually read her verses – theoretically, they may have derived their knowledge from hearsay, or from the epigrams of Martial in praise of Sulpicia – her poetry apparently enjoyed some fame in late antiquity and was perhaps still widely read.

From the same period a poem of seventy hexameters has come down to us under her name. This curious 'satire', which almost certainly dates from the early fifth century AD, denounces the expulsion of philosophers from Rome by Domitian in AD 88–9 or 93–4. It is a literary pastiche borrowing words and expressions from various authors.[80] Apart from the hint that Sulpicia composed poetry in various metres (among which are the iambic trimeters of her surviving fragment), the author of the literary fake does not add to our knowledge of Sulpicia's life or poetry. He (or perhaps, she) was aware that Sulpicia lived during the reign of Domitian, and Calenus is mentioned, but apparently only to try to convince the reader that Sulpicia was the author. The reason for the attribution of this poem to Sulpicia remains obscure; as far as we know, Sulpicia wrote love poetry, which makes the attribution of a political 'satire' attacking Domitian and forecasting his imminent death a surprising one.[81] Yet, it is another indication that in the early fifth century she still enjoyed some renown as a poetess.

It is, of course, almost impossible to judge Sulpicia's place in Latin literature from two problematic lines only, even if supplemented with Martial's poems in praise of her. Yet, some tentative conclusions may be drawn. The directness of her verses, her erotic theme and vocabulary, and her supposed use of various metres place her in the tradition of Roman love poets such as Catullus.[82] However, there are great differences between her poetry and that of the male love poets of the late republic and the Augustan period. First, Sulpicia writes about married love instead of the promiscuous love-affairs celebrated by these poets.[83] Further, instead of assigning a Greek pseudonym to her beloved as was the convention in Latin love poetry, she calls him by his real Roman name – or so we suppose. Third, she keeps away from mythological themes and perhaps also from mythological adornment. Instead, she focusses on a direct description of physical love.

These differences show that she went her own way, though indebted to the tradition of Latin love poetry; however, we cannot exclude the possibility that her verses resembled other poetry of her time now lost. The directness with which she conveys her feelings and the absence of mythological themes recall her name-sake, Sulpicia the elegist. Also in her revelation of a woman's erotic feelings and sexual love (though in her case it is restricted to marital love) she resembles the earlier poetess, but Sulpicia Caleni seems to have been more outspoken in her description of sexual intimacy. Both adopt a marked female perspective in a male genre; that this was far from typical of all poetry written by women will appear from the work of the last two female poets to be discussed, Julia Balbilla and Terentia, to whom we may turn now.

Julia Balbilla

Four Greek epigrams inscribed on the left leg and foot of one of the Memnon Colossi (plate 4) in Egyptian Thebes form a record of an otherwise unknown poetess of Greek descent, Julia Balbilla.[84] She accompanied the emperor Hadrian and his wife Sabina on their great journey around the eastern provinces from AD 128 onwards which led them to Egypt in AD 130. In this land of wonders, so popular with Roman tourists, the imperial company made the tour of the many Egyptian attractions such as the pyramids, the temples and the tombs of the Valley of the Kings. On 19 and 20 November at sunrise they visited the 'singing' Colossus of Memnon at Thebes to hear his voice.[85]

The so-called Colossus of Memnon was a huge seated statue of the Pharaoh Amenophis III, which was ruined by an earthquake in 27 BC leaving only the pedestal with the lower parts of the legs and the hands resting on the knees in place. At sunrise, because of expansion of the stone caused by the sudden rise in temperature, the broken statue used to produce a sound, which was believed to be the voice of the statue. In the Graeco-Roman tradition the name of the mythical *heros* Memnon, son of Eos and Tithonos, was given to the mutilated statue and it was said that with this sound 'Memnon' greeted his mother Dawn. Regarded as one of the wonders of Egypt, the 'singing' statue attracted many visitors, who left records of their admiration (sometimes even amounting to religious adoration) in numerous inscriptions on the legs and feet of the statue. Septimius Severus, who in AD 199–200 visited Egypt with his family, was also impressed, and ordered the restoration of the statue. However, as a consequence of the restoration the statue lost its 'voice' and therewith its attraction to the ancient tourists; from that moment it fell into oblivion.[86]

The four poems of Julia Balbilla, which total forty-five lines and are all that is left of her poetry, are inscribed on the left leg and foot of the statue. The muti-lated condition of the poems today, due to erosion by the wind and the sand of the desert, raises some problems in interpreting the texts. These difficulties are of minor importance to our inquiry and therefore they will not be discussed here.[87]

The three epigrams grouped together on the left leg (plate 5) were inscribed by one and the same hand, probably on 20 November. They commemorate the

Plate 4 One of the Colossi of Memnon in Egyptian Thebes; the legs and feet of the statue
are covered with inscriptions. Photo Carla van Battum.

imperial visits to Memnon. They are carved with care in good lettering at a
height of about one and a half metres above the base of the statue, a place which
was made clearly visible by the rays of the rising sun. Apparently special care was
taken to underline their importance. The epigrams are written in elegiac distichs,

165

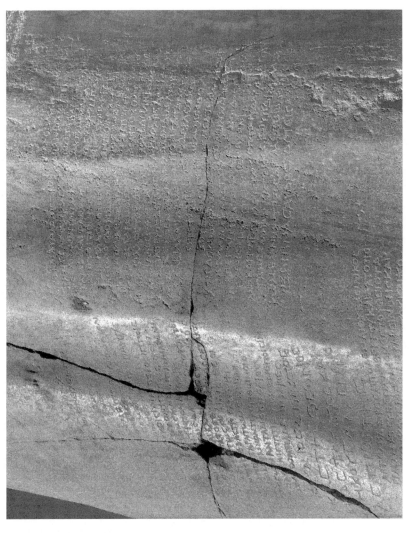

Plate 5 Three poems by Julia Balbilla (Bernand (1960) nos 28–30) inscribed on the left leg of the Colossus of Memnon. Photo Carla van Battum.

the hexameters neatly arranged vertically with indentation of the pentameters. Each epigram is preceded by a short preface in prose explaining the occasion. The fourth poem, inscribed on the left foot of the statue, commemorates Balbilla's own experience of hearing Memnon, and contains two dates: 20 and 21 November 130. The inscription shows a different hand and, like most inscriptions on the foot, it is written in larger and more deeply carved letters than those on the leg, possibly to compensate for its less conspicuous place. Like the other three poems it is written in elegiac distichs, but it is shorter and has no preface. On the instep of the left foot, a place clearly visible in the light of the rising sun, the empress Sabina commemorated her visit by a short inscription in prose.[88]

The topmost poem on the left leg, the one that was inscribed first, deals with Hadrian's visit. It is introduced with the words: 'By Julia Balbilla, when the emperor Hadrian heard Memnon' and describes in six distichs Memnon's three-fold greeting of Hadrian and Hadrian's own commemoration of the event (which is lost). The poem reads:

> Memnon the Egyptian, I have been told, speaks from his Theban stone
> when warmed by the rays of the sun. But when he saw Hadrian, the all-
> powerful ruler, he greeted him even before the first rays of the sun as well
> as he could. But when Titan traversing the sky with his white horses held
> the second mark of the hours in his shadow, Memnon again sent out his
> voice sharp-toned as of beaten bronze; for joy, he also uttered a third cry.
> Then the emperor Hadrian himself also greeted Memnon amply and on
> a stele he left verses for posterity reporting all he had seen and heard.
> Clear to all it became how much the gods loved him.[89]

The second poem is inscribed partly under and partly to the right of the first and is preceded by the words: 'When I had come together with the empress Sabina to Memnon'. It is the longest of her poems, written to mark Sabina's visit to Memnon, at which Balbilla herself was present. The poem does not seem to form a unity and has long been regarded as consisting of two separate poems. After six lines in which Balbilla invokes Memnon and implores him to greet Sabina with his chant, a 'mythical' part follows in which the impious Persian king Cambyses is held responsible for the mutilation of Memnon and is punished for it (lines 7–10). The last part of the poem (lines 11–18), which is only loosely connected with the preceding lines, speaks of Balbilla's elevated ancestry. W. Peek has pointed out that by its composition in three parts, an invocation of Memnon, a narrative part and a conclusion, the poem shows hymnic features, but the lines about her own ancestry are out of place in a hymn.[90]

The third poem, consisting of four distichs, is inscribed under the second. It is introduced by the words: 'Since we had not heard Memnon on the first day' and explains the failure of the previous day by Memnon's eagerness to see the lovely Sabina again, thus neatly turning what may be regarded as an insult into a compliment. Balbilla asks Memnon not to stay silent again, threatening him with the emperor's wrath, and Memnon obeys, shuddering with fear of the might of the great Hadrian.[91]

Balbilla's last and shortest poem, inscribed on Memnon's left foot, has no preface. It seems to have been composed hastily and carelessly as it consists of seven lines, three distichs followed by a single pentameter, and contains other errors which, however, may be due to the stonecutter. Unlike the other poems it is written in the first person and commemorates Balbilla's visit to Memnon on the previous day (in the company of the empress Sabina) and her hearing his 'divine voice'. In contrast to the more or less official reports of the imperial visits on the leg of the statue, this seems to be a private poem recording her own experience. It resembles other private inscriptions on the statue (most of which, however, are in prose) in its emphasis on the name and the company of the visitor, and the date and the hour of the visit. Its main significance lies in the exact date it provides.[92]

Attempts have been made to reconstruct the events on the basis of these poems. According to Bernand[93] the imperial company visited Memnon for the first time on 19 November, but failed to hear his voice. On 20 November they returned, first Sabina with Julia Balbilla and then, slightly later, Hadrian and his company. They were all greeted by Memnon: Sabina and Balbilla at the first hour and Hadrian at the second. Hadrian is even said to have been greeted three times, a poetic exaggeration of Balbilla's, who wanted to disguise the painful experience of Memnon's silence on the first day of their visit. In fact, Memnon probably only 'spoke' twice in Hadrian's presence, as is attested by the inscription of one of the other persons present.[94] The following day, according to Bernand, Julia Balbilla returned to the statue alone. She recorded this in her fourth poem, but was careful enough to devote two lines of this short poem to her visit in the company of the empress Sabina in order to avoid giving offence.

Though Bernand's detailed reconstruction of the sequence of events is well argued, it is not wholly convincing, nor does it provide the only possible solution.[95] Moreover, it seems doubtful whether the sequence of events can be reconstructed from poetic reflections like these. Balbilla did not mean to produce an exact record of what happened. Her aim was to commemorate the imperial visit to the Colossus of Memnon in a way pleasing to the emperor and his wife and demonstrating her own poetic ability and erudition. Therefore, she flattered both Hadrian and Sabina exuberantly. Hadrian is portrayed as the master of the universe, the beloved of the gods, whose wrath causes even the godlike Memnon to shudder with fear.[96] Sabina is mentioned more affectionately; in Balbilla's poems she figures not only as the 'august spouse of the sovereign Hadrian' but also as 'our beloved empress', and attention is drawn to her lovely appearance. Balbilla was clearly on more intimate and affectionate terms with Sabina than with Hadrian.[97]

In the judgement of most modern scholars Balbilla's poems are 'mediocre' or even 'atrocious'.[98] This harsh judgement is partly caused by their baroque, rather overwrought style, which, though not uncommon at the time, seems priggish in the eyes of the modern reader. Also her flattery of the imperial couple, though in keeping with the ideas of the godlike ruler current at the time in the eastern part of the empire, may seem embarrassing to modern readers, and her deification and personification of the statue, portraying it as sensitive to Sabina's beauty and as in awe of Hadrian's might, slightly ridiculous. Further defects for which her poetry is criticized are its artificial and lifeless images, its tedious sequence of paratactic sentences and its lack of balance and unity. Yet, the modern verdict seems too harsh when we compare it to male amateur poetry of the time, much of which was hardly less mediocre.[99]

Though, of course, they are not great poetry, Balbilla's verses are notable for two things: the erudition she displays and her curious use of the Aeolic dialect. As regards her erudition, she clearly enjoys demonstrating her learning in both Greek and Egyptian traditions and literature. For example, she mentions both the Egyptian name of the Colossus and the Greek myths concerning Memnon, and she cleverly connects the Egyptian myth that Cambyses mutilated the Colossus with Herodotus' tale of the killing of Apis by this Persian king and his subsequent death.[100]

The second distinctive trait of her poetry is her use of a highly unusual dialect: all four poems are written in imitation of the Aeolic-Lesbian dialect of about 600 BC and are larded with other rare, archaic words, most of them derived from Homer. For a woman living in the Roman world of the second century AD such a choice of dialect seems surprising and probably also amazed (and impressed) her contemporaries: in spite of the archaizing fashion in the literature of the time, her use of the Aeolic dialect is unique in second-century Greek poetry.[101] Her ability to write in an obsolete dialect, though sometimes faulty and resulting in hyper-Aeolisms, demonstrates her literary skill and her knowledge of archaic Greek poetry. But there must have been another, more specific reason to write her poems in a pseudo-archaic Lesbian dialect: Sappho. Though the theme of Balbilla's verses has no connection with Sappho whatsoever, her artificial re-creation of the archaic Aeolic dialect indicates her ambition to pose as a second Sappho. It seems to be a deliberate and ambitious attempt to follow in the footsteps of, and pay tribute to, the greatest poet of her sex, Sappho.

Who was Julia Balbilla, and in what capacity did she take part in the imperial voyage? From her second poem it may be inferred that she stemmed from a high-ranking family. She apparently took great pride in her elevated ancestry, and her vanity led her to devote some lines to it in one of her poems:

> For pious were my parents and grandfathers: Balbillus the Wise and king Antiochus; Balbillus, the father of my mother of royal blood and king Antiochus, the father of my father. From their line I too draw my noble blood, and these verses are mine, pious Balbilla.[102]

Though some problems remain, this provides us with the following genealogy.

Her father, C. Iulius Antiochus Epiphanes, was a son of the last ruling king of Commagene, Antiochus IV.[103] Her mother, who is not mentioned by name, but who has been identified with Claudia Capitolina, was the daughter of 'Balbillus the Wise'. This Balbillus has been identified with Tib. Claudius Balbillus, prefect of Egypt under Nero and a learned man; he was probably the same man as the friend and court-astrologer of Claudius, Nero and Vespasian.[104] Thus, Julia Balbilla stemmed from a distinguished family: on her father's side she was descended from the royal dynasty of Commagene and on her mother's side from one of the highest equestrian magistrates. Moreover, Balbilla's elder brother, C. Iulius Antiochus Epiphanes Philopappus, was adlected into the senate by Trajan *inter praetorios* and was *consul suffectus* in AD 109.[105]

Despite her foreign background Julia Balbilla was probably born and bred in Rome, where her grandfather lived as a hostage from about AD 72 onwards. Though her brother was a consul, Balbilla herself was probably not of senatorial rank: since her father was not a member of the senate, she had not inherited senatorial dignity, and we have no information about a possible marriage that might have given her senatorial rank. As hers was a wealthy and well-educated family of mixed equestrian and senatorial status she did, of course, belong to the Roman élite. At the time of her trip to Egypt she was an elderly woman and, as no husband is mentioned, possibly a widow.

Her position in the company of Sabina is unclear; she is usually called a friend or a lady-in-waiting of the empress, vague terms to disguise our ignorance of their relationship.[106] In some respects her encomiastic poetry and her unequal relation with the imperial couple resemble those of a Greek court-poet. As court-poets usually did, she accompanied her patroness on her voyage and commemorated her experiences in poetry; her affectionate tone when writing about the empress suggests a personal relationship of some intimacy. Stemming from a wealthy family of high social rank, she was, of course, no professional poet in need of free lodging or financial support, but neither were some of the more wealthy Greek poets.[107]

In view of her wealth and status her position may perhaps be regarded as the female counterpart of a (male) *comes* of an emperor, who accompanied the emperor on a journey or expedition. As Balbilla's father and her grandfather had been *comites* of emperors, she would continue what was almost a family tradition.[108] Yet, such a position is highly unusual for a woman and her precise relation to the imperial couple cannot be decided. We may only conclude that she was a learned poet from a wealthy high-ranking family whose poems demonstrate not only her pride in her ancestry and in her closeness to the imperial family, but also her erudition and her ambition to write poetry in the dialect of Sappho. The four poems inscribed on the Colossus of Memnon are all that is left of her work; they are rare surviving examples of poetry written by upper-class women in an age well known for its literary dilettantism among the Roman élite.[109] In this she showed as much poetic ambition and as little poetic talent as many of her male colleagues.

170

Terentia

The one surviving poem of the last female poet to be discussed here is of a different kind: in comparison to the other three she seems to be a mere versifier. Terentia was of senatorial rank and a daughter and sister of consuls. She toured Egypt at about the same time as Julia Balbilla, possibly in the suite of the emperor or his wife, and left record of her visit in a short verse-inscription commemorating her deceased brother, D. Terentius Gentianus.[110] The Latin poem, which consists of six hexameters as we have it now but which may originally have been longer, was inscribed on the polished surface of one of the pyramids of Gizeh, probably that of Cheops, near Memphis. In 1335 a German pilgrim, Wilhelm von Boldensele, saw it and, as it was one of the few inscriptions he could read (most of the others were written in hieroglyphs or in Greek and other languages), he copied it. Apparently in his days the original limestone coating of the great pyramids, which was covered with countless hieroglyphs and inscriptions by Greek and Roman travellers, was still largely intact, though the inscriptions seem to have been worn through erosion by the sand. In the following centuries the pyramids were used as quarries for the neighbouring city of Cairo and the outer casing, which consisted of a fine-grained limestone, was removed from one pyramid after the other. Only at the top of the Pyramid of Chephren is there a portion of the original Tura limestone coating remaining intact today. With the coating the inscriptions have disappeared; they are lost to us except for this one poem by Terentia, saved by Von Boldensele, and two Greek inscriptions which have come down to us in other ways.[111] Terentia's poem, as we have it, reads:

> I saw the pyramids without you, my dearest brother, and here I sadly shed tears for you, which is all I could do. And I inscribe this lament in memory of our grief. May thus be clearly visible on the high pyramid the name of Decimus Gentianus, who was a pontifex and companion to your triumphs, Trajan, and both censor and consul before his thirtieth year of age.[112]

The inscription was partly worn and must have been hard to read, as Von Boldensele had difficulty in understanding its meaning and his copy is probably incomplete. It ends abruptly and the name of the author is lacking. We do not know how many lines are missing, but that it was written by a woman, the sister of the deceased, is certain because of the feminine ending of 'maesta' (line 2) and because of the fact that she addresses him as her brother in the first line of her poem.[113] As her brother's *gentilicium* was Terentius, her name must have been Terentia.

There is no indication when and in whose company Terentia visited Egypt. As her father and her brother, whose career we can trace from epigraphy till AD 120, had been on friendly terms with Trajan and Hadrian, it is usually supposed that she joined the imperial trip to Egypt in 130, but this is hard to reconcile with the story in the *Historia Augusta* that Terentius Gentianus had eventually fallen into disfavour with Hadrian, who regarded him as a rival to the throne and hated him for his popularity in the senate. We do not know the date of Gentianus' fall from favour, which may, after all, never have taken place (or perhaps refers to another Terentius Gentianus), nor do we know whether Gentianus was executed or compelled to commit suicide. But if he fell from favour with Hadrian and was eventually killed, it would have been odd for Terentia to inscribe these verses for her brother as a member of the imperial company.[114] Therefore, we must conclude that either the *Historia Augusta* is wrong about Gentianus' disgrace or Terentia did not take part in the imperial journey, but inscribed her commemorative verses during a private visit to Egypt after Hadrian's death.[115] Terentia's poem expresses genuine sorrow for her brother's early death, but it also displays her great pride in his brilliant career, which she makes even more brilliant by changing his rank of *censitor* (of Macedonia) to *censor* (line 6). As is to be expected she does not write about his possible disgrace, but it is to be noted that she ignores Hadrian in the preserved part of the poem, though she does mention Trajan.

The poem is no literary masterpiece; it seems to be an occasional poem by an upper-class woman who, like so many of her class and time, dabbled in poetry in her leisure-time. As regards its content the poem shows a mixture of elements. In its description of the career of the deceased and of the grief of the relative he leaves behind it is reminiscent of a (metrical) epitaph, but it also contains a conventional theme found in tourists' records of their visits to the great monuments of Egypt: the wish that their loved ones could share the experience.[116] Terentia's poem is of special interest to us because of the erudition it displays and because of the (literary) pretension in inscribing a poem on one of the great pyramids of Egypt.[117] Though it is composed rather clumsily and has little poetic value, it bears witness to her education and her poetic aspirations by its reminiscences of verses of Horace, Ovid and, perhaps, Catullus. The second verse of her poem recalls the words of Ovid, and possibly those of Catullus, about the death of a brother: like Ovid Terentia writes that all a relative can do is shed tears for the deceased. The third verse is an adaptation of a verse in one of the odes of Horace, spoken by the Danaid Hypermnestra to her husband and nephew Lynceus, son of Aegyptus, a myth that bears many references to Egypt and death.[118]

We may conclude that Terentia was well read and that she took pride in showing it. By alluding to the work of famous poets of the Augustan age and by inscribing her poem on one of the great pyramids she demonstrates her self-confidence: her poem was meant for eternity. Though she was a literary dilettante, for whom there is no place in the history of Roman literature, her poem is of some value to us; it demonstrates once more that among upper-class women of the time there were serious and ambitious amateur poets.

Some concluding remarks may be made. As we have seen, the work of the four female poets discussed above differs widely; it has come down to us in various ways and is also of a very different kind. Therefore, to our initial question, whether female poets differed significantly from male ones in style, genre, subject-matter and in respect of their audience, no simple answer can be given. On the one hand we have the two Sulpiciae: ambitious poets, who worked in the male genre of love poetry and attained professional standards in it; their verses were read by men and, probably, women. Their poetry shows a marked female perspective. The unusual way in which Sulpicia the elegist handled conventional elegiac themes, her preoccupation with a woman's reputation and with the 'female' themes of rumour and gossip, and her inversion of elegiac gender roles show her to have been acutely aware of her unique position as a female love poet in an all-male genre. Also Sulpicia Caleni wrote about love from the woman's point of view but, since so little of her poetry is left, we cannot judge it in any detail. This 'female perspective' did not earn them contempt or exclusion from the literary tradition; on the contrary, their skilful adaptation of the rules of the genre seems to have been appreciated, since their work was read and transmitted at least until the fifth century (Sulpicia Caleni) or even up to the present day (Sulpicia the elegist).

The poetry of Julia Balbilla and Terentia, however, is of a totally different kind. Both were literary dilettantes and wrote occasional verse (i.e. poetry for specific occasions) instead of love poetry; neither of them was especially concerned with 'female' themes or a female perspective. By inscribing their poems on a public monument they gave publicity to them, but, as far as we know, neither ever 'published' poetry. Unlike the verses of the Sulpiciae, the poems of Julia Balbilla and Terentia survived by chance, those of Balbilla because the monument on which they were carved withstood the ages, and the poem of Terentia because it was accidentally copied by a visiting pilgrim. Yet, whereas the poems of Julia Balbilla reflect her ambition to meet professional standards and are written in commemoration of a public occasion, the imperial visit to Memnon, Terentia seems inexperienced and of little talent; besides, her theme is private sorrow.

To summarize, the work of these four female poets does not represent a uniform 'female voice' but rather four different 'literary voices' of women. Therefore, we cannot conclude that in Roman society poetry by women was characterized by a specific style or subject-matter distinctive from that of male poetry; and even less that this supposed difference from male poetry would have excluded women poets from the literary tradition. On the contrary, the female perspective adopted in the work of the Sulpiciae generally seems to have been appreciated. The poems of Julia Balbilla and Terentia, on the other hand, may give an impression of their endeavours in amateur poetry such as was fashionable among the élite of their days, but like that of most of their male peers it survived only by chance. However, if we may judge from the shaky evidence of a mere four female poets there is one conspicuous difference between male and female poetry: the choice of genre. As far as we know women only wrote short elegies and epigrams on love and occasional themes. In the traditional hierarchy of literary genres these were less valued than the more serious poetic genres, such as epic, tragedy, didactic poetry and lyric poetry.[119] Though, of course, men also worked in these genres (writing epigrams was highly fashionable among upper-class amateur poets during the empire), it is their *restriction* to the minor genres that marks the special position of women. Since these poems were only rarely published they had less chance of survival, and as they were considered more frivolous than poems composed in one of the major genres, they were more likely to provoke mixed feelings. This brings us to our third and last question.

Mixed feelings: Roman attitudes towards women writing poetry

The Roman judgement of upper-class women writing poetry was far from uniform. Like educated women generally (chapter 3) they were regarded with mixed feelings. In this section some contradictory judgements about upper-class women writing poetry will be discussed and an attempt will be made to discover the reasons for this ambivalent attitude. As is the case with other questions posed in this study, the scanty evidence does not allow definitive conclusions.

We shall start with two notorious women of the late republic, Sempronia and Clodia Metelli, who allegedly wrote verses, and then compare the mainly negative judgement of them to the praise bestowed by the love poets on the poetic gifts of their *puellae*. To throw light on the complicated relation between poetry and life, and on the possible influence of the praise of the poetic talent of the *puellae* of love poetry on upper-class women who had similar talents, a digression is added about the question whether the *puellae* of love poetry were meant to depict real individuals or were fictitious. A brief discussion of the custom of comparing a woman's poetry with that of Sappho closes this section.

As we have seen, the notorious Sempronia of Sallust's *Bellum Catilinae* was praised in ambiguous terms for her ability to write verses.[120] Though Sallust mentions it among her accomplishments, his complex portrait of her puts her talents in a doubtful light, associating them with a life of luxury and sexual libertinism. Since we have no other evidence of Sempronia than Sallust's biassed portrait, it is hard to distinguish reality from fiction, but as she was a well-educated woman from an erudite family it would not be surprising if she actually wrote verses, – which then must have circulated since Sallust knew of them. Sallust's portrayal of her talents in poetry, music and dance, however, is malicious because they were presented as similar to those of the well-educated courtesan.

With even greater malice, Cicero in his *Pro Caelio* calls Clodia Metelli an 'old poetess of many plays'.[121] T. P. Wiseman takes Cicero's remark literally and believes that Clodia actually had some connection with the stage, assuming that she wrote mime; he argues that at this period mime was a fashionable entertainment dealing with the same subject-matter as love elegy.[122] However, I take it that

Cicero's remark should be regarded in the light of his defence of Caelius: he had much to gain by associating Clodia with the stage because of its bad reputation. Besides, Cicero puns on the double meaning of *fabula*, which means both 'play' and 'fictitious tale', in order to discredit her as a witness for the prosecution. Thus, the underlying meaning is 'an inveterate fabricator of many tales [i.e. lies]'. In a similar vein, in an attack against her brother, Cicero mentions her 'panto-mimic [or balletic] interludes', perhaps hinting at her marital interludes, her love-affairs. Therefore, his words should not be taken literally: they do not necessarily mean that she actually wrote mime or was a librettist of pantomime, as Wiseman believes; because of the strong sexual associations of the stage they must have been meant to blacken her.[123]

There is a striking similarity between the portrayal of Sempronia and Clodia Metelli in the work of Sallust and Cicero and literary *puellae* such as Catullus' Lesbia and Propertius' Cynthia.[124] Yet, they were judged very differently: the unconventional life of Sempronia and Clodia Metelli, which brought them into conflict with traditional standards, was used by Sallust and Cicero to cast doubt upon their morals, whereas a similar behaviour and comparable accomplish-ments earned the mistresses of love poetry nothing but praise of their poet-lovers. Their poetic gifts were extolled: their pseudonyms refer to Sappho (Catullus' Lesbia), to Apollo, the god of poetry (Propertius' Cynthia, Tibullus' Delia), or to a famous Greek poetess (Ovid's Corinna); and Propertius actually celebrates the poetry written by his Cynthia. How does this praise relate to the misgivings with which Clodia and Sempronia were regarded? Are we to believe that the *puellae* of love poetry were real women, as is usually believed of 'Lesbia', who is supposed to be the same woman as Clodia Metelli?[125] And should the pseudonym 'Lesbia' be taken to imply that Clodia Metelli did in fact write verses, which made Cicero call her an 'old poetess of many plays'?

This is not supported by the evidence; the assumption that the mistresses of love poetry conceal actual, and identifiable, women brings us onto very slippery ground.[126] This problem has already been touched upon in chapter 3 (p. 80), but as it has a bearing on our understanding of the Roman attitude towards women writing poetry it requires a somewhat fuller discussion here.

The mistresses of love poetry: reality or fiction?

If the historical truth about Sempronia is hard to discover in her literary portrait by Sallust, the uncertainty is even greater with the mistresses of the famous love poets of the late republic and the Augustan period. In antiquity the reality of these mistresses seems to have been taken for granted and Apuleius' remark that Clodia was the real name of Catullus' Lesbia, Hostia that of Propertius' Cynthia and Plania that of Tibullus' Delia has found wide acceptance in the past, leading to all sorts of, mainly fruitless, biographical speculation.[127] Apart from Clodia, who is generally, but not beyond doubt, equated with Clodia Metelli, these 'real' names are not very helpful. There is not much evidence for a reconstruction of the background of a Hostia or a Plania: all information on their lives, their social status and their relationships with their poet-lovers must be inferred from the poems of these poets themselves, which leads to circular reasoning. Moreover, 'biographical' details of these mistresses provided by the poets prove so inconsistent that it is impossible to determine the social and even the marital status of the *puellae*.[128] As a consequence, the belief in the reality of these *puellae*, which persisted for a long time, is now called in question. Some recent studies take the opposite view and argue that all women in love poetry are literary fictions not to be regarded as more or less realistic portraits of actual Roman women (let alone as pseudonyms of particular individuals). In this view, 'The Elegiac Woman' (with capitals to stress her abstract status as a narrative subject) is a 'literary construct' determined by poetic programmes and conventions; she is no flesh-and-blood woman, but a 'written woman'.[129]

Of course, poetry is not the same as autobiography, and the realist approach that attempts to detect the 'real' woman behind the pseudonym and to describe her life and outward appearance on the basis of the poems seems naive. Yet, the opposite view, which reduces these women to symbols of the creative process of writing or metaphors for the author's poetic ideals, is also unsatisfactory. Though it rightly attacks the simple and direct relation posited by the 'realists' between the poems and reality, the assumption that the women figuring in Roman elegy bear no relation whatsoever to real Roman women is unconvincing. In this view the dividing-line between literature and life seems drawn too sharply.[130]

To my mind, the problem is more intricate: usually there is a connection, though an indirect one, between poetry and the life and experiences of the poet. We may, therefore, assume that there was some sort of relationship between these 'literary' *puellae* and contemporary women. The nature of this relationship is unclear: it may range from a more or less direct connection between historical women and the *puellae* of love poetry to a more remote kind of relation in which the *puellae* are to be seen as projections of their authors' sentiments and ideals.

To find a more precise answer to this question, it must be taken into account that ancient readers never seem to have questioned the reality of the elegiac mistresses. This does not mean that we should believe that elegiac poetry comprises precise portrayals of identifiable women, but it does indicate that the women figuring in love poetry were sufficiently true to life to be convincing. We may assume that, to captivate their readers, the poets tried to make their poetical mistresses look real: their actions and feelings were to be convincing, though not necessarily exactly those of women they knew. A poet may combine the character and behaviour of several women and may infuse his own feelings and ideals into a 'portrait' of his mistress, provided she seems true to life; she should not be altogether alien to actual women of the time.

However, there may be more to it. As has been argued by Griffin, the relation between literature and life is reciprocal, life affecting literature and literature affecting life.[131] Therefore, we should not simply ask how far the *puellae* of love poetry were inspired by contemporary Roman women but also to what extent historical women were influenced by literary creations such as the *puellae* of the love poets. From other periods of history we know that a literary creation may have a powerful influence on the mind of its readers. Similarly, a mutual inter-action between literature and life is probable for Roman society. Thus, the free-dom, accomplishments and assertiveness of the *puellae* may have inspired Roman women to follow their example, and the praise bestowed by the poets on their accomplishments may well have affected the opinion of educated men – as we have already seen in the 'domestication' of the ideal of the *puella docta* during the empire (chapter 3, p. 81).

To narrow our inquiry to the poetic gifts of women, the interaction between literature and life may have been twofold: on the one hand, from real women who wrote poetry, such as Cornificia and Sulpicia, the authors of love poetry may have derived the conception of their beloveds' poetic gifts, and on the other, the example of the poetic skill of the *puellae* may have inspired real women to culti-vate a literary talent. In other words: the poetic ideal of a beautiful and sophisti-cated woman writing poetry may have contributed to the actual participation of women in the fashion of writing amateur poetry during the empire.

Since the last decennia of the republic and especially during the first two centur-ies AD it was fashionable among the members of the élite to write poetry (mainly epigrams of various kinds); even emperors tried their hand at it.[132] By writing clever short poems they demonstrated their literary skill and their knowledge of (Greek) culture. In comparison to the major genres such as epic, tragedy, lyric and didactic poetry, epigrams were easy to produce; one did not have to be a professional poet: any well-educated person might be expected to be able to compose a few verses.[133] Upper-class men wrote epigrams for their own amuse-ment and that of their friends: apart from recitations before an audience of friends and acquaintances or the sending of a small number of copies to close friends, these verses were usually not meant for publication, in contrast to their prose writings, which dealt with serious subjects such as oratory, history, law or agriculture.

Women too were affected by this new fashion – and were ridiculed for it by satirical authors such as Persius and Lucian.[134] Almost all their verses are lost. One line has been preserved by chance: the elder Seneca cites a hexameter written by a Vestal Virgin in praise of marriage and married life. 'How happy married women are! I may die if marriage is not sweet', she is reported to have written – and was accused of unchastity.[135] The name of this Vestal is not men-tioned, nor is anything known about her – she may even be fictitious – but in the excerpt of the discussion about her case in Seneca's *Controversiae* there is no sign of surprise that a Vestal should write verse.[136]

In the mainstream literary tradition women's participation was largely ignored but, as we have seen, some of their poems have survived, by chance, on stone. The poems of Julia Balbilla and Terentia, discussed above, may be taken as examples of what the work of female literary dilettantes could be like and demonstrate the pride women took in their poetry (and in their education, which is revealed in it).[137] In contrast to the ridicule and suspicion that women writing poetry met in some of the literary sources, the respect which Balbilla apparently won by her poems with the imperial family (since she was allowed to commemorate their visit to Memnon) and her pride in her work show that in her days writing poetry could be a respected activity for upper-class women. Such positive appraisal also appears from the fact that women writing poetry had their own, female, model of excellence and their supreme source of praise: Sappho.

In Sappho's footsteps

As we have seen, the four poems of Julia Balbilla inscribed on the Colossus of Memnon were remarkable for the Aeolic-Lesbian dialect, a highly unusual choice in the second century AD, with which she imitated Sappho.[138] Sappho's fame was great. Her poems were well known among educated people, not only from reading but also because they were sung at banquets.[139] Though, as is to be expected of great poetry, her poems appealed both to a male and a female public and influenced the work of male Roman poets (most notably Catullus), Sappho was felt to have a special significance for the poetry of women. Praised as the tenth Muse and the female counterpart of Homer, she personified the summit of women's poetry and as such she was a source of praise and inspiration for female poets; their poetry could receive no higher praise than a comparison with Sappho.[140]

As so little Latin poetry written by Roman women is left, we do not know whether women writing in Latin alluded to Sappho's poetry or imitated her metres or themes, but, as we shall see, despite the language difference the compliment of comparing their poetry to that of Sappho was current in the Roman world. As far as I know, it was introduced in Latin literature by the Roman love poets.[141] Their use of it does not necessarily imply actual imitation of Sappho's lyrics by the women in question; in most cases it seems to have been meant simply to praise a woman for her poetic talent.

In connection with this the pseudonyms of some of the mistresses of love poetry are telling. In choosing Lesbia as the name for his poetic mistress Catullus makes clear that Sappho was a source of inspiration for himself and at the same time he compliments the literary talent of his *puella*; yet, this pseudonym does not mean that 'Lesbia' was a poetess in the tradition of Sappho. Similarly, Ovid's choice of Corinna as the pseudonym of the *puella* of his *Amores* alludes to the famous Greek lyric poetess Corinna, but nowhere does Ovid suggest that his mistress wrote verses.[142] Such a general use of the compliment perhaps also underlies Catullus' praise of the unknown *puella* of his friend, the poet Caecilius, whom he calls 'more learned in poetry than the Sapphic Muse',[143] for no other reason (or so it appears) than her enthusiasm for Caecilius' poem – which, incidentally, in Catullus' eyes needed reworking. Though perhaps ironical, the compliment refers to her knowledge of and taste for poetry; but apart from the comparison with Sappho there is no evidence that she herself was a poet. Only Propertius actually speaks of the poetry of his *puella*, extolling, in a learned variation on the theme, her verses above those of the Greek poetess Corinna and perhaps Erinna: 'and when she challenges with her verses the writings of ancient Corinna and deems Erinna's poems no match for her own'.[144]

However, the comparison to Sappho also had a dubious side. Already in fourth-century Greek comedy the sensuality of Sappho's poetry had given rise to jokes about her alleged promiscuity, and her reputation for licentiousness continued in Rome side by side with her fame as a great poet.[145] This made the compliment rather awkward for respectable upper-class women. Therefore, when applying it to a woman they knew and respected, Roman poets took care to stress her chastity. Ovid, when praising 'Perilla's' poetry with a variation of the now habitual compliment: 'only the Lesbian poetess will surpass your work', mentions her 'chaste ways' and the constant presence of her mother. And the comparison is only vaguely hinted at by the *Amicus Sulpiciae* when picturing Sulpicia (the elegist) in the company of the Muses: 'no girl is more worthy of your choir', a compliment usually reserved for Sappho, the tenth Muse.[146] In a poem addressed to Canius Rufus, Martial praises his friend's fiancée, the otherwise unknown Theophila, with a variation on the theme. After describing her as a woman imbued with Greek culture and extolling her great knowledge of philosophy and her keen and 'unwomanly' judgement of poetry,[147] he speaks about her poetry as follows: 'Your Pantaenis, though well known to the Pierian choir, would not rank herself too much above her. Sappho, the lover, praised a poetess: more chaste is Theophila and not more learned was Sappho.' These difficult lines, which introduce what is wrongly believed to be an unknown poetess called Pantaenis into the comparison, are a variation on the same theme: Theophila matches Sappho in learning and beats her when it comes to chastity.[148] The most flattering description is found in his epigram in praise of Sulpicia Caleni. Here Martial introduces a variation by suggesting that Sulpicia not only equals Sappho but even surpasses her in learning, beauty and chastity: 'With her as your school-mate, or with her as your teacher, you would have been more learned, Sappho, and chaste; but had he seen her together with you and at the same time, hard Phaon would have loved Sulpicia.'[149] This seems to be as far as the compliment can possibly go, and drawn out to such a length that it seems stale.

Whether women wrote verses that were up to professional standards, as the two Sulpiciae did, or merely dabbled in poetry, Sappho ranked as the summit of poetic ability and thus provided a convenient compliment for a woman's poetic talent. In most cases no direct imitation of Sappho's poetry (metres, language or themes) can be pointed out; it was her reputation for poetic excellence and her gender that made her an ideal model. That the comparison with Sappho was desired by the women themselves is suggested by Lucian. In his satirical description of the miserable life of educated Greeks who had accepted a post in a wealthy Roman household, he makes fun of upper-class Roman women who wanted to seem educated: 'They count it as one among their embellishments if it is said that they are well educated, have an interest in philosophy and write songs not much inferior to Sappho's.'[150] As women writing poetry met with mixed feelings, they probably welcomed the precedent of a great poet of their own sex, who, whatever misgivings the sensuality of her verses provoked, was generally admired for poetic excellence.[151]

As we have seen, women writing poetry might be ridiculed by satirists, regarded with suspicion by traditional-minded authors, praised by the love poets or respected by some intellectuals during the empire. The reasons for these conflicting feelings are to be sought in the conflicting demands of class and gender (described in chapter 1). On the one hand, the ability to write verses was a sign of an upper-class education; on the other, such accomplishments were apt to raise suspicion with traditional-minded men, as they overstepped the boundaries set by custom for the upper-class *matrona*. By writing poetry an upper-class woman entered the domain of men, or that of women of doubtful morality such as the *puella docta* of love poetry. In addition to this, upper-class men had contradictory feelings about the writing of light poetry, the kind of poetry women wrote most: though a fashionable pursuit for one's leisure time, epigrams were considered to be somewhat frivolous. All this may have deterred women from writing, and publishing, poetry. Nevertheless, the greater appreciation of writing epigrams among upper-class men during the first two centuries AD seems also to have extended to women; they were accorded their own gender-specific praise: a comparison with Sappho. If we may judge from the poems of Julia Balbilla and Terentia inscribed on the great Egyptian monuments female amateur poets of the upper classes were as proud of their poetic achievements as were the men of their class.

Conclusions

What have we learned about the place of upper-class women in Roman literary life? First the positive results. As we gather from the sparse evidence, female poets did have a place, though a very modest one, in Roman literary life. They wrote elegies and epigrams according to the style and fashion of their days and took pride in their poetry, which they circulated, and perhaps published, or inscribed on stone. Women's poetry does not seem to have differed significantly from that of men in style and poetic technique, but a female poet might show her gender by adopting the dialect of Sappho or a marked female perspective: she might focus on women's feelings of love and play with the 'female' themes of gossip and reputation instead of using the military and political metaphors of male poetry. This female perspective may have gained women poets a female audience (for which we have no evidence), but it did not lose them their male public. Thus, to return to the second question posed in the introduction to this chapter, there are no indications that women's poetry was marginalized because of its female perspective, a particular use of language or a distinctive subject-matter.

Yet, as compared to male poets (and to female poets in the Greek world), the evidence for female poets in Rome is remarkably scanty. What may have been the cause? Were Roman women less given to writing poetry or was the manuscript tradition (the copying of texts through the ages as opposed to the fortuitous preservation of writings) less friendly to their work than to that of men? To this question no single answer can be given; it seems that several interrelated factors were responsible for the small number of female poets known to us. Below I shall list some of the impediments women might meet when writing (or publishing) poetry, and try to propose possible reasons for the almost total loss of their work in the manuscript tradition.

Women's virtual absence from literary coteries   Though not formally excluding women, male literary coteries did not often admit them; as we have seen, very few women (all related to male poets or patrons) may have gained admittance and it remains unclear whether they were accepted on equal terms with male poets or occupied only a marginal position. Mingling with male friends outside family circles was regarded as inappropriate for any respectable upper-class woman, and this may have deterred them from seeking admittance. Women's virtual absence from such male groups of literary friends must have isolated them from literary life and severely restricted their opportunities for circulating and publishing their poetry.

Women's restriction in poetic genre   As we have seen, female poets differed from male ones in respect of the genre they favoured. Unlike men, they occupied themselves, as far as we know, exclusively with love poetry and epigram. We never hear of a woman choosing one of the major genres, writing an epic, a drama or a didactic poem on agriculture or the like. The reasons for this restriction can only be guessed. Conditions of publication and recitation, women's haphazard education and the exigencies of their lives may have prevented any attempts at a work of greater scope; besides, the subjects of war or agriculture may not have appealed to them. Women's orientation to the house and family may have favoured the writing of introspective poetry or, at least, poetry dealing with private concerns. Because of their shortness epigrams could be written on wax-tablets and recited at banquets or other social gatherings in which women participated. Besides, love poetry was, at the time, a new and somewhat subversive genre: the male poets defied traditional Roman values by presenting a political or military career as inferior to a life of love. They also inverted traditional gender roles by adopting the passive and subservient 'female' role in relation to the dominant mistress; thus they attacked traditional male and female values. It seems possible that such a 'counter-genre', which extolled the poetic talent of the *puella docta*, was actually more open to women.

The appreciation of women writing poetry   As we have seen, women writing poetry were regarded with mixed feelings in Roman society: the suspicions of traditional-minded authors clashed with the praise of the love poets. This ambiguity may have made it risky for an upper-class woman to write poetry and, more so, to publish it, at least during the republic. During the empire women were

181

affected by the fashion of writing amateur poetry which was current among the élite; it may have encouraged them to write verses. Most of this poetry, however, was never published.

The ideal of female reticence (see chapter 1)   The traditional values of chastity and domesticity prescribed a retired way of life for Roman women. Reticent and dignified behaviour was expected, especially of upper-class women, since they were not compelled to earn their livelihood (as most lower-class women had to), but could stay at home and uphold the austere values of their class. In writing and – particularly – in publishing poetry, especially love poetry, Roman upper-class women broke these rules and risked criticism from Roman traditionalists. This may have discouraged them from writing.

The exigencies of their class   As we saw above, much of the poetry written in the genres chosen by women was the work of upper-class amateurs: it was written for recitation among friends and not for publication. Women seem to have conformed to this aristocratic restraint, perhaps especially because it agreed with traditional ideals of female behaviour just mentioned. Thus, the amateurism favoured by their class may have kept them from publication.

The influence of family   It can hardly be a coincidence that almost all poetesses of whom we know more than merely their names appear to have been members of cultured families: their fathers, husbands, brothers or uncles were patrons of poetry or wrote poetry themselves. As we have seen, the encouragement of male relatives was essential to their own poetic activity. Participation in literary coteries seems to have depended on the literary connections of their male relatives, and as publication was effected mainly through literary friends and acquaintances, such connections were essential to the publication, and thus to the survival, of their work. This must have severely reduced the opportunities for all women who did not come from such cultured families.

Women's haphazard education (see chapter 2)   The ability to write poetry was closely connected with education. As the teaching of poetry was the domain of the *grammaticus*, 'grammatical' education must have been essential, at least for the learned poetry current in Roman antiquity, but rhetorical training was also desirable, as Latin poetry was profoundly influenced by rhetoric. As we have seen, women's education was haphazard; it depended on the traditions, interests and standing of their families, their place of residence and the like, much more than that of the men of their class. Girls living in small towns, even if they belonged to the local upper class, seem to have had less opportunity for receiving a good literary education than boys. The result was that highly educated women were far fewer than men.

The influence of their place of residence   Most literary activity was concentrated in Rome and the survival of a literary work was closely bound up with its circulation, and appreciation, among the public of the capital.[152] As Rome offered the best opportunities, writers from various parts of the empire flocked to the capital to study and to start a career as a writer. Unlike male poets, most of whom came from the Italian municipalities and the provinces,[153] educated women from these

Italian towns and the provinces hardly had any opportunity to move to Rome – unless they married a man who lived, or went to live, in Rome. This reduced the opportunities for those women who resided outside the capital, and it is no coincidence that both Sulpiciae, the only poetesses whose work is partly preserved in the manuscript tradition, lived in Rome. Thus, a place of origin outside Rome strongly diminished the chances of survival of their work, much more than for men.

The hazards of transmission   In order to survive, a literary work had to be copied throughout the ages. Numerous factors, such as changes in public taste and in the choice of books used for education, but also sheer hazard, influenced the survival of verses. Simplifying grossly, one might say that the more copies in circulation, the better chance a work had to survive; therefore works used in education were in a favourable position – and among these there were no works written by women.

These are some of the causes, but there were others. As public libraries played an important role in the conservation and emendation of literary texts, works included in them had a better chance of survival. With the exception of the six poems by Sulpicia the elegist – which were probably placed in a public library together with the poems of other members of the coterie of Messalla and subsequently incorporated in a *codex*[154] – there is no indication that any female poet ever found her way into a Roman public library. In view of their apparent restriction to epigram and love poetry, it seems likely that the œuvre of women was usually small and consisted of short poems; this was probably not enough to occupy a complete papyrus roll, and that, in turn, prevented their preservation in the form of a separate *corpus*. It is telling that the surviving poetry of Greek female poets (such as Anyte, Erinna and Nossis), apart from some chance papyrus finds, is found mainly or exclusively in the *Anthologia Palatina*, a collection of epigrams of a great number of authors. But for this anthology their small volumes of epigrams would have been lost. Had such an anthology been made of Latin epigrams of our period (the *Anthologia Latina* contains mainly poetry of the early sixth century AD), we might perhaps have some epigrams of Cornificia, Perilla, Sulpicia Caleni or other Roman women now not even known by name.

To summarize, we may conclude that women wrote less than men mainly because of the exigencies of their daily life, their domestic and social obligations and the haphazard nature of female education; further, that they published even less of what they wrote because of the ideal of female reticence, the ambiguous attitudes to women poets, the amateurism expected of members of their class and their virtual exclusion from male literary coteries. Besides, their opportunities for writing and publishing were highly dependent on the literary connections of their male relatives and their place of residence. This accumulation of factors has proved to be devastating for women's poetry. Not only did women have fewer opportunities than men, but the few they had, depended on chance without any relation to their literary talent. Therefore, it seems likely that it was not the best poets who survived, but those who had the best chances.

As regards the survival of the work of the probably small number of women who actually published their poetry, we cannot tell whether or not the transmission of manuscripts dealt less kindly with their work than with that of men: only a few names of lost women poets are known, and we cannot tell how many more there once were. We know that much poetry written by men has been lost: as can be learned from the history of Roman literature, a great number of male poets are known to us only by name and – we may suspect – of even more not even the names are known. It seems unwarranted to ascribe the loss of women's poetry to their supposed 'female voice'. Though some women poets (notably the two Sulpiciae) differed from male poets in their use of language and in their female perspective, not all poetesses did so: in the poems of Julia Balbilla and Terentia no female traits can be detected. Yet, as we have seen, in the struggle for survival the work of women was particularly vulnerable: the probably small quantity of their work and their restriction to the slighter genres prevented the publication of it as a separate *corpus* and its inclusion in a public library; therefore, it seems doubtful whether any Roman woman poet (with the exception of Sulpicia the elegist, whose poetry was copied as part of a larger *corpus*) met the criteria for selection when the papyrus rolls were replaced by the more durable *codices* in late antiquity.

6

WOMEN AND WRITING: PROSE

In prose women were even more obscure than in poetry. We have hardly any trace of prose-writing by an upper-class woman. No Roman woman is known to have written a work of oratory, or history, or a treatise on some practical subject (such as farming). As far as we know they restricted themselves to letter-writing; a remarkable exception was Agrippina Minor, who is said to have written, and published, her memoirs, but we know of no other woman following her example. Neither is there any indication that Roman women kept diaries, a genre in which women have excelled in other periods of history. The only report that comes near to it is an intimate account of martyrdom by a well-educated young Christian woman of a high-ranking family in Roman North Africa, Vibia Perpetua. Though she falls outside the religious and geographical scope of this study and, for that reason, will not be discussed here, she is an extremely interesting case: here we have a young upper-class woman (about 20 years of age and presumably of decurial class) with a thorough, pagan literary education who manifests herself in a narrative of the events leading up to her execution in the arena in AD 203. Her account moves us by the immediacy with which she expresses her feelings and visions and is also of interest because of her distinctly female point of view: her worry about her baby, her preoccupation with breast-feeding and her own body, her anguish about the suffering of her father, her love for her deceased brother and the vivid description of her inner feelings and conflicts. Despite male attempts to rewrite and reinterpret her narrative, her account had great authority among Christian parishioners: once a year, on the anniversary of her martyrdom, her narrative was read aloud in the North African churches before an audience of male and female listeners. For once, there is a female voice that could not be ignored.[1]

It has recently been suggested that ancient women wrote novels, but there is no evidence for this and the arguments, which are based on the prominent role women played in ancient novels and the sympathetic description of their lives, are not convincing. Though it is, of course, possible (but hard to prove) that some novels, unknown to us now, were written by women, it seems highly unlikely that the names of some of the authors of ancient novels that have been preserved conceal female writers. Moreover, since most ancient novels are Greek, and probably stemmed from the Greek cities of the eastern Mediterranean, the question of a possible female (pseudonymous) authorship falls outside the geographical scope of this study.[2]

In the present chapter I shall deal first with the (lost) memoirs of Agrippina and then discuss women's participation in letter-writing, their attention to style, the question whether letters written by women differed from those by men in style or content and the reasons why so little of their writing is left. A chronological survey of women's activities in the field of writing (both poetry and prose) and a tentative assessment of women's place in Roman literature conclude this chapter.

As in the preceding chapter, chronological order will not always be followed. Therefore, the dates of the main figures are given here: our evidence starts with the 'Cornelia fragments' which are said to be from a letter written by Cornelia, the mother of the Gracchi, in the late second century BC. Special attention will be paid to the lost letters of the female correspondents of Cicero (first century BC) and of the younger Pliny (at the turn of the first and second centuries AD); further, to the letters of Claudia Severa found at Vindolanda (about AD 100), to the letter of Plotina to the Epicureans of Athens (AD 121) and to the (lost) letters of Domitia Lucilla, the mother of Marcus Aurelius (second century AD).

The memoirs of the younger Agrippina

The only Roman woman who is known to have written, and published, her memoirs is Agrippina Minor. Tacitus drew on them for an anecdote about her mother, Agrippina Maior, who asked Tiberius for permission to marry again, which, however, he refused. Tacitus concludes: 'This incident, not reported by any writers of annals, I found in the memoirs of her daughter Agrippina, who, when mother of the emperor Nero, recorded for posterity her life and the vicissitudes of her family.'[3] Apparently, Agrippina wrote her memoirs, describing not only her own life but also that of her family. She did so with a reading public in mind, indicated as 'posterity' by Tacitus, and, therefore, she must have published them; at any rate, copies were put into circulation and were still available when Tacitus wrote his Annals about sixty years later.

What was the character of these memoirs? Since they are lost, there is not much to go on. Yet, in calling her memoirs *commentarii*, Tacitus indicates their genre and style. Autobiographical *commentarii*, which were the kind of *commentarii* Tacitus must have had in mind, were a typically upper-class, male genre. Originating from notes kept by magistrates and provincial governors referring to their campaigns and political activities, they were produced during the republic by ambitious politicians of the nobility, who recorded their achievements in order to boost their own *dignitas* and that of their descendants. Such political autobiographies might be written, and published, to further the author's reputation or as a justification for some (controversial) act or event: the author could give his own version of it or could embellish his, perhaps underestimated, role in some achievement. The *commentarii* were a sub-literary genre: though written for a public they pretended to be nothing but rough notes for others to turn into full history (or, as some writers of *commentarii* hoped, an epic) and, therefore, they were usually written in a plain, factual style.[4]

In this male political tradition Agrippina is said to have written her memoirs. This was unexpected for a woman, but as the great-granddaughter of Augustus, the sister of the emperor Caligula, the wife of the emperor Claudius and the mother of the emperor Nero her position was a very unusual one. Moreover, in writing her autobiography she could follow the example of at least three of her male relatives: Augustus, Tiberius and Claudius all wrote accounts of their lives.[5] Yet, no other upper-class woman is recorded as having done so; she seems to have been the only female author in an all-male genre. As regards the style of her work we may guess that, apart from possible peculiarities, she adopted the plain, factual style which was characteristic of the genre,[6] but we cannot say much about its content. Our lack of information has led to wild speculations that her memoirs were a 'chronique scandaleuse', full of malice and slander written to blacken the reputation of her enemies. With this in mind a host of scurrilous anecdotes, found in the works of Tacitus and other authors, were assigned to them.[7] Obviously, the belief that they were a 'chronique scandaleuse', which is not in keeping with the character of *commentarii*, seems inspired by the prejudice that this is the kind of work women were apt to write rather than by any evidence.

Judging from the self-justification proper to *commentarii*, we may, perhaps, assume that Agrippina's account aimed at retaining (or regaining) the regard she considered her due by publishing her own version of the events of her life and family. In this respect, Agrippina had ample reason to write her memoirs: her role in the accession of her son Nero and her unprecedented display of political power – she received embassies, attended a meeting of the senate (though hidden behind a curtain) and had herself escorted by lictors – made her, to say the least, a controversial person.[8] Moreover, her hold on Nero wavered in the later years of her life; she may have wanted to make him (and posterity) understand how much he owed to her, and perhaps to defend her own claim to power: through the female line she was a great-granddaughter of Augustus and thus more directly related to this much-venerated founder of imperial power than Claudius and his descendants; Nero owed his throne to her alone.[9] The story of Tiberius' refusal of her mother's plea to be allowed to remarry may have suited her purpose in that it showed, once more, how badly her mother had been treated by the hated Tiberius. Agrippina Maior's popularity as a granddaughter of Augustus and the wife of Germanicus, and the undeserved persecution she and her children suf-fered from Tiberius, may have led Agrippina Minor to use her mother's memory to win sympathy, and perhaps she adduced the example of her mother's political involvement in support of her own ambitions.[10]

As nothing is left of her memoirs, it is useless to speculate about their content. Yet, I may perhaps venture a general remark: though written in the tradition of a male, political genre Agrippina's memoirs seem to have displayed a distinct interest in traditionally female concerns. Obviously, the standard contents of autobiography, the *cursus honorum* and military exploits, were not open to her. Instead, she seems to have focussed on family matters. Moreover, the story about her mother's wish to remarry, not found by Tacitus in the reports of annalists, shows a particular occupation with female experience (which, of course, does not preclude a keen eye for the political implications of such a marriage). This 'female perspective' is confirmed by the only other reference to her memoirs that is preserved. In a discussion of breech birth, which was con-sidered a bad omen, the elder Pliny writes: 'Nero also, who was emperor a short time ago and whose entire rule showed him the enemy of mankind, is stated in his mother Agrippina's writings to have been born feet first.'[11] Apparently, Agrippina considered details of Nero's birth of importance for her memoirs (whether she was aware of the ominous interpretation of such births cannot be made out). Though family matters were not wholly absent from the memoirs of men, Agrippina's apparent interest in marriage and childbirth reflects her own particular conditions and must have distinguished her memoirs from those of men.

As regards the reception of her memoirs, not much can be said. Autobiographi-cal *commentarii* were usually written for a male reading public of (aspiring) politi-cians. We do not know what readers Agrippina had in mind, but in view of the contents (which, if they really reflected her life and that of her family, must have consisted of a mixture of politics and family matters) a somewhat wider public, including women, may have been interested in them. We only know for certain that they were read by Tacitus (who in spite of his negative opinion of Agrippina refers to them without hostility) and by the elder Pliny; like most *commentarii*, they were eventually lost.

Letter-writing

In Roman society letter-writing was part of everyday life among the educated: letters were a common form of communication both for brief notes and for longer messages about political issues or private affairs. For example, as appears from the collections of their letters, Cicero and Fronto used to write or dictate letters at any time of the day, and the frequency of their exchange is baffling.[12] Letters were mostly written with ink on papyrus, tied into a roll and sealed, but short notes written to persons nearby were sometimes scratched on wax-tablets[13] and then erased for the reply. In some regions letters were written in ink on thin leaves of wood, for example, the ink leaf tablets found in Vindolanda in northern Britain. To facilitate the exchange of letters, high-ranking families had secretaries among their slaves to dictate to and couriers to deliver their letters with speed; besides, travellers were asked to carry letters.

As appears from references to their letters, upper-class women wrote and received letters almost as frequently as the men of their class. They wrote letters on all kinds of subjects varying from love to political advice. Depending on the circumstances, the contents of the letter and the addressee, they would write in their own hand or dictate to a scribe.[14] Like the men of their class, upper-class women might write and receive letters at any time of the day or even night: at a banquet, when travelling, in the theatre or at the games, or when making their toilet.[15] They issued and received written invitations, exchanged greetings and family information, and discussed private, financial or even political affairs. During the republic and the early principate upper-class women were expected to keep their husbands informed when they were abroad (in the army, on duty in the provinces or exiled) about the political situation in Rome and their private affairs.[16]

Cicero's correspondence provides a lively picture of the constant flow of letters not only between himself and his friend Atticus, his brother Quintus and other male relatives and acquaintances, but also between himself and his wife Terentia, his second wife Publilia and his daughter Tullia, between Cicero's son Marcus and Terentia and Tullia, between his sister-in-law Pomponia and her son Quintus, and from Atticus' wife Pilia to Cicero's brother Quintus, from Atticus to Tullia, from Terentia to Atticus, from Attica to her father Atticus, from the entire family to Tiro and also, it seems, from Terentia to Quintus' wife (Atticus' sister) Pomponia.[17] Though no letters written by these female correspondents have come down to us, we can partly reconstruct the contents of some of them from the letters of Cicero himself. For instance, Cicero's letters to Terentia, most of them written when he was abroad during the many crises in his life (his exile in 58–57 BC, his abhorred governorship of Cilicia in 51–50 BC and the civil war between Caesar and Pompey in 49–48 BC) show that Terentia kept him informed of affairs in Rome, discussed financial problems with him, encouraged him and gave him advice with regard to his return, for which he yearned so much. He depended very much on her information and support, and repeatedly asked her to write as often and as fully as possible.[18]

As appears from Cicero's letters, his female correspondents covered a wide range of topics including politics, finance, the management of property and family affairs. When we compare these topics with the subject-matter of the letters of the younger Pliny to women, those in Pliny's letters seem narrower, falling mainly under the headings of finance and family affairs (among which is advice about the education of children).[19] Of course, Pliny's letters were literary compositions carefully arranged with regard to elegance and social convention, but this narrowing of subject-matter may also reflect the 'domestication' of upper-class life during the empire. Moreover, since women now usually accompanied their husbands during their long terms of duty in the provinces instead of staying in Rome to look after their interests, there was less need to discuss political affairs in their letters.[20]

Though upper-class women wrote freely and frequently, there seems to have been an unwritten rule about whom they could write to without damaging their reputation. Conventions of propriety seem to have narrowly circumscribed the range of male correspondents restricting them to relatives and some close family friends.[21] Thus, according to our sources, letters between spouses form the bulk of the correspondence in which women were involved; in the second place come letters between women and other close male relatives (mainly sons and fathers) and, less frequently, between women and more distant male relatives.[22] Letters between men and women whose relationships did not belong to one of these categories easily gave rise to suspicion. Thus, Cicero's correspondence with Caerellia, whose relationship to him is unclear, was criticized for its supposed licentiousness. In spite of her being an elderly woman, the historian Dio accused Cicero, through his opponent Q. Fufius Calenus, of a sordid relation with Caerellia:

> Who does not know that you put away your first wife who had borne you two children, and in your extreme old age married another, a mere girl, in order that you might pay your debts out of her property? And yet you did not keep her either, since you wished to be free to have with you Caerellia, whom you debauched though she was as much older than yourself as the girl you married was younger, and to whom, old as she is, you write such letters as a jester and babbler might write if he were trying to start an amour with a woman of seventy.
>
> (Dio 46.18.3–4; Loeb trans., modified)[23]

This invective, in which he mingles fiction with fact, probably derives from the tradition of denunciation of Cicero which started during his lifetime or shortly after his death (an example is the Pseudo-Sallustian *Invectiva in Ciceronem*). Though Cicero's letters to Caerellia had been published, Dio seems not to have read them himself, but Quintilian apparently did, since he quotes from one of them when dealing with humorous expressions:

> I may also add the words used by Cicero in a letter to Caerellia to explain why he endured the supremacy of Caesar so patiently: 'These ills must either be endured with the courage of Cato or the stomach of Cicero', for here again the word 'stomach' has a spice of humour in it.
>
> (Quint. 6.3.112; Loeb trans.)[24]

The point of Cicero's joke is not entirely clear: perhaps he puns on the dual meaning of *stomachus* as the seat of irascibility (punning on his own touchy temper) and that of swallowing an affront (he must 'stomach' Caesar's dictatorship) while in self-mockery he opposes the strength of his *stomachus* to Cato's more elevated *animus* (referring to his suicide at Utica). Cicero's witty reply to Caerellia's apparent question about his acquiescence in Caesar's tyranny shows the correspondence to have been intimate in tone, sophisticated in a light-hearted way and, at least partly, political in substance. The fact that Cicero's letters to

Caerellia were published after his death (and read by Quintilian) shows them to have been considered of interest to a wider public.[25]

As our knowledge of women's letters is mainly based on the remarks of their male correspondents whose writings have been preserved, we hardly know of letters exchanged between women.[26] Yet, there can be little doubt that they exchanged letters not only with male relatives and some family friends but also, and perhaps even more frequently, with female relatives and friends. Being mostly of a private nature these letters are usually ignored in our sources. Fortunately, on the fringes of the Roman empire, in the wet soil of northern Britain and the dry sand of the Egyptian desert,[27] several letters exchanged between women have been preserved which may give us some idea of their contents.

Among the ink leaf tablets found at Vindolanda at Hadrian's Wall in northern Britain four letters are preserved of the 'archives' of Sulpicia Lepidina, the wife of Flavius Cerialis, prefect of the Ninth Cohort of Batavians at Vindolanda around AD 100.[28] Three of them were written to her by Claudia Severa, wife of another auxiliary officer named Aelius Brocchus, who was stationed at some other place along the northern frontier, and one by an unknown woman, who was perhaps called Paterna. A letter by another unknown woman, called Valatta, to Cerialis mentions Lepidina as an intermediary for some favour or concession which she asks from Cerialis.[29]

Two of Claudia Severa's letters have been preserved relatively well: in the first she invites Sulpicia Lepidina to come and visit her for her birthday, and the second announces her own planned visit to Sulpicia Lepidina. Both letters were dictated to a scribe, but Severa added a few words and greetings in her own hand. They provide the earliest known examples of a woman's handwriting in Latin. Her hand is 'somewhat clumsy' according to the editors[30] in comparison with the elegant hand of her scribe, but her style shows clear attempts at refinement and elegance of expression. The letter inviting Lepidina to her birthday, which is very well preserved, reads:

> Claudia Severa to her Lepidina greetings. On 11 September, sister, for the day of the celebration of my birthday, I give you a warm invitation to make sure that you come to us, to make the day more enjoyable for me by your arrival, if you are present (?). Give my greetings to your Cerialis. My Aelius and my little son send him (?) their greetings.
> [in her own hand:] I shall expect you, sister. Farewell, sister, my dearest soul, as I hope to prosper, and hail.
> (trans. Bowman and Thomas (1994) no. 291)[31]

The other letter is incomplete, but the contents can partly be gathered from what is left: Severa has asked her husband to allow her to visit her friend Lepidina. According to a possible reading she has something to discuss with Lepidina face-to-face. She will travel, possibly together with someone else, in whatever way she can and lodge at a place called Briga. In this letter Severa promises further letters to Lepidina about her coming visit, thereby indicating that there was a regular correspondence between them. The greeting at the end is again in her own hand: 'Farewell my sister, my dearest and most longed-for soul'.[32]

These letters throw an unusual light on a lively correspondence between female friends. Remarkably enough, these women were living at the edge of the Roman world and their families had only fairly recently acquired Roman citizenship. As is to be expected, they were not the consorts of ordinary soldiers, but of equestrian officers who lived with their wives and children[33] in the *praetorium*. The intimate tone and the social content of the letters may perhaps be taken as an illustration of what letters between upper-class women in Rome and Italy may have been like. Birthday invitations and (holiday) visits, which, to judge from what is preserved of their correspondence played an important role in the social life of Roman women at the northern frontier, probably had the same importance for women in Rome.[34] In contrast with women's letters addressed to men, which, as we have seen, dealt mostly with politics, the administration of property, legal matters (such as a lawsuit or a will) or family affairs (such as the choice of teachers for the children), those between female relatives and friends dealt with the *minutiae* of women's life outside or on the margins of the male social sphere and were therefore ignored in our sources.

Language and style

So far, we have dealt with the social purpose of the letters of upper-class women and with their subject-matter and addressees. We have seen that upper-class women were in the habit of writing letters (almost?) as frequently as the men of their class, though in the choice of their male correspondents they were restricted by rules of propriety. During the republic they seem to have written on a relatively wide range of topics, including politics, but during the empire the subject-matter tended to be mostly of a private nature. As apart from the disputed letter of Cornelia (to be discussed below) hardly any letter of a Roman woman survives, we do not know how much care they took about style. Did they embellish their letters with elegant turns of phrase according to the literary standards of the time? Were their letters appreciated for their style and read by a wider public than the original addressee? Or did women's letters show a distinctive language and style, different from those of men?

Strictly speaking, being prose, letter-writing was preliminary to rhetorical tuition, from which women were, as a rule, excluded (for some exceptions see chapter 2, pp. 24f.). Yet, it seems reasonable to assume that any upper-class woman who had received a full course of tuition from a grammarian would be able to write private letters according to the standards of the time, but our sources hardly give any information on the style of their letters. In reviewing the meagre evidence I shall, therefore, focus on two points only: first, the question whether or not women's letters met, or were expected to meet,

contemporary (male) standards of letter-writing, and second, what factors influenced their style of writing, a question closely bound up with the issue of
whether or not their letters differed from those of men as regards language or
style.

Living up to male standards

Among the educated, careful composition in letter-writing was highly valued:
(male) authors expressed admiration for beauty and warmth of expression or for
contents that rose above trivialities; in the course of the principate letter-writing
even came to be regarded as a literary genre of its own. Among the rules of
letter-writing brevity, simplicity and clarity were especially recommended. As for
their language and style, letters had to steer a middle course between the ornate
and the popular and to show elegance without ostentation; they were to reflect
the *sermo cotidianus* of the educated.[35]

What was the place of upper-class women in all this? Did their letters meet
these standards, or did letters written by women show a distinct style believed to
be typically female? In trying to answer these questions I shall start with the
disputed letter of Cornelia, the mother of the Gracchi, the only woman in our
period whose letters are known to have been published. As we have seen, she was
the earliest Roman woman praised for her excellent style of writing and speaking.
Cicero and Quintilian admired her letters for their eloquence,[36] but their publication – and the interest Cicero and Quintilian took in them – seems to have been
not only a matter of style; it must have been at least partly due to her prominence
as the mother of the Gracchi and the daughter of Scipio Africanus. This may
perhaps explain why, though eloquent letters were surely written also by other
upper-class women, only those of Cornelia were 'published'.[37]

This brings us to the question of the authenticity of the so-called 'Cornelia
fragments', two fragments of a letter which have been transmitted in some of the
manuscripts of Cornelius Nepos under the heading: 'excerpts from a letter of
Cornelia's, mother of the Gracchi, from the book of Cornelius Nepos on the
Latin Historians'.[38] They purport to be two fragments of a letter written by
Cornelia to her son Gaius in 124 BC, in which she strongly opposes his plan to
stand for the tribunate and warns him not to continue the revolutionary policy of
his brother Tiberius, which had led to disaster. Most likely they stem from Nepos'
lost life of Gaius Gracchus, which, apparently, was included among the 'Latin
Historians'.[39] The authenticity of the fragments has been hotly debated for more
than a hundred and fifty years, but without conclusive results. The discussion has
been complicated by emotional arguments about the supposed relation between a
(Roman) mother and her son, the psychology of women and the behaviour
expected of a woman of Cornelia's standing. Consequently, widely divergent
views have been brought forward: some scholars believe the letter to be authentic,
written by Cornelia herself in an admirable and forceful style demonstrating
her impressive personality and motherly concern, while others condemn it as a

manifest forgery unworthy of Cornelia's learned style and personality, and incompatible with her political views.[40]

The discussion deals with the style and the content of the letter, which are not always clearly distinguished. As regards its style, there are two main questions: do language and style agree with a date around 124 BC, and, if so, do they agree with what we may gather to have been the personal style of Cornelia? An affirmative answer to the first question does not, of course, prove Cornelia to be the author of the letter, since it does not rule out the possibility that it could be a contemporary fake. The second question is even more difficult to answer because of the lack of comparative material; in any case, her authorship cannot be proved just by pointing out that the style of the letter is impeccable. As for its content, the debate centred on Cornelia's opposition to the political activities of her son, which were felt to conflict with the support she gave him according to other sources. Also, the vehemence with which Cornelia upbraids her only surviving son in this letter seemed incompatible with accepted notions about her maternal devotion.

Some modern authors have tried to evade the problem by choosing a middle way between false and authentic. N. Horsfall,[41] for instance, believes that the discussion is based on a misconception. Instead of deciding between authentic and false one should study, according to his view, how far this letter of Cornelia's (or a contemporary of hers) may have been reworked by Nepos or his source, since it was customary to quote a speech or a letter in an adapted form. However, his arguments are not entirely convincing and the vexed question of the identity of the original author is left unanswered.[42]

Let us, therefore, turn to the letter itself. It consists of two separate fragments, which are generally assumed to belong to a single letter, though they are very different in tone and style.[43] In the first passage, the shorter of the two, Cornelia weighs the glory of revenge on one's enemies against the welfare of the state as a whole, arguing that the welfare of the state should come first. The second passage is more emotional. Here she violently reproaches Gaius for causing her severe trouble by pursuing the same political course as his brother and canvassing for the tribunate instead of respecting the desire of his mother to enjoy a quiet old age:

> I would take a solemn oath that apart from those who killed Tiberius Gracchus no enemy has given me so much trouble and so much pain as you in this matter, who ought to undertake the part of all the children I have ever had, and to make sure that I should have as little worry as possible in my old age, and that, whatever your schemes might be, you should wish them to be agreeable to me, and that you should count it a sin to take any major step against my wishes, especially considering I have only a little part of life left. Cannot even that brief span of time aid me in preventing you from opposing me and ruining our country? Where will it all end? Will our family ever cease

from madness? Will bounds ever be set to it? Shall we ever cease to dwell on affronts, both causing and suffering them? Shall we ever begin to feel true shame for confounding and harassing our country? But if that is quite impossible, when I am dead, then seek the Tribunate. Do what you like as far as I am concerned, when I am not there to know it. When I am dead, you will offer funerary sacrifices in my honour and invoke me as your hallowed parent. At that time will you not be ashamed to seek the intercession of those hallowed ones whom, when they were alive and present, you abandoned and deserted? May Jove above not let you persist in this nor let such lunacy enter your mind! But if you do persist, I fear that through your own fault you will encounter so much trouble throughout your whole life that at no time you will be able to rest content.

(Nepos, fr. 2; trans. Kenney (1982) 146, modified)[44]

In this letter 'Cornelia' opposes Gaius' plans with great force, using severe moral pressure and even threats to divert him from his course. Her insistence on the respect due to her as a mother and on his obligation to obey her wishes is not incompatible with Roman notions about maternal authority.[45] The strongly dominant personality speaking from the letter and her political involvement agree with what we know of Cornelia from other sources, but, as has been noticed before, the political attitude shown in this letter stands in striking contrast to the support Cornelia gave her sons according to most other sources – though one or two testimonies seem to suggest that she may have opposed her sons' policy.[46] In this letter the writer severely criticizes the policy of both Tiberius and Gaius, calling it madness and the country's ruin. This criticism has been explained as an attempt (of slightly later date) to separate the famous Cornelia from her sons ideologically and to claim her for the optimate cause. The letter would then be a falsification of a later date published by someone who favoured the optimate cause; thus, it would be part of a posthumous revaluation of Cornelia which also led to the statue erected for her.[47]

However, if the letter, as we have it, is not by Cornelia but by an unknown forger of later date, how did it, falsely attributed to her, find its way into the works of Nepos? H. U. Instinsky suggests that Nepos may have found it in the work of a historian from the period shortly after Cornelia's death who inserted (fictitious) letters to enliven his work.[48] To this it may be objected that Nepos, who was a friend of Cicero's, must have known her published letters and would have detected a manifest forgery. Since he admits this letter into his work, it is unlikely to have been in sharp contrast to her extant letters; consequently, the critical attitude towards Gaius' revolutionary policy may well have been Cornelia's own. In view of her noble descent this is not implausible, perhaps even likely: she may have desired a more conventional career for her talented sons.[49] Thus, even if Nepos reworked the letter of Cornelia or incorporated an earlier counterfeit into his work, it cannot have deviated too far from her actual political views or from her style of writing. With her published letters still extant, Nepos is likely at least to have kept to the flavour of the original.

Theoretically, there is another possibility, namely that the letter is a fabrication of much later date, which somehow slipped into the manuscripts of Nepos between Nepos' time and the edition of selected works of Nepos by the grammarian Aemilius Probus in the fifth century AD. The letter might then have been part of a rhetorical exercise in impersonation representing Cornelia writing to her son Gaius on the eve of his tribunate, which in the end proved fatal. Though this may perhaps account for the excessive anxiety of 'Cornelia' (since the letter would have been written *post factum*), it seems hard to reconcile this assumption with the language of the letter, which, according to most scholars, points to a date at the end of the second century BC: its old-fashioned words and expressions are lexically close to those of Plautus, Cato and the older Roman poets and the directness of the style resembles Cato's speeches.[50] Though it is not wholly impossible that a good forger of the imperial period was capable of writing in impeccable Latin of the second century BC, it seems unlikely that he would have deviated so much from the prevailing representation of Cornelia as a supporter of her sons' policy.

Thus, the balance seems to be somewhat in favour of the genuineness of the fragments, but we have to admit that their authenticity cannot be established beyond doubt. Let us, nevertheless, have another look at the style of the fragments. Is this compatible with the *doctissimus sermo* attributed to Cornelia by Quintilian? The similarity in tone and expression to Cato's speeches, the Graecisms, the figures of speech and the forensic vigour of the letter, which gives it a speech-like quality, point to a thorough education, for which, as we have seen, Cornelia was known.[51] Yet, some stylistic imperfections in the letter have led to conflicting opinions. For instance, the repetition of rhetorical questions, four of them introduced by *ecquando*, is regarded by Instinsky, who argues against the authenticity of the letter, as overdone, whereas A. S. Gratwick, who believes the letter to be genuine, regards this and other minor stylistic imperfections as spontaneous outbursts and proof of her powerful style, comparable to Cato's.[52]

Though style cannot prove authenticity, the fragments can, to my mind, be fully understood as parts of a private letter written by a woman who was trained, as Cornelia seems to have been, in the rhetoric of the time. The slight stylistic imperfections and incongruities as well as the severe rebuke of her son may be explained by the privacy of the letter; they do not exclude the possibility of a public display of support. If so, the letter must have been published after her death and inserted, possibly slightly reworked, by Nepos in his life of Gaius. Yet, even if false, the letter is not without value: in order to ring true it must have reflected current opinion about her personality and style of writing. As is evident from the uncertainty concerning its authenticity, the letter shows no particular style or idiom that may be called characteristic of a woman.[53] That such a letter was believed to be by a woman may be taken as an indication that the stylistic standards of letter-writing were the same for men and women.

In short, the language and style of the letter attributed to Cornelia did not
noticeably differ from those of the men of her time and class, but she may, of
course, have been exceptional. Therefore, to answer the question posed above
(*viz.* whether the letters of women met contemporary standards of letter-writing
or showed a distinctive style or language), I shall first deal with some precepts
given by Ovid (and by the emperor Augustus) for the style of women's letters and
then discuss certain remarks by the younger Pliny on actual letters written by
women. We shall see that everything suggests that the same standards
were applied to the letters of men and those of women, and that at least some
upper-class women lived up to these standards.

In his *Ars Amatoria* Ovid laid down precepts on how to write love-letters.
Women were advised to avoid the overly rhetorical as well as the boorish and to
choose graceful, but familiar words: 'Let the words you write be elegant, girls,
but familiar and in common use: plain speech gives pleasure; how often has a
message inflamed a doubting lover, or some barbaric phrase done harm to a fair
shape.'[54] In agreement with ancient rules of letter-writing Ovid wanted wom-
en's love-letters to be refined, but not too far removed from everyday speech.
Men were given the same advice; eloquence was to be appreciated, but they
should avoid using 'affected words' or a declamatory style.[55] A similar advice
(but not meant for writing love-letters) is found in Augustus' letter to his granddaughter Agrippina as quoted by Suetonius, in which he exhorts her 'to take
care not to write and talk affectedly'. This shows that, like Ovid, Augustus
wanted women (like men) to refrain from the use of affected or unfamiliar
words.[56]

So much for stylistic recommendations. In the, unfortunately sparse, descriptions of women's letters in the literary sources, there are no indications that
women used (or were believed or expected to use) a distinct style or language in
their letters. Rather, the same standards were set, and adhered to, irrespective of
the gender of the writer. In his published collection of letters the younger Pliny
comments on the style of certain letters written by the wife of his friend Pompeius Saturninus, which, to his mind, closely resembled the language of Plautus
or Terence.[57] As we have seen (chapter 2, pp. 31f.), these letters were probably
exercises in literary composition demonstrating her virtuosity in using the language and vocabulary of these admired old authors and the success of her husband in teaching her. Pliny's (feigned?) uncertainty about their authorship – he
probably wanted to flatter his friend by expressing his doubts that such letters
could actually have been written by his wife – indicates that their style did not
betray the gender of the writer.

To judge from what Pliny writes to his own wife her letters were of a different
nature, but the same stress is laid on style and elegance of expression. If we may
believe Pliny, their frequent correspondence when Calpurnia was in Campania
for the sake of her health was full of endearments and tender complaints about
their separation. Both claim to find comfort only in reading each other's letters
over and over again, which in Pliny's case actually fans the fire of his longing: 'for

how amiable must her conversation be, whose letters have so much charm?'.[58] The *suavitas* of Calpurnia's letters refers not only to her affectionate words but also to her pleasant style. As *suavitas* may be used to characterize the writing and speaking of both men and women, it does not indicate a typically female style; in fact, it is appropriate for the letters of both Pliny and Calpurnia.[59]

Pliny's words show that letters by women were appreciated for a good style following ancient rules of letter-writing or contemporary fashion, just like those of men. In his opinion, such literary letters by women were exceptional (one wonders how exceptional) and highly praiseworthy. As we have seen, other upper-class men, such as Cicero, Quintilian, Ovid and Augustus, also appreciated letters from women written in elegant Latin. We may infer that the appreciation and prestige such letters earned for their author stimulated women to pay attention to style. Should we, therefore, conclude that there was no difference whatsoever in style and language between the letters of men and women? Or were matters more complicated and did differences, if they existed, depend not so much on the gender of the writer as on other factors? In the following I shall deal with three factors that influenced the style of women's letters: social status, context and addressee.

Social status

A polished letter was a mark of a good education and, therefore, of high social status. It was expected as a matter of course among the members of high society and imitated by those of less elevated descent who aspired to a higher status. In this respect women do not seem to have differed from men: by writing elegant letters according to the rules of the day they could demonstrate their high social status, or try to lay claim to a higher status than was rightfully theirs. A mock example of such a claim is found in an imaginary letter of early date, the quaint love-letter of a young slave girl, Phoenicium, in one of the comedies of Plautus. It forms a marked contrast to the desired simplicity of letters as sketched above. I quote part of it:

> Phoenicium to her lover Calidorus, through this medium of wax and wood and letters, sends her dearest wishes, and longs to have her own dearest wish from you, longs for it with tears in her eyes, with mind and heart and soul all tremulous. [...] Now all our days and ways of love and dear familiarity, mirth and merriment, converse and kissing, o so sweet, all the cuddling of beloved bodies close, all the soft little bites of sweet little lips, all the fond little squeezing and teasing of breasts – all these delights of mine and yours, will be torn away, torn asunder, ended for eternity, unless I find my salvation in you, or you yours in me.
>
> (Plaut. *Pseud.* 41–4 and 64–71; Loeb trans., modified)[60]

Part of the fun of this letter lies in the contrast between the low status of the girl and the exuberant style of her letter, which bristles with unusual or invented words.[61] By accumulating uncommon words and long-winded phrases Plautus makes fun of the slave girl's aspiration to use the language of the educated classes.

Another way of showing one's education was to write letters in Greek or to sprinkle them with Greek expressions. This was meant to show that the writer and the addressee were educated in 'both languages', as was typical of the education of the Roman élite from the late republic onwards.[62] Though none of her letters is preserved, Marcus Aurelius' mother Domitia Lucilla may be taken as an example of such upper-class bilingualism: the two Greek letters which the orator Fronto, her son's tutor in Latin rhetoric, addressed to her may be regarded as a compliment to her education.[63] The letters belong to what seems to have been a regular correspondence between them (unfortunately, they are the only ones left); they are long and elaborate Greek compositions rather than personal communications. This holds especially for the first one, which is wholly taken up by Fronto's excuse for not having written for some time because he was busy preparing a speech for the emperor (Antoninus Pius). The letter consists almost entirely of similes, a rhetorical device of which Fronto was particularly fond: he compares himself with a hyena, a snake, a spear, a ship, a line and a certain painter to illustrate his single-mindedness, or rather, as he himself calls it, his incapacity to do more than one thing at a time (in this case, writing a speech for the emperor and a letter to Domitia Lucilla). The second letter, which as preserved is not complete (breaking off in the middle of the third paragraph), is written for Domitia's birthday, the celebration of which Fronto's wife Gratia attended. Though it starts on a personal note (he regrets that he is unable to come because of his consulship[64]), the main part of the letter is taken up by a long string of elaborate compliments to Domitia Lucilla: in her all traditional virtues proper to womankind, and not a single vice, were united.

In view of such elaborate and mannered Greek letters the end of his first letter comes as a surprise; in a tone of self-deprecation he asks her forgiveness for his poor Greek: 'If any word in this letter be obsolete and barbarous, or in any other way unsatisfactory, or not entirely Attic, pay no attention to it, but only, I beseech you, to the intrinsic meaning of the word'; [65] he compares himself to Anacharsis the Scythian who, though a barbarian as regards his deficiency in speaking Attic, was a wise man. This may sound like a *topos* to us, and a mere compliment to Domitia's education, but Fronto's uncertainty seems real: he encloses his letter in a letter to Marcus Aurelius asking him to correct his Greek before handing it to his mother:

> I have written your mother a letter, such is my audacity, in Greek, and enclose it in my letter to you. Please read it first, and if you detect any barbarism in it, for you are fresher from your Greek than I am, correct it

and so hand it over to your mother. I should not like her to look down on me as a barbarian.

(Fronto, *Ad M. Caes.* 1.8.7; Loeb trans., modified)[66]

Fronto's misgivings as regards his command of Greek were probably due to his provincial descent: born at Cirta in Roman North Africa as a member of the educated provincial élite he clung tenaciously to linguistic purity both in Latin and in Greek, trying to obliterate his provincial background and identifying himself completely with Graeco-Roman culture.[67] Compared to his own rather rigid attitude towards Greek culture Fronto probably admired the easy familiarity with Greek and Latin culture of the aristocratic Domitia Lucilla, who had been educated in 'both languages' from early childhood onwards; but one wonders whether she appreciated his mannered style, since according to her son she was given to a simple style of life.[68]

As we have seen, the ability to be eloquent in Greek was a source of pride, especially to those who came from the provinces, like Fronto. This also held for women. For example, the wealthy North African widow Aemilia Pudentilla was noted for her ability to write excellent Greek letters, which, as her second husband Apuleius scornfully remarks, were 'Greek' to his persecutors.[69] This mastery of Greek confirms her upper-class standing. Further off from the centre of Graeco-Roman culture an ability to write elegant Latin might serve a similar purpose, as may be inferred from the letters of Claudia Severa at Vindolanda (see pp. 191ff.). Severa's use of uncommon words and expressions (such as 'diem sollemnem natalem', 'interventu tuo', 'sperabo te' and 'ita valeam' in no. 291), which give her letter a somewhat archaic flavour, shows that she tried, though not quite successfully, to express herself elegantly in the language of the educated. Because of the insufficiency of our knowledge of spoken Latin at the time it is unclear whether, or to what extent, her use of uncommon words and unexpected syntax is to be explained by the influence of the spoken language or by an over-eagerness to write what she regarded as polished Latin. At any rate, she stretched the possibilities of the language and, like Phoenicium in Plautus' comedy, showed herself to be less well educated than she pretended to be. As a woman of non-Roman descent, whose family had received Roman citizenship during the reign of Claudius, she was probably eager to demonstrate her Latin education by means of the pedantic and somewhat archaic expressions she had learned at school. In this respect, her style seems determined more by her non-Roman background and her aspiration to a high social status than by her gender.[70]

Context and addressee

As we have seen, social status, or an aspiration to a high social status, may have influenced the style of women's letters, but this may also hold for letters written by men. However, when reading the letter of Phoenicium, quoted above (p. 198), one wonders whether Plautus merely mocked her misuse of upper-class language or if he also made fun of what was believed to be a typically female way of speaking and writing. To answer this question and to tackle the problem of the possible existence of a distinctive 'female speech' in Rome, we have to consider the use of diminutives in the letter, a feature which up to the present day is associated with the language of women in popular belief.[71] Are we to assume that the use of diminutives was, or was believed to be, a characteristic of 'female speech' in Rome? Surprisingly, it was not: though Roman sources occasionally depict women as using diminutives, there is no evidence of a female preference for them. For instance, even when allowance is made for the fact that on the stage men speak more than women, most diminutives in Latin comedy are used by men.[72]

This outcome may seem unexpected but is explained by the context in which men use, or are presented as using, diminutives, namely in erotic scenes, in conversations with or about children and in the intimacy of the family. A good example of the last-mentioned is a brief conversation between Marcus Aurelius and his mother noted down in one of his letters to Fronto, his teacher of Latin rhetoric; in it Marcus Aurelius uses diminutives to express his affection no fewer than three times:

> I had a long chat with my *little* mother as she sat on the bed. My talk was this: "What do you think my Fronto is now doing?" Then she: "And what do you think my Gratia is doing?" Then I: "And what do you think our *little* sparrow, the *little* Gratia, is doing?"
>
> (Fronto *Ad M.Caes.* 4.6.2; Loeb trans., modified)[73]

Thus, the use of diminutives appears to be determined by the context, the (gender of the) addressee and the intimate relationship of the speaker to the addressee, not by the gender of the speaker. The letter of Plautus' Phoenicium is a similar case: writing to her lover, Phoenicium uses diminutives in the two lines in which she describes their love-making; clearly, their use is prompted by the language of love rather than the gender of the alleged writer of the letter.[74]

Recent studies of women's speech in modern languages by sociolinguists have come to the same conclusion: no correlation exists between (female) gender and the use of diminutives. In fact, in itself gender is found to account for very few differences in the use of language, most observed differences being the result of a correlation between gender and other social factors, such as age, social status and the (gender, age or social status of the) addressee; the last aspect in particular has often been found to be decisive.[75]

An instance of the influence of the gender of the addressee is found in the letters of Claudia Severa at Vindolanda, cited above: her Latin differs in some respects from that of most letters written by men at Vindolanda. For instance, her elaborate greetings at the end of her letters containing expressions of endearment such as 'soror, anima mea . . . karissima' (no. 291) and 'mea soror karissima et anima ma [sc. mea] desideratissima' (no. 292) indicate an intimacy and intensity of feeling which is lacking in the usual *vale frater* at the end of the letters of most men at Vindolanda. Apart from her use of endearments, Severa's letters show what have been called 'polite modifiers', words used to tone down an imperative or, as in this case, a request. As terms of endearment and polite modifiers were felt to be typical of women in antiquity and are listed by J. N. Adams among the characteristics of 'female speech' in Latin comedy, these elements might tempt us to label her letters as 'typically female'.[76] However, other letters by women lack polite modifiers and do not show such a profusion of endearments, so it seems better to explain their use here by the influence of the gender of the addressee and of the nature of the relationship between writer and addressee than by the gender of the author. In other words, this may have been common between women friends, but is certainly not typical of women's letters in general.

A very different case of the influence of the addressee, by a process called 'attenuation' (i.e. adaptation to the style of speaking of the addressee to show that one belongs, or wishes to belong, to his or her social group), is found in a Greek letter written by Plotina about the question of who should succeed as the head of the Epicurean school.[77] This long, conversational letter to the Athenian Epicureans was inscribed in marble together with her petition (in Latin) to Hadrian and with Hadrian's reply; it shows her mastery of Greek, which she fashioned according to the style of speaking of the addressees, thus demonstrating her familiarity with, and perhaps even her membership of, the Epicurean school. Examples of the adjustment of her style to her addressees are: the spirited opening of her letter with its emphasis on friendship (one of the characteristics of Epicureanism): 'From Plotina Augusta to all her friends greetings! We have now what we were so eager to obtain'; further, her solidarity with the addressees appearing from the use of 'we' instead of 'you' throughout the letter and perhaps also, towards the end of her letter, the accumulation of philosophical nouns ending in -*ma*, which, according to H. Temporini, is reminiscent of the style of Epicurus.[78]

To these examples may be added some of the letters discussed above which, though less markedly, show the influence of context and addressee on language and style, namely the rhetorical style of Cornelia's letter, the archaizing fashion of the letters of the wife of Pompeius Saturninus (who himself was inclined to use archaisms) and Calpurnia's amorous and charming letters to her equally amorous husband. Clearly, we cannot simply speak of 'female speech' or of a 'typically female' style of writing in Roman society (or in modern society). Matters are far more complicated: context, social class and age of both 'speaker' and addressee, and the gender of the addressee, interact with the gender of the speaker (or writer) in influencing the style and language used.[79] Most letters by women addressed to men were probably adjusted in subject-matter, language and style to male standards (though we may expect letters between the sexes to have differed slightly from letters between men only, since presumably men also adjusted their speech somewhat when addressing women[80]). If anywhere, it is in letters between women, of which, unfortunately, we have very few examples, that elements of a possible 'female speech' may be detected, but even there other factors (for example, the age and social status of writer and addressee) may override the influence of gender.

Why are nearly all letters written by women lost?

Innumerable letters must have been written by women, yet only very few have been preserved, and those merely by chance and not because they were copied through the ages or included in the work of historians (with the possible exception of the letter by Cornelia). Of course, most letters written by men are also lost, but whereas some of their letters are preserved in the work of a biographer or a historian, or in individual collections of letters, those written by women were invariably ignored: in the great collections of letters of Cicero and Fronto, and those of the pagan and Christian epistolographers of the fourth and fifth centuries AD, all of which include a considerable number of letters addressed to women, hardly a single letter written by a woman is found.[81]

What is the cause of this almost total loss? Are we to suspect malicious intent or is it due to mere chance? Is it perhaps because the letters of women circulated less widely than those written by men? According to A. Rousselle it was due to malice, rather than to chance, that women's letters were lost.[82] When discussing the great epistolographers of the fourth and fifth centuries AD she suggests that the loss of nearly all letters of their female correspondents was caused by the difference in the way men and women treated the letters they received: letters written by women were not collected with the same care by their male correspondents as those written by men. In other words: according to Rousselle women dutifully preserved the letters they received from male correspondents and, therefore, could hand them over for publication, but men usually disposed of the letters they received from women, though they often kept those from men. Besides, she believes, women did not keep copies of their own letters, whereas men often did. This difference between men and women led, she believes, to the almost complete loss of the letters of women.

In suspecting malice rather than chance as the cause of the loss of women's letters Rousselle even goes so far as to blame male letter-writers for allowing the 'fond letters' of their female friends to be lost. However, there is no evidence for this theory and no compelling reason to believe, with Rousselle, that men wilfully disposed of the letters they received from their female correspondents. There may have been other reasons why the letters of women were excluded from published collections. Rather than trying to explain the loss of these letters by a single cause, it seems better to consider a combination of interrelated factors, which reinforced one another in causing the loss. The following list of possible factors is by no means a comprehensive one; it is meant to give a tentative indication of the circumstances that may have led to the almost total loss of the letters written by women.

The private character of women's letters   As far as we know, women mostly wrote private letters expressing their personal feelings and experiences. Though such letters might sometimes contain political information, like Terentia's letters to Cicero during his exile, they were essentially of a private character and meant exclusively for the addressee. In this respect women of the imperial family formed an exception: at times they wrote more or less official letters to cities or communities, for example, the letter of Plotina to the Athenian Epicureans or that of Julia Domna to the Ephesians.[83] We know of no such letters written by other upper-class women. Besides, no letters of recommendation by them have been preserved, nor have any literary letters, such as those of the younger Pliny, written by women ever been published, or discourses on philosophical topics such as the *Epistulae Morales* of the younger Seneca, or verse-epistles, like those of Ovid or Statius. Because of the private nature of the daily life of women their letters were mostly of a personal kind.

The reluctance to publish private letters, especially those of women   In order to protect the privacy of the writer and because of the triviality of their contents private letters were, as a rule, kept from publication; notable exceptions are the collections of letters of Cicero and Fronto, which were published after their death. Because of the modesty and the retired way of life expected of women (see chapter 1) the publication of a private letter written by a woman was considered offensive. For example, Apuleius scolds his persecutors for having publicly quoted from a letter of Pudentilla to her son, for such behaviour is, as he repeatedly asserts, disrespectful of her modesty.[84] Thus, modesty may have prevented women from to circulating, and publishing, their own letters, and feelings of propriety may have prompted men to exclude letters from women from eventual publication.

Women's restriction in the choice of male correspondents   As we have seen, women were restricted in their choice of male correspondents: for reasons of propriety their correspondents were mainly – though, of course, not exclusively – limited to other women and to male relatives. Letters to male relatives are apt to be of a private nature and since, moreover, the letters between women, which may have formed the bulk of their correspondence, fell outside male attention, women's letters are usually ignored by our sources.

The style of their letters   Rousselle remarks that the loss of women's letters cannot be satisfactorily explained by any inferiority of style due to a lack of schooling.[85] Above we saw that the same standards were applied to the letters of men and to those of women, and that at least some upper-class women are reported to have written letters in an excellent style. As far as we know, the letters written by women did not differ significantly from those of men as regards style and language; only letters exchanged between women may have shown some distinctive traits. During the principate letter-writing came to be taught at the schools of rhetoric and, in an elementary form, also by grammarians. We may assume that a polished style of letter-writing was within the reach of upper-class women who were fortunate enough to receive a full education in grammar. But, as we saw in chapter 2, the education of women, even of those of the upper classes, varied a great deal and depended on the inclinations and circumstances of the family to a much greater extent than that of men of their class. This makes it risky to generalize, and though it seems reasonable to assume that many upper-class women were able to compose a well-written letter according to the standards of their days, we cannot be certain that all were.

The selection of letters for preservation   No one keeps all letters received; everyone makes his (or her) own choice about which to keep and which to discard. Though Rousselle goes too far when she assumes that men wilfully discarded the letters they received from women while mostly keeping those of men, the custom of selecting letters for preservation may have worked against those written by women. It seems reasonable to assume that both men and women kept letters they thought important or which had some emotional value. Though this may occasionally have included letters of women, for instance, those of mothers (such as the letters of Aemilia Pudentilla which were dutifully preserved by her elder son Pontianus) or wives, their chance of being preserved was much smaller than that of the letters of important public persons, who were invariably men.[86]

The habit of making copies of one's own letters   The decision to make copies depended on the store one set on them. A distinction according to gender, though not as rigid as suggested by Rousselle, seems possible. We know that some men kept copies of some of their letters,[87] often with an eye to later publication, and that women – as far as we know – were not in the habit of composing letters for publication. Yet, though we have no evidence of it, it would be absurd to assume that women never kept copies of their own letters.

The public status of the author of the letters   This must have been decisive for the publication of letters. For example, it was not the style of writing, but the supreme position of the emperor Marcus Aurelius together with the fame of his correspondent (the orator Fronto) that lent interest to their correspondence and, similarly, the public reputation of a man like Cicero imparted a particular value to even his most casual letters and, therefore, his correspondents carefully hoarded them. In this light, it is not surprising that, though after Cicero's death his letters to Terentia and Caerellia were recovered for publication,[88] those written by Terentia and Caerellia themselves were ignored and are, consequently, lost.

The publication of collections of letters   Ancient collections usually contain the letters of a single person, who published his letters himself (as the younger Pliny did) or whose letters, in the case of Cicero and Fronto, were collected and published after their death by friends, heirs or others; the publication was based on copies kept by the author, or on letters recovered from the recipients (who might add copies of their own letters). Though letters of correspondents may be included, they are usually few in number. However, in the collection of Fronto those of Marcus Aurelius are exceptionally numerous, probably because Fronto's descendants were proud of his close relationship with the emperor. The publication of letters of correspondents is not always directly related to the care with which they had been preserved by the recipient. For example, we know that Cicero carefully stored Atticus' letters, pasted together in rolls, and that Atticus did the same with those of Cicero. Yet, though Cicero's letters to Atticus were published (probably long after the death of both correspondents), not a single letter by Atticus is included: all his letters are lost.[89]

To summarize, we have found that the loss of nearly all letters written by women seems due to a combination of causes, all directly or indirectly connected with gender. The mainly private sphere of women's lives and their restriction in respect of male addressees limited the scope of their letters: they probably dealt mainly, though not exclusively, with private matters, and these were probably considered too trivial to be of wider interest. The unwillingness to publish private letters of women, for reasons of propriety, further reduced their chance of survival. It is probably no coincidence that the disputed letter of Paula and Eustochium published in the collection of Jerome is no more than a stylistically polished idealization of the holy places, devoid of personal details. As, by tradition, women were excluded from political life, it was unlikely that their letters, no matter how well written or erudite they might be, were preserved by the recipients and posthumously published – the political involvement and public reputation of Cornelia makes her a telling exception to this rule. Discarded by recipients and excluded from published collections, the letters of women are irretrievably lost.

Women and writing: a chronological survey

In this chapter, as in the preceding one, I have dealt with women's writing thematically, without paying much attention to chronology. Of course, the long period covered does not make it likely that things remained unchanged, but the evidence is insufficient to detect a chronological development with any degree of certainty. Yet, to make up for this lack the main evidence is summarized here in a chronological order and an attempt is made to delineate possible trends and developments.

Our earliest data concern letters: in the second century BC Cornelia, the mother of the Gracchi, is said to have written letters in an excellent style which were published and read by orators such as Cicero and Quintilian. Of course, Cornelia was an exceptional woman, both because of her political involvement and because of her extraordinary family, but she was not the only well-educated woman of her time. Letter-writing must already have been a normal occupation of upper-class women in the second century BC and stylistic excellence may be expected also from such upper-class women of slightly later date as Laelia, daughter of the orator C. Laelius, and her daughters, who were praised by Cicero for their eloquence and purity of diction.[90]

In the first century BC there is somewhat more evidence, mainly in connection with the female correspondents of Cicero – though none of their letters is left. Now poetry enters the scene. Four names are known: Cornificia, Sempronia, Sulpicia the elegist and, around the turn of the century, Ovid's Perilla. The fact that six poems of Sulpicia have been preserved and that Cornificia's epigrams probably survived into the fourth century AD may be regarded as a token of the appreciation of their poetry. Circumstances seem to have become more favourable to the verses written by women than they had been before: Hellenistic poetry inspired new genres, love elegy and epigram, which because of their brevity and emphasis on personal feelings were more accessible to women poets than, for instance, epic and didactic poetry. Moreover, the poetry of Catullus and Roman love elegy defied traditional Roman values and extolled women for qualities totally different from the domestic virtues of the Roman *matrona*. Lastly, Greek poetry provided Roman women with famous Greek examples, such as Sappho, Corinna and Erinna, models of female poetic excellence, to whom Roman women might be compared as a compliment to their poetic endeavours.

As we saw in chapter 3, the first two centuries AD were notable for a greater interest in education among upper-class circles; this extended also to the education of the women of these classes: the once dubious accomplishments of the *puella docta* were now appreciated – at least, in a chaste married wife. As apart from the study of poetry some preliminary writing exercises in prose became part of the curriculum of the *grammaticus*, the widening opportunities for education may have enabled more and more upper-class women to learn how to compose short poems and to write their letters according to the literary standards of the time.

Fortuitous finds of poems written by Julia Balbilla and Terentia, dating from the Hadrianic period, show that women participated in the fashion of writing amateur poetry which flourished among the upper classes in the first two centuries AD. In cultured upper-class circles the writing of amateur poetry was regarded as an asset not only for men, but – under certain conditions – also for women. As regards the publication of their poetry in this period, we only have Sulpicia Caleni (first century AD), whose direct description of physical love shows that frankness and a distinct female perspective could be appreciated in verses written by a woman, but Martial's vigorous defence of her reputation as a chaste *univira* suggests that women writing poetry – at least the kind of poetry Sulpicia wrote – still provoked mixed feelings.

Writing letters remained common among women, as in the centuries before. Attention was paid to the use of correct language and style, in newly romanized areas also, as is illustrated by the Latin letters exchanged between two women at the northern frontier of Roman Britain (around AD 100). Moreover, it was not only orators and men of letters who composed well-written letters as an exercise in style; so did the anonymous wife of one of the friends of the younger Pliny. Finally, the first century AD provides our only evidence of a Roman woman writing, and publishing, her memoirs: Agrippina Minor.

In the late second and early third centuries the decline of Roman literature leaves us in the dark about women's writing. Yet, in this period, but outside the scope of this study, we have the unique work of Perpetua, who described the events of her last days before her execution as a Christian martyr with remarkable candour and directness of emotion. This work written by a young North African woman, who had apparently been given a thorough upper-class Latin (and perhaps Greek) education, warns us against assuming too readily that the general silence of our sources reflects an actual lack of women's writing at the time. But for the extraordinary events of her life and the fact that her 'prison diary' was preserved by the editor (for theological reasons probably not her own),[91] we would never have heard of her, nor would we have believed that such a work could be written by a provincial woman of her age.

When assessing the place of women in Roman literature the most striking feature is their restriction as regards genre: epigram, elegy, letters and memoirs seem to be the only genres in which they wrote, though it cannot be ruled out (the evidence being too scarce) that some women may also have contributed to other genres. In the traditional hierarchy of literary genres these four were the minor ones, letter-writing and memoirs even being rated as sub-literary. Women's restriction as to genre seems, at least partly, due to the circumstances under which they lived: their exclusion from public functions, and thus from first-hand experience in political, juridical and military life, may have barred them from writing history, oratory, epic and other major genres. As upper-class women led their lives – or, at least, were supposed to lead their lives – within the small circle of the family, their subject-matter was apt to be restricted to private concerns. This does not mean that their letters, or poems, were written without regard for the rules of the genre or consisted of artless emotional outpourings, as has been wrongly said of the poetry of Sulpicia the elegist: on the contrary, the preserved poetry shows that they were well aware of the poetic rules and the tradition of the genre.

Other barriers that may have prevented women from writing or, at least, from writing a work of greater volume and scope are, as we have seen, the exigencies of their lives as upper-class women, wives and mothers, their more haphazard education, the ambiguous appreciation of women writing, and publishing, a work of literature and their virtual exclusion from literary coteries, public recitation and the channels of publication. For writing and publishing a work of literature women were dependent on the circumstances of their family much more than men. Whereas men of talent could, to some extent, create their own opportunities by moving to Rome and joining a literary coterie, this was virtually impossible for women; their opportunities were to a large extent determined by the literary contacts of their male relatives and the place where they happened to live. Because of all this, the number of female authors must have been smaller by far than that of male authors and their work of more limited scope. Finally, the manuscript transmission seems to have worked against the writings of women, because the small volume (elegy, epigrams) or private nature (letters, memoirs) of their work hampered publication and preservation in the usual format of the papyrus roll. Thus, the limitations of their lives and social position, their preference for, or perhaps rather, their restriction to, the less valued or even sub-literary genres, and the small volume of their work relegated them to literary obscurity.

CONCLUSIONS

In this study I have investigated the education of upper-class women in Roman society, a subject that has been largely ignored in modern scholarly literature. In order to determine the place of Roman upper-class women in the world of the educated I have tried to reconstruct their opportunities to acquire an education, the impediments they faced, the level of education they could reach and the judgement on educated women in Roman society. Separate chapters are devoted to their role as patronesses of literature and learning and to their written work. Though occasionally I have included some women from the Latin-speaking western provinces, I have focussed on Rome and Italy.

For information on the education of upper-class women I have studied the literary sources and – less systematically – the epigraphic and archaeological evidence. Admittedly, the evidence is slight and haphazard, sometimes tantalizingly so. But, though it does not permit us to quantify or to trace a chronological development with any degree of certainty, the accumulation of the evidence and the careful consideration of the contexts permit certain conclusions as regards the education of upper-class women.

The point of departure was the discussion of those few upper-class women whose education is explicitly mentioned in the sources. In order to find out how common the education of such women may have been, the relative importance of the factors influencing their opportunities is studied: the period they lived in, their domicile, wealth and class, the disposition and the circumstances of their families, their age at marriage and their marital state. Second, the moralizing and critical remarks about educated women in our sources formed the starting-point for the analysis of Roman upper-class attitude towards them. Third, I have questioned the reticence of our sources as regards the education of women and I have tried to understand what is implied, though left unspoken, and what is hidden for reasons of propriety. In the following the main results of each chapter are summarized.

In chapter 1 the social position of upper-class women is briefly sketched. The study of three aspects of their position that seemed most relevant (their place within the family at the different stages of their lives, their relation to the three

210

leading *ordines*, and the norms and rules prescribing the behaviour of the upper-class *matrona*) shows that their social position was ambiguous and contradictory: it was determined both by integration (for example, in the social life of the family and in some of the priviliges and constraints of their class) and by segregation (for example, as regards tasks, female values and the public career associated with their class) and, besides, by the contradictory demands of class and gender.

The position of an upper-class woman within her family, discussed in the first section of the chapter, reflects this ambiguity: as a wife and mother she occupied a position of authority in her house and participated fully in the social life of her family, yet, there was also a marked segregation along gender lines as regards most tasks and daily activities. A woman's life was defined by her family and by the various roles she had within the family much more than that of a man, and her close association with the house and family caused her life to be mainly occupied with family concerns. Even so, her life was not confined to her house. Thanks to her wealth and to the blurring of the social and political spheres in Roman society, a woman from a leading Roman family might extend her influence and authority well outside her house and, occasionally, she might even interfere – though mostly indirectly – in political matters.

The second aspect of the social position of upper-class women, their relation to the three leading *ordines*, is also ambiguous. Since they were bound to the élite orders in an indirect way (through their fathers or husbands), their relation to these orders was uncertain: though they shared some of the advantages, they were excluded from the active public life associated with these orders and, consequently, they were lower in esteem than most men of their class (though usually having precedence over men of lower rank). Thus, on the one hand, upper-class women were associated with the *ordo* they were born into or were married into, but on the other, as a sex they were set apart: whatever their rank, they were excluded from a political, military, juridical or administrative career and their segregation from public life was made manifest to all by Augustus' arrangement of the seating in the (amphi)theatre, where women were relegated to the highest rows. Their uncertain relation to class was, to some extent, counterbalanced by the, rather puzzling, *ordo matronarum*, an assembly of upper-class (read: senatorial) women formed on the model of the male senatorial order: in it women organized themselves, celebrated festal occasions and banqueted, took joint action in matters concerning them, laid out rules for behaviour, internal hierarchy and the concomitant symbols of status, and competed for status among themselves. By this pseudo-order the women of the senatorial class marked themselves off from women of the other classes.

In contrast with the *de facto* sociability and freedom of movement of upper-class women, the norms and rules prescribing the behaviour of the *matrona* – the upper-class woman in her most valued role of wife and mother – were highly restrictive: chastity, modesty, frugality, reticence and domesticity were the main values governing her behaviour and continued to be so, despite changes in the life and legal status of women, during our entire period. Though adding to her position of respect and authority within the family, these norms, at least in theory, limited her activities to what contributed to the prestige and welfare of her family. Thus, to be accepted, women's ventures into the male public domain of, for instance, politics had to be unobtrusive and for the good of the family (or the state), the traditional channels of female influence being of a private nature, such as family councils and personal influence with male relatives. The strain between these restrictive norms and the manifold demands made on upper-class women in daily life manifests itself in various aspects of their lives, but here I have confined myself to the field of education. Though women's intrusion into this traditionally male field was bound to provoke criticism, the numerous demands made on upper-class women in Roman society necessitated at least a certain minimum of education. Moreover, a literary education in 'both languages' was a mark of wealth and status distinguishing members of the upper class from those of the lower classes. As a consequence, men of the leading classes were likely to have ambivalent feelings as regards the education of women, on the one hand stimulating, at least to some extent, their education within their own families and on the other hand criticizing that of women in general.

The ambiguity of the social position of upper-class women and the contradictory demands of class and gender, their dependence on the circumstances of their families and the norms restricting their behaviour define the scope of this inquiry. In chapter 2 I studied their opportunities to receive an education and the impediments they faced. Starting from the education of men, about which far more is known, it is argued that the usual three-stage division of Roman education (elementary, grammatical, rhetorical) cannot be used in the discussion of the education of women. As upper-class women were expected to marry young (in their early or mid-teens), a division into pre-marital education and education during, or after, marriage is more appropriate. As regards their pre-marital education the, admittedly meagre, evidence allows two inferences. First, as the education of upper-class girls lacked the clear-cut objective of that of the boys of their class (preparation for a public career), their education was bound to be more haphazard and more dependent on individual circumstances. Generally speaking, wealth, high rank, a tradition of learning in the family and the presence of a private library favoured the education of female members of a family, whereas, conversely, we may assume that less ample family resources were spent on the education of sons only. As a consequence, there must have been great differences in education between upper-class girls, much more than between upper-class boys. Second, the early age at which women usually married must have left most of them only half educated at the time of their marriage. Thus, to become fully educated, upper-class girls had to continue their education after their wedding-day.

The second part of this chapter investigates the opportunities that married women had to continue their education. Unlike girls, some of whom went to school together with boys (though most upper-class girls seem to have received home-tuition), adult women were excluded from the more formal institutions of education: they were not allowed to attend the school of a *rhetor*, or that of any other public teacher, and they were by tradition excluded from public libraries; for them there was no 'grand tour' to Greece to study with Greek philosophers and even the grammar stage of their education had to be passed in the privacy of their homes. Therefore it is not surprising to find that the influence of their family, especially that of the father and husband, was decisive for their education. In the works of Greek and Roman moralists such as Plutarch and the younger Pliny and in the archaeological evidence of the imperial period (mainly sarcophagi) we find women reading and studying under the guidance of their husbands. This was considered the most appropriate way: the husband's moral guidance and his superior education was thought to prevent his wife from forming untoward ideas of her own. Yet, we cannot generalize and assume that this was the standard practice in upper-class circles; in more or less the same period a more old-fashioned husband, the elder Seneca, prohibited his wife from studying because of notions of female propriety.

Apart from tuition by her husband, a married upper-class woman who wanted to continue her education might find several ways open to her: she could continue her education with the help of a private tutor (though the moralizing sources are suspicious of such contacts), devote herself to self-study by reading books from the family library or from her own collection, profit from discussions with her son(s) or her sons' teachers, or listen to an exposé of a learned protégé. Since women participated fully in the social life of their families, they could also add to their education by attending social gatherings of various kinds, such as dinners that provided cultural entertainment, or plays, mimes and ballets in the theatre. There is no certainty as regards the presence of women at recitations, apart from that of female relatives of the poet or the host. It should be emphasized that any of the above ways *might* be open to a married woman of the upper classes, but that they were not necessarily all open to all upper-class women in daily practice; much depended on the disposition of the husband, the presence of teachers or of a family library and on other personal circumstances. Thus, the education of a woman was essentially haphazard, both in her youth and in adult life. Therefore, the few women with an excellent education who are known to us, all of them stemming from wealthy and prominent families, cannot be taken as representative of upper-class women in general; rather, they indicate the level of education an upper-class woman *could* attain if wealth and the disposition of her family, together with her own circumstances and inclination, favoured such an education. Second, apart from moral philosophy, which in certain circles during the empire was included in the education of girls for its moral effects and which was considered appropriate as a consolation for widows and for mothers who were bereaved of a son, a woman's intellectual interest in adult life was largely determined by her course in 'grammar', which dealt with the study of poetry (if she had followed such a course).

The third chapter deals with the aims of the education of upper-class women and with ancient opinions on educated women. In the first part of this chapter

213

I have broached the question why upper-class women were given an education though the public career for which such an education usually prepared was denied them. What aims are expressed in our sources and what aims, though unspoken, may we suspect? The aims expressed in our sources can be classed under two headings: the acquisition of virtue and what may be called 'the ideal of educated motherhood'. The former is advocated by moral philosophers such as Musonius Rufus and Plutarch and by moralists such as the younger Pliny. In their view the education of women served a moral end: education in general, but especially a training in philosophy, was considered to breed moral virtues such as modesty, industry and self-restraint. By a training in philosophy a woman would become a chaste and prudent wife, a dignified and self-controlled *matrona* and a competent mother. Though Musonius Rufus has been called a feminist by some, he was far from being one; on the contrary, by regarding education as a means of making women into better housewives and mothers he reaffirms traditional female virtues. By stressing the domestic virtues of educated women, Musonius Rufus and Plutarch defended female education against critics who objected that education made women arrogant and presumptuous. Thus, the acquisition of virtue was not the original, or the actual, reason for the education of women; rather, it provided a justification for women's education which supported traditional notions. However, this justification may, of course, have influenced public opinion and thereby the opportunities for women's education.

In a similar way certain authors propagated the 'ideal of educated motherhood', of which Cornelia, the mother of the Gracchi, was exemplary. Although her excellent education was probably due to the wealth and prominence of her family, later authors justify it by referring to the favourable effect it was believed to have had on the education of her sons. In this view the education of women was appreciated in so far as it enabled women to supervise the education of their sons, to choose good teachers for them and to set an example by a first-rate style of speaking and writing. Thus, both aims expressed in our sources reaffirm traditional female virtues, justifying the education of women because of the traditional end it was believed to serve: to make women into better wives and mothers.

Apart from these two justifications, other motives for educating women may be gathered from our sources though they are not explicitly mentioned as such: *viz.* the social role of the upper-class *matrona* and family prestige. As we saw in chapter 1, the manifold demands made on upper-class women in Roman society necessitated a minimum of education: to administer their property women had at least to be able to read and write, and in entertaining guests and at other social occasions a literary education must have facilitated their contacts with their social peers. Second, education was a sign of high rank because of the time and money it involved. Giving not only one's sons but also one's daughters an extensive (and expensive) education was proof of wealth and high social status. During the republic women from leading upper-class families like Cornelia, the mother of the Gracchi, and Laelia, the daughter of Gaius Laelius, maintained the prestige of their families not only by their adherence to traditional virtues, but also by the purity of their diction, which betrayed an excellent education. Symbols of status have a tendency to spread downwards: during the principate also less elevated (though well-to-do) families copied the life-style of the higher ranks and took pride in the education of their womenfolk – as appears from wall-paintings and sarcophagi which depict women holding book-rolls, pencils or writing-tablets.

The ambiguous attitude found in Roman society towards educated women is discussed in the second part of this chapter. Though a sign of wealth and high social status, the education of upper-class women was not universally approved of; the Roman attitude towards educated women was highly ambiguous, varying from praise to sharp criticism. These conflicting feelings, which coexisted in one and the same period and might even be apparent in one and the same person, reveal the tension between status and expediency on the one hand and ideals of female propriety and traditional morality on the other. The latter coincide with the Roman distrust of Greek education and the moral laxity to which this was thought to lead, a prejudice that was especially strong during the republic. In their judgement of educated women most authors put morality first; their approval of women's education was, at best, a conditional one: it was accepted as long as the women concerned observed traditional rules and put their education in the service of their family, just as the virtuous women of the past were said to have done.

In defiance of traditional morality, Roman love poets of the Augustan period praised the *puella docta*, a young woman of loose sexual morals skilled in the Greek educational triad of poetry, music and dance. More traditional-minded authors, however, ignored in their writing the education of the women they respected, whereas they might exploit the cultural accomplishments of a female adversary to throw doubt upon her morals. However, in the course of the principate the ideal of the *puella docta* was 'domesticated' and, stripped of its sexual connotations, it was incorporated in the ideals of married life. This, and the pride in women's education among wider circles of the well-to-do, bears witness to a greater *de facto* acceptance of it. However, traditional virtues remained essential for their reputation and women were judged first and foremost as wives and mothers. When it was not justified by traditional or moral aims, their education might be held up for ridicule or abuse; it was feared to lead to a life of luxury and moral depravity, or to make a woman arrogant, meddlesome and unbearable. Thus, despite occasional female intrusions into the field, education remained a male privilege: women venturing into this domain in a modest and unassuming way might be praised as 'honorary men', but too great a devotion to or ostentation arising from learning was scorned as undesirable 'male' behaviour. In this way, the notion that education was the field of men was kept intact. In spite of the greater *de facto* acceptance during the empire, education remained precarious for women: though adding to their social prestige and to that of their family, it threatened their reputation. To avoid censure it had to be modestly subordinated to the ideal of the chaste and dedicated *matrona*.

The same circumstances are found in the discussion of patronesses of literature and learning in chapter 4: to be acceptable, their intrusion into the male
domain of patronage had to be counterbalanced by a strict adherence – at least
outwardly – to traditional female values. As regards their numbers and the scope
of their patronage, women played only a minor role in Roman cultural patronage: no more than five upper-class women and eight or nine women belonging to
the imperial family can, with varying degrees of certainty, be called patronesses
of literature or learning, and most of them exercised patronage only on a modest
scale. In discussing the evidence special attention is paid to their motives, the
conditions which favoured patronage and the impediments they faced, but also to
the services they exchanged with their protégés and the terms in which they were
praised.

As regards the conditions favouring women's patronage, Cornelia, the mother
of the Gracchi, who is the earliest Roman patroness of literature and learning we
know of, set an example. Her extraordinary wealth and education, her high social
status and authority as an elderly widow of a leading family and the tradition of
patronage in her family foreshadow the conditions favouring the patronage of
imperial women such as Octavia and Antonia. Moreover, the praise of Cornelia
as a paragon of old-fashioned Roman virtue and motherhood indicates the complexity of the praise of women, which is a consistent feature during the whole of
our period.

As regards the impediments women met, there are three aspects of their social
position that hampered them in exercising patronage of literature and learning:
the retired way of life expected of them, which clashed with the public role of the
patron, the lack of a public career or position, which limited the support they
could offer, and, third, the uncertain command of their wealth, which might be
limited by the legal or social control of a guardian or male relatives. In these
respects the women of the imperial family were exceptional: because of their
public position, their closeness to the emperor and the independent control of
their wealth they could secure great rewards for their protégés, including privileges and appointments. Thus, both in their own right and by mediating with the
emperor they could be powerful patronesses. Yet, in spite of their prominent
position they also had to comply with traditional female virtues, disguising their
activities as a patron under the veil of a modest and self-effacing wife or devoted
mother. As a consequence, they usually did not exploit their privileged circumstances to the full and, though they were wealthy and well educated, and exercised the public role of patrons, they were praised in conventional terms as loyal
wives or devoted mothers.

Women's outward compliance with these traditional rules and the conventional terms in which they were praised obscure their activities as patrons for
us. But it also had two other effects which at first sight may seem contradictory: it
impeded their full participation in the male field of patronage (or, for that matter,
education), but at the same time it allowed them to play at least some role in it in
the disguise of the devoted wife, mother or widow. It is only under this condition,

the strict observance of traditional rules, that women could venture into the male domain of patronage without damaging their reputation. This underlies the acceptance of the patronage of imperial women such as Octavia, Antonia and Plotina, and is responsible for the bad reputation of Agrippina Minor (though it is her self-interested intrusion into the field of politics rather than into that of education that caused her downfall); it also holds for the four non-imperial patronesses attested in the works of Martial and Statius. The example of one of them, Argentaria Polla, moreover, shows that women were well aware of such traditional notions and could use them to their own advantage: by commissioning poems in honour of Lucan Argentaria Polla not only honoured her deceased husband – thus incidentally showing herself to be a devoted widow – but also asserted her social status as the widow of a senator and a famous poet.

This brings us to the motives of upper-class women in patronizing men of letters or learning, apart from, self-evidently, their personal inclination. In the case of Cornelia and in that of the imperial women, patronage of literature and learning was to some extent bound up with their prominent position as members of the imperial, or of a leading republican, family. It cannot be dissociated from their political influence, which, however, was much more risky for their reputation, and from the tradition of patronage in their families. By exercising patronage of men of literature or learning these women lived up to the cultural tradition of their families as far as the limitations of their sex allowed, thus maintaining the status and prestige of their families.

The motives of the non-imperial patronesses of Martial and Statius, however, are, at least partly, found in the 'inconsistency' of their status: they were wealthy and well-educated women but, in spite of a senatorial marriage, they belonged to the fringes of the Roman élite because of their provincial or municipal extraction and their non-senatorial birth. Patronage of poets enabled them to reduce this inconsistency and heighten their prestige in upper-class circles by displaying their wealth and education and by being publicly praised for their adherence to pristine Roman virtues. Thus, they showed themselves to be committed both to the moral values and to the literary culture of the Roman upper classes.

In the last chapters, 5 (about poetry) and 6 (about prose), the perspective is shifted from the writings of men *about* educated women to the writings of these women themselves. Here, if anywhere, educated women should speak for themselves. Unfortunately, very little work written by women is preserved. This has given rise to the question whether this dearth is due to the rarity of female authors in Roman society or to accidental loss, or perhaps wilful suppression, of their work. In order to give an answer that explains both problems (*viz.* the rarity of female authors and the almost total loss of their work), I have tried to reconstruct the place of upper-class women in the literary life of their time. Three questions guide the presentation of the evidence: what place did women occupy in Roman literary circles and production? Did female writers differ from male ones in style, genre, subject-matter, or in respect of their audience? And what was the Roman attitude to female writers?

Summarizing the main results, we may say that women had a place, though a very modest one, in Roman literary life: some of them wrote short poems in the style and fashion of their days and their letters were a match for those of men in style and in frequency. Women's obscurity in Roman literary life and the almost total loss of their work were caused by a number of interrelated factors which are closely bound up with gender. First, the virtual exclusion of women from literary coteries (with very few exceptions) isolated them from literary discussions and criticism, and barred them from the main channels of 'publication'. Second, their choice of genre and subject-matter appears to have been much more restricted than that of men: as far as we know, women wrote only love poetry, epigrams, letters and memoirs, genres that mostly draw on the author's private feelings and experience. In the traditional hierarchy these were minor genres, letters and memoirs being even 'sub-literary'. Within these genres no significant difference in style or poetic technique can be pointed out between male and female work, though some writings by women (for instance, the poems of Sulpicia) display a distinctly female perspective and may have appealed to a female audience (which is not to say that they did not appeal to a male audience). Third, the Roman attitude to women writers was ambivalent, since by writing, and even more by publishing, women broke with the traditional female virtues of modesty and reticence. In spite of occasional praise of a woman's work, writing and publishing literary work, especially love poetry, remained a dubious activity for upper-class women.

Apart from these points, some other factors, which differ somewhat in their effect on the activities of women in poetry (chapter 5) and prose (chapter 6), hampered their writing and contributed to the subsequent loss of their work. Their haphazard education, the ideal of female reticence, the exigencies of their lives as upper-class women, and their domestic and social obligations reduced the number of women who possessed the necessary education and talent, and enjoyed enough leisure and encouragement, to write a work of literature. Moreover, their opportunities to write and, even more so, to publish were highly dependent on the literary connections and approval of their male relatives and also on their place of residence (a work circulating in Rome and appreciated by a Roman audience had the best chance of survival).

As far as poetry is concerned, women only wrote love poetry and occasional verse (mostly epigrams), minor genres which, though highly fashionable among amateur poets of their class, were rarely published. Women may have readily conformed to this aristocratic restraint, particularly as it agreed with traditional notions. Moreover, the small size of their œuvre (probably too small to fill a papyrus roll) hampered publication and preservation as a separate *corpus*. The few writings of women that were published in the end had little chance of survival, because, with the exception of Sulpicia's poems, none of them were included in the public libraries or used in education.

As regards prose, the situation is even worse. Women's restriction to the sub-literary genres (letters and memoirs) is partly explained by the circumstances in which they lived: their exclusion from a public career and their lack of rhetorical training (*pace* some rare exceptions) barred women from writing oratory, history, or any other prose-genre, since prose-writing was closely connected with rhetorical education. On the other hand, they wrote letters almost as frequently as men did, and one woman (Agrippina Minor) is known to have written, and published, her memoirs, thus venturing into the male field of autobiography. Although the letters of several women were admired for their good style, only those of Cornelia, the mother of the Gracchi, were published (all are now lost with the exception of a – disputed – letter transmitted in the work of Nepos) and no letters written by women were included in the published collections of Cicero or Fronto. The private character of their lives and letters, the restrictions applied to their choice of male addressees for reasons of propriety and the reluctance to publish letters of women all contributed to the almost total loss of letters written by women.

In summary, we have to admit that Roman upper-class women occupied only a very minor and inconspicuous place in the world of the educated. As their education did not serve the purpose of preparing them for a public career, it depended on the circumstances and disposition of their families much more than that of men. Yet, though little known, their participation in education, patronage and literature is significant, as it shows that they could move beyond the concerns of house and family into the male-dominated world of literary studies. In Roman society women's education was controversial, entailing both prestige and problems. Since, in Roman thought, education and literary culture were inextricably linked with high birth and a high social position, the elevated station of women of the upper classes favoured a good education. Yet, this tended to bring them into conflict with the traditional rules of female behaviour, and open participation in the male field of learning threatened a woman's moral reputation. These contradictory demands of class and gender obliged upper-class women to observe great discretion in the field of learning; they had to mask their activities under the veil of devoted wifehood, motherhood and widowhood. The traditional terms in which they are praised obscure their activities in the field of education, but this should not mislead us: as has been made clear in this study, the conventional praise of women in Roman sources does not do justice to the complexity of their lives.

NOTES

INTRODUCTION

1 See, respectively, E. Rawson (1985) 48, B. Rawson (1992) 40 and Hillard (1992) 40.

2 Standard works on Roman education such as Marrou (1965) and Clarke (1971) largely ignore the education of women, and Bonner (1977) only occasionally pays attention to it. In his study of ancient literacy Harris (1989) 252 suggests that women of the Roman élite 'may have been virtually as literate as men', but he does not pursue the problem of their education any further. In the nineteenth century Friedländer collected some of the literary evidence: see Friedländer, L. (1919⁹) *Darstellungen aus der Sittengeschichte Roms in der Zeit von August bis zum Ausgang der Antonine*, Leipzig: Hirzel Verlag, vol. 1, pp. 268–9 and 294–8, and earlier still, in 1796, Alexander, W. *The History of Women from the Earliest Antiquity to the Present Time*, Philadelphia: J. H. Dobelblower (repr. New York: AMS Press 1976), pp. 32–66, devoted a chapter to 'female education', in which in a mere thirty-four pages he dealt with the education of women in ancient Egypt, Phoenicia, Babylon, Persia, Greece, Rome, the Scandinavian countries, medieval Europe, sixteenth- and seventeenth-century France, Asia, Africa and China, and North America up to his own days. For a historiographical survey of the study of ancient women in the nineteenth and twentieth centuries, see Blok, J. (1987), 'Sexual asymmetry: a historiographical essay', in Blok and Mason (1987) 1–57; for recent trends see also Rawson, B. (1995) 'From "daily life" to "demography"', in Hawley and Levick (1995) 1–20.

3 For the gradations in the status of the three leading orders, see, e.g., Garnsey and Saller (1990) 112–25, Jacques and Scheid (1990) 303–13 and Raepsaet-Charlier (1982); for the internal hierarchy among *decuriones*, Dyson (1992) 204–5. For the superior morality claimed by the upper classes as distinguishing them from the rest of society and legitimizing their privileged position, see, e.g., Edwards (1993) 24ff. For knights sharing the same (literary) culture and education as senators, see Demougin (1988) 754–64; for the Italian élite, see Wiseman (1983). Though 'class' is a somewhat inadequate term for the senatorial, and – to an even higher degree – for the equestrian and decurial orders, because of the great variation in wealth, status and career between their members, it is used in this study for the sake of convenience.

4 For working women, see chapter 2, n. 18. As the overwhelming majority of the women who were trained for a profession seem to have been of slave or freed status, a word of caution is needed here. It seems possible that the freeborn lower classes, apart from the very poor, were in the habit of keeping their daughters at home while their sons were taught a trade (note, for instance, the absence of freeborn girls in apprenticeship documents from Roman Egypt, Bradley (1991) 108). As we shall see (chapter 3, pp. 72ff.; for an example, see also p. 83), during the empire some well-to-do 'middle-class' or sub-élite families imitated the élite in giving their daughters a literary education.

NOTES

5 According to the estimation of Raepsaet-Charlier (1982) 460 and *FOS*, p. X, n. 35, about 15–20 per cent of the senatorial women of the first two centuries of the empire are known to us, though often only very slightly; of the imperial family almost all women are recorded, though of some of them we only have their names. Very little is known (mainly from inscriptions) of the much more numerous women of the equestrian and decurial classes. This disproportion in the attention of the literary sources is reinforced by the fact that most evidence comes from Rome: unlike equestrians (and, it goes without saying, members of the decurial élite), all senators and their families lived in Rome for much of their lives (though, of course, many of them also had houses elsewhere and estates in the countryside): see *Dig.* 1.9.11 and 50.1.22.6; for senatorial property (including their houses in the capital) during the republic, see Shatzman (1975), and for the empire, see Mratschek-Halfmann (1993); for their domicile in Rome as well as their local ties, see Eck, W. (1997), 'Rome and the outside world: senatorial families and the world they lived in', in Rawson and Weaver (1997) 73–99.

6 To keep this study within reasonable limits I shall not devote a separate chapter to the study of philosophy by women or to their incidental display of rhetorical proficiency, but some of the relevant evidence is presented in the chapters on education (chapters 2 and 3).

1 THE SOCIAL POSITION OF UPPER-CLASS WOMEN

1 The terms *doctae sorores* or *virgines*, learned sisters or maidens, do not indicate women but the Muses: see, e.g., Catull. 65.2; Tib. 3.4.45 (Lygdamus); Ovid *Trist.* 2.13 (cf. *Trist.* 3.2.4: 'docta . . . turba' and *AA* 3.411–12: 'doctis . . . Musis'), Mart. *Ep.* 1.70.15, 9.42.3 (cf. 10.58.5–6 'doctas . . . Pieridas'). Also other terms that might have been used to denote an adult learned woman, such as *femina* or *mulier docta*, are hardly ever found in Roman literature. The two examples I know of are irrelevant: Ovid mentions a *femina docta* in *AA* 3.320, clearly as a synonym to *puella docta*, and the grammarian Remmius Palaemon when giving the declination of *doctus* writes: 'the ablativus ends on "is", thus *doctis viris*, learned men, and *doctis mulieribus*, learned women' ('ablativum in is, ab his doctis viris et ab his doctis mulieribus'; *Ars Gramm.*, p. 533.15–16 ed. H. Keil, Leipzig 1868). For the *puella docta* see chapter 3, pp. 79ff. and chapter 5, pp. 175ff.

2 For learned women in the Middle Ages see, for instance, Dronke (1984) and, also for other periods, Labalme (1980). For Roman women there was no freedom of choice comparable to that of the fifteenth-century Italian Alessandra Scala: 'Shall I marry, or devote my life to study?': see King (1980). The only alternative to marriage was to be chosen as a Vestal Virgin – of whom there were only six at a time; but the Vestals were not especially noted for their learning.

3 Hopkins (1974) 110; see also Rawson (1985) 38 and 98–9 and D'Arms (1970) 70–2, 156–8 and 165–7; on the change in Roman attitude towards education in the early imperial period, see Wallace-Hadrill (1983) 26ff. and Zanker (1995) 193ff. For an extensive discussion of *otium* in Roman life and of the mixed feelings it provoked, see André, J. M. (1966), *L'Otium dans la vie morale et intellectuelle romaine des origines à la époque Augustéenne*, Paris; see also Toner, J. P. (1995), *Leisure and Ancient Rome*, Cambridge: Polity Press, esp. pp. 22–33; for leisure honourably filled with intellectual pursuits (*otium honestum*) among equestrians, see Demougin (1988) 751–64. For education as a mark of distinction Bourdieu's much-quoted concept of 'symbolic capital' seems relevant (Bourdieu, P. (1977) *Outline of a Theory of Practice*, Cambridge: Cambridge University Press, pp. 171–97 and Bourdieu, P. (1992) *The Logic of Practice*, Cambridge: Polity Press, pp. 112–21): the acquisition and development of education and intellectual achievement required, as was recognized by Lucian *Somnium* 1, 'great labour, much time,

221

considerable expense, and a conspicuous social position' (παιδεία μὲν καὶ πόνου πολλοῦ καὶ χρόνου μακροῦ καὶ δαπάνης οὐ μικρᾶς καὶ τύχης δεῖσϑαι λαμπρᾶς); the 'symbolic capital' thus achieved (by a transformation of economic capital into 'cultural' capital) distinguished members of the upper classes from the uneducated masses. For *paideia* and literary knowledge as a form of symbolic capital by which men of the Roman élite distinguished themselves from their less well-educated peers and from members of the other classes, see Gleason (1995) XX–XXI, 140, 162 and 164–5; in reaction to Hopkins she rightly stresses 'the vast amount of effort expended by aristocrats on developing their rhetorical skill precisely in order to be "good without seeming to try"' (p. XX, n. 9).

4 In a letter of the younger Pliny (*Ep.* 7.24) Ummidia Quadratilla, an elderly lady of senatorial rank, is reported to have said that 'as a woman, being condemned to the leisure prescribed to her sex, she used to amuse herself with playing draughts or watching her mimes' ('solere se ut feminam in illo otio sexus laxare animum lusu calculorum, solere spectare pantomimos suos').

5 For the *vir doctus* see, for instance, Cic. *Brut.* 114: 'doctus vir et Graecis litteris eruditus' and *Part. Or.* 90, where 'humanum et politum' is opposed to 'indoctum et agreste'. For more examples of the use of *doctus* to indicate a man's erudition, culture and civilized conduct (*humanitas*) see *TLL* 1752–3; on the honour and admiration for a man who had enjoyed higher education see, e.g., Lucian *Somn.* 11–12; for the relation between education and moral qualities cf. the well-known expression *vir bonus dicendi peritus* (Sen. *Contr.* 1 *pr.* 9–10; Quint. 12.1.1), which denotes the admired combination of eloquence and moral excellence. As regards the qualification *docta*, there seems to be a disparity between the literary texts, in which it is mostly a dubious qualification when used for an upper-class woman (like the notorious Sempronia, who is called *docta* in Sall. *Cat.* 25: see chapter 3, pp. 84f.), and the inscriptions, where it is used as a compliment (for some examples, see chapter 3, n. 71). This may be explained by differences of class and time, the inscriptions mostly honouring women of the lower (freedmen) classes and dating from the imperial period, when the qualification *docta* – under certain conditions – lost some of its dubious aspects (see chapter 3, p. 81).

6 Especially helpful were, apart from the studies and articles mentioned in the following notes, Treggiari (1991) on Roman marriage and the social life of upper-class matrons; Dixon (1990) and (1992b) on the Roman mother and the Roman family; Gardner (1990) on the juridical position of upper-class women; and the volumes of Bradley (1991), Rawson (1991) and (1992), and Rawson and Weaver (1997) on women's role and position within the family. For a useful survey of both Greek and Roman women, quoting many sources, see Fantham, E. *et al.* (1994) *Women in the Classical World: Image and Text*, Oxford and New York: Oxford University Press.

7 Hallett (1984b).

8 For the customary discrimination against daughters in Roman testamentary practice, see Champlin, E. (1991) *Final Judgments: Duty and Emotions in Roman Wills, 200 B.C.–A.D. 250*, Berkeley: University of California Press, pp. 114–20: daughters consistently received a smaller share of the inheritance than sons; for discussion, see van Bremen (1996) 243–5 and 250–1.

9 On the age of girls at first marriage, see Hopkins (1965): modal age of (pagan) marriage 12–15 years. Shaw (1987), Treggiari (1991) 39–43 and 398–403, and Saller (1994) 25–42 argue for an age in the late teens or about 20 for first marriages of girls of the other classes, but agree that girls of the senatorial class usually married about five years earlier; see also Rawson (1991) 27. On the dedication of toys (Pers. *Sat.* 2.70 and Lact. *Div. Inst.* 2.4.13: to Venus; Pseudo-Acro ad Hor. *Sat.* 1.5.65f.: to the *Lares*) and the wedding as a rite of passage, see Treggiari (1991) 180 and Wiedemann (1989) 149. For the special costume of the Roman bride which marked her transitional state, see La

Follette, L. (1994) 'The costume of the Roman bride', in Sebesta and Bonfante (1994) 54–64.

10 For the age at first marriage of upper-class men, see Saller (1987): 25 years at average; Syme (1987) records examples of a more varying practice. Treggiari (1991) 402 suggests that Augustus' marriage legislation may have reduced the age-gap between husband and wife in a first marriage, as his laws on marriage encouraged upper-class men to marry (and become fathers) before the age of 25. In a woman's subsequent marriage her own choice could be decisive: for instance, Cicero's daughter Tullia, together with her mother, chose P. Cornelius Dolabella for a (third) husband against the express wishes of Cicero (see Dixon (1992a)).

11 For a detailed description of the negotiations preceding the choice of a marriage-partner and the criteria applied, see Treggiari (1991) 83–180: for a *digna condicio* (a suitable match) both partners had to be equal in birth, wealth and social rank, but good looks, character and moral virtues were also considered, as were the position and morals of their families. In the choice of a husband, his career and education and, in that of a wife, chastity, a modest demeanour, compliance and a kindly disposition were additional qualifications. For an illuminating example of the subordination of the individual to the family's interests see Bradley, K. R. (1991) 'A Roman family', in Bradley (1991) 177–204 about the marriage between Cicero's younger brother Quintus and Atticus' sister Pomponia, which, though it was notoriously unhappy, continued for twenty-five years thanks to the joint efforts of Cicero and Atticus, who set great store on their *affinitas* established by this union. For the ideal of matrimonial *concordia*, see chapter 2, pp. 33f.

12 For the social role and daily routine of women in married life, see Treggiari (1991) 414–27; for an example of their financial activity, see the dealings of Cicero's wife and daughter in Dixon (1992a); see also the section on women's letters in chapter 6 (pp. 188ff.). For women's integration in the Roman house, see Wallace-Hadrill (1988) and (1994), who explains the absence of gender-differentiation by the dominant role played by status in comparison to gender and age, and Mols (1994) 123; for the spatial dimension to Roman family life, see also George, M. (1997) 'Repopulating the Roman house', in Rawson and Weaver (1997) 299–319. The presence of women at dinner parties is discussed in chapter 2 (pp. 42ff.). For the political involvement of women which followed from their position as daughters, wives and mothers of men of politics, see, e.g., Dixon (1983), Purcell (1986) and Fischler (1994); for the problems caused by their intrusion into the male domain of politics, see chapter 3, p. 127. For the custom of women accompanying their husbands to the provinces, see Marshall, A. J. (1975) 'Roman women and the provinces', *AncSoc.* 6: 109–29 and by the same author (1975) 'Tacitus and the governor's lady: a note on Annals iii.33–4', *G & R* 22: 11–18; see also Raepsaet-Charlier, M.-Th. (1982) 'Epouses et familles de magistrats dans les provinces romaines aux deux premiers siècles de l'Empire', *Historia* 31: 56–69.

13 When Livia, as a widow, planned to invite the senate and the equestrians with their wives to a banquet in honour of an image which she had dedicated in her house to Augustus, she was prevented from doing so by Tiberius, who himself entertained the men while she feasted the women (Dio 57.12.5; for other examples: Dio 55.2.4 and 8.2). This division according to gender applied also to the entertainment of slaves and dependants: when Cicero's brother Quintus wanted to provide a banquet for the servants of his estate at Arcanum, he asked his wife Pomponia to invite the women, while he himself invited the men (Cic. *Att.* 5.1; see also *Att.* 2.3.4: Cicero inviting Atticus and Terentia inviting his sister Pomponia); of course, at the dinner itself Pomponia was expected to recline with her husband (which she refused to do because she and Quintus were again engaged in one of their matrimonial quarrels). Mixed dinners, at which the male guests were accompanied by their wives, were the norm in Roman society. See, for

instance, Cic. *Att.* 4.12, Tac. *Ann.* 11.2.2, Suet. *Cal.* 36.2, Lucian *Merc. Cond.* 15 and 29; for more examples, Yardley, J. H. (1991) 'The symposium in Roman elegy', in Slater (1991) 149–55, Treggiari (1991) 414 and 420ff.; see also chapter 2, pp. 42ff.

14 Dixon (1990) preface, 1–7, 109ff., 121, 131 and 141ff.: the main role of the Roman mother of the upper classes was that of disciplinarian, supervising the moral and intellectual education of her children and transmitting Roman culture and traditional morality; see also chapter 3, pp. 68ff.

15 For the status and authority of upper-class widows, especially with adult sons, see Dixon (1990) 6–7, 31, 35, 41–2, 47–50, 66–7, 168ff. and Treggiari (1991) 498–501. Walcot, P. (1991) 'On widows and their reputation in antiquity', *SO* 66: 5–26 is super-ficial; Lightman and Zeisel (1977) 19–32, especially pp. 27f., to my mind underestimate the regard paid to upper-class widows in pagan Rome by assuming that widowhood became respectable only in Christianity. For the political power exercised through sons, see, for instance, Seneca *Cons. Helv.* 14.2, who complains of mothers who, unlike Helvia, 'make use of a son's power with a woman's lack of self-control, who, because they cannot hold office, seek power through their sons' ('quae potentiam liberorum muliebri impotentia exercent, quae, quia feminis honores non licet gerere, per illos ambitiosae sunt'). Some widows of the imperial family held their own official recep-tions receiving 'the senate', or 'the most prominent men' and others in their houses: see Dio 57.12.2 (Livia); 78.18.2–3 (Julia Domna) and Tac. *Ann.* 13.18 (Agrippina Minor). The bleak picture of the position of widows painted by Krause, J. U. (1994) *Witwen und Waisen im römischen Reich I: Verwitwung und Wiederverheiratung*, Stuttgart: Steiner (HABES 16), Krause, J. U. (1994) *Witwen und Waisen im römischen Reich II: Wirtschaftliche und gesellschaftliche Stellung von Witwen*, Stuttgart: Steiner (HABES 17) and Krause, J. U. (1995) *Witwen und Waisen im römischen Reich III: Rechtliche und soziale Stellung von Waisen*, Stuttgart: Steiner (HABES 18) does not hold for the upper classes: see my review in *AC* 65 (1996) 508–11 and in *AC* 66 (1997) 627–9. For wealthy widows acting as bene-factresses to their cities and receiving public honour, see the example of Ummidia Quadratilla, who built an amphitheatre and a temple, and repaired a theatre, in her native city of Casinum (Plin. *Ep.* 7.24, *CIL* X 5183 = *ILS* 5628, *AE* (1946) 174); for widows 'pushed into positions of prominence' by the death of their nearest male relatives in the Greek East, see Bremen, R. van (1994) 'A family from Sillyon', *ZPE* 104: 43–56 and Bremen, R. van (1996) 18, 108ff., 189, 217, 232, 260f. and 271. For the problem of the *tutela* of women and the measure of independence they had in the control of their finances, see chapter 4, pp. 101f.

16 With few exceptions (the Vestal Virgins and, from the legislation of Augustus onwards, women *sui iuris* who had borne three or more children) women *sui iuris* had to have a guardian, like children under age, but in contrast with the *tutela* of a (male) child, which ended when he came of age, that of a woman was for life. For *tutela* and the legal incapacity of Roman women, see Gardner (1990) 5–29 and (1993) 85–109; see also chapter 4, pp. 101f.

17 From *Dig.* 1.9.8, 10 and 12 (Ulpian) we may conclude that women either inherited senatorial rank from their fathers or acquired it by marrying a man of senatorial rank. When (re-)marrying a man of inferior status they lost their senatorial dignity with the exception of those few who were allowed to keep their rank by imperial decree. It is uncertain whether this rule concerning the loss of senatorial dignity, which apparently had force of law in Ulpian's days, was of recent date or simply confirmed earlier practice or rules. Raepsaet-Charlier argues that the loss of senatorial dignity of women in case of a mésalliance can be attested from about the middle of the second century AD onwards (when women of senatorial rank were granted the title *clarissima*) and may be ascribed to legislation by the emperor Marcus Aurelius: see, e.g., Raepsaet-Charlier (1981), Raepsaet-Charlier, M.-Th. (1983) 'A propos de Julia Soaemias, Aelia

Gemellina et Vedia Phaedrina', *RIDA* 30: 185–92 and *FOS*, pp. 1–14. In her opinion, the question whether it reflected still earlier rules or practice is an academic one, as women of senatorial rank only very rarely married beneath their class before this time. Chastagnol, A. (1979) 'Les Femmes dans l'ordre sénatorial: titulature et rang social à Rome', *RH* 103 (262): 3–28 and Alföldy (1986) 194–8 ascribe the loss of rank to a regulation of Caracalla; Alföldy suggests that the possible loss of senatorial dignity did not really matter before the title *clarissima* was used to denote a woman of senatorial rank, but this seems unconvincing since there were other ways to distinguish senatorial women from those of inferior rank. For the question whether 'mixed' marriages (between members of the senatorial order and men or women of inferior rank, mostly of the equestrian, and sometimes decurial, order) were common or not, see Raepsaet-Charlier (1992) and (1994), who says that in the early empire 'mixed' marriages were extremely rare (especially when the woman was of superior rank), but became somewhat more common in the second and third centuries AD.

18 Raepsaet-Charlier (1981), (1982) and *FOS* 1–14 argues that from the time of Augustus onwards women belonged to the senatorial order by birth (legal testimony pointing to hereditary distinction of them from that time onwards). For instance, Augustus' legislation prohibiting people of senatorial rank from marrying freedmen or (children of) actors included daughters, granddaughters and great-granddaughters of senators (in the male line); see *Dig.* 23.2.44. Like women of the senatorial order, the women of equestrian families were regarded as part of the equestrian élite and thus liable to the same prohibitions: on the inscription found at Larinum (Tiberian period) the daughters, granddaughters and great-granddaughters of both senators and *equites* were prohibited from performing on stage or in the arena (see Levick (1983) and Lebek (1990)); for equestrian birth extending to women, see *Dig.* 40.10.4 (Ulpian). For the social status of women within the *ordo equester*, see Demougin (1988) 555–68 and 657–76.

19 Unlike 'class' and 'rank', which denote objective economic and socio-political positions, 'status' is used in this study in the sense of prestige enjoyed by someone on the basis of a complex combination of criteria such as birth, rank, wealth, political office, marriage, achievement, education and moral excellence: see Hopkins (1974) 105 and Garnsey and Saller (1990) 118–23.

20 *Dig.* 1.9.1 *pr.*: 'consulari feminae utique consularem virum praeferendum nemo ambigit. Sed vir praefectorius an consulari feminae praeferatur, videndum. Putem praeferri, quia maior dignitas est in sexu virili' (trans. Watson, A. (1985) *The Digest of Justinian*, Philadelphia: University of Pennsylvania Press).

21 Some examples: Plaut. *Cist.* 23ff.; Liv. 10.23.10: 'Volgata dein religio a pollutis, nec matronis solum sed omnis ordinis feminis' ('Afterwards the cult was degraded by polluted worshippers, not matrons only but women of every order'). Incidentally, this text also shows that in the eyes of Livy it was quite conceivable that women marrying beneath them lost their rank: Verginia, a patrician, was excluded by the matrons from the ceremonies of Pudicitia Patricia because of her marriage to a consul of plebeian birth. Val. Max. 5.2.1: the grant of status symbols to the *ordo matronarum*; Val. Max. 8.3.3: *ordo matronarum* denoting the 1,400 wealthiest women of Rome taxed by the triumvirs in 42 BC; Liv. 34.7.1: wealthy *matronae* affected by the prohibitions of the *Lex Oppia* of 215 BC, which restricted their use of gold, purple and carriages, are contrasted in the speech of Valerius with 'the other orders' (*alii ordines* – the male élite orders are meant) enjoying these privileges. For *matronae* acting as a group in public, for instance, in mourning (Liv. 2.7.4; 2.16.7; 22.7.7), contributing their gold to the state (Liv. 5.25.8–9) and protesting, see also Hemelrijk (1987).

22 Whereas male virtues (*virtus, gravitas, dignitas* and *auctoritas*) were manifested in the fulfilment of public duties and responsibilities, women's virtues were of a private, domestic

kind. Yet, male and female virtues were regarded as complementary: see, for instance, Liv. 10.23.7 (in the words attributed to Verginia): 'even as the men of our state contend for the prize of valour, so the matrons may vie for that of modesty' ('quod certamen virtutis viros in hac civitate tenet, hoc pudicitiae inter matronas sit') and Plin. *NH* 7.120, who presents as parallel cases the choice of the best man by the senate and that of the most chaste woman by the 'vote of the matrons' (*matronarum sententia*).

23 Cf. Val. Max. 5.2.1: as a reward for their successful intervention with Coriolanus the senate decreed that the *ordo matronarum* was granted the right to wear *vittae*, purple dress and gold ornaments (besides the *stola*). Liv. 5.25.9: in reward for their contribution of gold to the state the senate granted the *matronae* the right to drive in four-wheeled carriages to religious ceremonies and to the games and in two-wheeled carriages on festal and working days ('ut pilento ad sacra ludosque, carpentis festo profestoque uterentur'). The recovery of these symbols of rank was the aim of the women publicly protesting against the *Lex Oppia* in 195 BC; see Hemelrijk (1987). During the empire official permission from the senate was needed for the use of the *carpentum* within the city; see Dio 60.22.2: Messalina was granted this privilige by a vote of the senate; see also Suet. *Claud.* 17.3; for Agrippina Minor using the *carpentum* within the city, see Tac. *Ann.* 12.42.3. For the Roman concept of *ordo*, see Cohen, B. (1975) 'La Notion d'"ordo" dans la Rome antique', *Bull. Assoc. Budé* 4th ser.1: 259–82. For male senatorial dress, see Talbert, R. J. A. (1984) *The Senate of Imperial Rome*, Princeton, N.J.: Princeton University Press, pp. 216–20; see also Stone, S. (1994) 'The toga: from national to ceremonial costume', in Sebesta and Bonfante (1994) 13–45. For the *ordo matronarum* and women's organizations, see also Purcell (1986).

24 In a fragment of a lost work on marriage by the younger Seneca a woman complains to her husband about her inferior status within the *conventus* in comparison to that of certain other women: 'that woman appears in public with richer dress, and this one here is honoured by all; poor me, I am despised in the gathering of women' ('illa ornatior procedit in publicum, haec honoratur ab omnibus, ego in conventu feminarum misella despicior', Sen. *De Matrimonio* fr. XIII.49 (Haase) = Hier. *Adv. Iov.* 1.47). Suet. *Galb.* 5 mentions a quarrel at the *conventus matronarum* between Agrippina Minor and the mother-in-law of the later emperor Galba. In *SHA Elegab.* 4.3 the *conventus matronalis* is reported to have met on the Quirinal on certain festal days and 'whenever a matron was presented with the insignia of a "consular marriage" – bestowed by the early emperors on their kinswomen, particularly on those whose husbands were not nobles, in order that they might not lose their noble rank' ('si umquam aliqua matrona consularis coniugii ornamentis esset donata, quod veteres imperatores adfinibus detulerunt et iis maxime quae nobilitatos maritos non habuerant, ne innobilitatae remanerent'); see also n. 17 above. *CIL* VI 997 (= *ILS* 324) is a dedication of the empress Sabina to the *matronae*, later renewed by Julia Domna; it perhaps stemmed from a building in which they met. For the competition of status in the *consortia matronarum*, see Hier. *Ep.* 22.16. Some Italian municipalities seem to have had similar organizations of women (possibly of decurial class); for example, the *curia mulierum* of Lanuvium is mentioned in *CIL* XIV 2120 (= *ILS* 6199) as receiving a benefaction (a double banquet) alongside the decurions and the Augustales; for more examples see Purcell (1986) 84–5.

25 *SHA Elegab.* 4.4: 'senatus consulta ridicula de legibus matronalibus: quae quo vestitu incederet, quae cui cederet, quae ad cuius osculum veniret, quae pilento, quae equo, quae sagmario, quae asino veheretur, quae carpento mulari, quae boum, quae sella veheretur, et utrum pellicia an ossea an eborata an argentata, et quae aurum vel gemmas in calciamentis haberent'. On the problem of this *senaculum* or *mulierum senatus* see Straub, J. S. (1966) '*Senaculum, id est mulierum senatus*', in *Historia-Augusta-Colloquium* 3 (1964–5), Bonn: Habelt, pp. 221–40, who believes that the *senaculum* was a building which may have been established by the emperor for the gatherings of senatorial

women; his suggestion that the passage in the *SHA* is inspired by Jerome's ridicule of the 'senate' of Christian women meeting in his days is not convincing. The emperor Gallienus was said to have 'invited the matrons into his council' (*SHA Gall.* 16.6: 'matronas ad consilium suum rogavit'), and in the early empire Claudius was said to have received an embassy 'in the presence of the matrons' (*Act. Isid.* col. ii. 7–8: παρουσῶν δὲ καὶ τῶν ματρωνῶν), but we cannot tell whether this refers to some organization of *matronae* (for the *Acta Isidori* see Musurillo (1954) 19ff.). The emperor Aurelian is credited with the plan to restore the senate (the building?) to the matrons, giving pride of place to priestesses among them: 'He had planned to restore to the matrons their senate, or rather *senaculum*, with the provision that those should rank first therein who had attained to priesthoods with the senate's approval' (*SHA Aur.* 49.6: 'Senatum sive senaculum matronis reddi voluerat, ita ut primae illic quae sacerdotia senatu auctore meruissent') and Jerome, in a letter to Marcella (*Ep.* 43.3), mentions the *senatus matronarum* as meeting daily, though he probably means a congregation of Christian women; see also *Ep.* 108.33, where he praises Paula as *Romani prima senatus*. The elder Pliny ridicules the *mulierum . . . senatusconsultum* (Plin. *NH* 37.85) which settled the question as to which gemstone was supreme.

26 That this division of society was a common one is reflected by descriptions of what was regarded as a mixed crowd: see, for instance, Stat. *Silv.* 1.6.43–4 (about a banquet given by the emperor Domitian): 'One table serves every order alike, children, women, people, knights and senators' ('una vescitur omnis ordo mensa/ parvi, femina, plebs, eques, senatus'; see also Stat. *Silv.* 1.2.233–5). Note that these groups are each called an *ordo*; this 'order' of women differs from the 'order' of matrons discussed above in that (at least in theory) it includes women of all ranks.

27 For Augustus' regulation of seating in the theatre and amphitheatre, see chapter 2, pp. 45ff.

28 For the moral behaviour expected of the respectable married Roman woman, see, e.g., Treggiari (1991) 183–261, who discusses the ideals and realities of marriage on the part of both partners, and von Hesberg-Tonn (1983) and Williams (1958); see also Lightman and Zeisel (1977) for the ideal of the *univira*. The younger Seneca praises the retired way of life of his aunt Helvia with the following words: 'throughout the sixteen years during which her husband was governor of Egypt she was never seen in public, never admitted a native to her house, sought no favour from her husband, nor suffered any to be sought from herself. And so a province that was gossipy and ingenious in devising insults for its rulers . . . respected her as a singular example of blamelessness . . . It would be much to her credit if she had won the approval of the province for sixteen years; that she had escaped its notice is still more.' (Sen. *Cons. Helv.* 19.6: 'per sedecim annos, quibus Aegyptum maritus eius optinuit, numquam in publico conspecta est, neminem provincialem domum suam admisit, nihil a viro petit, nihil a se peti passa est. Itaque loquax et in contumelias praefectorum ingeniosa provincia . . . velut unicum sanctatis exemplum suspexit. . . . Multum erat, si per XVI annos illam provincia probasset; plus est, quod ignoravit'; for her old-fashioned modesty and her retired way of life, see also 19.2–5).

29 Ovid. *AA* 1.31–2: 'Este procul, vittae tenues, insigne pudoris / quaeque tegis medios, instita longa, pedes.' Mart. *Ep.* 1.35.8–9 speaks of 'stolatum . . . pudorem' and Val. Max. 8.3 of 'the modesty befitting the stola' (*verecundia stolae*). In view of the austerity of the dress and its association with chastity and respectability the translation 'Odysseus in petticoats' for Caligula's nickname for Livia, 'Ulixes stolatus', (Suet. *Cal.* 23.2; translated by J. C. Rolfe in the Loeb edition) is off the mark. For Augustus' legislation on marriage and adultery, see Mette-Dittmann (1991), Baltrusch (1989) 162–89 and Treggiari (1991) 60–80 and 277–98 with further references. For the distinctive dress of the *matrona* and its connotation of matronly chastity, see Zanker (1990) 167–70, Scholz

(1992) and Sebesta (1994) 48–50. For female *infamia* marked by the *toga*, see Gardner (1990) 32, 129, 245 and 251–2.

30 Plin. *NH* 33.40 (in a section about the use of gold): 'etiamne pedibus induetur atque inter stolam plebemque hunc medium feminarum equestrem ordinem faciet?'. For a similar description of male equestrian rank, see *NH* 33.29: 'a third order, intermediate between the common people and the senate' ('tertium ordinem mediumque plebei et patribus'). For gold ornaments on women's shoes or on their sandal-straps, see *SHA Elegab.* 4.4, where this was subject to regulation of the so-called 'women's senate'; like gold on the shoes of men it was probably not simply meant as a decoration but signified the wealth and rank of the woman wearing it. As regards the confusion about the exact meaning of *matrona* the definition given by Festus is not very helpful: 'matronas apellabant eas fere quibus stolas habendi ius erat' ('they called *matronae* those women more or less who had the right to wear the *stola*'; Festus, p. 112 Lindsay). Aul. Gell. *NA* 18.6', in a discussion of the right meaning of the words *matrona* and *materfamilias*, shows that already in antiquity there was uncertainty about the meaning and proper use of these terms. For the suggestion that the social rank of a woman might be indicated by stripes woven into her *stola*, see Zanker (1990) 169 and Scholz (1992) 25–6. For the shift in meaning of *stola*, used exclusively of senatorial women from the Flavian period to the end of the second century AD, see Scholz (1992) 13–20. In inscriptions of the late second and third centuries AD the titles ματρῶνα στολᾶτα and *femina stolata* seem to apply to (landowning) women married to equestrians: see Holtheide, B. (1980) 'Matrona Stolata – Femina Stolata', *ZPE* 38: 127–31.

2 THE EDUCATION OF UPPER-CLASS WOMEN: OPPORTUNITIES AND IMPEDIMENTS

1 For a detailed discussion of these passages, see chapter 3, p. 78 (Cornelia) and pp. 84ff. (Sempronia).

2 Rawson (1997) and Rawson (1997) 'Representations of Roman children and childhood', *Antichthon* 31: 74–95 draws attention to a discrepancy between Latin literature and visual art in this respect, visual art showing a growing taste for representations of children (mostly boys) during the empire.

3 The most comprehensive account of ancient education still is that of Marrou (1965), but Clarke (1971) is clearer in the discussion of its social implications; for the place of education in Greek and Roman society see also Christes (1975). Bonner (1977) gives a detailed description of Roman education, but is somewhat outdated in his social judgements; for intellectual life in the late republic, see Rawson (1985).

4 For grammarians and the grammatical curriculum, see Clarke (1971) 11–28, Bonner (1977) 47–64 and 189–249, Rawson (1985) 117–31 and 267–81; though 'grammar' is, of course, a misleading translation to denote the curriculum of the *grammaticus*, it will be used here for reasons of convenience. For the *progymnasmata*, preliminary exercises graded in order of difficulty which prepared for the study of rhetoric, see Quint. 1.9, Clarke (1971) 25–6 and 36–9, and Bonner (1977) 250–3. In the early empire the Latin grammarians usually taught the elementary exercises and the rhetorician the more difficult ones. Quint. 2.1.1–3 deplores the tendency, apparent in his days, for grammarians to take over all preliminary exercises (not only the elementary ones), thus encroaching on the field of the teacher of rhetoric.

5 For the 'grand tour' to the Greek world, see Bonner (1977) 90–6, Clarke (1971) 76–7 and Rawson (1985) 9–13.

6 On the obscure terminology and the lack of clearness in the distinction between the *magister* and the *grammaticus*, see Harris (1989) 234–5. On variations in age: Clarke (1971) 6, Kleijwegt (1991) 90 and 117–20; also Bonner (1977) 136–7 allows for some

variation in the age of pupils attending a *grammaticus* or a rhetorician. Quint. 1.1.15–24 criticizes the custom of waiting until the child was 7 years old before starting elementary education. Some examples of youthful students: Cicero's nephew Quintus received rhetorical training at the age of 12 or 13 (see Cic. *Q. fr.* 3.1.14 and 3.3.4 and Bonner (1977) 30) and Quintilian's elder son had studied both Greek and Latin literature before he died at the age of 9 (Quint. 6 *proem.* 9–11); but these boys can hardly be called average pupils.

7 For the ideals of early Roman education within the family, see Plut. *Cat. Ma.* 20; Tac. *Dial.* 28; Bonner (1977) 3–19; Marrou (1965) 339–55. The personal involvement of the father (and, for that matter, the mother), the emphasis on discipline and moral training and the father's attempt to form his sons after his own image were characteristic.

8 For the *artes liberales* see Clarke (1971) 2–5 and Rawson (1985) 117. Dialectic, though always considered as one of the *artes liberales*, is in a somewhat unusual position as it is also regarded as a part of philosophy. Being vocational subjects, medicine and architecture are usually excluded, though they were included by Varro in the nine books of his *Disciplinae*. For the modest role of mathematics in Roman education, see Bonner (1977) 77–9, Clarke (1971) 45–54 and Rawson (1985) 156; its teaching was mostly left to professional mathematicians or to philosophers.

9 For the introduction of schools of Latin rhetoric, see Clarke (1971) 30–2, Bonner (1977) 65–6 and 71, Christes (1975) 159; see also Wallace-Hadrill (1983) 30–8. The grammarian Q. Caecilius Epirota (*RE* 3 Caecilius 53 col. 1201, *PIR*² C 42), a freedman of Atticus and the former tutor of his daughter, was, according to Suet. *Gramm.* 16, the first to start reading Virgil and other recent poets at his school; see Quinn (1982) 110–12, also Clarke (1971) 19–20 and Bonner (1977) 213.

10 For the separation between the *grammaticus Graecus* and the *grammaticus Latinus* in the early empire, see Bonner (1977) 57. For the decrease of the importance of Greek in Roman education, see Marrou (1965) 379ff. and Rawson (1985) 318. Clarke (1971) 14–16 and Bonner (1977) 44–5 suggest that Roman children generally grew up as bilinguals because of the presence of Greek slaves (especially nurses and pedagogues). However, though presumably many Romans were able to speak a sort of pidgin-Greek, this should, to my mind, not be confused with the knowledge of the Greek language and literature that was part of the education of the upper classes. Despite the Hellenizing fashion of the later first and second centuries AD (see Wallace-Hadrill (1983) 175–89 and Boatwright (1987) 202–12), fluency in both languages and erudition in Greek literature were rare outside the upper classes.

11 For literary erudition as a mark of distinction of the upper classes see, e.g., Hopkins, K. (1991) 'Conquest by book', in Beard *et al.* (1991) 142–4, Kleijwegt (1991) 83–8, Harris (1989) 250–1, Jones (1986) 149ff. and Leppin, H. (1992) 'Die Laus Pisonis als Zeugnis senatorischer Mentalität', *Klio* 74: 234–5; see also chapter 1, n. 3. For education as one of the channels of upward social mobility, see Hopkins (1974).

12 For the chairs of Latin and Greek rhetoric at Rome, see Suet. *Vesp.* 18. Quintilian was the first Latin rhetorician to receive such a state appointment, with a salary of 100,000 sesterces a year: see Clarke (1971) 8–9, Bonner (1977) 161 (and 146–62 on fee-paying and paid appointments in general). For Pliny's help in founding a school in Comum and his financial contribution to it, see *Ep.* 4.13 (discussed on pp. 25f.); he mentions in passing that in other municipalities teachers were hired publicly (*Ep.* 4.13.6: 'multis in locis . . . in quibus praeceptores publice conducuntur'); see also Gell. *NA* 16.6.1–12 (the pretentious grammarian of Brundisium), Harris (1989) 241–2 and Dyson (1992) 192. However, these things seem to have happened only occasionally and they are far from constituting an established education system. For libraries, see pp. 53ff.

13 Whereas less wealthy families depended on (elementary and 'grammar') schools to educate their children, upper-class families had a choice between schools and private

tutors. Though home-tuition seems to have been the rule among the upper classes, Quint. 1.2 prefers schools to private tuition for upper-class boys too; see also Dio 52.26.1. According to Suet. *Gramm.* 3 there were more than twenty ('grammar') schools in Rome by the end of the republic; for schools in the late republic and the first two centuries of the empire, see Harris (1989) 233–48.

14 For an optimistic view, see Marrou (1965) 389ff.; see also Bonner (1977) 34 and Dyson (1992) 190–1 (about educational facilities in municipal Italy). For criticism of this optimism, see Harris (1989) 175–284, especially pp. 233ff.; also Kleijwegt (1991) 76–83. Reactions to Harris' book, collected in Beard *et al.* (1991), do not seriously challenge his low estimate of literacy, but disagree with other aspects, for instance, with the functions of writing as described by Harris; cf. Beard's contribution on the 'symbolic' functions of writing and her ideas about a 'literate mentality', Beard, M. (1991) '*Ancient literacy* and the function of the written word in Roman religion', in Beard *et al.* (1991) 35–57. Bowman, A. K. (1991) 'Literacy in the Roman empire: mass and mode', in Beard *et al.* (1991) 119–31, contends that, though Harris is, of course, right in saying that full literacy of the masses of the population in the Roman empire never existed, this does not contradict the fact that Roman society during the late republic and the empire was thoroughly dependent on writing. Even if only a minority of the population may have been fully literate, writing was the basis of the organization of society in all its facets, and thus it deeply influenced also the lives of illiterate and semi-literate persons.

15 For literacy and gender in the ancient world: Harris (1989) 22–4, also 48, 67, 96, 103, 106–8, 110, 114, 140, 143, 173, 239–40, 252–3, 262–6, 270–1 and 279–80. Duncan-Jones (1977) notes that age-rounding (which he takes for an indication of illiteracy) was more frequent among women than among men, especially in the servile classes.

16 For a belief in equal opportunities, see Marrou (1965) 391 and 400; also Bonner (1977) 27–8, 107, 135–6 is optimistic; against this view, Harris (1989) contends that there was a low level of literacy among women in the Roman empire.

17 For complete literacy among the Roman upper classes, probably including women, see Harris (1989) 248–53; also Dyson (1992) 191. For a discussion of the reasons why illiteracy would probably be rare among upper-class women during our period, see chapter 3, pp. 71ff.

18 For working women (most of them of freed or servile status; see n. 4 of the introduction to this study), see Kampen (1981a), Treggiari (1976), Bradley (1991) 13–36 (on *nutrices*) and 103–24 (on child-labour, including some female slaves), Evans (1991) 117–65, and Gardner (1990) 233–55; Joshel, S. R. (1992) *Work, Identity, and Legal Status at Rome: A Study of the Occupational Inscriptions*, Norman: University of Oklahoma Press, is a thought-provoking study of the use of occupational inscriptions for the social history of muted groups (here working people, among whom working women).

19 For the age of upper-class girls at marriage, see chapter 1, n. 9.

20 Most evidence comes from Rome during the late republic and the principate. See, for example: Hor. *Sat.* 1.10.91, 'I bid you howl amidst the high-backed chairs of your female pupils' ('discipularum inter iubeo plorare cathedras') used contemptuously for bad poets or literary men and implying that the education of girls was taken less seriously than that of boys; Ovid *Trist.* 2.369–70 about Menander, 'he is usually read by boys and girls' ('solet hic pueris virginibusque legi'), refers to the teachings of a *grammaticus*, but may imply home-tuition; the story of early republican Verginia attending school when she was of (nearly) marriageable age, as told by Dion. Hal. 11.28.3 and Liv. 3.44.4 ('virginem adultam') and 6 (the *litterarum ludi* in the forum; thus, strictly speaking, elementary education), may perhaps be taken as evidence for the practice in Livy's and Dionysius' own days – at least, they do not find it unusual for a grown girl to attend school; other texts are Juv. 14.209, 'this is what every girl learns

before her ABC' ('hoc discunt omnes ante alpha et beta puellae'); Mart. *Ep.* 3.69.8, 'a pueris debent virginibusque legi' (about the poetry of a certain Cosconius, which is fit for schoolboys and girls); Mart. *Ep.* 8.3.15–16, a *magister* reading poetry (epic and tragedy, which were part of the curriculum of a *grammaticus*) to a 'grown girl and a well-behaved boy' ('grandis virgo bonusque puer'); Mart. *Ep.* 9.68.2 about the *ludi magister* (of the elementary school) who is called 'hated by both boys and girls' ('invisum pueris virginibusque'). Apuleius *Met.* 9.17 mentions a baker's wife (*pistoris uxor*) and a wife of a *decurio* who had been at school together. On the basis of Martial's *Ep.* 8.3.15–16 Bonner (1977) 136 believes that some girls after receiving home-tuition for the elementary phase of their education would be sent to a 'good grammar school to complete their education'. This is unconvincing; it rather seems that girls might attend school both at the elementary and, less frequently, at the grammar level, possibly continuing school until puberty. For inscriptions (epitaphs) testifying to girls' proficiency in various fields of education, see chapter 3, n. 71.

21 For the *paedagogus* of Attica, who was about 5 or 6 at that time, see Cic. *Att.* 12.33; for her studies in grammar, see p. 36. It is unclear whether her pedagogue actually taught her himself. The word *paedagogus* is mostly used for a child-minder, who accompanied the child to school and supervised his (or her) studies and morals, but he sometimes also acted as an elementary teacher himself: see Bonner (1977) 37–45. For some inscriptions mentioning a *paedagogus* of a girl, see *CIL* VI 2210 (= *ILS* 4999), 6327, 9754 and 33787, *CIL* X 6561; for *paedagogi* of girls see also Bradley (1991) 47–8 and 51–5, who on the basis of inscriptions rather boldly assumes that about one girl to every two boys had a pedagogue; however, not all these pedagogues were teachers. For representations of girls receiving lessons on *sarcophagi* or *columbaria* from Rome, see Marrou (1938) no. 1 (a girl reading before a teacher, late republic or early empire), 8 (a girl being taught by a woman, perhaps her mother, in the presence of a Muse), and 13 (a girl at her writing-lesson supervised by her mother in the presence of some Muses, first half of the third century AD). These girls were not necessarily all from families without sons. Minicia Marcella (Plin. *Ep.* 5.16) will be discussed more fully in chapter 3 (pp. 60f.).

22 Strabo 14.1.48 (650). According to Strabo, who himself had been a pupil of Aristodemus, he taught both rhetoric and grammar in his home-town: the former in the morning and the latter in the evening. But 'at Rome, when he was in charge of the children of Pompey the Great, he was content with the teaching of grammar' (ἐν δὲ τῇ Ῥώμῃ τῶν Μάγνου παίδων ἐπιστατῶν ἠρκεῖτο τῇ γραμματικῇ σχολῇ). The three children of Cn. Pompeius Magnus and his third wife Mucia were: Gnaeus, born about 79 BC (*RE* 21 Pompeius 32 cols 2211–13), their younger son Sextus (*RE* 21 Pompeius 33 cols 2213–50) and their only daughter Pompeia (*RE* 21 Pompeia 54 cols 2263–4). See also *Dig.* 32.62: 'the male sex always includes the female' ('semper sexus masculinus etiam femininum sexum continet').

23 Plut. *Quaest. Conv.* 9.1.3 (*Mor.* 737B): τὸν διδάσκαλον τῆς θυγατρὸς ἀπόδειξιν διδόντα βιβλίου κομισθέντος ἐνδοῦναι τῇ παιδὶ τοιαύτην ἀρχήν: ἤλυθες ἐκ πολέμου, ὡς ὤφελες αὐτόθ᾽ ὀλέσθαι. The line is from Hom. *Il.* 3.428. Though the tactless quotation was probably not premeditated, one wonders what little Pompeia may have thought of her father, who had been away for more than four years campaigning in the East and on his return in 62–61 BC straight away divorced her mother, Mucia.

24 Homer was usually studied as the first author in the Greek 'grammar' course at Rome: cf. Clarke (1971) 18, Bonner (1977) 212–13 and Quint. 1.8.5; the *Iliad* would be read first. Without additional information we cannot be more precise about Pompeia's level of education at the time: διδάσκαλος is used for an elementary teacher, but also for a teacher of more advanced education (Harris (1989) 235). Her proficiency in reading Homer is indicative of the 'grammar' phase, but in home-tuition the distinction

between these two phases may have been vague. As Pompeia was probably conceived after her father's return from Spain in 71 BC, she was not yet 10 years old when he returned from the East; in 59 BC she was engaged to Faustus Sulla, the son of the dictator, and eventually married him in 54 or 53 BC. Because of her long engagement Marshall (1987) suggests that she may have been born as late as 68 or 67 BC and, therefore, was not of marriageable age until the middle 50s BC, but this would make her only 6 or 7 years old at the time of her father's return from the East, which seems incredibly young for reading Homer in the way she did.

25 Suet. *Gramm.* 17. The freedman M. Verrius Flaccus (*RE* 8 Verrius 2 cols 1636–45), a well-known *grammaticus* and a prolific writer, was famous for his method of teaching: he stimulated his pupils by making them compete with each other in writing on set subjects and by putting up prizes for the victor.

26 Cf. Suet. *Aug.* 64.2: 'Filiam et neptes ita instituit, ut etiam lanificio assuefaceret vetaretque loqui aut agere quicquam nisi propalam et quod in diurnos commentarios referretur.' His grandsons, however, he taught 'reading, swimming and the other elements of education, for the most part himself, taking special pains to train them to imitate his own handwriting' (64.3: 'Nepotes et litteras et natare aliaque rudimenta per se plerumque docuit, ac nihil aeque elaboravit quam ut imitarentur chirographum suum'). In the education of his grandsons Augustus seems to have imitated the ideals of early Roman education, such as that of the elder Cato: see Plut. *Cat. Ma.* 20 and n. 7 above.

27 See, e.g., Ovid *Met.* 15.834: 'exemploque suo mores reget'. For his simple style of living, see Suet. *Aug.* 73, who relates, among other things, that at home he used to wear simple clothes 'made by his sister, wife, daughter or granddaughters'; for Augustus setting the example of traditional morality see also Zanker (1990) 164–70.

28 Julia: Macr. *Sat.* 2.5.2: 'litterarum amor multaque eruditio, quod in illa domo facile erat'. Agrippina Maior: Suet. *Aug.* 86: 'quadam epistula Agrippinae neptis ingenium conlaudans: "Sed opus est", inquit, "dare te operam, ne moleste scribas et loquaris"' (Malcovati, H. (1962⁴) *Imperatoris Caesaris Augusti Operum Fragmenta*, Torino: In Aedibus Paraviae, p. 18, no. 25). Suetonius quotes from this letter to Agrippina in his discussion of Augustus' rhetorical preference and his criticism of both the archaizing tendency and the ornate style fashionable at the time; therefore, his praise of his granddaughter's 'talent' (*ingenium*) should be taken to refer to her rhetorical talent. Tiberius when censuring her for her outspokenness was said to have done so by quoting a Greek verse: see Tac. *Ann.* 4.52.2 and Suet. *Tib.* 53.1. For Suetonius' access to the letters of Augustus, see Wallace-Hadrill (1983) 91–6.

29 For Augustus' style of speaking and writing, see Suet. *Aug.* 86, Bardon (1940) 7–14 and Rawson (1985) 319. As has been said above (n. 25), the *grammaticus* of her brothers, M. Verrius Flaccus, set his pupils exercises in prose-composition, perhaps the *progymnasmata* which, strictly speaking, belonged to the field of the rhetorician (see above, n. 4). Of course, in the case of home-tuition the transition between the teachings of the grammarian and the rhetorician would be fluid. Whether Verrius Flaccus also taught Agrippina and Julia cannot be ascertained.

30 For the education of Paula, see Hier. *Ep.* 107.4 and chapter 3, p. 63. She was expected to learn her alphabet with the help of a set of ivory letters, as was advised by Quintilian (Quint. 1.1.26). A lively view on what actually went on in schools in late antiquity is offered by the *hermeneumata*, 'school colloquies' dating from the third and fourth centuries AD, which present school scenes and other scenes from the daily life of children: see Dionisotti (1987). As regards the grammatical curriculum, girls seem to have read the same authors as boys, such as Homer (Plut. *Mor.* 737B), Menander (Ovid *Trist.* 2.369–70), epic and tragedy (Mart. *Ep.* 8.3). In the fourth century AD we find the 12-year-old Maria, daughter of Stilicho and Serena, under her mother's guidance never ceasing 'to

unroll the writers of Rome and Greece' ('Latios nec volvere libros / desinit aut Graios, ipsa genetrice magistra'; only Homer and Sappho are mentioned by name): see Claudian *Epithal.* 232ff.

31 Unfortunately, there is no direct information about her education during girlhood. For a detailed discussion of Cornelia, see chapter 3, pp. 64ff., where biographical details are also provided; for her patronage of Greek men of learning, see chapter 4, pp. 97f.; for her (disputed) letter, see chapter 6, pp. 193ff.

32 For early Roman upbringing of girls: Bonner (1977) 7–8; on pp. 12–25 he describes changes in the education during the period in question.

33 As we have seen (p. 19), in the period before the great Latin poetry was written, *grammatici* taught chiefly Greek poetry. The literary education of Cornelia, like that of most men of her family, was to a large extent based on Greek literature – which explains her ease in dealing with Greek scholars and with the tutors of her sons later in life.

34 Suet. *Gramm.* 4 and Clarke (1971) 11. Cornelia's excellent education may not have been as exceptional as Harris (1989) 173 suggests; Laelia, the eldest daughter of the orator C. Laelius (*cos* 140 BC), seems to have received a similar education in Latin rhetoric: see below n. 51 and chapter 3, pp. 76f.

35 For girls attending school see n. 20 above; for inscriptions praising (sub-élite) girls for their education or their proficiency in various cultural accomplishments, see chapter 3, n. 71. For education in the liberal arts as a regular part of the upbringing of a girl of a well-to-do family in the Hadrianic period, see *Dig.* 27.2.4 (Julianus). Also for the Greek world an increase in literacy and educational opportunities for women has been noted in the Hellenistic and Roman periods: see Pomeroy (1977), Cole (1981) and Pomeroy, S. B. (1981) 'Women in Roman Egypt: a preliminary study based on papyri', in Foley (1981) 303–22.

36 Marrou (1965) 364 suggests that music-lessons were appreciated for girls, but see chapter 3, pp. 81ff.

37 See in this chapter, for instance, the anonymous woman addressed by Nicomachus (pp. 38ff.), Seneca's mother Helvia (pp. 40f.) and Cicero's friend Caerellia (p. 55).

38 For Julia Domna see chapter 4, pp. 122ff. However, there are no indications that she studied rhetoric as a girl. For the well-known speech of Hortensia, see Quint. 1.1.6, Val. Max. 8.3.3 and App. *BC* 32–3; see also Hemelrijk (1987). Her proficiency in rhetoric seems due to an inherited talent, and to the influence and example of her father, rather than indicating a trend for girls to receive rhetorical education. Another exception may have been Nero's last wife, Statilia Messalina (*FOS* 730, *PIR*[1] S 625), who, according to the scholiast on Juvenal 6.434, was known for her eloquence ('she applied herself to practising rhetoric to the point of studying the art of declamation', 'consecata est usum eloquentiae usque ad studium declamandi').

39 According to Dyson (1992) 55 and 96–8 the integration of the Italian municipalities into the Roman system was completed by Octavian. Dyson, S. L. (1992) 'Age, sex, and status: the view from the Roman rotary club', *EMC/CV* 36 n.s. 11: 369–85 suggests that in the Italian municipalities upper-class women, as a rule, played a larger role in public life than they did in Rome. Because they had fewer opportunities than men for emigration, their control of landed resources, their political connections and their social status made them more important in their home-town. For honorary inscriptions for women in the towns of Roman Italy, see Forbis (1990).

40 Though a freedman's son, Horace received his grammar education in Rome and not at his native Venusia; see Hor. *Sat.* 1.6.76–8: 'to be taught those studies that any knight or senator would have his own offspring taught' ('docendum/ artis, quas doceat quivis eques atque senator/ semet prognatos'). Also Sen. *Cons. Helv.* 6.2 speaks of 'a desire for liberal studies' ('liberalium studiorum cupiditas') as one of the reasons for migration

from the *municipia* and *coloniae* to Rome. However, many of the great poets came to Rome at a more advanced age, which presupposes a solid literary education in their home-towns or in a larger centre in the neighbourhood; see [Suet.] *Vita Vergil.* 1–8: Virgil, a native of Mantua, studied in Cremona till he assumed the *toga virilis*, then in Milan, and from there he moved to Rome. Wiseman (1983) contends that in many Italian towns literary culture flourished at an earlier date than in Rome. For local education and the old-fashioned life-style of the Italian municipalities, see Dyson (1992) 190–3 and 198.

41 Plin. *Ep.* 4.13. As the boys whose education is discussed were still under age (*praetextati*), it seems most likely that the tuition by a *grammaticus* is meant in this letter; also the emphasis on the moral education of the boys points in this direction; see Harris (1989) 242, n. 359: 'the point of the endowment was probably to allow the hiring of a well-qualified *grammaticus*'. However, Sherwin-White (1966) 289 assumes that a *rhetor latinus* is meant. The word *praeceptor* does not help us in this matter, as it may be used both for a teacher of grammar and for a teacher of rhetoric: for instance, in Plin. *Ep.* 3.3 *praeceptor* is used first for a teacher of grammar, as contrasted to the *rhetor latinus* (3.3.3), but at the end of the letter it denotes the rhetorician. Kleijwegt (1991) 80–2, while admitting that it is unclear whether the study of grammar or rhetoric is meant, calls it a 'grammar school' (p. 82). In an inscription of unknown date (*CIL* V 5278) a *grammaticus* is honoured by the municipality of Comum with the *ornamenta decurionalia*. Was he perhaps a grammarian appointed at the school founded by Pliny?

42 Harris (1989) 242: 'the leading citizens'. Pliny calls the father of one of the boys who studied in Milan *municeps* (fellow-citizen, *Ep.* 4.13.3) without adding his rank; but note that the same word *municeps* is used for his friend, Romatius Firmus, who was a *decurio* (*Ep.* 1.19). However, some of the fathers may have been well-to-do and ambitious merchants or even freedmen.

43 For the census qualification for decurions in Comum, see Plin. *Ep.* 1.19. For Verrius Flaccus, see above, n. 25. Also Quintilian earned 100,000 sesterces a year in his state appointment as a Latin rhetorician: see Suet. *Vesp.* 18.

44 In a letter to Calpurnia Hispulla Pliny writes about his wife: 'who, brought up by your hands and trained in your precepts, has seen only what is pure and moral in your company' (*Ep.* 4.19: 'tuis manibus educatam, tuis praeceptis institutam quae nihil in contubernio tuo viderit nisi sanctum honestumque'); for Calpurnia see pp. 32f. For a similar emphasis on the moral education of a girl, see chapter 3, p. 64. For old-fashioned values and traditions surviving in country districts and provincial towns, see, for instance, Tac. *Ann.* 3.55.4 and *Agr.* 4.2, Plin. *Ep.* 1.14.6 and Mart. *Ep.* 11.16.8. The proverbial chastity of country girls is called into question by Juv. 6.55ff.

45 For the Roman association of illiteracy and ignorance with rusticity, see Harris (1989) 17 and 191; Duncan-Jones (1977) notes that accuracy of age-information on tomb-stones (which he regards as a sign of literacy) deteriorated with the increasing distance from the provincial capital.

46 For the gradations of status within the élite and their sharing the same literary culture, see p. 2 of the introduction to this study.

47 For Attica's pre-marital education, see p. 22. Because of the adoption of her father, Titus Pomponius Atticus, by his maternal uncle Q. Caecilius (see Varro *RR* 2.2.2 and Nepos *Att.* 5.1), she is usually referred to as (Caecilia) Attica by the ancient authors (for instance, in Cicero's letters) rather than as Pomponia, but see *PIR*[1] P 573 and *RE* 21 Pomponia 78 cols 2350–1. She was born in 51 BC and married M. Vipsanius Agrippa (*RE* 9A Vipsanius 2 cols 1226–75) about 37 BC; see Nepos *Att.* 12.1–2. Treggiari (1991) 94 mentions their marriage as an example of intermarriage between senators and *equites*. For her daughter Vipsania Agrippina, see *FOS* 811.

48 Val. Max. 6.1.3 in his section about Roman chastity (*de pudicitia Romanorum*). For Pontius

Aufidianus: *RE* 22 Pontius 19 col. 36. The example of the daughter of Pontius Aufidianus follows on the famous legends of Lucretia and Verginia (6.1 and 2). For suspicions of a love-affair in which a tutor was involved, see also Suet. *Gramm.* 14 and 16. *Dig.* 27.2.4 (Julianus) about an orphaned girl whose ward was forced by her kinsmen to furnish money 'in order that she might be instructed in the liberal arts' ('ut liberalibus artibus institueretur') suggests that, at least in the Hadrianic period, training in the liberal arts formed an accepted part of a wealthy girl's upbringing.

49 For Calpurnia see pp. 32f. For Aemilia Pudentilla see chapter 6, p. 200. She was well educated in both Latin and Greek: see Apul. *Apol.* 30.11, 82.2, 83.1, 84.2, 87.5–6 and 98.8. On the outskirts of the Roman empire, in Vindolanda at Hadrian's Wall in northern Britain, the letters of Claudia Severa, a Romanized woman of equestrian rank, testify to her literacy and to her desire (but limited capacity) to write good Latin. See chapter 6, pp. 191f, 200 and 201f.

50 For Cornelia see chapter 3, pp. 64ff.; for the library, see p. 54. Macrobius *Sat.* 2.5.2 acknowledges the influence of an educated household on the education of girls when he writes that the great erudition of Augustus' daughter Julia was 'not hard to come by in her home' ('in illa domo facile erat').

51 For instance, Hortensia, daughter of the famous orator Q. Hortensius Hortalus, is praised by Quint. 1.1.6 and Val. Max. 8.3.3 for the oration she delivered before the triumvirs in 42 BC (see also App. *BC* 32–3). Both authors ascribe her proficiency to the influence of her father (see Val. Max. 8.3.3: 'Revixit tum muliebri stirpe Q. Hortensius verbisque filiae aspiravit', 'Q. Hortensius was reborn in the female line and came to life again in his daughter's words'). For more examples of girls displaying their fathers' talents, see chapter 3, n. 152. For eloquence running in a family, see Laelia, the daughter of the orator C. Laelius (*cos* 140 BC); she was noted for the excellence of her speech, which, according to Quint. 1.1.6, 'reproduced the elegance of her father's language' ('Laelia C. filia reddidisse in loquendo paternam elegantiam dicitur'), and this was said not only of herself, but also of her daughters and granddaughters. The men of the family all being famous orators, these women reflected their fathers' proficiency (see Cic. *Brut.* 211 and 252, and *De Or.* 3.45; Quint. 1.1.6 and chapter 3, pp. 76f.). Laelia's female descendants were highly educated also in the generations after that of her granddaughters: Cornelia, the wife of Pompey, with whom we opened this chapter, was Laelia's great-great-granddaughter. For the importance of the family background for the education of women in the Greek world, see also Bowie (1994) 439. For the influence of family on women's reading habits, see pp. 52f.

52 For mothers supervising the moral and intellectual education of their sons, see chapter 3, pp. 68f.; for mothers educating their (grand)daughters see, for instance, Seneca encouraging his mother Helvia to take care of the moral instruction of her granddaughter Novatilla, who had just lost her own mother (Sen. *Cons. Helv.* 18.7–8) and Calpurnia Hispulla guiding the moral education of her orphaned niece (Plin. *Ep.* 4.19). For mothers and daughters generally, see Dixon (1990) 210–32. In Christian antiquity, perhaps owing to a more rigid segregation of the sexes, the role of the mother in the supervision of both the moral and the intellectual education of her daughter is more often emphasized, the mother acting as both her daughter's model and her teacher; see Hier. *Ep.* 107.9: 'te habeat magistram' and 128.4: 'timeat ut magistram'. Claud. *Epith.* 230–5 elaborates upon the role of Serena, the wife of Stilicho, in educating her daughter Maria: '[Maria] was listening with rapt attention to the discourse of her saintly mother, drinking in that mother's nature and learning to follow the example of old-world chastity: nor does she cease under that mother's guidance to unroll the works of Latin or Greek writers, all that old Homer sang, or Thracian Orpheus, or that Sappho set to music with Lesbian quill' ('divinae fruitur sermone parentis / maternosque bibit mores exemplaque discit / prisca pudicitiae Latios nec volvere libros / desinit aut

Graios, ipsa genetrice magistra, / Maeonius quaecumque senex aut Thracius Orpheus / aut Mytilenaeo modulatur pectine Sappho'); see also Greg. of Nyssa, *Life of Macrina* 3.

53 Some examples: Caesar's daughter Julia was about 20 when she married Pompey; see Marshall (1987) 92. Agrippina Maior (born around 14 BC) was about 18 when she married Germanicus in AD 4 or 5; for the date of her marriage, see Lindsay, H. (1995) 'A fertile marriage: Agrippina and the chronology of her children by Germanicus', *Latomus* 54: 3–4; and Antonia Minor was nearly 20 when she married Drusus; see Treggiari (1991) 402.

54 As we have seen (p. 22), Pompeia (Pompey's daughter) read Homer before she was 10 years old.

55 For Agrippina Maior see p. 23. McKechnie (1994) argues that Perpetua's competence in rhythmical prose suggests that she was educated at least to the completion of a full grammar course including the preliminary exercises in rhetoric. For Vibia Perpetua see also chapter 6, p. 185 with n. 1; for her age at marriage, see Shaw (1993) 12.

56 Plin. *Ep.* 1.16.6: 'Legit mihi nuper epistulas; uxoris esse dicebat. Plautum vel Terentium metro solutum legi credidi: quae sive uxoris sunt, ut affirmat, sive ipsius, ut negat, pari gloria dignus est, qui aut illa componat aut uxorem, quam virginem accepit, tam doctam politamque reddiderit.' For Pompeius Saturninus, an erudite man of equestrian rank who wrote oratory, history and poetry in an archaizing style, see Sherwin-White (1966) 103; for his wife's letters see also chapter 6, p. 197; for the archaizing tendency of the empire, see Williams (1978) 306–12.

57 For Calpurnia, see *RE* 3 Calpurnius 130 col. 1407, *PIR*² C 326; *FOS* 177. She was Pliny's second (*FOS* 177) or third (Sherwin-White (1966) 559–60) wife. The marriage took place around AD 104, when Pliny was in his early forties and Calpurnia probably in her early or mid teens: see Plin. *Ep.* 8.10 and 11 (about her miscarriage): 'puellariter nescit' and 'culpa aetatis'. Her grandfather, the *eques* L. Calpurnius Fabatus (*RE* 3 Calpurnius 34 col. 1371; *PIR*² C 263, Demougin (1992) 613–14 no. 713), was still alive; he died about AD 111–12 when Pliny was governor of Bithynia. For Calpurnia and her family, see McDermott, W. C. (1971–2) 'Pliny the younger and inscriptions', *CW* 65: 84–5 and Syme (1991) 509–10.

58 For Calpurnia Hispulla, see *RE* 3 Calpurnia 132 col. 1407, *PIR*² C 329. Raepsaet-Charlier, M. T. (1993) 'Nouvelles recherches sur les femmes sénatoriales du Haut-Empire romain', *Klio* 75: 265 no. 418 identifies her with Hispulla (*FOS* 418), the wife of Q. Corellius Rufus (*cos suff.* in AD 78) and the mother of the younger Pliny's correspondent Corellia Hispulla (*FOS* 268; Plin. *Ep.* 3.3), but Syme (1985) 348 and (1991) 508–10 believes that Calpurnia Hispulla was the daughter of Corellius Rufus' wife's sister. In Pliny's letters Calpurnia Hispulla lives with her father, and no husband is mentioned. She was a close friend of Pliny's and arranged her niece's marriage to him, for which Pliny thanks her in a letter (*Ep.* 4.19).

59 Plin. *Ep.* 4.19: 'Accedit his studium litterarum, quod ex mei caritate concepit. Meos libellos habet, lectitat, ediscit etiam. Qua illa sollicitudine, cum videor acturus, quanto, cum egi, gaudio adficitur! Disponit, qui nuntient sibi, quem adsensum, quos clamores excitarim, quem eventum iudicii tulerim. Eadem, si quando recito, in proximo discreta velo sedet laudesque nostras avidissimis auribus excipit. Versus quidem meos cantat etiam formatque cithara non artifice aliquo docente, sed amore, qui magister est optimus.' See also Stat. *Silv.* 3.5.65 about his stepdaughter singing his verses: *mea carmina flectit*.

60 For her letters, see Plin. *Ep.* 6.4 and 7, who praises them for their *suavitas* (see also chapter 6, pp. 197f.). For her finding consolation in his works: Plin. *Ep.* 6.7: 'you write . . . that to console yourself for my absence you hold my writings and often put them in my place by your side' ('scribis . . . quod pro me libellos meos teneas, saepe etiam in vestigio meo colloces').

61 In agreement with contemporary ideals Pliny emphasizes the *concordia* of their marriage (*Ep.* 4.19). He also praises her *caritas, castitas, acumen, frugalitas* (*Ep.* 4.19) and *pietas*
(*Ep.* 10.120). For a study of these terms, see Maniet, A. (1966) 'Pline le Jeune et
Calpurnia', *AC* 35: 149–85. For other letters to or about Calpurnia: Plin. *Ep.* 4.1; 6.4;
6.7; 7.5; 8.10; 8.11; 10.121; he also briefly mentions her in *Ep.* 5.14.8; 8.19.1 and
9.36.4. For Pliny's concept of the ideal wife, see Shelton (1990).
62 It would be interesting to know what became of Calpurnia and her literary interest
after Pliny's death around AD 112, when she was left a childless widow in her early
twenties and likely to remarry – but at that date we have already lost track of her.
63 It is much debated whether during the empire there was an increase in romantic
feelings between husband and wife and a growing sentimentalization of Roman family
life; see, for instance, Veyne (1978), Dixon (1991) 99–113 and (1992b) 69–70 and 83–
90, and Treggiari (1991) 229–61 on *conjugalis amor*. To my mind, one cannot compare,
as Treggiari and Dixon do, the relation between Cicero and Terentia to that of Pliny
and Calpurnia. Apart from occasional outbursts of sentiment, mainly during his exile
or other crises, the relationship between Cicero and Terentia looks like a business
partnership; there is a much greater equality, a much greater freedom of action and a
much greater emotional distance between them than appear in Pliny's letters to his
wife. Whatever the truth of his description of his family life, Pliny's letters show that in
his time an emotional, and even passionate, attachment between husband and wife was
acceptable and perhaps even socially desirable among the senatorial élite. This may
well have been new; before his time open demonstration of an emotional attachment
seems to have been limited to the lower classes and sexual passion was restricted to
relations outside marriage; see the Roman love elegy. Of course, this does not mean
that before Pliny's time senatorial marriages were usually bad or emotionally cold; only
that it was regarded as undignified for a senator to display emotional and sexual
feelings for his wife, as in the anecdote about Cato Maior, who expelled from the senate
a man who kissed his wife in the presence of his daughter, and who prided himself that
he only embraced his wife when a loud peal of thunder occurred (Plut. *Cat. Ma.* 17);
an old-fashioned attitude to marriage is still to be found in the fragments of Seneca's
De Matrimonio (Sen. fr. 13.84–5; Haase). For the contemporary political ideal of *concordia* in the imperial family propagated on the legends of coins, see, e.g., Temporini
(1978).
64 Plut. *Praecepta Coniugalia* 48 (*Mor.* 145B–146), discussed in chapter 3, pp. 62f. Plutarch
himself had an educated wife, whom he addressed in a consolation for the death of
their infant daughter Timoxena (the *consolatio ad uxorem, Mor* 608B–612B). She was said
to have written a work, 'On love of self-adornment' (περὶ φιλοκοσμίας); see Plut.
Praec. Coni. 48 (*Mor.* 145A); see also Bowie (1994) 439.
65 Philo *Leg. Gai.* 319–20 assumes that Augustus instructed his wife Livia. Though this was
her second marriage, Livia was only 19 when she married Augustus who was five years
her elder. In a lost work 'on marriage' (*de matrimonio*) Seneca ascribes Terentia's 'wisdom' to Cicero's influence: see Sen. fr. 13.61 (Haase): 'coniunx egregia et quae de
fontibus Tullianis hauserat sapientiam'.
66 For instance, Apul. *Apol.* 73.1, 'non nihil a me in communibus studiis adiuvantur', 'they
are helped very much by me in their common studies', seems to imply that Apuleius
helped both his future wife Aemilia Pudentilla and her younger son Sicinius Pudens
with their studies. In Porph. *Marc.* 4ff. Porphyrius pictures himself as both the husband
and the teacher of his wife Marcella. In an epitaph (*ILS* 1259) the fourth-century
Paulina praises her husband Praetextatus for being her teacher and mentor in religious
matters; see Lefkowitz, M. (1983) 'Wives and husbands', *G & R* 30: 44–6. Augustinus in
his *Soliloq.* 1.10.17, a discussion between himself and his *ratio*, shows that the ideal still
existed in his days when he describes the model wife as one who is 'pretty, modest,

obliging, educated, or easily educable by you, bringing you just enough dowry – since you despise riches – to make her no kind of burden on your cultivated leisure' ('pulchra, pudica, morigera, litterata, vel quae abs te facile possit erudiri, adferens etiam dotis tantum, quoniam contemnis divitias, quantum eam prorsus nihilo faciat onerosam otio tuo'; translation by Clark (1993) 135). In the fifth century AD Sidonius Apollinaris encouraged Hesperius not to let the thought of his coming marriage distract him from his studies, reminding him 'that in the old times of Marcia and Hortensius, Terentia and Tullius, Calpurnia and Pliny, Pudentilla and Apuleius, Rusticiana and Symmachus, the wives held candles and candlesticks for their husbands while they read or composed' (Sid. *Ep.* 2.10.5: 'quod olim Marcia Hortensio, Terentia Tullio, Calpurnia Plinio, Pudentilla Apuleio, Rusticiana Symmacho legentibus meditantibusque candelas et candelabra tenuerunt').

67 The feathers on their heads are a reminiscence of their mythical victory over the Sirens in a musical contest: see Pausanias 9.34.2 and Wegner (1966) 111–17.

68 For examples see, e.g., Marrou (1938) nos 20, 79–81, 83–5 and 94–102 with the wife in the 'Polyhymnia pose' (no. 102, dated about AD 250–60, belonged to a L. Pullius Peregrinus, centurion and knight; see *ILS* 2669 = *CIL* VI 3558), 108–9 and Zanker (1995) 253–67; for other examples (from the early third century onwards) see Koch, G. and Sichtermann, H. (1982) *Römische Sarkophagen*, Munich: Beck, pp. 197–206; Koch, G. (1993) *Sarkophage der römischen Kaiserzeit*, Darmstadt: Wissenschaftliche Buchgesellschaft, pp. 82–4 and Wegner (1966) 129–38 (late second to fourth century AD); for Polyhymnia, who on sarcophagi is not the Muse of dance, or pantomime, but the Muse of speech and poetry, see Wegner (1966) 95ff. (with Beilage 4 and 5). For Christian examples of a man reading to his wife, who listens while praying (*orans*), see Marrou (1938) nos 86–7 and 91–2. In the Christian era the scheme was also used to represent Christ teaching the church (symbolized by a veiled woman); see Marrou (1938) no. 51 and Zanker (1995) 269. For symbolism of conjugal virtues on Roman sarcophagi of the later second and third centuries AD, see Kampen (1981b).

69 Suet. *Gramm.* 16: 'cum filiam patroni nuptam M. Agrippae doceret, suspectus in ea et ob hoc remotus'. *RE* 9A col. 1247 and Syme (1989) 143 suggest that the incident may have been trumped up in order to facilitate Agrippa's divorce from Attica when a better marriage offered itself: in 28 BC Agrippa married Octavian's niece, the elder Marcella (*FOS* 242). However, these two events are not necessarily connected; Attica had perhaps died before 28 BC; see Leon, E. F. (1962) 'Note on Caecilia Attica', *CB* 38: 35–7 (Leon's attempt to date Attica's birth in 55 instead of 51 BC is unconvincing). For Attica's education as a girl, see pp. 22 and 27; for her tutor Epirota, see above n. 9.

70 A claim to moral responsibility is found in the epitaph of Pudens (*CIL* VI 9449 = *ILS* 1848), who was a freedman of M. Aemilius Lepidus and the *grammaticus* and *procurator* (manager) of his daughter, Aemilia Lepida (*FOS* 30, *PIR*² A 421), during her marriage to Germanicus' son Drusus. On his epitaph, erected by a student of his, Pudens is made to speak in defence of himself: 'I guided her morals; as long as I lived, she remained the daughter-in-law of Caesar' ('moresq(ue) regebam / dum vixi mansit Caesaris illa nurus'). Aemilia Lepida's alleged adulteries with Seianus (Dio 58.3.8) and with a slave (Tac. *Ann.* 6.40) apparently necessitated such a posthumous self-defence by her grammarian. Incidentally, here we have a married woman who, like Attica, probably continued to attend the lessons of the grammarian who taught her when she was a girl (he was her father's freedman). Because of his close relationship with both male and female members of a family a grammarian could act as a go-between, sometimes to his own undoing; see Suet. *Gramm.* 14 about the *grammaticus* Curtius Nicias, who lost favour with Pompey because 'when he had brought a note from Memmius to Pompey's wife with an adulterous proposal, he was betrayed by her' ('cum codicillos Memmi ad Pompei uxorem de stupro pertulisset, proditus ab ea').

71 For an example, see Suet. *Gramm.* 19: the *grammaticus* Scribonius Aphrodisius was bought and set free by the former wife of Octavian, Scribonia (*RE* 2A Scribonia 32 col. 891). We do not know whether she employed him for her own education or for that of one of her children. Before her marriage to Octavian (by whom she became the mother of Julia) she had already been married twice and she had one or perhaps two sons and one daughter (the Cornelia in whose praise Propertius wrote his elegy 4.11); see Syme (1989) 247–9 and 255–7, Leon, E. F. (1951) 'Scribonia and her daughters', *TAPhA* 82: 168–75 and Scheid, J. (1975) 'Scribonia Caesaris et les Julio-Claudiens', *MEFRA* 87: 349–75. For restrictions in women's legal capacity to buy and sell, see chapter 4, pp. 101f. and the literature quoted there.

72 Sen. *Cons. Marc.* 4–5.

73 Lucian *Merc. Cond.* 25: 'it will make people think him a devoted student of Greek learning and in general a person of taste in literary matters' (δόξει γὰρ ἐκ τούτου καὶ φιλομαθὴς τῶν Ἑλληνικῶν μαθημάτων καὶ ὅλως περὶ παιδείαν φιλόκαλος); for Lucian's *De Mercede Conductis* see Jones (1986) 78–84 and 149ff. and Swain (1996) 312ff.

74 Lucian *Merc. Cond.* 36: καίτοι φορητὰ ἴσως τὰ τῶν ἀνδρῶν. αἱ δὲ οὖν γυναῖκες – καὶ γὰρ αὖ καὶ τόδε ὑπὸ τῶν γυναικῶν σπουδάζεται, τὸ εἶναί τινας αὐταῖς πεπαιδευμένους μισθοῦ ὑποτελεῖς συνόντας καὶ τῷ φορείῳ ἑπομένους· ἐν γάρ τι καὶ τοῦτο τῶν ἄλλων καλλωπισμάτων αὐταῖς δοκεῖ, ἢν λέγηται ὡς πεπαιδευμέναι τέ εἰσιν καὶ φιλόσοφοι καὶ ποιοῦσιν ᾄσματα οὐ πολὺ τῆς Σαπφοῦς ἀποδέοντα – διὰ δὴ ταῦτα μισθωτοὺς καὶ αὗται περιάγονται ῥήτορας καὶ γραμματικοὺς καὶ φιλοσόφους, ἀκροῶνται δ᾽ αὐτῶν – πηνίκα; γελοῖον γὰρ καὶ τοῦτο – ἤτοι μεταξὺ κομμούμεναι καὶ τὰς κόμας παραπλεκόμεναι ἢ παρὰ τὸ δεῖπνον· ἄλλοτε γὰρ οὐκ ἄγουσι σχολήν. πολλάκις δὲ καὶ μεταξὺ τοῦ φιλοσόφου τι διεξιόντος ἡ ἅβρα προσελθοῦσα ὤρεξε παρὰ τοῦ μοιχοῦ γραμμάτιον, οἱ δὲ περὶ σωφροσύνης ἐκεῖνοι λόγοι ἑστᾶσι περιμένοντες, ἔστ᾽ ἂν ἐκείνη ἀντιγράψασα τῷ μοιχῷ ἐπαναδράμῃ πρὸς τὴν ἀκρόασιν.

75 Lucian *Merc. Cond.* 33–4.

76 For Nicomachus of Gerasa see Levin (1975) 8–10, Haase (1982) *passim* and Barker (1989) 245–7. For the text of the *Enchiridion* I refer to the edition of Jan, C. von (1962) *Musici Scriptores Graeci*, Hildesheim: Olms (1st edition Leipzig 1895), abbreviated as *MSG*; for an English translation, see Barker (1989) 245–69 and Levin (1994); the *RE* 17 Nikomachus 21 cols 463–4 discusses Nicomachus' better-known *Introductio Arithmetica*, but does not even mention the completely extant *Enchiridium Harmonicum*.

77 See Haase (1982) 159–318, an extensive chapter on 'die Adressatin der musiktheo-retischen Lehrschrift'; on pp. 137ff. he argues that it is a real letter addressed to this lady, not a literary dedication. Though it is not mentioned explicitly that she was *Roman*, this seems most likely. Unlike Greek women Roman upper-class women trav-elled extensively, both by themselves (with a following) and with their husbands; see, e.g., Treggiari (1991) 426–7 and chapter 1, n. 12. For the high status of the unknown addressee of this treatise, see Levin (1975) 17: 'a member of the imperial aristocracy'. McDermott (1977) 192–203 not very convincingly tries to show that the unknown addressee was the empress Plotina, but Temporini (1978) 162 is rightly sceptical. For Nicomachus' humble way of addressing her, see Nicomachus *Ench.* 1 (*MSG* 237.17), 'most noble and august lady' (ἀρίστη καὶ σεμνοτάτη γυναικῶν), ch. 3 (*MSG* 242.14), 'noblest of women and best lover of beauty' (σεμνοτάτη γυναικῶν καὶ φιλοκαλωτάτη), ch. 12 (*MSG* 265.3–4), 'with your accustomed great kindness and thoughtfulness for your friends' (κατὰ τὸν ἡμερώτατόν σου τρόπον καὶ κοινῶν νοημονέστατον); Levin (1975) 17 brackets κοινῶν, but *contra* Haase (1982) 161–287. Haase (1982) 290–2 argues that the plural ὑμᾶς (chapter 1; *MSG* 238.12) denotes the following of this high-born lady.

78 For references to the journey of his addressee and his own travels, see the introductory chapter (1) of the *Enchiridion*.

79 Nicomach. *Ench.* 1 (*MSG* 237.15–238.12): πᾶσαν ὅμως ἐπιρρωστέον ἐστί μοι σπουδὴν σοῦ γε κελευούσης, ἀρίστη καὶ σεμνοτάτη γυναικῶν, κἂν αὐτὰ ψιλὰ τὰ κεφάλαια χωρὶς κατασκευῆς καὶ ποικίλης ἀποδείξεως ἐκθέσθαι σοι κατ᾽ ἐπιδρομήν· ἵνα ὑπὸ μίαν ἔχουσα αὐτὰ σύνοψιν ἐγχειριδίῳ τε ὡσανεὶ χρωμένη τῇ βραχείᾳ ταύτῃ ὑποσημειώσει ὑπομιμνήσκῃ ἐξ αὐτῆς τῶν ἐν ἑκάστῳ κεφαλαίῳ κατὰ πλάτος λεγομένων τε καὶ διδασκομένων. Θεῶν δὲ ἐπιτρεπόντων αὐτίκα μάλα σχολῆς λαβόμενος καὶ τῆς ὁδοιπορίας ἀνάπαυσιν σχὼν συντάξω τέ σοι μείζονα καὶ ἀκριβεστέραν εἰσαγωγὴν περὶ αὐτῶν τούτων καὶ πλήρει τὸ λεγόμενον συλλογισμῷ διηρθρωμένην καὶ ἐν πλείοσι βιβλίοις, καὶ διὰ τῆς πρωτίστης ἀφορμῆς ἀποπέμψω, ἔνθα ἂν διάγειν ὑμᾶς πυνθανώμεθα. For his taking her request as an order: σοῦ γε κελευούσης (*MSG* 237.16) and ἐπέταξας (*MSG* 265.2). The promised work is lost. Nicomachus refers to it several times in his *Enchiridion*; see *MSG* 242.11–7; 260.4ff.; 261.17–18; 264.1–2; 265.5ff. In his introduction to Bower, C. M. and Palisca, C. V. (eds) (1989) *Fundamentals of Music: Anicius Manlius Severinus Boethius*, New Haven: Yale University Press, pp. XXIV–XXIX Bower convincingly argues that the first four books of the *De Institutione Musica* of Boethius are a free Latin translation of this lost Εἰσαγωγὴ μουσική of Nicomachus; see also Bower, C. M. (1978) 'Boethius and Nicomachus an essay concerning the sources of *De Institutione Musica*', *Vivarium* 16: 1–45. The *Excerpta ex Nicomacho* (*MSG* 266–82) may represent extracts from this lost work; for an English translation of the fragments, see Levin (1994) 189–97.

80 Nicomach. *Ench.* 12 (*MSG* 265.1–8): Τῆς δὲ γραφῆς τοιαύτης τῇ ἐπείξει συγγινώσκουσα – σύνοισθα γὰρ, ὅτι ἐν αὐτῇ τῇ ὁδεύσει μοι ἐπέταξας παντοίως μετεώρῳ – κατὰ τὸν ἡμερώτατόν σου τρόπον καὶ κοινῶν νοημονέστατον ἀπόδεξαι μὲν ὡς ἀπαρχήν τινα καὶ ἐξευμενισμόν, προσδέχου δὲ θεῶν ἐπιτρεπόντων πληρεστάτην καὶ παντοίως ἐντελεστάτην τὴν περὶ αὐτῶν τούτων τεχνολογίαν αὐτίκα μάλα σοι ὑπ᾽ ἐμοῦ πεμφθησομένην μετὰ τῆς πρώτης ἀφορμῆς.

81 Ch. 1, *MSG* 238.12–15: τὴν δὲ ἀρχὴν ἐκεῖθέν ποθεν ποιήσομαι ῥᾴονος ἕνεκα παρακολουθήσεως, ὅθεν καὶ ἡνίκα ἐξηγούμην σοι περὶ αὐτῶν τούτων τὴν τῆς διδασκαλίας ἐποιησάμην ἀρχήν. From the use of the imperfect ἐξηγούμην (*MSG* 238.14) Levin (1975) 18 infers that Nicomachus' instruction had consisted of 'protracted discussions' and she suggests that he had taught his unknown mistress arithmetic and geometry before entering upon the subject of harmonics, but Barker (1994) 59 seems to imply that she had only once heard him lecturing on the subject. However, in my opinion ἡνίκα ἐξηγούμην σοι suggests that he had been her teacher.

82 Cf. *MSG* 237.16: σπουδὴν σοῦ γε κελευούσης.

83 For examples of undue attribution of musical discoveries to Pythagoras and for the Aristoxenian sources and terminology used in the *Enchiridion*, see the extensive annotation of the English translation by Barker (1989); see further Burkert, W. (1972) *Lore and Science in Ancient Pythagoreanism*, Cambridge, Mass.: Harvard University Press (on pp. 375–8 he discusses the physical impossibility of Pythagoras' alleged musical discoveries in a smithy, *Enchiridion* chapter 6).

84 See Levin (1975); on p. 14 she calls the treatise 'a sophisticated example of Pythagorean partisanship'. She believes (pp. 87ff.) that Nicomachus' misquotation from Plato's *Timaeus* (ch. 8 of the *Enchiridion*; *MSG* 250.6–11) was deliberate, in order to extoll Pythagoras, but see Barker (1989) 259f., n. 60 for a different interpretation.

85 Barker (1994) believes that the *Enchiridion* bridged the gap between the mathematically sophisticated treatises of the 'Pythagorean' kind, which were designed for a public of specialists, and the empirical approach of the Aristoxenian writings taught at school. Thus, the *Enchiridion* aimed at the generally educated amateur who was familiar with the apparatus and terminology of the Aristoxenian tradition of harmonics (having learned them at school), but as an adult was drawn to the intellectually more

demanding Pythagorean approach with its mathematical and metaphysical speculations.

86 Levin (1975) 18 assumes that Nicomachus instructed her in arithmetic and geometry (subjects which usually preceded the study of harmonics) as well as in musical theory.

87 For a possibly similar relation, see Diogenes Laertius 3.47 speaking to the unknown female addressee of his 'Lives and doctrines of the philosophers': 'Now, as you are an enthusiastic Platonist, and rightly so, and as you eagerly seek out that philosopher's doctrines in preference to all others, I have thought it necessary to give some account of the true nature of his discourses, the arrangement of the dialogues, and the method of his inductive procedure, as far as possible in an elementary manner and in main outline, in order that the facts I have collected respecting his life may not suffer by the omission of his doctrines. For, in the words of the proverb, it would be taking owls to Athens, were I to give you the full particulars' (Loeb trans.) (Φιλοπλάτωνι δέ σοι δικαίως ὑπαρχούσῃ καὶ παρ' ὁντινοῦν τὰ τοῦ φιλοσόφου δόγματα φιλοτίμως ζητούσῃ ἀναγκαῖον ἡγησάμην ὑπογράψαι καὶ τὴν φύσιν τῶν λόγων καὶ τὴν τάξιν τῶν διαλόγων καὶ τὴν ἔφοδον τῆς ἐπαγωγῆς, ὡς οἷόν τε στοιχειωδῶς καὶ ἐπὶ κεφαλαίων, πρὸς τὸ μὴ ἀμοιρεῖν αὐτοῦ τῶν δογμάτων τὴν περὶ τοῦ βίου συναγωγήν· γλαῦκα γὰρ εἰς Ἀθήνας, φασίν, εἰ δέῃ σοι τὰ κατ' εἶδος διηγεῖσθαι); see also Diog. Laert. 10.29 and chapter 4, n. 119.

88 For Helvia see *RE Suppl.* 12 Helvia 22 cols 426–9. For her early education, Sen. *Cons. Helv.* 2.4 and 16.3: 'soundly trained in an old-fashioned and strict household' ('bene in antiqua et severa institutam domo'). For her moral virtues, her loyalty to her family, her chastity, frugality, fertility and modesty, see Sen. *Cons. Helv.* 2.4, 14.3 and 16.3–4. Her marriage and that of her (half-)sister suggest that her family was wealthy and of some standing.

89 M. T. Griffin (1976) 32 believes that the elder Seneca when returning to Rome at some date before AD 5 left his wife Helvia in charge of the family estates (*Cons. Helv.* 14.3), and Seneca himself tells us that his aunt (and not his mother) brought him to Rome when he was a small child (*Cons. Helv.* 19.2). However, we find his mother conversing and studying with him (*Cons. Helv.* 15.1). For Seneca's family background, see also Griffin, M. T. (1972) 'The elder Seneca and Spain', *JRS* 62: 1–19.

90 She had left only two days before Seneca's banishment: see Sen. *Cons. Helv.* 15.2–3. The younger Seneca wrote his *consolatio ad Helviam* addressed to her when he lived in Corsica as an exile (between AD 41 and 49). At that time she had apparently returned to Rome (see 15.3 and 18.9).

91 Sen. *Cons. Helv.* 17.3–4: 'sed quantum tibi patris mei antiquus rigor permisit, omnes bonas artes non quidem comprendisti, attigisti tamen. Utinam quidem virorum optimus, pater meus, minus maiorum consuetudini deditus voluisset te praeceptis sapientiae erudiri potius quam imbui!'

92 Sen. *Cons. Helv.* 17.4: 'thanks to your keen mind, you imbibed more than might have been expected in the time you had; the foundations of all disciplines have been laid' ('Beneficio tamen rapacis ingenii plus quam pro tempore hausisti; iacta sunt disciplinarum omnium fundamenta'). The elder Seneca was opposed to philosophy (see Sen. *Ep.* 108.22: '(pater) philosophiam oderat') and had tried to keep his son, the younger Seneca, from conceiving too great a passion for it, but for different reasons (probably political ambition for his son); see M. T. Griffin (1976) 45–6. For Seneca's motives for opposing his wife's studies, see Sen. *Cons. Helv.* 17.4 and chapter 3, pp. 77f.

93 Sen. *Cons. Helv.* 15.1: 'Ubi conloquia, quorum inexplebilis eram? Ubi studia, quibus libentius quam femina, familiarius quam mater intereram?'

94 Sen. *Cons. Helv.* 17.4. For liberal studies as a defence against fortune, see *Cons. Helv* 17.1–3 and 5. For Seneca's advice to his mother to return to her studies: *Cons. Helv.* 17.3–5.

95 Nepos *Vir. Ill. praef.* 6–8: 'Quem enim Romanorum pudet uxorem ducere in convivium? Aut cuius non mater familias primum locum tenet aedium atque in celebritate versatur? Quod multo fit aliter in Graecia; nam neque in convivium adhibetur nisi propinquorum, neque sedet nisi in interiore parte aedium, quae gynaeconitis appellatur, quo nemo accedit nisi propinqua cognatione coniunctus.' Apart from literary sources on Roman dining habits and the kinds of entertainment involved much can be learned from the remains of Roman houses and their *triclinia*, especially from Pompeii, Herculaneum and other Campanian towns and from villas in the neighbourhood; see also *RE* 7A Triclinium cols 92–101 and Dunbabin (1991). For the absence of gender-differentiation in Roman houses, see Wallace-Hadrill (1988), reprinted in Wallace-Hadrill (1994) 3–61; also chapter 1, p. 9. Walker, S. (1983) 'Women and housing in classical Greece: the archaeological evidence', in Cameron and Kuhrt (1983) 81–91, seems too rigid in distinguishing male and female spheres in Greek houses; for a more subtle approach, see Jameson, M. (1990) 'Private space and the Greek city', in Murray, O. and Price, S. (eds) (1990) *The Greek City: From Homer to Alexander*, Oxford: Clarendon Press, pp. 171–95; for male and female spheres in classical Athens, see also Cohen, D. (1989) 'Seclusion, separation, and the status of women in classical Athens', *G & R* 36: 3–15, Cohen (1991) and Just (1994). For the contrast between Greeks and Romans as regards gender distinctions in housing and at dinner parties, see also Cic. *Verr.* 2.66 and Vitr. 6.7.2–4; Murray, O. (1990) 'Sympotic history', in Murray (1990) 6.

96 For reclining at dinner as a traditional male prerogative, see Isidor. *Etym.* 20.11.9 (from Varro's *De Vita Populi Romani*) and Val. Max. 2.1.2; for some, rather arbitrary, examples of upper-class *matronae* reclining at dinner in mixed company (including stories about the opportunities for adultery offered by drinking in such a company): Cic. *Att.* 5.1, *Fam.* 9.26.2 (about the freedwoman and actress Volumnia Cytheris, who reclined at a dinner where Cicero was present, who was shocked); Ovid. *Am.* 1.4, *AA* 1.229ff. and 3.749ff.; Juv. 6.434; Plin. *NH* 14.141; Suet. *Aug.* 69.1, *Calig.* 24, 25.1 and 36; *CIL* IV 7698b; Plut. *Amat.* 16 (*Mor.* 760A); Dio 48.44.3; for love-affairs in the context of *convivia*, see Yardley, J. C. (1991) 'The symposium in Roman elegy', in Slater (1991) 149–55. The traditional ideal of women sitting at dinner returns in late antiquity; see Rossiter, J. (1991) 'Convivium and villa in late antiquity', in Slater (1991) 206. For children of both sexes sitting at dinner, see Suet. *Claud.* 32 about Claudius' own children and the sons and daughters of distinguished men sitting at the foot of the couches 'after old-fashioned custom' ('more veteri') and Tac. *Ann.* 13.16; on the age for reclining, see Booth, A. (1991) 'The age for reclining and its attendant perils', in Slater (1991) 105–20. Reclining was a sign not only of their coming of age but also of their class: lower-class people sat at table: see, e.g., Dunbabin (1991) 136.

97 For a description of Roman dinner habits, see Balsdon (1969) 32–54. For stories about gladiatorial shows and decapitations during dinner illustrating the decadence and cruelty of the host: Liv. 39.43.3 (a story about the cruelty of L. Quinctius Flamininus); Suet. *Calig.* 32.1; *SHA Verus* 4.8–9, *Elag.* 25.7; Tac. *Ann.* 12.57 (Claudius' banquet at the Fucine lake); Athen. *Deipn.* 4 (153F); Liv. 9.40.17 (a 'custom' attributed to the Campanians), Strabo 5.4.13 (250); Sil. 11.51–4. For excesses and cruelty at dinner, see Paul, G. (1991) 'Symposia and deipna in Plutarch's Lives and in other historical writings', in Slater (1991) 157–69; according to D'Arms (1990) 314 ancient authors in associating dreadful events with dinner parties were fascinated by the connection of opposite poles.

98 For theatrical entertainment, see Jones (1991). For scholarly discourse during dinner: (a caricature) Lucian *Merc. Cond.* 35 (a rhetorician) and 14–18 (a newly hired philosopher invited for his first dinner at the house of his wealthy employer); Tac. *Ann.* 14.16 (philosophers); Suet. *Tib.* 56 (grammarians); *SHA Al. Sev.* 34.6–8 (Ulpian); for cultural entertainment, see also Aul. Gell. *NA* 1.22.5, 2.22.1 and 3.19.1; Juv. 11.179–82 (Homer and Virgil read at a simple dinner party); Plin. *Ep.* 3.5.11 and 6.31.13; Nepos *Att.* 14.1;

Plut. *Mor*. 673B; *SHA Hadr*. 26.4 (tragedies, comedies, Atellan farces, sambuca playing, readers or poets).

99   Plut. *Quaest.Conv*. 7.8 (*Mor*. 711A–13F); for the singing of poetry (Anacreon, Sappho and 'some erotic elegies of more recent poets') see also Aulus Gellius *NA* 19.9.4. For Atticus' dinners see Nepos *Att*. 14.1 ('neque umquam sine aliqua lectione apud eum cenatum est'); for Pliny's preference: Plin. *Ep*. 3.1.9 (about his friend Vestricius Spurinna): comedy; *Ep*. 1.15.2: comedians, a reader and a singer; *Ep*. 9.17: a frugal dinner with a reader, a musician and an actor is contrasted with a vulgar dinner with mimes, clowns and jesters; *Ep*. 9.36.4: a book read, a comedy and music; see also *Epp* 5.19 and 8.1 on readers. New comedy, especially Menander, but also Plautus and Terence, was considered suitable for performance or recitation at dinner; in fact, according to Plut. *Quaest. Conv*. 7.8 (*Mor*. 712B–D) Menander was so much a part of symposia that one could do more easily 'without wine than without Menander' (Plut. *Mor*. 712B); see also Plut. *Comp. Arist. Men*. 3 (*Mor*. 854B–C) and Fantham, E. (1984) 'Roman experience of Menander in the late republic and early empire', *TAPhA* 114: 299–309. It is a matter of debate whether excerpts or whole plays were performed at dinner: see Jones (1991) 193.

100 Plin. *Ep*. 9.36.4: 'Cenanti mihi, si cum uxore vel paucis, liber legitur; post cenam comoedus aut lyristes.' *SHA Pertinax* 12.7: 'when he dined without guests, he would invite his wife and Valerianus, who had been a teacher together with him, in order that he might have a literary conversation' ('cum sine amicis cenaret, adhibebat uxorem suam et Valerianum, qui cum eodem docuerat, ut fabulas litteratas haberet'). P. Helvius Pertinax (emperor in AD 193) was of humble birth and for a short period had been a grammarian; for his wife, see *FOS* 383. However, the fact that almost the same words are used in a portrait of the dinner-habits of Alexander Severus (*SHA Sev. Al*. 34.6) throws doubt on this story. For other examples, see Plin. *Ep*. 4.1: Pliny plans to celebrate the dedication of a temple at Tifernum Tiberinum with a public banquet, which he will attend together with Calpurnia; Lucian *Merc. Cond*. 15 mentions in passing that the rich man's wife was present at the numerous dinner entertainments. Plutarch *Quaest. Conv*. 7.8.4 (*Mor*. 712F) complains about the habit of the masses (οἱ πολλοί) of watching scurrilous farces during dinner in the presence of women and young children; see also Juv. 11.165: Spanish dancing-girls performing at dinner before young brides and their husbands.

101 She also made them perform in public: see Plin. *Ep*. 7.24 (a letter announcing her death in AD 107 at the age of almost 80). Pliny praises her for the excellent upbringing she gave her grandson, C. Ummidius Quadratus, who was a friend of Pliny's, but he mildly criticizes her passion for actors and the stage: 'She kept a company of pantomime-players and treated them with greater indulgence than becomes a lady of her standing, but Quadratus never watched them either in the theatre or at home, nor did she invite him to be present. Once when asking my attention for her grandson's studies, she told me that since, as a woman, she was condemned to the leisure prescribed to her sex, she used to amuse herself with playing draughts or watching her mimes, but whenever she wanted to do the one or the other she always told her grandson to be off and to busy himself with his studies' ('Habebat illa pantomimos fovebatque effusius quam principi feminae convenit. Hos Quadratus non in theatro, non domi spectabat; nec illa exigebat. Audivi ipsam, cum mihi commendaret nepotis sui studia, solere se ut feminam in illo otio sexus laxare animum lusu calculorum, solere spectare pantomimos suos; sed, cum factura esset alterutrum, semper se nepoti suo praecepisse, abiret studeretque'). For Ummidia Quadratilla: *FOS* 829, *PIR*[1] V 606. *RE* 9A Ummidia 3 cols 600–3 is criticized and supplemented by Syme, R. (1962) 'Missing persons III', *Historia* 11: 154–5 and Syme (1968) 150–1; see also Syme, R. (1968) 'The Ummidii', *Historia* 17: 72–105. Though living mainly in Rome she acted

as a generous benefactress to her native town, Casinum, where she donated a temple and an amphitheatre (*ILS* 5268 = *CIL* X 5183). She also repaired the theatre of Casinum (*AE* 1946: 174). *CIL* VI 10096, the epitaph of Eucharis, an actress and dancer who was the freedwoman of a certain Licinia, may perhaps point to a similar habit on the part of Licinia.

102 For all-male banquets, see, e.g., Hor. *Sat.* 2.8, Mart. *Ep.* 10.48 and Plut. *Quaestiones Conviviales*. Since for a variety of reasons not all male guests took their wives along with them to a dinner party (not all of them may have been married), men must have outnumbered women at most dinner parties. Though upper-class women living on their own (for instance, widows) could invite guests of both sexes (see Treggiari (1991) 414–27), they do not, as a rule, seem to have attended dinner parties on their own; yet, Cic. *Q. fr.* 3.1.19 seems to imply that Pomponia, Cicero's sister-in-law, dined out ('cum Pomponia foris cenaret') when her husband was in Gaul.

103 As we have seen in chapter 1, reticence and modesty were among the traditional virtues of the *matrona*. Plautus *Poen.* 32 tells the women among his audience to watch his play while remaining silent, even when laughing: 'matronae tacitae spectent, tacitae rideant'. The drunken conversation of the freedwomen Fortunata and Scintilla, reclining with their husbands after dinner in the *Cena Trimalchionis* (Petron. *Sat.* 67, 69, 70, 72) ridicules their vulgarity (in Petr. *Sat.* 74–5 Fortunata is put in her place by Trimalchio), and Propertius' Cynthia reciting his poetry when drinking together with him after dinner (Prop. 2.33.38) can hardly be taken as an example of a traditional Roman *matrona*. Perhaps we may compare the prescribed behaviour of women at table with that of men of inferior rank, who in the presence of their superiors had to be silent: see Juv. 5.125–7. Notions of rank and status were very important at Roman banquets and the order of reclining, and sometimes the quality of the food served, expressed (and confirmed) the social hierarchy among the guests. Women were not directly involved in the social differentiation of the banquet, as they shared the rank, and the couch, of their husbands. For ideas of convivial equality as compared to (the very unequal) convivial reality, see D'Arms (1990).

104 Juv. 6.434–9 and 445–7: 'Illa tamen gravior, quae cum discumbere coepit / laudat Vergilium, periturae ignoscit Elissae, / committit vates et comparat, inde Maronem / atque alia parte in trutina suspendit Homerum./ Cedunt grammatici, vincuntur rhetores, omnis / turba tacet . . . /nam quae docta nimis cupit et facunda videri / crure tenus medio tunicas succingere debet, / caedere Silvano porcum, quadrante lavari.'

105 Juv. 6.446–7. According to the Schol. Iuv. 6.447 women were excluded from the worship of Silvanus ('quia Silvano mulieres non licet sacrificare') and a *quadrans* was a man's fee to the baths (women being charged more, up to double the price men usually paid). For Juvenal depicting her as a rhetorician, see 6.438–40 and 448–50. Thus, in this portrait Juvenal ridicules not only the 'bluestocking' who intrudes into a male field, but also the pretentious grammarian, or rhetorician, who dominates table-talk with his tiresome monologues; in grammatical training the comparison between Homer and Virgil (Juv. 6.435–7) was one of the favourite topics.

106 It was probably thought funny to portray a woman in the role of a grammarian or a rhetorician just because it was an unexpected departure from the rules. Reekmans (1971) argues that Juvenal ridicules those who do not keep to the rules and duties imposed by social rank and position, and makes fun of life in the capital by reversing the traditional hierarchy of social categories such as extraction, wealth, gender and age.

107 For *recitationes* see *RE* 1A *recitatio* cols 435–46; Williams (1978) 303–6, Kenney (1982) 11–12, Quinn (1982) 83–8 and 140–65, White (1974) 43–4 and (1993) 60–3, Rawson (1985) 51–2, Harris (1989) 225–6 and Nauta (1995) 91ff. Its introduction was ascribed

by the elder Seneca (*Contr.* 4 *praef.* 2) to Asinius Pollio, who would have been 'the first of all Romans to recite his works to an invited audience' ('primus enim omnium Romanorum advocatis hominibus scripta sua recitavit'), but the custom of recitation was, in fact, older. For a lively account of the practice see Plin. *Ep.* 1.13; for Augustus listening to recitations of various kinds, Suet. *Aug.* 89.3. Guillemin, A. M. (1937) *Le Public et la vie littéraire à Rome*, Paris: Les Belles Lettres, pp. 98–100, distinguishes three types of literary recitations: (1) privately for a group of friends, (2) in a theatre for the general public, (3) in an auditorium for an invited audience.

108 Was it at such occasions, or at more private ones (for instance, during dinner), that Pompey's wife Cornelia 'was accustomed to listen to philosophical discourses with profit' (Plut. *Pomp.* 55: λόγων φιλοσόφων εἴθιστο χρησίμως ἀκούειν)?

109 For Pliny reciting in his *cubiculum*, see Plin. *Ep.* 5.3.11; for the use of the *cubiculum* for the reception of intimate friends, see Wallace-Hadrill (1988) 59 and Clarke, J. R. (1991) *The Houses of Roman Italy 100 B.C.–A.D. 250: Ritual, Space, and Decoration*, Berkeley: University of California Press, p. 13. Pliny more than once mentions recitations of poetry and, occasionally, of a speech (*Ep.* 5.12; for a list of passages referring to recitations, see Sherwin-White (1966) 421). He always recited to a select group of friends; see *Ep.* 8.21 (Pliny read his poetry to his friends at dinner for two days in succession; to enable his guests to write down their comments during the reading he had placed writing-tables before their couches) and *Ep.* 9.34.

110 For the recitation by Calpurnius Piso: Plin *Ep.* 5.17.5. For Pliny's wife Calpurnia: 'When I recite my works, she sits nearby, concealed behind a curtain' (*Ep.* 4.19; see above n. 59).

111 Tac. *Ann.* 13.5: 'so that she could station herself at a newly-added door in the rear, shut off by a curtain thick enough to conceal her from view but not to debar her from hearing' ('ut adstaret additis a tergo foribus velo discreta, quod visum arceret, auditum non adimeret'). The meeting of the senate possibly took place in the library of the palace: see Tac. *Ann.* 2.37.2. For the senate as an exclusively male preserve, where women were not allowed to enter, see Tac. *Ann.* 14.11 (about Agrippina) and Dio 57.12.3 (about Livia). The first woman who is said to have entered the senate was the mother (or grandmother) of the emperor Elegabalus (*SHA Elegab.* 4.1–2; 12.3; 14.6 and 18.3), but this is reported as a deplorable breach of rules.

112 In my view B. Rawson (1991) 20 is too confident in her opinion that 'Pliny's young wife must have been only one of many who attended literary readings, participated in literary discussions, and probably wrote for their own enjoyment.' For a more cautious approach see E. Rawson (1985) 52.

113 For Octavia's presence at Virgil's reading to Augustus, see Servius *Ad Aen.* 861 and Donat. [Suet.] *Vita Verg.* 32; also chapter 4, n. 35. Clutorius Priscus' unfortunate and premature recitation of a poem about the – as he believed – forthcoming death of Drusus took place in the house of P. Petronius Turpilianus 'in the presence of the latter's mother-in-law Vitellia and many ladies of rank' ('Vitellia coram multisque inlustribus feminis', Tac. *Ann.* 3.49). However, this occurred at a social gathering and was not a formal recitation.

114 Starr (1987) 213–14 argues that private recitations took place before a small group of friends and were closed to outsiders. It seems unlikely that women formed a regular part of such groups. For literary coteries, see chapter 5, pp. 147ff.

115 Roman public entertainment falls outside the scope of this study. For a survey, see Balsdon (1969) 244–339. For various aspects of the Roman theatre, see Slater (1996).

116 For female presence at plays and recitations of poetry see Plaut. *Poen.* 28–35; see also Ter. *Hec.* 35; Cic. *Tusc.* 1.37: *mulierculae et pueri* impressed by verses from an (unknown) tragedy. Suet. *Ner.* 32.3: a matron dressed in purple (which was forbidden by Nero)

among the audience at one of Nero's recitals; see also Quinn (1982) 145–58. Ovid. *Trist.* 2.501: girls and matrons viewing obscene mimes; Mart. *Ep.* 2.41: a girl with bad teeth is advised to avoid mime (which would make her laugh) and choose tragedy instead. For Statius' wife and the theatre see Stat. *Silv.* 3.5.16 and 91–2. Mime was often criticized for its scurrilousness, but Mckeown, J. C. (1979) 'Augustan elegy and mime', *PCPhS* 25: 71–84 believes that in the days of Augustus it was a sophisticated genre which influenced Roman elegy. For pantomime, see Jory, E. J. (1996) 'The drama of the dance: prolegomena to an iconography of imperial pantomime', in Slater (1996) 1–27.

117 Though acting was an occupation for women of the lower classes and entailed *infamia*, some upper-class women (and men) performed on the stage (and in the arena). For the *senatusconsultum* from the time of Tiberius forbidding them to do so, see Levick (1983) and Lebek (1990). For women acting as benefactresses, see, for instance, Ummidia Quadratilla (n. 101 above), who donated an amphitheatre to her native town, repaired its theatre and privately kept a troupe of pantomime players whom she also had perform in public. Agusia Priscilla from Gabii financed public games in the second century AD in honour of her priesthood: see *CIL* XIV 2804.

118 For segregation in the seating during the republic, see Rawson (1987) 90–1, who deals with the special seating of *equites* and senators on pp. 102ff.; for the introduction of reserved seats for senators see also Ungern-Sternberg, J. von (1975) 'Die Einführung spezieller Sitze für die Senatoren bei den Spielen (194 v. Chr.)', *Chiron* 5: 157–63. Vitruvius' remark (*Arch.* 5.3.1) about citizens watching the games (in the theatre) *cum coniugibus et liberis* is unclear in this context; perhaps he did not mean that they were actually sitting together or perhaps he refers to possible mixed seating among people of sub-equestrian rank during the republic. Yet, Rawson (1987) 90 draws attention to a *cuneus* (a wedge of seats) reserved 'for women' already in the theatre of Capua built around 100 BC: see *ILLRP* 713: 'cuniu(m) muliereb[us]'. Perhaps the segregation of seating by rank was not always strictly applied as the laws were repeatedly renewed: see Hopkins (1983) 17, n. 25.

119 For Augustus' seating arrangements, see Suet. *Aug.* 44. Applying what seems to have been a mixture of political and moral criteria he gave front seats to senators and among the common people he assigned separate rows to married men and their own *cuneus* to boys under age (with their *paedagogi* in the adjacent section). Further, dressing was regulated distinguishing the various ranks: senators wore their distinctive dress and the *plebs* in the *cavea media* had to wear white togas, those not wearing the toga (slaves, non-citizens and the urban poor, the *plebs sordida*) being restricted to the back rows, in the *summa cavea*; see Edmondson (1996). As regards women 'he would not allow women to view even the gladiators except from the upper seats, though it had been the custom for men and women to sit together at such shows' ('Feminis ne gladiatores quidem, quos promiscue spectari sollemne olim erat, nisi ex superiore loco spectare concessit', Suet. *Aug.* 44), implying that before his time they were segregated only at the theatre. For a detailed discussion of the evidence, see Rawson (1987); on pp. 83, 85 and 89–91 she deals with the seats reserved for women; for social hierarchy within the *cavea*, see Edmondson (1996) 84ff.; see further Hopkins (1983) 17–18 and Kolendo, J. (1981) 'La Répartition des places aux spectacles et la stratification sociale dans l'Empire Romain: à propos des inscriptions sur les gradins des amphithéâtres et théâtres', *Ktema* 6: 301–15.

120 See Edmondson (1996) 99–100. Baltrusch (1989) 140 believes that segregation according to gender was not strictly adhered to, but he bases this on the not very trustworthy dissertation of Bollinger, T. (1969) *Theatralis Licentia: die Publikumsdemonstrationen an den öffentlichen Spielen in Rom der früheren Kaiserzeit und ihre Bedeutung im politischen Leben*, Winterthur: Schellenberg (for critique of Bollinger's argument, see Rawson

(1987) 91). However, the evidence is not entirely consistent; for instance, Petron. *Sat.* 126, when taken literally – Rawson (1987) 91, n. 43 chooses not to take it thus – would suggest mixed seating in the front rows reserved for senators and in the fourteen rows reserved for knights. At certain occasions mixed seating seems to have been allowed, or even encouraged, as done mischievously by Caligula at the *Ludi Palatini*; see Jos. *AJ* 19.86 (see also *AJ* 19.75, where Roman nobles are said to have watched the plays of the *Ludi Palatini* together with their wives and children; the *plebs* seems to have been excluded); for mixed seating as an occasional element of *libertas*, see Rawson (1987) 112–13.

121 For the proximity of the *pullati* (the poor people, slaves and foreigners, who did not wear the toga) to the women's seats, see Calpurnius Siculus' description of the herdsman Corydon climbing to the rear of the wooden amphitheatre (probably that of Nero): 'we came to the seats, where the drably dressed [i.e. togaless] crowd watched the shows from between the chairs of the women' (Calp. Sic. *Ecl.* 7.26–7: 'venimus ad sedes, ubi pulla sordida veste / inter femineas spectabat turba cathedras'). Edmondson (1996) 93 infers from this text that they sat on high-backed chairs (*cathedrae*), but notes that this word might also be used for the enclosures in which the women sat. For the seating arrangements of women see Rawson (1987) 89–91 and Edmondson (1996) 88–93. Seating arrangements of women at the rear of the theatre are also found in the cities of the Greek East (exceptions were made for priestesses and important female office-holders who had seats at or near the front; see van Bremen (1996) 155–6. In Rome and Italy exceptions (apart from the Vestals and imperial women) were rare. Dio 71 [72] 31.2 relates that after the death of the empress Faustina, the wife of Marcus Aurelius, 'the most influential women' (τὰς γυναῖκας τὰς δυνάμει προεχούσας) were to sit at Faustina's place in the theatre around her gold statue, which was carried in a chair into the theatre. A seat of honour could be awarded to an individual for special services or merits, and from a decree of the decurions at Cumae (Tiberian date) we know of one case which included a woman in this honour: the mother of a local notable was granted a *locum lecticae* in the amphitheatre (from which she could see the shows while reclining, we may presume), though strictly speaking the text does not say where exactly her seat was located (was she sitting, or reclining, alongside her son?): see *AE* 1927 no. 158 line 3, Edmondson (1996) 93, n. 105 and Rawson (1987) 110, n. 162. No subdivisions among women's seats can be traced in the inscriptions indicating seating arrangements, such as *ILLRP* 713 (from Capua: 'cuniu(m) muliereb[us]') and *CIL* XI 4206 (from Interamna: 'in muliebrib[us] aeramentis'), as both merely indicate a section 'for women'. These inscriptions also indicate that segregation by gender at the theatre was not restricted to the capital and in some Italian towns antedated Augustus' regulations.

122 Also at public banquets, which were sometimes given by an emperor in a theatre or amphitheatre and which were accompanied by theatrical entertainment, women are mentioned as a separate, and undifferentiated, group: see Stat. *Silv.* 1.6.43–5 (about a banquet of Domitian in the amphitheatre) who sums up, in ascending order of prominence, groups which normally could be clearly distinguished among the audience by their separate places: 'One table serves every order alike, children, women, people, knights and senators: freedom has loosened the bonds of awe' ('una vescitur omnis ordo mensa, / parvi, femina, plebs, eques, senatus / libertas reverentiam remisit'). Here, in a reversal of normal practice (the occasion was the Saturnalia), a fictitious equality is enacted; Statius' emphasis on freedom and equality of the seating arrangement at Domitian's banquet is due to his desire to flatter the emperor. For 'theatre-dinner' and the ideal of convivial equality see Jones (1991) 194 and D'Arms (1990) 308–9.

123 The *cavea* widens upwards and the upper part of the theatre and amphitheatre

NOTES

therefore offers more space than the lower, but as the *summa cavea* often contains fewer rows than the *media cavea*, it did not hold more spectators. For discussion of the seating and calculation of the number of spectators who could be seated per *cuneus* and *maenianum* in the amphitheatre, see Golvin, J.-C. (1988) *L'Amphithéâtre romain: essai sur la théorisation de sa forme et de ses fonctions*, Paris: Boccard, pp. 341ff. For a reconstruction of the seating in the Flavian amphitheatre at Rome, see Edmondson (1996), fig. 21; the women would be seated in the *maenianum summum in ligneis*, the upper gallery, which was vertically divided into separate sectors and had wooden seats. A similar arrangement seems likely for the theatre.

124 Gunderson, E. (1996) 'The ideology of the arena', *ClAnt* 15.1: 123ff., observes that in the amphitheatre (and, I take it, in the theatre) the two leading orders (senators and knights) were over-represented in the seating arrangements as compared to their actual numbers. Yet, even this specifically reserved space was sometimes overcrowded. Gunderson describes the seating at the arena as an 'ideological map' of the social structure of Roman society; see also his comments on pp. 124 and 142 on the 'literal marginalization' of women by the seating arrangements, which he connects with their exclusion from politics.

125 For some examples: Cat. 36 implies that Lesbia had read his verses about her (not necessarily the Annals of Volusius); see also Tib. 1.2; 1.5; 1.6 (addressed to Delia) and 2.4 (to Nemesis); Prop. 1.8a.40, 1.11.19, 2.13.11ff., 2.24a.21, 2.26a.25–6, 2.33.38, 3.2.1–2 (Cynthia reading, reciting or listening to his poetry); a wider female public, mainly composed of *puellae* in love, is implied by Prop. 1.9.11ff. (in love-affairs love poetry is more effective with women than epic), 2.34.57–8, 3.2.9–10 (*turba puellarum*), 3.3.19–20 and 3.9.45. Further Ovid *Am.* 2.1.5 (*virgo*) and 37–8, 2.4.19–21, 2.11.31–2, 3.1.27, 3.8.5–7; *AA* 1.31–4, 3.1–2, *Rem. Am.* 813–14 (the third book of Ovid's *Ars Amatoria* and his *Medicamina Faciei* are addressed to a female public); *Trist.* 1.6 (to his wife), 2.5–6, 2.243–56, 2.303–4. For love poetry offered to a girl (or obscene poetry attached to her door): Prop. 1.16.9–10, Ovid. *Am.* 3.1.53–8; for poetry as a birthday gift or a gift for the Matronalia: Tib. 3.1 (Lygdamus to Neaera), Tib. 4.2 and 4.6 (to Sulpicia). For the theme of conquering a beloved through poetry, see also Stroh (1971); that this was a literary *topos* is clearly shown by Calp. Sic. *Ecl.* 3.42 (the poetry of the shepherd Lycidas praised by his rural mistress). On the other hand, poets often complain that their beloved did not appreciate their poems as much as they had wished: Tib. 2.4.13–20 (Nemesis does not care for Tibullus' poems), Ovid. *Am.* 1.8.57ff., 3.1.58 and 3.8.1–8, *AA* 2.273–86 (only *doctae puellae*, a *rarissima turba*, appreciate poetry) and Prop. 4.5.54. For Martial's female audience, see Mart. *Ep.* 3.68.1: *matrona*, 3.69.5: *iuvenes facilesque puellae*, 3.86.1: *casta*, 5.2.1: *matronae puerique virginesque*, 7.88.4: *casta puella*, 11.15 (women of old-fashioned morals) and 16. No social standing of the female public is mentioned in our sources, but it seems not restricted to the upper classes. This raises the problem of literacy among women of the sub-élite, especially since ancient books made greater demands on a reader than modern ones, because of the handwriting, the lack of punctuation and the errors inevitably made by the copyists. However, we should not forget that much literature was recited: poems might also be sung and in wealthy households literature was recited by a professional *lector*; see Starr, R. J. (1991) 'Reading aloud: *lectores* and Roman reading', *CJ* 86: 337–43.

126 For women addressed in philosophical treatises, see Seneca's *Consolationes* addressed to Marcia and to his mother Helvia, Nicomachus' *Enchiridion* and Diogenes Laertius' address to an unknown female Platonist (Diog. Laert. 3.47); later in the third century AD Porphyrius wrote his Πρὸς Μαρκέλλαν, an *epistula moralis* addressed to his wife. In Christian circles we have Tertullian's moral treatise addressed to his wife (*Ad Uxorem*). For women's interest in philosophical works, see Cic. *Att.* 13.21a.4–5 and

13.22.3 (Cicero's *De Finibus* surreptitiously copied by Caerellia) and Horace's caricature of a wealthy elderly woman ostentatiously displaying her Stoic booklets (*Epod.* 8).
Pliny *Ep.* 5.16.3 praises the young Minicia Marcella for her studiousness and intelligence in reading (he does not specify what she read). For girls and women reading the
school authors see Plut. *Mor.* 737B: Pompeia reading Homer with her tutor; Prop.
2.1.49–50 (mockingly): Cynthia rejecting the *Iliad* because of Helen; Juv. 6.434ff.: a
caricature of a woman displaying her knowledge of Homer and Virgil, and 6.483–4:
a woman reading the *acta diurna*; Ovid. *Trist.* 2.255–66 (in self-defence): even reading
such time-honoured poets as Ennius or Lucretius may harm women's morals; *Trist.*
2.369–70: boys and girls reading Menander; Mart. *Ep.* 8.3.15–16: epic and tragedy
being read at school to boys and girls. Varro dedicated his *Res Rusticae* to his wife
Fundania and mentioned more than fifty Greek treatises on agriculture for her to
consult in case he had omitted something she might wish to know; see Varro *RR*
1.1.1–4 and 7–11.

127 Exceptions do, of course, occur: Martial playfully exhorts young brides 'who want to
please their husband alone' to read Sulpicia, a contemporary poetess of erotic verses
addressed to her husband; see Mart. *Ep.* 10.35.1–2: 'Omnes Sulpiciam legant puellae
/ uni quae cupiunt viro placere' (for Sulpicia Caleni see chapter 5, pp. 160ff.). According to Statius the (amateur) poems of his patron L. Arruntius Stella were learned by
heart by *iuvenes* and *puellae* throughout the city (Stat. *Silv.* 1.2.172–3) and won him the
love of Violentilla, a wealthy Neapolitan widow (Stat. *Silv.* 1.2.197ff.), but, of course,
Statius is flattering his patron.

128 See, for instance, Prop. 1.9.11: 'in love Mimnermus' verse is more powerful than
Homer' ('plus in amore valet Mimnermi versus Homero'), in a piece of advice to an
epic poet in love: 'lay aside your gloomy books and sing what every girl would wish to
hear', i.e. love poetry (1.9.13–14: 'tristes istos compone libellos, / et cane quod quaevis
nosse puella velit'); see also Prop. 2.34.31–2 and 43–6.

129 Ovid. *AA* 1.31–4: 'Este procul, vittae tenues, insigne pudoris / quaeque tegis medios,
instita longa, pedes. / Nos venerem tutam concessaque furta canemus, / inque meo
nullum carmine crimen erit.' See also *AA* 2.599–600, 3.611–16, *Rem. Am.* 385–6, *Am.*
2.1.3–4; *Trist.* 2.243–52 and 303–4, *Pont.* 3.3.50ff.; that his poetry was read by
upper-class women as well is shown by *Trist.* 2.253–4 and 307–8. For the moral
legislation of Augustus on marriage and adultery, see Mette-Dittmann (1991),
Treggiari (1991) 60–80 and 277–98 with further references. As we have seen in chapter 1, p. 15, the *vittae* and the *instita* were, together with the *stola*, the marks of upper-
class Roman *matronae*; for a woman's clothing as a sign of her rank and position, see
Scholz (1992).

130 Martial suggests that upper-class *matronae*, even those who were outwardly chaste,
preferred his erotic poetry to the dull work of serious poets, whose verses Martial
mockingly calls suitable for virgins only – but not very much to their taste: Mart. *Ep.*
3.68, 3.86 and 11.16.9–10 refer to 'chaste' girls and matrons eagerly reading his
naughty verses; Mart. *Ep.* 11.2.2 warns girls of old-fashioned morals against reading
his poetry; Mart. *Ep.* 3.69.7–8, 5.2, 11.15.1–2 talks about chaste poems suitable for
old-fashioned girls and matrons. Also *Priap.* 8 suggests that matrons were especially
keen on reading pornographic poetry.

131 Obviously, I am only concerned here with female readers. For a survey of the reading
public in ancient Rome, see Kenney (1982) 3–32 on 'books and readers in the Roman
world' and Quinn (1982). For the audience of historians and writers of political
biography, *in casu* Suetonius, see Wallace-Hadrill (1983) 23–5 and Momigliano, A.
(1978) 'The historians of the classical world and their audience: some suggestions',
ASNP ser. 3 vol. 8: 59–75; the younger Pliny was studying Livy at the moment of the
eruption of Vesuvius; see Plin. *Ep.* 6.20. On bias and unconscious assumptions in

modern assessments of the ancient reading public of the novel, see Stephens (1994) 405–18.

132 See Bowie (1994) 453. Apart from Petronius' *Satyricon* and Apuleius' *Metamorphoses* the novel was a Greek genre which flourished in the first three centuries AD. As a consequence, the discussion of the question of who read the ancient novels centres on the Greek-speaking eastern provinces of the Roman empire (see, e.g., Hägg (1983) 81–108). We do not know how frequently Greek novels (or, possibly, Latin translations of them; see Bowie (1994) 457, n. 55) were read by educated Romans in Rome, Italy and the Latin-speaking western provinces.

133 Egger (1988) briefly discusses the theory of a mainly female readership of the ancient novel and throws light on the tacit assumptions underlying much of the argument. For a recent defence of a predominantly female readership, see Hägg (1983) 90–1 and 95–6. For an assessment of the possibilities for 'female identification' and female interest in the novel, see Egger, B. (1994) 'Women and marriage in the Greek novels: the boundaries of romance', in Tatum (1994) 260–80. Comparing the ancient novel with modern popular romantic fiction much read by women such as the Bouquet or Harlequin series, she suggests that the emotional and erotic power of the heroines together with the restricted gender role in the novel (more restricted, in fact, than that of contemporary female readers) would have appealed to female readers, but again, such arguments seem hardly convincing.

134 For a discussion of the meagre ancient evidence of the readers of novels, see Wesseling (1988) 67–9. The only reference to a female reader is given by the novel-writer Antonius Diogenes (about AD 100), whose work has survived only in Photius' summary (see Hägg (1983) 118–21): 'he dedicated the novel to his sister Isidora because of her great interest' (τῇ ἀδελφῇ Ἰσιδώρᾳ φιλομαθῶς ἐχούσῃ τὰ δράματα προσφωνεῖ, Photios *Bibl.* 111a–b); for the dedication, see Bowie (1994) 437. Most ancient testimonies about the novel are deprecatory; see, for instance, *SHA Albin.* 12.12, in which the preference of Clodius Albinus (one of the emperor-pretenders after the death of Pertinax) for reading novels (called 'old-wives' songs', *neniae aniles*), especially the work of Apuleius, is ridiculed; or see Macrob. *Somn. Scip.* 1.2.7–8, who calls them 'nursery stories' (*nutricum cunae*). Such pronouncements show that novels were regarded as trivial also by certain ancient critics, but this cannot be used as an argument for a predominantly female public.

135 For this view see, for instance, Bowie (1994), who provides an excellent discussion of earlier opinions; see also Stephens (1994), who by examining the remains of novels in Roman Egypt reaches the same conclusion (that novelists wrote for a limited audience of educated men from the upper classes). Wesseling (1988) argues that the ancient novels are 'multi-level writings' offering entertainment to different groups of people: though in the first place aimed at well-educated persons of the the upper classes, the novel probably also appealed to the less educated because of its exciting and romantic adventures. Even illiterates could become acquainted with episodes from them through social readings. Harris (1989) 228 believes that novels were 'the light reading of a limited public possessing a real degree of education'. Lefkowitz (1991) 212 says (without evidence) that women formed 'a large part of the audience' when novels were read aloud, but Bowie (1994) and Stephens (1994) 409 do not believe that public readings of novels took place.

136 Fom certain details of language in the narrative of the North African martyr Vibia Perpetua, which is included in the *Passio SS. Perpetuae et Felicitatis* (see chapter 6, n. 1), Dronke (1984) 285–6, n. 58 concludes that, before her conversion to Christianity, Perpetua had read Apuleius' *Metamorphoses*. For other literary influences in her writing (Virgil's *Aeneid* and Tibullus), see Dronke (1984) 11.

137 Yet, Sirago, V. A. (1983) *Femminismo a Roma nel Primo Impero*, Soveria Mannelli:

Rubbettino, p. 148 boldly states that Ovid's poetry cannot be understood without a female audience. For the theme of *servitium amoris*, see Lyne (1979); for Catullus playing the female role in his poetry, Wiseman (1985) 121f.

138 For the great range of poets studied with a grammarian, see Bonner (1977) 212–49; for example, Statius' father, who was a grammarian, taught not only Homer and Hesiod, but also Epicharmus, Pindar, Ibycus, Alcman, Stesichorus, Sappho, Callimachus, Lycophron, Sophron, Corinna, and other poets not mentioned by name; see Stat. *Silv.* 5.3.146–62. Upper-class women may have gained additional familiarity with poetry by singing choral poetry in choirs of boys and girls: see, e.g., Hor. *C.* 3.1.4; 4.6.31ff.; *C.S.* 6; *Ep.* 2.1.132–3; see also chapter 3, p. 81. Kenney (1982) 9 remarks that women 'formed a not inconsiderable part of the literate public' and were a separate class of readers as they 'had not been through the mill of contemporary rhetoric'.

139 For epigrams addressed and presented to female patrons, see chapter 4 (Antonia, Poppaea, Agrippina Minor, Argentaria Polla, Mummia Nigrina, Sabina and Marcella). Women's preference for writing elegies and epigrams is discussed in chapter 5.

140 Music: Ovid *AA* 3.311–28; dance: *AA* 3.349–52.

> Let the Muse of Callimachus and of the Coan bard be known to you, and the old drunkard's Teian strains; let Sappho too be known (for who more wanton than she?), or he whose sire is deceived by crafty Getan's cunning. And you should be able to read a poem of tender Propertius or something of Gallus or of you, Tibullus; and the fleece that Varro told of, famous for its tawny hairs, a cause of complaint to your sister, Phrixus; and Aeneas the wanderer, origin of lofty Rome, a work than which none more famous has appeared in Latium. Perhaps too my name will be joined to theirs, nor will my writings be given to Lethe's waters; and someone will say, 'Read the elegant poems of our master, wherein he instructs the rival parties; or from the three books marked by the title of "Loves" choose out what you may softly read with docile voice; or let some Letter be read by you with practised utterance; he first invented this art, unknown to others.'
>
> (Ovid *AA* 3.329–48; Loeb trans.)

> Sit tibi Callimachi, sit Coi nota poetae, / sit quoque vinosi Teïa Musa senis; / nota sit et Sappho (quid enim lascivius illa?), / cuive pater vafri luditur arte Getae. / Et teneri possis carmen legisse Properti, / sive aliquid Galli, sive, Tibulle, tuum; / dictaque Varroni fulvis insignia villis / vellera, germanae, Phrixe, querenda tuae; / et profugum Aenean, altae primordia Romae, / quo nullum Latio clarius extat opus. / Forsitan et nostrum nomen miscebitur istis, / nec mea Lethaeis scripta dabuntur aquis: / atque aliquis dicet 'nostri lege culta magistri / carmina, quis partes instruit ille duas: / deve tribus libris, titulus quos signat Amorum, / elige, quod docili molliter ore legas: / vel tibi composita cantetur Epistola voce: / ignotum hoc aliis ille novavit opus'.

Also Prop. 2.34.31–2 mentions Philetas and Callimachus as poets liked by girls. In the *Remedia Amoris*, a guide for those who want to cure themselves of love, Ovid gives a list of poets to be avoided that is almost identical: see Ovid *Rem. Am.* 757–66, warning against reading the *teneros poetas* (757): Callimachus, Philetas, Sappho, Anacreon, Tibullus, Propertius, Gallus and Ovid himself.

141 However, Ovid *Am.* 2.4.19–20 imagines a girl comparing the literary merits of Callimachus with those of Ovid, and Philodemus praises a certain Flora in spite of her *ignorance* of Sappho, which apparently required comment; see *AP* 5.132.7: 'and if she is Oscan and Flora and does not sing Sappho' (εἰ δ᾽ Ὀπικὴ καὶ Φλῶρα καὶ οὐκ

ᾄδουσα τὰ Σαπφοῦς); see chapter 5, n. 141. On performance of poetry, see Wiseman (1985) 124–9 and Quinn (1982) 83–93 and 140–67; see also Willams (1978) 304f.; for the poems of Sappho and Anacreon being sung at banquets, see Plut. *Quaest. Conv.* 7.8.2 (*Mor.* 711D) and Aul. Gell. *NA* 19.9.4. The libretti of pantomime derived from such authors as Virgil and Ovid, but Lucan, Statius and other poets also wrote them; see Sen. *Suas.* 2.19 and Juv. 7.87; for Ovid's poems presented in the theatre with dancing; see Ovid *Trist.* 2.519–20 and 5.7.25–6; for Virgil's *Aeneid*, Suet. *Ner.* 54. The younger Pliny takes pride in the fact that his amateur verses were put to music by his wife (see *Ep.* 4.19) and that they were also 'sung, and set to the cithara or lyre by Greeks who have learnt Latin out of love for my little book' (*Ep.* 7.4: 'cantatur etiam et a Graecis quoque, quos Latine huius libelli amor docuit, nunc cithara nunc lyra personatur').

142 For the poetry of Anacreon presented to Antonia Minor, see *AP* 9.239; see also chapter 4, p. 109. For Sulpicia the elegist, see chapter 5. Compare also Sempronia (Sall. *Cat.* 25.2, cited briefly at the beginning of this chapter): her accomplishments consisted in a similar combination of music, dance and poetry to that recommended by Ovid in *AA* 3.311–52. In late antiquity we find Maria, the marriageable daughter of Stilicho, reading Homer and Sappho, as well as other authors not mentioned by name, under her mother's guidance; see Claudian *Epith.* 232ff.

143 Quint. 1.8.5–12.

144 For the complete list, see Quint. 10.1.20ff. For the Greek elegiac poets: 10.1.58. Sappho and Anacreon are missing in 10.1.61. However, in 10.1.69 he mentions Menander, in 10.1.85f. Virgil, and in 10.1.87 Varro of Atax. In 10.1.88 Ovid is criticized for his lack of seriousness even when writing an epic; for the Augustan love poets, see 10.1.93.

145 In Mart. *Ep.* 14.183–96 (epigrams accompanying Saturnalian gifts of books) we meet another list. Martial distinguishes gifts of the rich from those of the poor (*Ep.* 14.1.5: 'gifts of rich and poor alternate', 'divitis alternas et pauperis'), and includes (more or less alternately; the alternation has been partly disturbed in the transmission of the work) both serious works and trifles: the pseudo-Homeric *Batrachomyomachia*, Homer's *Iliad* and *Odyssey*, the Pseudo-Virgilian *Culex*, Virgil, Menander's *Thaïs*, (a volume of) Cicero, the first book of Propertius, Livy (complete or an epitome?), Sallust, Ovid's *Metamorphoses*, Tibullus, Lucan, Catullus, and Calvus' 'On the use of cold water'. The serious works, those by Homer, Virgil, Cicero, Livy, Sallust and Lucan, here presented as gifts of the rich, are typical upper-class male reading; the frivolous works: the *Batrachomyomachia*, the *Culex*, those by Menander, Propertius, Ovid, Tibullus, Catullus and Calvus (?), though professedly gifts of poor men, partly coincide with the reading-list for women as recommended by Ovid.

146 Quinn (1982). For the fashion of reading and writing epigrams and other 'light' poetry among upper-class men and the mixed feelings which such 'frivolous' pursuits provoked, see chapter 5, pp. 177f.

147 For invectives against old women, who are ridiculed for their appearance and their sexual insatiability, see Richlin (1992a) 109–16; Juvenal and Martial scoff at aged women for speaking Greek, the language of love at Rome (Griffin (1976) 87–105; see Mart. *Ep.* 10.68 and Juv. 6.184ff., especially 191–4: 'All this might be pardoned in a girl; but will you, who are hard on your eighty-sixth year, still talk in Greek? That tongue is not decent in an old woman's mouth' ('dones tamen ista puellis: / tunc etiam, quam sextus et octogensimus annus / pulsat, adhuc Graece? non est hic sermo pudicus / in vetula').

148 See Seneca's *consolationes* addressed to Marcia and Helvia; for Livia turning to the philosopher Areius for consolation, see Sen. *Cons. Marc.* 4.2–5.6; for other examples of women interested in philosophy, see also Cicero's elderly friend Caerellia (p. 55), the

anonymous woman addressed by Nicomachus (pp. 38f.) and Augustus' sister Octavia, to whom the Stoic philosopher Athenodorus dedicated a work (chapter 4, p. 106). For philosophy as a respectable pursuit for an upper-class woman and a safe haven against sorrow, see, e.g., Sen. *Cons. Helv.* 17.3–18.1. Also for men of their class philosophy was a respectable occupation of their leisure time, an occupation which even Propertius envisages for his old age; see Prop. 3.5.23–46: a catalogue of philosophical and scientific themes which will bring pleasure to his old age. An exception is Hor. *Epod.* 8. 15–16, where an aged upper-class woman is ridiculed: 'quid quod libelli Stoici inter sericos/ iacere pulvillos amant?' ('What if Stoic booklets like to lie between your silk pillows?'). The context is an invective against a repulsive, but wealthy, old woman of high birth, who tries to seduce the poet. Esler, C. C. (1989) 'Horace's old girls: evolution of a topos', in Falkner, T. M. and de Luce, J. (eds) (1989) *Old Age in Greek and Latin Literature*, New York: State University of New York Press, p. 178, contends that Horace is unable to believe that a woman can enjoy the intellectual satisfaction of studying philosophy in old age, as men did. But that is not the issue here; it is her sexual appetite that is ridiculed.

149 Some examples: Plut. *Pomp.* 55 (quoted at the start of this chapter) about Pompey's wife Cornelia, who in spite of her studies was free of such faults, and Sen. *Cons. Helv.* 17.4: Seneca's father forbidding his wife to study because of the ostentatiousness such studies would lead to. For ridicule of ignorant Roman women misinterpreting Plato's *Republic* as an excuse for their promiscuity, see Epictetus fr. 15 (= Stob. 3.6.58): 'At Rome the women have in their hands Plato's *Republic*, because he insists on community of women. For they pay attention only to the words, and not to the meaning of the man' ('Εν 'Ρώμη αἱ γυναῖκες μετὰ χεῖρας ἔχουσι τὴν Πλάτωνος πολιτείαν, ὅτι κοινὰς ἀξιοῖ εἶναι τὰς γυναῖκας· τοῖς γὰρ ῥήμασι προσέχουσι τὸν νοῦν, οὐ τῇ διανοίᾳ τἀνδρός). Though the anecdote should not be believed to represent the reading habits of women (for the same misinterpretation, but attributed to false philosophers, see Luc. *Fugit.* 18), it does show that women who studied philosophy met with prejudice. Musonius Rufus fr. III, in a treatise propagating 'that women too should study philosophy' (ὅτι καὶ γυναιξὶ φιλοσοφητέον), defends himself against possible allegations (lines 54–8) that philosophy makes women arrogant and causes them to neglect their households; on the contrary, it makes women into better (house)wives and mothers.

150 For Ovid's poems addressed to his wife, see *Trist.* 1.6; 3.3; 4.3; 5.2; 5.5; 5.11; 5.14 and *Pont.* 1.4; 3.1. Ovid's relegation to Tomis is usually – and to my mind rightly – accepted as a historical fact: see, e.g., Syme (1978) 76ff. and 215–29. I disagree with Hofmann, H. (1988) 'Ovidius Elegiacus et Epicus: over enkele hoofdlijnen van het moderne Ovidius-onderzoek', *Lampas* 21 4/5: 320–32, who says that Ovid's stay in Tomis is merely a poetic *topos*; for a sensible discussion, see Holzberg, N. (1997) *Ovid: Dichter und Werk*, Munich: Beck, pp. 35–7. For Statius' *Ecloga ad Uxorem*, see *Silv.* 3.5. Other examples of wives (and, possibly fictitious, mistresses) addressed in poetry are: Tib. 1.2, 1.5, 1.6 (to Delia), 2.4 (to Nemesis), 3.1 (Lygdamus to Neaera) and Lucan's lost *Adlocutio ad Pollam* (Stat. *Silv.* 2.7.62–3); for another female relative: Ovid. *Trist.* 3.7 (to Perilla).

151 Though professedly Varro wrote his entire treatise on agriculture for his wife (Varro *RR* 1.1.1–4), in fact only the first book on agriculture proper is dedicated to her, while the second book on animal husbandry and the third on villa pasturage are dedicated to friends, respectively Turranius Niger and Pinnius (Varro *RR* 2 *praef.* 6; 3.1.9; Rawson (1985) 137). For his extensive bibliography of Greek treatises on agriculture, see Varro *RR* 1.1.7–11. It seems inserted mainly to impress his readers, and some of the authors may have been mere names to him: according to J. Heurgon of the Budé edition (1978) XXVIII he copied his bibliography from the Greek translation of the

work of Mago of Carthage, which he mentions in his list. He also promises his wife a Latin bibliography (in 1.1.7), but this is not included. These and other inaccuracies indicate that the work is probably a hasty compilation of three unfinished treatises; this is confirmed by his own statement about the hurry he was in because of his age: he was in his eightieth year when he composed his *Res Rusticae*, dedicated to Fundania in 37 BC; see Varro *RR* 1.1.1. For Fundania see *RE* VII Fundania 8 col. 293; her father, the senator C. Fundanius (*RE* VII Fundanius 1 cols 291–2), is one of the interlocutors of the first book of the *Res Rusticae*.

152 Stat. *Silv.* 3.5.33–6 (in a poem addressed to his wife Claudia): 'tu procurrentia primis / carmina nostra sonis totasque in murmure noctes / aure rapis vigili; longi tu sola laboris / conscia, cumque tuis crevit mea Thebais annis'. For the harmony of their marriage see lines 22–51. Claudia is compared with Penelope (3–11) and other heroines (45–9) and is an exemplary mother besides (lines 54–61). For her sharing his victory and defeat in poetic contests see lines 28–32. The picture of their marriage accords with contemporary ideals of matrimonial *concordia*: see above, p. 33. For a discussion of the poem, see Vessey, D. W. T. (1976/7) 'Statius to his wife: *Silvae* III.5', *CJ* 72: 134–40.

153 Stat. *Silv.* 3.5.63–5; see also chapter 3, p. 83. Claudia and her daughter are examples of well-educated women among the sub-élite, belonging to what perhaps may anachronistically be called the upper middle class. For other (possibly fictitious) examples of women reading the poetry of their husbands or lovers, see Cat. 35 about the learned girlfriend of the poet Caecilius (see chapter 5, p. 178), and Martial praising the literary judgement of the learned Theophila (chapter 5, p. 179), fiancée of the poet Canius Rufus, in *Ep.* 7.69.5–6: 'that work shall live, whatever it be, you let pass through these ears, so little womanlike or common is her judgement' ('vivet opus quodcumque per has emiseris aures; tam non femineum nec populare sapit'); I do not agree with the interpretation of Hallett (1992) 103 and 119, who believes that these lines refer to Theophila's own writings. The words 'aures' and 'sapit' point to a good ear for, and a keen judgement of, poetry. In Augustan love poetry the importance of the judgement of the mistress seems to be a *topos*, involving both her literary judgement and the power of poetry to persuade her to yield to the poet's love. For Cynthia's judgement of Propertius' poetry, see Prop. 2.13.7 and 11–15: 'me iuvet in gremio doctae legisse puellae, / auribus et puris scripta probasse mea. / haec ubi contigerint, populi confusa valeto / fabula: nam domina iudice tutus ero' ('Let it be enough satisfaction for me that I recite my poems in the arms of a learned girl and that her unspoiled ears cherish them. When this happens to me, I say farewell to the confused comments of the public; I feel safe in the judgement of my mistress').

154 For speeches see Plin. *Ep.* 4.19 about his wife Calpurnia reading and rereading his writings; see also p. 32f. I take it that her enthusiasm concerns his entire œuvre. Plin. *Ep.* 3.10: at the request of Vestricius Spurinna and his wife Cottia, Pliny sent them his speech in honour of the couple's deceased son before it was published, and asked for the couple's criticism. From the names of Cottia's slaves Solin, H. (1990) *Namenpaare: Eine Studie zur römischen Namengebung*, Helsinki: Societas Scientiarum Fennica (Comm. Hum. Litt. 90) 65–6 infers that she must have been a well-educated woman; for Cottia see *FOS* 298. In the *Life of Terence* it is said to have been common gossip (see also Cic. *Att.* 7.3.10 and Quint. 10.1.99) that Scipio Africanus and C. Laelius aided Terence with his writings:

> once at his villa at Puteoli C. Laelius was urged by his wife to come to dinner at an earlier hour than common on the Kalends of March [i.e. the Matronalia], but he begged her not to interrupt him. When at last he entered the dining-room at a late hour, he said that he had seldom written

more to his own satisfaction; and on being asked to read what he had written, he declaimed the lines of the 'Heautontimoroumenos'.

(Suet. *Vita Ter.* 3; Loeb trans.)

C. Laelium quondam in Puteolano Kal. Martis admonitum ab uxore temperius ut discumberet petisse ab ea ne interpellaret, seroque tandem ingressum triclinium dixisse, non saepe in scribendo magis sibi successisse; deinde rogatum ut scripta illa proferret pronuntiasse versus qui sunt in 'Heautontimorumeno'.

Though the anecdote, which is attributed to Nepos, is probably fictitious (for a discussion of the supposed collaboration between Terence, Scipio and Laelius, see Gruen (1992) 197–202), the matter-of-fact account of a husband reading his newly composed work to his wife rings true.

155 For Marcia see *FOS* (Cremutia) Marcia 301, *PIR²* M 256, *RE* 14 Marcia 116 cols 1603–4. For her father, A. Cremutius Cordus, see *PIR²* C 1565; *RE* 4 Cremutius 2 cols 1703–4; Syme (1958) 337–8, 517 and 546, Manning (1981) 29–30; MacMullen (1975) 19–20. In his historical work he had praised Brutus and called Cassius the last of the Romans, and was prosecuted for treason at the instigation of Sejanus. For the ancient sources about his trial, his spirited defence and the fate of his work, see especially Tac. *Ann.* 4.34–5, Dio 57.24.2–4 and Sen. *Cons. Marc.* 1.2–4.

156 Sen. *Cons. Marc.* 1.3–4 gives the full credit to Marcia: 'you recovered for the benefit of men that genius of your father [...] and the books which that bravest hero had written with his own blood you restored to their place among the memorials of the nation. You have done a very great service to Roman scholarship' ('ingenium patris tui ... in usum hominum reduxisti ... ac restituisti in publica monumenta libros quos vir ille fortissimus sanguine suo scripserat. Optime meruisti de Romanis studiis'). Dio 57.24.4 mentions also other people: 'his daughter Marcia as well as others had hidden some copies' (ἄλλοι τε γὰρ καὶ μάλιστα ἡ θυγάτηρ Μαρκία συνέκρυψεν αὐτά), and Tac. *Ann.* 4.35 just remarks: 'copies remained, hidden and afterwards published' ('manserunt, occultati et editi'). For censorship and bookburning during the principate, see Pinner (1958) 44 and Marshall (1976) 262–3. For Caligula's permission to republish the works of Cremutius Cordus, see Suet. *Cal.* 16. Marshall (1976) 262–3 suggests that his books were restored to the public libraries. For the removal of the passages 'which brought him to his ruin' see Quint. 10.1.104 ('circumcisis quae dixisse ei nocuerat'). According to Seneca Marcia had inherited her love of learning from her father; see Sen. *Cons. Marc.* 1.6: 'studia, hereditarium et paternum bonum'. Incidentally, Seneca's *Consolatio ad Marciam* itself is a compliment to her education.

157 Plin. *Ep.* 7.19. For Fannia see *FOS* 259; *PIR²* F 118; *RE* 4 Clodius 69 col. 107 and *RE* 6 Fannius 22 col. 1995. She belonged to one of the foremost families of the so-called 'Stoic opposition' against the imperial regime, most of whom suffered for it with their lives. Her father Thrasea Paetus was forced to commit suicide by Nero in AD 66, her grandfather Caecina Paetus had killed himself at the orders of Claudius in AD 42, her husband Helvidius Priscus was executed during the reign of Vespasian about AD 75, and his son Helvidius Priscus the Younger, Fannia's stepson, was killed by Domitian in AD 93. The women of her family were noted for their loyalty and their courage. Her mother Arria Minor (*FOS* 159) and grandmother Arria Maior (*FOS* 96) had shared the conviction and the hard life of their husbands, and Fannia proved herself loyal and courageous: twice she followed her husband into exile and the third time she was banished because of the biography. Pliny knew her and her family well; she figures in several of his letters; see 3.11, 3.16 (a description of the courageous behaviour and suicide of her grandmother Arria Maior, as told by Fannia), 7.19 and 9.13. For her husband Helvidius Priscus see *PIR²* H 59, *RE* 8 Helvidius 3 cols 216–21, Syme (1958)

556ff. For the so-called Stoic opposition see MacMullen (1975) 1–94, Brunt, P. A. (1975) 'Stoicism and the principate', *PBSR* n.s. 30: 7–35 and Wirszubski, Ch. (1950) *Libertas as a Political Idea at Rome during the Late Republic and Early Principate*, Cambridge: Cambridge University Press, pp. 138–50.

158 Plin. *Ep.* 7.19. Together with Fannia her mother Arria Minor was banished, as was Gratilla, the wife of Arulenus Rusticus, who had published a eulogy on Arria's husband Thrasea Paetus and was condemned to death for it (Tac. *Agr.* 2, Plin. *Ep.* 3.11.3, Suet. *Dom.* 10.3–4). The women probably assisted in providing the material for both eulogies. For the liability of women to be indicted before the senate for treason, see Marshall (1990).

159 For Ovid's complaints see, e.g., Ovid *Trist.* 3.14.37f. and 5.12.53f. For more references see Marshall (1976), especially pp. 252, 255 and 257. For Martial longing for the libraries (and audience) at Rome, see Mart. *Ep.* 12 *praef.*

160 See, e.g., Mart. *Ep.* 2.8, Cic. *Q. fr.* 3.4.5 and 3.5.6; see also Marshall (1976) 253–4 and 260, Clift (1945) 18–19, Pinner (1958) 31ff., Reynolds and Wilson (1974) 22, Rawson (1985) 42–5, Kenney (1982) 17–18, and Harris (1989) 224ff.

161 Starr (1987) argues that in Cicero's days copying from a manuscript in the possession of its author or the author's friends was the main channel of circulation of literary texts. This limited the public to a narrow circle consisting of the author's friends and his friends' friends. The increasing importance of bookshops in the first century AD broadened the public for a literary work and, according to Starr, is an indication that the hold of the traditional aristocracy on the circulation of literature declined.

162 For books, book production and libraries in the Roman world, see Birt (1882), *RE* 3 cols 415–24 'Bibliotheken', 939–71 'Buch' and 973–85 'Buchhandel', Clark (1909) 12–43, Boyd (1915), Kenyon (1932) 73–86, Clift (1945) 5–39, Pinner (1958) 30ff., who seems rather optimistic about the extent of commercial book production in Rome, Thompson (1962) 27–51, Platthy (1968), Reynolds and Wilson (1974) 18–37, Marshall (1976) 252–64, Kenney (1982) 3–32, Quinn (1982) 125–8, Fehrle (1986), and Blanck (1992) 120ff.

163 For friends and visiting scholars working in the library of Lucullus see, e.g., Plut. *Luc.* 42 and Cic. *Fin.* 3.2.7f.; for the relation between book collecting and patronage see Marshall (1976) 256–8. For the library of Aemilius Paullus, see Plut. *Aem.* 6.5 and 28.6, Isid. *Etym.* 6.5.1; for that of Lucullus, see Plut. *Luc.* 42, Cic. *Fin.* 3.2.7f. (Cicero and Cato working in it), Isid. *Etym.* 6.5.1; and that of Sulla, see Plut. *Sull.* 26, Cic. *Att.* 4.10.1 (Cicero may have bought some books from this library from Sulla's son Faustus, who had to sell part of his household goods because of debts; see Plut. *Cic.* 27.6); for more references to these and other Greek libraries brought to Rome and to the Greek scholars who followed them, see *RE* 3 col. 416, Marshall (1976) 257–60 and Fehrle (1986) 14–29.

164 For Atticus helping Cicero to build up his library, see, e.g., Cic. *Att.* 1.7, 4.4a.1, 4.5.4, 4.8.2, 13.32.2 and for Cicero borrowing from the libraries of Atticus and other friends: Cic. *Att.* 2.4.1, 2.20.6, 4.14.1, 13.8, 13.31.2, 13.32.2, 13.33.2; for Cicero's libraries: Cic. *Att.* 2.6.1 and 12.3.1; *Fam.* 7.23.3 and 13.77.3. For private libraries in this period see further Marshall (1976) 252–60, Blanck (1992) 152–60 and 179ff., *RE* 3 col. 416, Clark (1909) 22–6, Clift (1945) 12–22, Thompson (1962) 34–5.

165 For a library as an essential asset to the political élite, see Vitruvius *Arch.* 6.5.2; in 1.2.7 and 6.4.1 he mentions the library as a normal part of a villa. For an example of a suburban library, see Mart. *Ep.* 7.17. Pliny the Elder must have owned a vast library to be able to extract about two thousand volumes for his *Naturalis Historia*; see Plin. *NH praef.* 17 and Clift (1945) 27–8; for the library of the younger Pliny in his Laurentine villa, see Plin. *Ep.* 2.17.8. For mockery of luxurious libraries owned by ignorant nouveaux riches, see, e.g., Sen. *Tranq.* 9.4–10, Lucian *Ind.*, Petr. *Sat.* 48.4, Juv. 2.4–7 and, at a later date, Auson. *Ep.* 7.

166 Hor. *Epod.* 8.15–16; see also n. 148 above.

167 Marshall (1976) 258 believes that Scipio and his brother Q. Fabius Maximus would not have split up the library and that it remained at the disposal of Scipio Aemilianus; according to him, it formed a major attraction to the so-called Scipionic Circle (for doubts about the existence of such a circle, see Zetzel (1972)). We may be reminded of Polybius' story (Pol. 31.23.4) that the friendship between himself and Scipio Aemilianus started with a loan of books. We do not know whether the library remained within the family at Scipio Aemilianus' sudden death; if he left no will, his wife Sempronia, who was probably married to him *in manu*, may have inherited at least part of it, and so may Cornelia, who was the sister of his adopted father and thus related to him by agnatic ties, but he may have left the library to someone by will. As Cornelia was widowed at an early age she may (also) have inherited the library of her husband for the education of her sons. For Cornelia's patronage see Plut. *CG* 19 and chapter 4. For the transmission of libraries by legacy see Paul. *Sent.* 3.6.51, *Dig.* 32.52 and 33.7.12.34 and the example of the poet Persius, who left his money to his mother and his sister, but his books to his friend and teacher L. Annaeus Cornutus (see Suet. *Vita Persi* 7).

168 Varro *RR* 1.1.7–11; for Fundania, see p. 52. For Varro's library in his villa at Casinum, see Cic. *Fam.* 9.4 and Varro *RR* 3.5.9, the 'museum'; it was plundered in 43 BC when Varro was proscribed by Antonius and a considerable number of his writings were destroyed; see Gell. *NA* 3.10.17 and Cic. *Phil* 2.104–5, but see also Rawson (1985) 41. Clift (1945) 21 suggests that Octavia may have inherited this confiscated library after Antonius' death and may have passed on the books to the public library she dedicated to the memory of her son, Marcellus: see chapter 4. For Calpurnia's literary studies, see Plin. *Ep.* 4.19 and p. 32; for Pliny's library in his Laurentine villa see *Ep.* 2.17.8, and also Guillemin, A.-M. (1929) *Pline et la vie littéraire de son temps*, Paris: Les Belles Lettres, pp. 113–27.

169 For Attica see p. 36. For an attempt to reconstruct the contents of Atticus' library from Cicero's correspondence, see Clift (1945) 13–16, also Blanck (1992) 156. Clift (1945) 20–1 assumes that Attica inherited her father's private library; for her inheriting her father's correspondence, see chapter 6, n. 89.

170 For Perilla, see Ovid *Trist.* 3.7.4: 'inter libros Pieridasque suas'. Ovid's (fictitious) mistress Corinna is advised to stay at home, read her books (*libellos*) and make music, rather than undertaking a dangerous voyage by sea: Ovid *Am.* 2.11.31–2. A slave woman called Onomaste (*CIL* VI 4434: 'Onomaste/ Laricis/ a bybliot') may have been a librarian of Antonia's; see Kokkinos (1992) 61. For Helvia see pp. 40f.

171 For Caerellia see *RE* 3 Caerellius 10 col. 1284; Austin, L. (1946) 'The Caerellia of Cicero's correspondence', *CJ* 41: 305–9 is somewhat speculative as regards Caerellia's background. For Cicero's letters mentioning her see Cic. *Att.* 12.51.3, 14.19.4, 15.1.4, 15.26.4; *Fam.* 13.72. Since Cicero calls her *necessaria mea*, which means that she was his 'friend' or 'relative', in *Fam.* 13.72.1 and does not mention her before 46 BC, the year of his marriage with Publilia (*FOS* 660, *RE* 23 Publilius 17), we may perhaps suppose that she was a friend, or a relative, of Publilia's or her family. For her attempt to advise him in his dealings with Publilia after their divorce, see *Att.* 14.19.4 and 15.1.4; for her lending him money see Cic. *Att.* 12.51.3 and 15.26.4. For their correspondence which was still extant in Quintilian's days, see Quint. 6.3.112 and chapter 6, p. 190. It was lost afterwards and in Dio's time it had given rise to unfounded speculations about their relationship; see Dio 46.18.4 and Auson. *Cent. Nupt.* 10 (ed. S. Prete, p. 169 line 12).

172 Cf. Cic. *Att.* 13.21a.4–5: 'Caerellia, inspired of course by love of philosophy, is copying from your people [or "your copies"]; she has those very books De Finibus' ('Caerellia, studio videlicet philosophiae flagrans, describit a tuis; istos ipsos "de

finibus" habet'): see also *Att.* 13.22.3: 'Caerellia had some things she could only have got from you' ('Caerelliam quaedam habere, quae nisi a te habere non potuerit'). For her library, see Clift (1945) 13, n. 40.

173 Sid. Ap. *Ep.* 2.9.4: 'qui inter matronarum cathedras codices erant, stilus his religiosus inveniebatur, qui vero per subsellia patrum familias, hi coturno Latiaris eloquii nobilitabantur'. Clark (1993) 136 argues that Christianity reinforced traditional differences, upper-class girls being educated in 'Scripture and selected commentators' only, whereas boys were given a formal rhetorical training; see also Rousseau, Ph. (1995) '"Learned women" and the development of a Christian culture in late antiquity', *SO* 70: 116–47.

174 A *cathedra* is a high-backed, cushioned chair normally used by women; see e.g., Calp. Sic. 7.26: 'femineas . . . cathedras,' Prop. 4.5.37, Juv. 6.91: 'molles . . . cathedras' and 9.52 (a sign of effeminacy), Mart. *Ep.* 3.63.7 and 12.38.1. *Cathedra* was also used for the chair of a teacher; see Juv. 7.203.

175 For Caesar's plans to found a public library see Suet. *DJ* 44. For the library of Asinius Pollio (*RE* 1 Asinius 25 cols 1589–1602), see Plin. *NH* 7.115 and 35.10, Isidor. *Etym.* 6.5.2.

176 For the Palatine library of Augustus see, e.g., Suet. *Aug.* 29 and Dio 53.1.3; for Octavia's foundation see chapter 4, p. 105; for that of Matidia, see chapter 4, pp. 120f. For public libraries in Rome and Italy, see *RE* 3 cols 418–19, Clark (1909) 12–22, Boyd (1915) 3–20, Kenyon (1932) 80–3, Clift (1945) 22–33 and 36–9, Pinner (1958) 55ff., Thompson (1962) 30–4, 38 and 82–3, Marshall (1976) 261–3, Fehrle (1986) 62–70, Kenney (1982) 23–4, Blanck (1992) 160–7 (Rome) and 168–9 (the Italian municipalities and the western provinces).

177 Examples are the foundations of Octavia and Matidia mentioned in the preceding note. In an inscription on a statue-base found in the temple of Vesta in Rome the equestrian Q. Veturius Callistratus thanked the *Virgo Vestalis Maxima*, Campia Severina, that 'he was made supervisor of the finances of the Augustan libraries through her recommendation' *CIL* VI 2132 = *ILS* 4928, dated about AD 240: 'suffragio eius factus proc(urator) rat(ionum) summ(arum) privatarum bibliothecarum Augusti n(ostri)'. It concerns an equestrian procuratorship dealing with the supervision of the financial management of the imperial libraries, which Campia Severina must have obtained for him by recommending him to the emperor.

178 For students and scholars working and conversing in public libraries, see, e.g., Gell. *NA* 11.17.1f., 13.20.1 and 19.5.4. In certain circumstances books could be borrowed; see Gell. *NA* 19.5, *SHA Aur.* 1.7 and Fronto *Ad M. Caes.* 4.5.2 (Haines I, pp. 178–9). For the social function of the public library see, e.g., Thompson (1962) 86; for a *schola* belonging to the library of Octavia: Plin. *NH* 35.114 and 36.28 (*curia*), Clark (1909) 12–14. For meetings of the senate in the Palatine library, see Suet. *Aug.* 29 and Tac. *Ann.* 2.37.3; the *decuriones* of Suessa Aurunca apparently met in the library founded by Matidia; see *CIL* X 4760. For the library's function as a public record-office, see, e.g., Gell. *NA* 11.17.1f., *SHA Tac.* 8.1; Clark (1909) 19, Boyd (1915) 31–40 and Fehrle (1986) 69. For imperial censorship exercised through public libraries, Ovid's *Ars Amatoria* being the most notorious case, see Marshall (1976) 261–4, Ovid *Trist.* 3.1.59ff. and *Pont.* 1.1.5ff.

179 For the lists of meeting-places, see Ovid *AA* 1.67–262 and 3.387–96, *Trist.* 2.279–300; see also Prop. 4.8.75–8. Yet, Ovid's omission does not mean that women were actively excluded from public libraries and elsewhere he professes that public libraries made literary works accessible to everybody (see Ovid *Trist.* 2.420: 'publica facta patent'). Starr's remark (1987) 216, n. 23 may be quoted here: 'it is not clear how genuinely public the Roman public libraries were. I suspect that, while they may not have actively excluded the lower class, they probably did not need to.' Does the same hold for women?

3 THE EDUCATION OF UPPER-CLASS WOMEN:
AIMS AND OPINIONS

1 Plin. *Ep.* 5.16, an epistolary *laudatio funebris* for Minicia Marcella (*RE* 15 Minicia 29 col. 1845; *PIR*² M 631; *FOS* 552). She was the younger of the two daughters of C. Minicius Fundanus from Ticinum: *cos suff.* AD 107, *RE* 15 Minicius 13 cols 1820–6, *PIR*² M 612, *FOS* 551 *sub* Minicia, Syme (1968) 149 and Syme, R. (1991) 'Minicius Fundanus from Ticinum', in Birley, A. R. (ed.) (1991) *Roman Papers VII*, Oxford: Clarendon Press, pp. 603–19, and Statoria Marcella (*PIR*¹ S 648; *FOS* 733). By a fortunate chance Minicia's urn and epitaph were found in the family tomb at Monte Mario outside Rome in 1881: *CIL* VI 16631 = *ILS* 1030: 'D(is) M(anibus) Miniciae Marcellae Fundani f(iliae) v(ixit) a(nnos) XII m(enses) XI d(ies) VII'. There is a slight discrepancy between Pliny's letter which says that she was nearly 14 ('nondum annos XIIII impleverat'), and the inscription, which gives 12 years, 11 months and 7 days as her age at death. Goold, G. P. (1963), in a review of S. E. Stout's critical edition of Pliny's letters (Bloomington, 1962) in *Phoenix* 17: 144, proposes to emend the age mentioned in the letter to XIII, but Sherwin-White (1966) 347 observes that it is better to accept the discrepancy, as all manuscripts agree on the number 14: after all, Pliny may have been mistaken. The epitaph of Minicia's mother, Statoria Marcella (*CIL* VI 16632), was found in the same tomb as that of her daughter. As she is not mentioned in Pliny's letter she must have died before her daughter.

2 Plin. *Ep.* 5.16.3: 'How she loved her nurses, her pedagogues and her teachers, each one for his respective service to her. How studiously and intelligently did she devote herself to her reading!' ('Ut nutrices, ut paedagogos, ut praeceptores pro suo quemque officio diligebat! Quam studiose, quam intelligenter lectitabat!') The *nutrices, paedagogi* and *praeceptores* probably represent the three successive stages in her upbringing: the *nutrix* nurturing her as a small child, the *paedagogus* guiding her elementary instruction, and the *praeceptor* her more advanced studies in 'grammar' and the liberal arts; for the *praeceptor*, see chapter 2, n. 41 and below n. 7.

3 For moral precepts taken from the poets, see Bonner (1977) 172–6. Quint. 1.8.4 advises the young to read texts that are morally elevating; see also Hor. *Ep.* 2.1.130ff.; for the link which was felt to exist between culture and conduct, see, e.g., Apuleius *Met.* 10.2: 'he had a young son who was well instructed in literature and therefore noted for his sense of duty and modesty' ('habebat iuvenem filium probe litteratum atque ob id consequenter pietate, modestia praecipuum'); among the rewards of higher education Lucian *Somn.* 10 mentions temperance, justice, piety and steadfastness. For the emphasis on moral training in Roman education and on the moral merit of the teacher see also, e.g., Plin. *Ep.* 2.18 and 3.3 (who says that the ideal teacher should possess *severitas, pudor* and *castitas*), Quint. 1.2.3f. and Tac. *Dial.* 28. There was always a certain fear that a teacher might corrupt his pupils, both boys and girls; in the epitaph of the schoolmaster Philocalus in Capua Philocalus prides himself on the fact that he behaved 'with the utmost chastity towards his pupils' (*CIL* X 3969 = *ILS* 7763: 'summa cum castitate in discipulos suos').

4 For the ideal of the *puer senex* and the motif of *mors immatura* in literature and funerary inscriptions, see Kleywegt (1991) 123–31, Carp, T. (1980) '*Puer senex* in Roman and mediaeval thought', *Latomus* 39: 736–9, Kampen (1981b) 53–5 and Marrou (1965) 197–207; for such motifs in Pliny's letter about Minicia Marcella, see Wiedemann (1989) 92–3. Similarly Fronto, in a letter about the illness of Marcus Aurelius' 2-year-old-daughter Anna Galeria Faustina, calls her 'gravis et prisca femina' ('a serious and old-fashioned lady'); see Fronto *Ad M. Caes.* 4.12.5 (= Haines I, pp. 208–9). Compare also the precocious learning and the fortitude in facing death for which Quintilian praised his son, who died at the age of 9 (Quint. 6 *praef.* 11).

5 Plin. *Ep.* 5.16.2: 'iam illi anilis prudentia, matronalis gravitas erat et tamen suavitas puellaris cum virginali verecundia'.

6 Plin. *Ep.* 5.16.9: 'He has lost a daughter who resembled him as closely in manners as in person and was her father's living image in every way' ('Amisit enim filiam, quae non minus mores eius quam os vultumque referebat, totumque patrem mira similitudine exscripserat'). The resemblance of a daughter to her father – and not, as we might expect, to her mother – is a recurring compliment in Roman literature: see Hallett (1984b) 338–43. Cicero, when missing his beloved daughter Tullia during his exile, calls her 'the very replica of myself in face, speech and spirit' and praises her filial affection, modesty and talents: Cic. *Q. Fr.* 1.3.3: 'qua pietate, qua modestia, quo ingenio? Effigiem oris, sermonis, animi mei'. For the importance of daughters and the relation between fathers and daughters in Roman upper-class families, see Hallett (1984b). For Fundanus' studiousness and erudition, see Plin. *Ep.* 5.16.8: 'eruditus et sapiens, ut qui se ab ineunte aetate altioribus studiis artibusque dediderit' ('He is an erudite and wise man, who has devoted himself from his earliest youth to the higher studies and arts'). He was a friend of Pliny's and the addressee of *Ep.* 1.9, 4.15, 6.6 and probably 7.12.

7 The fact that *praeceptores* (plural) are mentioned points to tuition in several specialized fields, not only grammar. In view of their father's interest in philosophy and the liberal arts, it seems likely that he had them instructed in these fields. Endurance in illness is one of the things Minicia may have been taught by a Stoic philosopher.

8 Minicius Fundanus was a friend of Plutarch's and the main speaker in his *Coh. Ira* (in *Mor.* 455F he mentions his wife and daughters); when young, he had attended the lectures of the Stoic philosopher Musonius Rufus (*Coh. Ira* 1, *Mor.* 453D). Fundanus is also mentioned in Plutarch's *Tranq. An.* (*Mor.* 464E); for Fundanus, see also Jones (1972) 58.

9 Musonius Rufus fr. IV: εἰ παραπλησίως παιδευτέον τὰς θυγατέρας τοῖς υἱοῖς. The title is usually translated as 'Should daughters receive the same education as sons?' (see, e.g, Lutz (1947) 43; Eyben and Wouters (1975) 186). But, as we shall see, Musonius did not advocate an identical education for boys and girls. Musonius Rufus, who was of equestrian rank, was born at Etruscan Volsinii around AD 30 and died before AD 101/2 (*RE* 16.1 cols 893–7; *PIR*² M 753; Demougin (1992) 605–6); for the collection of his treatises and shorter fragments see Hense, O. (ed.) (1905) *C. Musonii Rufi Reliquiae*, Leipzig: Teubner; for text, translation and commentary, see Lutz (1947), Geytenbeek (1963), Eyben and Wouters (1975) and Jagu (1979). Apart from the times he went into exile – in AD 62 he followed Rubellius Plautus into exile, in AD 65/6 he was banished by Nero to Gyaros and at an unknown date he was again banished by Vespasian – he lived mostly in Rome. He was greatly admired by the younger Pliny (see *Ep.* 3.11), and by other upper-class Romans, for his eloquence and moral integrity.

10 The twenty-one discourses preserved in Stobaeus seem to have been published by a certain Lucius (see Jagu (1979) 9–10 and 20, Lutz (1947) 6–8 and Geytenbeek (1963) 8–12), an unknown man, who may have been Musonius' pupil during his exile on the island of Gyaros. Despite being a Roman, Musonius probably lectured in Greek, which was the language of philosophy. For the question in how far 'Lucius' gives a true account of Musonius' ideas, see Lutz (1947) 24–6.

11 For φρόνησις see lines 2–14 and 72–7; for δικαιοσύνη lines 14–18 and 83–6; for σωφροσύνη lines 18–25 and 77–8, and for ἀνδρεία lines 25–37 and 78–83. In fr. III 'that women too should study philosophy' (ὅτι καὶ γυναιξὶ φιλοσοφητέον) the first of these virtues (φρόνησις) is replaced by good management of the household (line 18).

12 See Flacelière, R. (1962) 'D'un certain féminisme grec', *REA* 64: 115 and Jagu (1979)

14–15; also Geytenbeek (1963) 51–62 and Eyben and Wouters (1975) assume that Musonius advocated 'equal rights' for women.

13 Fragment IV, lines 86–92. This may perhaps account for the rather careless use of 'same' and 'similar' throughout the treatise: cf. τὴν αὐτὴν παιδείαν (lines 1 and 39) and παιδευτέον παραπλησίως (in the title and lines 71–2).

14 Fragment IV, lines 94–7: καὶ οὐ τοῦτο βούλομαι λέγειν, ὅτι τρανότητα περὶ λόγους καὶ δεινότητά τινα περιττὴν χρὴ προσεῖναι ταῖς γυναιξίν, εἴπερ φιλοσοφήσουσιν ὡς γυναῖκες (translation by Lutz (1947) 49 with some adjustments); see also fr. III, lines 59–65.

15 Lines 15–16 and 50–71. Too much has been made of Musonius' remark about the interchangeability of duties (lines 60–6). Geytenbeek (1963) 60 even concludes that Musonius 'deletes [. . .] the opposition between masculine and feminine tasks', but also in fr. III, 'that women too should study philosophy', he accepts the traditional distinction between male and female tasks; in both treatises the chief aim of the study of philosophy is to make women into better (house)wives and mothers.

16 Boatwright (1991) 538–40 relates the retiring and submissive attitude of imperial women during the reign of Trajan and Hadrian to the ideals expressed by men like Musonius Rufus, Pliny and Plutarch; for these women see chapter 4, pp. 116ff.

17 In fr. III, ὅτι καὶ γυναιξὶ φιλοσοφητέον, Musonius is very outspoken about the importance of domestic tasks for women (lines 18–20, 48–54 and 70–2) and of their role as loving and unselfish wives and mothers (lines 33–41), dismissing the allegation of a fictitious interlocutor that women studying philosophy become arrogant and neglect their household duties (lines 54–8, cited on p. 87).

18 Plut. *Praec. Coni.* 48 (*Mor.* 145B–6A); for Plutarch's views on marriage, see Treggiari (1991) 224–6 and Patterson, C. (1992) 'Plutarch's "Advice on marriage": traditional wisdom through a philosophic lens', *ANRW* II 33.6: 4709–23. For the identification of Pollianus with L. Flavius Pollianus Aristio (*PIR*² F 339), son of T. Flavius Soclarus (*PIR*² F 369), who was a friend of Plutarch's, and Eurydice with Memmia Eurydice, see Bowersock, G. W. (1965) 'Some persons in Plutarch's Moralia', *CQ* n.s. 15: 267–70. He argues that they were the parents of Flavia Clea, priestess at Delphi and recipient of Plutarch's *De Iside et Osiride* and *Mulierum Virtutes.* Also another treatise, attributed to Plutarch, propagates the education of women: 'that a woman, too, should be educated' (Plut. *Mor.* fr. 128–33 Sandbach: ὅτι καὶ γυναῖκα παιδευτέον). The small fragments preserved do not deal with women's education and, therefore, are not discussed here.

19 Plut. *Mor.* 145C: καθηγητὴς καὶ φιλόσοφος καὶ διδάσκαλος. For the harmful ideas developing in women's minds when left to themselves, see Plut. *Mor.* 145 D–E: ἂν γὰρ λόγων χρηστῶν σπέρματα μὴ δέχωνται μηδὲ κοινωνῶσι παιδείας τοῖς ἀνδράσιν, αὐταὶ καθ᾽ αὑτὰς ἄτοπα πολλὰ καὶ φαῦλα βουλεύματα καὶ πάθη κυοῦσι.

20 Plut. *Mor.* 145E–F; most examples stem from the Greek world and deal with female relatives of philosophers and kings of the old days, who were praised for their wisdom and courage. The Roman examples, Claudia Quinta (who vindicated her chastity when she received Cybele in Rome; see, e.g., Liv. 29.14.12, Ovid *Fast.* 4.305–28, Cic. *Har. Resp.* 27) and Cornelia, illustrate the virtues of chastity and simplicity.

21 Plut. *Praec. Coni.* 48 (*Mor.* 145C): τὰ δὲ τοιαῦτα μαθήματα πρῶτον ἀφίστησι τῶν ἀτόπων τὰς γυναῖκας· αἰσχυνθήσεται γὰρ ὀρχεῖσθαι γυνὴ γεωμετρεῖν μανθάνουσα, καὶ φαρμάκων ἐπῳδὰς οὐ προσδέξεται τοῖς Πλάτωνος ἐπᾳδομένη λόγοις καὶ τοῖς Ξενοφῶντος. ἂν δέ τις ἐπαγγέλληται καθαιρεῖν τὴν σελήνην, γελάσεται τὴν ἀμαθίαν καὶ τὴν ἀβελτερίαν τῶν ταῦτα πειθομένων γυναικῶν, ἀστρολογίας μὴ ἀνηκόως ἔχουσα.

22 For the stereotype of female credulity, see, e.g., Strabo 7.3.4 (about religion), Tac. *Ann.* 14.4.1 and Plut. *Pyth. Or.* 25 (*Mor.* 407C), who ranks women with lower-class men as

prone to credulity. For the relation of magic and the uneducated generally, Flinterman (1995) 64–5.

23 Hier. *Ep.* 107.4ff., dated in AD 403. Laeta, a Roman lady of senatorial rank (*RE* 12 Laeta 7 cols 451–2), had a pagan father, the pontifex Publilius Ceionius Caecina Albinus (*RE* 3 Ceionius 30), a man of great learning, but she was brought up as a Christian by her Christian mother. She married the Christian Julius Toxotius and desired to give their daughter Paula a good Christian upbringing. In his letter of instruction Jerome propagated the same method of learning to read and to write as was earlier prescribed by Quint. 1.1.20ff. For her companion Paula was to be given a girl who was *gravis, pallens, sordidata, subtristis* (Hier. *Ep.* 107.9) and her meals were always to leave her hungry (*Ep.* 107.10).

24 From Plato onwards the capacities of girls and women and their education had been a topic of philosophical debate and some of Musonius' notions about the education of women and the equality of virtues are found already in Plato, the early Stoa, Epicureanism and the Cynics: see Geytenbeek (1963) 53–62, Eyben and Wouters (1975) and Jagu (1979) 14–15 and 31–3. On Greek views, especially those of Plato, on women's education, see also Lefkowitz (1990) and Hawley, R. (1994) 'The problem of women philosophers in ancient Greece', in Archer *et al.* (1994) 70–86. In the view of the Greek physician Soranus education helped to bring girls safely through the dangerous years of puberty because it distracted their attention from their corporal maturation and suppressed premature desires; see Soranus *Gyn.* 1.33.4. For education as a useful occupation of otherwise wasted years, see Quint. 1.1.16–19.

25 Sen. *Cons. Helv.* 18.8: 'nunc mores eius compone, nunc forma; altius praecepta descendunt, quae teneris imprimuntur aetatibus. Tuis adsuescat sermonibus, at tuum fingatur arbitrium; multum illi dabis, etiam si nihil dederis praeter exemplum.' In *Cons. Marc* 16.1 he argues for moral equality between men and women and in *Cons. Helv.* 17.3–5 he advises his mother Helvia to study philosophy as a refuge from sorrow.

26 Sen. *Const. Sap.* 14.1: 'Quid refert . . . quot lecticarios habentem, quam oneratas aures, quam laxam sellam? Aeque inprudens animal est et, nisi scientia accessit ac multa eruditio, ferum, cupiditatium incontinens'; for his view of women as a prey to emotion and irrationality see also Sen. *De Ira* 3.24.3. For Seneca's contradictory views on women: Manning (1973), Eyben and Wouters (1975) 193; Geytenbeek (1963) 57–8.

27 This may be inferred from the – not very prominent – hostile tradition about Cornelia, which is connected with her involvement in the political activities of her sons. Very hostile is the account of App. *BC* 1.20, which suggests that together with her daughter Sempronia she murdered her son-in-law Scipio Aemilianus because of his resistance to the reforms of her sons. The story is fictitious, but relations between Scipio Aemilianus and Cornelia were probably strained for several reasons; see, e.g., Astin (1967) 36 and 226–41, Bernstein (1978) 53ff. and Barnard (1990) 389. Other accounts, such as Sen. *Cons. Helv.* 16.6, Plut. *TG* 8.5 and *CG* 4.3–4 and 13.2, are ambivalent or show hostile traits in the contemporary opinion about her which were mainly connected with the political alignment of her sons; see also Bernstein (1978) 44–5. For the hostile tradition regarding the Gracchi, which is found in Latin authors such as Cicero and stems from the senatorial opposition to their policy in their own days, see Scardigli (1979) 63.

28 For the ancient sources about Cornelia see *RE* 4 Cornelia 407 cols 1592–5. Plut. *Mor.* 145F and Aelian *VH* 14.45 mention her as a model of Roman female virtue (and Juv. 6.166–9 mocks her as a haughty and conceited woman because of her pride in her virtuousness). Her marriage was reputed to have been harmonious, as appears from the romantic (but, of course, fictitious) tale that Tiberius Gracchus, when given the choice, chose to die before his wife: see, e.g., Plut. *TG* 1.2–3, Plin *NH* 7.122, Val. Max. 4.6.1 (in his section on conjugal love), Cic. *Div.* 1.36 and (sceptical) 2.62. Plutarch reports that as a widow she turned down a marriage proposal from a reigning Ptolemy (*TG* 1.4).

NOTES

Rawson, E. (1975) 'Caesar's heritage: Hellenistic kings and their Roman equals', *JRS* 65: 154 assumes that the Ptolemy mentioned by Plutarch was Ptol. VI Philometor, who reigned from 180 to 145 BC, but Carcopino (1928) 77, Scullard, H. H. (1951) *Roman Politics 220–150 B.C.*, Oxford: Clarendon Press, p. 236 and Briscoe, J. (1969) 'Eastern policy and senatorial politics 168–146 BC', *Historia* 18: 49–51 suppose that it was Ptolemy VIII Euergetes II Physcon, who reigned with interruptions from 170 to 116 BC and visited Rome in 162 and 154 BC. Günther, L. M. (1990) 'Cornelia und Ptolemaios VIII: zur Historizität des Heiratsantrages', *Historia* 39: 124–8 argues that the proposal was not historical and that Plutarch's story of Cornelia rejecting it had a propagandistic aim: it served to underline the integrity of Cornelia and her family. For the Roman ideal of the *univira*, which in its traditional sense also comprised fidelity to the husband after his death, see, e.g., Williams (1958) 16–29, Lightman and Zeisel (1977) 19–32, von Hesberg-Tonn (1983), Dixon (1985b) 358–61 and (1990) 22 and Treggiari (1991) 233–5.

29 For Cornelia as the devoted mother see Plut. *TG* 1.4–5, Cic. *Brut.* 104 and 211, Tac. *Dial.* 28, Quint. 1.1.6; for the Roman ideal of motherhood see Dixon (1990). The well-known story in Val. Max. 4.4 *praef.*, in which she calls her children her jewels, is usually cited as proof of her disdain for jewelry and of her dedication to her children. The story is almost certainly fictitious, since a nearly identical story is told of the wife of Phocion (Plut. *Phoc.* 19.3). The difference between Cornelia calling her children her ornaments and the wife of Phocion describing her husband in that way is perhaps connected with the difference between the Greek and the Roman conception of female loyalty; see also Barnard (1990) 387. In Sen. *Cons. Marc.* 16.3 and *Cons. Helv.* 16.6 Cornelia figures as the mother enduring hardship without complaint, a model of self-control held up for suffering mothers like Marcia and Helvia. For her exemplary self-control, see also Plut. *CG* 19.

30 As regards the question whether she approved of the political course taken by her sons or opposed it, the ancient sources conflict: see, e.g., Plut. *TG* 8.5 and *CG* 4.2–4, 13.2, App. *BC* I.20, Diod. Sic. 34.25.2, Cic. *De Or.* 3.214, Dio 24.83.8, and the so-called 'Cornelia fragments' in Nepos (fr. 59 Marshall), discussed in chapter 6, pp. 193ff. For modern discussion see, e.g., Stockton (1979) 25–6 and 116–17, Förtsch, B. (1935) *Die politische Rolle der Frau in der römischen Republik*, Stuttgart: Kohlhammer, pp. 56–72 (for bias in her work, see Vos, M. de (1990) 'De emancipatie van de Romeinse vrouw als historiografische constructie', *Tijdschrift voor Vrouwenstudies* 43: 290); Kreck (1975) 47–105 (who distinguishes a popular and an optimate view on Cornelia) and Barnard (1990) 389–90.

31 Moir (1983) 143 argues that Cornelia was born around 195 BC, believing that Plut. *TG* 4.3, who calls Cornelia 'unmarried and unbetrothed' (ἀνέκδοτον καὶ ἀνέγγυον) when her father died, shows that she was of marriageable age in 183 BC. However, this is not convincing: the fact that she was unmarried at that time does not mean that she was of marriageable age. The *terminus ante quem* for Cornelia's marriage is the birth of her eldest son, Tiberius Gracchus, in 163–2 BC. Pliny *NH* 7.57 is a source of confusion here. In a discussion of the fertility of couples he writes 'aliaeque feminas tantum generant aut mares, plerumque et alternant, sicut Gracchorum mater duodeciens, Agrippina Germanici noviens' ('some women have only female or only male children, though usually the sexes come alternately – for instance, in the case of the mother of the Gracchi this occurred twelve times, and in that of Germanicus' wife Agrippina nine times'). This has usually been interpreted to mean that Cornelia gave birth to boys and girls alternately; on the assumption that Tiberius Gracchus was her eldest son since he had his father's *praenomen* (possibly with one daughter before him), a date of marriage as late as 165 BC has been proposed. This date leaves Cornelia hardly twelve years to bear twelve children, as her husband Tiberius Gracchus died around 154 BC.

263

Against this opinion Moir (1983) suggests that 'plerumque et alternant' means that six daughters were followed by six sons, the change of sex taking place only once and not at every single birth. This interpretation requires a much earlier date of marriage – she suggests 181/0 BC – which fits well with her estimate of Cornelia's birth in 195 BC. I wonder, however, if Cicero would have called Cornelia *adulescens* (*Div.* 1.36) at her husband's death, if she was 41 at the time. In my opinion, Carcopino's suggestion (1928) 71–4 is more convincing: Pliny means to say that Cornelia bore children of both sexes (without even assuming equal numbers: the other example, Agrippina Maior, had six boys and three girls), thus producing a kind of family which with good reason can be described as occurring 'usually' (*plerumque*). Carcopino's estimate of Cornelia's date of marriage in 176/5 (p. 66) provides Cornelia with nearly twenty-two years to bear twelve children. Strictly speaking, Plutarch suggests that all twelve children were still alive and in her care (and, therefore, under age) at her husband's death (*TG* 1.3 and 5), which necessitates a date of marriage around 170 BC, but one should perhaps not rely too much on Plutarch's rather sketchy account for details of chronology. When her husband died in 154 BC she must have been in her thirties, still comparatively young. She remained a widow for the rest of her life, during which she suffered the murder of both her famous sons, and lived to old age in her villa at Misenum. Her daughter Sempronia probably survived her, since in 101 BC she was called upon to unmask an imposter, who posed as Tiberius' son (Val. Max. 3.8.6). The fact that Cornelia is not named in this instance is usually taken as an indication that she had died before 101 BC; see *RE* 4 Cornelia 407 col. 1595; *contra* Moir (1983) 139–40. Seneca *Cons. Marc.* 16.3, however, claims that all Cornelia's children died before her, but this may have been a mistake; also in the *Cons. Helv.* 16.6 he wrongly assumes that Tiberius and Gaius survived all other children, thereby overlooking Sempronia, who outlived both. In her last years, Plut. *CG* 19 tells us, she spoke of her sons with detachment and without showing sorrow as though they belonged to ancient history. Consequently some people believed that her mental capacities were affected by old age, which is vigorously denied by Plutarch. Although his report does not inform us of her age, she apparently outlived her sons for several years. Thus, we may assume that she lived to be over 70 or perhaps even reached 80.

32 For Scipio Africanus, see Scullard (1970); for his philhellenism also Gruen (1992) 242–3. Before his death, early in 183 BC, Africanus had agreed to give each of his daughters an enormous dowry of 50 talents (which is more than 1,300,000 HS per person; see Boyer (1950) 172 and 176), half of which was to be paid by his wife Aemilia, who had been appointed as his *heres*, at their marriage; the other half was liable for payment at her death, which occurred in 162 BC, and was duly paid by her heir Scipio Aemilianus (Pol. 31.27). For an instructive discussion of this matter see Boyer (1950) 172–8 and Dixon (1985a) 147–70.

33 For Aemilia see *RE* 1 col. 592 Aemilia 179; Dixon (1985a) 151ff.; Barnard (1990) 384–7; for her display of wealth: Pol. 31.26. For Aemilius Paullus see, e.g., Astin (1967) 15. He had acquired a whole staff of tutors from Greece to educate his children and after his conquest of Macedonia he allotted his sons as their part of the booty a choice of the books from the library of Perseus (Plut. *Aem.* 6.5 and 28.6, Plin *NH* 35.135, Isid. *Etym.* 6.5.1). For this library, see chapter 2, p. 54.

34 He was her natural cousin through her mother, her adoptive nephew through his adoption by her brother Publius and her son-in-law through his marriage to her only surviving daughter Sempronia, though he was of about the same age as Cornelia herself. He was the central character in Cicero's *De Republica* and *De Senectute*, and the *De Amicitia* dwells on his friendship with Laelius, but see Zetzel (1972). For Scipio Aemilianus see, e.g., Astin (1967), who includes a sound discussion of the so-called Scipionic Circle (pp. 294–306), which has been given undue importance by some

scholars, e.g., Brown, R. M. (1934) *A Study of the Scipionic Circle*, Scottdale, Pa. (Iowa Studies in Classical Philology, vol. 1). Against 'literary circles' at this period see also Gold (1987) 8 and 183, n. 32. Gruen (1992) 197–202 rejects his supposed patronage of Terence and (pp. 224–6) the so-called Scipionic Circle.

35 For P. Cornelius Scipio see *RE* 4 cols 1437–8 Cornelius 331, Astin (1967) 12–14 and Scullard (1970) 238. For his eloquence see, e.g., Vell. Pat. 1.10.3 and Cic. *Brut.* 77; for his historical work in Greek see Cic. *Brut.* 77. Because of his ill-health he was debarred from high office and therefore he was inconspicuous in public life and consequently also in history.

36 For Cornelia's choice of Greek teachers see Cic. *Brut.* (100 and) 104; for her contact with Greek scholars, Plut. *CG* 19; for her eloquence in Latin, e.g., Cic. *Brut.* 211 and Quint. 1.1.6. For her education, see also chapter 2, pp. 24f.

37 For Gracchus senior (*cos* 177) see *RE* 2A Sempronius 53 and Bernstein (1978) 39–42 and 210. For the considerable disparity in age between Gracchus and Cornelia see Plut. *TG* 1.2, Plin. *NH* 7.122 and Cic. *Div.* 1.36. He was born between 220 BC (*RE* 2A Sempronius 53 col. 1404 followed by Bernstein (1978) 26 and Moir (1983) 141) and 208 BC (Carcopino (1928) 70) and was noted for his brilliant public career and for his personal integrity (Plut. *TG* 1).

38 As a mother's authority was strengthened by widowhood, at least when she was well-born and wealthy like Cornelia, a second marriage was probably not very attractive. Therefore, Cornelia's real motives for not remarrying may have been other than the loyalty to her deceased husband attributed to her in most ancient sources. For the status and authority of a wealthy widowed mother, see chapter 1, p. 10.

39 Her marriage to Scipio Aemilianus took place before Scipio set off for Carthage in 147 BC: see Plut. *TG* 4.4, Bernstein (1978) 55 and Stockton (1979) 24–5. Carcopino (1928) 77 argues that in view of Scipio Aemilianus' campaigns abroad they were probably married in 152 BC or slightly earlier. For this marriage which was childless and notoriously unhappy, see Liv. *Ep.* 59, App. *BC* 1.20, Oros. 5.10.10 and Astin (1967) 235–6.

40 As a mother could not exercise true *tutela*, a *tutor* must have been nominally in control; see Gardner (1990) 14–22. Only in late antiquity was the right of *tutela* sometimes conferred on a mother if she swore not to remarry; see Dixon (1990) 64–5.

41 Plut. *TG* 1.4: 'Cornelia took charge of the children and of the estate, and showed herself so discreet, so good a mother, and so magnanimous, that Tiberius was thought to have made no bad decision when he chose to die instead of such a woman' (Κορνηλία δὲ ἀναλαβοῦσα τοὺς παῖδας καὶ τὸν οἶκον, οὕτω σώφρονα καὶ φιλότεκνον καὶ μεγαλόψυχον αὑτὴν παρέσχεν ὥστε μὴ κακῶς δόξαι βεβουλεῦσθαι τὸν Τιβέριον ἀντὶ τοιαύτης γυναικὸς ἀποθανεῖν ἑλόμενον). Cic. *Brut.* 211: 'in gremio . . . matris' and Tac. *Dial.* 28: 'gremio ac sinu matris'. Education by the parent was idealized as the way of bringing up children in of the good old days, Bonner (1977) 10–19.

42 Cic. *Brut.* 211: 'Legimus epistulas Corneliae matris Gracchorum; apparet filios non tam in gremio educatos quam in sermone matris'; similarly Quint. 1.1.6: 'We are told that the eloquence of the Gracchi owed much to their mother Cornelia, whose highly educated way of speaking is preserved also for later generations in her letters' ('Gracchorum eloquentiae multum contulisse accepimus Corneliam matrem, cuius doctissimus sermo in posteros quoque est epistolis traditus'); Hier. *Ep.* 107.4 mentions Cornelia as one of the exemplary mothers of pagan Rome: 'We are told that the eloquence of the Gracchi was largely due to the way in which their mother talked to them as children' ('Gracchorum eloquentiae multum ab infantia sermo matris scribitur contulisse'). For her careful education of her sons see also Tac. *Dial.* 28 and Plut. *TG* 1.5: 'These boys Cornelia brought up with such care and such ambitious hopes that, although by common consent no Romans have ever been more naturally gifted, they

were considered to owe their virtues even more to education than to nature' (οὕτω φιλοτίμως ἐξέθρεψεν ὥστε πάντων εὐφυεστάτους Ῥωμαίων ὁμολογουμένως γεγονότας πεπαιδεῦσθαι δοκεῖν βέλτιον ἢ πεφυκέναι πρὸς ἀρετήν).

43 Cic. *Brut.* 104, about Tiberius: 'Fuit Gracchus diligentia Corneliae matris a puero doctus et Graecis litteris eruditus. Nam semper habuit exquisitos e Graecia magistros, in eis iam adulescens Diophanem Mytilenaeum Graeciae temporibus illis disertissimum.' See also Cic. *Brut.* 100: Gaius' teacher Menelaus of Marathus.

44 Cic. *Brut.* 104, 125 and 211, Quint. 1.1.6, Tac. *Dial.* 28.6, and Plut. *TG* 1.5. Cicero, who on the whole is rather negative about the Gracchi because of their political course (see Scardigli (1979) 63), concedes that they possessed great eloquence (see, e.g., his remarks in *Rab. Post.* 14–15, *Font.* 39, *Brut.* 103–4, 125–6, *De Or.* 1.154 and *Har. Resp.* 41), which to his mind they owed both to Cornelia's influence and to their natural talents.

45 In a section on Roman bronze statues Plin. *NH* 34.31 mentions the statue erected for 'Corneliae Gracchorum matri, quae fuit Africani prioris filia. Sedens huic posita soleisque sine ammento insignis in Metelli publica porticu, quae statua nunc est in Octaviae operibus.' Plutarch also mentions the statue in *CG* 4.3: 'later they [i.e. the people] erected a bronze statue of her with the inscription "Cornelia, mother of the Gracchi"' (ἧς γε καὶ χαλκῆν εἰκόνα στήσας ὕστερον ἐπέγραψε Κορνηλίαν μητέρα Γράγχων). Flory (1993) 290, following Coarelli (1978) 13–28, believes that Plutarch gives the original inscription (in Greek translation) 'as it was at the time of the statue's erection' (which Coarelli dates around 100 BC) and that it was recut in the Augustan period to include the name of her father. However, Plutarch's rather loose statement cannot be used as evidence for an inscription of the second or first century BC; moreover, as will be argued in the next note, the existence of a statue of Cornelia before the Augustan period (and, therefore, of an earlier inscription) seems highly unlikely. Judging from his rendering of the inscription it seems more likely that Plutarch had not seen the statue himself. It may already have been lost in Plutarch's days; perhaps it was burnt in the fire of the Porticus Octaviae in AD 80: Bernoulli, J. J. (1882) *Römische Ikonographie I: Die Bildnisse berühmter Römer (mit Ausschluss der Kaiser und ihrer Angehörigen)* Stuttgart: Spemann, p. 73 draws attention to the traces of fire on the surface of the base. Coarelli (1978) 20, however, believes that the statue survived even the fire of AD 191 and that the Severan inscription 'opus Tisicratis', which he connects with the statue of Cornelia and not with a subsequent reuse of the base, had been added during the restoration of the *porticus* in AD 203.

46 Honorific statues of women like Cloelia (an equestrian statue!) and other legendary women (see Plin. *NH* 34.28–9; see also Liv. 2.13, Plut. *Publ.* 19.5, *Mul.Virt.* 14 (*Mor.* 250F), *Quaest. Rom.* 30 (*Mor.* 271E); see Kajava (1989) 123–4) have never been confirmed by finds and must be discarded as fictions. Both Plutarch and Pliny are vague as regards the date of the erection of the statue. In his discussion of Gaius' conflict with M. Octavius in which Cornelia successfully interfered (123 BC), Plutarch says that the people 'later' (ὕστερον) erected a bronze statue in her honour. The elder Pliny connects his account with (probably unhistorical) utterances of Cato the Elder in 184 BC. Considering the many inaccuracies in Pliny's work his remark that the Porticus Metelli (built from 146 BC onwards and dedicated in 131 BC) was where the statue was first located is not above suspicion. Yet, Coarelli (1978) 13–25 dates the erection of the statue around 100 BC and argues that its placement in the Porticus Metelli was an act of deliberate provocation (the Metelli were political opponents of the Gracchi); he is followed by Flory (1993). Kajava (1989) 119–31, especially p. 121, suggests a date shortly after the death of Gaius in 121 BC or slightly later, thus connecting the statue with the statues that were set up spontaneously for the Gracchi by the people according to Plutarch *CG* 18.3. However, as even in the Greek East honorific statues of Roman

senatorial women date only from the first century BC onwards (see Kajava (1990b) 95ff.), the presence of a public honorific statue of Cornelia in Rome before the time of Augustus seems highly unlikely.

47 *CIL* VI 31610 (=10043) = *ILS* 68 = *ILLRP* 336 = *Inscriptiones Italiae* XIII.3.72 (with a photograph), now in the Museo Nuovo, catal. epigr. 6969. For a discussion of this base and its inscriptions (the inscription of Cornelia, generally accepted to be of Augustan date; the Severan inscription above it reads: 'opus Tisicratis') see Kajava (1989) 125ff., Coarelli (1978) 14ff. and Kreck (1975) 66–70. In epigraphic usage *mater* is indispensable here; a sole genitive after the affiliation usually denotes the woman's husband. For a discussion of this anomaly see Kajava (1989) 127–8. The only parallel (Val. Max 6.7.1: 'Aemilia . . . mater Corneliae Gracchorum') is, according to Lewis, R. G. (1988) 'Some mothers . . .', *Athenaeum* 66: 198–200, to be explained by its context. I do not think, however, that the omission of *mater* is satisfactorily explained by assuming that there was a group of mother-figures as Lewis suggests (p. 200); rather it seems to be a convenient short cut which, because of her fame, was thought to be sufficient. Also the sole use of 'Africanus' to denote her father is uncommon (but cf. Vell. Pat. 2.7.1: 'Cornelia, Africani filia' and Plin. *NH* 34.31), but may be explained by his fame. If the inscription is not a fake of recent date – and apart from this anomaly there is no reason to suppose so – we must assume that Cornelia was sufficiently well known for this inscription to be understood; see Kajava (1989) 130.

48 Suet. *Aug.* 31.5. Hallett, J. (1985) 'Queens, *princeps* and women of the Augustan élite: Propertius' Cornelia-elegy and the *Res Gestae Divi Augusti*', in Winkes, R. (ed.) (1985) *The Age of Augustus*, Louvain-la-Neuve (Archaeologica Transatlantica V), pp. 82–3 suggests that the statue was erected by Augustus as a tribute to the ancestress of his stepchildren (the children of his former wife Scribonia), the virtuous Cornelia (see Prop. 4.11) and her brother P. Cornelius Scipio, and may have been connected with the consulship of the latter in 16 BC, but this seems insufficient to explain the erection of the statue.

49 See chapter 4, n. 45.

50 See Coarelli (1978) 26–7 and Kajava (1989) 128f. For the reflection in art of Augustus' restoration of traditional morality, see Zanker (1990) 161ff. Coarelli (1978) 20–1 and Kajava (1989) 127 suggest that Cornelia's statue was modelled upon the (lost) seated Aphrodite of Phidias, which is supposed to have been the model for many statues of seated women down to the fourth century AD and which according to Pliny *NH* 36.15 also stood in the Porticus Octaviae. However, there seems to be no good reason to assume that Cornelia was modelled upon this statue; it may just as well be suggested that she was modelled upon statues of more appropriate goddesses like Hestia, Cybele or Demeter.

51 Cf. Plut. *Quaest. Rom.* 30 (*Mor.* 271E), who regards sandals as a symbol of love of one's home. Varro mentions wearing 'shoes without straps' (*sine fasceis calciamenta*) as one of the signs of the simple life in the countryside during his youth; see Varro in his 'on the education of children', *Catus, de Liberis Educandis* fr. 19. For sandals see Goldman, N. (1994) 'Roman footwear', in Sebesta and Bonfante (1994) 105–11.

52 For her grand style of living and her patronage of Greek scholars in her Campanian villa, see chapter 4, pp. 97ff. For her political role, see n. 30 above and the discussion about the so-called 'Cornelia fragments', chapter 6, pp. 193ff.

53 Similarly, in early twentieth-century America the trained and disciplined mind which was thought necessary to educate children served as a justification for a college education for girls: see Rothman, S. M. (1978) *Woman's Proper Place: A History of Changing Ideals and Practices, 1870 to the Present*, New York: Basic Books, pp. 97–8 and 106–8.

54 For Octavia and Antonia Minor see chapter 4, pp. 104ff.

55 For the authoritative role and the *disciplina ac severitas* expected of the ideal Roman mother see Dixon (1990); see also chapter 1, p. 10. This sub-section centres on the role

of mothers as educators of sons; for their role in the education of daughters see chapter 2, n. 52.

56 Tac. *Dial.* 28: 'Nam pridem suus cuique filius, ex casta parente natus, non in cellula emptae nutricis, sed gremio ac sinu matris educabatur, cuius praecipua laus erat tueri domum et inservire liberis. Eligebatur autem maior aliqua natu propinqua, cuius probatis spectatisque moribus omnis eiusdem familiae suboles committeretur; coram qua neque dicere fas erat quod turpe dictu, neque facere quod inhonestum factu videretur. Ac non studia modo curasque, sed remissiones etiam lususque puerorum sanctitate quadam ac verecundia temperabat. Sic Corneliam Gracchorum, sic Aureliam Caesaris, sic Atiam Augusti praefuisse educationibus ac produxisse principes liberos accepimus.' For the vices of contemporary education, see Tac. *Dial* 29.

57 Bonner (1977) 15. For Aurelia, see *RE* 2 Aurelia 248 col. 2543, Cic. *Brut.* 252: the purity of Caesar's Latin was formed *domestica consuetudine*; Plut. *Caes.* 9–10 characterizes her as a woman of strict respectability. For Atia, the mother of Augustus and of his sister Octavia, see *RE* 2 Atia 34 cols 2257–8; after the death of her husband C. Octavius she remarried, but the influence of the stepfather on Octavian's education seems to have been small. For Atia's careful and strict education of her son, see Nic. Dam. *Vit. Caes.* 3–6 (*F. Gr. H.* IIA 90, fr. 127 Jacoby); see also Dixon (1990) 172–3 and Parker, E. R. (1946) 'The education of heirs in the Julio-Claudian family', *AJPh* 67: 29–50. For Iulia Procilla: *FOS* 454; *PIR²* I 693.

58 Tac. *Agr.* 4.2–3: 'Mater Iulia Procilla fuit, rarae castitatis. In huius sinu indulgentiaque educatus per omnem honestarum artium cultum pueritiam adulescentiamque transegit . . . Memoria teneo solitum ipsum narrare se prima in iuventa studium philosophiae acrius, ultra quam concessum Romano ac senatori, hausisse, ni prudentia matris incensum ac flagrantem animum coercuisset.'

59 For Agrippina Minor checking Nero's passion for philosophy see Suet. *Ner.* 52.1; for Domitia Lucilla's interference with her son's eagerness to follow the life of a philosopher: *SHA M.A.* 2.6 (for Domitia Lucilla *FOS* 329, *PIR²* D183, *RE* 5 Domitia 105 cols 1518–19; see also n. 60 below). Also Julia Mamaea (*PIR²* I 649), the widowed mother of Alexander Severus, was known for her excellent education of her son (Herodian 5.7.5) and allegedly turned her son's attention from philosophy and music to other pursuits: *SHA Alex. Sev.* 14.5 (for her beneficial influence see also 66.1). For Antonia's and Livia's protest against the subject of Claudius' historical writing see Suet. *Claud.* 41.2. A passion for philosophy was thought incompatible with political life and the dignity of a Roman senator or ruler: see Griffin, M. and Barnes, J. (eds) (1989) *Philosophia Togata I: Essays on Philosophy and Roman Society*, Oxford: Clarendon Press, pp. 19–22. For the Greek roots of these objections to philosophy, see Flinterman (1995) 205ff.

60 Dixon (1990) 170–4 assumes that mothers successfully interfered with their sons' studies *in spite of* their exclusion from formal education, taking this as a sign of their authority over them. However, their undeniable authority was backed by their education. Though we do not know details of the education of all upper-class women mentioned in this sub-section, we know that, for instance, Agrippina Minor was so well-educated that she wrote and published her autobiography (see chapter 6, pp. 186ff.) and chose Seneca as a tutor for her son Nero (Tac. *Ann.* 12.8; Dio 60.32.3). Also Julia Mamaea was respected for her education (see chapter 4, n. 127) and capable of choosing good teachers for her son (Herodian 5.7.5). Domitia Lucilla, Marcus Aurelius' widowed mother, who checked her son's philosophical leanings, was thoroughly educated in both Greek and Latin, as may be inferred from Fronto's long and erudite Greek letters to her (see chapter 6, pp. 199f.). The Athenian orator Herodes Atticus, who was to be one of her son's tutors in Greek oratory, had lived for a time in her father's house during her youth (Fronto *Ad M. Caes.* 3.2 = Haines I, pp. 60–1).

61 Cic. *Brut.* 210, in a discussion about the importance of home training for the future orator: 'It does certainly make a great difference what sort of speakers one is daily associated with at home, with whom one has been in the habit of talking from child-hood onwards, how one's father, one's attendant, one's mother too speaks' ('magni interest quos quisque audiat cotidie domi, quibuscum loquatur a puero, quem ad modum patres paedagogi matres etiam loquantur'). Also Quint. 1.1.6 makes sure that mothers are included: 'As regards parents, I should like to see them as highly educated as possible, and I do not speak only of fathers' ('In parentibus vero quam plurimum esse eruditionis optaverim, nec de patribus tantum loquor'), though he also attaches much value to the correctness of speech of nurses, who took care of children in their earliest years (Quint. 1.1.4–5). Vitr. *Arch.* 6 *praef.* 4 expresses gratitude to both his parents for his liberal education and Martial *Ep.* 9.73.7–8 mockingly reproaches his parents for giving him grammatical and rhetorical training, which, in his view, was less profitable than the occupation of a cobbler: 'But me my foolish parents taught paltry letters: what is the use of teachers of grammar and rhetoric to me?' ('at me litterulas stulti docuere parentes: / quid cum grammaticis rhetoribusque mihi?').

62 Education by a widowed mother did not always turn out successfully: see *SHA Q.T.* 14.1 about the usurper Bonosus (late third century AD): 'he lost his father when a child, and being reared by his mother, a very brave woman, he learned nothing of literature' ('parvulus patrem amisit atque a matre fortissima educatus litterarum nihil didicit). Nero, who lost his father at the age of 3, and whose mother Agrippina was banished in his early youth as well, was brought up very badly by his aunt Domitia Lepida (*FOS* 319), who gave him, according to Suet. *Nero* 6.3, 'a dancer and a barber' as tutors ('sub duobus paedagogis saltatore atque tonsore'). His fortunes changed with the return of his mother from exile. A widowed mother could consult her son's guardian, or a family friend, about the teachers to be chosen for him: for example, the widowed Corellia Hispulla (*FOS* 268; *PIR*² C1296) had employed home tutors for the grammatical educa-tion of her son. When he was to enter the rhetorical phase she sought Pliny's advice for the best tutor in Latin rhetoric: Plin. *Ep.* 3.3.3. More examples of a successful education of sons by widowed mothers: Sertorius, who was brought up by his widowed mother, was thoroughly trained in law and rhetoric, Plut. *Sert.* 2; the young Pliny pursued his studies under the watchful eye of his widowed mother, Plinia Secunda: Plin. *Ep.* 6.20; Marcia's son was educated well under her constant guid-ance, Sen. *Cons. Helv.* 24.2; the well-educated North-African widow Aemilia Puden-tilla had taught her ne'er-do-well son Sicinius Pudens to speak a little Greek, Apul. *Apol.* 98.8.

63 See, for instance, Dixon (1992a) and (1992b) 49–50; see also chapter 4, pp. 101f.

64 For example, Marcus Aurelius' praise of his mother, Domitia Lucilla, is expressed in conventional terms emphasizing her 'abstention not only from doing ill, but even from the very thought of doing it; and furthermore to live the simple life, far removed from the habits of the rich' (ἀφεκτικὸν οὐ μόνον τοῦ κακοποιεῖν, ἀλλὰ καὶ τοῦ ἐπὶ ἐννοίας γίνεσθαι τοιαύτης· ἔτι δὲ τὸ λιτὸν κατὰ τὴν δίαιταν καὶ πόρρω τῆς πλουσιακῆς διαγωγῆς, *Med.* 1.3; she is also mentioned in *Med.* 1.7.2 and 9.21), though, in fact, she was a very wealthy, well-educated and politically influential woman (for her great wealth, see *RE* Suppl. 15 cols 1523–4; Mratschek-Halfmann (1993) 366–7 no. 299 and Birley (1966) 25–6; for her effective political support, see, for instance, *SHA Did. Jul.* 1.3 and Champlin (1980) 109). Also Fronto in one of his Greek letters addressed to her (*Epist. Graec.* 2.2 = Haines I, pp. 148–9) praises her as possessing 'all virtues and accomplish-ments befitting a woman' (ἁπάσας τὰς γυναικὶ πρεπούσας ἀρετὰς καὶ ἐπιστήμας), but nowhere does he mention her excellent education and her versatility in Greek, which is only implied by the care with which he wrote his Greek letters (Fronto *Epist. Graec.* 1 and 2) addressed to her and his anxiety that she might detect barbarisms in

them (see also Fronto *Ad M. Caes.* 1.8.7 = Haines I, pp. 124–5); see also chapter 6, pp. 199f.

65 For the ideal of companionship and harmony in marriage and the notion of the husband as a teacher of his wife, see chapter 2, pp. 31ff.

66 For a brief survey of the social position of upper-class women, see chapter 1. For an illustrative example of the financial activities and duties of upper-class women and the financial, political and moral support they were expected to give their husband when exiled, see the case-study of Cicero's wife Terentia (and his daughter Tullia) by Dixon (1992a); for a brief discussion of how far upper-class women could control their finances independently, see chapter 4, pp. 101f. For women's letters, see chapter 6, pp. 188ff. Against, among others, Harris (1989), McDonnell (1996) stresses the frequency with which upper-class men (and, perhaps slightly less frequently, women of the same class) chose to write in their own hands and the legibility of their handwriting, despite the presence of readers and secretaries of the servile class in upper-class households.

67 For the education of Laelia, the elder daughter of C. Laelius (*cos* 140 BC), see chapter 2, n. 51 and chapter 3, pp. 76f.

68 See Plut. *Cat. Ma.* 18.3 speaking about the resentment of Cato's taxation of luxuries: 'for most people think themselves robbed of their wealth if they are prevented from displaying it, and it is the superfluities, not the necessities of life, which really afford the opportunity for such display' (πλούτου γὰρ ἀφαίρεσιν οἱ πολλοὶ νομίζουσι τὴν κώλυσιν αὐτοῦ τῆς ἐπιδείξεως, ἐπιδείκνυσθαι δὲ τοῖς περιττοῖς, οὐ τοῖς ἀναγκαίοις). For the 'unproductive expenditure of time' as a mark of high social status, see Veblen, Th. (1899/1994) *The Theory of the Leisure Class*, Harmondsworth: Penguin, p. 45. As has been explained above (see the sub-section entitled 'The ideal of educated mother-hood'), the usefulness of Cornelia's education as regards the education of her sons is an invention of later date and should not be regarded as the actual reason for her extensive education.

69 As we saw in the preceding chapter, wealth, class and family greatly influenced women's opportunities for education, women of the imperial family and those of the leading senatorial families having the best chances: imperial women such as Augustus' sister Octavia and her daughter Antonia, Agrippina Maior and Agrippina Minor, Plotina, Sabina (chapter 4) and Marcus Aurelius' mother Domitia Lucilla (chapter 6, pp. 199ff.) were highly educated, culminating in the great erudition of Julia Domna and the women of her family. In a letter to his mother Julia Mamaea, Severus Alexander is said to have written about his sister (*SHA Max. Duo* 29): 'but I fear that my sister, educated in the refinements of Greek culture, could not endure a barbarian father-in-law, however much the young man himself may seem handsome and learned and imbued with Greek elegance' ('sed timeo, ne soror mea Graecis munditiis erudita barbarum socerum ferre non possit, quamvis ipse adulescens et pulcher et scholasticus et ad Graecas munditias eruditus esse videatur'). Though the existence of this sister is contested, the letter shows that – at least to the writer of this part of the *Historia Augusta* – education and culture were appreciated as a matter of course for the women of Severus' family.

70 Mart. *Ep.* 12.97.3: 'dives, nobilis, erudita, casta'. Also Ov. *AA* 2.282 (below n. 94) and Lucian's mockery in *Merc. Cond.* 36 of Roman upper-class women who wished to be acknowledged as πεπαιδευμέναι indicate that education brought prestige during the empire, also to women. For the regard for education during the principate, see, e.g., Wallace-Hadrill (1983) 26ff., Zanker (1995) 193–272, Mratschek-Halfmann (1993) 14–20; see also chapter 2, n. 11. Illustrative of the rising appreciation of education for women during the empire is the change in the image of Mary, mother of Christ, whose learning was upgraded in the mid-third century to rival that of contemporary upper-class (Christian) women. She was praised for studying the scriptures, which resulted, in subsequent art, in the scenes of the Annunciation with Mary reading: see Vogt, J.

(1974) *Ancient Slavery and the Ideal of Man*, Oxford: Blackwell, pp. 146ff., especially 158–9, and Lane Fox, R. (1988) *Pagans and Christians in the Mediterranean World from the Second Century AD to the Conversion of Constantine*, Harmondsworth: Penguin, p. 311.

71 See, for instance, *CIL* VI 9693 (*CLE* 1136): a certain Euphrosyne is praised as 'docta, opulenta, pia, casta, pudica, proba'; *CIL* VI 10096: the freedwoman of Licinia, the actress Eucharis, who died at the age of 14, is praised in her long epitaph as 'docta erodita omnes artes'. *CIL* VI 12652: Homonoea, a freedwoman who died before her twentieth birthday, 'quam Pallas cunctis artibus erudiit'; *CIL* VI 18324: had the 7-year-old Dionysia lived on, 'doctior in terris nulla puella foret'; *CIL* VI 20674: Julia Secunda, aged 11, 'doctrinaq(ue) super legitimam sexus sui aetatem praestantissimae'; *CIL* VI 21846: Magnilla, 7 years old, is called 'super annos docta'; *CIL* VI 25808: a girl, not yet married and deceased at the age of 15, is called 'erudita omnibus artibus'; *CIL* VI 33898 (*ILS* 7783): Euphrosyne, who died at 20, was 'docta novem musis' and 'philosopha'; *AE* (1916) 56: Ianuaria, 15 years old, 'cunctas artes perbibit'. For girls receiving lessons, and girls and women reading and writing on sarcophagi or *columbaria* from Rome, see Marrou (1938) no. 1, 8, 13, 68, 71 (the tomb of a freedwoman called Claudia Italia, *CIL* VI 15482, showing the deceased woman with a book-roll in her hand opened at the last 'page', a symbol of death, on which is inscribed: πάσης μουσικῆς μετέχουσα), 72, 84, 89, 102, 103, 106, 111 (Christian), 154, 156, 157, 163, 165, 167 (Christian), 192 and 193; see also Amedick, R. (1991) *Die Sarkophage mit Darstellungen aus dem Menschenleben: Vita Privata*, Berlin: Mann (ASR 1, 4), p. 66. Most of the epitaphs seem to have been erected for (Greek) freedwomen who may have received their training as slaves, but the sarcophagi also show freeborn girls of well-to-do families. The formulaic and stereotypical words of praise should, of course, not be taken literally: these girls and young women were not, all of them, departed geniuses. But the pride in their education, though partly reflecting professional pride, demonstrates that they had adapted themselves to upper-class values and ideals.

72 Six pictures of this type are listed by Schefold (1957) 130, 158, 168, 171–2, 202 and 249; see further Helbig (1868) nos 1422–6, Harris (1989) 263, n. 459, Stemmer, K. (1992) *Casa dell' Ara massima (VI 16, 15–17)*, Munich: Hirmer, pl. 154ff., *Pompeii: pitturi e mosaici*, Rome: Istituto della Enciclopedia Italiana, vol. V (1994) 878 no. 40, vol. VI (1996) 486 and 621, vol. VII (1997) 572. For paintings of women, most of them finely dressed, reading papyrus rolls, see Helbig (1868) nos 1866–8 and Birt (1976) 162–7. The two portraits discussed here are in Naples, National Museum inv. nos 9084 (the so-called portrait of Sappho, of Claudian date) and 9058. The pensive beauty of the first-mentioned lady and her writing implements are responsible for the romanticizing interpretation that she was a poetess ('Sappho'). The latter painting is sometimes identified with the *studiosus iuris* Terentius Neo and his wife; see Della Corte, M. (1926) 'Publius Paquius Proculus', *JRS* 16: 145–54, but Thompson (1979) 78–85 argues that the portrait is Julio-Claudian, probably of the time of Tiberius, and therefore cannot represent Terentius Neo. For the interpretation of the woman as a young housewife pondering over her household expenses, see Curtius, L. (1929) *Die Wandmalerei Pompejis: eine Einführung in ihr Verständnis*, Leipzig: Seemann, pl. 11 and 12 and pp. 378–81, and Kraus, T. (1973) *Lebendiges Pompeji*, Cologne: DuMont, pls 213 and 214; this interpretation can be dismissed out of hand since trivialities of this kind were not commonly portrayed. A recent interpretation of the tondo as representing a portrait of Ovid has been rightly dismissed by Heintze, H. von (1995) 'Nicht puella docta, sondern Ovid? Zum Tondo aus Pompeji im Nationalmuseum von Neapel, Raum LXXVII, Inv.-no. 9084', *Gymnasium* 102: 223–4.

73 See Thompson (1979) 81. The original location of this famous portrait cannot be determined. In the eighteenth century the tondo was cut out of some Pompeian wall-painting. For its possible counterpart, a tondo of a young man holding a papyrus roll,

see Naples inv. no. 9085, Helbig (1868) 1420; for a plausible reconstruction of the wall, see Allroggen-Bedel, A. (1975) 'Herkunft und ursprünglicher Dekorationszusammenhang einiger in Essen ausgestellter Fragmente von Wandmalereien', in Andreae, B. and Kyrieleis, H. (eds) (1975) *Neue Forschungen in Pompeji und den anderen vom Vesuvausbruch 79 n. Chr. verschütteten Städten*, Recklinghausen: Bongers, pp. 118–19.

74 In the place in which the portrait was found, which may not have been its original setting (see Thompson (1979) 78–9), a small painting of Amor and Psyche was painted above the couple, symbolizing their love (Naples inv. no. 9195, Schefold (1962) 137, *Pompeii: pitturi e mosaici*, Rome: Istituto della Enciclopedia Italiana, vol. VI (1996) 487). Though this confirms the obvious identification of the portrayed as a married couple, it does not imply that the writing implements symbolize their marriage-contract.

75 For the use of a *titulus* or *index*, which was usually white, green (see Helbig (1868) 1420) or red, as on our painting, see Birt (1976) 115, 226 (fig. 146, a red *titulus*) and 237–9, and Blanck (1992) 83ff. Cicero when arranging his private library ordered slaves to add title-slips made of pieces of parchment (he calls them by their Greek name, σιττύβαι) to his books; see Cic. *Att.* 4.4a, 4.5 and 4.8. For a red label, see also Ovid *Trist.* 1.1.7 and Mart. *Ep.* 3.2.11. For inscribed labels on paintings, see Birt (1976) 115, 189 (fig. 124: Homerus) and 239 (fig. 156: Homerus and fig. 157: Plato) and Thompson (1979) 79.

76 For the various uses of writing-tablets, see Harris (1989) 193–4. Schefold (1962) 136f. assumes that the diptych is the attribute of the Muse Calliope and the book-roll that of Clio, but Wegner (1966) 94–101 shows that the attributes of the Muses are to some extent interchangeable: Calliope and Clio may be holding a book-roll, writing-tablets, a musical instrument or nothing at all. On sarcophagi a book-roll may also symbolize the 'book of life', and when closed, or opened at the last page, it means death, but this is, of course, inappropriate for a family portrait in a private house. Zanker (1995) 204 argues that the form of these portraits derives from the portraits of poets in public libraries and that, therefore, the women portrayed pose as amateur poets, but this seems to stretch the evidence too far.

77 See Harris (1989) 147 fig. 5: 'well-to-do middle class' and 263; see also McDonnell (1996) 469. The original location of the portrait of the couple (Naples Museum, inv. 9058) was, according to Schefold (1957) 168, on the wall of an exedra off the atrium of a rather modest house; for the location of the other portraits, see Schefold (1957) 130 (atrium), 158 (triclinium), 171–2 (atrium), 202 (triclinium) and 249 (ala); for that of the portrait of 'Sappho' see n. 73 above. However, we should be cautious in drawing conclusions from this as, according to Thompson (1979) 78–9, the place in which a portrait is found is not necessarily its original location. For the close connection between housing and social status, see Wallace-Hadrill (1988) and (1994); also Saller, R. P. (1984) *'Familia, domus*, and the Roman conception of the family', *Phoenix* 38: 336–55, especially 349ff. For a useful differentiation between 'representative' and 'residential' rooms in wealthy houses and for the connection between the architecture and decoration of representative rooms (such as the atrium) and the social status of the proprietor of the house, see Mols (1994) 122–7 and 146–8.

78 See, e.g., Harris (1989) 147 fig. 5: 'Writing as a sign of status' and 252, Ling, R. (1991) *Roman Painting*, Cambridge: Cambridge University Press, pp. 158–9 and McDonnell (1996) 469. The theme may have been influenced by Greek art (see Harris (1989) 107–8 and 163), but it should not be regarded as a mere convention without any relation to reality: since these portraits were found in Roman houses and represent Roman women, they may be used to illustrate Roman views on educated women.

79 For Julia see p. 80 of the present chapter; for Poppaea see chapter 4, p. 115.

80 It is, of course, doubtful how far the Roman idealized view of the past is trustworthy; Cornell, T. J. (1991) 'The city-state: the construction of an ideology', in Molho, A., Raaflaub, K., Emlen, J. (eds) (1991) *City-states in Classical Antiquity and Medieval Italy:*

Athens and Rome, Florence and Venice, Stuttgart: Steiner, pp. 53–69 convincingly argues that the ideology of the *mos maiorum* was created in response to changing realities. For the preservation of conservative social morality and the idealization of Rome's past, see also Lind, L. R. (1979) 'The tradition of Roman moral conservatism', in Deroux (1979) 7–58.

81 For the contempt for Greek culture, typical of the Roman of the old type, see Cic. *De Or.* 2.265 (about his grandfather), Plut. *Cat. Ma.* 22 and Marius' anti-aristocratic speech in Sall. *BJ* 85.32; such ignorance of, or contempt for, Greek learning was often pretended, and in many cases it can be shown to have coincided with a thorough knowledge of Greek culture; see Gruen (1992) 223–71. For Cicero's own ambivalence as regards Greeks and Greek culture, see Guite, H. (1962) 'Cicero's attitude to the Greeks', *G & R* 9: 142–59. For the complicated relation between Roman feelings of moral superiority and the cultural superiority of the Greeks, see Edwards (1993) 92–7.

82 For Tullia, see *RE* 7A Tullia 60 cols 1329–36; Cicero's extraordinary love of his daughter gave rise to much speculation already in antiquity (for charges of incest, see Dio 46.18.6 and Pseudo-Sall. *Inv. Cic.* 2); see Hallett (1984b) 133–4. For his interest in the education of his son Marcus (*RE* 7A Tullius 30 cols 1281–6) and his nephew (son of his brother Quintus and Atticus' sister Pomponia) Quintus (*RE* 7A Tullius 32 cols 1306–12) see, e.g., Cic. *Q. Fr.* 2.4.2; 2.14.2; 3.1.7; 3.3.4; *Att.* 4.15.10; 8.4.1; *Part. Or.* 1.1–2. Since Tullia entered upon her first marriage about 63 BC, the bulk of Cicero's letters were written when Tullia was already a married woman, which may partly account for his silence on her education.

83 Cic. *Q. Fr.* 1.3.3: 'effigiem oris, sermonis, animi mei'; see also a fragment of Cicero's *Consol.* in Lactantius *Inst.* 1.15.20, in which he calls Tullia *doctissima*. The resemblance of a daughter to her father was a recurring theme in Roman literature, as we have seen in the example of Minicia Marcella discussed on pp. 60f.; for more examples, see Hallet, (1984b) 338–43, also Fronto *Ad M. Caes.* 5.53 = Haines I, pp. 250–1. Yet, this does not necessarily mean that the compliment was untrue.

84 Cic. *Brut.* 211: 'Auditus est nobis Laeliae C. f. saepe sermo; ergo illam patris elegantia tinctam vidimus et filias eius Mucias ambas, quarum sermo mihi fuit notus, et neptes Licinias, quas nos quidem ambas, hanc vero Scipionis etiam tu, Brute, credo, aliquando audisti loquentem. Ego vero ac libenter quidem, inquit Brutus; et eo libentius, quod L. Crassi erat filia.' Cicero's use of *loqui* instead of *dicere* suggests that the speech of the women is known to him from private conversation (as we would expect), not from their speaking in public. Also Cic. *Brut.* 252 mentions the oratorical qualities of the Laelii and Mucii, which were trained by *domestica consuetudine*. For Laelia, the elder daughter of the orator C. Laelius (*cos* 140 BC), see *RE* 12 Laelia 25 col. 418; she was born in 150 BC or a little earlier and married the eminent jurist Q. Mucius Scaevola, the Augur (*cos* 117 BC), to whom Cicero at the start of his career (about 90 BC) attached himself for the study of civil law when Scaevola was already an old man (Cic. *Brut.* 306, *Am.* 1). For the Muciae, see *RE* 16 Mucia 26 and 27. The younger Mucia (*RE* 16 Mucia 27 cols 448–9) married the outstanding orator L. Licinius Crassus (*cos* 95 BC), under whose guidance Cicero was educated as a boy (Cic. *De Or.* 2.2); she became the mother of two daughters, both called Licinia (*RE* 13 Licinia 183 and 184 cols 497–8), the elder of whom married P. Scipio Nasica and became the mother of two sons, the one called L. Licinius Crassus Scipio because of his adoption by his maternal grandfather, the orator L. Licinius Crassus, and the other Q. Caecilius Metellus Pius Scipio Nasica (*cos* 52 BC), because of his adoption by Q. Caecilius Metellus Pius (*cos* 80 BC), who was related to him through his paternal grandmother, Metella. He was the father of Cornelia, the fifth wife of Pompey the Great: see pp. 78f. For Cicero's appraisal of the education of Cornelia, the mother of the Gracchi, see pp. 64ff.

85 Cic. *De Or.* 3.45: 'Equidem cum audio socrum meam Laeliam – facilius enim mulieres

incorruptam antiquitatem conservant, quod multorum sermonis expertes ea tenent semper quae prima didicerunt – sed eam sic audio ut Plautum mihi aut Naevium videar audire: sono ipso vocis ita recto et simplici est ut nihil ostentationis aut imitationis afferre videatur; ex quo sic locutum esse eius patrem iudico, sic maiores, non aspere, ut ille quem dixi, non vaste, non rustice, non hiulce, sed presse et aequaliter et leniter.' Also Quint. 1.1.6 praises Laelia's speech as the living image of that of her father's: 'Laelia, the daughter of C. Laelius, is said to have reproduced the elegance of her father's language in her own speech' ('et Laelia C. filia reddidisse in loquendo paternam elegantiam dicitur').

86 For Helvia see chapter 2, pp. 40f.

87 Sen. *Cons. Helv.* 17.4: 'propter istas, quae litteris non ad sapientiam utuntur sed ad luxuriam instruuntur, minus te indulgere studiis passus est'. For the elder Seneca's 'old-fashioned strictness' (*antiquus rigor*) as regards his wife's studies and his too great concern for ancestral customs (*maiorum consuetudini deditus*), see Sen. *Cons. Helv.* 17.3–4. His provincial origin may have been partly responsible for this; see chapter 2, n. 44.

88 Plut. *Pomp.* 55 (also cited at the beginning of chapter 2): ἐνῆν δὲ τῇ κόρῃ πολλὰ φίλτρα δίχα τῶν ἀφ' ὥρας. καὶ γὰρ περὶ γράμματα καλῶς ἤσκητο καὶ περὶ λύραν καὶ γεωμετρίαν, καὶ λόγων φιλοσόφων εἴθιστο χρησίμως ἀκούειν. καὶ προσῆν τούτοις ἦθος ἀηδίας καὶ περιεργίας καθαρόν, ἃ δὴ νέαις προστρίβεται γυναιξὶ τὰ τοιαῦτα μαθήματα. For Cornelia see *RE* 4 Cornelia 417 cols 1596–7. She was the daughter of Q. Caecilius Metellus Pius Scipio Nasica (*cos* 52 BC) and Aemilia Lepida (*RE* 1 Aemilia 166 col. 591). She stemmed from a highly aristocratic family: her father was a Scipio by birth and a Metellus Pius by adoption. Born about 70 BC, Cornelia was married in 55 BC to P. Licinius Crassus, son of the triumvir, to be widowed by his death at Carrhae in Parthia in 53 BC. In early 52 BC she married Pompey, who, as was common gossip at the time, was old enough to be her father (Plut. *Pomp.* 55).

89 Her literary education probably comprised both Greek and Latin literature, as she was well-versed in Greek in adult life; for a discussion of how common such an education may have been, see chapter 2. During the civil war between her husband and Caesar she was brought to safety together with Pompey's son Sextus to Mytilene on Lesbos (Plut. *Pomp.* 66), where, according to Lucan, she was very popular (Luc. *Phars.* 8. 151–8).

90 For the idealized and romanticized portrayal of Cornelia's love, anxiety and suffering because of the defeat and death of Pompey, see Plut. *Pomp.* 74–80 and Luc. *Phars.* 5. 722–815; 8. 40–158, 577–92, 637–62; 9. 51–116; see also Bruère, R. T. (1951) 'Lucan's Cornelia', *CPh* 46: 221–36. She is described as the exemplary *univira* in spite of her two marriages (Luc. *Phars.* 8.156f. praises her *pudor, probitas, castitas* and *modestia*), who, though innocent, blamed herself for bringing disaster on her husbands. In the Middle Ages she lived on as a model of conjugal love and of the plaintive, but courageous widow; see Moos, P. von (1975) 'Cornelia und Heloise', *Latomus* 34: 1024–59.

91 For the inversion of conventional gender roles in Roman love poetry see, for instance, Hallett (1984a); for the theme of *servitium amoris*, see Lyne (1979).

92 For the Greek educational triad, see Beck (1975) 55. For the literary and musical education of Greek women of the Hellenistic period, Pomeroy (1977). The ideal (and the term) of the *docta puella* is found mainly in the poetry of Propertius and Ovid and less explicitly in that of Tibullus; for the accomplishments of the love poets' mistresses, see Lilja (1965) 133–43.

93 For Cynthia as a *docta puella*, see Prop. 1.7.11; 2.11.6; 2.13.11ff. (see chapter 2, n. 153). For her literary and musical accomplishments and their importance to Propertius as a source of love, see also Prop. 1.4.13; 2.30.37–40 (Cynthia as one of the Muses); 3.20.7; see also Catul. 86 and Petron. fr. 31 Bücheler. For her musical accomplishments: Prop. 1.2.28; 1.3.42; 2.1.9–10; 2.3.19–20; for her grace when dancing: Prop. 2.3.17–18;

2.19.15; for her appreciation of her lover's poetry: Prop. 2.24a.21; 2.26a.25–6; 2.33.38 (Cynthia reading and reciting his poetry); 3.2.2; for her gift of writing poetry: Prop. 1.2.27–30; 2.3.21–2; for her charming conversation: Prop. 1.2.29–30.

94 For Corinna's appreciation of Ovid's poetry: Ovid. *Am.* 3.8.5 and 7 (she, nevertheless, prefers a wealthy lover), but in *Am.* 3.1.58 she is called *barbara* for 'drowning' his poem in water. He tries to dissuade her from taking a planned sea-voyage, advising her to keep to her normal way of life: 'The safer course is fondly to keep your couch, to read your books, to sound with your fingers the Thracian lyre' (Ovid. *Am.* 2.11.31–2: 'Tutius est fovisse torum, legisse libellos, / Threiciam digitis increpuisse lyram'). For other *doctae puellae* in Ovid's poetry: Ovid. *Am.* 2.4.17ff. (in which he calls their accomplishments rare), 2.10.6 and *AA* 2.281–3, in a complaint about the lack of appreciation of poetry among girls: 'Yet there are learned women too, a scanty number; and others are not learned, but wish to be so. Let either sort be praised in poems' ('Sunt tamen et doctae, rarissima turba, puellae; / altera non doctae turba, sed esse volunt./ Utraque laudetur per carmina'). For their accomplishments in music, poetry and dance: Ovid *AA* 3.311–52; for the erotic attraction of women making music or dancing: *Am.* 2.4.25–32 and, in the present chapter, pp. 81ff. A *docta puella* reciting her lover's poetry and singing him songs also figures in Pseudo-Virgil *Lydia* 6–7 and 24–5: 'non ulla puella / doctior in terris fuit'. For the, possibly ironical, compliment Catullus pays to the girlfriend of his friend, the poet Caecilius: 'more learned in poetry than the Sapphic Muse' (Catul. 35.16–17: 'Sapphica puella/ Musa doctior'), see chapter 5, pp. 178f.

95 Apart from Gallus' Lycoris, who has been identified with the Greek freedwoman and actress Volumnia Cytheris (*RE* 9A Volumnia 17 col. 883) and Catullus' Lesbia, who may have been modelled upon Clodia Metelli or one of her sisters, women of senatorial rank, there are no clear indications of the social status of the love poets' mistresses. Williams (1968) 525–42 believes that most of them were women of reasonably high social standing and Rawson (1992) 29 states that Roman love poetry was 'almost all inspired by adulterous affairs with temporarily deserted, upper-class wives', but the evidence does not warrant this conclusion. White (1993) 90 has recently taken up the old idea that these women belonged to the 'demi-monde'. The complicated relation of these mistresses with contemporary reality is discussed in chapter 5, pp. 175ff.

96 For Clodia see chapter 5, pp. 174f; for Sempronia see pp. 84ff. For the similarity between the portraits of Clodia in Cicero's *Pro Caelio* and Sempronia in Sallust's *De Coniuratione Catilinae* and those of Lesbia and Cynthia, see n. 126 below. Of course, the moral reputations of Clodia and Sempronia are also attacked in a more direct way by Cicero and Sallust.

97 Ovid, who calls the poetess 'Perilla' *doctissima* (*Trist.* 3.7.31) and praises her learned poetry and rare mental gifts (*Trist.* 3.7.12 and 14), takes care to stress her chastity (3.7.13: 'mores . . . pudicos') and describes her as habitually sitting in the company of her mother or amid her books (3.7.3–4). The poetess Sulpicia, described as a *docta puella* by the unknown *amicus Sulpiciae* (Tib. 4.2.24 and 4.6.2), is emphatically portrayed as true to one man. Similarly, Martial praises his friend's learned fiancée Theophila for her chastity: comparing her with Sappho he writes: 'castior haec [i.e. Theophila] et non doctior illa fuit' (Mart. *Ep.* 7.69.10; see chapter 5, p. 179) and in *Ep.* 10.35 the poetess Sulpicia Caleni is portrayed as *docta* and *pudica*; see chapter 5, p. 162.

98 Griffin (1976), (1977) and (1985) 1–64, discussed in chapter 5, pp. 176f.

99 For Julia see *RE* 10 Julia 550 cols 896–906, *PIR*² I 634, *FOS* 421. For the conflicting stereotypes applied to Julia in the ancient sources, see Richlin, A. (1992) 'Julia's jokes, Galla Placidia, and the Roman use of women as political icons', in Garlick *et al.* (1992) 65–91. Syme, R. (1974) *The Roman Revolution*, Oxford: Oxford University Press, pp. 425–7 suggests that Augustus' motives for banishing her in 2 BC were mainly political, her promiscuity serving as a convenient pretext, but Raditsa, L. F. (1980) 'Augustus'

legislation concerning marriage, procreation, love affairs and adultery', *ANRW* II 13: 290–5 and Ferrill, A. (1980) 'Augustus and his daughter; a modern myth', in Deroux, C. (ed.) (1980) *Studies in Latin Literature and Roman History*, vol. II, Brussels (coll. Latomus 168), pp. 332–46 argue against the 'conspiracy myth'.

100 Macr. *Sat.* 2.5.2: 'cum alioquin litterarum amor multaque eruditio, quod in illa domo facile erat, praeterea mitis humanitas minimeque saevus animus ingentem feminae gratiam conciliarent'. For Julia's popularity, see also Suet. *Aug.* 65.3 and Dio 55.13.1.

101 For the language and imagery of love poetry in his letters, see *Ep.* 6.4, 6.7, 7.5 (the theme of the 'excluded lover'); see also Shelton (1990); for the changing views on married life during the empire, see chapter 2, p. 33; the literary conventions of Augustan love poetry were adopted by later authors like Statius, Sulpicia Caleni and the younger Pliny while writing of their married love.

102 For praise of Calpurnia's accomplishments together with her *frugalitas* and *castitas* see Plin. *Ep.* 4.19, discussed in chapter 2, pp. 32ff.; in *Ep.* 6.7 Calpurnia finds consolation for their temporary separation in her husband's works. For Calpurnia's role as the submissive wife, see also the fifth-century author Sidonius Apollinaris, who numbers Calpurnia among the examplary wives who 'held candles and candlesticks for their husbands while they read and studied' (Sid. *Ep.* 2.10.5: 'legentibus meditantibusque candelas et candelabra tenuerunt'). Another example of a wife praised for her learning as well as her chastity is Argentaria Polla (see chapter 4, pp. 129ff.), who is called both *docta* and *casta* by Statius (*casta*: Stat. *Silv.* 2.7.62; *docta*: 2.7.83). Statius also praises his own stepdaughter both for her talent for music, dance and poetry and for her compliance with traditional female virtues, such as chastity and modesty (Stat. *Silv.* 3.5.63–7; see p. 83).

103 As music and dance are only indirectly connected with the subject of this study, they will be surveyed here only in so far as they were appreciated, or censured, in upper-class women. For further reading I refer to the exhaustive studies of Wille (1967) and (1977); see also Comotti, G. (1989) *Music in Greek and Roman Culture*, Baltimore and London: Johns Hopkins University Press, pp. 48–56.

104 Nep. *Epam.* 1: 'ne alienos mores ad suos referant, neve ea quae ipsis leviora sunt pari modo apud ceteros fuisse arbitrentur. Scimus enim musicen nostris moribus abesse a principis persona, saltare vero etiam in vitiis poni; quae omnia apud Graecos et grata et laude digna ducuntur'.

105 For some examples of Roman girls and women singing and dancing at religious ceremonies and on festive days see Cat. 34.2, Liv. 27.37, Ovid. *Trist.* 2.23f., Hor. *C.* 2.12.13–20, 3.1.4: 'virginibus puerisque cano' (choral poetry sung by a choir of boys and girls), 4.6.31ff., *C.S.* 6, Suet. *Cal.* 16.4, Dio 59.7.1, at the funeral of Augustus: Suet. *Aug.* 100.2 (children of both sexes of the leading families), for upper-class women singing dirges and eulogies at the funeral of an emperor: Herodian 4.2.5. For the modesty to be displayed by a matron when dancing see Hor. *Ep.* 2.3.231–3, who compares the uneasy feelings of the personified 'tragedy' among satyr-plays to the bashfulness of a matron feeling ashamed when asked to dance on festal days. For Greek reserve in connection with dancing, see, e.g., Plut. *Mor.* 145C; for Greek and Roman attitudes towards the dance, see also Jory, E. J. (1996) 'The drama of the dance: prolegomena to an iconography of imperial pantomime', in Slater (1996) 20–7.

106 Roman moralists and traditionalists contrast music and dance of the good old days with that of their own time. See, for instance, Cicero's praise of the *iucunda severitas* of the music of the days of Naevius and Livius Andronicus in his *Leg.* 2.15.39 as opposed to his contempt for contemporary music (and dance) in, for instance, *Mur.* 13; *Off.* 1.150; *Cael.* 35; *Pis.* 10.22; *Cat.* 2.23, but see for a more positive assessment *De Or.* 3.87. Sen. *Tranq.* 17.4 contrasts the soft, effeminate dances of his own time with the manly way of ancient dancing and Quintilian in his defence of the value of a musical

training for the orator (1.10.9–33) makes an exception for the 'emasculated' music of his own days (1.10.31). As there is hardly any evidence of early Roman music (or, for that matter, dance), it is uncertain in how far Roman music was indigenous: Wille (1967) and (1977) emphasizes the indigenous element, but Griffin (1976) 95 doubts whether music free of Greek influence ever existed at Rome.

107 Macr. *Sat.* 3.14.7: 'docentur praestigias inhonestas, cum cinaedulis et sambuca psalterioque eunt in ludum histrionum, discunt cantare, quae maiores nostri ingenuis probro ducier voluerunt: eunt, inquam, in ludum saltatorium inter cinaedos virgines puerique ingenui. Haec cum mihi quisquam narrabat, non poteram animum inducere ea liberos suos homines nobiles docere sed cum ductus sum in ludum saltatorium, plus medius fidius in eo ludo vidi pueris virginibusque quinquaginta, in his unum – quod me rei publicae maxime miseritum est – puerum bullatum, petitoris filium minorem annis duodecim, cum crotalis saltare quam saltationem impudicus servulus honeste saltare non posset'.

108 Macr. *Sat.* 3.14.5: 'matronae etiam saltationem non inhonestam putabant sed inter probas quoque earum erat saltandi cura dum modo non curiosa usque ad artis perfectionem'. Also *Sat.* 3.14.6: 'nobilium vero filios et, quod dictu nefas est, filias quoque virgines inter studiosa numerasse saltandi meditationem'.

109 Sen. *Q.N.* 7.32.3: 'privatum urbe tota sonat pulpitum: in hoc viri, in hoc feminae tripudiant; mares inter se uxoresque contendunt uter det latus mollius'. Also Horace expresses dismay at the lascivious dances performed by Roman girls, which, in his opinion, lead to adultery (Hor. *C.* 3.6.21–32) and Juvenal ridicules the musical zeal of upper-class women and insinuates sexual motives (Juv. 6.379–97 and O.19; as is to be inferred from line 385 his censure is aimed especially at women of the nobility).

110 For the association of Greece with effeminacy and the Roman claim to moral superiority, see Edwards (1993) 22–5 and 92–7; on Greek laxity corrupting Roman morals, see also the opinion of a Greek, Pol. 31.25.4–5. For the reproach of effeminacy directed against male performers of music and dance, see, for instance, Sen. *Contr.* 1 *praef.* 8 and Edwards (1993) 82. The younger Seneca presents the craze for voluptuous dancing as a sign of the moral corruption of his time (*Q.N.* 7.32.3; see also *Ep.* 90.19).

111 Most of the female professional musicians and dancing-girls were slaves or freedwomen: see, e.g., Treggiari (1976) 91 and Wille (1967) 315–24, Eichenauer, M. (1988) *Untersuchungen zur Arbeitswelt der Frau in der römischen Antike* (Europäische Hochschulschriften 3, vol. 360) Frankfurt-on-Main: Lang, pp. 64–79 (for the defects of this study, see the review by K. Thraede in *BJ* 192 (1992) 639–42). They did not all come from the Greek-speaking provinces: there were the famous dancing-girls from Cadiz in Spain, the popularity of whose lascivious dances is often referred to by Roman moralists as the culminating-point of the licentiousness of their time; see Plin. *Ep.* 1.15, Mart. *Ep.* 1.41.12, 3.63.3, 5.78.26–8, 6.71.1–2, Juv. 11.162–4 and Stat. *Silv.* 1.6.71.

112 For instance, Sempronia, in Sallust's portrait of her in *Cat.* 25, was 'able to play the lyre and dance more skilfully than a respectable woman need, and had many other accomplishments which minister to voluptuousness' ('psallere saltare elegantius quam necesse est probae, multa alia, quae instrumenta luxuriae sunt'); for Sempronia, see pp. 84ff. Macrobius *Sat.* 3.14.5 comments: 'he [Sallust] censures the lady not because she knew how to dance but because she was such a very good dancer' ('Semproniam reprehendit non quod saltare sed quod optime scierit').

113 Prop. 2.3.17–20: 'quantum quod posito formose saltat Iaccho,/ egit ut euhantes dux Ariadna choros,/ et quantum, Aeolio cum temptat carmina plectro,/ par Aganippeae ludere docta lyrae'. See also Prop. 1.2.27–8, 1.3.42, 2.1.9–10, 2.22.4–6, and Ovid. *Am.* 2.4.25–32 and 2.11.31–2, *AA* 3.315–28 and 349–52; inversely Ov. *Rem. Am.* 333–6, see also Pseudo-Virgil *Lydia* 6–7 and 24–5. Horace, though censuring Greek

dancing in freeborn Roman girls, praises it in women who by their Greek names and the erotic context of his remarks may be classed as professional musicians or *meretrices* of slave or freed status; see Hor. *C.* 3.9.9–10, 4.11.33–6, 4.13.7.

114 This assimilation of music (and, more hesitatingly, dance) in Roman society led to a widespread musical dilettantism in which certain emperors took the lead. Nero was severely criticized for his undignified performances; for a discussion of Nero as an 'acting emperor', see Edwards, C. (1994) 'Beware of imitations: theatre and the subversion of imperial identity', in Elsner, J. and Masters, J. (1994) *Reflections of Nero: Culture, History and Representation*, Chapel Hill and London: University of North Carolina Press, pp. 83–97. However, by the time of the boyhood of Titus a musical education seems to have been accepted in court circles; see Wallace-Hadrill (1983) 181; the musical education and accomplishments of Titus and, later, Hadrian are mentioned without disapproval (Suet. *Tit.* 3.2 and *SHA Hadr.* 14.8–9). For upper-class dilettantes see Wille (1967) 336–57.

115 For examples of epitaphs praising women's musical accomplishments, see, e.g., *CLE* 1282 (= *CIL* VI 10131), 1301 (= *CIL* VI 17050) and 1302; it should be noted that some of the women praised for their musical skills on epitaphs may have been professional musicians. A series of sarcophagi of the late second and early third centuries AD depict the deceased couple, the wife playing the lyre (in some cases accompanied by Muses) and the husband reading; this shows that no social stigma was attached to lyre-playing for women at that time; on the contrary, it was a source of prestige; see Zanker (1995) 256, Marrou, H. (1933) 'Deux sarcophages romains relatifs à la vie intellectuelle', *RA* sixth series, 1: 163–80, esp. 173ff. (I am not convinced by his Pythagorean interpretation of these sarcophagi); for more examples of women playing the lyre, or another musical instrument, on sarcophagi, see Marrou (1938) 154 71.

116 Stat. *Silv.* 3.5.63–7: 'Sic certe formaeque bonis animique meretur; / sive chelyn complexa petit seu voce paterna/ discendum Musis sonat et mea carmina flectit/, candida seu molli diducit brachia motu/ ingenium probitas artemque modestia vincit'. As we see in the case of Statius' stepdaughter, who was the daughter of a professional musician (a singer or a cithern-player: van Dam (1984) 1) or poet (Hardie (1983) 59), a girl of modest descent might receive an education comprising some poetry, training in music (singing and lyre-playing) and dancing.

117 Plin. *Ep.* 4.19; see chapter 2, pp. 32ff. and chapter 3, p. 81, in which apart from praising Calpurnia's accomplishments he stresses the chastity, frugality and modesty of his wife and the harmony of their marriage.

118 Dio 75.14.5 relates that Plautilla, the daughter of Plautianus, Septimius Severus' praetorian prefect, had 'Roman citizens of noble birth' (ἀνθρώπους ... εὐγενεῖς Ῥωμαίους) as her teachers of music, who, moreover, were castrated for the purpose. To have upper-class men (instead of freedmen or men of the lower classes) as teachers of music for his daughter and to have them, though adult men, castrated at that, is, of course, a (fictitious?) example of Plautianus' lawlessness and power, which is illustrated by Dio also in numerous other anecdotes; but the story also shows that Plautianus wished to give his daughter an élite education, which included musical training. In his letter of advice about the education of little Paula, Jerome prescribes that she should be deaf to all musical instruments (Hier. *Ep.* 107.8), which implies that musical education was a normal part of the education of upper-class girls in his days.

119 For Pompey's wife Cornelia, see Plut. *Pomp.* 55 and p. 78. Against dancing, see also Plut. *Praec. Coni.* 48 (*Mor.* 145C): 'Studies of this sort [i.e. philosophy and the concomitant subjects], in the first place, divert women from all untoward conduct; for a woman studying geometry will be ashamed to be a dancer' (τὰ δὲ τοιαῦτα μαθήματα πρῶτον ἀφίστησι τῶν ἀτόπων τὰς γυναῖκας· αἰσχυνθήσεται γὰρ ὀρχεῖσθαι γυνὴ γεωμετρεῖν μανθάνουσα).

120 For Sempronia see Sall. *Cat.* 25 and 40.5, *RE* 2A Sempronia 103 col. 1446. She was married to D. Junius Brutus (*cos* 77 BC) and was the mother (or stepmother) of D. Junius Brutus Albinus, one of the assassins of Caesar. Syme (1964) 133–5 suggests that she was the daughter of a Sempronius Tuditanus (*RE* 2A Sempronius 89), thus making her an aunt to Fulvia, the wife of Clodius, Curio and Antonius, but this is not certain; see Paul (1986) 10. The suggestion of Münzer, F. (1920/1963) *Römische Adelsparteien und Adelsfamilien*, Stuttgart: Metzler, pp. 272f. that she was a daughter of C. Gracchus is generally rejected. The rather meagre evidence of Sempronia's participation in the conspiracy (Sall. *Cat.* 40.5) has given rise to the question why this elaborate portrait of her is included; for a discussion of this problem see, among others, Paul (1986) 10, Boyd (1987) 183–4 and Wilkins (1994) 86ff. with references to earlier studies.

121 Sall. *Cat.* 24.3: 'Ea tempestate plurimos cuiusque generis homines adscivisse sibi dicitur, mulieres etiam aliquot, quae primo ingentis sumptus stupro corporis toleraverant, post, ubi aetas tantummodo quaestui neque luxuriae modum fecerat, aes alienum grande conflaverant'.

122 Sall. *Cat.* 25: 'Sed in eis erat Sempronia, quae multa saepe virilis audaciae facinora commiserat. Haec mulier genere atque forma, praeterea viro liberis satis fortunata fuit; litteris Graecis et Latinis docta, psallere saltare elegantius quam necesse est probae, multa alia, quae instrumenta luxuriae sunt. Sed ei cariora semper omnia quam decus atque pudicitia fuit: pecuniae an famae minus parceret, haud facile discerneres: lubido sic accensa, ut saepius peteret viros quam peteretur. Sed ea saepe antehac fidem prodiderat, creditum abiuraverat, caedis conscia fuerat, luxuria atque inopia praeceps abierat. Verum ingenium eius haud absurdum: posse versus facere, iocum movere, sermone uti vel modesto vel molli vel procaci; prorsus multae facetiae multusque lepos inerat'.

123 See esp. Sall. *Cat.* 5.1–8, but note that in his orations (*Cat.* 20 and 58) and in the description of Catiline's courageous death in the final battle (*Cat.* 60) Sallust presents a more positive view. For Sempronia as a female counterpart to Catiline, see, among others, Paul (1986) and Boyd (1987) 185, who argues that Sempronia is 'both Catiline's complement and his ironic reverse', as she transgresses female boundaries by her *virilis audacia*, whereas he is an example of effeminacy. For Sempronia's 'masculinity' see p. 90.

124 For the ambiguities in Sallust's presentation of Catiline, see Wilkins (1994) and Hunink, V. (1998) 'Het tegenwicht van Sallustius', *Lampas* 31.1: 40–55. Paul (1986) 14–15 relates the positive elements of Sempronia's portrait to the Roman *laudatio funebris*, which for men traditionally comprised praise of his *genus, honores, res gestae, virtutes* and, from the late republic onwards, also of his education, and for women emphasized their family relationship and matronal virtues; cf. Kierdorf, W. (1980) *Laudatio Funebris: Interpretationen und Untersuchungen zur Entwicklung der römischen Leichenrede*, Meisenheim am Glan: Hain (Beiträge zur klassischen Philologie 106), pp. 112–16 and 121–6.

125 Sallust uses the word *mulier* when speaking of her; in contrast with *femina* or *matrona*, *mulier* is used pejoratively for a woman of her rank; see Adams, J. N. (1972) 'Latin words for "woman" and "wife"', *Glotta* 50: 234–55; for Sallust's use of the words *homo* and *mulier* to abuse the aristocratic adherents of Catiline's conspiracy, see Santoro L'Hoir (1992) 56–9 and 60–2. Her accomplishments, especially those in music, dance and facile conversation, are compared to those of the *hetaira*; see also Paul (1986) 15–16; for the reproof of dancing too well, see also Macr. *Sat.* 3.14.5. For the similarity between Sallust's portrait of Sempronia and Propertius' Cynthia, see Williams (1968) 541. The erotic connotations of the words *procax, facetiae* and *lepos* (*Cat.* 25.5) add to the suggestion of moral laxity; see Seager, R. (1974) '*Venustas, lepidus, bellus, salsus*: notes on the language of Catullus', *Latomus* 33: 891–4. For Sallust's association of women and *luxuria*, see Boyd (1987).

126 There is a striking similarity between the portraits of Clodia Metelli, who in Cicero's *Pro Caelio* is portrayed as a gifted but degenerate aristocratic woman, of Sempronia and of the empress Poppaea. The Schol. Bob. 135 (Stangl) on Cic. *Sest.* 116: 'who knows all the pantomimic interludes of his sister' ('qui omnia sororis embolia novit') says that Clodia was 'given to dancing more extravagantly and immoderately than befitted a *matrona*' ('Clodiam . . . studiosam fuisse saltandi profusius et immoderatius quam matronam deceret'; translation by Wiseman (1985) 27–8), which may be a confused recollection of Sallust's portrait of Sempronia in *Cat.* 25.2 ('saltare elegantius quam necesse est probae'), but may also point to a standard charge of ancient criticism of cultured and unconventional women. According to Syme (1958) 353 and Boyd (1987) 184 Sallust's Sempronia formed a model for Tacitus' portrait of the empress Poppaea (*Ann.* 13.45–6; for Poppaea Sabina chapter 4, p. 115), both women being described as aristocratic, cultured, clever and beautiful, but morally depraved; against this, Fischler (1994) 120 argues that the portraits are independent of each other, both displaying 'an inversion of the standard attributes of the Roman Matron'.

127 Hillard (1992) 55. Compare the obscene verses about Clodius and Clodia chanted in the theatre by Milo's supporters, Cic. *Q. Fn.* 2.3.2. Skinner (1982) 200–8 argues that allegations of sexual misconduct were used by Catullus and Cicero as political metaphors; for instance, Cicero employed the *topos* of incest between Clodius and Clodia as a metaphor for political collaboration between them. According to Dixon, S. (1992) 'The enduring theme: domineering dowagers and scheming concubines', in Garlick *et al.* (1992) 209–25 women who sought, or gained, power in the public realm were stereotyped either as 'scheming concubines' who exercised power through their dangerous sexuality, or as 'domineering dowagers'; see also Hillard (1992).

128 For invectives against women who were politically prominent (aimed at discrediting their male relatives or associates), see Hillard (1989) and (1992). For invectives against women generally: Richlin (1984) and Lefkowitz (1981) 32–40. An example of the arbitrary use of sexual invectives against political opponents is the sexual abuse of the paragon of virtue, Cornelia, mother of the Gracchi, that can be inferred from the defence of her son Gaius (Plut. *CG* 4.4).

129 Sen. *Cons. Helv.* 17.4; see n. 87 above. Note that the elder Seneca (according to his son) objected to the *luxuria* of (some) educated women, as Sallust did in his portrait of Sempronia. Though here translated as 'ostentatious display' *luxuria* also has the connotations of 'extravagance' and 'voluptuousness'; thus, the sexual reputation of educated women also comes into play. For the many connotations of this word and its association with Greek culture, see Isager, J. (1993) 'The Hellenization of Rome: *luxuria* or *liberalitas*?', in Bilde, P. G., Nielsen I. and Nielsen, M. (eds) (1993) *Aspects of Hellenism in Italy: Towards a Cultural Unity?*, Copenhagen: Museum Tusculanum Press (Acta Hyperborea 5), pp. 257–75.

130 Lucian *Merc. Cond.* 34–6; see chapter 2, pp. 37ff.

131 Mart. *Ep.* 10.68, Juv. 6.185–200. Both maliciously restrict the Greek words uttered by Roman women to words of love: ζωή καὶ ψυχή (Juv. 6.195) and κύριέ μου, μέλι μου, ψυχή μου (Mart. *Ep.* 10.68.5), the bedroom language of a Greek courtesan (Mart. *Ep.* 10.68.7–12, Juv. 6.194–200). They add to the disgrace of these women by presenting them as upper-class (Mart. *Ep.* 10.68.2 and 12: Laelia living in the *vico . . . patricio* will, however she tries, never be called a 'Lais', a famous Corinthian courtesan) and elderly (Juv. 6.192: a woman of 85). The women are ridiculed for aping Greek ways and Greek speech to attract lovers, which is especially ridiculous for elderly women. For Greek as the language of love, see also Lucr. 4.1160–9. For the suggested use of (fake) learning to attract lovers, see also the wealthy, elderly woman with her Stoic books among her silk pillows, ridiculed by Horace (*Epod.* 8.15–16; see chapter 2,

n. 148). Here, invective against educated women is combined with the standard characteristics of invective against wanton and repulsive old women; see, e.g., Richlin (1992a) 67–8 and 109–16.

132 Mus. Ruf. fr. III. 54–8: ὅτι αὐϑάδεις ὡς ἐπὶ πολὺ καὶ ϑρασείας εἶναι ἀνάγκη τὰς προσιούσας τοῖς φιλοσόφοις γυναῖκας, ὅταν ἀφέμεναι τοῦ οἰκουρεῖν ἐν μέσοις ἀναστρέφωνται τοῖς ἀνδράσι καὶ μελετῶσι λόγους καὶ σοφίζωνται καὶ ἀναλύωσι συλλογισμούς, δέον οἴκοι καθημένας ταλασιουργεῖν. For Cornelia, see Plut. *Pomp.* 55 (see p. 78).

133 Juv. 6. 448–56: 'non habeat matrona, tibi quae iuncta recumbit, / dicendi genus aut curvum sermone rotato / torqueat enthymema, nec historias sciat omnes, / sed quaedam ex libris et non intellegat. odi / hanc ego quae repetit volvitque Palaemonis artem / servata semper lege et ratione loquendi / ignotosque mihi tenet antiquaria versus / nec curanda viris opicae castigat amicae / verba: soloecismum liceat fecisse marito'. For Juvenal's ridicule of educated women (Juv. 6. 434–56), see also chapter 2, pp. 43f. The *historiae* (line 450) do not denote history in our sense, but the 'stories' of *grammatici* explaining allusions to (mythical or historical) persons, places or events in literary texts (Quint. 1.8.18; Bonner (1977) 237ff.). Juv. 6. 242–5 depicts women who in a sort of topsy-turvy world dictate the arguments to the great jurist Celsus. They pretend to be even better at law (an exclusively male field by tradition) than the great Celsus and show an arrogance which a male jurist would not dare to permit himself.

134 Mart. *Ep.* 2.90.9–10: 'sit mihi verna satura, sit non doctissima coniunx, / sit nox cum somno, sit sine lite dies'. Mart. *Ep.* 11.19: 'Quaeris cur nolim ducere, Galla? diserta es, / saepe solaecismum mentula nostra facit'. This verse contains word-play on *diserta* ('eloquent') and *soloecismus* ('solecism', 'slip in syntax'), committed by the speaker's genitals, apparently because of his abhorrence of a learned woman. Mart. *Ep.* 12.97.3 ridicules a man who has married the ideal Roman wife, *dives, nobilis, erudita, casta*, but seeks enjoyment in the love of boys.

135 See Richlin (1984) and (1992a). She defines sexual invective as male, aggressive and controlling boundaries: satire is concerned with power and social hierarchy and is aimed at those who oppress the satirist (for instance, patrons, nobles or the wealthy in general) and at those whom he feels he ought to dominate, such as women, freedmen, 'pathic' (i.e. passive) homosexuals, foreigners, and other 'out-groups'. By exposing these groups to abuse the male narrator asserts his own normality and dominance, and thus reinforces the desired social norms.

136 For the political involvement of upper-class women in the late republic and the stereotypes applied to them, see, e.g., Dixon (1983), Hillard (1989) and (1992); for the power and images of Roman imperial women, see, for instance, Fischler (1994) and Purcell (1986). For the relation between female power and sexual invective, see also Skinner (1983) about Clodia Metelli.

137 Similar suspicion of educated women together with propagation of women's traditional role is found in the song about the 'seven duties of women' by the Dutch popular song-writer Koos Speenhoff (1869–1945), which was popular at the time of the movement for women's suffrage. Translated (in prose) the first couplet, which reveals contemporary prejudices about educated women, reads: 'The first duty of every woman is never to make a display of her learning. This does not suit love-making: a kiss is but a kiss. What good does it bring to torture her pretty little head with a book? A woman who thinks when speaking never speaks what she thinks.' ('De eerste plicht van elke vrouw/ Is nooit geleerd te doen./ Dat komt bij liefde niet te pas,/ Een zoen is maar een zoen./ Wat geeft het of ze met een boek / Haar lieve hersens krenkt / Een vrouw die denkt bij wat ze zegt, / Zegt nimmer wat ze denkt.' Schreijer, C. (1980) *Sara, je rok zakt af: vrouwenliedboek*, Amsterdam: Sara, p. 57). Apart from rejection of women's learning, her six remaining duties are to love her husband,

to dress well, to be obedient, to indulge the whims of her husband, to be quiet and to be a good cook, not surprisingly all for the benefit of her husband.

138 This implies a hierarchy in which 'male' virtues were held to be superior to 'female' ones (just as men were considered to be superior to women). This hierarchy was further strengthened by the tendency to contrast 'male' virtues with bad 'female' traits. Accordingly, 'masculinity' was always praised in men, and under certain conditions also in women; it was associated with courage, steadfastness, rationality and self-control, whereas the opposite concept, that of 'femininity', was usually despised: it was associated with timidity, credulity, extravagance, licentiousness, irrationality, love of luxury and, in general, a lack of self-control which made women an easy prey to passions. Thus, for a man to display 'female' behaviour was always wrong: in fact, effeminacy was one of the worst taunts, associated with 'pathic' (i.e. passive) homo-sexuality, moral degeneracy, cowardice, and political and social weakness. To compare a man to a woman or to call him 'effeminate' was to humiliate him. For a discussion of 'effeminacy' in Roman thought see Edwards (1993) 63–97, and for the taunt of effeminacy in Roman invective, see Richlin (1992a) 85ff. and 136–9. For 'masculinity' as something that had to be achieved, also by men, see Gleason (1995).

139 Lucretia: Val. Max. 6.1.1 ('cuius virilis animus maligno errore fortunae muliebre corpus sortitus est'); for the legend of Lucretia see also Liv. 1.57–60, Sen. Cons. Marc. 16.2, Dion. Hal. 4.64–8 and RE 13 Lucretia 28 cols 1692–5. Not only did her courage surpass female standards, but she also committed suicide in a typically masculine way, by using a metal weapon: see van Hooff, A. J. L. (1990) From Autothanasia to Suicide: Self-killing in Classical Antiquity, London: Routledge, p. 50. About Cloelia (RE 4 Cloelia 13 cols 110–11), who, according to legend, was honoured for her 'courage, unprec-edented in a woman' (Liv. 2.13.11: 'novam in femina virtutem'; see also Val. Max. 3.2.2) with an equestrian statue (see, e.g., Liv. 2.13.6–11, Plin. NH 34.28–9), Seneca remarks in his Cons. Marc. 16.2: 'on account of her signal courage we all but inscribed Cloelia among male heroes' ('Cloeliam ... ob insignem audaciam tantum non in viros transcripsimus') and Plut. Mul. Virt. 14 (Mor. 250F) reports that the Etruscan king Porsenna admired 'her strength and daring as above that of a woman' (τὴν ῥώμην ... καὶ τὴν τόλμαν αὐτῆς ὡς κρείττονα γυναικὸς), which made her worthy of a gift (i.e. a horse) 'fitting for a warrior' (ἀνδρὶ πολεμιστῇ πρεπούσης); for her 'male' mind contrasted with the 'womanish soul' of certain degenerate young men, see Cic. Off. 1.61.

140 For Porcia see RE 22 Porcia 28 cols 216–18. I am not concerned with the question whether or not the account of her suicide is historically true, only with the way in which she is made to exemplify both 'male' and 'female' virtues. For praise of her 'masculine' virtues see Dio 44.13, Plut. Brut. 13 (her rising above pain) and 23; for her alleged suicide by swallowing pieces of burning coal, metal being denied her: Dio 47.49.3, App. BC 4.136, Plut. Brut. 53 (who gives two versions of her death), Val. Max. 4.6.5, who comments that she imitated her father's manly suicide in spite of her feminine spirit: 'muliebri spiritu virilem patris exitum imitata' and even surpassed his example by the novelty of her death. Val. Max. 3.2.15 in his section de fortitudine praises her for having nothing womanly in her character, 'minime muliebris animi', as does Plut. Cat. Min. 73.4 for her 'male courage' (ἀνδρείας). For her feminine virtues, see, for instance, Plut. Brut. 13, who calls her φιλόστοργος ('of an affectionate nature') and φίλανδρος ('fond of her husband'). Generally she is described as a loyal, chaste and affectionate wife and daughter (e.g., Plut. Brut. 13 and 53; Val. Max. 4.6.5). For another example of a woman's bravery that 'exceeded the limits of her sex', see Tac. Ann. 16.10–11 about the courageous suicide committed by Antistia Pollitta (FOS 72) together with her father, L. Antistius Vetus, and her grandmother. She had been the wife of Rubellius Plautus, who in AD 62 was murdered at Nero's command. In

defence of her father she cried out at Nero 'in a threatening tone which went beyond her sex' ('sexum egressa voce infensa clamitabat'; Tac. *Ann.* 16.10.4).

141 Sen. *Cons. Helv.* 16.2: 'non potest muliebris excusatio contingere ei, a qua omnia muliebria vitia afuerunt'; see for the same argument also 16.1 and 5; for his enumeration of the female vices which his mother lacked, see 16.3–4. As examples for his mother he adduces 'women whose conspicuous bravery has placed them in the rank of great men' ('feminas, quas conspecta virtus inter magnos viros posuit', *Cons. Helv.* 16.5), such as Cornelia, the mother of the Gracchi. Freedom from female weaknesses seems to be a stock element in his praise of women he respected, for in his *Cons. Marc.* 1.1 Seneca also praises Marcia as having overcome female weakness: 'you were as far removed from womanish weakness of mind as from all other vices' ('tam longe ab infirmitate muliebris animi quam a ceteris vitiis recessisse'; in the same section he mentions her *robur animi*, strength of mind, and her *virtus*, courage); in 1.5 he says that 'the greatness of your mind forbade me to take your sex into account' ('haec magnitudo animi tui vetuit me ad sexum tuum respicere'). The examples of self-control he holds up for Marcia are all male (*Cons. Marc.* 12.6–15.4). For 'female weakness' and *muliebris* as an adjective of contempt, see Manning (1973), Santoro L'Hoir (1992) 80–3, Vidén (1993) 110–29, *TLL muliebris* cols 1568–9.

142 Sen. *Ep.* 95.20–1: 'Maximus ille medicorum et huius scientiae conditor feminis nec capillos defluere dixit nec pedes laborare; atqui et capillis destituuntur et pedibus aegrae sunt. Non mutata feminarum natura, sed victa est; nam cum virorum licentiam aequaverint, corporum quoque virilium incommoda aequarunt. Non minus pervigilant, non minus potant, et oleo et mero viros provocant; aeque invitis ingesta visceribus per os reddunt et vinum omne vomitu remetiuntur; aeque nivem rodunt, solacium stomachi aestuantis. Libidine vero ne maribus quidem cedunt, pati natae, di illas deaeque male perdant! Adeo perversum commentae genus inpudicitiae viros ineunt. Quid ergo mirandum est maximum medicorum ac naturae peritissimum in mendacio prendi, cum tot feminae podagricae calvaeque sint? Beneficium sexus sui vitiis perdiderunt et, quia feminam exuerant, damnatae sunt morbis virilibus'. The translation here is that of C. Edwards (1993), pp. 87–8. For other examples of women ridiculed for imitating male behaviour: Juv. 6.242–5 (women engaging in law), 6. 246–67, especially 253–4 (female gladiators), 6.398ff. (women attending men's meetings) and 6.419–33 (women visiting the baths by night, taking physical exercise and displaying male drinking habits); see also Mart. *Ep.* 1.90, 7.67 and 7.70 about Lesbian women usurping the male role in sexual matters as well as in other fields, such as physical exercise, massage and drinking habits.

143 See Edwards (1993) 137ff.: the parallel drawn by some Roman moralists between the predilection for building luxurious houses and a disinclination to have children; both were felt to be 'unnatural'.

144 For Sallust's portrait of Sempronia, see Sall. *Cat.* 25 and pp. 84f.

145 In his rhetorical portrait of her she is accused of domineering, 'masculine' behaviour and sexual licentiousness: Cic. *Cael.* 67: *imperatrix*; see also *Cael.* 62: *mulier potens*; see also his use of the word *quadrantaria* (*Cael.* 62), which hints at her reputation as a pennywhore and to her nickname *quadrantaria Clytaemnestra* (Plut. *Cic.* 29.4 and Quint. 8.6.53), but also implies her masculinity as she is presented as paying the usual fee for the men's bath (a *quadrans*); in *Cael.* 1, 37–8, 48–9, 50 and 57 she is equated with a *meretrix*. For Cicero's treatment of Clodia in his *Pro Caelio* see Ramage, E. S. (1984) 'Clodia in Cicero's pro Caelio', in Bright, D. F. and Ramage, E. S. (eds) (1984) *Classical Texts and their Traditions: Studies in Honor of C. R. Trahman*, Chico, Calif.: Scholars Press, pp. 201–11; for the theme of 'role-reversal' in Cicero's portrait of Clodia and Clodius 'masculinizing' Clodia and 'effeminizing' Clodius, see Santoro L'Hoir (1992) 23 and Geffcken, K. A. (1973) *Comedy in the Pro Caelio*, Leiden (Mnemosyne, Suppl. 30),

pp. 37–41. For a sound assessment of Clodia's role and political influence, see Skinner (1983) and Hillard (1989) 170–3.

146 For Fulvia's masculinity, see Plut. *Ant.* 10.3: οὐ ταλασίαν οὐδὲ οἰκουρίαν φρονοῦν γύναιον and ἄρχοντος ἄρχειν καὶ στρατηγοῦντος στρατηγεῖν βουλόμενον ('who wished to rule a ruler and command a commander'); Vell. Pat. 2.74.3: 'nihil muliebre praeter corpus gerens'. Plut. *Ant.* 30.2 calls her meddlesome and headstrong: πολυπράγμονα and θρασεῖαν; for more references, see *RE* 7 Fulvia 113 cols 281–4. For her involvement in male undertakings, especially military affairs, see Hallett, J. P. (1977) '*Perusinae glandes* and the changing image of Augustus', *AJAH* 2: 151–71; for her ambitions and her influence on the careers of her husbands, Babcock, C. L. (1965) 'The early career of Fulvia', *AJPh* 86: 1–32. For the masculine power of Agrippina Minor: Tac. 12.7.3 ('adductum et quasi virile servitium'); for her fierce and ambitious character, depicted in masculine terms, see Kaplan (1979). For her breach of custom by involving herself publicly in political and military affairs: Tac. *Ann.* 12.37, 12.42, 13.5 and 14.11. She is depicted as presiding over a naval show at lake Fucinus wearing a military cloak woven with threads of gold: Tac. *Ann.* 12.56.3 (chlamyde aurata); see also Dio 60.33.3 and Plin. *NH* 33.63.

147 For Agrippina Maior, see *PIR*¹ V 463, *FOS* 812. In her obituary Tacitus characterizes her as a woman who could not bear anyone to be equal to her, was hungry for power and had overcome female vices by her masculine ambitions ('aequi inpatiens, dominandi avida, virilibus curis feminarum vitia exuerat', *Ann.* 6.25.2). For her inheriting her father's and her maternal grandfather's capacity for political and military leadership, see Hallett (1984b) 339–40; for her heroic defence of a bridge over the Rhine as she assumed the duties of a general see Tac. *Ann.* 1.69.1: 'femina ingens animi munia ducis ... induit'; for her resemblance to her father Agrippa and her grandfather Augustus and her pride in her noble ancestry: Tac. *Ann.* 1.40.3; for her popularity, Tac. *Ann.* 3.4.2: 'they styled her the glory of her country, the only true descendant of Augustus, the peerless model of ancient virtue' ('decus patriae, solum Augusti sanguinem, unicum antiquitatis specimen appelarent'). As to her female virtues, she was praised for her fecundity, chastity and love of her husband (Tac. *Ann.* 1.33: 'castitas' and 'amor mariti'; 1.41.2: 'a wife of notable fertility and splendid chastity', 'insigni fecunditate, praeclara pudicitia'; 4.12: 'pudicitia ... impenetrabili'). For Tacitus' ambiguous portrayal of Agrippina Maior, see Kaplan (1979) and Vidén (1993) 38–43.

148 Roman prejudice in respect of the mind and abilities of women is connected with the curious notion (also to be found in Roman law) of the supposed emotional instability of women (*infirmitas sexus*). The terms *infirmitas*, *levitas* or *imbecillitas* of women were employed from the time of Cicero onwards to explain the origin of the *tutela mulierum*, which was in steady decline during that period; see Dixon (1984); see also Gardner (1990) 21. From physical weakness it came to be used as a literary commonplace to denote women's weakness of character. Women were supposed to be emotionally weak and unrestrained, easily given to weeping and excessive mourning, and this defect was thought to affect their judgement as well. For some examples, see Cic. *Mur.* 27 about women's *infirmitas consilii*, Sen. *Cons. Marc.* 1.1, who assumes that the usual *infirmitas muliebris animi* had not affected Marcia, Val. Max. 9.1.3: 'imbecillitas mentis', Liv. 3.48.8: because of their *imbecillus animus* women were prone to lose self-control when mourning, Seneca *Contr.* 1.6.5: 'imbecillitas', Gaius 1.144: 'propter animi levitatem' (however, this is rejected by Gaius in 1. 190), Dig. 22.6.9 *pr.*: 'propter sexus infirmitatem'.

149 For some examples of the comparison of women with the socially inferior as regards rationality and judgement see Mart. 7.69.6 about Theophila: 'so little womanlike or common is her judgement' ('tam non femineum nec populare sapit'), which puts

women (with the exception of Theophila) on a par with men of the lower classes; Sen. *Cons. Polyb.* 6.2: 'yet what is so base and so womanish as to give oneself over to be utterly consumed by sorrow?' ('quid autem tam humile ac muliebre est quam consumendum se dolori committere?') and *Cons. Marc.* 7.3, where he connects women, barbarians and the uneducated generally in being prone to mourning; for credulity as a fault of both women and the uneducated lower classes, see above n. 22.

150 Philo *Leg. Gai.* 320: ἀρρενωθεῖσα τὸν λογισμόν. For Philo's view on 'male' and 'female', see Baer, R. A. (1970) *Philo's use of the Categories Male and Female*, Leiden: Brill (Arbeiten zur Literatur und Geschichte des Hellenistischen Judentums 3), pp. 40ff. Similarly Dio 62.2.2 says about Boudicca, queen of the Britons, that she 'possessed greater intelligence than women usually have' (μεῖζον ἢ κατὰ γυναῖκα φρόνημα ἔχουσα). For education as a means of overcoming 'female' irrationality, see Sen. *Const. Sap.* 14.1 (n. 26 above). For the notion of 'female' irrationality in classical Greece, see Just (1994) 164–5; Isomachus' wife is complimented for her 'masculine mind': ἀνδρικήν . . . διάνοιαν (Xen. *Oec.* 10.1). Lefkowitz (1990) argues that in the view of, for instance, Plato, women needed education because of the innate untrustworthiness of their minds: education served to make women think like men. To possess 'a male mind', then, was praised in women as it served the benefit of men.

151 Mart. *Ep.* 7.69.6. I take Hor. *Ep.* 1.19.28, 'mascula Sappho', to refer to Sappho's extraordinary poetic ability – which is complimented as masculine – rather than to her alleged sexual preference.

152 For Hortensia, see Val. Max. 8.3.3, cited in chapter 2, n. 51. For Laelia, see Quint. 1.1.6, chapter 2, n. 51 and pp. 76f. For Tullia: Cic. *Q. fr.* 1.3.3 and above n. 83. For Minicia Marcella: Plin. *Ep.* 5.16.9: see pp. 60f. For these and other examples, see Hallett (1984b) 338–43 and (1989) 62–9; see also the younger Pliny's praise of his wife as worthy of her father and grandfather (and her aunt): Plin. *Ep.* 4.19.

153 Juv. 6.445–7: 'thirsting to be deemed both wise and eloquent, she ought to tuck up her skirts knee-high, sacrifice a pig to Silvanus and take a penny-bath' ('nam quae docta nimis cupit et facunda videri, / crure tenus medio tunicas succingere debet, / caedere Silvano porcum, quadrante lavari'), see chapter 2, p. 44 and chapter 3, pp. 87f.

154 Val. Max. 8.3.1: 'quia sub specie feminae virilem animum gerebat, Androgynen appellabant'. For an exhaustive discussion of Maesia, see Marshall, A. J. (1990) 'Roman ladies on trial: the case of Maesia of Sentinum', *Phoenix* 44: 46–59, who believes that the nickname is meant to satirize her usurpation of the male role in court. However, though Valerius Maximus in his introduction to his section on 'women pleading their own cause or that of others before the magistrates' is critical of women speaking in public (which he judges incompatible with female modesty), his account of Maesia's defence shows admiration of her proficiency (she spoke *diligenter* and *fortiter*).

155 See, for instance, King (1980) 75–80; see also Labalme, P. H. (1980) 'Women's roles in early modern Venice: an exceptional case', in Labalme (1980) 129–52 about Elena Cornaro, whose prodigious learning earned her the laudatory description: 'in ea praeter sexum nihil muliebre' (NB: cf. the scornful remark of Vell. Pat. 2.74.3 about Fulvia, 'nihil muliebre praeter corpus gerens'). For early Christian thinkers the 'masculinity' of women and the assimilation of the sexes was an ideal and a symbol of salvation. However, this did not make women of the early church the equals of men; it was only by denying their sex that Christian women could aspire to spiritual equality: Meeks, W. A. (1974) 'The image of the androgyne: some uses of a symbol in earliest Christianity', *HR* 13: 165–208, Cameron, A. (1980) 'Neither male nor female', *G & R* 27: 60–8 and Aspegren, K. (1990) *The Male Woman: A Feminine Ideal in the Early Church*, Stockholm: Almquist & Wiksell (Acta Universitatis Upsaliensis. A, Women in Religion 4). The female martyr Vibia Perpetua writing about her dream-vision of a

boxing-match with an Egyptian opponent remarked: 'I was stripped naked and became a man' ('expoliata sum et facta sum masculus': *Passio SS. Perpetuae et Felicitatis* 10.7), which is interpreted by Dronke (1984) 14 as a desire to strip herself 'of all that is weak, or womanish, in her nature'; for other interpretations, see Shaw (1993); see also Miles (1991) chapter 2: ' "Becoming male": women martyrs and ascetics'.

156 *Contra* Raepsaet-Charlier (1994), who objects to the practice of treating the last centuries of the republic and the principate indiscriminately and emphasizes the social and political differences between the two periods. However, for matters of mentality like those treated here, such a rigid division is, to my mind, misleading. On the problem of historical change and periodization, see Dixon, S. (1997) 'Continuity and change in Roman social history: retrieving "family feeling(s)" from Roman law and literature', in Golden, M. and Toohey, P. (eds) *Inventing Ancient Culture: Historicism, Periodization, and the Ancient World*, London: Routledge, pp. 79–90.

157 The growth in interest in the education of women in the late first and the second century AD as compared to earlier periods coincides with an increase in interest in family life and a greater prominence of children in visual art; see Rawson (1997). We may surmise that this reflects a higher valuation of women and children in the Trajanic–Antonine period and that this may have contributed to the increased educational opportunities for girls and women at the time and to a greater interest in their individual achievements in the field of education.

158 See Gruen (1992), who, focussing on the third and second centuries BC, objects to the usual dichotomy between philhellenism on the one hand and nationalism and conservatism on the other.

159 The same probably holds for Laelia and the women of her family, discussed on pp. 76f.

160 For Roman ambivalence regarding Greek culture, see Rawson, E. (1992) 'The Romans', in Dover, K. J. (ed.) (1992) *Perceptions of the Ancient Greeks*, Oxford: Blackwell, pp. 1–28, Edwards (1993) 22–4 and 92–7, Gruen, E. S. (1990) *Studies in Greek Culture and Roman Policy*, Leiden: Brill (Cincinnati Class. Stud. n.s. 7), Balsdon, J. P. V. D. (1979) *Romans and Aliens*, London: Duckworth, pp. 30–58 and Wardman, A. (1976) *Rome's Debt to Greece*, London: Paul Elek. For the change in opinion in the course of the first century AD and the appreciation of (Greek) education during the empire as testified by numerous portraits of upper-class men posing as poets and intellectuals, see Zanker (1995) 193–272.

4 PATRONESSES OF LITERATURE AND LEARNING

1 Plut. *CG* 19: Καὶ μέντοι καὶ ἡ Κορνηλία λέγεται τά τ᾽ ἄλλα τῆς συμφορᾶς εὐγενῶς καὶ μεγαλοψύχως ἐνεγκεῖν, καὶ περὶ τῶν ἱερῶν, ἐν οἷς ἀνηρέθησαν, εἰπεῖν, ὡς ἀξίους οἱ νεκροὶ τάφους ἔχουσιν. Αὐτὴ δὲ περὶ τοὺς καλουμένους Μισηνοὺς διέτριβεν, οὐδὲν μεταλλάξασα τῆς συνήθους διαίτης. Ἦν δὲ καὶ πολύφιλος καὶ διὰ φιλοξενίαν εὐτράπεζος, ἀεὶ μὲν Ἑλλήνων καὶ φιλολόγων περὶ αὐτὴν ὄντων, ἁπάντων δὲ τῶν βασιλέων καὶ δεχομένων παρ᾽αὐτῆς δῶρα καὶ πεμπόντων. For Cornelia, see chapter 2, pp. 24f. and chapter 3, pp. 64ff.; for the letter attributed to her, see chapter 6, pp. 193ff.

2 For the wealth and patronage of culture of Hellenistic (mainly Ptolemaic) queens, see Pomeroy (1984) 3–40. On feelings of equality, or even superiority, on the part of members of the Roman republican nobility towards Hellenistic kings, see Rawson, E. (1975) 'Caesar's heritage: Hellenistic kings and their Roman equals', *JRS* 65: 148–59: conquering Roman generals, such as Cornelia's father Scipio Africanus, dealt with Hellenistic kings on an equal footing or even as superiors. The story that Cornelia turned down a marriage proposal from a reigning Ptolemy – see Plutarch *TG* 1.4 and chapter 3, n. 28 – fits in with this picture.

3 Oros. 5.12.9 tells us that she went to live at Misenum after the death of Tiberius in 133 BC, but D'Arms (1970) 9 believes that Misenum may well have been her chief residence from the death of her husband in 154 BC onwards. For the change in villa life in Campania about the middle of the second century BC and the establishment of *villae expolitae* which were not productive estates but solely built for the pleasure of their owners, see D'Arms (1970) 1–17: Cornelia's family seems to have played an important part in the early phase of this leisured villa life. Her father had a villa in Liternum (which may have been productive as a farm) to which he withdrew after his political decline; her uncle Aemilius Paullus probably owned a luxury villa at the Greek town of Velia and her son-in-law Scipio Aemilianus possessed several estates in the area; for their property, see also Shatzman (1975) 243–4 and 246–50. For the luxurious seaside villas of Campania and the refined *otium* and Greek scholars connected with Campanian villa life from the time of Cornelia onwards, see D'Arms (1970) and Zanker (1990) 35–41.

4 For the patronage of men of learning by members of her family, see chapter 3, p. 65. After the death of Scipio Aemilianus (who was a Scipio by adoption) in 129 BC she was the only one of the descendants of Scipio Africanus Maior to continue the family tradition and to earn great public esteem and distinction. Her brothers were inconspicuous in public life because of ill-health and early death (Publius) or ill-favour (Lucius; *RE* 4 Cornelius 325 cols 1431–3), and of her sister, the elder Cornelia, almost nothing is known. In contrast to them the younger Cornelia was a grand public figure; also the hostility that she provoked may be regarded as proof of her prominence.

5 For her wealth and that of her family see Boyer (1950) 172–8, Dixon (1985a) and the discussion of Cornelia in chapter 3, pp. 64ff. As both her father and her husband had died she was *sui iuris*; though she was formally in need of a guardian to control her finances, the interference of a *tutor* who was no close relative was often minimal (for more details see pp. 101f.). For her good choice of teachers, Cic. *Brut.* (100 and) 104; for her possible library and the relation between private libraries and patronage of (Greek) scholars during the republic when good private libraries were scarce and public libraries did not yet exist, see Marshall (1976) 256–8 and chapter 2, pp. 54f.; cf. the fine library of Lucullus which was open to his friends and clients (Plut. *Luc.* 42) and Piso's patronage of the Greek poet and philosopher Philodemus, who lived in his villa and, as it seems, had his own library there; see Bloch, H. (1940) 'L. Calpurnius Piso Caesoninus in Samothrace and Herculaneum', *AJA* 44: 485–93. Some scholars seem also to have lived in Cornelia's villa for some time: Plut. *CG* 19.2 speaks of Greeks and men of letters who 'were always around her' (ἀεὶ ... περὶ αὐτὴν ὄντων) and distinguishes visiting and resident friends (19.3: τοῖς ἀφικνουμένοις καὶ συνοῦσι) who enjoyed her pleasant conversation.

6 Plutarch's source for this description is unknown. For a discussion of the sources of Plutarch's 'Lives of the Gracchi' and a positive assessment of their reliability, see Scardigli (1979) 61–73.

7 See Saller (1982), (1983) 255 and (1989), Wallace-Hadrill (1989a); see also Garnsey and Saller (1990) 148–59 and Jacques and Scheid (1990) 319–24. For a different view of the role of patronage versus merit and seniority, cf. Alföldy (1986) 139–61, especially 149ff. For the role of the emperor as the great patron and the concept of brokerage, see Saller (1982) ch. 2.

8 Saller (1982) 10; for collective patronage see, e.g., Harmand, L. (1957) *Un aspect social et politique du monde romain: le patronat sur les collectivités publiques des origines au Bas-Empire*, Paris (Publ. de Clermont, 2e serie Fasc. 2); the formal co-optation of a patron of a community is discussed by Nicols, J. (1980) 'Tabulae patronatus: a study of the agreement between patron and client-community', *ANRW* II 13: 535–61 (one woman included); see further Nicols, J. (1980) 'Pliny and the patronage of communities', *Hermes* 108:

365–85 and Nicols, J. (1988) 'Prefects, patronage and the administration of justice', *ZPE* 72: 201–17; for patronage of provinces, see, e.g., Nicols, J. (1990) 'Patrons of provinces in the early principate: the case of Bithynia', *ZPE* 80: 101–8. For the relation between patronage and euergetism, see Wesch-Klein, G. (1990) *Liberalitas in Rem Publicam: private Aufwendungen zugunsten von Gemeinden im römischen Afrika bis 284 n. Chr.*, Bonn: Habelt (Antiquitas I, vol. 40); on pp. 46–8 she focusses on women as benefactresses. For patronage of collegia (mainly of the eastern provinces), see van Nijf, O. M. (1997) *The Civic World of Professional Associations in the Roman East*, Amsterdam: Gieben, ch. 2.

9 See Saller (1982) 1 and (1989). To this definition Wallace-Hadrill (1989b) adds that it is a voluntary association. Saller (1982) VII excludes the patronage of a former master over his freedmen as this was obligatory and thus differed fundamentally from the other types (cf. Wallace-Hadrill (1989a) 76–7 and Fabre, G. (1981) *Libertus: recherches sur les rapports patron-affranchi à la fin de la république romaine*, Rome: Coll. Ecole Française de Rome 50).

10 As the terms *patronus* and *cliens* were felt to be somewhat humiliating for the client, straightforward indications of patronage are rare in ancient literature (but not in epigraphy: see Saller (1982) 10); generally the language of *amicitia* is preferred. According to Saller (1982) 9 'the use of *patronus* in the literature of the early Empire was restricted to legal advocates, patrons of communities and ex-masters of freedmen'. For a discussion of the terminology used see, e.g., Saller (1982) 7–39 and (1989); White (1978) and (1993) 27–34 proposes to use the vocabulary of friendship in studies of Roman literary patronage, but this seems rather misleading; see also Saller (1983) 256 and Nauta (1995) 15–19. However, in the following I occasionally use the term 'poet-friend' to denote a literary protégé.

11 See Saller (1989) 60; on patronage of the career of the sons of senatorial and equestrian families by senior aristocrats, see also White (1982) 59.

12 Plin. *Ep.* 3.21 (on the death of Martial) calls *pecunia* (money) and *honores* (office) the traditional rewards for the fame and immortality a poet confers on cities or individuals; for a patron of literature, see also *Ep.* 8.12. Saller (1982) 26ff. distinguishes public and private aspects of a patron's role (*pecunia* deriving from the patron's private resources and *honores* from his public position), which, however, according to him were inextricably interwoven. White (1978) 90–1 provides a list of material benefits any rich man's friend (not only a poet) might receive, including privileges or sinecures. White (1982) 61–3 calls attention to the 'increasingly mercenary ways of talking about poetry' in the second half of the first century AD. For Martial and Statius expecting some (financial) recompense from those to whom they sent poems and eulogies, see, e.g., Mart. *Ep.* 5.18, 36 and 59, where small gifts and eulogies are regarded as 'hooks' to extract a greater recompense; see also Saller (1983).

13 There has been a discussion between White (1978), slightly revised in White (1993) 5–14, and Saller (1982) 28 and (1983) as to which kind of support was more important to the poets: material support or non-material backing. Because of the equestrian status of most Latin poets of the early empire White suggests that publicity and other non-material backing was the most important benefit a patron could bestow, and that material gifts were not essential to the poet's subsistence. In response to this, Saller rightly stresses the importance of gifts, money and landed property to the leisure and livelihood of the poets, even when they were *equites*, and gives many examples of valuable gifts. We should take into account that there were great differences in economic circumstances within the equestrian order – see, e.g., Mratschek-Halfmann (1993) 140–52 – and that some scholars, or poets, such as perhaps Martial (see Saller (1983) 251), may have achieved equestrian status only because of a gift or favour of a patron (*contra* White (1993) 5–14). To many poets equestrian status seems to have meant

sufficiency without surplus and an additional income was needed to maintain an upper-class life-style: see also Nauta (1995) 52f. and Sullivan (1991) 56 (about Martial). For literary patronage generally, see Gold (1982) and (1987), and Williams (1978) 272–312.

14 To many poets of a later period Maecenas was such an ideal patron – see, e.g., *Laus Pisonis* 233ff., Mart. *Ep.* 1.107.3–4, 8.56.5, 11.3.10, 12.4.1–4, Juv. 7.94. See also Saller (1983) 247–8 and Gold (1987) 4.

15 See Plin. *Ep.* 3.21.6: 'gloria et laus et aeternitas'; for the bestowal of fame and immortality as one of the services rendered by a poet to his patron(s), see, e.g., White (1993) 21–2 and 71–2, and Nauta (1995) 37–9 and 137–9.

16 See Saller (1982) 22. Garnsey and Saller (1990) 149 and 152–4 distinguish three categories of exchange relationship: patrons and clients, patrons and protégés (or superior and inferior friends) and equal friends; literary patronage is mainly concerned with the second type of relationship.

17 For some recent discussions of female patronage, mainly the civic type which does not concern us here, see Nicols, J. (1989) 'Patrona civitatis: gender and civic patronage', in Deroux, C. (ed.) *Studies in Latin Literature and Roman History V*, Brussels (coll. Latomus 206), pp. 117–42, Forbis (1990) and Kajava (1990a). MacMullen, R. (1980) 'Women in public in the Roman empire', *Historia* 29: 210–12, MacMullen (1986) and Dyson (1992) 208–9 also discuss some patronesses. For the Greek East, see the stimulating article by van Bremen (1983) and her recent book, van Bremen (1996).

18 See Hardie (1983) 41 and White (1993) 89.

19 This brief discussion of the *tutela* of women relies heavily on the excellent survey by Gardner (1990) 5–29; see also Crook (1992) and Gardner (1993) 84–109. For Cornelia's dowry, see Boyer (1950) 172–8 and Dixon (1985a).

20 For Terentia's financial dealings, see Dixon (1992a). Because of the usual difference in age between husband and wife men were relatively advanced in age when they became fathers and more than 50 per cent of the women marrying *sine manu* may have lost their fathers by their late teens: see Saller (1987).

21 See Dixon (1992a). Because of the strict separation of property between husband and wife in non-*manus* marriages a wife who was still a *filiafamilias* and thus incapable of possessing property in her own right might run into great financial difficulties: her husband was not legally obliged to maintain her at his own expense, perhaps not even to devote the fruits of her dowry to her maintenance (though, in practice, this seems to have been the normal behaviour; see Treggiari (1991) 332–40); see Crook, J. A. (1990) '"His and hers": what degree of financial responsibility did husband and wife have for the matrimonial home and their life in common in a Roman marriage?' in Andreau, J. and Bruhns, H. (eds) (1990) *Parenté et stratégies familiales dans l'antiquité romaine: actes de la table ronde des 2–4 octobre 1986*, Rome: Ecole française de Rome, pp. 153–72. Dixon (1992a) 104–5 suggests that apart from his dotal payments to her husband Dolabella, Cicero had provided for his daughter by a 'separate, regular payment for her everyday expenses', probably by settling some property on her. For the separation of property between husband and wife, see also Gardner (1990) 71–7 and Treggiari (1991) 365–96.

22 For the decline of the *tutela mulierum* see Gardner (1990) 5–29 and Dixon (1984); see also Gardner (1993) 89–97.

23 Van Bremen (1996) chs 7 and 8.

24 Their importance is permanent throughout the empire and cannot be explained by ascribing it to the character, or failings, of individual emperors: though some emperors were especially known (or rather notorious) for the influence of their female relatives, imperial women might be influential under almost all emperors; cf. Saller (1982) 64–5; Fischler (1994) argues that the political influence of women of the imperial family resulted from the socially accepted role of upper-class matrons fulfilling family

responsibilities. For the public power and status of imperial women see also MacMullen (1986) 434 and Purcell (1986). For the emperor as a patron 'to outbid all rivals' see Garnsey and Saller (1990) 180; for imperial *beneficia* and the importance of the emperor's relatives and friends in distributing them, Saller (1982) ch. 2.

25 For the 'brokerage' of high-ranking senators securing *beneficia* from the emperors for their protégés, see Saller (1982) 74ff. and Leunissen, P. M. M. (1993) 'Conventions of patronage in senatorial careers under the principate', *Chiron* 23: 101–20. Though functioning as a mediator the patron-broker received part of the credit and gratitude from the recipient of the *beneficium*. Consequently, a failure was felt to be a blow to his prestige but in case of success he increased his own *dignitas*, since a favour bestowed at his request was regarded as a sign of imperial esteem. The letters of Pliny the Younger provide many examples of such 'brokerage': see, e.g., *Ep.* 2.9, 3.8, 6.6, 10.4 and 10.26, displaying Pliny's anxiety for the success of his clients, which was of importance for his own *dignitas*, and, e.g., *Ep.* 10.11, 10.12, 10.13 and 10.94, in which he refers to the indulgence of the emperor as regards earlier requests in order to justify his present entreaty.

26 For the role of the emperor in spreading culture, see Wallace-Hadrill (1983) 175–89. For Greek poets and philosophers at the court of Augustus, see Bowersock (1965) 30–41 and 122–39; for Nero's literary patronage, his encouragement of a literary revival and his eventual failure, see Morford, M. (1985) 'Nero's patronage and participation in literature and the arts', *ANRW* II 32.3: 2003–31, who also points out that under Tiberius, Caligula and Claudius imperial literary patronage was of a much more limited kind. For Domitian's patronage of literature, see Coleman, K. M. (1986) 'The emperor Domitian and literature', *ANRW* II 32.5: 3095–111, Hardie (1983) 45–9 and Nauta (1995) 306–97. For differences in the extent of the literary patronage between individual emperors, see further Williams (1978) 297–303.

27 For the anecdote, see Macr. *Sat.* 2.4.31. For gifts of cash or property, appointments, privileges and other rewards to poets and scholars because of the dedication of a literary work to the emperor or other services (such as teaching and advising), see Bowersock (1965) 30–41 and 122–39 (for Augustus), White (1993) 15–16 (with n. 22), Saller (1983) 249; for the intellectual entourage of the emperor in general, see Millar (1977) 83–101 and 491–506, who remarks that the presentation of a literary or scholarly work to the emperor procured a privileged form of access; see also Hardie (1983) 45. That risks were also involved may be illustrated by the over-eager Clutorius Priscus (Tac. *Ann.* 3.49 and Dio 57.20.3), who, spurred on by the great sum of money he had received from Tiberius for his elegy on the death of Germanicus, started writing a poem on Drusus' death when he heard of his illness. When Drusus did not die, Clutorius paid with his life for this anticipation of his death.

28 For Octavia see *RE* 17 Octavia Minor 96 cols 1859–68; she lived from about 69 to 11 BC. Balsdon (1977) 66–74 and 80 summarizes the events of her life.

29 Vitr. *Arch.* 1 *praef.* 2–3: 'cum eis commoda accepi, quae, cum primo mihi tribuisti recognitionem, per sororis commendationem servasti. Cum ergo eo beneficio essem obligatus, ut ad exitum vitae non haberem inopiae timorem, haec tibi scribere coepi'. Apart from the cramped construction of the sentence the words 'commoda' and 'recognitionem' are problematic. F. Granger in the Loeb edition translates 'commoda' with 'advancement' and 'recognitionem' with 'surveyorship' and believes that Octavian prolonged Vitruvius' job as a surveyor by the recommendation of Octavia. Saller (1982) 50 takes this as an extreme example of the priority of patronage over merit in securing jobs: 'here, if anywhere in the administration, one might have expected considerations of technical competence to outweigh patronage'. This suggestion, however, is doubtful: as Vitruvius was a competent and experienced military architect, who had already served Julius Caesar in this capacity, it seems unlikely that he needed a recom-

mendation to keep the job he was doing. According to Marsden (1971) 3, who believes that Vitruvius received a pension, experienced military architects 'were relatively rare and tended to be retained in the same jobs for long periods'. Therefore, I prefer the translation of Ph. Fleury in the Budé edition (1990): 'avec eux je reçus des gratifications; après me les avoir d'abord accordées, tu en continuas le renouvellement sur la recommendation de ta sœur'. In this translation 'recognitionem' denotes the temporary review of the list of benificiaries of gratifications, which led to the continuation of Vitruvius' name on the list. Thus, his gratifications were continued by the recommendation of Octavia and Vitruvius was allowed to retain them for the rest of his life as a personal *beneficium* from the emperor. As Vitruvius had reached an advanced age at the time and was not rich enough to live off his wealth (see *Arch.* 2 *praef.* 4 and 6 *praef.* 4–5), it seems possible that he was allowed to retire while keeping his income.

30 For the sake of convenience I shall henceforth refrain from distinguishing between Octavian and Augustus when denoting her brother, calling him Augustus also before he received the title in 27 BC. For Augustus' fondness for his sister, see Plut. *Ant.* 31.1 and Suet. *Aug.* 61; for her influence with her brother, see Dio 47.7.4–5; she also supported the interests of Antony's friends by intervening for them with her brother; see Plut. *Ant.* 54.2. Augustus' high regard for her appears from her successful mediation in Tarentum – see Plut. *Ant.* 35, App. *BC.* 5.93ff. – and from his mourning and funeral oration at her death: see Ovid. *Cons. Liv.* 442 and Dio 54.35.4–5. In the case of Vitruvius, the distinction between political and cultural patronage may seem blurred, but Rawson (1985) 47, n. 42, to my mind rightly, regards it as patronage of learning. Though architecture in ancient Rome was not generally considered to belong to the *artes liberales*, Vitruvius easily qualified as a man of letters because of his wide learning (see, e.g., Vitr. 1.1.2–18 and 6 *praef.* 1–4). Cichorius (1922) 271–9 suggests that Octavia was a patroness not only of Vitruvius but also of Athenaeus Mechanicus, who dedicated a work on siege-machinery to Octavia's son Marcellus, but I have not found any indication of this.

31 Plut. *Marc.* 30.6: 'In his honour and to his memory Octavia, his mother, dedicated the library, and Caesar the theatre, which bear his name' (εἰς δὲ τιμὴν αὐτοῦ καὶ μνήμην Ὀκταβία μὲν ἡ μήτηρ τὴν βιβλιοθήκην ἀνέθηκε, Καῖσαρ δὲ θέατρον ἐπιγράψας Μαρκέλλου). See also Zanker (1990) 151 and Gros, P. (1976) *Aurea Templa: recherches sur l'architecture religieuse de Rome à l'époque d'Auguste*, Rome: Ecole française de Rome (BEFAR 231) pp. 81–4. Both the *porticus* and the library (with its books) burnt down in the great fire of Rome in AD 80 (Dio 66.24.2). Augustus appointed the grammarian Melissus, a freedman of Maecenas, as the head of the libraries; see Suet. *Gram.* 21. *CIL* VI 2347 (= 4431 = *ILS* 1971), 2348 (= *ILS* 1972), 2349 (= 5192 = *ILS* 1970) are epitaphs of public slaves *a bybliothece latina* and *a bibliotheca graeca* of the Porticus Octaviae. For Marcellus, Octavia's only son by her first marriage (to C. Claudius Marcellus) and designated by Augustus as his successor, see *PIR*² C 925 and *RE* 3 Claudius 230 cols 2764–70.

32 Dio 49.43.8, a rather casual remark; he is followed by Clark (1909) 12–14, Kenyon (1932) 80, Pinner (1958) 55, Thompson (1962) 31 and Marshall (1976) 261. Also Suet. *Aug.* 29.4 is often quoted as evidence in support of the view that the *porticus* and the library were built by Augustus in honour of his sister, despite the fact that Suetonius does not mention the library.

33 For this view, see Boyd (1915) 8–10 and Fehrle (1986) 64.

34 Thus, Marsden (1971) 5. It seems unlikely that the adjacent theatre of Marcellus was meant, as this was built by Augustus and dedicated about ten years after Marcellus' death. Ovid. *AA.* 1.69–70: 'ubi muneribus nati sua munera mater / addidit'. Also *Trist.* 3.1.69 refers to the library of the 'Porticus Octaviae' but does not mention who founded it. Clift (1945) 21 suggests that Octavia may have donated the books which her late husband Antony had confiscated when looting Varro's library in 43 BC (Gell. *NA* 3.10.17).

35 Following the example of Augustus, who wanted only the best writers to write about him (Suet. *Aug.* 89), she may have found the self-seeking commemoration of Marcellus by many (minor) poets and artists rather tasteless. For Propertius' poem mourning the death of Marcellus, see Prop. 3.18. For Virgil's commemoration of Marcellus; see *Aen.* 6.860–86, especially 883. For Octavia weeping at his recitation of the sixth book of the *Aeneid*, see Servius *Ad Aen.* 861; for her fainting, Donatus *Vita Verg.* 32: 'it is said that when he reached the verses about her son, "You shall be Marcellus" [*Aen.* 6.883], she fainted and was with difficulty revived' ('ad illos de filio suo versus, "tu Marcellus eris" defecisse fertur atque aegre focilata est'). According to an interpolation in the manuscript of Donatus she gave Virgil 10,000 (see White (1993) 148, n. 64) sesterces per verse in return for Virgil's tribute to her son: 'dena sestertia pro singulo versu Virgilio dari iussit' (Brummer, I. (1912) *Vitae Vergilianae*, Leipzig: Teubner, p. 27.6–7). Also Servius *Ad Aen.* 861 seems to refer to some financial reward (apparently in unstamped bullion) for Virgil: 'qui pro hoc aere gravi donatus est, id est massis' ('for this he received a present of unstamped bullion').

36 Plut. *Publ.* 17.5: Τοῦτον τὸν ἄνδρα Μούκιον ὁμοῦ τι πάντων καὶ Σκαιόλαν καλούντων Ἀθηνόδωρος ὁ Σάνδωνος ἐν τῷ πρὸς Ὀκταουίαν τὴν Καίσαρος ἀδελφὴν καὶ Ὀψίγονον ὠνομάσθαι φησίν.

37 See Cichorius (1922) 281–2, who bases his conclusion on the fact that Plutarch mentions the addressee instead of the title of the book. Though admittedly this may point to a *consolatio* (cf., e.g., Seneca's *Consolatio ad Marciam*), Plutarch's careless reference does not exclude the possibility that it was a work of a different kind. Bowersock (1965) 34 adopts Cichorius' conclusion without questioning and assumes that the work dedicated to Octavia was of the same kind as Areius' consolation of Livia at the death of her son Drusus in 9 BC; like Athenodorus, the Platonist Areius of Alexandria was a court philosopher and a teacher of Augustus (see Bowersock (1965) 33–4, 39–41 and 123). Areius' consolation of Livia, however, seems to have consisted of a speech, not a written *consolatio*, though he may have published his speech afterwards; cf. Seneca *Cons. Marc.* 4.2–5.6 (Areius comforting Livia by talking to her); see also Temporini (1978) 165; *contra* Bardon (1940) 11. For *consolationes* in general see, e.g., Kassel, R. (1958) *Untersuchungen zur griechischen und römischen Konsolationsliteratur*, Munich: Beck (Zetemata 18). Examples of *consolationes* addressed to women are the *Consolationes ad Marciam* and *ad Helviam* (unusual in consoling his mother for his own exile) by Seneca and the *Consolatio ad Uxorem* by Plutarch (to console his wife for the death of their daughter).

38 For Athenodorus see *PIR*² A 1288, *RE* Suppl. V cols 47–55 and Demougin (1992) no. 48; see also Rawson (1985) 81–2 and 295. The evidence on Athenodorus' residence in Rome is confused. According to Bowersock (1965) 32 and Cichorius (1922) 279–80 he came to Rome in 44 BC, but Hijmans, B. L. (1975) 'Athenodorus on the categories and a pun on Athenodorus', in Mansfeld, J. and Rijk, L. M. de (eds) *Kephalaion: Studies in Greek Philosophy and its Continuation Offered to Professor C. J. de Vogel*, Assen: Van Gorcum, p. 106 argues for a date as early as 50 BC. In Rome he became a teacher and adviser of Octavian, who also employed him in political matters concerning the Greek world by sending him on a political mission to Tarsus. He died in Tarsus in his eighties (Pseudo-Lucian *Macrobioi* 21). As Strabo 14.674–5 connects his arrival in Tarsus with the fall of Antony (Athenodorus was to expel Boethus, whom Antony had appointed ruler of Tarsus), he must have arrived in Tarsus shortly after 30 BC. Cichorius (1922) 279–82 and Bowersock (1965) 32–4, 39 and 48 do not specify the date of Athenodorus' return to Tarsus. They seem to believe that Athenodorus was still living in Rome in 23 BC, which is very unlikely.

39 In Latin literature Mucius Scaevola, who after failing to kill Porsenna held his right hand in the fire, showing stoical indifference to physical pain, figured as an example of

courage and endurance; see Liv. 2.12.8–13.2, Seneca *Ep.* 24.5 and Val. Max. 3.3.1, who opens his section *de patientia* with Mucius Scaevola. In Christian literature he served as an example of pagan courage and was compared to Christian martyrs (Augustine *Civ. Dei* 5.14).

40 Her first husband Marcellus died when she was pregnant, but a *consolatio* for the death of a husband is unusual; moreover, Octavia married Antony within a year. For her dignified behaviour despite Antony's rude treatment, see, for instance, Plut. *Ant.* 53, 54 and 57; for her despair at the outbreak of the civil war between Antony and Augustus: Plut. *Ant.* 54 and 57. After Marcellus' death she was inconsolable; she is described by Seneca (*Cons. Marc.* 2.4–5) as an example of a woman unable and even unwilling to stop mourning and closing her ears to every attempt at consolation: 'She spurned the poems that were written to glorify the memory of Marcellus and all other literary honours, and closed her ears to every form of consolation' ('carmina celebrandae Marcelli memoriae composita aliosque studiorum honores reiecit et aures suas adversus omne solacium clusit').

41 In 35 BC Livia and Octavia were granted exceptional privileges: freedom of *tutela*, the sacrosanctity of the tribunes and the erection of public statues for them; see Dio 49.38.1, Purcell (1986) 85ff. and Flory (1993).

42 Octavia stayed in Athens with Antony during the winters of 39–8 and 38–7 BC and probably also during the intervening summer; she visited Athens again during the winter of 36–5 BC and perhaps part of the summer of 35 BC. According to Plutarch *Ant.* 57 she was much loved and honoured by the Athenians, and both she and Antony were worshipped as 'beneficial gods' (Θεοὶ Εὐεργέται); see Raubitschek, A. E. (1946) 'Octavia's deification at Athens', *TAPhA* 77: 146–50, who believes that she was identified with Athena Polias; for the inscription see also AE (1952) 199 and Kajava (1990) 71. It has been suggested that she attended lectures in Athens, but this cannot be proved; see Rawson (1985) 47, n. 40. Though Octavia accompanied Antony to the festivals of the Greeks, he attended the 'discussions and lectures of the public teachers' only in the company of two friends and attendants, according to App. *BC* 5.76 (Plut. *Ant.* 33 does not mention Octavia's presence at either of these occasions). For her intelligence see Plut. *Ant.* 31.2; in 35.3 and 54.2 Plutarch presents her language as balanced and controlled. Cichorius (1922) 278, somewhat overstating Octavia's importance, calls her the 'Mittelpunkt eines regen geistigen Lebens'.

43 Priscianus *Inst.* X.47 (ed. H. Keil II, p. 536 (Leipzig 1855)): 'Maecenas in Octaviam: pexisti capillum naturae muneribus gratum.' Priscianus quotes this sentence because of his interest in the perfect *pexisti* (from *pecto*). For the rhythm, see *RE* XIV Maecenas col. 223. Maecenas was notorious for his affected style and rhythm: see, for instance, Bardon (1956) 17–18, who convincingly rejects emendations that eliminate Octavia as the addressee. Because of its diction and rhythm the line may have been taken from a poem praising Octavia's beauty, or perhaps from a more general eulogy of her person written in rhythmic prose.

44 For Augustus' patronage of culture, see Suet. *Aug.* 84–9 and Bowersock (1965) 30–41 and 122–39; for his patronage of Virgil, see, e.g., Suet. *Vita Verg.* 12, 17, 31–2. Virgil's fourth *ecloga*, expressing his hope for the birth of a son, was perhaps recited at the marriage of Antony and Octavia; see Goold, G. P. (1992) 'The voice of Virgil: the pageant of Rome in Aeneid 6', in Woodman, T. and Powell, J. (eds) *Author and Audience in Latin Literature*, Cambridge: Cambridge University Press, pp. 110–12.

45 Apart from her own children: three children by her first husband C. Claudius Marcellus (M. Claudius Marcellus and Claudia Marcella Maior and Minor), and two daughters by her second husband M. Antony (Antonia Maior and Minor; Plut. *Ant.* 35 mentions a third pregnancy, but no third child is known); she reared 'in a noble and magnificent manner' (Plut. *Ant.* 54.2) most of Antony's children by his other wives:

NOTES

possibly his daughter Antonia from his marriage to his cousin Antonia; further, his two sons, Marcus and Iullus Antonius, by Fulvia (though the former was with his father for much of the time) and his three children, the twins Alexander Helios and Cleopatra Selene and Ptolemaeus Philadelphus, by Cleopatra: see Plut. *Ant.* 35, 54, 57 and 87. For Antony's marriages and children, see Bradley (1991) 133–5. As regards the injurious behaviour of Antony she showed remarkable patience: see, for instance, Plut. *Ant.* 53, 54 and 57; for her beauty, intelligence and dignity, see Plut. *Ant.* 31.2, who is very kindly disposed towards her.

46 Plut. *Ant.* 35, 53, 54, Dio 48.54.3 and App. 5.93ff. describe her efforts to keep peace between Antony and Augustus, and Plut. *Ant.* 54 and 57 her despair at her eventual failure: she was very upset by the outbreak of civil war and afraid of being regarded as one of its causes. Seneca *Cons. Marc.* 2.3–5 depicts the promising personality of Marcellus, his prospect of succeeding Augustus and Octavia's jealousy and hatred of Livia because of her sons (whose chances of succession had been increased by Marcellus' death). Frustrated hope was probably the reason for her excessive and even aggressive mourning, as painted by Seneca.

47 *AP* 9.239: Βύβλων ἡ γλυκερὴ λυρικῶν ἐν τεύχει τῷδε / πεντὰς ἀμιμήτων ἔργα φέρει χαρίτων / Ἀνακρείοντος, ἃς ὁ Τήιος ἡδὺς πρέσβυς / ἔγραψεν ἢ παρ' οἶνον ἢ σὺν Ἱμέροις. / δῶρον δ' εἰς ἱερὴν Ἀντωνίη ἥκομεν ἠῶ / κάλλευς καὶ πραπίδων ἔξοχ' ἐνεγκαμένη. Lines 3 and 4 are regarded as a late interpolation by most editors, but are accepted by Gow and Page (1968) II: 217. The words παρ' οἶνον and σὺν Ἱμέροις in line 4 refer to the convivial and the amatory poetry of Anacreon.

48 We do not know the occasion or the year of this gift. According to Gow and Page II (1968) 217 it may have been her birthday or perhaps some other occasion, for instance, the Saturnalia, but probably not her wedding-day. The rather mercenary way of dealing with poetry, with a view to financial recompense, resembles that of Martial (see *Ep.* 5.18, 36 and 59; see also pp. 128ff.).

49 For Crinagoras of Mytilene see *RE* XI cols 1859–64, Cichorius (1922) 306–23, Gow and Page (1968) II: 210ff., Bowersock (1965) 33, 36f. and 123–4 and Williams (1978) 129–38. He was a man of high esteem in his native town and took part in two embassies sent by his city to Julius Caesar in 48–47 and in 45 BC. His association with Augustus probably dates from his third embassy in 26–25 BC to Spain where Augustus was recovering from an illness. After his return from Spain he remained in Rome as a court-poet and a companion to Augustus for a considerable time, probably even for the rest of his life, and commemorated in his epigrams events in the lives of many members of the imperial family, for instance, Augustus (*AP* 9.291 and 419), Tiberius (*A. Pl.* 61), Germanicus (*AP* 9.283), Marcellus (*AP* 6.161 and 9.545), Antonia Minor (*AP* 6.244 and 345; 9.239) and Cleopatra Selene, the daughter of Antony and Cleopatra (*AP* 7.633 and 9.235). He died around AD 20 aged over 80; see Gow and Page (1968) II: 212. White (1993) 201ff. draws attention to the fact that whereas the living relatives of Augustus were only rarely and cautiously introduced into the Latin poetry of the time, Greek epigrammatists wrote 'court-poetry', responding in verse to events in the public and private life of the imperial family.

50 For Antonia Maior, who was born in 39 BC, see *RE* I Antonia 113 col. 2640 and *PIR*² A 884; by her marriage to L. Domitius Ahenobarbus she was the mother of two daughters, Domitia and Domitia Lepida, and one son, Gnaeus Domitius Ahenobarbus who became the father of the emperor Nero. For Antonia Minor see *RE* I Antonia 114 col. 2640, *PIR*² A 885 and *FOS* 73; for a comprehensive study of her on the basis of literary sources as well as the rich archaeological evidence, portraits, coins, inscriptions and papyri concerning her, see Kokkinos (1992); she was born in 36 BC and married Nero Claudius Drusus about 18 BC. For a girl of her class she married late: she was 18 years old, or perhaps even somewhat older; see Treggiari (1991) 402. After the death of

NOTES

Drusus in 9 BC she refused to remarry although the emperor urged her to do so; see Jos. *AJ* 18.180 and Treggiari (1991) 500; perhaps the fact that she had already borne three children strengthened her position. She lived with her mother-in-law Livia (Val. Max. 4.3.3, Tac. *Ann.* 13.18) and remained a widow till her death in AD 37.

51 Plut. *Ant.* 87.3: τὴν δὲ σωφροσύνῃ καὶ κάλλει περιβόητον Ἀντωνίαν. Gow and Page (1968) II: 217 accept the identification; see also Kokkinos (1992) 118–19.

52 *AP* 6.244: Ἥρη Ἐληθυιῶν μήτηρ, Ἥρη δὲ τελείη, / καὶ Ζεῦ γινομένοις ξυνὸς ἅπασι πατήρ, / ὠδῖνας νεύσαιτ' Ἀντωνίῃ ἵλαοι ἐλθεῖν / πρηείας μαλακαῖς χερσὶ σὺν Ἠπιόνης, / ὄφρα κε γηθήσειε πόσις μήτηρ θ' ἑκυρή τε· / ἣ νηδὺς οἴκων αἷμα φέρει μεγάλων. Gow and Page (1968) I: 205 and II: 221 accept the identification with Antonia Minor.

53 *AP* 6.345: Εἴαρος ἄνθει μὲν τὸ πρὶν ῥόδα, νῦν δ' ἐνὶ μέσσῳ / χείματι πορφυρέας ἐσχάσαμεν κάλυκας / σῇ ἐπιμειδήσαντα γενεθλίῃ ἄσμενα τῇδε / ἠοῖ νυμφιδίων ἀσσοτάτη λεχέων. / καλλίστης στεφθῆναι ἐπὶ κροτάφοισι γυναικός / λώϊον ἢ μίμνειν ἠρινὸν ἠέλιον.

54 Antonia Minor was born on 31 January; her sister, the elder Antonia, was born in summer. For winter-roses, apparently a novel gift imported from Egypt, see Mart. *Ep.* 6.80 and 13.127. For the identification with Antonia Minor, see Bowersock (1965) 36, Kokkinos (1992) 11 and (more cautiously) Gow and Page (1968) II: 216.

55 Crinagoras probably stayed in Rome approximately between 26 BC and his death around AD 20; Antonia lived in the imperial palace for almost all her life. *AP* 6.345 may have been the earliest poem addressed to her dating from the year of her marriage. *AP* 6.244, about the birth of one of her children, must be dated before 11 BC; the date of *AP* 9.239 cannot be established.

56 For Thallus, see *RE* Va Thallos 2 col. 1226, Cichorius (1922) 356–8, Gow and Page (1968) II: 410–13. His *gentilicium* is mentioned in the title to *AP* 7.188. Cichorius' conjecture is accepted by Bowersock (1965) 141, D'Arms (1970) 85–6 and *PIR*² A 885.

57 *AP* 6.235, according to Gow and Page (1968) II: 411, is written in honour of Germanicus; however, Cichorius (1922) 356–7 assumes that it deals with Caligula.

58 For Honestus see *RE* VIII cols 2269–70, Cichorius (1922) 362–5, Gow and Page (1968) II: 301–9. For the identification of the Honestus of the Garland of Philip with the Honestus of the inscribed epigrams in Boeotia, see Gow and Page (1968) II: 301–9.

59 Honestus XXI [C2]: ἡ δοιοὺς σκήπτροισι θεοὺς αὐχοῦσα Σεβαστή / Καίσαρας εἰρήνης δισσὰ λέλαμπε φάη· / ἔπρεψεν δὲ σοφαῖς Ἑλικωνιάσιν πινυτόφρων / σύγχορος, ἧς γε νόος κόσμον ἔσωσεν ὅλον. Translation by Gow and Page (1968) I: 277; see also Gow and Page (1968) II: 308–9.

60 Cichorius (1922) 362–5; his conclusion that Antonia Minor was Honestus' patroness is accepted by D'Arms (1970) 85–6 and Bowersock (1965) 141 (however, according to Jones (1970) 251, n. 67, who himself favours an identification with Livia, Bowersock has told him that he would now repudiate the identification with Antonia). Also Temporini (1978) 28–9 believes, on chronological grounds, that only Antonia Minor can be meant. Kokkinos (1992) 42, 88–9 and 92–3, while accepting the identification with Antonia Minor, suggests two alternative identifications for the Caesars: her son Germanicus and her son-in-law, the younger Drusus, or her grandson Caligula and her son Claudius; both seem doubtful. In support of the identification of the Augusta with Antonia he draws attention to the two lighted torches depicted on the reverse of some coins of Antonia which he connects with the 'twin torches of Peace' in line 3 of the poem; however, the legend on the coins refers to a priesthood of the cult of Augustus. According to Gow and Page (1968) II: 308 Cichorius' interpretation is 'perhaps just possible', but they prefer to identify the Augusta with Livia. For Antonia's exposure of the plot of Sejanus see Jos. *AJ* 18.180f., Dio 66.14, Kokkinos (1992) 25–7; *contra* Nicols (1975).

295

61 Shortly after his accession in March AD 37 her grandson Caligula honoured her with the privileges formerly granted to Livia, among which was the title of Augusta (Suet. *Calig.* 15, Dio 59.3.3–4; there is no evidence to support the suggestion of Kokkinos (1992) 93 that Tiberius offered the title to her but that she declined). Less than two months after Caligula's accession she died, allegedly driven to suicide by him (Suet. *Calig.* 23, Dio 59.3.6). Antonia is said to have declined the title of Augusta during her lifetime, but was honoured as such after her death especially since her son Claudius reintroduced her title (Suet. *Claud.* 11); see Temporini (1978) 28–9 and Flory (1997) 122–3. For an inscription from Asia Minor calling her Antonia Sebaste see *AE* (1982) 891. Cichorius' interpretation of line 4 as alluding to the conspiracy of Sejanus has been rejected by Nicols (1975), but is accepted by Kokkinos (1992) 42 and 91ff.

62 See Temporini (1978) 28–9, n. 115, who gives several examples: for instance, Julia, the daughter of Augustus, who never officially bore the title of Augusta, was honoured in an inscription from the temple of Venus at Paphos as θεὰν σεβαστὴν (see *IGR* III 940 and Nicols (1975) 52). Other female members of the imperial family were referred to as Augusta in Greek provincial inscriptions far in advance of their official reception of the title.

63 Tiberius Gemellus, the son of Antonia's daughter Livilla and Tiberius' son Drusus, and Caligula were both grandsons of the emperor Tiberius: Tiberius Gemellus by blood and Caligula by adoption (being the son of Tiberius' nephew and adopted son, Germanicus). Tiberius Gemellus was younger than Caligula and lacked the necessary political and military support to stand his ground against him. For Caligula and Tiberius Gemellus as joint heirs to Tiberius, see Suet. *Tib.* 76 and *Calig.* 14, Philo *Leg. Gai.* 4, Dio 59.1f. Temporini (1978) 28–9 draws attention to a contemporary inscription from Corinth which honours Antonia Minor and Tiberius Gemellus as Augusta and Caesar; see also Kokkinos (1992) 46.

64 Several other identifications have been proposed, but even the most plausible among them – Augustus' daughter Julia with her sons Gaius and Lucius, or his wife Livia with her husband Augustus and her son Tiberius – are open to objections. For the identification of the Augusta with Julia, see, e.g., the first editor of the epigram, Jamot, P. (1902) 'Fouilles de Thespies: le Monument des Muses dans le Bois de l'Hélicon et le poète Honestus', *BCH* 26: 129–60, esp. 153f. and *BE* 68 (1955) no. 119; for the identification with Livia (with Augustus and Tiberius as the Caesars), see Gow and Page (1968) II: 308 and Jones (1970) 249–55; Nicols (1975) 53 suggests Livia with her grandsons Germanicus and Tiberius' son Drusus.

65 For Antonia's great wealth see, e.g., Dio 51.15.7, D'Arms (1970) 85–6 and Kokkinos (1992) 70ff. (discussing her possessions in Egypt). The account of Antonia's patronage of Agrippa I, the son of her friend Berenice of Judaea, shows that she could provide substantial support both financially and politically; for this and for her influence with Tiberius, see Jos. *AJ* 18.143, 164–7, 179–204, 236, Syme (1989) 141 and Kokkinos (1992) 25, who stresses her importance and (political) influence as the leading woman at court and gives many examples of inscriptions erected in her honour by beneficiaries (pp. 43ff.). Her one possible rival, her daughter-in-law Agrippina Maior (*FOS* 812), a powerful woman with strong political ambitions, had fallen into disfavour with Tiberius and in AD 29 was banished to Pandateira, where she died four years later. Antonia closely supervised the education of her sons even when they were adults, dissuading Claudius from writing a history of the civil war (Suet. *Claud.* 41.2). Crinagoras' gift of five books of poetry to her (*AP* 9.239) bears witness to her literary interest.

66 For her long widowhood, beauty and traditional virtues, see, e.g., Val. Max. 4.3.3, Jos. *AJ* 18.180, Plut. *Ant.* 87.3, Ovid *Cons. Liv.* 299ff.; see also Kokkinos (1992) 15–16. Eck *et al.* (1996) 244 point out that Antonia was praised in a decree of the senate of AD 20 for her *sanctitas morum* and for the fact that she married only once (lines 140–2) – though the

latter conflicted with the Augustan marital laws. Apart from her own three children she supervised the education of many young foreign princes and princesses, such as the children of Cotys, the murdered king of Thrace, and Agrippa I of Judaea (for more examples, see Kokkinos (1992) 25), and, after the death of Livia in AD 29, her grandson Caligula and his sister Drusilla (Suet. *Calig.* 10 and 24); for her possible care of some of Germanicus' children during his lifetime, see Kokkinos (1992) 17–18 and 83. Her harsh treatment of her son Claudius, openly displaying her contempt for him because of his physical disability and his supposed weakness of mind (Suet. *Claud.* 3.2), may remind us of the fact that the Roman ideal of motherhood differed from ours in its emphasis on severity and the role of the mother as disciplinarian (see also chapter 3, pp. 68ff.). His grandmother Livia, with whom Claudius lived for some time (Dio 60.2.5), behaved in a similarly harsh fashion towards him.

67 Syme (1989) 347 seems to believe that Octavia herself enlisted Nestor of Tarsus (an Academician who eventually succeeded Athenodorus as governor of Tarsus) as a teacher of her son Marcellus, but this is not said explicitly by Strabo (14.675).

68 See also van Bremen (1983) and van Bremen (1996) for wealthy and prominent bene-factresses and female office-holders in the cities of the Greek East in the Roman period who were praised in conventional terms emphasizing traditional female virtues and their roles as wives and mothers. Against this, Forbis (1990) argues that, in contrast with the conventional praise for women which is the rule in the literary sources, the vast majority of honorary inscriptions dedicated to upper-class women in the Italian muni-cipalities openly praise them for their public munificence, just like men. Even so, in her recent book she gives some clear examples of benefactresses praised in traditional terms emphasizing their chastity and their domestic virtues; see Forbis (1996) 85–7.

69 *CIL* VI 10230 (= *ILS* 8394): 'Quibus de causeis quom omnium bonarum feminarum simplex similisque esse laudatio soleat, quod naturalia bona propria custodia servata varietates verborum non desiderent, satisque sit eadem omnes bona fama digna fecisse, et quia adquirere novas laudes mulieri sit arduom, quom minoribus varietatibus vita iactetur, necessario communia esse colenda, ne quod amissum ex iustis praecepteis cetera turpet. Eo maiorem laudem omnium carissima mihi mater meruit, quod modes-tia probitate pudicitia opsequio lanificio diligentia fide par similisque ceterreis probeis feminis fuit, neque ulli cessit virtutis laboris sapientiae periculorum' (though the Latin text is not wholly understandable at all points, the overall meaning seems clear enough). For the funeral eulogy for Murdia, see also Gardner (1990) 55. A comparable example of conventional praise for a woman, who as appears from her funerary inscription had led a very unconventional life, is the so-called *Laudatio Turiae*: *CIL* VI 1527, 31670, 37053 (= *ILS* 8393) lines 30ff.: see Durry, M. (1950) *Eloge funèbre d'une matrone romaine (éloge dit de Turia)*, Paris: Les Belles Lettres, and Wistrand, E. (1976) *The So-called Laudatio Turiae: Introduction, Text, Translation, Commentary*, Göteborg: Acta Univer-sitatis Gothoburgensis.

70 For Livia see *PIR*[2] L 301, *RE* XIII cols 901–24, Balsdon (1977) 63–96, especially 90–5. For her status, her political power (and patronage) and her public building, see Purcell (1986), Boatwright (1991) 519f., Flory (1997) 113–22; see further Saller (1982) 65, Temporini (1978) 95 n. 426; her power is apparent in the role she played in saving Plancina from prosecution; see Eck *et al.* (1996) 87f., 224ff. and 240ff. Apart from Tacitus, whose venomous portrait of her may be regarded as an indication of her power, she is portrayed by others as a woman of keen political insight who was con-sulted by Augustus on political matters (see, e.g., Suet. *Aug.* 84, *Claud.* 4; for her human-izing influence on him: Dio 58.2.3 and the fictitious dialogues between Livia and Augustus in Dio 55.14–22 and Sen. *Clem.* 1.9.6). For her philanthropic activities: Dio 57.16.2 (assistance to fire victims) and 58.2.3 (payment of dowries). Though she was wealthy and well educated, there are no indications that she ever exercised literary

patronage: Areius' consolation of her at the death of her son Drusus (Sen. *Cons. Marc.* 4.2–5.6) and the disputed *Consolatio ad Liviam*, wrongly ascribed to Ovid, cannot count as evidence. The *Consolatio ad Liviam* is probably a forgery of much later date; see, e.g., Richmond, J. (1981) 'Doubtful works ascribed to Ovid', *ANRW* II 31.4: 2744–83 and Balsdon (1977) 80; but Schrijvers, P. H. (1988) 'A propos de la datation de la *consolatio ad Liviam*', *Mnemosyne* 41: 381–4 argues that it was written in AD 20 (after the death of Germanicus) and recited to the imperial family.

71 See Castritius, H. (1969) 'Zu den Frauen der Flavier', *Historia* 18: 492–502.

72 Tac. *Ann.* 12.8: 'At Agrippina . . . veniam exilii pro Annaeo Seneca, simul praeturam impetrat, laetum in publicum rata ob claritudinem studiorum eius, utque Domitii pueritia tali magistro adolesceret et consiliis eiusdem ad spem dominationis uterentur.' For Agrippina Minor, see chapter 6, pp. 186ff.; see also Saller (1982) 57 and M. T. Griffin (1976) 59–66; for Agrippina turning Nero from philosophy: Suet. *Ner.* 52; for her political ambitions, see, e.g., Griffin (1984) 23–33 and 38–40 and, generally, Barrett (1996).

73 For Leonidas of Alexandria, see Cichorius (1922) 365–8 and Page (1981) 503–41. *AP* 9.344 = Page (1981) 525–7 seems autobiographical. Poems addressed to Nero (*AP* 6.321 and 328, 9.352), to Nero's mother Agrippina (*AP* 6.329), to his wife Poppaea (*AP* 9.355) and to Vespasian (*AP* 9.349) bear witness to his connections at the court and their duration.

74 *AP* 6.329: Ἄλλος μὲν κρύσταλλον, ὁ δ᾿ ἄργυρον, οἱ δὲ τοπάζους / πέμψουσιν, πλούτου δῶρα γενεθλίδια· / ἀλλ᾿ ἴδ᾿ Ἀγριππείνη δύο δίστιχα μοῦνον ἰσώσας, / ἀρκοῦμαι δώροις, ἃ φθόνος οὐ δαμάσει (trans. Loeb). See also Page (1981) 519–20.

75 *AP* 9.355: Οὐράνιον μίμημα γενεθλιακαῖσιν ἐν ὥραις / τοῦτ᾿ ἀπὸ Νειλογενοῦς δέξο Λεωνίδεω, / Ποππαία, Διὸς εὖνι, Σεβαστιάς· εὖαδε γάρ σοι / δῶρα τὰ καὶ λέκτρων ἄξια καὶ σοφίης (trans. Loeb, modified). See also Page (1981) 535–6. As Poppaea received the title of Augusta after the birth of her daughter in AD 63, this poem must have been written between AD 63 and her death in AD 65.

76 For Poppaea, see *FOS* 646, *RE* XXII Poppaea Sabina cols 85–91, *PIR*¹ P 630, Balsdon (1977) 124–9, Griffin (1984) 100–4. For her intelligence: Tac. *Ann* 13.45: 'sermo comis nec absurdum ingenium'; the resemblance is also noticed by Page (1981) 535. Tacitus portrays her as an ambitious and amoral adulteress though he allows for her beauty, intelligence, wealth and the distinction of the maternal side of her family; see Tac. *Ann.* 13.45–6, 14.1 and 59–64, 15.61.2 and 16.6–7. According to Syme (1958) 353 she was modelled on Sallust's Sempronia. For σοφία used to denote the knowledge of astrology, see *AP* 9.80, a mock-poem of Leonidas on the folly of astrologers. For Poppaea's dealings with astrologers, see Cramer (1954) 128–30.

77 Tac. *Hist.* 1.22: 'Poppaea's boudoir had contained many astrologers, the worst possible instruments to be used in imperial marriage' (or 'to achieve marriage with a princeps') ('Multos secreta Poppaeae mathematicos, pessimum principalis matrimonii instrumentum, habuerant'). Though astrologers were looked upon with suspicion by traditional-minded Romans as dangerous persons who were apt to stir up public unrest and though on several occasions they were expelled from Rome, many Romans were fascinated by astrology. For the notoriety and popularity of astrologers (*astrologi, mathematici* or *Chaldaei*) in the leading circles of Rome during the empire, see Cramer (1954) and MacMullen (1975) 128–62; for mockery of women interested in astrology: Juv. 6.553–91.

78 Smallwood, E. M. (1959) 'The alleged Jewish tendencies of Poppaea Sabina', *JThS* n.s. 10: 329–35 gives some examples of political patronage by Poppaea. For her support of Flavius Josephus, who by her εὐεργεσία (her intercession with Nero) obtained the release of some Jewish priests from captivity in AD 64 and received large presents from her as well, see Jos. *Vita* 13–16. Her support of Josephus should be regarded as political

patronage and not as literary patronage, since Josephus had not yet established himself as a writer at the time. Smallwood is rightly sceptical as regards Poppaea's supposed Jewish sympathies, which have been inferred from her intercession with Nero on behalf of a Jewish embassy (see, e.g., Jos. *AJ* 20.189–96, especially 195); for a different point of view see Williams, M. H. (1988) Θεοσεβὴς γὰρ ἦν – The Jewish tendencies of Poppaea Sabina', *JThS* n.s. 39: 97–111. For her political involvement, see also Tac. *Ann.* 15.61.2.

79 Jos. *Vita* 429: καὶ πολλὰ δὴ τοῦ καίσαρος γυνὴ Δομετέα διετέλεσεν εὐεργετοῦσα με.

80 Weinreich, O. (1940–1) 'Martials Grabepigramm auf den Pantomimen Paris (XI,13)', *SHAW* 31: 3–24 suggests that Martial's *Ep.* 11.13, a belated epitaph for the famous actor Paris, who had been put to death by Domitian in AD 83 because of his alleged intrigue with the empress Domitia Longina (Suet. *Dom.* 3.1, Dio 67.3.1), was commissioned by Domitia for Paris' grave-monument after Domitian's death (for this view, see also Kay, N. M. (1985) *Martial Book XI: A Commentary*, London: Duckworth, p. 95). However, the poem does not give any indication that Domitia was its commissioner or that she was in any way involved in Paris' burial (Vinson, M. P. (1989) 'Domitia Longina, Julia Titi, and the literary tradition', *Historia* 38: 431–50 believes the story about Domitia's affair with Paris to be false). It seems more likely that the epitaph was written by Martial out of gratitude for past *benificia* on the part of Paris; see Hardie (1983) 52 and 63, Nauta (1995) 6.

81 For Domitia Longina, see *FOS* 327, *PIR²* D 181, *RE* V Domitia 103 cols 1513–16, Jones, B. W. (1992) *The Emperor Domitian*, London: Routledge, pp. 32–8; see also Syme (1970). Most of our sources indulge in gossip about her adulteries (see, e.g., Suet. *Tit.* 10.2 and *Dom.* 3.1, Dio 67.3.1) or about her alleged complicity in the murder of Domitian (Suet. *Dom.* 14.1 and Dio 67.15.2–4); however, there is another side to Domitia Longina: she was the daughter of the able and popular general Corbulo (who fell victim to Nero) and herself a wealthy and well-educated woman who supported the writer Flavius Josephus. Though she outlived her imperial husband for more than twenty-five years, she continued to call herself 'the wife of Domitian' (*CIL* XV 548a–9d, on brick stamps).

82 For the imperial women of the period of Trajan and Hadrian, see Boatwright (1991). To explain their modest role as compared to the power and autonomy of earlier imperial women such as Livia and Agrippina Maior and Minor, she draws attention to the childlessness of Plotina and Sabina, to the break with a strictly dynastic monarchy, and to the more modest descent of the women of Trajan's and Hadrian's families: less highly born, less wealthy and less well-connected than the women of the Julio-Claudian dynasty, they enjoyed less power and autonomy.

83 For Plotina, see *PIR¹* P 509, *RE* XXI Pompeia 131 cols 2293–8, *FOS* 631 and chapter 6, p. 202.; see also Temporini (1978). For the dossier, see *IG* II² 1099, *Syll.³* 834 (the Greek letter), *ILS* 7784 (the Latin part); Smallwood (1966) no. 442; see also Oliver (1989) no. 73, Temporini (1978) 162–7, Castner (1988) 51–5 and Graindor, P. (1934) *Athènes sous Hadrien*, Cairo: Boulac, pp. 203–7. What survives is: scanty remains of a text in Greek, only five letters of which are left; the date, the heading 'a Plotina Augusta' and her letter to Hadrian in Latin which is nearly complete; Hadrian's brief reply in Latin to Popillius Theotimus, the head of the school, and Plotina's long letter in Greek to the Epicurean school, which breaks off towards the end. For the date (AD 121), see Temporini (1978) 167. For translations of the Greek letter see Wilhelm, A. (1899) 'Ein Brief der Kaiserin Plotina', *JÖAI* 2: 270–5, Oliver (1989) 177–8 and Castner (1988) 53.

84 *ILS* 7784: '[Quod studium meum] erga sectam Epicuri sit, optime scis, d[om]ine. Huius successioni a te succurrendum [est; nam quia n]on licet nisi ex civibus Romanis adsumi diad[o]chum, in angustum redigitur eligendi [facultas. Rogo e]rgo nomine Popilli Theotimi, qui est modo diado[c]hus Athenis, ut illi permittatur a te et Graece

[t]estari circa ha[n]c partem iudiciorum suorum, quae ad diadoches ordinationem pertinet, et peregreinae condicionis posse substituere sibi successorem, s[i i]ta suaserit profectus personae; et quod Theotimo concesseris, ut eodem iure et deinceps utantur fut[uri] diadochi sectae Epic[u]ri, eo magis, quod opservatur quotiens erratum est a testatore circa electionem [di]adochi, ut communi consilio substituatur a studiosis eiusdem sectae qui optimus erit: quod facilius fiet, si e[x] compluribus eligatur' (trans. Alexander, P. J. (1938) 'Letters and speeches of the Emperor Hadrian', *HSCPh* 49: 160–1, modified). The first words of Plotina's letter are lost and have been restored as 'quod studium meum'. Though, of course, this restoration is not beyond doubt (McDermott (1977) 200, n. 32 suggests 'quae sententia mea'), a comparable expression of her feelings towards the Epicurean school seems likely.

85 Millar (1977) 504 suggests that perhaps there was no specific rule of this kind, but that as Popillius Theotimus, then head of the school, was a Roman citizen, he was obliged to make his will in Latin and to leave property and succession of the school to a Roman citizen. Temporini (1978) 166 suggests that Popillius' successor may have been the *peregrinus* Heliodorus, who was perhaps identical with the like-named friend and confidant of Hadrian (*SHA Hadr.* 16.10); see now Follet, S. (1994) 'Lettres d' Hadrien aux Epicuriens d'Athènes (14.2–14.3.125): *SEG* III 226 + *IG* II² 1097', *REG* 107: 158–71.

86 The formality of Plotina's request appears from the fact that she addresses him as *domine*. For *libelli* and *subscriptiones*, written petitions to the emperor and his answers subscribed under the petitions, see Millar (1977) 240–52 (for Hadrian's *subscriptio* to Popillius Theotimus, see p. 504). Because of the fact that Hadrian's reply refers to Popillius Theotimus in the third person though bearing his name in the address, Williams, W. (1986) 'Epigraphic texts of imperial subscripts: a survey', *ZPE* 66: 207, n. 34.2 suggests that it is not a regular imperial rescript but an announcement by Hadrian of the imperial *beneficium* granted to Popillius Theotimus which was excerpted from an imperial *commentarius beneficiorum*.

87 *Syll.*³ 834 (line 6): τῶι ὡς ἀληθῶς εὐεργέτηι καὶ πάσης π[α]ιδείας κοσμητῆι ὄντι.

88 *Syll.*³ 834 (lines 6–8): σε[βα]σμιωτάτωι αὐτοκράτορι, ἐμοὶ δὲ προσφιλεστάτω[ι] κατὰ πάντα καὶ ὡς διαφέροντι κυρίωι καὶ ὡ[ς ἀ]γαθῶι τέκνωι.

89 Dio 69.10.3a: πολλὰ παρ' ἐμοῦ αἰτήσασα οὐδενὸς ἀπέτυχεν and τοιαῦτα ᾔτει οἷα οὔτε ἐβάρει με οὔτε συνεχώρει ἀντειπεῖν; cf. Fronto *Ad Am.* 1.3 (= Haines I, pp. 280–1) for a similar display of modesty in asking favours. For Hadrian's high regard for Plotina and his mourning at her death, see Dio 69.10.3 and *SHA Hadr.* 12.2.

90 Dio 68.5.5: τοιαύτη μέντοι ἐνταῦθα ἐσέρχομαι οἵα καὶ ἐξελθεῖν βούλομαι. He adds that throughout Trajan's reign she conducted herself in such a way as to incur no censure.

91 In a highly speculative article McDermott (1977) identifies Plotina with the unnamed lady to whom the Neopythagorean philosopher and mathematician Nicomachus of Gerasa addressed his *Enchiridion Harmonicon*, a manual on musical theory and Neopythagorean philosophy (see chapter 2, pp. 38ff.). However, the identification is not convincing; see Temporini (1978) 162, n. 705, who also refutes the attempt of Oliver, J. H. (1975) 'The empress Plotina and the sacred thymelic synod', *Historia* 24: 125–8 to prove that Plotina was patroness of an association of musical artists meeting at Nîmes.

92 Cf. Boatwright (1991). For, at least partly, biassed stories about her political influence with Trajan and her role in Hadrian's adoption by Trajan, see *SHA Hadr.* 2.10, 4.1, 4 and 10, Dio 69.1.2–4; for her beneficial influence, *Epit. Caes.* 42.20–1; see also Temporini (1978) 78–86, 120–60 and 179–81, McDermott (1977) 197–8 and 201–2, and Boatwright (1991) 530–2. For her alleged Jewish sympathies see Musurillo (1954) 44–8 and 161–78, Smallwood, E. M. (1976) *The Jews under Roman Rule: From Pompey to*

NOTES

Diocletian, Leiden: Brill, pp. 390–2 and Temporini (1978) 90–100 about an early third-century Greek papyrus (P. Oxy. 1242) which describes a Greek and a Jewish delegation before Trajan presenting their views on disturbances between Greeks and Jews in Alexandria. Plotina is accused of favouring the Jews and influencing Trajan and his *consilium* in this respect. If a historical event underlies this account – which is far from certain as it concerns a propagandistic pamphlet from a later period showing a strong Greek bias – it must have taken place before AD 113, probably between AD 107 and 113.

93 Plotina is praised for her modesty, simplicity and high moral integrity by Dio 68.5.5, Plin. *Ep.* 9.28.1 and *Pan.* 83–4; see also Temporini (1978) 176–81 and Boatwright (1991) 530–2. *Sanctitas* (moral purity) – and its Greek equivalent σεμνότης – seems to have been the main characteristic used for her in our sources; see Plin. *Ep.* 9.28.1: 'sanctissima femina' ('the most irreproachable of women') and Plin. Pan. 83.5: 'quid enim illa sanctius, quid antiquius?' ('where could a more irreproachable woman be found or a woman of more old-fashioned virtue?'). With its connotation of social distance and reserve it seems one of the stock epithets in praising traditional virtues both among high-class Roman women – see Plut. *Ant.* 31 (about Octavia) and Bernand (1960) no. 29.6 (Julia Balbilla about the empress Sabina) – and men; see Plin. *Ep.* 10.1: 'imperator sanctissime' (about Trajan). For her letter to the Epicureans see also chapter 6, below.

94 For Sabina see *RE* Suppl. XV Vibia no. 72b cols 909–14, *PIR*[1] V 414, *FOS* 802, Balsdon (1977) 139–40, Carandini (1969) 57–101, Boatwright (1991). Born between AD 83 and 86, she married Hadrian in AD 100 and died in AD 137. For the unhappiness of her marriage, see, e.g. *SHA Hadr.* 11.3 and 23.9, *Epit. Caes.* 14.8. Numerous portraits of her have been preserved, studied by, e.g., Carandini (1969), who draws attention to a 'ritratto filosofico' of Sabina in Athens, dated about AD 128–9, an idealized portrait of Sabina as a woman of culture (pp. 78 and 164, figs 110–12).

95 For Julia Balbilla and her poetry see chapter 5, pp. 164ff. For Sabina's inscription in prose, see Bernand (1960) no. 32.

96 For some examples, see Treggiari (1991) 424, Temporini (1978) 92–3; see further Macr. *Sat.* 2.5.3 and 6 (the difference between the following of Livia and Augustus' daughter Julia) and Tac. *Ann.* 3.9.2 (the female following of Plancina); cf. Plin. *Pan.* 83.7 praising Plotina for her moderation in the number of her attendants ('quam parca comitatu').

97 *SHA Hadr.* 11.3: 'quod apud Sabinam uxorem iniussu eius familiarius se tunc egerant quam reverentia domus aulicae postulabat'. The sentence continues with the remark that, had he been a private citizen, he would have sent away Sabina too because of her irritability.

98 For the date and place of their dismissal, see Syme (1958) 779, and Syme, R. (1980) 'Guard prefects of Trajan and Hadrian', *JRS* 70: 68–9 and (1981) 'The travels of Suetonius Tranquillus', *Hermes* 109: 108–17, Halfmann (1986) 90–2; also Wallace-Hadrill (1983) 1 and 6 briefly discusses the affair and suggests that it may have been a normal replacement.

99 For the *b[y]bl[i]otheca M[ati]diana* see *CIL* X 4760 = *ILS* 6296; see also Duncan-Jones (1974) 31 and 228, n. 637 and Boatwright (1992) 31; the inscription is dated in AD 193. For the honorific inscriptions on statue-bases in Suessa Aurunca see *CIL* X 4744–7; see also *CIL* X 3833.

100 For Matidia the Younger see *PIR*[2] M 368, *RE* Suppl. XV cols 131–4, *FOS* 533, Temporini (1978) 22, 40–1, 46, 150 and Boatwright (1991) and (1992). W. Eck in *RE* Suppl. XV cols 131–2 argues that her father was a L. Mindius and not L. Vibius Sabinus, who was probably the father of her sister Vibia Sabina; see also PIR[2] 366 (stemma), 367 and 368 'Mindia Matidia', Boatwright (1991) 517 and (1992) 24; but

other scholars – see, e.g., Syme (1958) 795 and Balsdon (1977) 136 – call her Vibia Matidia; *FOS* 533 mentions both possibilities without preference for either. She was probably born before AD 85 and died in the 160s during the reign of Marcus Aurelius; see Fronto *Ad Am.* 1.14 (= Haines II, pp. 98ff.), *Ad Marc. Caes.* 2.16 and 17 (= Haines II, pp. 94ff.).

101 Typical is *CIL* X 4745, inscribed for her by the Suessani during the reign of Antoninus Pius in which she is called 'the daughter of (the elder Matidia) Augusta, grand-daughter of the deified Marciana Augusta, sister of the deified Sabina Augusta, maternal aunt of the emperor Antoninus Pius, Augustus, father of his fatherland', 'Aug(ustae) fil(iae), divae Marcianae Aug(ustae) nepti, divae Sabinae Aug(ustae) sorori, imp(eratoris) Antonini Aug(usti) Pii p(atri) p(atriae) materterae'. For more examples see Boatwright (1992) 23, who emphasizes the very close interrelation of the imperial women in the Trajanic-Hadrianic period. Though the exemplary harmony between these imperial women is stressed in the literary sources (see, for instance, Plin. *Pan.* 83–4), the emphasis on Matidia's female relations on honorary inscriptions can, to my mind, be explained satisfactorily by the fact that they formed Matidia's connection with the imperial house, since she herself was not directly related to the emperor. For Marciana, Matidia the Elder, and her daughters living with Trajan and Plotina in the imperial palace, see Boatwright (1992) 23 and Temporini (1978) 187–8.

102 It has led to Syme's rather harsh verdict that she was 'a dim, ignored, and perhaps oppressed female: no sign that she ever married' (Syme (1958) 231, n. 7); also Boat-wright (1991) 517 and (1992) 27 assumes that she did not marry. However, for a woman, and especially for a woman of her class, life-long celibacy was highly unusual; see Treggiari (1991) 83–4.

103 For her extraordinary wealth and her independent control of it, see Boatwright (1991) 522–4 and 528 and (1992) 24ff.; though the independence of her control seems likely both because of the decline of the control of the *tutor* in the second century AD and the lack of close male relatives, it is not known whether or not she was officially granted the right to dispense with a guardian. She endowed an alimentary foundation for boys and girls, the *Variani alumni*, with a large gift in her will: see Fronto *Ad Am.* 1.14 (= Haines II, pp. 98ff.) and Duncan-Jones (1974) 31, 171, 228, n. 637. A milestone at Suessa Aurunca bearing her name shows that she had seven miles of road built (*AE* (1991) no. 492); for the library in Suessa Aurunca, see n. 99 above. Her generosity is associated with that of her mother on an inscription from their native Vicetia (*CIL* V 3112 = *ILS* 501: 'ex liberalitate Matidiarum'); for Vicetia, see also *CIL* V 3111. For the connection of the Matidii with Vicetia in northern Italy, see Alföldy, G. (1980) 'Ein Senator aus Vicetia', *ZPE* 39: 266 and Temporini (1978) 186.

104 Kajava (1990a) 34 points out that members of the imperial family only very rarely acted as patrons of individual municipalities, mentioning as an exception the case of Vibia Aurelia Sabina, one of the daughters of Marcus Aurelius. Matidia may have been a similar exception. For the comparison with Pliny, see Duncan-Jones (1974) 31, who calls her 'Pliny's main rival in public generosity' as regards Italian communities, calculating that Pliny spent about 5 million sesterces on *alimenta*, a school, a library, a temple and baths for local communities (pp. 17–32). For the great costs of a library see, e.g., Marshall (1976) 255. By comparison: Pliny spent 1 million sesterces on the foundation of a library in his native town of Comum and another 100,000 on the maintenance costs: see Duncan-Jones (1974) 27 and 31, Plin. *Ep.* 1.8.2, *CIL* V 5262 = *ILS* 2927, *AE* (1947) 65.

105 Fronto *Ad Ant. Imp.* 2.1 (= Haines I, pp. 300–1) Marcus Aurelius to Fronto: 'our little daughters are at present lodging with Matidia in the town, so that they cannot come to me in the evening because of the chillness of the air' ('parvolae nostrae nunc apud Matidiam in oppido hospitantur: igitur vespera ad me ventitare non possunt propter

aurae rigorem'). For the problems concerning her will see Fronto *Ad Marc. Caes.* 2.16
and 17 (= Haines II, pp. 94ff.), *Ad Am.* 1.14 (= Haines II, pp. 98ff.), Champlin (1980)
71–2. For her abstinence from politics, see Boatwright (1992) 26f.

106 Fronto *Ad Marc. Caes.* 2.16 (= Haines II, pp. 96–7): 'summo genere, summis opibus
nobilissima femina de vobis optime merita'.

107 For Plotina see Plin. *Pan.* 83.6: 'illa nihil sibi ex fortuna tua nisi gaudium vindicat'. For
Hadrian's funeral oration for Plotina praising the reasonableness of her requests, see
Dio 69.10.3a (quoted above n. 89). For Hadrian's funeral speech for Matidia the Elder
see *CIL* XIV 3579; in it Hadrian praises his mother-in-law for her beauty, modesty,
chastity, devoted motherhood and her long widowhood, in which she was faithful to
the memory of her husband; like Plotina she sought nothing from his position but
selfless pleasure (line 30: 'gaudere fortuna mea maluit quam frui'), but even more
modest than Plotina, she asked no favours from him (lines 27–8). For both funeral
speeches, see Temporini (1978) 168–73.

108 See Temporini (1978) and Boatwright (1987), (1991) and (1992) 21 and 26.

109 For her public funeral see Fronto *Ad Marc. Caes.* 2.16 (= Haines II, pp. 96–7) and
Boatwright (1992) 26–7. Boatwright (1991) 524 tentatively connects Matidia's greater
financial freedom and her more noticeable generosity with her more distant ties to the
throne.

110 Philostr. VA 1.3: μετέχοντι δέ μοι τοῦ περὶ αὐτὴν κύκλου – καὶ γὰρ τοὺς ῥητορικοὺς
πάντας λόγους ἐπήνει καὶ ἠσπάζετο – μεταγράψαι τε προσέταξε τὰς διατριβὰς
ταύτας καὶ τῆς ἀπαγγελίας αὐτῶν ἐπιμεληθῆναι, τῷ γὰρ Νινίῳ σαφῶς μέν, οὐ μὴν
δεξιῶς γε ἀπηγγέλλετο. For a discussion of the authenticity of these memoirs,
see Flinterman (1995) 79–86, who believes that they are a pseudepigraphic
Neopythagorean work from the second or early third century AD. For Julia
Domna, see *FOS* 436, *PIR*² I 663, *RE* X Iulius 566 cols 926–35. Balsdon (1977) 150–6
summarizes the main events of her life.

111 See Bowersock (1969) 101–9; for an exponent of the 'romantic' view on Julia Domna's 'circle of savants' see, e.g., Platnauer, M. (1918/1965) *The Life and Reign of the
Emperor Lucius Septimius Severus*, Rome: L'Erma di Bretschneider, pp. 144–5, who
lists as members her sister Julia Maesa, her nieces Julia Soaemias and Julia Mamaea,
Arria (a female friend of Galenus who was interested in philosophy – see below n.
119), Galenus himself, Diogenes Laertius, Serenus Sammonicus, Aelian, Oppian, the
jurists Papinian, Ulpian and Paulus, Antipater of Hierapolis, Athenaeus the Deip-
nosophist, Apollonius of Athens, Heracleides of Lycia, Hermocrates, Alexander of
Aphrodisias and Philostratus, thus including almost all known intellectuals of the
time. The evidence only tells us that Philostratus was a member, and also Philiscus of
Thessaly, who is strangely omitted by Platnauer. For the identity of the dedicatee of
the *Vitae Sophistarum*, see Avotins, I. (1978) 'The date and the recipient of the *Vitae
Sophistarum* of Philostratus', *Hermes* 106: 242–7, who convincingly identifies him with
Gordian I and is followed in this by Flinterman (1995) 26–7. Gordian's supposed
membership of Julia's circle is based on a discussion about the sophists between
Philostratus and Gordian in the temple of Apollo at Daphne near Antioch, the residence of Julia Domna at the time (Philostr. *VS* 480).

112 Dio 75.15.6–7: καὶ οὕτω καὶ ἐς τὰ ἄλλα πάντα ὁ Πλαυτιανὸς αὐτοῦ κατεκράτει ὥστε
καὶ τὴν Ἰουλίαν τὴν Αὔγουσταν πολλὰ καὶ δεινὰ ἐργάσασθαι· πάνυ γὰρ αὐτῇ ἤχθετο,
καὶ σφόδρα αὐτὴν πρὸς τὸν Σεουῆρον ἀεὶ διέβαλλεν, ἐξετάσεις τε κατ' αὐτῆς καὶ
βασάνους κατ' εὐγενῶν γυναικῶν ποιούμενος. καὶ ἡ μὲν αὐτή τε φιλοσοφεῖν διὰ
ταῦτ' ἤρξατο καὶ σοφισταῖς συνημέρευεν·

113 For Plautianus' rise to power and his eventual downfall, see *PIR*² F 554 and Birley
(1988) 107, 131, 137, 141, 154, 161–3 and 221 no. 32. For Julia Domna's political
influence during the reign of her son Caracalla, who, among other things, left her in

charge of the imperial correspondence, see Dio 77.18.3 and 78.4.2–3. For her accompanying Septimius Severus (and later Caracalla) on his journeys and military expeditions, see Halfman (1986) 90–2 and Birley (1988) 76f., 115f., 129, 146, 191. The unprecedented number of honorific titles she enjoyed both during the reign of Septimius Severus and during that of Caracalla indicates her public prominence: apart from the title Augusta, which was given her in AD 193, she was granted, for instance, the title *mater castrorum* in AD 195, which had been held only by the younger Faustina before her, and she was the first to be honoured with the title *mater castrorum et senatus et patriae*; see Temporini (1978) 5–6, 35, 47, 63, 66 and 78 and Williams, M. G. (1902) 'Studies in the lives of Roman empresses', *AJA* 6: 259–305. Also her identification with Athena Polias – see Oliver, J. H. (1940) 'Julia Domna as Athena Polias', *HSCPh* Suppl. I (Athenian Studies presented to W. S. Ferguson), pp. 521–30 – may point to her influence with the emperor (which she used in favour of the Athenians).

114 For a discussion of the date of Philostratus' introduction into the circle of Julia Domna and his presence in the entourage of the empress in (possibly) Britain, (certainly) Gaul and (probably) during her last years in Nicomedia and Antioch, see Flinterman (1995) 19–22.

115 See, e.g., Bowersock (1969) 5; Flinterman (1995) 25 draws attention to the fact that Philostratus uses the imperfect tense when speaking about Julia Domna (*VA* 1.3). He suggests that Philostratus may have received the commission to write the biography during the imperial visit to Tyana in AD 215.

116 Bowersock (1969) 106 seems over-critical as regards Julia Domna's possibilities as a patroness when he says that Philostratus, though belonging to her circle, 'got nowhere'. Though Philostratus does not seem to have received one of the chief rewards open to a Greek sophist, the chair of rhetoric at Athens or an appointment as *ab epistulis Graecis*, he may have been satisfied with the prestige and benefits yielded by his position at the imperial court; see Anderson (1986) 5–6.

117 Philostr. *VS* 622: καὶ προσρυεὶς τοῖς περὶ τὴν Ἰουλίαν γεωμέτραις τε καὶ φιλοσόφοις εὕρετο παρ' αὐτῆς διὰ τοῦ βασιλέως τὸν Ἀθήνησι θρόνον.

118 Philostr. *VS* 622 (see n. 117).

119 The female addressee of his work – see Diog. Laert. 3.47 (cited in chapter 2, n. 87) and 10.29 – is usually identified either with Julia Domna or with a certain Arria, an upper-class woman interested in philosophy and a friend of Galen, who cured her of a stomach disease (*De Theriaca ad Pisonem* 2, Kühn 14.218–19), but, of course, Diogenes Laertius' work may have been addressed to an unknown woman. In view of the fact that it lacks a dedication, it seems possible that Diogenes wrote it at the instigation of Julia Domna, but finished it after her death and omitted the dedication. However, in addressing the unknown woman no title of deference is used such as would have been expected if an empress were involved. Millar, F. (1964) *A Study of Cassius Dio*, Oxford: Clarendon Press, pp. 19–20 suggests that Dio's deferential attitude towards Apollonius of Tyana in 67.18.1–2 (as contrasted with 77.18.4, written after Julia Domna's death) perhaps betrays the influence of Julia Domna's admiration for the legendary sage. However, this does not prove membership of her circle; and if Barnes, T. D. (1984) 'The composition of Cassius Dio's *Roman History*', *Phoenix* 38: 240–55 is right in dating the composition of the entire work during the reign of Severus Alexander, Millar's suggestion is undermined.

120 Galen *De Comp. Med. Sec. Loc.* I (Kühn 12.435): βασιλικαὶ γυναῖκες ἢ οἱ βασιλεῖς αὐτοὶ προστάττουσιν ἡμῖν, adding that he was not in the position to refuse such a request (οἷς οὐκ ἔνεστιν ἀρνεῖσθαι), though he apparently considered it beneath his dignity as a physician. Ilberg, J. (1905) 'Aus Galens Praxis: ein Kulturbild aus der römischen Kaiserzeit', in Flashar, H. (ed.) (1971) *Antike Medizin*, Darmstadt:

Wissenschaftliche Buchgesellschaft (Wege der Forschung 221), pp. 395–7 dates this work during the reign of Septimius Severus. Nutton, V. (1987) 'Galen's philosophical testament: "On my own opinions"', in Wiesner, J. (ed.) *Aristoteles: Werk und Wirkung*, vol. II, Berlin: de Gruyter, pp. 27–51 (esp. 46–9) and Nutton, V. (1988) *From Democedes to Harvey: Studies in the History of Medicine III*, London: Variorum Reprints, pp. 315–24 convincingly argues that Galen did not die in AD 199 or 200, as is traditionally assumed, but lived beyond AD 210, and perhaps even 215, thus eliminating the main argument of Bowersock (1969) 106 against Galen's membership of Julia Domna's circle; see also Swain (1996) 430–2. I thank Dr H. F. J. Horstmanshoff for these references. For the prestige of Galen, his philosophical interest and his position as a court-physician, see Bowersock (1969) 59–75.

121 Philostr. *Ep.* 73, dismissed by Bowersock (1969) 104–5 as spurious, but convincingly defended as genuine by Jones (1972) 131–2, Anderson, G. (1977) 'Putting pressure on Plutarch: Philostratus' *Epistle 73*', *CPh* 72: 43–5 and Penella (1979) 161–8. For a brief discussion of its contents, see Anderson (1986) 4–5 and 276–7. One *caveat* remains: though Philostratus' authorship of the letter seems certain, it is not beyond doubt that the letter was actually sent to Julia Domna; like many other letters of his collection it may have been a literary exercise, perhaps written after her death (this is with more reason to be expected for *Ep.* 72, which castigates Caracalla for murdering his brother). Yet, even so it seems likely that it more or less reflects the interests and subjects discussed between them.

122 For the compliment implied in mentioning Aspasia, see Anderson (1986) 277 and Flinterman (1995) 23, n. 110. The compliment of praising a woman's mind by comparing her to Aspasia was not new. In a similar way, but more explicitly, Lucian had praised Pantheia, the mistress of Lucius Verus, by comparing her to Aspasia (and to other female models of excellence such as Sappho and the Diotima of Plato's *Symposium*); see Lucian *Im.* 17 and Jones (1986) 75–7; for Aspasia see now Henry, M. M. (1995) *Prisoner of History: Aspasia of Miletus and her Biographical Tradition*, Oxford: Oxford University Press.

123 *Ep.* 73: πεῖθε δὴ καὶ σύ, ὦ βασίλεια, τὸν θαρσαλεώτερον τοῦ Ἑλληνικοῦ Πλούταρχον μὴ ἄχθεσθαι τοῖς σοφισταῖς, μηδὲ ἐς διαβολὰς καθίστασθαι τοῦ Γοργίου. εἰ δὲ οὐ πείθεις, σὺ μέν, οἷα σου σοφία καὶ μῆτις, οἶσθα, τί χρὴ ὄνομα θέσθαι τῷ τοιῷδε, ἐγὼ δὲ εἰπεῖν ἔχων οὐκ ἔχω. As he does not reveal which epithet is to be used for Plutarch (he perhaps refrains from mentioning it out of deference to the empress), his joke is not completely understood; Anderson (1986) 277 calls it 'a typically cryptic Gorgiasm of his own'.

124 Bowersock (1969) 106–9.

125 Dio 77.18.3: 'she held public receptions for all the most prominent men, precisely as did the emperor' (ἠσπάζετο δημοσίᾳ πάντας τοὺς πρώτους καθάπερ καὶ ἐκεῖνος) and 'devoted herself more and more to the study of philosophy with these men' (ἡ μὲν καὶ μετὰ τούτων ἔτι μᾶλλον ἐφιλοσόφει). For her advice and her appointment to handle the routine imperial correspondence see Dio 77.10.4; 77.18.2–3 ('to receive petitions and to have charge of his correspondence in both languages, except in very important cases', τὴν τῶν βιβλίων τῶν τε ἐπιστολῶν ἑκατέρων, πλὴν τῶν πάνυ ἀναγκαίων, διοίκησιν αὐτῇ ἐπιτρέψας) and 78.4.2–3. For her royal retinue and the praetorian guard attending on her, see Dio 78.23.2. For an assessment of her political power during Caracalla's reign see Dio's account of her reaction to the death of Caracalla (Dio 78.23–4): when her intrigues to become sole ruler had come to nothing, she preferred dying to losing her power (in 78.24.2 Dio calls it ἀρχή) and returning to a life as a private person.

126 For the kind of favours and honours bestowed on sophists by emperors, see Bowersock (1969) 30ff., Anderson (1993) 30–5, Millar (1977) 83–101 and 491–506. Flinterman

(1995) 41–4 distinguishes three categories: appointment to positions suitable to their rhetorical and literary qualities (such as *ab epistulis Graecis* or *advocatus fisci*), appointment to other posts of an equestrian or senatorial career and, third, gifts, ceremonial honours or an appointment to the imperial chair of rhetoric in Athens or the chair of Greek rhetoric in Rome. We know nothing of Julia conveying one of the first two categories of favours to her scholarly friends, but the third category was clearly within her power.

127 Eusebius *Hist. Eccl.* 6.21.3–4; see also Orosius *Adv. Pagan.* 7.18.7; the similarity is noted by Bowersock (1969) 108. For Julia Mamaea see *PIR*² I 649; she is reported to have educated her son, Alexander Severus, in an excellent way; see *SHA Alex. Sev.* 3.1–5 and 66.1, Herodian 5.7.5 and, less favourably, 6.1.1ff. She was also addressed by Hippolytus, who was a presbyter, and perhaps bishop, at Rome; see Richard, M. (1963) 'Quelques nouveaux fragments des Pères Anténicéens et Nicéens', SO 38: 79–80.

128 As we have seen (n. 41 above), Octavia and Livia were granted freedom of *tutela*. It has been argued that all imperial women had freedom of *tutela*, being granted the privileges of the Vestals including the financial ones (see Boatwright (1991) 520), but this is not certain.

129 Even the emperor's concubine might be courted by men of learning: see Lucian's *Imagines* and *Pro Imaginibus*, which were written in praise of Pantheia, the mistress of Lucius Verus at his court in Antioch (Jones (1986) 75–7).

130 Dio is kindly disposed towards Julia Domna in his work, sympathizing with her because of the emnity of Plautianus (75.15.6–7), her sorrow at the murder of her son Geta (77.2.2–6) and her hatred of her cruel and savage son Caracalla (78.23.1 and 24.1); in his obituary of her (78.24) he describes her as an unhappy woman despite her lofty station. Bowersock (1969) 108, to my mind, somewhat misjudges Dio's appreciation of her when he emphasizes his remark that Caracalla owed his craftiness partly to his mother (Dio 77.10.2); this remark seems a shorthand version of his more detailed judgement on Caracalla's vices as deriving in part from those of the Syrians, from whom he was descended on his mother's side (Dio 77.6.1a). On the whole, Dio speaks with sympathy of Julia Domna, contrasting her studiousness and sensibility with the cruelty and lawlessness of her son Caracalla. Repeatedly (e.g., 77.18) her interest in sophistic oratory and philosophy or her prudent advice is contrasted with the cruelty, lawlessness and licence of her son Caracalla. Dio's acceptance of imperial rule and the apparently good relations between Julia Domna and members of the senatorial order (as compared to the insulting behaviour of Caracalla towards members of the senatorial order) may have disposed Dio kindly towards Julia Domna, but Herodian also is mainly sympathetic: see 4.3.8–9. However, the *Historia Augusta* follows a more critical tradition: *SHA Sev.* 18.8: adultery and conspiracy against Severus; *SHA Sev.* 21.7 and *Car.* 10.1–4: incest with her son Caracalla (she is wrongly called his stepmother). Penella, R. J. (1980) 'Caracalla and his mother in the *Historia Augusta*', *Historia* 29: 382–4 suggests that the critical tradition on Julia Domna was probably due to Plautianus and draws attention to the 'Neronization' of Caracalla in the *Historia Augusta* (which appears from his alleged incest with his mother and his portrayal as a would-be matricide).

131 Nicomachus' *Enchiridion Harmonicon* (discussed in chapter 2, pp. 38ff.) and Diogenes Laertius' 'Lives of the Eminent Philosophers' (above n. 119) are addressed to unknown women. As both philosophical works lack a dedication, the relationship between these authors and the high-ranking women they addressed cannot be ascertained. Nicomachus' remarks about his former teaching of the unknown lady seems to point to a position as a house-philosopher teaching for a regular payment in a Roman family (as many Greeks did in his days), rather than to patronage. I also

exclude (*pace* White (1975) 284) Pliny's elderly friend Ummidia Quadratilla (*FOS* 829; see chapter 2, n. 101), who acted as a benefactress to her native city by building a temple and an amphitheatre, and who owned a troupe of pantomime players. Her wealth and social prominence would surely have allowed her an important role as a patroness of literature and learning had she chosen to be one, but we have no such information.

132 For the decline of the 'great patron' during the empire, the emperor taking over as the major source of patronage, see, e.g., Hardie (1983) 41–9 and White (1975). In the Domitianic period, which concerns us here, numerous complaints about the stinginess of patrons in Martial's epigrams and Juvenal's satires (see Nauta (1995) 1–11) demonstrate their disappointment that, apart from that of the emperor, patronage on a grand scale had ceased to exist. The emperors could not tolerate the self-glorification typical of the great aristocratic patrons of earlier periods. According to Saller (1983) and White (1978) 77 Martial's complaints do not point to a general decline of patronage from the Augustan or Neronian age onwards. Apart from the emperor numerous wealthy men, many of whom were amateur poets themselves, were sought as patrons by an increasing number of poets trying to gain a livelihood from wealthy patrons. For changes in literary patronage from the republican period up to the time of Hadrian, see Williams, G. (1982) 'Phases in political patronage of literature in Rome', in Gold (1982) 3–27. According to White (1982) 61–2 and Hardie (1983) 72 there was a growing professionalism among poets of the time causing increasingly mercenary ways of talking about poetry. For literary dilettantism among the Roman aristocracy of the time, see chapter 5, n. 132.

133 For Statius' non-imperial patrons see White (1975), Hardie (1983) 58–72 and Nauta (1995) 183–304; for those of Martial, see also Sullivan (1991) and Nauta (1995) 37–181. White (1974) 50 and (1975) 297 counts about 140 *amici* of Martial, at least 60 of whom according to him may have been his patrons. The four patronesses of Martial and Statius are: Argentaria Polla (Stat. *Silv.* 2.7, Mart. *Ep.* 7.21–3 and 10.64), Mummia Nigrina (Mart. *Ep.* 4.75 and 9.30), Sabina (Mart. *Ep.* 10.93) and Marcella (Mart. *Ep.* 12.21 and 31).

134 White (1974). For books and publication in antiquity see chapter 5, pp. 147f.

135 For recitations, see chapter 2, pp. 44f.

136 See White (1974), who argues that the *libelli* are private drafts of poems, or 'private brochures', as he calls them, which circulated informally prior to the publication of the books; his view is accepted by, among others, Sullivan (1991) 4–5. Despite criticism of White's view by, for instance, Nauta (1995) 104–16, his theory is convincing; see also White, P. (1996) 'Martial and pre-publication texts', *EMC/CV* 40 n.s. 15: 397–412, in which he defends his brochure hypothesis against criticism. Apart from this specific meaning, a *libellus* in Martial's poetry may also mean 'a small book': see, e.g., Mart. *Ep.* 7.17.6 and 10.74.7, or in a juridical context 'petition' (Mart. *Ep.* 8.82); for a discussion of the meanings of *liber* and *libellus* see also Sage, E. T. (1919) 'The publication of Martial's poems', *TAPhA* 50: 168–76. Because of these different meanings of the word *libellus*, the decision of White (1974) to use *libellus* as a technical term is perhaps somewhat confusing, yet this does not detract from the importance of his general argument.

137 I adopt this term from White (1993) 22. For the publicity-value of published poetry, see White (1974) 48ff. and (1993) 21–2; see also Nauta (1995) 37–9 and 137–9. It is well illustrated by Martial's epigram 4.31, in which he teases a woman longing for such publicity by withholding her name till the very end of the poem and then giving the Greek equivalent only, or so it seems. For the honour of having one's name published see also Mart. *Ep.* 5.15, 5.60 (in which he refuses to mention his enemy's name and thereby denies him lasting fame) and 12.61.

138 I exclude from discussion Claudia Rufina and Sempronia (*pace* White (1975) 284): Claudia Rufina is praised (but not addressed) by Martial in a poem (*Ep.* 11.53) which extols her beauty, marriage and childbearing. Though she is also praised for her sophistication (having succesfully adapted herself to Graeco-Roman culture in spite of her British origin), there is nothing to prove that she acted as a patroness: no wealth is mentioned, no *libellus* is offered to her and no respectful term of address, such as *regina* or *domina*, or vocabulary of patronage is used. Possibly the poem was written for someone else. If Claudia Rufina is the same person as Claudia Peregrina (Mart. *Ep.* 4.13) married to Martial's friend the centurion Aulus Pudens, as is suggested by Balsdon (1977) 202, the poem may well have been written for him. Sempronia is addressed in what seems to me to be a mock-epigram of condolence (Mart. *Ep.* 12.52) for the death of her husband, a poet and orator called Rufus (probably not the same as Martial's friend, the poet Canius Rufus): instead of focussing on the wife's mourning Martial relates her willing abduction by a lover followed by her eventual return to her husband. Both Rufus (a very common name: see Nauta (1995) 40–5 on real and fictional Rufuses in Martial's poetry) and Sempronia seem to be fictitious characters in this satiric epigram ridiculing women's vices. I also exclude the poetess Sulpicia Caleni (Mart. *Ep.* 10.35 and 38) for reasons mentioned elsewhere (see chapter 5, n. 68) and the wealthy Violentilla (*FOS* 809), the wife of one of Statius' and Martial's most important patrons, the senator and amateur poet L. Arruntius Stella (*PIR*[2] A 1151, *RE* II Arruntius 26 cols 1265–6; for his patronage, see White (1975) 267–72 and Nauta (1995) 149–53 and 198–200). Martial's epigrams in praise of her (translating her name in Greek as Ianthis; see Mart. *Ep.* 6.21, 7.15 and 50) and Statius' praise of her in his *epithalamium* (*Silv.* 1.2) were probably written to please her husband, though it is not impossible that she joined her husband in generosity to poets: she is praised by Statius for her wealth as well as for her mind (Stat. *Silv.* 1.2.121–2) and is said to have been won over by Stella's poems (Stat. *Silv.* 1.2.197ff.; see also Mart. *Ep.* 1.7 and 7.14.5), which may be taken as an indication for her taste in poetry. Of course, the countless women addressed in Martial's poetry in an erotic context, famous women from past ages and fictitious ones, are not discussed here.

139 Statius *Silv.* 2 *praef.* 22–4: 'Cludit volumen Genethliacon Lucani, quod Polla Argentaria, rarissima uxorum, cum hunc diem forte consuleremus, imputari sibi voluit.' The text contains several difficulties which have been discussed elsewhere and do not concern us here. The main difficulty lies in 'consuleremus', for which many conjectures have been suggested. According to White (1975) 281–3 'consuleremus diem' is anomalous. He supports its emendation to 'coleremus' (for this and other emendations, see van Dam (1984) 61–2). 'Colere diem' should then be understood as 'celebrare diem', so that the translation according to White (1975) 283 runs as follows: 'This is a poem which Argentaria Polla happened to ask me to compose for her on an occasion when we were celebrating the anniversary of his birth.' However, this emendation does not give a better reading than the somewhat unusual construction of 'consuleremus diem'. The conclusion that Statius, present at the celebration of the anniversary of the deceased Lucan, should unexpectedly be asked for a poem seems awkward, even considering the contemporary fashion of writing inpromptu poems. It seems more likely that, when planning the celebration, she commissioned Statius to compose a poem in commemoration of her late husband. Therefore, I agree with Buchheit (1960) 231, n. 4: 'Die handschriftlich gut bezeugte Lesart *consuleremus* genießt sprachlich wie sachlich gegenüber zahlreichen, etwas übereilten Konjekturen [. . .] unbedingten Vorrang.'

140 For the pun on her *gentilicium*, see Nisbet (1978) 7 and Hardie (1983) 70; the adjective *argentarius/a* refers to silver, money and banking activities. Van Dam (1984) 61: 'Polla wanted to have it known that she ordered the poem and paid for it.' According to

White (1982) 62 the frequent use of the verb *imputare* by first-century poets is proof of their increasing preoccupation with money. However, *imputare* may also be used metaphorically: see Stat. *Silv.* 2.7.30. In a similar vein, Statius may not have meant his pun to be taken literally, but may have wished to 'credit' Argentaria Polla with his poem. Nevertheless, his poem put her under an obligation to reciprocate.

141 M. Annaeus Lucanus (*PIR*² A 611, *RE* I Annaeus 9 cols 2226–36), born in AD 39, was compelled to put an end to his life in 65 because of his involvement in the conspiracy of Piso against Nero. For the celebration of the birthday of a dead person, see Nisbet (1978) 10 and Hardie (1983) 115–16; Argetsinger, K. (1992) 'Birthday rituals: friends and patrons in Roman poetry and cult', *ClAnt* 11: 175–93 does not discuss birthday celebrations of deceased persons. Though keeping anniversaries of dead persons is well attested in the ancient world and poetry may sometimes have been involved, the *Genethliacon Lucani* is without parallel in Latin literature; see van Dam (1984) 450–2, who argues that it partly derives its originality from the fact that Statius mixes elements of the *consolatio* in the genre of the *genethliacon*.

142 See also White (1975) 280 and Nauta (1995) 73, but *contra* van Dam (1984) 455, who argues that Martial and Statius would have mentioned the fact. As the second book of the *Silvae* contains datable poems from AD 89 onwards, Lucan's fiftieth anniversary in AD 89 seems to me to be the most likely date for which the poem was composed.

143 Statius *Silv.* 2.7, Mart. *Ep.* 7.21–3. Of course, they may not have been the only poets to commemorate the occasion.

144 For an analysis of this poem see Buchheit (1960) 231–41, Hardie (1983) 115–18 and van Dam (1984) 450ff. In the *encomium* of Lucan, which makes up the largest part of the poem (lines 24–106), lines 81–8 are written in praise of his widow Polla; in 120–3 Lucan is asked to beg the gods for one day with Polla, an allusion to the myth of Protesilaos and Laodameia; 124–35 describe Polla's veneration of her dead husband and her spiritual communion with him. Statius ends the poem in an optimistic vein, wishing her to be consoled and henceforth enjoy happiness and peace of mind: let grief be turned into adoration. In the last fifteen lines of the poem (120–35) Polla is the main subject.

145 Stat. *Silv.* 2.7.85–6: 'forma, simplicitate, comitate / censu, sanguine, gratia, decore'; 2.7.83: 'doctam atque ingenio tuo decoram'; 2.7.62: 'castae'; 2 *praef.* 23: 'rarissima uxorum'. The epithet *docta* was, as we have seen (chapter 3, pp. 79ff.), potentially doubtful, associating her with the loose life of the *puella docta*, but Statius' words about her chastity and her veneration of her deceased husband place her firmly among the respectable wives and widows.

146 See Buchheit (1961). The epigrams (Mart. *Ep.* 7.21–3) were commissioned by Polla for the same occasion; see, e.g., Buchheit (1960) 245–7, and afterwards incorporated in his seventh book, published in AD 92.

147 Buchheit (1961), Hardie (1983) 115–18; for birthday customs see also *RE* 7 cols 1143–4 and Cairns, F. (1971) 'Propertius 3,10 and Roman birthdays', *Hermes* 99: 149–55.

148 Martial addresses her twice, stressing her relation with Lucan and her veneration of him after his death: Mart. *Ep.* 7.21.1–2: 'Haec est illa dies quae . . . / Lucanum . . . tibi, Polla, dedit' ('This is the day which gave Lucan to you, Polla') and 7.23.3–4: 'tu, Polla, maritum/ saepe colas et se sentiat ille coli' ('May you, Polla, often revere your husband, and may he feel that he is revered').

149 See Mart. *Ep.* 7.23.2 and Stat. *Silv.* 2.7.35 and 80; to praise a Latin epic poet as a second Virgil is, of course, a commonplace; for another example, see Nauta (1995) 144. For more similarities between the three epigrams of Martial and Statius' *Genethliacon Lucani*, see Buchheit (1960) 245–6 and Hardie (1983) 70–1 and 115–18.

150 Hardie (1983) 70–1; in the preface to his second book of *Silvae* (see above n. 139) Statius perhaps refers to such a conversation when describing the occasion when she asked for

a poem for Lucan's anniversary: 'when we happened to be considering the celebration of the day'. For a discussion of literary requests and direction of a poet's work by friends or patrons in the Augustan period, see White (1993) 64–91, who argues that suggestions offered by friends and patrons did not usually amount to detailed instruction; however, on pp. 82–4 he mentions occasional verse as a genre more liable to direction than other genres.

151 Statius *Silv.* 2.7.62–3: 'then by a charming address you shall bestow fame and glory upon chaste Polla' ('hinc castae titulum decusque Pollae / iocunda dabis adlocutione'). Lucan's *Adlocutio ad Pollam* is lost and not mentioned elsewhere. It may have been part of his *Silvae* – see, e.g., Hardie (1983) 60 – but *contra* Buchheit (1960) 236, n. 4. Nisbet (1978) 5 suggests that the *Adlocutio ad Pollam* may have been the model for Statius' address to his wife Claudia (*Silv.* 3.5). Statius probably chose this poem to take a central place in his review of Lucan's poetry (2.7.54–80), omitting some better-known works, to please Polla; see also van Dam (1984) 478.

152 Sid. Ap. *Ep.* 2.10.6, writing in the fifth century AD, gives a (fictitious) list of women of pagan antiquity assisting their famous poet-husbands or lovers in their work: 'Corinna often helped her Naso to complete a verse, and so it was with Lesbia and Catullus, Caesennia and Gaetulicus, Argentaria and Lucan, Cynthia and Propertius, Delia and Tibullus' ('saepe versum Corinna cum suo Nasone complevit, Lesbia cum Catullo, Caesennia cum Gaetulico, Argentaria cum Lucano, Cynthia cum Propertio, Delia cum Tibullo'). This list serves to remind his addressee, who was on the point of getting married, that the company of women does not hinder one's studies. As Sidonius knew his Statius (see *Carm.* 9.226–9), he may have invented the story on account of the word *docta* in *Silv.* 2.7.83; see Nisbet (1978) 4–5.

153 Stat. *Silv.* 2.7.124–31. The reality of this portrait has been contested: for a discussion see van Dam (1984) 502–5.

154 See Hardie (1983) 50, M. T. Griffin (1976) 253 and 292, Saller (1983) 251, Sullivan (1991) 3–4 and 317 and Nauta (1995) 80: when he came to Rome in AD 64, Martial became a protégé of the family of the Annaei and may have received his estate at Nomentum from Seneca or his heirs. Martial refers favourably to Lucan and Seneca in several epigrams: *Ep.* 1.61, 4.40, 7.21–3, 7.44, 10.64, 12.36, 14.194. For the great number of Spaniards among Martial's connections, see, e.g., Sullivan (1991) 1–2 and 16ff.

155 Mart. *Ep.* 10.64: 'Contigeris regina meos si Polla libellos, / non tetrica nostros excipe fronte iocos. / Ille tuus vates, Heliconis gloria nostri, / Pieria caneret cum fera bella tuba, / non tamen erubuit lascivo dicere versu / "Si nec pedicor, Cotta, quid hic facio?" ' (the translation of the last line is by Sullivan (1991) 70–1). For the dates of publication of Martial's books see Sullivan (1991).

156 Mart. *Ep.* 10.64.6. The verse, Lucan fr. 10 (Morel), is usually said to have belonged to his lost epigrams, Cotta being tentatively identified with the profligate Aurelius Cotta (*PIR*[2] A 1486), but Dr V. Hunink drew my attention to the fact that *pedicor*, denoting the passive homosexual role, is highly offensive. No Roman aristocrat would ever say this about himself – though he might say it about someone else as an insult. Therefore, it is highly unlikely that the subject of the fragment is Lucan himself; rather it must have been a figure in a mime. For the sexual term and sexual *mores*, see Adams (1982) 2, 123–5 and 217, and Wiseman (1985) 10–14.

157 See, e.g., Nauta (1995) 17–18, White (1978) 81 and (1993) 29–30 with n. 47 and Saller (1983) 251–2. White (1975) 285 argues that it has a strong emotional force and was considered humiliating by dependants. For examples of *rex* and *dominus* as titles of respect to a patron in Martial's work, see Mart. *Ep.* 1.112, 2.18, 2.68, 3.7, 4.83, 5.19, 5.22, 6.88, 10.10, 10.96, 12.60. For Horace's use of *rex* to address Maecenas (e.g., *Epist.* 1.7.37), see Gold (1987) 129.

158 For her patronage see, e.g., Nisbet (1978) 1–11, Nauta (1995) 67, 73–4, 159, 210–12, 232, Sullivan (1991) 40, 49, 70, 102, 123, 125, 192, 317; White (1975) includes her among the six patrons whom Martial and Statius shared.

159 For Argentaria Polla see *FOS* 90, *PIR*² A 1039, *RE* 2 Argentaria 2 col. 706. Polla, in republican times a female *praenomen*, was used as a *cognomen* by the early principate; see Kajava, M. (1994) *Roman Female Praenomina: Studies in the Nomenclature of Roman Women*, Rome: Institutum Romanum Finlandiae (Act. Inst. Rom. Finl. vol. 14), pp. 126–31, who points out that it was not used by members of the high aristocracy: the senatorial Pollas of the imperial period were mostly daughters of respectable Italian or provincial families who had recently entered the senate or women who had received senatorial status through marriage. For her connection with Marcus Argentarius, see Nisbet (1978) 5–7; Hardie (1983) 4 calls her the 'probable daughter of the Greek epigrammatist and rhetorician Marcus Argentarius' and van Dam (1984) 455 cautiously suggests that the declaimer might be her grandfather; for this view see also Sullivan (1991) 40 and Nauta (1995) 210. The connection is rejected, for lack of evidence, in *FOS* 90. It is usually assumed that Argentarius the declaimer is the same man as M. Argentarius the epigrammatist whose work has partly survived in the Greek Anthology, but this is not certain (*PIR*² A 1038 doubts the identification); for a detailed discussion, see Small, S. G. P. (1951) 'Marcus Argentarius: a poet of the Greek Anthology', *YClS* 12: 67–145 (esp. 67–78).

160 Castillo (1982) 477 and 481 assumes that she was of Greek origin, but he is not followed in this by Halfmann (1979). For her possible Spanish extraction see Dardaine, S. (1983) 'La *Gens* Argentaria en *Hispania* (La femme de Lucain avait-elle une origine hispanique?)', in *Mélanges de la Casa de Velázquez* 19.1: 5–13, who draws attention to inscriptions mentioning Argentarii in Baetica, the region from which Lucan also stemmed. For the acquaintance between Argentarius the declaimer and the elder Seneca, see Sen. *Contr.* 9.3.12–13.

161 Lucan stemmed from a very wealthy and distinguished family in Corduba in the province of Baetica. Argentaria Polla's family, though less distinguished, may have been respectable and well-to-do; see Statius' praise of her wealth and lineage (*Silv.* 2.7.86). Sussman, L. A. (1978) *The Elder Seneca*, Leiden: Brill (Mnemosyne suppl. 51), p. 30, n. 62 counts this marriage as one of the 'shrewd marriages' of the Annaei assuming (without evidence, unfortunately) that Argentaria Polla was a wealthy lady before her marriage. For Roman prejudice against provincials, see below nn. 199, 204; see also Tac. *Ann.* 14.53.5 about Lucan's uncle Seneca, who humbly declared himself to be 'born in the station of a knight and a provincial' ('equestri et provinciali loco ortus'). Lucan's father M. Annaeus Mela (*PIR*² A 613), a brother of Seneca and a very wealthy man, by his own choice stayed a knight throughout his life (he was *eques Romanus dignitate senatoria*). Lucan became a friend of Nero's and at the Neronia of AD 60 he sang Nero's praises in public. Possibly as a reward Nero advanced him to senatorial rank.

162 In *RE* I col. 2228 it is assumed that Lucan and Argentaria Polla were married at, or shortly after, AD 60. If Argentaria was about 15 years old when she married, she was about 19 or 20 at the time of Lucan's death. For the average age of girls at marriage, see chapter 1, n. 9.

163 Nisbet (1978) 5 rather carelessly assumes that after Lucan's death she 'retired to her husband's property on the Bay of Naples', ignoring the fact that with his father still living Lucan was not *sui iuris* and thus legally incapable of owning property or making a will. At his death his wealth fell to his father, causing the latter's death, according to Tacitus (*Ann.* 16.17.4–5), as Nero coveted his riches. At his death in AD 66 Mela tried to protect his own and his son's possessions from confiscation by leaving a large sum to Tigellinus, but it is unknown whether he was successful. Bradley, K. R. (1978)

Suetonius' Life of Nero: An Historical Commentary, Brussels (coll. Latomus 157), p. 187 distinguishes four possible heirs of Mela's and Lucan's fortunes: Pompeia Paulina (*FOS* 630), Seneca's wife, who died within a few years after his suicide; Argentaria Polla; Iunius Gallio (*PIR*² I 757), who, however, killed himself shortly after the death of Seneca in AD 65, and his daughter Novatilla (*FOS* 50); see Sen. *Cons. Helv.* 18.7–8; he strangely omits Mela's wife (and Lucan's mother) Acilia, who survived her husband (Tac. *Ann.* 15.56 and 71). Of these persons Argentaria Polla is the only one known to have lived till the end of the century. It does not seem probable that Argentaria's possible inheritance was seriously impeded by the restrictions imposed by the Lex Voconia, as this law was regularly circumvented (for a discussion of the Lex Voconia see Gardner (1990) 170–8, Crook (1992) and Evans (1991) 72–82), but the probable childlessness of her marriage seriously restricted her legal capacity to receive under wills (see the next note).

164 Vidman, L. (1982) *Fasti Ostienses*, Prague: Acad. Scient. Bohemoslav., p. 98 suggests that A]nnius Mela (*PIR*² M 446), *consul suffectus* of AD 103, may have been Lucan's son, Annius being a misspelling of Annaeus, but *FOS* 90 is rightly sceptical: if Lucan and Argentaria had a son, he would have been mentioned by Statius or Martial. For women of childbearing age remarriage was the norm: under the Augustan marriage laws childless widows who had not remarried within a year (later two years) were penalized by limitations on their ability to receive inheritances and legacies under wills: see, e.g., Humbert (1972) 76–180, Treggiari (1991) 60ff. and 501f., Gardner (1990) 77–8 and 178–9, Mette-Dittmann (1991) 132–86 and Wallace-Hadrill, A. (1981) 'Family and inheritance in the Augustan marriage laws', *PCPhS* 207 (n.s. 27): 58–80. For remarriage see also Bradley, K. R. (1991) 'Remarriage and the structure of the upper-class Roman family', in Rawson (1991) 79 98 and Parkin (1992) 132–3.

165 Sid. Ap. *Carm.* 23.165–6: 'quid quos duplicibus iugata taedis/ Argentaria pallidat poetas'. The word 'pallidat' in line 166 is usually taken to mean 'makes pale (with love)', thus identifying the poets with the husbands (see next note). According to the Loeb and the Budé edition these verses allude to Lucan and Statius both as poets and as husbands and also Vessey, D. W. T. (1974) 'Sidonius, Polla and two poets', *CB* 50: 37–9 assumes that the poets of line 166 must be the same persons as the husbands, but, of course, he dismisses Statius as her supposed second husband. Because of its obscurity the line 'Argentaria pallidat poetas' (the reading of the Codd.) is usually emended to 'Argentaria Polla dat poetas', meaning 'the poets, whom Argentaria Polla presents to us', referring to her patronage.

166 Nisbet (1978) 5–7 suggests that 'pallidat' is a pun on the name Argentaria, referring to the pale colour of silver, or to the *nitor* of silver as contrasted with the *pallor* of the poets. For the idea that writing poetry and studying lead to paleness, see Juv. 7.97, Persius *prol.* 4, *Sat.* 1.26 and 124, 5.62, Mart. *Ep.* 7.4, Plin. *NH* 20.160, Quint. 1.2.18 and 7.10.14. 'Pallidat' may be understood in the sense that Argentaria makes her poets pale (with love of her money, we should understand: see Hor. *Sat.* 2.3.78: 'argenti pallet amore'), thus referring to her patronage. If so, the translation reads: 'What about the poets whom the twice-married Argentaria makes pale?' Yet, problems remain, as only one of these poets was her protégé (Statius), the other (Lucan) being her husband.

167 Nisbet (1978). The identification is accepted by Hardie (1983) 4: 'the almost certain fact of the remarriage of Lucan's widow Polla Argentaria [. . .] to Pollius Felix, the Hellenising Campanian and patron of Statius' and p. 60; van Dam (1984) 454–5 more cautiously remarks that 'this possibility cannot be ruled out'; Nauta (1995) regards it as a 'plausible hypothesis'. The *RE* keeps them apart (*RE* 2 Argentaria 2 col. 706 and *RE* XXI Polla 2 cols 1407–8), and so does the *PIR* (*PIR*² A 1039 and *PIR*¹ P

407). For Pollius Felix see *RE* XXI Pollius 2 cols 1419–22, *PIR*[1] P 419, Nisbet (1978) 3, Hardie (1983) 67–8, D'Arms (1970) 126 and 220f., van Dam (1984) 192–3. He was an important patron to Statius, who dedicated not only two poems to him (*Silv.* 2.2: a poem describing Pollius' Surrentine villa, and *Silv.* 3.1: about the temple of Hercules built by Pollius on the precincts of his villa), but also his third book of *Silvae* (*Silv.* 3 *praef.*). *Silv.* 4.8 is addressed to Pollius' son-in-law, Julius Menecrates, congratulating him on the birth of his third child.

168   For Statius mentioning Polla or alluding to her presence see *Silv.* 2.2.9f., 107, 143, 144f., 147f. and 151ff.; 3.1.87, 159ff. and 179; 4.8.13f. For Pollius' poetry and the Epicurean motifs and symbols in Statius *Silv.* 2.2, see Nisbet (1978) and Nauta (1995) 300–3. Polla is called 'elegant' ('nitida' 2.2.10) and is praised for her 'youthful charm' ('iuvenilis gratia', 2.2.10); in 2.2.143ff. her harmonious marriage is extolled, and in 2.2.148–50 her serenity. Line 2.2.147, 'tuque, nurus inter longe [*or* longae] . . . praecordia curae', is corrupt (a fusion of two lines). The lacuna between 'longe' and 'praecordia' has been plausibly filled with the words 'praedocta Latinas/ parque viro mentem cui non' by Hardie, W. R. (1904) 'Notes on the *Silvae* of Statius', *CR* 18: 158, referring to her education and to the intellectual equality of the couple; for this and other proposals, see van Dam (1984) 275–6. In the other poems she is praised in a similar vein: 'nitida', 3.1.87, 'venerabilis', 3.1.159, 'placida', 3.1.179, 'benigno . . . sinu', 4.8.13f., but they more clearly show her to be a middle-aged woman (3.1.161) taking care of the grandchildren (3.1.179 and 4.8.13–14). The age of the two Pollas is compatible: all poems in which a Polla figures were composed between AD 89 and 95, so that, even if Argentaria Polla was in her late teens when Lucan died (which is about the youngest we may assume), she was nearly 50 in AD 95, a middle-aged woman like Polla Pollii.

169   Stat. *Silv.* 2.2.151–4: 'non tibi sepositas infelix strangulat arca/ divitias avidique animum dispendia torquent/ faenoris: expositi census et docta fruendi/ temperies'. Translation by Nisbet (1978) 7. For the implication that Polla Pollii was a patroness of letters herself, see Nisbet (1978) and Hardie (1983) 156 and 176.

170   This is rather exceptional: as is observed by Nisbet (1978) 2, Statius generally ignores the wives of his addressees, Abascantus' wife Priscilla (Stat. *Silv.* 5.1: an *epicedium*; *RE* XXIII Priscilla 2; *PIR*[1] P 705) and Statius' mother (mentioned, not by name, in *Silv.* 5.3.240f.) being exceptions. However, Nisbet fails to mention Violentilla (*FOS* 809), wife of Statius' patron Arruntius Stella, who figures prominently in Stat. *Silv.* 1.2 (an *epithalamium*).

171   Statius depicts her, according to Nisbet (1978) 4, as 'a Laodameia to her dead husband and a Penelope to her living one'; see Stat. *Silv.* 3.5.45–54; see also Burck, E. (1986) 'Statius an seine Gattin Claudia', *WSt* 20: 215–27. His wife's friend Priscilla is called *univira*, though married twice, and is praised for her love and devotion to her second husband, as if she were his virgin bride (Stat. *Silv.* 5.1.45–56). For the ideal of the *univira* and the contemporary frequency of remarriage see Humbert (1972) 76–180. On pp. 102–12 and p. 122 he discusses examples of women praised for their love and fidelity to two successive husbands (e.g., Statius' wife) and argues that second marriages were not felt to be incompatible with the ideals of marriage; see also Treggiari (1991) 249.

172   For detailed criticism on several of Nisbet's interpretations of *Silvae* 2.2 and 2.7, see van Dam (1984) 62, 276–8, 454–5, 504–6.

173   For the latter view, see D'Arms (1970) 221 and (1974) 111, who mentions as a possible father an Augustalis at Puteoli (*CIL* X 1574), but *contra* Nisbet (1978) 3–4 and Hardie (1983) 67–8: a member of the local aristocracy. As wealthy sons of freedmen were sometimes admitted to town councils (Garnsey and Saller (1990) 114), he may have been both.

174 Raepsaet-Charlier (1994) 195 doubts Argentaria's possible remarriage to Pollius Felix for this very reason. Nisbet (1978) 4 ignores the problem, simply assuming that: 'After Lucan's suicide Polla might have felt no desire to marry again into a great political family.' For the problem whether or not a woman of senatorial rank lost her rank when marrying a man of inferior status, see chapter 1, n. 17. For the first century AD this is uncertain.

175 See Raepsaet-Charlier (1992) 35 and 42. It is perhaps no coincidence that Statius *Silv.* 4.8.59–62 expresses the hope that Pollius' grandchildren by his daughter will be admitted to the senate (the two boys) or marry a man of senatorial rank (the girl). Because of *Silv.* 4.8.13–14 ('quaeque sibi genitos putat attollitque benigno / Polla sinu') Nisbet (1978) 3 assumes that the grandchildren are those of Pollius by an earlier marriage, but this seems unnecessary. Polla, 'who counts them her own sons as she raises them to her loving bosom', may have been as close with them as if they were her own children (instead of her grandchildren); see also Van Dam (1984) 280. The father of the children, Julius Menecrates (*PIR*[2] I 430), being an *eques*, Polla may have been their nearest relative of (former) senatorial rank.

176 This might have been the case if she had not succeeded to some of the fortunes of Lucan or his family (see above n. 163). Even if she stemmed from a respectable and well-to-do (but not senatorial) family, Pollius' wealth may well have allowed her to live in greater affluence than she would have been able to afford herself. This may have made up for her the possible loss of senatorial dignity. However, all this remains hypothetical.

177 See n. 21 above. Similarly, in discussing joint office-holding and joint benefactions of husband and wife in the cities of the Greek East in the Roman period van Bremen (1996) chs 5 and 9 argues that each partner contributed separately out of his or her own funds to the benefaction, which was in a real sense a 'joint venture'.

178 D'Arms (1974) 111 suggests that Polla Pollii may not have been of free birth, but there is no evidence for this.

179 In view of what we have discussed this is perhaps not very likely, but note that Statius *Silv.* 2.7.86 (who, of course, may be exaggerating) praises her for her wealth and lineage (*censu, sanguine*).

180 For her importance as a patroness of Statius, see Hardie (1983) 59–60 and 67, who, following Nisbet's identification of her with Polla Pollii, calls her 'Statius' main Neronian link'. For her patronage of Martial, see White (1975) 284–6 and 291, who assumes that Martial and Polla knew each other only slightly and suggests that their association went no further than the celebration of Lucan's birthday; *contra* Sullivan (1991) 4, 102 and 317.

181 But, of course, Martial's books of epigrams appeared only from AD 86 onwards.

182 White (1975) 285 draws attention to the fact that the first line of Martial's poem to Argentaria Polla (*Ep.* 10.64.1: 'Contigeris, regina, meos si Polla libellos') resembles that of a similar poem to the emperor (Mart. *Ep.* 1.4.1: 'Contigeris nostros, Caesar, si forte libellos'), which, however, he takes for a sign of the formality of their contact. For Martial taking liberties with patrons of greatly superior status, see Nauta (1995) 59–60 and 149–50.

183 Statius' remark (in the preface to his second book of *Silvae*, see above n. 139) about Argentaria Polla asking for a poem places her request in the context of their common discussion of the coming celebration, and Martial's epigram introducing one or more copies of his poetry sent to Argentaria Polla (*Ep.* 10.64, see p. 131) and asking for a benevolent reading suggests that he valued her literary judgement.

184 See above n. 150.

185 Direct reference to her education is only found in Statius *Silv.* 2.7.83: 'doctam atque ingenio tuo decoram'. Hints are given by Statius (*Silv.* 2.7.62–3), who mentions

Lucan's *Adlocutio ad Pollam* giving her fame and prestige (*titulum decusque*) instead of other, better-known works of Lucan, and by Martial's request for a benevolent reading of his poetry and his quotation of Lucan's scurrilous verse in a poem addressed to her (*Ep.* 10.64) which shows that she was a woman of the world, whose literary judgement was of importance to him. Asserting the 'literary identity' of the patron was, according to Nauta (1995) 276–80, one of the main functions of Statius' *Silvae*, but, as we see here, in the case of a female patron praise of her literary interests or abilities was expressed in more guarded terms.

186 This is not to say that male patrons are always easily recognized as such; the poets' praise of, for instance, their friendship or their moral excellence may hide their patronage from us, but generally the praise of men is more varied than that of women, and praise of their poetry, their wealth, their lavish villas, their collection of bronzes or, more clearly, their generosity may hint at acts of patronage.

187 White (1975) 284–6 and 291.

188 Tac. *Ann.* 16.17: 'He was the father of Lucanus, a fact that greatly contributed to his fame' ('Annaeum Lucanum genuerat, grande adiumentum claritudinis').

189 Mart. *Ep.* 4.75.3–4: 'you wish to share with your husband your father's wealth, glad that your husband should be partner and sharer with you' ('te patrios miscere iuvat cum coniuge census, / gaudentem socio participique viro'). As we have seen (n. 21), this was highly unusual, the property of husband and wife in a non-*manus* marriage being strictly separated. Gifts between husband and wife were not legally valid, only few gifts being excepted from this rule, for instance, when the wife's money enabled the husband to meet the census qualification of the senatorial or equestrian order, to obtain office, or to celebrate games: see Dig. 24.1.40–2 and Ulp. *Reg.* 7.1 (most of it a relaxation of the rule by the emperor Antoninus Pius). For the separation (and mixing) of property between husbands and wives see Gardner (1990) 71–7 and Treggiari (1991) 365–96, who remarks that despite the legal separation of property in non-*manus* marriages the idea of sharing was an important feature of Roman ideology of marriage. One wonders what practice underlies Martial's praise of Nigrina. She may, for instance, have shared her inheritance in daily life, though legally it remained hers (or perhaps she allowed her husband to be co-heir in her father's will), or she may have contributed substantially from her inheritance to the costs of her husband's career (cf. Mart. *Ep.* 10.41: a woman divorcing her husband because of the great expenses involved in his career). Treggiari (1991) 251, however, suggests that Martial's poem refers to *societas omnium bonorum* (community of property) arranged by Nigrina. This sharing of property between husband and wife which had been the rule in *manus* marriages was highly uncommon in a marriage without *manus* and thus a sign of exceptional generosity.

190 For Mummia Nigrina, see *PIR*[2] M 714, *RE* XVI Mummius 28 col. 534, *FOS* 558; Syme (1983) 372–4. For her wealth, see Mratschek-Halfmann (1993) 341 no. 224. For the epitaph of one of their slaves see *CIL* VI 27881, dating from AD 87. As the female slave of *CIL* VI 27881 was their shared property, they must have been married at that time.

191 For the life and career of L. Antistius Rusticus, see *PIR*[2] A 765, *RE* I Antistius 41 col. 2558, Suppl. VI col. 7 and XII col. 88, Alföldy, G. (1969) *Fasti Hispanienses: senatorische Reichsbeamte und Offiziere in den spanischen Provinzen des römischen Reiches von Augustus bis Diokletian*, Wiesbaden: Steiner, pp. 160–1, Birley, A. R. (1981) *The Fasti of Roman Britain*, Oxford: Clarendon Press, pp. 269–70, Castillo (1982) 474 and 493 no. 25, Eck (1970) 66, 103, 133, 142ff., 146, Syme (1983). These scholars vary a little as regards the dates of Antistius' career, but this does not concern us here.

192 Martial emphatically extols her among *Latin* wives; see Mart. *Ep.* 4.75.1: 'O, blessed in soul, Nigrina, and blessed in husband, and among Latin wives the chiefest glory' ('O

felix animo, felix, Nigrina, marito / atque inter Latias gloria prima nurus'). For her patronage of Martial, see Castillo (1982) 493 no. 25, Mratschek-Halfmann (1993) 341 no. 224 and Nauta (1995) 67; Sullivan (1991) 34 and 191 leaves the question undecided.

193 Mart. *Ep.* 10.93: 'Si prior Euganeas, Clemens, Helicaonis oras / pictaque pampineis videris arva iugis, / perfer Atestinae nondum vulgata Sabinae / carmina, purpurea sed modo culta toga. / Ut rosa delectat metitur quae pollice primo, / sic nova nec mento sordida charta iuvat.' The last line of the poem probably refers to stains left on the paper of the roll by the chin when it was rolled up. Against White (1974), Nauta (1995) 126 argues that 'nondum vulgata ... carmina' (lines 3–4) is no evidence that the poem introduces a private collection of as yet unpublished poetry for Sabina. He argues that it is 'an advance copy of the published book', but this seems to stretch Martial's words too far. The identity of Clemens is unknown; I see no reason to assume with Sullivan (1991) 49 that he was Sabina's husband.

194 For more examples see White (1974) 56 and (1993) 41 with n. 19. Sullivan (1991) 49 counts Sabina among the new patrons Martial acquired during the last years of his stay in Rome.

195 Plin. *Ep.* 3.21; he quotes from Mart. *Ep.* 10.19.

196 For Terentius Priscus see *RE* Va Terentius 63 cols 667–8 and *PIR*[1] Terentius 62; for his patronage of Martial, see, for instance, Hardie (1983) 56, Nauta (1995) 13, 66–7, 71–2 and 112, Sullivan (1991) 52–5. For their contact in Rome see, for instance, Mart. *Ep.* 6.18, 8.45 and perhaps also 9.77; Martial dedicated book 12, or the *libellus* which formed the core of it, to him (12 *praef.* and 12.1, 4, 14 and 62). In 12.4 he emphasizes Priscus' significance as a patron by comparing him with Maecenas. Terentius Priscus gave him not only literary encouragement but also substantial material support which allowed him the leisure to write: 'tu das ingenuae ius mihi pigritiae' ('you give me the free man's right to laziness', Mart. *Ep.* 12.4.6), thereby qualifying as his Maecenas (Saller (1983) 251 and Nauta (1995) 13 suggest that he gave Martial an estate). Note the resemblance between *Ep.* 1.107.3–4, where Martial asks in vain for the *otium* Maecenas used to provide for his poets and *Ep.* 12.4.1–2, where Priscus is described as the new Maecenas. For complaints about his lack of *otium* when living in Rome, see, e.g., Mart. *Ep.* 1.107, 5.20, 10.58 and 10.70. I see no reason to distinguish a father and a son in Martial's Terentius Priscus; see also Jones (1972) 60, n. 74 and Nauta (1995) 66–7, n. 93.

197 Mart. *Ep.* 12.31.7: 'these are the gifts of my lady' ('munera sunt dominae'). For *dominus* and *rex* as titles of deference to a patron see above n. 157. For his leisurely life in Spain see Mart. *Ep.* 12.18 and 68.

198 For Marcella and her patronage of Martial, see Saller (1983) 256, Hardie (1983) 56, Sullivan (1991) 26, 54, 122, 183–4 and Nauta (1995) 67. In the past Marcella has wrongly been called Martial's wife; against this see, for instance, Sullivan (1991) 26 and Nauta (1995) 67, n. 95.

199 Mart. *Ep.* 12.21: 'Municipem rigidi quis te, Marcella, Salonis / et genitam nostris quis putet esse locis? / Tam rarum, tam dulce sapis. Palatia dicent, / audierint si te vel semel, esse suam; / nulla nec in media certabit nata Subura / nec Capitolini collis alumna tibi; / nec cito ridebit peregrini gloria partus, / Romanam deceat quam magis esse nurum. / Tu desiderium dominae mihi mitius urbis / esse iubes: Romam tu mihi sola facis.' The only indication of her age is the word *nurus* meaning young (married) woman or daughter-in-law. As no husband is mentioned, she was probably not married. The compliments on her refinement resemble those paid to Claudia Rufina (11.53), who is praised for her successful adaptation to Graeco-Roman culture in spite of her British background. This seems to have been a standard device to compliment those who were well educated despite their provincial background. Mart. *Ep.* 14.99

pays the same compliment to a 'barbarian' British basket turned Roman: 'but Rome now prefers to call me her own' ('sed me iam mavolt dicere Roma suam').

200 Mart. *Ep.* 12 *praef*: 'the audience of my fellow-citizens . . . that refinement of critical judgement, that inspiration of the material, the libraries, the theatres, the parties, where pleasure is unconscious of being work' ('civitatis aures . . . illam iudiciorum subtilitatem, illud materiarum ingenium, bibliothecas theatra convictus, in quibus studere se voluptates non sentiunt').

201 See nn. 199, 204. Unlike a gift of money a *benificium* in kind, such as the estate Marcella gave to Martial, could be mentioned in poetry without being considered bad manners; see Hardie (1983) 46.

202 Though there was no legal bar to a senatorial career for competent members of the provincial nobility and many local notables, especially of the romanized Spanish provinces, entered upon a senatorial career under the Flavians, in the first two centuries AD men of provincial background formed a minority in the senate and were only gradually accepted into the Roman aristocracy. Senators from the romanized western provinces, Gallia Narbonensis and parts of Spain (for instance, Baetica), preceded senators from the eastern and African provinces and were more easily assimilated. For (the integration of) provincial senators, see Alföldy (1986) 118ff., Le Roux, P. (1982) 'Les Sénateurs originaires de la province d'*Hispania citerior* au haut-empire romain', *Tituli* 5: 439–64; Devreker, J. (1980) 'La Composition du sénat romain sous les Flaviens', in Eck, W., Galsterer, H. and Wolff, H. (eds) *Studien zur antiken Sozialgeschichte: Festschrift Fr. Vittinghoff*, Cologne: Boehlau (Kölner historische Abhandlungen, 28) pp. 257–68, Sherwin-White, A. N. (1973²) *The Roman Citizenship*, Oxford: Clarendon Press, pp. 259ff. Castillo (1982) 465–519 contends that in the first century AD senators from the Spanish province of Baetica formed a relatively closely knit group, marrying mainly women from the same province, *contra* Raepsaet-Charlier (1994) 185, n. 110. The existence of 'ethnic' groups in cosmopolitan Rome is illustrated by the striking predominance of Spanish contacts among Martial's friends and patrons.

203 For the concept of status inconsistency, see, e.g., Goffman, I. W. (1957) 'Status consistency and preference for change in power distribution', *American Sociological Review* 22.3: 275–81 and Hornung, C. A. (1977) 'Social status, status inconsistency and psychological stress', *American Sociological Review* 42: 623–38; for a relation between status inconsistency (or 'dissonance' as it is called by Hopkins) and social mobility in Roman society, see Hopkins (1974) 103–20, who believes that aristocratic women 'lived in a competitive salon culture' (p. 118); see also White (1975) 284. Though I would prefer to avoid an anachronistic term such as 'salon', upper-class women may well have competed for prestige among themselves. In such a competition I suggest (slightly modifying the criteria of male status given by Hopkins (1974) 105) that descent, marriage, rank, wealth, education, style of living and moral excellence formed the criteria by which women's social status was judged. In his discussion of comic non-conformity to the rules of traditional hierarchy in the work of Juvenal, Reekmans (1971) 141–4 briefly discusses status inconsistency. In a similar way, Nauta (1995) 280ff. argues that many of Statius' *Silvae* may be interpreted as a defence of a patron whose position was in some way contested, or as an advertisement of his patron's ambitions, wealth or culture, but he does not mention Argentaria Polla in this respect.

204 For cultural prejudice against provincial and municipal men see *SHA Hadr.* 3.1, where Hadrian reading a speech to the senate 'provoked laughter by his somewhat countrified accent' ('agrestius pronuntians'). This accent, according to Boatwright (1987) 204–5, was due to his youth in Spain. The African emperor Septimius Severus was said to have 'retained an African accent even to his old age' (*SHA Sev.* 19.9: 'Afrum

quiddam usque ad senectutem sonans'), but, according to the same work, he was greatly embarrassed at the poor Latin of his sister (*SHA Sev.* 15.7: 'vix Latine loquens ac de illa multum imperator erubesceret'). Also the question posed to Tacitus by a Roman knight whether he was an Italian or a provincial, 'Italicus es an provincialis?' (Plin. *Ep.* 9.23.2), is explained by Syme (1958) 619 as referring to his Transpadane or Narbonensian accent. For the existence of a Roman accent typical of the capital, see Cic. *De Or.* 3.44: 'vox Romani generis urbisque propria' as distinct from a provincial accent (*peregrinum*); see also Cic. *Arch.* 26 (about poets from Corduba): 'pingue quiddam sonantibus atque peregrinum'. For embarrassment about his provincial background, see the letters of Fronto, especially *Ep. Graec.* 8.1 (Haines I, pp. 20–1), *Ep. Graec.* 1.5 (Haines I, pp. 136–7), *Ad M. Caes.* 1.8.7 (Haines I, pp. 124–5) and *Ad M. Caes.* 2.6.2 (Haines I, pp. 142–3) in which he calls himself 'a breathing barbarian' ('opicum animantem'); for these examples see also chapter 6, pp. 199f. Also Martial, who often takes pride in his native country, is afraid to send to the city a book which is not merely 'from Spain, but Spanish' (Mart. *Ep.* 12. *praef.*: 'ne Romam . . . non Hispaniensem librum mittamus sed Hispanum'). For prejudices against, and the gradual assimilation of, municipal men in the Roman élite, see D'Arms, J. H. (1984) 'Upper-class attitudes towards *viri municipales* and their towns in the early Roman Empire', *Athenaeum* 62: 440–67. Inversely, the prejudice against provincials appears from the hyperbolic praise of successful adaptation to Roman culture in spite of a provincial background; see, e.g., Stat. *Silv.* 4.5.45–6 about Septimius Severus (perhaps an ancestor of the emperor) from Leptis Magna in northern Africa: 'neither your speech, nor your dress is Punic, yours is no stranger's mind: Italian are you, Italian!' ('non sermo Poenus, non habitus tibi, / externa non mens: Italus, Italus') and Martial's praise of Marcella (*Ep.* 12.21) and Claudia Rufina (*Ep.* 11.53).

205 In Forbis' collection of 482 honorary inscriptions from Italian municipalities (excluding Rome) which record language of praise, 71 inscriptions (15 per cent) were erected for women, but only a minority of them were indicated as patronesses; see Forbis (1996) 243.

206 To some extent, the relation between the empress and upper-class women was similar to that between the emperor and upper-class men; this, for instance, is expressed in the term *princeps femina* used for Livia in the *Cons. Liv.* 356 (wrongly ascribed to Ovid). For emperors propagating certain ideals of behaviour, for instance, by means of the themes and legends on coins on which empresses were equated with Vesta, Ceres or Juno, while the legends emphasized their *fecunditas, pudicitia, pietas* or the *concordia* of the imperial family, see, e.g., Giacosa, G. (1977) *Women of the Caesars: Their Lives and Portraits on Coins*, Milan: Arte e Moneta, Temporini (1978), Kokkinos (1992) 87ff., Kleiner, D. E. E. (1992) 'Politics and gender in the pictorial propaganda of Antony and Octavian', *EMC/CV* 36 n.s. 11: 357–67, Flory, M. B. (1996) 'Dynastic ideology, the Domus Augusta, and imperial women: a lost statuary group in the Circus Flaminius', *TAPhA* 126: 287–306, Varner, E. R. (1995) 'Domitia Longina and the politics of portraiture', *AJA* 99: 187–206, Fittschen, K. (1982) *Die Bildnistypen der Faustina Minor und die Fecunditas Augustae*, Göttingen: Vandenhoeck & Ruprecht (Abh. Ak. Wiss. Göttingen, Phil.-Hist. Kl. 3, vol. 126), and Lusnia (1995).

207 See Lusnia (1995); see also Kampen, N. B. (1991) 'Between public and private: women as historical subjects in Roman art', in Pomeroy (1991) 218–48.

5 WOMEN AND WRITING: POETRY

1 For the poems of Sulpicia, see pp. 151ff.; for an illuminating survey of the assessment of her poems, and their assignment to Tibullus or Ovid, in earlier scholarship, see, e.g., Lowe (1988), Santirocco (1979) 229–30 and Parker (1994) 40.

2 In the study of ancient literature attempts to find a 'female voice' and a 'lost tradition' of female authors have not been very frequent; for a recent example, see Skinner (1993), who applies Showalter's concept of 'gynocritics' to the poems of Sappho to demonstrate a female 'subculture' and a 'woman-specific discourse' in her texts ('gyno- critics' is defined as: the investigation of the 'history, styles, themes, genres and struc- tures of literature by women': see Showalter, E. (1985) 'Toward a feminist poetics', in Showalter, E. (ed.) *The New Feminist Criticism: Essays on Women, Literature and Theory*, New York: Pantheon, pp. 125–43); for pertinent criticism of this approach, see Weedon, C. (1987) *Feminist Practice and Poststructuralist Theory*, Oxford: Blackwell, pp. 152ff. For an excellent discussion of Sappho as a female poet, see Winkler, J. J. (1990) *The Constraints of Desire: The Anthropology of Sex and Gender in Ancient Greece*, New York: Routledge, pp. 162–87 on 'Double consciousness in Sappho's lyrics'. For a rather prejudiced example of looking for a 'lost tradition', see Wilson-Kastner, P. *et al.* (1981) *A Lost Tradition: Women Writers of the Early Church*, Lanham: University Press of America.

3 Shaw (1993) 16, n. 41; for Perpetua see chapter 6, n. 1.

4 I do not want to restrict myself, as is usually done, to those very few women whose work has been (partly) preserved; see, for example, McIntosh Snyder (1989), who in her chapter on 'Women writers in Rome' (pp. 122–36), though stating her intention to do otherwise, devotes her attention almost exclusively to the poetry of Sulpicia, the dis- puted letter of Cornelia and the speech held by Hortensia to the triumvirs in 42 BC (taking the Greek version of Appian *BC* 4.32–3 for a 'reasonably close paraphrase of her speech').

5 As is discussed in greater detail on p. 148, publication is an anachronistic notion when used for Roman times, since the distinction between work circulating among friends and acquaintances and work formally 'published' was vague; see, for instance, Kenney (1982) 15–22 and Starr (1987).

6 Most poetesses whose names have come down to us belonged to the senatorial class, but of some of them the social rank is unknown. The extensive literary education they must have had for writing verses suggests that they came from well-to-do families, but the Greek names of some may imply that they were, or were descended from, freed slaves. Perhaps the Greek *cognomen* of the shadowy poetess Memmia Timothoe indicates such a status; she will not be discussed here. Isidor. of Sevilla *Etym.* 1.39.17 tells us that she lived at the time of Ennius and was the first among the pagans to compose hymns to Apollo and the Muses ('Hymnos ... apud gentiles prima Memmia Timothoe fecit in Apollinem et Musas, quae fuit temporibus Ennii longe post David').

7 See, for instance, White (1993). I do not wish to revive the controversial notion of literary circles here; by 'coterie' I mean a loose group of friends who discussed literary matters and who read (or listened to) and criticized each other's work; for glimpses of such literary friendships see, for instance, Catul. 50.1–6, Ovid *Pont.* 3.5.39–40 and Plin. *Ep.* 5.12.

8 For this brief summary of publication in Roman times I lean heavily on Starr (1987), whose exposition of the gradually widening circles in which literary texts circulated is highly instructive; for the fluid and informal nature of ancient publication, see also Kenney (1982) 10–22 and Reynolds and Wilson (1974) 18–37. For the custom of sending (or reciting) speeches, poems or other literary products to friends and patrons before publication, see Plin. *Ep.* 1.2 and 8, 2.5, 3.10, 13, 15 and 21; 4.14, 18 and 27; 5.3, 10 and 12; 6.21, 7.4, 17 and 20; 8.3, 7, 15, 19 and 21; 9.1, 4, 8, 16, 18, 20, 25, 26, 28, 29 and 31; see also Sherwin-White (1966) 42–5; for the importance of friends and patrons in publicizing a poet's work, see, e.g., White (1978) and (1993) 41. Though 'publication' is a somewhat misleading term in view of its modern connotations, it is used here for the sake of brevity.

9 For some examples see Davis, N. Z. (1980) 'Gender and genre: women as historical writers, 1400–1820', in Labalme (1980) 153–82.

10 Her father, Q Cornificius, was a 'new man' in the senate; see *RE* IV Cornificius 7 col. 1624. Wiseman (1971) 227 no. 139 believes that he originated from Lanuvium, but Rawson (1978) 196 doubts this.

11 Hier. *Chron.* under the year 41 BC; see ed. R. Helm, p. 159: 'Cornificius poeta a militibus desertus interiit, quos saepe fugientes galeatos lepores appellarat. Huius soror Cornificia cuius insignia extant epigrammata'. For Q Cornificius see *RE* IV Cornificius 8 cols 1624–30 and Rawson (1978). He pursued a military and political career as a partisan of Caesar's, but later chose the side of the senate; he was killed in 42 BC in a fight with T. Sextius, the Antonian governor of Africa Nova.

12 For this view, see, e.g., Rawson (1978) 191. For Suetonius as one of the sources for Jerome's 'Chronicle', see *Chron.*, p. 6 (ed. R. Helm): 'admixta sunt plurima, quae de Tranquillo et ceteris inlustribus historicis curiossissime excerpsi'.

13 He was a friend of Cicero's, who calls him a *doctus homo* (*Fam.* 12.17.2; for his wealth see *Att.* 12.14.2), and the recipient of a number of surviving letters from him in the period 46–43 BC (*Fam.* 12.17–30), and also a friend of Catullus', who addresses him in a poem asking him for a consolation, probably in verse (Catul. 38). For his poetry, see Ov. *Trist.* 2.436 (erotic verse). Part of a line (a hendecasyllable) has come down to us in Macr. *Sat.* 6.4.12. He also wrote an epyllion on Glaucus in hexameters, see Macr. *Sat.* 6.5.13 for a fragment. For his poetry see further Courtney (1993) 225–7, Lyne (1978) and Rawson (1978) 188–90 and 201.

14 *CIL* VI 1300a = *ILLRP* 439: 'Cornificia Q. f. Cameri (uxor) / Q. Cornificius Q. f. frater / pr(aetor) augur'; this Camerius has been identified with the Camerius of Catullus 55 by Rawson (1978) 190. The Cornificia of the inscription must be the poetess, unless she had a sister of the same name who was married to a Camerius; see for the identification also Wiseman, T. P. (1976) 'Camerius', *BICS* 23: 15–17. As her brother Q Cornificius was praetor in 47 or 45 BC, the inscription must date from after that date. Wiseman (1969) 58 and Rawson (1978) 190–1 suggest that our Cornificia was also the same as the Cornificia whom Cicero rather contemptuously called 'quite an old woman and more than once married' (*Att.* 13.28.4: 'vetulam sane et multarum nuptiarum') in 45 BC when telling Atticus that she rejected the noble M. Iuventius Thalna (*RE* X Iuventius 27 cols 1370–1 identifies him with the Iuventius of Catullus, another possible link with the friends of Catullus) as a husband because she found him not wealthy enough. But the identification cannot be proved and Wiseman (1971) 52 more cautiously identifies Cicero's Cornificia with 'his [i.e. Cornificius'] sister or his aunt'. For Cornificius' library and copyists see *Fam.* 12.17.2; also Clift (1945) 13.

15 Apul. *Apol.* 10: 'Ticidam . . . quod quae Metella erat Perillam scripserit'; Ovid. *Trist.* 2.437–8: 'et quorum libris modo dissimulata Perillae / nomine, nunc legitur dicta Metella suo'. These lines are obscure and partly corrupt (e.g., instead of 'Perillae' most MSS read 'per illos'). Courtney (1993) 228–9 translates: 'and those poets in whose books Metella, lately celebrated under the fictitious name of Perilla, is now celebrated by her real name', but different interpretations have been given (cf., e.g., G. Luck in his commentary on the *Tristia* (Heidelberg, 1977, vol. II, p. 144), who takes it that Metella, celebrated under a pseudonym in the poetry of her admirers, now wrote poetry herself under her own name. However, this hypothesis seems too shaky to include a Metella among our poetesses). For the identification of this Metella with Caecilia Metella, possibly the daughter of Clodia Metelli and the wife of P. Cornelius Lentulus Spinther, see Wiseman (1974) 188–91.

16 Ovid. *Trist.* 3.7.3–4: 'You will find her sitting in the company of her sweet mother or amid books and the Pierian maidens she loves' ('aut illam invenies dulci cum matre sedentem, / aut inter libros Pieridasque suas'). For sitting with her mother as a symbol

of chastity, cf. Tib. 1.3.83–8, where Delia is portrayed sitting with her mother and toiling at her woolwork till late at night, like a chaste Lucretia (Liv. 1.57).

17 For Perilla's fortune, which according to Ovid was modest though she deserved a great one, see Ovid *Trist.* 3.7.39: 'sunt tibi opes modicae, cum sis dignissima magnis'. In view of the common complaint of poverty by poets of the equestrian class, the modesty of her fortune should not be taken too seriously; it may well point to equestrian status. The assumption of Courtney (1993) 229 that she was a Greek freedwoman of Ovid's 'too unimportant socially to make concealment of her name necessary' seems unwarranted and is not in keeping with the tone of an equal and intimate relationship throughout the poem. Hallett, J. (1990) 'Contextualizing the text: the journey to Ovid', *Helios* 17.2: 191 in calling her 'a female poetic protégée' leaves her class and the origins of her relationship to Ovid in the dark. For their acquaintance from her early youth onwards, see 3.7.17: 'teneris in virginis annis'. Their cordial relation is emphasized in lines 5–6: she will immediately drop whatever she is doing when she receives a letter from Ovid, and in line 45 she is mentioned among the things he longs for most in exile, along with his fatherland and his home: 'caream patria vobisque domoque'. In *FOS* 860 Perilla is tentatively identified with Ovid's stepdaughter; for this stepdaughter, see Ovid *Pont.* 4.8.11–12 and 90 and Syme (1978) 79, 89–90 and 145. For the identification of Perilla as his stepdaughter, see also Nagle, B. R. (1980) *The Poetics of Exile: Program and Polemic in the Tristia and Epistulae ex Ponto of Ovid*, Brussels: Latomus (Coll. Latomus 170), p. 150.

18 Compare his expression in *Trist.* 3.7.18 ('utque pater natae', referring to 'Perilla') with his description of his stepdaughter in *Pont.* 4.8.11 ('almost my daughter', 'mihi filia paene'; in line 90 he calls himself 'almost the father-in-law' 'socero paene', of her husband). For Perilla as a *puella docta*, cf. *Trist.* 3.7.12: 'doctaque . . . carmina . . . Canis', 14: 'raras dotes ingeniumque' and 31: 'doctissima'. For her modesty: 13: 'mores . . . pudicos'; for her beauty, see lines 13, 33 and 37. In view of the dubious reputation of the *puella docta* poets were apt to stress the modesty of accomplished female relatives; cf., for instance, Statius' portrayal of his stepdaughter (Stat. *Silv.* 3.5.63–7) cited in chapter 3, p. 83. The *cognomen* of the son of Ovid's anonymous stepdaughter, Nerullinus, suggests that her name may have been Nerulla (but *FOS* 860 is sceptical), since during the empire the *cognomen* of a child was often derived from the family name of the mother.

19 It might be supposed that 'Perilla' is a fictitious person, or a metaphor for Ovid's own poetic career, but this is not supported by the tone of the poem and seems unlikely in view of the reality of the other addressees of the *Tristia* (though none of them is mentioned by name); see Syme (1978) 76–7.

20 Ovid. *Trist.* 3.7.17–18: 'primus id aspexi teneris in virginis annis, / utque pater natae duxque comesque fui'. For her talent and his discovery of it, see lines 14–18. For their common pursuit of composing learned verse; see lines 11–12: 'studiis communibus . . . / doctaque . . . Carmina'.

21 For Ovid himself as a young poet working on his poetry under the guidance of a (senior) friend or patron, see *Pont.* 1.7.27f., 2.3.77f.: Messalla as the *dux* of his talent, 2.4.13–18: a friend listening to and criticizing his newly composed poetry, and 4.12.23–6: his old friend Tuticanus encouraging Ovid and criticizing his poetry (see line 23: 'you gave me kindly encouragement, you were my guide and comrade' 'tu bonus hortator, tu duxque comesque fuisti'); in *Trist.* 4.10.119 the Muse is addressed in the same way: 'tu dux et comes es'; see also Hor. *Ars Poetica* 438–52 for the importance of the critical remarks of a friend prior to publication of poetry.

22 *Trist.* 3.7.23–6: 'Dum licuit, tua saepe mihi, tibi nostra legebam; / saepe tui iudex, saepe magister eram: / aut ego praebebam factis modo versibus aures, / aut, ubi cessares, causa ruboris eram.'

23 This is unclear: cf. Ovid. *Trist.* 3.7.11–12: 'say to her: "are you too still devoted to our

common pursuit of singing learned verse, though not in your father's fashion?"' ('tu quoque, dic, studiis communibus ecquid inhaeres, / doctaque non patrio carmina more canis?'). In the second line the obscure 'non patrio . . . more' is open to various interpretations: Perilla may have composed her poetry in Greek instead of her native Latin (cf. *Pont.* 4.13.33: 'non patria . . . scripta Camena' 'not written in the language of my native Muse', for a poem by Ovid written in Getic), she may have written poetry that was non-erotic, if we take 'patrio more' to denote Ovid's erotic poetry (this solution is perhaps corroborated by Ovid's wish in line 53 that a happier use of her art is granted her, an allusion to his exile to Tomis), or, not very likely, 'patrio more' may denote her biological father, who, in that case, must have been a poet of a different kind from his daughter. In his commentary on the *Tristia* G. Luck (Heidelberg 1977 vol. II, p. 200) suggests that it may also refer to the rarity of women's poetry in Roman society.

24 For her possible fear of writing poetry because of his exile see *Trist.* 3.7.21–2 and 27–30: 'Perhaps from the example of the injury that verse has done me you fear a repetition of the fate which has brought me punishment. Lay aside your fear, Perilla; only let no woman or any man learn from your writings how to love' ('Forsitan exemplo, quo me laesere libelli, / tu metuis poenae fata secunda meae. / Pone, Perilla, metum; tantummodo femina nulla / neve vir a scriptis discat amare tuis'). For the immortality of poetry contrasted with the transitory possessions of life (such as beauty and wealth) see line 33 to the end of the poem.

25 Around AD 12, about two years after the probable date of Ovid *Trist.* 3.7, Ovid's stepdaughter married P. Suillius Rufus (*cos suff.* AD 43 or 45; *PIR*¹ S 700, Ovid. *Pont.* 4.8 is addressed to him); they had at least one son, P. Suillius Nerullinus (*PIR*¹ S 699), who was born about AD 15, and a granddaughter, Suillia; see *FOS* 737. If they did not divorce beforehand, she endured long years of the exile of her husband, who was banished by Tiberius in AD 24 and only recalled by Caligula thirteen years later; she died before he was exiled for the second time in AD 58 (Tac. *Ann.* 13.43; for Suillius' career, see Syme (1970) 28–9 and 31–2).

26 Tib. 3.13–18 = 4.7–12; as the division of the third book of 'Tibullus' into a third and a fourth book dates from the fifteenth century, I shall refer to Sulpicia's poems by their place in the third book. In recent years Sulpicia's poetry has received much attention. I refer only to recent contributions relevant to the present study (they provide full references to earlier work on Sulpicia): Santirocco (1979), Currie (1983), Hinds (1987), Lowe (1988), Roessel (1990) and Parker (1994). For a discussion of the transmission and date of the poetry of the *Corpus Tibullianum* (also called the *Appendix Tibulliana*), see Tränkle (1990).

27 For a survey of the discussion of the authorship of the elegies now generally attributed to Sulpicia (3.13–18 = 4.7–12) and those assigned to the unidentified *auctor de Sulpicia* or *amicus Sulpiciae* (Tib. 3.8–12 = 4.2–6), see Lowe (1988) 194–7, Parker (1994) 40 and Santirocco (1979) 229–30; for the *amicus Sulpiciae*, see Hinds (1987) and Fredericks (1976). In contrast to the condescension with which Sulpicia's poetry was treated in the past, the authorship of Sulpicia has recently been doubted because the verses seem in certain respects 'too good to be true'; see Lowe (1988), who remarks that the poet 'seems suspiciously forthcoming with autobiographical identifiers' (p. 197, n. 22) and Currie (1983) 1758, who believes that the instances of reversal in her poetry may 'point to a literary game conducted by clever people within the Messalla coterie'. Hinds (1987) 46 suggests the possibility that Sulpicia's elegies may perhaps be a post-Ovidian response to the poetry of the *amicus Sulpiciae* instead of the other way round, but this is denied by Parker (1994) 53. In spite of these objections nearly all critics have eventually accepted the authorship of Sulpicia.

28 For prosopographical information on Sulpicia, see *FOS* 738, *PIR*¹ S 739, *RE* IVA Sulpicia no. 114 cols 879–80; in Tib. 3.16.4 = 4.10.4 she calls herself *Servi filia Sulpicia*.

For the long-drawn-out process of identifying the poetess Sulpicia with the niece of Messalla Corvinus, see Lowe (1988) and Parker (1994) 55, n. 2. For her father see *RE* IVA Sulpicius no. 96 cols 860–2, Syme, R. (1955) 'Missing senators', *Historia* 4: 69–70 and Syme (1981); for his erotic verses, Hallett (1992) 351. A possible sister (or, perhaps, aunt) married a Cassius and became mother of a daughter, Paula Cassia (*ILS* 3103, *RE* IVA Sulpicia no. 111 cols 878–9, Syme (1989) 206); for her brother: Frontin. *De Aq.* 99; see also Syme (1981) 425. Her mother Valeria (*RE* VIIIA Valeria 392 col. 244) is said to have rejected remarriage after her husband's death; see Hier. *Adv. Jovinian.* 1.46 (from Sen. *De Matrimonio* fr. 77 Haase), thereby conforming to the ideal of *univira*. For her maternal uncle Messalla, see *PIR*[1] V 90, *RE* VIIIA Valerius Messalla 261 cols 131–57, Syme (1989) 200–16. In Tib. 3.14.6 Sulpicia addresses him as *propinque*, 'my kinsman', and to judge from the same poem he may have had some authority over her. From this it has been concluded that he must have been her guardian, but this is uncertain; in view of the predominance of agnatic *tutela* before the reign of Claudius we would expect a (male) member of her father's family to be her guardian, but this was not compulsory; see Gardner (1990) 5–29. For Messalla's literary patronage, see Davies (1973).

29 For this view, see, among others, Luck (1959) 93–5 and 100–3, Davies (1973) 25 and Currie (1983) 1760.

30 For her intention to publish, see Santirocco (1979) 234–5, followed by Lowe (1988) 203–4, Hinds (1987) 43 and Roessel (1990) 248–9; this does not conflict with the possibility that the poems may have been published only after her death by an editor; see Parker (1994) 42. For the theme of winning a lover through poetry – a common theme in love elegy – see Stroh (1971).

31 3.13.1–4 and 7–10: 'Tandem venit amor, qualem texisse pudori / quam nudasse alicui sit mihi, Fama, magis. / Exorata meis illum Cytherea Camenis / attulit in nostrum deposuitque sinum. . . . Non ego signatis quicquam mandare tabellis, / me legat ut nemo quam meus ante, velim, / sed peccasse iuvat, vultus componere famae / taedet: cum digno digna fuisse ferar.' For other possible interpretations of the first two lines, see Tränkle (1990) 302–4.

32 The traditional view, that the poems of the *Appendix Tibulliana* were composed by members of Messalla's circle and published shortly after his death, is rejected by Tränkle (1990) 1–2, who argues that only Sulpicia's elegies date from the lifetime of Messalla, but that the other poetry preserved in the *corpus* is post-Ovidian, some of it perhaps even to be dated to the end of the first or the beginning of the second century AD. For a post-Ovidian date of the poems of the *amicus Sulpiciae*, see also Hinds (1987) 36–7. Parker (1994) 24 points to the inclusion of 3.19 (attributed to Tibullus) and 3.20, which he assumes to be leftovers from earlier published work, as an argument for a posthumous publication by an editor.

33 In her poem about the outing he planned for her birthday she addresses him with the words 'nimium Messalla mei studiose' (3.14.5), presenting his concern for her as excessive. For the role of the uncle in the upbringing of his sister's children, see Hallett (1984b), who, however, seems to make too much of the supposed contrast between the close emotional ties of the *avunculus* (maternal uncle) with the children of his sister and the allegedly more detached and severe role of the *patruus* (paternal uncle); for a less contrasting appraisal of the role of the *avunculus* and the *patruus* and more in general of relationships of kinship through paternal and maternal lines, see Saller, R. P. (1997) 'Roman kinship: structure and sentiment', in Rawson and Weaver (1997) 7–34. We may infer that being her mother's brother Messalla was expected to show that he was concerned about her, especially after she had lost her father.

34 For instance, the husband of Sulpicia Caleni (see pp. 160ff.) was probably a literary patron of Martial's.

35 Because of the firmly Roman context of her (Greek) poetry Julia Balbilla is included in our discussion of Roman female poets; the poems by Caecilia Trebulla (see below n. 109) on the same monument will not be discussed, as despite her aristocratic and Roman-sounding *gentilicium* no Roman upper-class background or connections can be shown to have existed. I shall also refrain from discussing the 'hymn to Rome' of the puzzling Greek poetess Melinno; see Stobaeus 3.7.12 (Hense III, p. 312, Berlin 1894), Lloyd-Jones, H. and Parsons, P. (eds) (1983) *Supplementum Hellenisticum*, Berlin: de Gruyter, no. 541 and n. 138 below, as too little is known of her to decide whether she fits into the geographical and chronological scope of this study; the assumption that south Italian Locri was her place of residence rests on the tenuous base of Nossis of Locri mentioning a Melinna (*AP* 6.353), and assumptions about her date vary from the fourth century BC to the second century AD.

36 The sarcasm is especially apparent in the first couplet: 'Gratum est, securus multum quod iam tibi de me / permittis, subito ne male inepta cadam', which may be translated thus: 'It is a fine thing that you feel free to allow yourself so much at my expense, so that I may not suddenly stumble in my misplaced naivety'. For a discussion of these difficult verses, see Lowe (1988) 200–1.

37 See Parker (1994), who gives two main reasons: first, he argues that the traditional division by O. Gruppe (in 1838), who assigned the first six poems about Sulpicia and Cerinthus (3.8–13) to the *auctor de Sulpicia* and the latter five (3.14–18; subsequent editors added 3.13) to Sulpicia herself, has no firm foundation. Second, the five poems now generally assigned to the anonymous *auctor de Sulpicia* are alternately written in the *persona* of a friend or fellow poet (3.8, 3.10 and 3.12) and as if Sulpicia herself were speaking (3.9 and 3.11). For one poet to take such alternate positions is unprecedented in Greek and Roman literature and Parker concludes that 3.9 and 11, written according to the convention of subjective love elegy, are what they pretend to be: poems by Sulpicia herself. Yet, they differ in style and length: 3.9 is twenty-four lines long and 3.11 twenty, whereas the six elegies generally attributed to Sulpicia consist of forty lines altogether.

38 For the division of Tib. 3.8–18 into two groups, see Gruppe, O. (1838) *Die römische Elegie*, Leipzig, vol. I, pp. 25–64, esp. 48–50; see also Parker (1994) 40 and above n. 37. For the biographical view, see, for instance, the commentary of Smith, K. F. (1913) *The Elegies of Albius Tibullus*, New York: American Book Company (reprinted in Darmstadt 1964), pp. 79–87; Luck (1959) 100–2 and 107–9 and Currie (1983); for a discussion of this view and of the earlier assignment of her poems to male pseudonymous poets, see, e.g., Santirocco (1979) 230 and 238, and Lowe (1988) 193–7. As has been observed by Lefkowitz (1981) 59–68 in her chapter on 'critical stereotypes and the poetry of Sappho', preconceived ideas about female artists often cause criticism of female poets to look remarkably alike, even when the poets are as different as Sappho and Emily Dickinson: instead of works of art their poems are regarded as mere emotional outpourings.

39 Already in the fifteenth century humanists identified Cerinthus with the name Cornutus, which is metrically equivalent, wrongly assuming that the Greek Κήρινθος ('bee-bread') derived from κέρας ('horn'). M. Caecilius Cornutus (*RE* III Caecilius 46 col. 1200, *PIR*² C 34), a friend of Messalla's and Tibullus' of senatorial rank, is addressed by the latter in two poems: Tib. 2.2.9 (in a poem for his birthday portraying him as happily married) and 2.3.1. Scheid, J. (1975) *Les Frères Arvales: recrutement et origine sociale sous les empereurs julio-claudiens*, Paris: PUF, pp. 35–40 and 95 accepts the traditional view that Cerinthus is M. Caecilius Cornutus, thus providing Sulpicia with a husband and a son who were *fratres Arvales*. He is followed in this by Raepsaet-Charlier (*FOS* 738). *Contra* Roessel (1990) 243–50, who argues that since Κήρινθος ('bee-bread') cannot be derived from κέρας ('horn'), the identification of Cerinthus with Cornutus

makes no sense; instead he stresses the poetic significance of the name through its association with bees, honey and wax (used for covering writing-tablets). Yet, as Santirocco (1979) 236, n. 23 rightly remarks, Roman readers may not have been so sensitive to the difference in quantity between the η and the ε. For a survey of opinions about the identity of Cerinthus, Santirocco (1979) 236–7, Currie (1983) 1754–5, Lowe (1988) 196 and Parker (1994) 56, n. 9; see also Syme (1989) 47 and 206.

40 Santirocco (1979) 234–5, followed by Hinds (1987) 43–4 and Lowe (1988) 203–5. Of course, we do not know whether the six poems were composed as a cycle or are the only ones preserved from a larger collection of poems. For the rearrangement see, e.g., Smith, K. F. (1913) *The Elegies of Albius Tibullus*, New York: American Book Company (reprinted in Darmstadt 1964), pp. 81–2; also Currie (1983) 1760–1 and Tränkle (1990) 300 attempt to reconstruct the chronology of the affair from her poetry. A curious example of rearrangement is found in a recent article of Merriam (1990), who proposes a reordering of the poems on the basis of the growing openness apparent in them (from ignorance and concealment of the affair to revelation).

41 Her poetic skill and stylistic sophistication are minutely described by Santirocco (1979) and Lowe (1988): verbal echoes, alliteration, assonance, intricate word-play, skilful treatment of the couplet as a unit of meaning, syntactical symmetry, framing devices, close relations between syntax and meaning, the device of paired poems, etc. In contrast with the traditional criticism of amateurism Lowe (1988) 205 now speaks even of 'an excess of intellectual control' and suggests that the obscure and difficult syntax and her fondness for multiple hypotaxis are more probably due to virtuosity and a habit of compressing her thoughts.

42 3.13.10: 'cum digno digna fuisse ferar', 'let it be told that we have been together, as a worthy woman with a worthy man'; for her youth see 3.18.3: 'iuventa'. For Sulpicia's class-consciousness, see Santirocco (1979) 233. Hallett (1989) 71 suggests that pride in birth or family connections may have been particularly strong among (upper-class) women since a woman's identity was to a large extent determined by her family; see for this matter more fully chapter 1.

43 3.16.3–4: 'sit tibi cura togae potior pressumque quasillo / scortum quam Servi filia Sulpicia'. The toga, worn by children and women who were *infames* such as prostitutes, is usually opposed to the long *stola* worn by respectably married women of the upper classes; see chapter 1, pp. 14f.

44 3.16.5–6: 'solliciti sunt pro nobis, quibus illa doloris / ne cedam ignoto maxima causa toro'. Various interpretations of these obscure lines have been given, cf. Santirocco (1979) 232–3 and Lowe (1988) 200–2. To my mind, the most plausible interpretation is that 'solliciti' refers to her relatives who care for her (in the first place her mother and her uncle) and not to potential rivals of Cerinthus and that 'ignoto toro' alludes to the low status of the spinning-girl and not to that of the shadowy Cerinthus (cf. Santirocco (1979) 232–3, Currie (1983) 1763–4 and Lowe (1988) 201; *contra* Tränkle (1990) 318–20).

45 Lowe (1988) 197, n. 22, who finds her 'suspiciously forthcoming with autobiographical identifiers'. For Messalla: 'Iam, nimium Messalla mei studiose, quiescas' (3.14.5) and 'propinque' (3.14.6).

46 For Sulpicia presenting herself as a *puella*: 3.14.3, 3.15.1 and 3.17.1. In 3.14 and 15 she poses as a *puella urbana* lacking rusticity, even hating the countryside (see, e.g., 3.14.4: 'Dulcius urbe quid est?'). Unlike most *puellae* of the love poets she has no *vir* to deceive, but her uncle's interference has to be dealt with, for instance, his (well-meant) plan for a trip to the countryside on her birthday (3.14), which would mean leaving Cerinthus behind.

47 This is defined by Skinner (1993) 132 as 'an organized way of seeing the world, constituted through language, that permits the individual to impose a coherent meaning on the circumstances and events of his or her life'.

48 Santirocco (1979) 234–5; see also above p. 152.

49 3.13.9: 'vultus componere famae'. Cohen (1991) 54–69 and 83–97 provides an illuminating discussion of 'the politics of reputation' (the expression is Cohen's) in ancient and modern Mediterranean societies and of the importance of keeping up appearances to avoid gossip.

50 3.13.1–2, translated above p. 152; for a different translation, see Lowe (1988) 203. For her 'sin': 3.13.9 ('peccasse').

51 3.13.5–6: 'mea gaudia narret, / dicetur siquis non habuisse sua'; cf. Catul. 5.2–3: 'rumoresque senum severiorum / omnes unius aestimemus assis'. For a similar sentiment: Prop. 2.30.13f.

52 The expression 'fuisse cum' (3.13.10) is colloquial and denotes sexual intimacy; cf. Ovid. *Am.* 2.8.27f., Santirocco (1979) 237; also 'nudasse' in 3.13.2, though used metaphorically, is part of the erotic word-play of the poem.

53 3.18.6: 'ardorem cupiens dissimulare meum'.

54 For her rather extravagant demonstration of repentance, see lines 3–4: 'if in my whole youth in my stupidity I have committed anything of which I admit to have been more repentant' ('si quicquam tota commisi stulta iuventa, / cuius me fatear paenituisse magis'). For her sexual vocabulary, see 3.18.1: 'fervida cura', 'burning passion' (*cura* is common in elegiac poetry; see Santirocco (1979) 237) and 3.18.6: 'ardorem', meaning 'passion' or 'ardent desire'; both expressions have a conspicuous place: at the end of the first verse and at the beginning of the last. *Mea lux*, to address the beloved, is common in love poetry; cf. for instance, Prop. 2.29.1. In short, to use the words of Hallett (1989) 71, Sulpicia 'breaks with respectable notions of femininity'.

55 For the metaphor of the *militia amoris*, see, e.g., Murgatroyd, P. (1975) '*Militia amoris* and the Roman elegists', *Latomus* 34: 59–79 and Cahoon, L. (1988) 'The bed as battlefield: erotic conquest and military metaphor in Ovid's *Amores*', *TAPhA* 118: 293–307. For the inversion of gender roles in Roman love poetry, see, e.g., Wiseman (1985) 121f., Wyke (1987b) 160ff., Hallet (1984a) and (1989) 72; see also Gold, B. K. (1993) 'But Ariadne was never there in the first place: finding the female in Roman poetry', in Rabinowitz and Richlin (1993) 85 and 90–1.

56 That they were of equal status is suggested by 3.13.10: 'digno digna'. The words 'ignoto . . . toro' in 3.16.6 are, to my mind wrongly (see above n. 44), taken by some as proof of Cerinthus' obscure birth, see, e.g., Tränkle (1990) 320. Also Boucher, J. P. (1976) 'A propos de Cérinthus et de quelques autres pseudonymes dans la poésie augustéenne', *Latomus* 35: 504–19 argues for an undistinguished background for Cerinthus, assuming, judging by his name, that he was a kind of gigolo, but Roessel (1990) 244 convincingly refutes Boucher's view on the meaning of the name 'Cerinthus'. Treggiari (1991) 121–2 argues that Sulpicia's poems were 'the preliminaries to a marriage which was socially a *digna condicio*', which seems to stretch the evidence too far, and Dixon (1992) 87 goes even further by believing that Sulpicia sings of married love.

57 Roessel (1990) suggests that the name 'Cerinthus' ('bee-bread', connected to both honey and wax) is ambiguous, denoting both her beloved and her writing material, which introduces a discussion about the reality of Cerinthus similar to that of the elegiac *puellae*; see pp. 175f.

58 Cf., for the conventional situation, Ovid *AA*. 1.276: 'vir male dissimulat, tectius illa cupit' ('the man dissembles badly: she conceals desire better').

59 3.14.1: 'invisus natalis' 'my hated birthday'; for more conventional birthday-poems in which the birthday is a joyful event, cf. Tib. 1.7 and 2.2. The 'odious country' (3.14.1: 'rure molesto') and the 'chilly river' (3.14.4: 'frigidus amnis' or 'Arnus') are unfit for a sophisticated *puella urbana* (3.14.3: 'dulcius urbe quid est?', 'what is more pleasant than the town?'). Her poem about her illness (3.17), which shows a 'calculated ambiguity between real fever and the heat of passion' (Santirocco (1979) 233; for the love-sickness

theme in the Garland, see Fredericks (1976) 765–8), inverts the conventional situation: as a rule (which is not always observed), the illness of his *puella* causes the love poet much anxiety; cf., e.g., Prop. 2.28 and 28a, and Luck (1959) 113, n. 2. Here, the poet-lover (who at the same time is the *puella*) is ill and the beloved seems indifferent. Yardley, J. C. (1990) 'Cerinthus' *pia cura* ([Tibullus] 3.17.1–2)', *CQ* n.s. 40: 568–70 argues that, like Catullus before her, Sulpicia applies the language of *amicitia* and the notion of reciprocal *benificia* to her love-affair. For the absence of *servitium amoris*, see Tschiedel, H. J. (1992) 'Die Gedichte der Sulpicia (Tib. 3.13–18) – Frauenlyrik?', *Grazer Beiträge* 18: 87–102; an indication of a more egalitarian relationship may be found in 3.13.10: 'digno digna'. For her inversion of conventional elegiac themes generally, see Currie (1983) 1756–8, Hallett (1989) 70–1, Merriam (1990) 97–8.

60 For gender reversals in Sulpicia's poetry, see Santirocco (1979) 237, Currie (1983) 1758, Hinds (1987) 43 and Roessel (1990) 247ff. As inversion of traditional values and roles was one of the characteristics of contemporary (male) love elegy Sulpicia conformed to the rules of the genre in this respect, but her position as a female author in a male genre and her use of female values and themes instead of male ones distinguish her poetry from that of male elegists.

61 See the studies mentioned in nn. 38 and 41 above. For her use of colloquialisms, see Santirocco (1979) 236, Parker (1994) 52; for some examples see also Bréguet, E. (1946) *Le Roman de Sulpicia: élégies IV 2–12 du 'Corpus Tibullianum'*, Geneva: Georg, pp. 43–9.

62 This has been demonstrated for the sixteenth-century Spanish nun, writer and (post-humously) saint Teresa of Avila by Weber (1990), who cogently argues that the 'sub-jective spontaneity' and 'feminine affectivity' ascribed to the writings of Teresa of Avila (because of her use of colloquialisms and her plain, unadorned style) were in fact a deliberate rhetorical strategy, by which, among other things, she made her work access-ible also to female readers, most of whom had not received a rhetorical training.

63 For the five poems of the so-called 'Garland of Sulpicia' (Tib. 3.8–3.12 = 4.2–4.6) see Fredericks (1976), Currie (1983) 1754–5, Hinds (1987) and Parker (1994). Hinds (1987) 36–7 adduces many examples of verbal similarity with Ovid and argues for a post-Ovidian date; for a date soon after Ovid, see also Tränkle (1990) 2–3. The poetry of this unknown poet is, to say the least, curious: three poems written in the person of a friend or an observer (3.8, 10 and 12) are interlaced with two poems in the person of Sulpicia herself (3.9 and 11).

64 See Skinner (1993) 137, who suggests that to male readers the female subject-position of Sappho's work offered 'a socially permissible escape from the strict constraints of masculinity', allowing them to 'play the other'.

65 For his elaboration of Sulpicia's inversion of the gender roles of elegy, see Hinds (1987) 30–46; for some examples see 3.11.17–20, esp. 'tectius optat' (line 17) and 'pudet' (line 18) portraying Cerinthus in the silent, modest role appropriate to a well-bred girl; see also 3.9.20, where Cerinthus is addressed as 'caste puer'. Also Sulpicia's threefold role as an upper-class girl, an elegiac *puella* and the poet-lover is apparent in the poetry of the *amicus*: she is presented as a young upper-class woman who has to conceal her love (see 3.11.7, 'furta'; 3.12.6: 'occulte' and 16: 'tacita . . . mente'), as a beautiful and sophisticated *puella*: 3.8.15 and 24; 3.10.1, 11 and 16; 3.11.3; 3.12.2 ('docta puella') and 9, and as the poet-lover in 3.9 and 11 (on the 'ambiguity of speaker' see Fredericks (1976) 770ff.; Parker (1994) assigns these two poems to Sulpicia herself). For verbal allu-sions to Sulpicia's poetry: 'mea lux' 3.9.15; cf. Sulpicia's 3.18.1 (though this expression is part of the regular language of love; cf., e.g., Catul. 68a. 132 and Prop. 2.29.1); 'dignior', 3.12.10, alludes to 'digna digno' in Sulpicia's 3.13.10; the 'credula turba' of 3.10.18 perhaps alludes to the 'solliciti' in Sulpicia's 3.16.5 and 3.9.24: 'recurre sinus' to 3.13.4: 'deposuitque sinum'; for themes adopted from Sulpicia's poems (but treated

in a more conventional way): illness (3.10; cf. Sulpicia's 3.17) and the paired birthday-poems (3.11 and 12; cf. Sulpicia's 3.14 and 15).

66 Lowe (1988) 193.

67 Mart. *Ep.* 10.35.1–4: 'Omnes Sulpiciam legant puellae / uni quae cupiunt viro placere; / omnes Sulpiciam legant mariti / uni qui cupiunt placere nuptae.'

68 For Sulpicia Caleni, see *RE* IV A Sulpicia 115 cols 880–2. For the comparison with Egeria see Mart. *Ep.* 10.35.13–14; as Egeria also figures in the late antique satire written under the name of Sulpicia, the *Conquestio Sulpiciae* (line 68), Parker (1992) 92, n. 24 and Richlin (1992b) 133–4 suggest that Egeria may have figured in Sulpicia's own poetry. Sullivan (1991) 49 believes that both Sulpicia and Calenus were Martial's patrons, but as only Calenus is addressed by Martial (in 10.38) and as he occupies an important place in the poem praising Sulpicia's poetry (10.35: his name is the last word of the poem), I take it that he (and not Sulpicia) was a patron of Martial's. Martial's use of his *cognomen* in addressing him may be regarded as a sign of their intimacy. Duret, L. (1986) 'Dans l'ombre des plus grands II: Poètes et prosateurs mal connus de la latinité d'argent', *ANRW* II 32.5: 3218–22 assumes, without ground, that Sulpicia is a pseudonym and that Calenus is a fictitious person.

69 Mart. *Ep.* 10.35 shows her alive, whereas 10.38 seems to have been written shortly after her death: lines 9–11 portray Calenus as counting his life by the fifteen years of his marriage alone and 12–14 state that he would prefer one day of his marriage restored to him by Fate (Atropos) to reaching four times the age of Nestor; see Parker (1992) 94–5 and Hallett (1992) 103 and 112. As book 10 of Martial's epigrams was published in two editions, the first in AD 95 and the second revised edition in AD 98, she may have died between AD 95 and 98. Richlin (1992a) 232, n. 4 and (1992b) 128–32 believes that 10.38 reflects a quarrel or a divorce instead of Sulpicia's death, which, however, contradicts Martial's description of the happiness of their marriage. Courtney (1993) 361 thinks that the poem celebrates an anniversary. If written shortly after Sulpicia's death the poem indeed seems unusually gay. However, to my mind, the last lines of the poem allow no other interpretation than that Sulpicia has died.

70 Schol. ad Juv. 6.537, published by Giorgio Valla in his Venetian edition of Juvenal in 1486. According to Parker (1992) 89–91, Valla found the fragment of Sulpicia in a now lost manuscript which contained a collection of scholia under the name of 'Probus', probably a manuscript of Juvenal's with a marginal commentary which ultimately derived from a late antique commentary on Juvenal (from the end of the fourth century AD). The mutilated condition of this manuscript may be responsible for the rather damaged text as transmitted by Valla. Reference to the fragment is strangely omitted by Merriam, C. U. (1991) 'The other Sulpicia', *CW* 84.4: 303–5. Parker (1992) 91 has pointed out that the iambic trimeters of the fragment (mentioned as one of her metres in the late antique *Sulpiciae Conquestio* 4–7) confirm its authenticity, as this information cannot be inferred from Martial. For the linen produced by the Cadurci, a Gallic tribe that was famous for it at the time, see Strabo 4.2.2, Plin. *NH* 19.8 and 13, Juv. 6.537 and 7.221.

71 Morel, W. (1963²), *Fragmenta Poetarum Latinorum Epicorum et Lyricorum*, Leipzig: Teubner, p. 134; Morel's reading is accepted by C. Büchner in his 2nd edition (1982) of the *Fragmenta Poetarum Latinorum Epicorum et Lyricorum*, Stuttgart and Leipzig: Teubner, p. 166 and in the 3rd edition (1995) of the same work by J. Blänsdorf (Stuttgart and Leipzig: Teubner, pp. 334–5). For a discussion of the transmission of the text, see Parker (1992) 89–91. For 'concubentem' and Pithoeus' emendation 'concubantem', see Levin, S. (1993) 'Overlapping verbs, *concubare* and *concumbere*', *CW* 87.2: 52.

72 Baehrens, A. (1886) *Fragmenta Poetarum Romanorum*, Leipzig: Teubner, p. 370. He is the only one to give the complete text of Valla ad Juv. 6.537 (*de cadurco*): 'membrum mulieris, inquit Probus, intellegitur, cum sit membri muliebris velamen; vel, ut alii, est

instita, qua lectus intenditur; unde ait Sulpicia: lux me cadurci dissolutis fasciis / nudam Caleno concubantem proferat' ('intenditur' is a correction for Valla's 'incenditur'; see Wessner, P. (1931/1967) *Scholia in Iuvenalem Vetustiora*, Stuttgart: Teubner, p. 108). This may be translated as: 'Probus says that the female genitals are meant, as it [i.e. *cadurcum*] is the covering of the female genitals. Or, as others say, it is the linen bed-girth, with which the bed is spread; whence Sulpicia says: "Let the light reveal me lying naked with Calenus when the bed-girth of Cadurcian linen has been loosened"' (cf. the translation by Parker (1992) 90; for *cadurcum* and *membrum muliebre* as sexual terms denoting the female genitals in late antique literature and glossaries, see Adams (1982) 46, 65–6 and 93). If this translation is right, the explanation of 'Probus' seems worthless, but also the alternative interpretation (*alii*, probably included in Valla's 'Probus'), though possibly correct, is puzzling. The meaning of the word *instita* ('bandage', 'girth') ranges from the interlaced cordings of the bedframe (usually of leather, wood or rope, but other material seems possible) to the disputed seam or straps of the *stola* of the *matrona* and the symbol of her respectability; see Scholz (1992) 88–93 and Sebesta (1994). Baehrens suggests *lux* as the missing subject of the fragment, which is perhaps supported by Mart. *Ep.* 10.35 and 38, where he mentions Calenus, the bed and the lamp ('lucerna' line 7) and Fulgentius 1 *praef.* 4 and 23 (ed. Helm, pp. 4 and 13); the emendation of 'dissolutis' for 'restitutis' was proposed in order to produce a text which is easier to understand. Other interpretations of Baehrens' text seem possible too. For example, the word *cadurcum* can also be used for the linen clothes Sulpicia may have been wearing, in combination with *fasciis* perhaps especially the breast-band (the *fascia pectoralis*). The translation would then read: 'Let the light reveal me lying naked with Calenus when the linen breastband has been loosened.'; cf. Mart. *Ep.* 11.104.7–8: 'fascia te tunicaeque obscuraque pallia celant: / at mihi nulla satis nuda puella iacet'. ('A breast-band, and a tunic, and opaque robes conceal you; but for me no girl lies naked enough'). For the breast-band (*fascia*, usually singular) see also Mart. *Ep.* 14.134, Ovid *AA* 3.274, *Rem. Am.* 338, Prop. 4.9.49.

73 Morel, W. (1963²) *Fragmenta Poetarum Latinorum Epicorum et Lyricorum*, Leipzig: Teubner, p. 134; Richlin (1992b) 128–32 takes *cadurcum* to indicate the duvet or bedlinen covering the bed and translates: 'If, the straps of [i.e. underneath] my duvet having been restored, [someone? something?] should show me lying naked with Calenus'. As she takes these lines for a fragment of a lost satire of Sulpicia instead of erotic poetry, her interpretation differs from that of most other scholars: in her opinion, the tone of the fragment is angry and suggests a break up of the marriage or a satirical description of marriage from a woman's point of view.

74 Parker (1992) 90 and 93; see also Hallett (1992) 105 and Courtney (1993) 361. In a short note Waterhouse, W. C. (1993) 'The words of the second Sulpicia', *CW* 87: 51 proposes to emend the usual reading 'cadurci' into 'cadurcum', which would make *cadurcum* (bed linen) the now missing subject of the verses.

75 *Pace* Richlin (1992b), who believes it is a satire: see above n. 73. The metre of Sulpicia's two surviving lines (iambic trimeters) also allows for the possibility that they are from a mime or from the spoken part of a drama, but as no such works are attributed to her this seems unlikely.

76 Mart. *Ep.* 10.35.8–9: 'sed castos docet et probos amores, / lusus delicias facetiasque', and in line 16 he calls her 'pudica'; for her ignoring mythological subjects see 10.35.5–7 (mentioning Medea, Thyestes, Scylla and Byblis, rather horrible examples of love and crime, as the subjects she shuns).

77 Mart. *Ep.* 10.38.6–7: 'o quae proelia, quas utrimque pugnas / felix lectulus et lucerna vidit' (translation by Richlin (1992b) 127). For these lines as an allusion to Sulpicia's own poetry see also Parker (1992) 92 and Courtney (1993) 361; for the theme of the bedroom lamp as a witness to love-making, see, e.g., Mart. *Ep.* 14.39. The happiness of

their marriage is commemorated by Mart. *Ep.* 10.38: the years are called *molles* (1), all days and nights of their marriage are marked with precious pearls (4–5: 'o nox omnis et hora, quae notata est/ caris litoris Indici lapillis!', 'o nights and hours, each marked with the little precious pearls of India's shore!', alluding to the custom of marking a happy day with a white stone and a bad day with a black one; cf. Mart. *Ep.* 9.52.5), 9–11: Calenus counts his life by the years of his marriage alone and 12–14: he would gladly sacrifice the prospect of a life four times the age of Nestor if Sulpicia were only one day restored to him. Parker (1992) 95 suggests also that Martial's choice of hendecasyllables for his poems in praise of Sulpicia may be an allusion to her own poems; cf. the *Sulpiciae Conquestio* 4.

78 Mart. *Ep.* 10.35.10–12: 'cuius carmina qui bene aestimarit, / nullam dixerit esse nequiorem, / nullam dixerit esse sanctiorem' (translation by Richlin (1992b) 126); see also line 20, 'puella'. For her conformity to the ideal of the *univira*, see also lines 19–21, in which it is said that Sulpicia would not accept even Jupiter, Bacchus or Apollo as a husband if Calenus were taken from her (a remote echo of Catullus poem 70 about Lesbia's preference for Catullus, as has been noted by Hallett (1992) 105). The echo of a poem about Lesbia in a poem about Sulpicia alludes to her role as the *puella* of love poetry.

79 When defending himself against the charge of immorality because of his licentious verses Ausonius, in the conclusion to his *Cento Nuptialis* (Prete 1978, p. 168.10), says about Sulpicia: 'prurire opusculum Sulpiciae, frontem caperare', the last-mentioned words indicating the frowning brow of the prudish; see also Richlin (1992b) 135. For the conventional claim of male poets of erotic poetry, 'my page is wanton, my life is chaste', see, e.g., Catul. 16.5–6, Ovid. *Trist.* 2.354, Mart. *Ep.* 1.4.8; for more examples Richlin (1992a) 2–13. Martial's defence of Sulpicia's reputation in 10.35 resembles this claim. Sid. Ap. *Carm.* 9.261–2 does (not) want to imitate, among others, 'non quod Sulpiciae iocus Thaliae / scripsit blandiloquum suo Caleno'. See further the late fifth-century author Fulgentius *Mythol.* 1 *praef.* 4 (p. 4 Helm): 'the wantonness of little Sulpicia' ('Sulpicillae procacitas') and 23 (p. 13 Helm) 'the gabbiness of Ausonian little Sulpicia' ('Sulpicillae Ausonianae loquacitas'; it seems that he knew Sulpicia from Ausonius). On the diminutive 'Sulpicillae' as contemptuous, see Parker (1992) 92, n. 22. For a discussion of the context of these passages, see Richlin (1992b) 134–7 (I do not agree with her conclusion that Sulpicia was a writer of satire).

80 *Conquestio Sulpiciae de statu rei publicae et temporibus Domitiani.* Sulpicia's name is mentioned only in the title, but the fact that Calenus is mentioned (in line 62) and the fact that the fictitious author lived during the reign of Domitian indicate that the *fabella* (line 2) pretends to be by Sulpicia Caleni. For a concise discussion of the date and the transmission of the text, see Reynolds, L. D. (ed.) (1983) *Texts and Transmission: A Survey of the Latin Classics*, Oxford: Clarendon Press, pp. 405–6. For an extensive discussion and edition of the text (with a German translation), see Fuchs, H. (1968) 'Das Klagelied der Sulpicia über die Gewaltherrschaft des Kaisers Domitian', *Discordia Concors: Festgabe für Edgar Bonjour zu seinem siebzigsten Geburtstag am 21. August 1968, vol. 1*, Basle and Stuttgart: Helbing & Lichtenhahn, pp. 32–47. Fuchs draws attention to the many literary borrowings from various Latin authors and argues that the poem cannot have been written before the fifth century AD. For further references, see Parker (1992) 92, n. 20; also Richlin (1992b) 132–4 briefly discusses the poem.

81 This poem is sometimes taken to suggest that Sulpicia was also known for satiric poetry; see Richlin (1992b), who calls her a 'lost Roman satirist' (n. 73 above). However, apart from the fact that a late antique 'satire' has been falsely attributed to Sulpicia, which would suggest that Sulpicia wrote not only love poetry, her arguments (the supposedly 'angry' tone of the surviving fragment, her vocabulary which would remind of Persius and Juvenal, and the fact that some authors of satires were named together with Sulpicia by Ausonius and Sidonius Apollinaris) are unconvincing.

82 For Sulpicia's use of a variety of metres, see the *Sulpiciae Conquestio* 4–6: hendecasyl-lables, iambic trimeters and scazons. The hendecasyllables of Martial's epigrams 10.35 and 38 perhaps allude to her poetry. Catullus uses iambic trimeters, the metre of Sulpicia's surviving fragment, in three of his poems (4, 29 and 52). Bardon (1956) 227 wrongly believes that Sulpicia wrote in elegiac distichs (he does not mention the pre-served fragment). In assessing her erotic vocabulary Parker (1992) 93–4 adds amatory words found in Martial's epigrams about her (10.35 and 38), such as *lusus, delicias, facetias, proelia, pugnas* and *felix lectulus*, to the words Sulpicia actually uses in her surviving fragment, arguing that with these words Martial echoes her poetry. This is perhaps possible, but on account of lack of evidence it remains highly speculative. Hallett (1992) 109–19 points out echoes of Propertius 2.15 both in Sulpicia's own fragment and in Mart. *Ep.* 10.35 and 38 and suggests that Sulpicia used Propertian language. Though Prop. 2.15.12–16 uses the words *nudus/a* and *concubuisse*, I think that it stretches the evidence too far to assume Propertian influence, as Hallett does, and her comparison between the couples, Calenus–Sulpicia and Propertius–Cynthia (and that between Martial's Sulpicia and Catullus' Lesbia on pp. 105–9), is, to my mind, far-fetched.

83 This may have been different in her days. For instance, the poet Lygdamus ((Tib.) 3.1–6), who is dated by Tränkle (1990) 1–3 at the end of the first century AD, wrote, or professed to write, love poetry to and about his wife Neaera (both names are pseud-onyms). However, Luck (1959) 102–6 believes that his use of *vir* (3.1.23) and *coniunx* (3.1.26 and 27) to denote himself and Neaera does not indicate that they were actually married. For the contemporary trend of adopting the language of love poetry when describing married love, see Dixon (1992b) 86–7 and chapter 3 above (p. 81).

84 For Julia Balbilla, see *PIR*² I 650, *RE* X Julia 559 cols 923–5, Cichorius (1922) 394–8, Cramer (1954) 82, 95, 136, 152–3, 161, 171–2 and 201.

85 For their journey, see Carandini (1969) 76–91, Cramer (1954) 171–3; for Egypt as a land of wonders, see Smelik and Hemelrijk (1984) 1938–45 on Roman tourists in Egypt and the Colossus of Memnon.

86 For ancient descriptions of the 'singing' statue of Memnon, see, e.g., Strabo 17.816, Plin. *NH* 36.58, Paus. 1.42.3, Juv. 15.5, Tac. *Ann.* 2.61, Philostr. *VA* 6.4, *Im.* 1.7, Lucian *Tox.* 27 and *Philops.* 33. For the visit of Septimius Severus, see *SHA Sev.* 17.4. For the religious adoration of 'Memnon', see Théodoridès, A. (1989) 'Pèlerinage au Colosse de Memnon', *CE* 64: 267–82. For a collection of the more than a hundred (!) Greek and Latin inscriptions on the Colossus of Memnon (with a French translation and commen-tary), see Bernand (1960).

87 The best edition (with a commentary and a French translation) is that of Bernand (1960) 80–98, nos 28–31, with the emendation of West, M. L. (1977) 'Balbilla did not save Memnon's soul', *ZPE* 25: 120; see further Peek (1934) 95–109, nos 1–4 (with a commentary and a German translation). A partial translation of the poems in English is given by Cramer (1954) 172–3, and two of Balbilla's poems are translated by West (1978) 107–8 and Bowie (1990) 62–3. Homeyer, H. (1979) *Dichterinnen des Altertums und des frühen Mittelalters*, Paderborn: Schoeningh provides a text and German translation of the poems of Julia Balbilla (pp. 100–5) and Caecilia Trebulla (pp. 107–9), but contains many mistakes. I shall refer to the poems according to their numbers in the edition of Bernand.

88 For the three epigrams on the left leg, see Bernand (1960) nos 28–30, especially pp. 83–4, for their conspicuous place, Bernand (1960) 10–12; for the fourth epigram: Bernand (1960) 96–8, no. 31. Sabina's inscription: Bernand (1960) 99–100, no. 32.

89 Bernand (1960) no. 28: Ἰουλίας Βαλ(β)ίλλης· ὅτε ἤκουσε τοῦ Μέμνο(νο)ς ὁ Σεβαστὸς Ἀδριανός. Μέμνονα πυνθανόμαν Αἰγύπτιον ἀλίω αὔγαι / αἰθόμενον φώνην Θηβαί(κ)ω ʼπυ λίθω. / Ἀδρίανον δ' ἐσίδων τὸν παμβασίληα πρὶν αὔγας / ἀελίω χαίρην εἶπέ (ϝ)οι ὡς δύνατον. / Τίταν δ' ὅττ' ἐλάων λεύκοισι δι' αἴθερος ἵπποις / ἐνὶ σκίαι ὡράων δεύτερον ἦχε μέτρον, / ὡς χάλκοιο τύπεντ[ο]ς ἴη Μέμνων πάλιν αὔδαν / ὀξύτονον·

χαίρω[ν κ]αὶ τρίτον ἆχον ἴη. / Κοίρανος Ἀδρίανο[ς τότ ἄ]λις δ᾽ ἀσπάσσατο καὖτος / Μέμνονα κὰν [στάλ]αι κάλλι[π]εν ὀψ[ι]γόνοις / γρόππατα σαμαίν[ον]τά τ᾽ ὄσ᾽ εὔιδε κὤσσ᾽ ἐσάκουσε. / Δῆλον παῖσι δ᾽ ἔγε [ν]τ᾽ ὢς (ϝ)ε φίλισι θέοι. Peek (1934) no. 1, *SEG* VIII no. 715. Translations of Julia Balbilla's poetry are my own. Bernand (1960) 80–6 extensively discusses problems of the text and earlier interpretations.

90 For this poem, see Bernand (1960) no. 29 ("Οτε σὺν τῇ Σεβαστῇ Σαβείνῃ ἐγενόμην παρὰ τῷ Μέμνονι) and the discussion on pp. 86–92; see also Peek (1934) 96–8, no. 2.

91 Bernand (1960) 93–6, no. 30 ("Οτε τῇ πρώτῃ ἡμέρᾳ οὐκ ἀκούσαμεν τοῦ Μέμνονος); Peek (1934) 98–9, no. 3, *SEG* VIII no. 717.

92 Bernand (1960) 96–8, no. 31 and Peek (1934) 99–100, no. 4. At the end of the poem two dates are mentioned: 20 and 21 November. Peek ascribes this to an error of the stonecutter, but Bernand argues that the second date, 21 November, was the day Balbilla heard Memnon alone, which, in his opinion, is commemorated in this poem. Though I agree with Bernand that Balbilla probably returned to the statue alone on that day, she does not explicitly describe hearing him alone or hearing him twice, once with Sabina and once alone. In my opinion she returned to the statue to commemorate privately her experience of the previous day; for comparable examples of private commemorations, most of them in prose, see Bernand (1960) nos 2, 4, 5, 8, 34, 35, 79.

93 Bernand (1960) 83–5 and 98.

94 Bernand (1960) no. 33; for discussion of the obscure expression that Memnon greeted Hadrian the first time 'as well as he could', ὡς δύνατον (no. 28.4), see Bernand (1960) 85.

95 Cramer (1954) 172–3 in a superficial treatment of Balbilla's poetry suggests that on the first day Memnon had kept silent only to Sabina and Balbilla, who had come to hear him together, which owing to the obscurity of the text remains equally possible. Both in Bernand's and in Cramer's reconstruction we need more days to account for the failure to hear Memnon on the first day on the one hand and the separate greetings to Hadrian (Bernand 28) and to Sabina and Balbilla (Bernand 29–32) on the other. As Memnon only performed at sunrise we may expect him to speak only once a day or perhaps twice briefly in succession. The latter may have happened at Sabina's visit; in her own commemoration of the event (Bernand no. 32) she writes that she heard Memnon twice during the first hour (for the hour see Bernand no. 31.4). Hadrian seems to have heard him twice in the second hour (Bernand no. 28.6 and no. 33). For other visitors who heard Memnon twice or even three times within an hour, see Bernand nos 9, 15, 18 and 47.

96 See Bernand no. 28.3 and 12, 30.5–8.

97 See Bernand no. 29.6: τὰν σέμναν ἄλοχον κοιράνω Ἀδριάνω; no. 30.2 speaks about the 'beautiful Sabina' (κάλα ... Σάβιννα) and her 'lovely appearance' (line 3, ἐράτα μόρφα), 31.3 about the 'beloved empress Sabina' (ἐράται βασιλήιδι ... Σαβίννᾳ).

98 Bowie (1990) 62; modern judgement of her poetry is mostly negative; see, e.g., Cramer (1954) 173, Peek (1934) 95–6, 101–2. Bernand (1960) 80–98 and West (1978) 106–7 are less negative.

99 For examples of Greek amateur poetry of the time see, e.g., Bowie (1989) and (1990).

100 Also Pausanias 1.42.3 gives both names: Memnon and Phamenoph. For the Egyptian name of the Colossus, see Bernand (1960) no. 29.3–4: 'Amenooth, the Egyptian king, as the priests say, who are expedient in the ancient myths' (Ἀμένωθ, βασίλευ Αἰγύπτιε, τὼς 'νέποισιν / ἴρηες μύθων τῶν παλάων ἴδριες) and no. 31.2: Φαμένωθ, both indicating King Amenophis III; for the myths concerning Memnon, see, e.g., Bernand no. 28.1–2; 29.1–2; 31.2; for the story about Cambyses mutilating the statue, Bernand no. 29.7–10. This tradition, which ascribed the destruction of the statue (which in fact had been caused by an earthquake) to the hated conqueror of

Egypt, Cambyses, is also attested in some other inscriptions on the Colossus; see Bernand nos 72 and 94 (by another woman poet, Caecilia Trebulla) and in Pausanias 1.42.3. The novelty of Balbilla's representation of this tradition lies in its connection with the death of Cambyses and his killing of Apis, which is told by, among others, Herodotus III.29, 30 and 64. For a discussion of the ancient tradition of Cambyses as the cruel tyrant and his killing of Apis, see Smelik and Hemelrijk (1984) 1864–9.

101 As far as I know, no other poet has written in Aeolic after Theocritus (third century BC), who composed four poems (nos 28–31) in the dialect of Sappho and Alcaeus; see Gow, A. S. F. (1950) *Theocritus*, vol. I, Cambridge: Cambridge University Press, pp. LXXVII–LXXX. For a detailed discussion of Balbilla's use of the Aeolic-Lesbian dialect (words, spelling and inflexion) and of words and expressions derived from Homer, see Bernand (1960) 84, 89–90, 95, 97–8 and Peek (1934) 96–102; for her posing as a second Sappho, West (1978) 106–8. Thumb, A. and Scherer, A. (1959²) *Handbuch der griechischen Dialekte*, Heidelberg: Winters, pp. 82–3 § 252 ascribe her errors in the archaic Lesbian dialect to mistakes in the teaching of contemporary grammarians.

102 Bernand (1960) no. 29.13–18: Εὐσέβεες γὰρ ἔμοι γένεται πάπποι τ' ἐγένοντο, / Βάλβιλλός τ' ὁ σόφος κ' Ἀντίοχος βασίλευς, / Βάλβιλλος γενέταις μάτρος βασιλήιδος, ἄμμας, / τῶ πάτερος δὲ πάτηρ Ἀντίοχος βασίλευς· / κήνων ἐκ γενέας κἄγω λόχον αἷμα τὸ κᾶλον, / Βαλβίλλας δ' ἔμεθεν γρόπτα τάδ' εὐσέβε[ος]. For a discussion of her descent, see Bernand (1960) 90–2. The mutilation of the text has led to other, less convincing, reconstructions; see, e.g., Peek (1934) 98, who believes that Balbillus was Balbilla's father and not her grandfather. According to Spawforth (1978) 249–60 Balbilla was also, more distantly, related to members of the leading élite of Greece, notably Herculanus of Sparta and Herodes Atticus of Athens.

103 For her father C. Iulius Antiochus Epiphanes, who, though no ruling king himself as the kingdom of Commagene was annexed in AD 72 by Vespasian and incorporated into Syria, bore the honorary title of king, see *PIR*² I 150, *RE* X Iulius 66 cols 159–63, *ad FOS* 441, Cramer (1954) 136–7, Halfmann (1979) 132 no. 36a, Sullivan (1977) 742 (stemma) and 795–6.

104 For Claudia Capitolina see *PIR*² C 1086, Halfmann (1979) 131–2 and Cramer (1954) 82. For the identification of the two Balbilli, the astrologer (*PIR*² B 38) and the prefect of Egypt in AD 55–9 (*PIR*² C 813), see, e.g., Cichorius (1922) 394–5, Bernand (1960) 90–1, Cramer (1954) 95 (stemma) and 115–39, Syme (1958) 508, n. 9, West (1978) 106, Demougin (1992) 447–9 no. 538. Balbillus (the prefect of Egypt) was termed by the younger Seneca 'an excellent man of most rare learning in every branch of studies' (Sen. *Q.N.* 4.2.13: 'virorum optimus perfectusque in omni litterarum genere rarissime'). Against the identification: *PIR*² B 38 and C 813 and *RE* III Claudius 82 col. 2679, Suppl. 4 col. 986 (stemma) and Suppl. 5 col. 59f.

105 For her brother Philopappus, see *PIR*² I 151, *RE* XX Philopappus 1 col. 75, Halfmann (1979) 46, 121, 131 no. 36 and Sullivan (1977) 796–7; see also Oliver, J. H. (1982) 'Roman senators from Greece and Macedonia', *Tituli* 5: 583. He was known for his literary and intellectual interest: Plutarchus addressed his treatise 'How to tell a flatterer from a friend' (*De adulatore et amico*) to Philopappus; see Plut. *Mor.* 48 E–F and 66C, and made him an interlocutor in his *Quaest. Conv.* (*Mor.* 628B). He may also be the Philopappus to whom the epic poet Capito addressed a work (see Athen. 8.350C); see also Cramer (1954) 152–3.

106 For her age, see Bernand (1960) 92, Spawforth (1978) 252, Cramer (1954) 152–3. She was probably born about AD 80 and lived till after AD 137. Lady-in-waiting: Cichorius (1922) 396, Bernand (1960) 92, Peek (1934) 102, Fein, S. (1994) *Die Beziehungen der Kaiser Trajan und Hadrian zu den 'litterati'*, Stuttgart and Leipzig: Teubner, pp. 112–14

assumes that she was part of the 'ständigen Gefolge' of the empress on the basis of the long-standing relation between her family and the imperial house, but suggests that the relation was not very intimate. Birley, A. R. (1997) *Hadrian: The Restless Emperor*, London: Routledge, p. 228 calls her 'the bosom friend of the Empress' and, surprisingly, suggests a lesbian relationship between them on the basis of the Lesbian dialect of Balbilla's poems (p. 251).

107 For Balbilla as a female court-poet, see also chapter 4, p. 119. For the social eminence of some of the Greek professional poets during the empire, see, e.g., Hardie (1983) 26–30.

108 For *comes*, first designating a man who had accompanied the emperor on a journey, but from the fourth century onwards a post or rank, see Millar (1977) 61 and 117–19; for the *comites Augusti* see also Halfmann (1986) 92–103. A *comes* was often a man of senatorial or equestrian rank, but also poets and men of learning could be *comites* of an emperor. Balbilla's father, Tib. Claudius Balbillus, seems to have been a *comes* of the emperor Claudius (see Demougin (1988) 746–51) and her possible great-grandfather Thrasyllus, poet and astrologer, is called a *comes* of Tiberius by Suet. *Aug.* 98.4; see also Halfmann (1986) 247 no. 23. Hadrian's use of *comes* and *con[tubernalis]* in his funerary oration for the elder Matidia (*CIL* XIV 3579) is probably metaphorical; according to Temporini (1978) 171 it refers to Matidia accompanying Trajan on his journeys.

109 The three Greek epigrams (iambic trimeters) inscribed on the Colossus of Memnon by a certain Caecilia Trebulla at about the same time as those of Julia Balbilla (Bernand (1960) 16–22 and 187–91, nos 92–4; West (1978) 105–6) will not be discussed here as, unfortunately, nothing is known about her. Despite her aristocratic-sounding *gentilicium* it cannot be decided whether she was an upper-class Roman woman travelling in Egypt as a 'tourist' like Julia Balbilla, or, perhaps, a well-educated woman of the upper-middle classes who lived in Egypt. Her unpretentious poems, nevertheless, testify to the spread of the fashion of writing poetry among women of the time; for an English translation, see Lefkowitz, M. R. and Fant, M. B. (1992²), *Women's Life in Greece and Rome: A Sourcebook in Translation*, London: Duckworth, p. 10.

110 For Terentia, see *RE* VA Terentia 97 cols 716–17; *FOS* 753. She was the daughter of D. Terentius Scaurianus (*RE* VA Terentius 68 cols 669–72, *PIR*¹ T 68), who had been a favourite of Trajan's and who was *consul suffectus* in AD 102 or 104. Terentia's brother, D. Terentius Gentianus (*RE* VA Terentius 48 cols 656–62; *PIR*¹ T 56), was *consul suffectus* in AD 116. Because of the *cognomen* Gentianus found in the nomenclature of the Hedii Lolliani in the second and third centuries AD it has been suggested that Terentia married L. Hedius Rufus Lollianus Avitus (*PIR*² H 39 and the stemma on p. 52), *consul suffectus* in AD 114 and proconsul of Asia under Hadrian. However, it is usually believed that another Terentia (*FOS* 754), an unknown daughter of her brother's, married the son of L. Hedius Rufus Lollianus Avitus with the same name (*PIR*² H 40; see also the stemma on p. 52), *consul ordinarius* in AD 144.

111 For Greek reports of the building of the pyramids and the hieroglyphs inscribed on them, see Herod. II.124–5 and Diod. Sic. 1.64. For the inscriptions on the pyramids, the mediaeval visitors and the demolition of the outer coating of the pyramids, see Mommsen in *CIL* III 21, Letronne (1848) 487–518 and especially Graefe (1984) and (1990). The demolition of the limestone coating started in the twelfth century with the small pyramids, in the second half of the fourteenth century the great Pyramid of Cheops followed and in the seventeenth century a start was made with the demolition of those of Chephren and Mykerinos. Only the coating was taken off because of the fine quality of its limestone. Some blocks may still be found in the mosques and other great buildings of Cairo, but most of them probably disappeared in the limekilns. Von Boldensele reports that the poem was inscribed on one of the two great pyramids (the

Pyramid of Cheops or that of Chephren); Graefe (1984) 574f. convincingly argues for that of Cheops. For the two Greek inscriptions that have come down to us, see Letronne (1848) 514–16, Graefe (1984) 570 and (1990) 14.

112 *CIL* III 21 and 6625, *ILS* 1046a, *CLE* 270, Smallwood (1966) no. 237b. For a discussion of the text, see *RE* VA Terentius 48b cols 657–8, Letronne (1848) 516–17, Graefe (1984) 570–4 and (1990) 14–15. The translation is my own. I follow Bücheler's reading of the text (*CLE* 270), who emended the text given by Mommsen (*CIL* III 21, *ILS* 1046a; based on Von Boldensele's copy with small emendations where the text was unintelligible) in two important respects: he reads 'sic' instead of 'sit' (line 4) and 'exstet' instead of 'esse' (line 6), thus providing a text that is understandable and written in correct Latin: 'Vidi pyramidas sine te, dulcissime frater, / et tibi, quod potui, lacrimas hic maesta profudi, / et nostri memorem luctus hanc sculpo querelam. / Sic nomen Decimi [G]entia[n]i pyramide alta, / pontificis comitisque tuis, Trajane, triumphis / lustra[que] sex intra censoris, consulis, exst[et.' Von Boldensele's copy is probably incomplete and not all corruptions can be emended with certainty. It is a pity that the name of Decimus Gentianus is one of the details that may have been difficult to read for him as the manuscripts of Von Boldensele's account give the meaningless 'centi anni' or 'centanni'. Mommsen's emendation to 'Gentiani' has been generally accepted. Some fifteenth-century pilgrims, who pretend to give their own transcription of the poem, probably copied that of Von Boldensele (see Graefe (1984) 571). However, Friedländer, L. (1874³) *Darstellungen aus der Sittengeschichte Roms in der Zeit von August bis zum Ausgang der Antonine*, Leipzig: Hirzel, vol. 2, pp. 256–7 proposes to adopt the reading 'pyramis' of one of these fifteenth-century pilgrims, Felix Fabri, instead of 'pyramide' in line 4 and suggests the emendation 'scit' for 'sit' reading: 'Scit nomen Decimi [G]entia[n]i pyramis alta, ', 'the high pyramid knows the name of Decimus Gentianus'. For our inquiry these variants and emendations are of no importance.

113 Most studies mentioning the poem assume that a sister of Terentius Gentianus' composed it, but Graefe (1984) 574 overlooking the feminine ending of the adjective 'maesta' (line 2), suggests that it may have been written by a brother of Gentianus.

114 For the view that Terentia accompanied Hadrian and Sabina on their trip to Egypt, see, e.g., Syme (1984) 50–1. Her brother Terentius Gentianus was a favourite of Trajan's and, at first, also of Hadrian's, and had a brilliant career attaining most ranks before the legal age: born about AD 89–90 he was successively a military tribune, quaestor, tribune of the people, praetor, legatus Augusti, *consul suffectus* (AD 116) and pontifex, and in AD 120 he governed Macedonia as a *censitor* (Syme (1984) 50, *CIL* III 1463 = *ILS* 1046, *AE* (1924) 57 and (1936) 97). We do not hear from him since and he apparently died before his sister's journey to Egypt. According to *SHA Hadr.* 23.5 he eventually fell into disfavour with Hadrian. This seems to have happened after Hadrian's tour of the provinces (see *SHA* 23.1: 'Peragratis sane omnibus orbis partibus', but perhaps the short period between his western and his eastern tour is meant) and may possibly be connected with Hadrian's illness in AD 136. Though the account of the *Historia Augusta* is usually accepted, it seems not impossible that Gentianus died from an unknown cause and that his early death gave rise to unfounded suspicions. Bücheler *CLE* 270 suggests that the Gentianus who fell into disfavour with Hadrian was a son of the Gentianus commemorated in this poem. For Gentianus' career, see, e.g., Syme (1984) 50–1, Eck (1970) 12, n. 54 and 184–90, and Schumacher, L. (1973) 'Prosopographische Untersuchungen zur Besetzung der vier hohen römischen Priesterkollegien im Zeitalter der Antonine und der Severer (96–235 n. Chr.)', Mainz (diss.), pp. 213–14.

115 Despite Augustus' prohibition Egypt was quite frequently visited by persons of senatorial rank who received imperial permission to visit their Egyptian possessions, see

Hohlwein, N. (1940) 'Déplacements et tourisme dans l'Egypte Romaine', *CE* 15: 253–78.

116 For similar expressions of regret for the absence of loved ones in the commemoration of a visit to the Colossus of Memnon, see Bernand (1960) nos 92, 98 and 99.

117 That it may have been regarded as presumptuous to draw attention to her brother's brilliant career by inscribing a memorial poem on an Egyptian pyramid may perhaps be inferred from the fate of C. Cornelius Gallus (the first prefect of Egypt, *RE* IV Cornelius 164 cols 1342–50), who was punished by Augustus among other things for having a list of his achievements inscribed upon one of the pyramids (Dio 53.23).

118 Cf. Ovid *Fast.* 5.472, in which the ghost of Remus speaks about the grief of his brother Romulus: 'quod potuit, lacrimas manibus ille dedit' ('he gave to my departed soul – 'twas all he could – his tears'). More remotely connected is Catul. 68.149–50, in which Catullus sends a poem to a friend as a consolation (for the loss of his wife?) and as a thank-offering for all that he has done for him: 'hoc tibi, quod potui, confectum carmine munus / pro multis, Alli, redditur officiis' ('This is my gift – 'twas all I could – composed in verse and meant as a token of gratitude to you, Allius, for your numerous services'). One of the themes of this complex poem is the grief of Catullus himself at the recent death of his brother. Hor. *Carm.* 3.11.51–2: 'et nostri memorem sepulcro / scalpe querellam' shows a striking verbal similarity to Terentia's: 'et nostri memorem luctus hanc sculpo querelam' (line 3). Horace's ode deals with the legend of Hypermnestra, who, disobeying her father's command, refused to slay her husband, and nephew, Lynceus. In Ovid *Her.* 14, Hypermnestra calls Lynceus her 'brother' (in lines 117, 122 and 130). In both poems, however, it is the woman who dies and who asks her husband (whom she also calls her 'brother') to inscribe an epitaph for her (Ovid *Her.* 14.128 and Hor. *Carm.* 3.11.51–2).

119 This also holds for other female poets discussed in this chapter, as far as we know their work; cf. Cornificia (epigrams). Perhaps an exception should be made for the hymns which were written by the puzzling (Greek) poetesses Memmia Timothoe and Melinno, but they are not discussed here (see resp. n. 6 and n. 138). As we have seen (p. 163), the satire attributed to Sulpicia Caleni is a composition of much later date falsely transmitted under her name; but because of the survival of only two lines of her work we cannot be sure of the genre(s) she worked in. According to Propertius 1.9.11ff. and 2.34.31ff. women preferred love poetry to epic, but this opinion may be caused by his own refusal to write an epic. In the traditional hierarchy of genres of Latin poetry epic was valued highest, immediately followed by tragedy, and didactic and lyric poetry were valued above elegy, epigram and satire. Lowest in esteem were mime and fable. For the poetic challenge of the dominant genre of epic by what were considered minor genres, see Sullivan, J. P. (1993) 'Form opposed: elegy, epigram, satire', in Boyle, A. J. (ed.) *Roman Epic*, London: Routledge, pp. 143–61.

120 For Sempronia see chapter 3, pp. 84ff.

121 Cic. *Cael.* 64: 'veteris et plurimarum fabularum poetriae' alluding to a mime; see also *Cael.* 65 and Wiseman (1985) 28. For Clodia Metelli, see *RE* IV Clodia 66 cols 105–7, Wiseman (1985) 15–53 and Skinner (1983). She was the elder sister of the notorious P. Clodius Pulcher and the wife of Q. Caecilius Metellus Celer (*cos* 60 BC), who died in 59 BC. She belonged to a family of the highest nobility which was connected with many of the most powerful families of Rome; see Wiseman (1985) 15–20. About her two sisters, the widow of Marcius Rex (*RE* IV Clodia 72 col. 108) and the notorious Clodia Luculli (*RE* IV Clodia 67 col. 107), much less is known.

122 Wiseman (1985) 26–38; Rawson (1985) 47, n. 41 is, to my mind rightly, sceptical.

123 Cic. *Sest.* 116: 'sororis embolia', 'the pantomimic interludes of his sister'; pantomimic or balletic interludes were performed between the acts of a play. Wiseman (1985)

27–8 imagines Clodia in the role of a librettist of pantomime, but according to the scholiast it refers to her dancing in it; cf. *Schol. Bob.* 135–6 (Stangl) and see chapter 3, n. 126. By referring to mime and pantomime Cicero associates Clodia with sexual licentiousness both because of the scurrilous contents of (panto)mime and because in mime the parts of women were often played by *meretrices*. For Cicero's invective against Clodia in his *Pro Caelio*, see also chapter 3, pp. 85 and 90. For a sobering assessment of Clodia Metelli, based on the letters of Cicero, see Skinner (1983).

124 Although the portraits of Sempronia and Clodia may to a certain extent be regarded as literary, they represent real women who were well known in their time and therefore they must have been sufficiently true to life. Wiseman (1985) 28 suggests that the theme of sexual immorality in the portraits of Sempronia by Sallust and that of Clodia by Cicero in his *Pro Caelio* may have been partly inspired by the type of the 'wealthy matron with the morals of a whore', a familiar character in contemporary mime. But apart from their supposed lack of morals Sempronia and, less explicitly, Clodia were known for much the same cultural and intellectual accomplishments as the *puellae* of the love poets, such as versifying, lyre-playing, dancing, and conversing with wit and facility. For similar (though rather far-fetched) comparisons between historical women and elegiac *puellae*, see Verdière, R. (1971) 'Un amour secret d'Ovide', *AC* 40: 623–48 about Ovid's Corinna and Maecenas' wife Terentia. Also Horace's 'Licymnia' (*Carm.* 2.12.13–28) has been identified with Maecenas' wife Terentia; see Syme (1978) 201 and Williams, G. (1962) 'Poetry in the moral climate of Augustan Rome', *JRS* 52: 35–8, who argues that Horace's ode praising Licymnia dancing, though intended as a compliment to Maecenas' wife Terentia, is determined by poetic convention and bears no relation to the realities of Terentia's life. The identification is rejected by Davis, G. (1975) 'The *persona* of Licymnia: a revaluation of Horace, *Carm.* 2.12', *Philologus* 119: 70–83.

125 For Lesbia as a pseudonym for one of the three sisters of the notorious P. Clodius Pulcher, see Wiseman (1985) 130–7. This identification is corroborated by Catullus' poems: Catullus portrays Lesbia as a noblewoman ranking above him; see Wiseman (1985) 158–64. Moreover, Catul. 79.1, 'Lesbius est pulcher', probably is a pun on the name of her brother, Clodius Pulcher; see, e.g. Skinner (1982) 197. The poem contains allusions to an incestuous relationship between Clodius and Clodia, which was common gossip at the time; see the obscene verses about Clodius and Clodia chanted in the theatre by Milo's supporters, Cic. *Q. F.* 2.3.2. Wiseman (1969) 52–5 argues that the charge of incest was first levelled at the youngest sister, Clodia Luculli (cf. Cic. *Mil.* 73, Plut. *Lucull.* 38, *Caes.* 10; in Plut. *Cic.* 29.4–5 all three of his sisters are included) and later transferred by Cicero to Clodia Metelli (see, for instance, Cic. *Cael.* 32, 36 and 78, *Dom.* 92, *Sest.* 16, 39 and 116, *Har. Resp.* 38 and 39); see also Skinner (1982) 205. For doubts about the identification with Clodia Metelli, see Wiseman (1969) 50–60, (1974) 104–14 and (1985) 1–2, 136, 211–18, who argues that at the time of the composition of Catullus' poetry, which he dates between 56 and 54 BC, Clodia Metelli was a widow whereas Lesbia is portrayed as a married woman. In his view, one of Clodia's younger sisters, the widow of Marcius Rex (since 61 BC) or the divorcee of Lucullus (since 66 BC), may have remarried at that date and, therefore, has a better claim to be the woman behind the pseudonym. However, there is no evidence of a remarriage and other scholars defend the traditional identification of Lesbia with Clodia Metelli; see, e.g., Skinner (1982) 197 and (1983) 274. 'Delia' and 'Cynthia' refer to Apollo because the island Delos was sacred to Apollo (hence Delius as one of the names of Apollo; see Tib. 3.4.79) and the Cynthos is the mountain on Delos (hence Apollo Cynthius; see Prop. 2.34.80). For Cynthia's poetry, see Prop. 1.2.27: 'cum tibi praesertim Phoebus sua carmina donet', 'so most of all, when Phoebus blesses you with his gift of song' and Prop. 2.3.21–2.

126 Apparently Sidonius Apollinaris thought so, as he wrote in his letter to Hesperius (*Ep.* 2.10.6) that 'Corinna often helped her Naso to complete a verse, and so it was with Lesbia and Catullus, Caesennia and Gaetulicus, Argentaria and Lucan, Cynthia and Propertius, Delia and Tibullus' ('saepe versum Corinna cum suo Nasone complevit, Lesbia cum Catullo, Caesennia cum Gaetulico, Argentaria cum Lucano, Cynthia cum Propertio, Delia cum Tibullo'); perhaps Sidonius Apollinaris took Mart. *Ep.* 8.73 (about the poetic inspiration provided by Cynthia, Lycoris, Nemesis, Lesbia, Corinna and Alexis for their poet-lovers) literally.

127 In AD 158 Apuleius defending his own use of pseudonyms (for boys) in his erotic poems gives, as though it were common knowledge, a list of famous pseudonyms of Latin love poetry: 'let them then accuse C. Catullus for calling Clodia Lesbia, and similarly Ticidas for writing Perilla instead of Metella, and Propertius because he names Cynthia and thereby conceals Hostia, and Tibullus because having Plania in mind he wrote Delia in his verses' (Apuleius *Apol.* 10: 'accusent C. Catullum, quod Lesbiam pro Clodia nominarit, et Ticidam similiter, quod quae Metella erat Perillam scripserit, et Propertium, qui Cynthiam dicat, Hostiam dissimulet, et Tibullum, quod ei sit Plania in animo, Delia in versu'). These 'real' names are metrically equivalent to the pseudonyms, as seems to have been the habit of Latin poets when choosing a pseudonym. The identifications are repeated in most of the older studies and commentaries. For a discussion of this view and of the identity and social status of the mistresses, see Lilja (1965) 23–30 and 35–42, who maintains that real women are hidden behind the poetical *personae* created by the poets (their poetry, in her view, is a mixture of real experiences and imagination). For a (somewhat prejudiced) survey of the biographical approach to Latin love elegy, see Wyke (1987a) 47–9 and (1989b) 113–17.

128 Cynthia, for example, has been called a freedwoman, a woman of noble family, a married woman, a *meretrix* and a foreigner; see Griffin (1985) 27–8. For a cautious attempt, see Syme (1978) 200–3: on pp. 202–3 he mentions a Hostius, an epic poet, who may have been Cynthia's (read Hostia's) *doctus avus* (Prop. 3.20.8) and suggests that Plania may have belonged to a 'Campanian family of some note in foreign commerce'. But all this is hypothetical. For a survey of various views on this matter, see Lilja (1965) 35–42, who suggests that the love elegists deliberately left the social status of their mistresses in the dark; see also Hinds (1987) 33. Hallett (1984a) defends the theory of inversion of contemporary reality in Latin love poetry, arguing that Latin love elegy challenged the reigning standards of behaviour by turning conventional gender roles upside down and ascribing to their mistresses qualities conventionally proper to Roman men. Yet, her approach is firmly 'realist': in her view the poets and their elegiac mistresses represented a 'counter-cultural' life-style. See also the discussion between A. Betensky and J. P. Hallett in *Arethusa* 6 (1973) 267–9 and 7 (1974) 211–19.

129 For this view see especially Wyke (1987a), (1987b), (1989a) and (1989b), who, speaking of the poetry of Ovid and Propertius, argues that poetic conventions and not biographical reality determine the 'construction' of the elegiac mistress. For example, Cynthia is not a poeticized girlfriend, but 'part of a poetic language of love' ((1989a) 35); no pseudonym for a woman of flesh and blood, but a poetic fiction and a 'symbol of her author's practice of writing' ((1987b) 173). Also Veyne, P. (1983) *L'Elégie érotique romaine: l'amour, la poésie et l'occident*, Paris: Seuil, pp. 9–23 draws attention to the ambiguity of 'Cynthia', both the heroine and the title of the book, and argues that she is a poetic fiction and a metaphor of Propertius' published books of poetry.

130 Rigorous application of this point of view makes historical inquiry impossible; see Versnel, H. S. (1990) *Ter Unus. Isis, Dionysus, Hermes. Three Studies in Henotheism: Inconsistencies in Greek and Roman Religion I*, Leiden: Brill, pp. 30–2.

131 Griffin (1976), (1977) and (1985) 1–64: with numerous examples Griffin elucidates the mutual interaction between 'literature' and 'life' and the intermingling of poetic motifs and actual behaviour: poetic motifs taken from the experiences of life and literature affecting actual behaviour (as, for instance, exemplified in the 'Propertian life' of Marc Antony; see Griffin (1977) 17–26 = (1985) 32–47; I do not agree with his opinion that the mistresses of love poetry are, in fact, *meretrices* raised to the level of art; see '*Meretrices*, matrimony and myth', in Griffin (1985) 112–41).

132 For the fashion of writing amateur poetry among upper-class men, see, e.g., Hor. *Epist.* 2.1.108–17; see also White (1975) and (1993) 24–5, Harris (1989) 222–3, Williams (1978) 275ff. and Hardie (1983) 41, 70, 72 and 172–4; for statues and portraits of upper-class Romans of the empire posing as poets, see Zanker (1995) 201ff. For some well-known examples of men of the senatorial class writing amateur poetry (mainly epigrams): Cicero (see, e.g., Plut. *Cic.* 2 and references to his poems in his letters such as *Q. Fr.* 2.9.1, 2.15a.2, 2.16.5, 3.1.11; see further Schanz-Hosius (1927) 535–8, Bardon (1952) 367) and Pliny, who refers to his hobby of writing light verse in many of his letters from the fourth book onwards: see, e.g., *Ep.* 5.3 and 7.4, in which he defends himself against attacks of frivolousness for writing verses and reciting them to friends (Sherwin-White (1966) 33); see also Apuleius *Apol.* 5–12; for a parody of the fashion: Petronius *Sat.* 55. Also some emperors composed poetry, e.g., Augustus (Suet. *Aug* 85; for his verses, see Bardon (1940) 14–22), Tiberius (Suet. *Tib.* 70), Nero (Suet. *Nero* 52, Tac. *Ann.* 13.3), Hadrian (*SHA Hadr.* 14 and 25; Bardon (1940) 393–424) and Marcus Aurelius (Fronto *Ad M. Caes.* 1.8.6 = Haines I, pp. 124–5 and 2.10.2 = Haines I, pp. 138–9).

133 For the connection between grammatical education and the writing of poetry, see, e.g., Suet. *Gramm.* 11 and White (1993) 287–8, n. 38. According to Nachtergael, G. (1980) *Dans les classes d'Egypte d'après les papyrus scolaires grecs*, Brussels: Ministère de l' éducation nationale (Documents Pédagogiques 23), pp. 24–5 Greek papyri show that at the end of their study of grammar pupils in imperial Egypt were expected to be able to write an epigram in the language and style of Homer.

134 For ridicule of literary dilettantism among upper-class women, see Lucian's *Merc. Cond.* 36. Persius *Prol.* 13 contemptuously calls the poets and poetesses of his days 'raven poets and magpie poetesses' ('corvos poetas et poetridas picas'), hinting at their love of money and their poor imitation of great poetry, but this may refer to professional poets (and poetesses, or should we believe them to be effeminate men?) who wrote poetry for money. Zanker (1995) 204 believes that the famous painted portrait from Pompeii of a Roman lady with a pencil and writing-tablets (see chapter 3, pp. 73ff. and plate 2) should be interpreted as a female amateur poet, but this seems unwarranted.

135 Sen. *Contr.* 6.8: 'Virgo Vestalis scripsit hunc versum: Felices nuptae! Moriar nisi nubere dulce est. Rea est incesti'.

136 H. Bornecque in the Budé-edition (1932) believes that the case may have been inspired by Livy's account of the Vestal Postumia (Liv. 4.44.11–12), who was accused of unchastity because she dressed well and talked rather more freely and wittily than a virgin should; and Bonner, S. F. (1969²) *Roman Declamation in the Late Republic and Early Empire*, Liverpool: Liverpool University Press, p. 33, suggests that Crassus' defence of the Vestal Licinia in 113 BC may have been its source, but neither of these Vestals is reported to have written verse. If the story is not fictitious, it seems more likely that Seneca, who was known for his prodigious memory, quoted a real case which happened during his lifetime.

137 With the exception of the poem by Terentia the *Carmina Latina Epigraphica* are not discussed here because of the scarcity of biographical data provided in the inscriptions and the complicated problem of the authorship of the poems: in most cases

certainty cannot be attained whether the person who set up the stone or had the poem inscribed (among whom were some upper-class women) was also the person who had composed the poem. For discussion of this problem see Zarker, J. W. (1958) 'Studies in the Carmina Latina Epigraphica', Ann Arbor (diss.), pp. 57–133 and Cugusi, P. (1985) *Aspetti letterari dei carmina latina epigraphica*, Bologna: Patron, pp. 21–90. Pikhaus, D. (1985) 'Literaire bedrijvigheid in de provincies: de *Carmina latina epigraphica* uit Romeins Afrika (Ie–VIe eeuw)', *Handelingen der Koninklijke Zuidnederlandse Maatschappij voor Taal- en Letterkunde en Geschiedenis* 39: 157–77 rejects the theory that the stone-cutters' workshops had manuals or handbooks with examples of poetry from which customers could select a poem suitable for the occasion. It seems possible, though hard to prove, that some upper-class women dedicating the inscription were also themselves the authors of the poems; see, for example, *CIL* I^2 3339, *CIL* VI 2160 and *CIL* IX 3158 (*commatica*: mixtures of prose and poetry). I thank Dorothy Pikhaus for these references.

138 For Julia Balbilla see pp. 164ff. Also several other Greek poetesses referred to Sappho's verses, or imitated her metre or dialect, as a poetic tribute to her, but with the exception of Julia Balbilla they do not concern us here. For Greek women poets (such as Erinna and Nossis) who recall Sappho's poetry in their language or themes or refer to her in some other way, see West (1978) 101–4 (though he seems too positive as regards possible Aeolisms in their poetry), Barnard, S. (1978) 'Hellenistic women poets', *CJ* 73: 204–13 and Skinner (1993). For a brief survey of Greek poetesses in the fourth century BC and the Hellenistic period, see Pomeroy (1977) 54–7. For allusions to Sappho in the poetry of Nossis, see Skinner (1991) 20–47, who argues that Sappho served as Nossis' main literary model. Later tradition associated these Greek women poets with Sappho by falsely presenting Lesbos or Mytilene as their place of birth, or by wrongly assuming that they were Sappho's pupils or contemporaries, which again indicates that there was felt to be a tradition of female poetry somehow connected with Sappho: Suidas s.v. Ἤριννα mentions 'Lesbian' as one of the possible nation-alities of Erinna and assumes that she was one of Sappho's companions, and the manuscripts of the Greek Anthology refer to her as 'Erinna the Mytilenaean' (cf. the lemma to *AP* 7.710). Also Nossis and Anyte were associated with Sappho: the lemma to *AP* 9.332 refers to Nossis as 'Nossis of Lesbos' and at *AP* 7.718 she is called 'the companion of Sappho of Mytilene' and in the lemma to *AP* 7.492 Anyte is called 'Anyte of Mytilene'. Also the Greek poetess Melinno seems to have taken Sappho as her model: her hymn to Rome, preserved by Stobaeus *Ecl.* 3.7.12 (III, p. 312 Hense), is composed in Sapphic stanzas (a metre obsolete in Greek poetry after the days of Sappho and Alcaeus, though revived in Latin poetry by Catullus and Horace) and contains reminiscences of Sappho's Lesbian dialect; see West (1978) 102–4 (*contra RE* 15 cols 521–3: 'Dorian'; Bowra, C. M. (1957) 'Melinno's hymn to Rome', *JRS* 47: 21–8 finds only faint echoes of the Lesbian dialect in her poem). As transmitted in the manuscripts her hymn is attributed to Melinno of Lesbos (!): Μελιννοῦς Λεσβίας εἰς Ῥώμην.

139 Cf. Plut. *Quaest. Conv.* 7.8.2 (*Mor.* 711D) and Aul. Gell. *NA* 19.9.4.

140 For Sappho as one of the Muses or the tenth Muse, see, e.g., *AP* 7.14 (the mortal Muse), and 407, 9.26 (a 'canon' of nine Greek poetesses portrayed as the nine worldly Muses), 66, 506 and 571, Catul. 35.16–17, Prop. 2.30.37ff.; also in Plut. *Amatorius* 18 (*Mor.* 762F) Sappho is associated with the Muses. For Sappho as the female counter-part of Homer, see *AP* 7.15: 'My name is Sappho, and I excelled all women in song as much as Maeonides [Homer] excelled men' (Οὔνομά μευ Σαπφώ. τόσσον δ' ὑπερέσχον ἀοιδὰν / θηλειᾶν, ἀνδρῶν ὅσσον ὁ Μαιονίδας), but also other Greek poetesses were occasionally compared to Homer: cf. *AP* 9.26 (Anyte) and 9.190 (Erinna). For Sappho's reputation in Greek and Roman literature, see, e.g., McIntosh

Snyder (1989) 4–13. For Sappho's influence on Catullus' poetry (notably his poem 51), see Wiseman (1985) 144–54 and Jenkyns, R. (1982) *Three Classical Poets: Sappho, Catullus and Juvenal*, London: Duckworth, pp. 20f. and 44–53.

141 In an inverse sense the compliment was played upon in a (Greek) poem of Philodemus of Gadara written in Rome about 70 BC (*AP* 5.132). In it Philodemus praises the physical qualities of an Italian girl named Flora (perhaps the same as the famous courtesan and once the mistress of Pompey) and excuses her lack of culture with the words: 'and if she is Oscan [i.e. uncultured] and Flora and does not sing Sappho' (εἰ δ' Ὀπικὴ καὶ Φλῶρα καὶ οὐκ ᾄδουσα τὰ Σαπφοῦς). I do not agree with the translation of the Loeb edition, which translates Ὀπικὴ as 'Italian'; since Ὀπικὴ has the connotation of 'barbarous' and 'uncultured'; cf. Juv. 3.207 and 6. 455, Plin. *NH* 29.14 and Fronto *Ad M. Caes.* 1.8.7 (Haines I, pp. 124–5). For a discussion of the poem see Cohen, S. J. D. (1981) 'The beauty of Flora and the beauty of Sarai', *Helios* 8: 41–53.

142 For 'Lesbia' as a complimentary pseudonym referring to Sappho, see, e.g., Lilja (1965) 142, Pomeroy (1977) 66, n. 40 and Wiseman (1985) 135–6. For Corinna's appreciation of poetry, see Ovid *Am.* 3.8.5–7.

143 Catul. 35.16–17: 'Sapphica puella/ Musa doctior'. The puzzling expression 'Sapphica Musa' may indicate the poetry of Sappho or refer to the custom of calling Sappho the tenth Muse. The anonymous girlfriend is depicted as head-over-heels in love with Caecilius from the moment she read his poem on Magna Mater, a poem which, according to Copley, F. O. (1953) 'Catullus 35', *AJPh* 74: 149–60, Catullus considers promising, but unfinished and in need of reworking. Therefore, his extravagant compliment to her poetic taste and judgement seems somewhat ironical. Fisher, J. M. (1971) 'Catullus 35', *CPh* 66: 1–5 takes the *puella* for a metaphor for the writing of love poetry.

144 Prop 2.3.21–2: 'et sua cum antiquae committit scripta Corinnae,/ carminaque Erinnes non putat aequa suis'. 'Erinnes' or 'Erinnae' is an emendation; the text 'quae quivis', transmitted in some of the manuscripts, is accepted in the Budé edition by D. Paganelli (Paris 1947, repr. 1961) who translates: 'je la vois se mesurer à l'antique Corinne et poétesse sans égale affirmer sa maîtrise'. Prop. 2.3.19: 'when she tries songs to the Aeolian lyre' ('Aeolio cum temptat carmina plectro') alludes to Sappho ('Aeolio' refers to the Aeolian poets, Sappho and Alcaeus), but, perhaps, Propertius does not portray Cynthia as writing poetry, but as singing Sappho's (or perhaps Alcaeus') poems to the lyre; also Prop. 2.30.37–40 representing Cynthia as one of the Muses, a compliment usually reserved for Sappho, perhaps indirectly compares her to Sappho.

145 For Sappho's reputation for licentiousness in both homosexual and heterosexual love, see, e.g., Dover, K. J. (1980) *Greek Homosexuality*, New York: Vintage Books, p. 174, McIntosh Snyder (1989) 8ff. and Skinner (1991) 36.

146 For Perilla, see Ovid. *Trist.* 3.7.20: 'sola tuum vates Lesbia vincet opus'. For her chastity: *Trist.* 3.7.13: 'mores . . . pudicos'; see also lines 3–4 portraying Perilla as usually to be found with her mother or amongst her books. For Sulpicia, see [Tib.] 3.8.24: 'dignior est vestro nulla puella choro'.

147 Mart. *Ep.* 7.69. The first line of the poem suggests that it was written to accompany a portrait of Theophila: 'this is Theophila your promised bride, Canius' ('Haec est illa tibi promissa Theophila, Cani'). For her knowledge of Greek culture and philosophy: 7.69.2–4; for her 'unwomanlike' literary judgement: 'non femineum . . . sapit' (line 6). For Canius, probably the poet Canius Rufus from Gades (also mentioned by Martial at, e.g., *Ep.* 1.61.9; 3.20; 7.87.2 and 10.48), see *PIR*[2] C 397 and *RE* III col. 1483; he was a many-sided writer who wrote elegies, epic, tragedies, fables and history; see Mart. *Ep.* 3.20.

148 Mart. *Ep.* 7.69.7–10: 'Non tua Pantaenis nimium se praeferat illi, / quamvis Pierio sit

bene nota choro. / Carmina fingentem Sappho laudabat amatrix: / castior haec et non doctior illa fuit'. The meaning of these puzzling lines, and especially the question to whom the words 'carmina fingentem' and 'illa' refer, are the subject of debate. According to the Budé edition by H. J. Izaac (Paris 1930), both refer to the unknown Pantaenis of the preceding verses, but Hallett (1992) 103, 108–9 and 119, who follows the translation of the Loeb edition by W. C. A. Ker, takes 'illa' as referring to Sappho while leaving the identity of 'carmina fingentem' undecided: 'a poetess'. Pantaenis is usually believed to be a Lesbian poetess and beloved of Sappho, unknown to us, or, because of the word 'tua' to denote Pantaenis which suggests a connection between Canius and Pantaenis, an unknown poetess admired by Canius. However, in my opinion, it seems more likely that Pantaenis was the 'title' of one of Canius' poems (cf. 'Dindymi domina' as the first words and 'title' of the poem of Catullus' friend Caecilius in Catul. 35.14). By alluding to a poem written by Canius in an epigram addressed to him, which praises the learning of his fiancée, Martial elegantly pays a compliment to both Canius and Theophila.

149 Mart. *Ep.* 35.15–18: 'hac condiscipula vel hac magistra / esses doctior et pudica, Sappho: / sed tecum pariter simulque visam / durus Sulpiciam Phaon amaret'.

150 Luc. *Merc. Cond.* 36: ἔν γάρ τι καὶ τοῦτο τῶν ἄλλων καλλωπισμάτων αὐταῖς δοκεῖ, ἢν λέγηται ὡς πεπαιδευμέναι τέ εἰσιν καὶ φιλόσοφοι καὶ ποιοῦσιν ᾄσματα οὐ πολὺ τῆς Σαπφοῦς ἀποδέοντα. For a quotation of the whole passage see chapter 2, pp. 37f. with n. 74.

151 Cf. Skinner (1991) 34: Sappho as an 'enabling precedent' for the eroticism in Nossis' poetry.

152 As regards the importance of a Roman audience for the survival of a literary work, see Kenney (1982) 10 and Dowden, K. (1994) 'The Roman audience of *The Golden Ass*', in Tatum (1994) 419–34.

153 Watts, W. J. (1971) 'The birthplaces of Latin writers', *G & R* n.s. 18: 91–101 shows that almost all (male) Latin writers of note were born in the Italian towns or the western provinces (Spain, Africa, Gaul) and at some time during their lives moved to Rome, where they wrote at least part of their work. For the survival of their work it was imperative that it addressed a Roman audience, not only a provincial one.

154 For the importance of public libraries for the preservation of literary texts, see Clift (1945) 25 and Kenney (1982) 23–7. The latter points out that the early monastic and cathedral libraries in Italy built up their collection of books by acquiring or copying books from the pagan public libraries of Rome. One of the bottlenecks in the transmission of literary texts was the gradual replacement of the papyrus roll by the more convenient parchment codex between the second and the fourth centuries AD; see also Reynolds and Wilson (1974) 30–3. The two main reasons for selecting a literary work for transcription into codex-form were, as has been argued by Kenney, that the work was available (for instance, a good copy in a public library) and that it was considered worth the trouble and expense of recopying. Of course, texts used in education or which were popular at the time easily fulfilled these requirements, but many other works, among which were those of women, did not and thus were lost.

6 WOMEN AND WRITING: PROSE

1 The most illuminating studies of Perpetua's *passio* are Shaw (1993) and Dronke (1984) 1–17. Though a Christian convert, Perpetua must have had a pagan upbringing: her father was a pagan, but one of her brothers had recently been converted to Christianity, like herself; according to the unknown editor of her narrative she was 'well born, well educated and respectably married' (*Passio* 2.1: 'honeste nata, liberaliter instituta, matronaliter nupta'). To my mind, the simplicity and directness of her

language, noted by all students of her *passio*, are not due to the lack of rhetorical schooling of her sex or the influence of oral communication on female writing, as has usually been suggested, but were chosen deliberately. The rhythm of her prose and its literary allusions (see Dronke (1984) 7ff.) suggest that she could have written in a more complicated style had she wished. As has been demonstrated for the writings of Teresa of Avila (see Weber (1990)), she may have deliberately opted for *sermo humilis*, a simple, unadorned style, which in her hands acquires an unusual literary quality. She probably recognized the power of simplicity in her narrative, or perhaps she renounced her pagan literary education when she converted to Christianity. For the authority of her *passio*, see Shaw (1993) 33–8 and McKechnie (1994) 279–80. In late antiquity (in the fourth century AD) we have the 'travel diary' of Egeria; see, for instance, Wilkinson, J. (1981²) *Egeria's Travels to the Holy Land*, Jerusalem: Ariel.

2 There are only two Latin novels known to us: the *Satyricon* of Petronius and the *Metamorphoses* of Apuleius (see Hägg (1983) 166–91), and their male authorship is certain. Hägg (1983) 96–7 seems to believe that some of the known novels may have been written by women under a male pseudonym, but in the absence of any evidence his arguments are less than convincing; for a sensible discussion of the problem, see Lefkowitz (1991), who, to my mind rightly, believes that the contents of a work are no reliable basis for determining the gender of its author (witness the sympathetic portrayal of women and their importance in Greek tragedy). On the methodological problems of trying to identify an author's gender, see Kraemer, R. S. (1991) 'Women's authorship of Jewish and Christian literature in the Greco-Roman period', in Levine (1991) 221–42. Bowie (1994) disproves the theory of a primarily juvenile and female readership of the ancient novel and shows it to have been a male upper-class genre, written by male authors (some possibly from the circles of practising sophists) and intended for an educated public consisting mainly of men; see chapter 2, pp. 48f. Also the pornographic writings attributed to (Greek) female authors will not be discussed here; see for example, the 'loose booklets of Elephantis' (Mart. *Ep.* 12.43.4: 'molles Elephantidos libelli'), illustrated pornographic works which appear to have been rather well known in Rome in the first century AD (Priap. 4 shows that they were illustrated and Tiberius had them in his villa at Capri; see Suet. *Tib.* 43). These and other sex manuals attributed to women are probably pseudonymous and may well have been written by men; see, e.g., Tsantsanoglou, K. (1973) 'The memoirs of a lady from Samos', *ZPE* 12: 183–95 and Parker, H. N. (1992) 'Love's body anatomized: the ancient erotic handbooks and the rhetoric of sexuality', in Richlin, A. (ed.) *Pornography and Representation in Greece and Rome*, New York and Oxford: Oxford University Press, pp. 90–111.

3 Tac. *Ann.* 4.53.3: 'Id ego, a scriptoribus annalium non traditum, repperi in commentariis Agrippinae filiae, quae Neronis principis mater vitam suam et casus suorum posteris memoravit'. The incident is told by Tacitus among the events of AD 26.

4 For autobiographical *commentarii* see Kenney (1982) 147–8 and Rawson (1985) 227–9.

5 Augustus: Suet. *Aug.* 85: *De Vita Sua* in thirteen books; Tiberius: Suet. *Tib.* 61.1: a *commentarius de vita sua* written *summatim breviterque*; Claudius: Suet. *Claud.* 41.3: *De Vita Sua* in eight books.

6 Lewis, R. G. (1993) 'Imperial autobiography, Augustus to Hadrian', *ANRW* II 34.1: 657 points out some peculiarities of language in the speech attributed to her by Tacitus (*Ann.* 13.21) and suggests that in composing this speech Tacitus may have imitated Agrippina's style as he knew it from her memoirs.

7 For an extreme example of this trend, see Clack, J. (1975) 'To those who fell on Agrippina's pen', *CW* 69: 45–53, who argues that passages in Juvenal dealing with the private life of the Claudians (such as his portrait of Messalina) which cannot be traced to any extant source are actually based on Agrippina's memoirs, a very speculative and,

to my mind, untenable assumption. More reasonably, Griffin (1984) 23, calling the memoirs a work of propaganda, suggests that various anecdotes favourable to Nero and Agrippina herself in Suetonius (*Nero* 6.1), Tacitus (*Ann.* 11.11.3) and the elder Pliny (*NH* 7.71) derive from these memoirs.

8 For Agrippina Minor, see *FOS* 426, *RE* X Iulia Agrippina 556 cols 909–15; for a narrative of her life: Balsdon (1977) 107–22 and, recently, Barrett (1996) (on pp. 198–200 he discusses her memoirs); for her (public display of) political ambitions, e.g., Tac. *Ann.* 12.37 and 42, 13.2 and 5, Dio 60.33.7, Griffin (1984) 23–33 and 38–40. For her 'masculine' behaviour see chapter 3, n. 146. For Tacitus' malicious portrayal of her: Syme (1958) 314 and 375–7.

9 For her unique position, see, e.g., Tac. *Ann.* 12.42.3, who calls her 'a woman who represents a unique example up to the present day as the daughter of an imperator [i.e. Germanicus] and as sister, wife and mother of an emperor' ('imperatore genitam, sororem eius, qui rerum potitus sit, et coniugem et matrem fuisse unicum ad hunc diem exemplum est'). That she was aware of this may be implied by the concluding words of Tacitus' account of the homage Caratacus paid her: 'she herself [i.e. Agrippina] proudly used to say that she was a partner in the empire which her ancestors had created' (Tac. *Ann.* 12.37: 'ipsa semet parti a maioribus suis imperii sociam ferebat'); see also the speech attributed to her by Tacitus in *Ann.* 13.21. For the importance of the female descendants of Augustus in transmitting legitimacy to the male rulers of the Julio-Claudian dynasty, see Corbier, M. (1995) 'Male power and legitimacy through women: the *domus Augusta* under the Julio-Claudians', in Hawley and Levick (1995) 178–93.

10 For Agrippina's use of her mother's image in art (sculpture) to support her claim to power, see Wood, S. (1988) '*Memoriae Agrippinae*: Agrippina the Elder in Julio-Claudian art and propaganda', *AJA* 92: 409–26.

11 Plin. *NH* 7.46: 'Neronem quoque paulo ante principem et toto principatu suo hostem generis humani pedibus genitum scribit parens eius Agrippina.' It seems reasonable to assume, as is generally done, that the text referred to here is her memoirs. In the index of Pliny's work (book 1) he mentions her among his sources for book 7 as 'Agrippina Claudi' (Agrippina the wife of Claudius).

12 At certain periods of his life Cicero wrote to Atticus almost every day, apart from his other correspondents; see, for instance, *Att.* 2.4–16 (written in April 59 BC), *Att.* 7.17–10.15 (written between February and early May 49 BC) and *Att.* 12.12–13.19 (written between March and June 45 BC). Such a frequency of correspondence did not occur only between friends or relatives when separated by a great distance (though Harris (1989) 229–30 suggests as much): according to Nepos *Att.* 20 Augustus (then still Octavian) was in the habit of writing to Atticus almost every day even when both were in Rome; but Augustus was known as a prolific letter-writer; see Wallace-Hadrill (1983) 94.

13 Such as Rectina's note to the elder Pliny imploring him to save her from the imminent danger caused by the eruption of Vesuvius (Plin. *Ep.* 6.16, 'accipit codicillos Rectinae Casci imminenti periculo exterritae'). Also, love-letters were generally written on wax-tablets, so that *cerae, codicilli* and other words indicating wax-tablets could be used as synonyms for love-letters; see, for instance, Ovid *AA* 1.437–8.

14 It seems that among men, and women, confidential letters and letters to intimate friends were often written in their own hand (or at least the closing greetings were). Examples were Cicero's letters to Atticus which he mostly wrote himself except in special cases (*Att.* 2.20.5, 2.23.1 and 8.13.1), though in later years he more often relied on the help of a scribe (except for confidential matters: see *Att.* 11.24.2). Quint. 1.1.29 confirms that *in epistulis secretis et familiaribus* people normally wrote in their own hand; according to McDonnell (1996) 474 letters to 'close relations, intimate friends, social

superiors, and persons one wanted to flatter' were usually written in one's own hand. For a woman's hand, see the 'archives' of Sulpicia Lepidina at Vindolanda in northern Britain (pp. 191f.); among Egyptian papyri, see, for instance, White, J. L. (1986) *Light from Ancient Letters*, Philadelphia: Fortress Press, no. 64 (a letter written by a certain Isidora in 28 BC, presumably in her own hand). According to Suetonius (*Calig.* 24.3), Caligula, when accusing his sisters falsely of a conspiracy against his life, 'made public letters in the handwriting of all of them' ('chirographa omnium ... divulgavit'); a woman's handwriting is mentioned also in Ovid *Am.* 2.2.6, *AA.* 3.493 and ridiculed in Plaut. *Pseud.* 23ff. As both men and women regularly relied on the help of a scribe, a woman's use of a scribe does not, in itself, prove her illiteracy (see Bowman (1994) 95; for the importance of dictating, see also Horsfall, N. (1995) 'Rome without spectacles', *G & R* 42: 49–56). For female secretaries and readers (slaves and freedwomen) working for women, see Günther, R. (1987) *Frauenarbeit – Frauenbindung: Untersuchungen zu unfreien und freigelassenen Frauen in den stadtrömischen Inschriften*, Munich: Fink, pp. 62–9 and Treggiari (1976) 77–9; for example, Antonia Minor used her freedwoman Antonia Caenis as her *a manu* (secretary); see Jos. *AJ* 18.182, Dio 65.14 and Suet. *Vesp.* 3.1.

15 See, for instance, Lucian *Merc. Cond.* 36 (quoted in chapter 2, p. 37): the discourse on chastity by a philosopher is interrupted while the woman pupil reads a note from her lover and quickly writes a reply; Prop. 3.16.1: a letter from his mistress reaching him at midnight; Plut. *Brut.* 5 and *Cat. Mi.* 24: a wanton love-letter of Servilia's delivered to Caesar (and read by him) in the middle of an important meeting of the senate; Macr. *Sat.* 2.5.6: Julia's neat reply to a letter of advice written by her father Augustus about her youthful companions at a gladiatorial show. Of course, such anecdotes are not to be taken at face value, but they confirm what we know of male letter-writers, such as Cicero, who wrote or dictated letters at any time and under all circumstances: cf., for instance, *Q. Fr.* 3.1.19 (dictated during dinner), *Fam.* 9.26.1 (copying a letter during a banquet) and *Fam.* 12.20 (written in the senate).

16 Thus, for instance, in Ovid's verse-epistles to his wife from exile, he expects her to work hard in his interest: see *Trist.* 1.6.5ff., 3.3, 4.3.71–2, 5.2.33ff., 5.5, 5.11, 5.14.15ff., *Pont.* 1.4, 3.1.31ff.; see also *Trist.* 1.3.79–102. For Terentia's efforts on behalf of her husband, see n. 18 below.

17 All twenty-four letters of book 14 of Cicero's *Ad Familiares* are addressed to Terentia (in 1–7, 14 and 18 Tullia is included as addressee) and are written in answer to her letters; see also n. 18. Other letters from Terentia to Cicero are referred to in *Att.* 3.5, 11.21 and 11.24. Letters written by Tullia to Cicero are referred to in *Att.* 10.2 (Tullia writing about Dionysius, the teacher of Marcus and Quintus), *Att.* 10.8.1 (Tullia's advice to await the outcome of civil war in Spain), *Fam.* 14.2.4 (Tullia telling him whom to write to when in exile) and *Fam.* 14.14 (from Cicero and his son to Terentia and Tullia). Publilia's letter to Cicero is mentioned in *Att.* 12.32, though he doubts whether it is her own. Correspondence between Pomponia and her son Quintus is mentioned in *Att.* 13.38, 13.39.1 and 13.41.1. A letter from Atticus to Tullia is referred to in *Att.* 11.24.1 and Terentia's letter to Atticus in *Att.* 7.26.3. Attica's writing to Atticus is mentioned in *Att.* 12.1; in *Att.* 5.11.7 Cicero confesses that he secretly read Pilia's letter to his brother Quintus: it was written with sympathy (συμπαθῶς). *Fam.* 16.11 is written to Tiro in the name of the entire family; in *Att.* 2.3 Cicero announces Terentia's (probably written) invitation of Pomponia for a brief holiday.

18 During Cicero's exile in 58–57 BC Terentia looked after his interests in Rome and kept him informed of his affairs encouraging him when he was depressed, telling him whom to thank or to write to, advising him about his safety and about his possible return, and discussing matters about slaves and property; she also seems to have given him financial support (*Fam.* 14.1.3–6, 14.2.2–4, 14.3.3–5 in response to three letters of Terentia's, 14.4.3–5). For his asking her to write as often and as fully as possible; see *Fam.* 14.2.4

and 14.3.5; as she worked hard for his return and managed his affairs in Rome he preferred her to stay there instead of joining him in exile (*Fam.* 14.3.5, 14.4.3). Also during his governorship of Cilicia she gave him 'a full and most painstaking account of everything' (*Fam.* 14.5.1: 'diligentissimeque a te perscripta sunt omnia'), and when he was away from home during the civil war she kept him informed on matters of finance and property (*Fam.* 14.6), politics (*Fam.* 14.8 and 14.14.2) and family affairs (*Fam.* 14.10, 14.14.2, 14.16, 14.18 and 14.21). These letters were of such importance to him that in *Fam.* 14.18 he asks her to establish regular letter-carriers so that he may receive a letter from her and Tullia every day, and in *Fam.* 14.21 he asks for letters 'saepissime' 'as often as possible'.

19 Plin. *Ep.* 1.4 to Pompeia Celerina, the mother of his deceased second wife, in praise of her villas, which he was allowed to use when on a journey; she had written a note to her servants there to make Pliny feel at home. *Ep.* 2.4 to the unknown Calvina, apparently an *adfinis* of him, about his financial support of her since her father had died in heavy debt. *Ep.* 3.3 to Corellia Hispulla, daughter of his friend Corellius Rufus, whose wife was probably remotely related to Pliny's wife Calpurnia (see chapter 2, n. 58), in which he advises her about a teacher of rhetoric for her son. *Ep.* 3.10 to Vestricius Spurinna and his wife Cottia in answer to their request to be allowed to read the life he had written in memory of their deceased son; he asks for a critical reading and comments. *Ep.* 4.19 to his wife's aunt Calpurnia Hispulla, a eulogy of his third wife Calpurnia, who had been brought up by her aunt. *Ep.* 6.4, 6.7 and 7.5 to his wife Calpurnia in Campania, letters full of love and anxiety because of her absence and her delicate health, in which he asks her to write to him twice a day (6.4). She apparently responded in the same vein, writing that she missed him badly and found consolation only in his letters (6.7). *Ep.* 7.14 to Corellia, sister of Corellius Rufus, a short note in answer to her offer to pay the full price when buying land from him instead of the reduced price suggested by Pliny. *Ep.* 8.11, addressed to Calpurnia Hispulla again, about his wife's miscarriage. Pliny seems to have arranged his letters to women carefully so as to have one letter to a woman in almost every book of his letters.

20 For the 'domestication' of upper-class life during the empire, see Veyne (1978). However, for women of the imperial family, family affairs merged with politics; see, for instance, Augustus' letters to Livia consulting her about the attitude to adopt towards Claudius (Suet. *Claud.* 4). Augustus took Livia's opinion very seriously: according to Suet. *Aug.* 84.2 he was in the habit of writing down what he wanted to say when he was going to have an important conversation with her. Further, the fictitious letters between Marcus Aurelius and his wife, Faustina the Younger (*SHA Av. Cas.* 9–11), about the rebellion of Avidius Cassius present her as involved in political matters. For upper-class women accompanying their husbands to the provinces during the empire, see chapter 1, n. 12.

21 So Syme (1985) 350–1 argues that with the exception of Cottia, who was addressed together with her husband, all female addressees of the younger Pliny were related to him in some way, however remotely (see n. 19 above). Clark (1993) 134 suggests that Jerome's extensive correspondence with women who were not relatives of his 'may well have been a factor in his being asked to leave Rome'.

22 For some examples of correspondence between spouses (apart from the correspondence between Cicero and Terentia and the verse-epistles from Ovid to his wife listed in n. 16 above) see, for instance, the younger Pliny's letters to his wife Calpurnia: Plin. *Ep.* 6.4, 6.5 and 7.5; Augustus' letters to his wife Livia consulting her on family matters: Suet. *Tib.* 51 and *Claud.* 4; letters between Antony and Fulvia (Plut. *Ant.* 10.4–5 and 30.2); Statius' verse-epistle to his wife: Stat. *Silv.* 3.5; a letter of complaint by an unknown wife to her husband: *SHA Hadr.* 11.6; the apocryphal letters of Marcus Aurelius and his wife, the younger Faustina, quoted in *SHA Av. Cas.* 9–11; an

apocryphal letter by Macrinus to his wife: *SHA Ant. Diad.* 7.5–7. Fictitious verse-epistles from women to their absent husbands or lovers in Propertius (4.3: Arethusa to Lycotas) and Ovid's *Heroides* reflect the habit of correspondence between spouses. For references to letters from women to other male relatives: Apul. *Apol.* 82.2: Aemilia Pudentilla to her son Pontianus (see also p. 200); Plut. *CG* 13.2: Cornelia to her son Gaius; Suet. *Claud.* 3.2: Livia admonishing her grandson Claudius in 'short, harsh letters' ('acerbo et brevi scripto'); Cic. *Att.* 9.6 and 9.9 mentions letters from a Clodia to her son-in-law Metellus (but see Shackleton-Bailey, D. R. (1968) *Cicero's letters to Atticus IV (49* BC), Cambridge: Cambridge University Press, p. 364) and Tac. *Ann.* 1.53 mentions a (doubt-ful) letter from Augustus' daughter Julia to her father.

23 Dio 46.18.3–4 (in his fictitious speech of Calenus against Cicero): τίς δ᾽ οὐκ οἶδεν ὅτι τὴν μὲν γυναῖκα τὴν προτέραν τὴν τεκοῦσάν σοι δύο τέκνα ἐξέβαλες, ἑτέραν δὲ ἐπεσηγάγου παρθένον ὑπεργήρως ὤν, ἵν᾽ ἐκ τῆς οὐσίας αὐτῆς τὰ δανείσματα ἀποτίσῃς; καὶ οὐδὲ ἐκείνην μέντοι κατέσχες, ἵνα Καιρελλίᾳ ἐπ᾽ ἀδείας ἔχῃς, ἣν τοσούτῳ πρεσβυτέραν σαυτοῦ οὖσαν ἐμοίχευσας ὅσῳ νεωτέραν τὴν κόρην ἔγημας, πρὸς ἣν καὶ αὐτὴν τοιαύτας ἐπιστολὰς γράφεις οἵας ἂν γράψειεν ἀνὴρ σκωπτόλης ἀθυρόγλωσσος πρὸς γυναῖκα ἑβδομηκοντοῦτιν πληκτιζόμενος. In the fourth century AD this invective was apparently well known since Ausonius in the closing episode of his *Cento Nuptialis* uses it as an excuse for his own naughty verses: 'In all his precepts Cicero's strictness is prominent, in his letters to Caerellia licence lurks' (*Cent. Nupt.*, p. 169, Prete: 'in praeceptis omnibus extare Tulli severitatem, in epistulis ad Caerelliam subesse petulantiam'). For Caerellia see chapter 2, p. 55. Her relationship to Cicero is unclear: in *Fam.* 13.72.1 Cicero calls her his *necessaria*, which, however, can be used both for a female relative and for a female friend.

24 Quint. 6.3.112: 'Etiam illud, quod Cicero Caerelliae scripsit reddens rationem, cur ille C. Caesaris tempora tam patienter toleraret, "Haec aut animo Catonis ferenda sunt aut Ciceronis stomacho"; stomachus enim ille habet aliquid ioco simile'. In Dio's days the letters may already have been lost.

25 Apart from his letters to Terentia (and family) in *Fam.* 14 his letters to Caerellia were the only ones addressed to a woman that have been published. They were probably recovered for publication from Caerellia (see *RE* 7A col. 1206), or perhaps from copies of his letters preserved by Cicero himself. Apart from political issues the letters may have dealt with philosophy, in which they shared an interest (see chapter 2, p. 55), but in view of their financial dealings and Caerellia's attempts to reconcile him with Publilia, they possibly treated also of finance and family matters. The date of the letter quoted by Quintilian, between the suicide of Cato in 46 BC and Caesar's death, agrees with the date of Cicero's references to Caerellia in his preserved letters. As far as we know, Caerellia's letters to Cicero were not published.

26 The casual remark in Ovid *Am.* 2.2.19 in which he asks the slave who is set as a guardian over a girl to pretend that the letter she reads comes from her mother (and not from a lover) is one of the few references to letters between women in the literary sources (see also Ovid *AA* 3.497–8 and below n. 34). Its casualness shows, as was to be expected, that such letters were common.

27 For some letters exchanged between women in Roman Egypt, see, for instance, Hunt, A. S. and Edgar, C. C. (1932) *Select Papyri I*, London: Heinemann, no. 134 (a daughter to her mother, third century AD) and 165 (an orphaned niece to her aunt, fourth century AD), Pestman, P. W. (1990) *The New Papyrological Primer*, Leiden: Brill, no. 40 (a daughter to her mother, early second century AD); for private letters of women in Greek and Roman Egypt, see also Cole (1981) 234–6. These and other letters from Roman Egypt fall outside the scope of this study.

28 For the correspondence of Sulpicia Lepidina and Claudia Severa in the Vindolanda tablets, see Bowman and Thomas (1994) 256–65 (nos 291–4); I shall refer to the

numbers of the letters in this edition. See further Bowman and Thomas (1987) 128–30
and 139–41, Cugusi, P. (1992) *Corpus Epistularum Latinarum*, Florence: Gonnelli (2 vols),
Appendix Vindolanda 137 γ,δ,ε and Birley, A. R. (1991) 'Vindolanda: notes on some
writing tablets', *ZPE* 88: 100–2; for the Latin of the Vindolanda tablets, see Adams
(1995).

29 The letters of Claudia Severa: Bowman and Thomas (1994) nos 291–3 (nos 291–2 are
quite well preserved, but no. 293 is only a scrap containing the closure of a letter in
Severa's own hand). The editors suggest that possibly no. 227 is a draft written by
Cerialis for his wife Lepidina, but as too little of the text is left I prefer to ignore it. For
the letter of Paterna see Bowman and Thomas (1994) no. 294. Paterna seems to be of
lower status (perhaps a dependant), as she calls Lepidina *domina* instead of *soror*, the title
of address used by women who were social equals and on intimate terms (like Claudia
Severa and Sulpicia Lepidina). The editors suggest that she promises to bring Lepidina
some medicine. For the fragmentary letter of the unknown Valatta, 'probably a
woman', see Bowman and Thomas (1994) no. 257: 'Valatta to her Cerialis, greetings. I
ask my lord that you relax your severity (?) and through Lepidina that you grant me
what I ask (?) . . .' ('Valatta [Ceriali suo] s[alutem.] rogo, domine, re[..]teritat[e]m
tuam [. . .] et per Lepidinam quod [. . .] mihi concedas'). Though the reading is not
altogether certain, this is a very interesting letter as it shows Lepidina mediating with
her husband on behalf of a female friend or dependant.

30 Bowman and Thomas (1987) 138, but in comparison to a professional scribe most
hands seem bad. Women were no exception in this: according to Quintilian (1.1.28–9)
upper-class people generally neglected their handwriting since they had scribes to
dictate their writing to; for some examples of bad handwriting, see Harris (1989) 249.
For the legibility of upper-class handwriting and the frequency with which members of
the upper classes wrote letters in their own hand, see McDonnell (1996).

31 For text, translation and commentary, see Bowman and Thomas (1994) no. 291. If
some uncertain readings are ignored, the text may be restored as: 'Cl(audia) Severa
Lepidinae [suae sa]l[u]tem. iii idus Septembr[e]s, soror, ad diem sollemnem natalem
meum rogo libenter facias ut venias ad nos iucundiorem mihi [diem] interventu tuo
factura si [venia]s. Cerial[em t]uum saluta. Aelius meus [eum] et filiolus salutant.
Sperabo te, soror. Vale, soror, anima mea, ita valeam, karissima et have'.

32 Bowman and Thomas (1994) no. 292. The closure is restored as: '[val]e, m[ea] soror
karissima et anima ma [sc. mea] desideratissima'.

33 That there were children in the *praetorium* at Vindolanda appears from archaeological
evidence (such as little shoes; see Driel-Murray, C. van (1995) 'Gender in question', in
Rush, P. (ed.) *Theoretical Roman Archaeology: Second Conference Proceedings*, Aldershot: Ave-
bury, pp. 3–21) and from the verse of Virgil (*Aen.* 9.473) written on the back of a draft
letter, probably a writing-exercise of a schoolchild; see Bowman and Thomas (1987)
130–2 and Bowman and Thomas (1994) no. 118. For their acquisition of citizenship: to
judge from her *gentilicium* Claudia Severa's family acquired citizenship during the reign
of Claudius (Bowman and Thomas (1994) 257), whereas that of Sulpicia Lepidina may
have been of even more recent date: the reign of Sulpicius Galba (Bowman (1994) 57).
The name of her husband, Flavius Cerialis, suggests that he was a first- or second-
generation Roman citizen: he may have been a son of a Batavian who received Roman
citizenship as a reward for his loyalty to Rome during the Batavian revolt (AD 69–70)
and who named his son after Q. Petillius Cerialis who suppressed the revolt; see Adams
(1995) 129.

34 Cf. Cic. *Att.* 2.3 (Terentia's invitation to Pomponia for a holiday visit); see also Fronto *Ad
M. Caes.* 2.9 (Haines I, pp. 146–7) and *Epist. Graec.* 2 (Haines I, pp. 146–51): a Greek
letter from Fronto to Domitia Lucilla, Marcus Aurelius' mother, on her birthday, at the
celebration of which Fronto's wife Gratia was present together with other women.

NOTES

35 For letter-writing and the ancient typology of letters, see Stowers, S. K. (1986) *Letter Writing in Greco-Roman Antiquity*, Philadelphia: Westminster Press, and Sherwin-White (1966) 1–11 and 42–5; also Peter, H. (1901) *Der Brief in der römischen Literatur: literargeschichtliche Untersuchungen und Zusammenfassungen*, Leipzig, *RE* Suppl. 5 s.v. Epistolographie cols 185–220 and Cugusi (1983) 105–35. For the usefulness of letter-writing as an exercise for the orator, see, for instance, Plin. *Ep.* 7.9.8: 'letters develop brevity and simplicity of style' ('pressus sermo purusque ex epistulis petitur'), also Cic. *Fam.* 9.21.1 and Quint. 9.4.19; on the composition of letters, see Plin. *Ep.* 1.1, 2.13.7, 3.20.11, 9.2, 9.28.

36 For Cornelia, see chapter 3, pp. 64ff.; for her excellent style of writing (and speaking), Cic. *Brut.* 211 and Quint. 1.1.6, and chapter 3, p. 66. Cicero (*Brut.* 211) actually appears to have read her letters and suggests that his interlocutors Atticus and Brutus had done the same. Quintilian (1.1.6) is generally assumed to have derived this passage from Cicero (see, e.g. Instinsky (1971) 184), but, to my mind, his rather vague statement as regards the transmission of the letters ('in posteros . . . est . . . traditus') does not preclude the possibility that they had been preserved down to his own time. Plut. *CG* 13.2 refers to Cornelia's letters to her son Gaius in connection with her political support for her son's cause, but his information appears to be second-hand only: 'for to this matter there are said to have been obscure allusions in her letters to her son' (λέγουσιν . . . ταῦτα γὰρ ἐν τοῖς ἐπιστολίοις αὐτῆς ᾐνιγμένα γεγράφθαι πρὸς τὸν υἱόν). For Cornelia's eloquence, see also Hier. *Ep.* 107.4.

37 As has been said in chapter 5, 'publication' is an anachronism when used for Roman times, since circulation among friends and 'publication' can hardly be distinguished. We do not know how widely Cornelia's letters circulated (perhaps they were used as models for instructing orators), or how many of them were 'published'. Yet, Instinsky (1971) 184–5 seems too sceptical when he doubts that they had been published at all (he suggests that they may have been known to Cicero by some personal connection). Barnard (1990) 390 says that Cornelia's only surviving daughter, Sempronia, 'is the person most often credited with publishing or even forging Cornelia's letters', but she fails to provide ancient evidence, or references to modern studies, to support her statement. Though Sempronia may perhaps have inherited her mother's archives after her death, this is not sufficient reason to assume that she was also her mother's publisher – if ever there was one.

38 'Verba ex epistula Corneliae Gracchorum matris ex libro Cornelii Nepotis de Latinis historicis excerpta' (Nepos fr. 59; ed. P. K. Marshall, Leipzig 1977). Barnard (1990) 390 wrongly assumes that the Cornelia fragments 'appear in nearly all his manuscripts'; for the manuscript tradition, see Marshall, P. K. (1977) *The Manuscript Tradition of Cornelius Nepos*, London: Institute of Classical Studies (*BICS* suppl. 37). In the earliest surviving manuscript, the late twelfth-century Wolfenbüttel Codex (also called the Codex Guelferbytanus, or A) the title added by the scribe who copied the fragments reads: 'Verba ex epistula Corneliae Gracorum matris ex eodem libro Cornelii Nepotis excerpta', referring to the life of Cato copied immediately preceding, which was one of the lives of the lost 'Latin Historians'. This manuscript was, probably indirectly, copied from the lost Codex Danielis written between the ninth and twelfth centuries (which did contain the Cornelia fragments), from which in the fifteenth century the other two main manuscripts, L (Leidensis) and P (Parcensis, lost in the First World War), were copied, and which was the basis of the Utrecht edition of 1542 (u). Of these manuscripts only A and the fifteenth-century Italian *codices* deriving from A contain the Cornelia fragments; L has only the life of Atticus, P only that of Cato, and u none.

39 Plut. *TG* 21 refers to a life of C. Gracchus by Nepos. Some scholars, such as, recently, Horsfall (1987) 232, have argued that a life of C. Gracchus would have been included by Nepos under the *Oratores*, not the *Historici*. However, as has been argued by Clift

349

(1945) 99–100, n. 69, the derivation from *De Latinis Historicis*, which is found in the manuscripts, should not be questioned: we do not even know for certain that Nepos wrote on orators, and since the lives of Atticus, Cato and, probably, Cicero were included among the 'Historians', C. Gracchus can be placed among them without too much difficulty (for references to his writings see Plut. *TG* 8.9 and Cic. *Div.* 1.36 and 2.62).

40 For a bibliography of the discussion up to 1921, see Stern, E. von (1921) 'Zur Beurteilung der politischen Wirksamkeit des Tiberius und Gaius Gracchus', *Hermes* 56: 273–4, who himself believes in the authenticity on psychological grounds. Instinsky (1971) provides an instructive survey of the debate starting with Ed. Meyer, who in the first edition of his history of the Gracchi in 1894 (see below n. 47) called the letter 'ein handgreifliches rhetorisches Machwerk', but was forced to revise his opinion, though reluctantly, in his second edition (cf. Meyer, E. (1924²) *Kleine Schriften* I, Halle: Niemeyer, pp. 368ff.) under the influence of the authority of philologists such as Norden and Wissowa. Surprisingly, A. S. Gratwick in Kenney (1982) 145–6 writes: 'the authenticity of the document has been much disputed, for no good reason at all', mentioning as evidence for his bold statement only Cicero (*Brut.* 211) and Leo, F. (1913) *Geschichte der römischen Literatur I: Die archaische Literatur*, Berlin: Weidmann, pp. 304ff. (for a critique of Leo's highly emotional arguments in defence of the authenticity of the letter, see Instinsky (1971) 180–1). However, Gratwick qualifies the certainty of his remark in the next sentence: '*if genuine*, this is the earliest extant prose-writing in any language by a woman' (my italics).

41 Horsfall (1987); he summarizes his point of view in Horsfall, N. (1989) *Cornelius Nepos: A Selection, including the Lives of Cato and Atticus*, Oxford: Clarendon Press, pp. 41–2; also Instinsky (1971) 183–4 prefers to speak of the 'Grad der Authentizität'.

42 See Horsfall (1987) 232, where he explains the habit of 'adapted citation' in the service of the stylistic unity of a work: a quotation is adapted 'to bring it into a degree of harmony with its textual environment'. However, on p. 233 he argues that the excerpts 'constitute unflawed specimens of the Latin prose of the second century BC', a view which is nowadays widely held, but which conflicts with his earlier statement. Also his attempt on p. 234 to find traces of reworking in the excerpts fails to convince. For a different view, see Cugusi (1983) 142.

43 The fragments are linked by the words 'eadem alio loco'. Since here it makes no difference whether the fragments stem from one or from two letters, I shall refer to them as if deriving from one letter; *contra* Bardon (1952) 91.

44 Nepos, fr. 2: 'Verbis conceptis deierare ausim, praeterquam qui Tiberium Gracchum necarunt, neminem inimicum tantum molestiae tantumque laboris quantum te ob has res mihi tradidisse, quem oportebat omnium eorum, quos antehac habui liberos, partis tolerare, atque curare ut quam minimum sollicitudinis in senecta haberem, utique quaecumque ageres, ea velles maxime mihi placere, atque uti nefas haberes rerum maiorum adversum meam sententiam quicquam facere, praesertim mihi cui parva pars vitae superest. Ne id quidem tam breve spatium potest opitulari, quin et mihi adversere et rem publicam profliges? Denique quae pausa erit? Ecquando desinet familia nostra insanire? Ecquando modus ei rei haberi poterit? Ecquando desinemus et habentes et praebentes molestiis insistere? Ecquando perpudescet miscenda atque perturbanda re publica? Sed si omnino id fieri non potest, ubi ego mortua ero, petito tribunatum; per me facito quod lubebit, cum ego non sentiam. Ubi mortua ero, parentabis mihi et invocabis deum parentem. In eo tempore non pudebit te eorum deum preces expetere, quos vivos atque praesentes relictos atque desertos habueris? Ne ille sirit Iuppiter te ea perseverare, nec tibi tantam dementiam venire in animum. Et si perseveras, vereor ne in omnem vitam tantum laboris culpa tua recipias, uti in nullo tempore tute tibi placere possis'.

45 Cf. Dixon (1990) 179 and 191, who remarks that 'the arguments she employs would today be deemed fit for psychiatric analysis', but were not regarded as improper in Roman antiquity. For a somewhat less vehemently reproachful attitude of a mother towards her son who did not live up to her expectations, see the Greek letter from Kophaena, a Christian woman in Egypt of the fourth century, to her son Theodulus: 'I wish you to know, as the merchant told you, that your mother Kophaena has been ill for thirteen months, and yet you have not written me even one letter although you know that I treated you better than my other children, and you did not think to send even a word to me when you learned that I was ill.' See Naldini, M. (1968) *Il Cristianesimo in Egitto: lettere private nei papiri dei secoli II–IV*, Florence: Le Monnier, no. 93 (trans. Rousselle (1993) 181).

46 In most sources Cornelia is pictured as supporting her sons and their policy: see, e.g., Plut. *TG* 8.5, *CG* 13.2 (though also her opposition is mentioned here) and 19.1, App. *BC* 1.20, Dio 24.83.8. Also those who defend the authenticity of the letter have noticed this discrepancy, but they try to explain it away by emphasizing Cornelia's anxiety for her only surviving son (e.g., Stern, E. von (1921) 'Zur Beurteilung der politischen Wirksamkeit des Tiberius und Gaius Gracchus', *Hermes* 56: 273–4), or by pointing to her typically feminine irrationality (Thiel, J. H. (1929) 'De Corneliae Epistula', *Mnemosyne* 57: 351ff.) or by a reinterpretation of the other sources in accordance with the tenor of the letter (e.g., Nipperdey, C. (1877) *Opuscula*, Berlin: Weidmann, pp. 95–118). For sources suggesting that she may have opposed the revolutionary policy of her sons, see Plut. *CG* 4.4 (her intervention in defence of Tiberius' former opponent M. Octavius) and 13.2, Diod. 34.25.2.

47 See Meyer, E. (1894) 'Untersuchungen zur Geschichte der Gracchen', *Festschrift zur zweihundertjährigen Jubelfeier der Universität Halle*, Halle: Niemeyer, p. 6, Carcopino (1928) 107 and Coarelli (1978) 25–6 (a political pamphlet); Instinsky (1971) 186–9 notes that, among other things, the use of the verbs *miscere* and *perturbare* to describe the political deeds of the Gracchi reflects the (slightly later) optimate view of the policy of the *populares*; to support his view he cites several examples from Cicero, who uses these terms to characterize certain speakers in his dialogues as optimates. Therefore, he believes, the terms cannot have been Cornelia's own. Also Horsfall (1987) 233 mentions the possibility that the letter is reworked by a 'historian sympathetic to optimate criticism of the Gracchi'. For the statue of Cornelia, see chapter 3, pp. 66f.

48 Instinsky (1971) 189, followed by Coarelli (1978) 26. Horsfall (1987) 233–4 suggests that there may have been two stages in the possible reworking of the original letter by Cornelia or a near contemporary of hers: by an unknown historian used by Nepos and by Nepos himself, but he finds no definite traces of the process.

49 After all, her father, her husband, her brother-in-law (P. Cornelius Scipio Nasica Corculum) and her son-in-law (Scipio Aemilianus) had all been consul twice. The (possibly apocryphal) story that Cornelia reproached her sons that she was known as the mother-in-law of Scipio Aemilianus and not yet as the mother of the Gracchi (Plut. *TG* 8.7) may be interpreted in this light. As Roman convention dictated that sons matched or exceeded their father's or ancestors' achievements, this must have been a heavy burden for the Gracchi. The argument that Cornelia's political view as expressed in the letter conflicts with the accounts of most other sources is not decisive, as these sources (Plutarch, Appian and Dio Cassius) are much later, *viz.* from a time when the Gracchi had been re-evaluated and were reckoned among the great men of the past; see *RE* 2A cols 1424f. about the later judgement on Tiberius Gracchus.

50 See, e.g., Horsfall (1987) 233, Gratwick in Kenney (1982) 147, Instinsky (1971) 183, Clift (1945) 102, Bardon (1952) 88–91 and Cugusi, P. (1970) *Epistolographi Latini Minores I, 2*, Turin: Paravia, pp. 65–73.

51 For a comparison to Cato, see Fraenkel, E. (1968) *Leseproben aus Reden Ciceros und Catos*,

Rome: Storia e Letteratura, pp. 161–3 and A. S. Gratwick in Kenney (1982) 146–7 and 152–4; on p. 147 he draws attention to her use of antithesis, anaphora and hendiadys. For the Graecisms (such as 'pausa' and the expression 'et habentes et praebentes'), see Clift (1945) 102. For Cornelia's education, see chapter 2, p. 24 and chapter 3, p. 66.

52 Instinsky (1971) 185–6 argues that the series of rhetorical questions is more fitting for a political speech (though superfluous even then) than for a private letter, but A. S. Gratwick in Kenney (1982) 146–7 and 152–4, comparing the letter to the speeches of Cato, suggests that Cornelia may have circulated copies of the letter to embarrass Gaius and make him obey her. Also Horsfall (1987) 234 believes that the excerpts derive from a public communication. However, I prefer to take it for what it appears to be: a private letter.

53 For studies of female speech in antiquity, see Adams (1984), who lists some character- istics, and, more cursorily, Gilleland, M. E. (1980) 'Female speech in Greek and Latin', *AJPh* 101: 180–3. Gratwick in Kenney (1982) 147 calls her style 'virile' and notes that she avoids diminutives, but we have no evidence that diminutives were characteristic of female speech in Rome at any period (for the diminutives in Plaut. *Pseud.* 66ff., see pp. 200f.).

54 Ovid. *AA* 3.479–82: 'Munda, sed e medio consuetaque verba, puellae, / scribite: ser- monis publica forma placet; / A! quotiens dubius scriptis exarsit amator, / et nocuit formae barbara lingua bonae!' Cf. also Juv. 6.233–4 about the corrupting influence of the mother-in-law: 'it is she who teaches her [daughter] to reply to a seducer's love- letters without coarseness or naive simplicity' ('illa docet missis a corruptore tabellis / nil rude nec simplex rescribere'). Ovid's restriction that his instructions were meant for freedwomen and courtesans, not for married women of the upper classes (*AA* 3.483: 'quamvis vittae careatis honore', 'though you lack the honour of the fillet'), should not be taken at face value: see chapter 2, p. 48. If his *Heroides* (verse-epistles written in the name of mostly legendary women to their absent husbands or lovers) may be taken as a poetic representation of the desired style of women's letters, they were to reach a highly sophisticated literary level indeed. For some references to women of various classes writing love-letters, see Mart. *Ep.* 3.63.9, 14.6, Ovid. *AA* 1. 483–4, 2.543, 3.469ff. and 621–30, *Am.* 1.11.19–24, 1.12.1–2, 2.2.6, 2.15.15–18, 2.19.41, 3.14.31, Plaut. *Asin.* 767 (alluding to the writing of love-letters) and *Pseud.* 41ff., Hor. *Ep.* 12.2 (an old woman ridiculed for sending love-letters), Tib. 2.6.45–6, Prop. 3.16.1, Juv. 6. 140–1 and 233–4, 14.29–30, Petron. *fr.* 30.14, Plut. *Brut.* 5 and *Cat. Mi.* 24. Brief, secret messages between lovers might be written with the finger in wine on the table, see Tib. 1.6.19–20, Prop. 3.8.26, Ovid. *AA* 1.571–2, *Am.* 1.4.20, 2.5.17–18, *Trist.* 2.454.

55 See Ovid. *AA* 1. 459–68: on the right use of eloquence and the avoidance of *verba molesta* (464) and a declamatory style; 467–8 show a verbal similarity to his advice to women, quoted above: 'sit tibi credibilis sermo consuetaque verba, / blanda tamen, praesens ut videare loqui' ('Your language should inspire trust and your words be familiar, yet coaxing too, so that you seem to be speaking to her in person').

56 Suet. *Aug.* 86: ' "Sed opus est", inquit, "dare te operam, ne moleste scribas et loquaris" ' (see chapter 2, p. 23); cf. Ovid's warning in *AA* 1.464 against the use of *verba molesta*. Augustus' daughter Julia easily met this requirement in her brief and elegant reply to her father's note reproaching her for her retinue of smart young men who compared badly with the grave elderly men in Livia's company: 'eleganter illa rescripsit: "et hi mecum senes fient" ' ('neatly she replied: "these men around me will one day be old men too" '; Macr. *Sat.* 2.5.6).

57 Plin. *Ep.* 1.16.6, quoted and discussed in chapter 2, pp. 31f.

58 Plin. *Ep.* 6.7: 'nam cuius litterae tantum habent suavitatis, huius sermonibus quantum dulcedinis inest!' In *Ep.* 6.4 Pliny asks her to write to him twice a day; *Ep.* 7.5 plays on the theme of the 'excluded lover' of love poetry.

59 For *suavitas* as a characterization of style see Maniet, A. (1966) 'Pline le Jeune et Calpurnia', *AC* 35: 157–61.

60 Plaut. *Pseud.* 41–4 and 64–71 (I omit the middle part of the letter (lines 51–9) which gives practical information important for the plot of the play, and the greetings at the end): 'Phoenicium Calidoro amatori suo / per ceram et lignum litterasque interpretes / salutem mittit et salutem abs te expetit, / lacrumans titubanti animo, corde et pectore. / . . . Nunc nostri amores mores consuetudines, / iocus ludus sermo suavisaviatio, / compressiones artae amantum corporum, /teneris labellis molles morsiunculae, / papillarum horridularum oppressiunculae, / harunc voluptatum mi omnium atque itidem tibi/ distractio discidium vastities venit, / nisi quae mihi in test aut tibist in me salus.' In lines 23ff. the girl's handwriting is mocked as barely legible, forming a stark contrast with the complicated phrases and novel words of the letter.

61 Nevertheless, her lover comments: 'it makes me feel that I am talking with her' (Plaut. *Pseud.* 62: 'mihi videor cum ea fabularier').

62 For education as a mark of social status, see chapter 3, pp. 72ff. From Livia and Augustus' sister Octavia onwards, imperial women (most of them of non-imperial, upper-class descent) show that a thorough education in both Greek and Roman literature and culture was expected of women of high standing and became increasingly a condition for a high status. For the use of Greek, see, for instance, Augustus' letters to his wife (Suet. *Claud.* 4), in which Greek words and Graecisms abound. Further, the ability of the empress Plotina to produce a well-written letter in Greek (see p. 202) points to a thorough education in 'both languages', which was expected of a woman of her standing. Though herself of provincial descent (she originated in Nîmes in Gallia Narbonensis) and from a family that had only recently entered Roman aristocracy, her education measured up to her elevated position as the emperor's wife.

63 Fronto *Epist. Graec.* 1 (Haines I, pp. 130–7) and 2 (Haines I, pp. 146–51), both written in AD 143; their contact dated from AD 138 (or earlier) when Fronto was appointed tutor of Latin rhetoric to her son Marcus. Many letters exchanged between Fronto and Marcus Aurelius contain greetings from or to Domitia Lucilla. She was also on intimate terms with Fronto's wife, Gratia; see *Ad M. Caes.* 2.8 (Haines I, pp. 144–7), 2.9 (Haines I, pp. 146–7), 4.6.2 (Haines I, pp. 182–3), 5.5 (Haines I, pp. 192–3), 5.31 (46) (Haines I, pp. 230–1) and *Epist. Graec.* 2 (Haines I, pp. 146–7). In a letter thanking Fronto for a well-written and affectionate letter Marcus Aurelius compares it to those of his mother; see Fronto *Ad M. Caes.* 2.2.2 (Haines I, pp. 114–15): 'I could venture to say that even she, who bore me and nursed me, never wrote me anything so delightful, so honeyed' ('Ausim dicere, quae me genuit atque aluit, nihil umquam tam iucundum tamque mellitum eam ad me scripsisse').

64 Fronto was *consul suffectus* for two months (July and August of AD 143), Birley (1966) 104ff. The *encomium* for the emperor mentioned in the earlier letter to Domitia Lucilla is his speech thanking Antoninus Pius for this honour.

65 Fronto, *Epist. Graec.* 1.5: εἴ τι τῶν ὀνομάτων ἐν ταῖς ἐπιστολαῖς ταύταις εἴη ἄκυρον ἢ βάρβαρον ἢ ἄλλως ἀδόκιμον ἢ μὴ πάνυ Ἀττικόν, μὴ τοῦτ', ἀλλὰ τοῦ ὀνόματός σε ἀξιῶ τὴν διάνοιαν σκοπεῖν αὐτὴν καθ' αὑτήν·

66 Fronto, *Ad M. Caes.* 1.8.7 (Haines I, pp. 124–5): 'Epistulam matri tuae scripsi, quae mea impudentia est, Graece, eamque epistulae ad te scriptae implicui. Tu prior lege et, si quis inerit barbarismus, tu, qui a Graecis litteris recentior es, corrige atque ita matri redde. Nolo enim me mater tua ut Opicum contemnat'. In his letter to Domitia Lucilla he even presents himself as inferior to Anacharsis in wisdom: 'I will compare myself, then, with Anacharsis, not, by heaven, in wisdom, but as being like him a barbarian. For he was a Scythian of the nomad Scythians, and I am a Libyan of the Libyan nomads' (*Epist. Graec.* 1.5: παραβαλῶ δὴ ἐμαυτὸν Ἀναχάρσιδι οὐ μὰ Δία κατὰ τὴν σοφίαν ἀλλὰ κατὰ τὸ βάρβαρος ὁμοίως εἶναι. Ἦν γὰρ ὁ μὲν Σκύθης τῶν

νομάδων Σκυθῶν, ἐγὼ δὲ Λίβυς τῶν Λιβύων τῶν νομάδων). In his 'discourse on love', *Epist. Graec.* 8.1 (Haines I, pp. 20–1) again in self-mockery, he calls himself 'in speech little short of a barbarian' (τὴν μὲν φωνὴν ὀλίγου δεῖν βαρβάρου).

67 Paradoxically, this shows him to be a true provincial: excessive pride in Graeco-Roman culture (at the expense of one's non-Latin heritage) and a tendency to indulge in rhetoric and mannerism were typical of Africa's educated classes in his days; see Champlin (1980) 5–19.

68 Marcus Aurelius praises his mother in his *Meditationes* 1.3 for her old-fashioned simplicity; in spite of her enormous wealth and high education, she is presented as a woman who lived the simple life of traditional female virtue. For Domitia Lucilla, see *PIR*[2] D183, *FOS* 329. She came from an extremely wealthy senatorial family and inherited most of her mother's large fortune. As an indication of her education in Greek it should be mentioned that the Athenian orator Herodes Atticus, later her son's teacher in Greek rhetoric, lived in her father's house for some time during her youth; see Fronto *Ad M. Caes.* 3.2 (Haines I, pp. 60–1); see also Birley (1966) 25–6, 33 and 78. As regards her taste, Marcus Aurelius, who himself preferred simple letters, writes in his *Meditationes* 1.7 (about Rusticus): 'to write letters without affectation (ἀφελῶς) like his own letter written to my mother from Sinuessa'.

69 Cf. Apul. *Apol.* 30.11: 'ni te dudum animadvertissem Graecam Pudentillae epistulam legere nequivisse' ('if I had not noticed long ago that you are unable to read Pudentilla's Greek letter') and 87.5: 'qui epistulam Pudentillae Graecatiorem legere non potuerat' ('who was unable to read Pudentilla's letter as the Greek was beyond him'); in 82.2, 83.1, 84.2 and 87.6 he quotes from her letter in Greek; for text and commentary, see now Hunink, V. (1997) *Apuleius of Madauros: Pro se de Magia (Apologia)*, Amsterdam: Gieben (2 vols). Apuleius ridicules Pudentilla's younger son, Sicinius Pudens, who was his formal accuser in the lawsuit of AD 158/9, for speaking only Punic since he had left his mother, a disgrace for a man of his birth and standing (Apul. *Apol.* 98.8). Of course, Apuleius may have exaggerated the lack of education of his opponents. For Pudentilla, her wealth and her family, see *PIR*[2] A 425, Corbier, M. (1982) 'Les familles clarissimes d'Afrique proconsulaire (Ier–IIIe siècle)', *Tituli* 5: 727–8, Gutsfeld, A. (1992) 'Zur Wirtschaftsmentalität nichtsenatorischer provinzialer Oberschichten: Aemilia Pudentilla und ihre Verwandten', *Klio* 74: 250–68 and Fantham, E. (1995) 'Aemilia Pudentilla: or the wealthy widow's choice', in Hawley and Levick (1995) 220–32; Hunink, V. (1998) 'The enigmatic lady Pudentilla', *AJPh* 119: 275–91 warns against the tendency to draw far-reaching conclusions regarding Pudentilla's wealth, life and character on the basis of the *Apology* of Apuleius alone and stresses the literary and rhetorical nature of the work.

70 Parallels for her vocabulary and syntax are found mainly in the plays of Plautus and Terence and in the letters of Cicero, the younger Pliny and Fronto; see Bowman and Thomas (1994) 257–62; see also Bowman (1994) 93–7. For elements of spoken Latin in the language of the Vindolanda tablets, see Petersmann, H. (1992) 'Zu den neuen vulgärlateinischen Sprachdenkmälern aus dem römischen Britannien: die Täfelchen von Vindolanda', in Iliescu, M. and Marxgut, W. (eds) *Latin vulgaire – latin tardif III: Actes du IIIème Colloque International sur le latin vulgaire et tardif*, Tübingen: Niemeyer, pp. 283–91. Adams (1995), who judges her letters 'elegant, colloquial, and syntactically correct' (p. 129), rejects the use of the term 'Vulgar Latin' for the Vindolanda Tablets, but allows for some influence from spoken varieties of the language. For the influence of spoken Latin, especially on spelling, see also Mann, J. C. (1971) 'Spoken Latin in Britain as evidenced in the inscriptions', *Britannia* 2: 218–24. Jackson, K. (1953) *Language and History in Early Britain: A Chronological Survey of the Brittonic Languages First to Twelfth Century A.D.*, Edinburgh: Edinburgh University Press, pp. 97–110 notes that the spoken Latin of Roman Britain was of a somewhat archaic nature as a result of the fact that the

native aristocracy had acquired it at school instead of picking it up from infancy. He ascribes the archaic flavour of this acquired language to the 'petrifying influence of the schoolmaster'.

71 Of the wide range of connotations of diminutives (such as nonchalance, contempt, sarcasm, irony, affection or lack of confidence) particularly the two last-mentioned are in popular opinion associated with women.

72 For a collection of examples, see Hanssen (1953). In Latin comedy slaves and old men are found to employ diminutives more frequently than other persons. Hanssen (1953) 5–102 plausibly explains this by pointing to the erotic context of their utterances. For diminutives in writing used by a woman, the sixteenth-century Teresa of Avila, as part of a deliberate rhetorical strategy, see Weber (1990) 11ff. and 91ff.

73 Fronto *Ad M.Caes.* 4.6.2 (Haines I, pp. 182–3): 'Deinde cum matercula mea supra torum sedente multum garravi. Meus sermo hic erat: Quid existimas modo meum Frontonem facere? Tum illa: Quid autem tu meam Gratiam? Tum ego: Quid autem passerculam nostram Gratiam minusculam?' For more examples, such as Cicero's use of diminutives when writing about his daughter Tullia (e.g., *Att.* 6.9: 'Tulliola', *Att.* 1.18 and *Fam.* 14.4.4.: 'filiola', *Att.* 4.15: 'pusilla') and about Atticus' daughter Attica (e.g., *Att.* 16.11.8), see Hanssen (1953) 163–226.

74 The diminutives in the letter are: 'labellis . . . morsiunculae / papillarum horridularum oppressiunculae' (Plaut. *Pseud.* 67–8).

75 See Thorne, B., Kramarae, C., Henley, N., (1983) 'Language, gender and society: opening a second decade of research', in Thorne, B., Kramarae, C., Henley, N. (eds) *Language, Gender and Society*, Rowley, Mass.: Newbury House, pp. 7–24. Brouwer, D. (1982) 'The influence of the addressee's sex on politeness in language use', *Linguistics* 20: 697–711 detects no significant relation between the sex of the speaker and the use of diminutives; instead, she finds a marked correlation between age and the use of diminutives, younger persons using them more often. Also, hardly any differences in speech were discovered between male and female speakers, but the gender of the addressee affected the use of polite forms (both men and women were politer when speaking to men). On the influence of the addressee on 'speech styles' see Giles *et al.* (1979).

76 For the endearments used in her letters, see Adams (1995) 120. For the ancient belief that endearments were typical of women, see, for instance, Donatus ad *Phorm.* 1005: 'nam feminarum oratio . . . blanda est' (for more examples, see Adams (1984) 47); for endearments used by women in Latin comedy, see Adams (1984) 47 and 68–73. Bowman and Thomas (1994) 258 point out that the expression *anima (mea)* is used frequently, but not exclusively, by or to women, whether as speakers or as addressees. For 'polite modifiers' in Latin comedy, used mainly when addressing other women, see Adams (1984) 55–67. Though Adams lists only verbs, I would argue for 'libenter' and the expression 'si venias' in Bowman and Thomas (1994) no. 291: 'rogo libenter facias ut venias ad nos, iucundiorem mihi [diem] interventu tuo factura si [venia]s', as these words are used to modify the urgency of her request. For modifiers and other possible characteristics of 'female speech', see also Smith, Ph. M. (1979) 'Sex markers in speech', in Scherer and Giles (1979) 109–46.

77 For Plotina's letters, dated AD 121: *IG* II² 1099, *Syll.*³ 834 (for the Greek letter), *ILS* 7784 (the Latin part only); see also chapter 4, pp. 116ff. The Latin letter of Plotina is nearly complete; the Greek letter breaks off after line 24; see also Oliver (1989) no. 73, Temporini (1978) 162–7 and Castner (1988) 51–5. For the term 'attenuation' see Giles *et al.* (1979) 369–70.

78 *Syll.*³ 834 (lines 1–2): Πλωτεῖνα σεβαστὴ πᾶσι τοῖς φίλοις χαίρειν. [Ἔ]χομεν οὗ τυχεῖν ἐσπεύδομεν. For her use of words ending in -μα, see Temporini (1978) 163–4: θρήσκευμα (*Syll.*³ 834: line 15), συναίσθημα (line 18), σέμνωμα (line 20), τήρημα

(line 20) and ἰδίωμα (line 23). That she was a genuine adherent of Epicureanism is argued by Temporini (1978) 162–7 and Castner (1988) 51–5.

79 Of course, this is still a rather crude simplification: for more factors influencing speech, such as ethnicity, personality, group membership, etc., see Scherer and Giles (1979) and the literature quoted there. I have not paid much attention to age as a determinant of speech, but I wonder whether the advanced age of both Cornelia and Plotina influenced the rather authorative style of their letters.

80 See also Adams (1995) 120.

81 Apart from the disputed letter of Cornelia transmitted in the work of Nepos, there is a letter in the correspondence of Jerome which is attributed to two female authors (Hier. *Ep.* 46: a letter of Paula and her daughter Eustochium from Jerusalem to their friend Marcella in Rome about their journey to the East in which they invite her to join them); the female authorship of this letter, which is doubted by some scholars – see, e.g., Kelly, J. N. D. (1975) *Jerome: His Life, Writings and Controversies*, London: Duckworth, p. 141 and Rouselle (1993) 182, n. 9 (but see p. 183 of the same work) – is convincingly defended by Dronke (1984) 17–19. For the number of letters to women in the collections of the emperor Julian, John Chrysostom, Basil, Jerome and Augustine, see Rousselle (1993) 182, n. 9.

82 Rousselle (1993) 179ff.

83 For Plotina's letter to the Epicureans, see chapter 4, pp. 116ff. and chapter 6, p. 202. For the letter of Julia Domna to the Ephesians which was inscribed on stone, see Oliver (1989) no. 265 (= *I.Eph.* 212): in this letter she expresses her sympathy with the request of the Ephesians to her 'dearest son' Caracalla (τοῦ γλυκυτάτου μου υἱοῦ) to obtain a third neocory (cf. the note to *SEG* 37 (1987) 886), adding as a special reason for her sympathy the leading intellectual role of the city; for the interpretation of the mutilated text, see also *AE* (1966) 430 and the reaction of Robert in *BE* (1968) 461, Lifshitz, B. (1970) 'Notes d'épigraphie grecque', *ZPE* 6: 57–60 (with Robert's comments in *BE* [1971] 580) and Robert, L. (1967) 'Sur des inscriptions d'Ephèse: fêtes, athlètes, empereurs, épigrammes', *RPh* 93: 44–64. Engelmann, H. (1983) 'Inschrift und Literatur', *ZPE* 51: 125–6 suggests a literary allusion to Xenophon (*Hell.* 3.4.17) to account for the uncommon word ἐργαστήριον in Julia Domna's letter.

84 Apul. *Apol.* 84.7–8, 85.1–6, 86.1–2, 87.8 and 100.8; of course, in her case secrecy is required even more because of the alleged topic of the letter, love.

85 Rousselle (1993) 183.

86 Some examples of the preservation of letters: Livia had kept the letters of Augustus in a *sacrarium* and threw them in Tiberius' face at a very unfortunate moment (Suet. *Tib.* 51). Wallace-Hadrill (1983) 94 suggests that unpublished letters of Augustus were kept in the imperial libraries. Letters in verse written by Sp. Mummius were preserved by his descendants: Cic. *Att.* 13.6.4 (= 6A). Aemilia Pudentilla's elder son Pontianus was in the habit of keeping all letters written to him by his mother (which after his death were left in the care of his *tabularius*), thus allowing Apuleius to make verifiable copies of them in his defence: see Apul. *Apol.* 70.8 (possibly a copy kept by Pudentilla herself), 78.6, 83.1 and 84.5: 'Fortunately Pontianus kept the letters of his mother unimpaired, as he was used to' ('Bene, quod integras epistolas matris Pontianus ex more adservavit'). For the preservation of documents, see also Plin. *NH* 13.83, who writes that, in a private archive, he had seen documents that were nearly two hundred years old, in the handwriting of Tib. and C. Gracchus.

87 See, for instance, Plin. *Ep.* 1.1, Cic. *Fam.* 7.25.1 and 10.31.6, *Att.* 8.9.1, 13.6.3 and 16.5.5. Incidentally, these instances show that Cicero did not systematically keep copies of his letters: he possibly intended to revise and publish a selection of them; see *Att.* 16.5.5 and *Fam.* 16.17.1 (the plan remained unfulfilled). For more examples: Rousselle (1993) 182–3.

88 They were probably recovered from the archives of the recipients, or, perhaps, Cicero (or Tiro) had kept copies of some of them. His letters to Caerellia, now lost (see *RE* 7A col. 1205), were presumably published separately.

89 For Atticus keeping Cicero's letters in volumes, see Nepos *Att.* 16.3–4. Nepos was allowed to use Atticus' unpublished collection of Cicero's letters in 34 BC and found it an invaluable source for the knowledge of the history of those times. For the care with which Cicero collected Atticus' letters, pasted together in rolls, see *Att.* 9.10.4: 'I unrolled the roll of your letters, which I keep under seal and preserve most carefully' ('evolvi volumen epistularum tuarum, quod ego sub signo habeo servoque diligentissime'). The date of the eventual publication of the letters to Atticus is disputed. Shackleton Bailey, D.R. (1965) *Cicero's Letters to Atticus. Vol. I: 68–59* BC, Cambridge: Cambridge University Press, pp. 59–73 argues that Cicero's letters to Atticus were published during Nero's reign. He assumes that Attica inherited them from her father and bequeathed them to her only daughter Vipsania Agrippina (*FOS* 811). Through Vipsania's marriage with the later emperor Tiberius and their son Drusus the letters may have found their way into the imperial archives. Of course, Cicero's collection of Atticus' letters may have been lost in the mean time.

90 For Laelia, her daughters and granddaughters, see chapter 3, pp. 76f.

91 See Miles (1991) 62.

TRANSLATIONS

Most translations in this book are based on the works listed below. Some of them are quoted unchanged, but most had to be modified. Other translations are my own.

Antologia Palatina, from *The Greek Anthology* I and II, trans. W. R. Paton, Loeb Classical Library, Cambridge, Mass.: Harvard University Press, 1959 and 1970, and from Gow, A. S. F. and Page, D. L. (eds) (1968) *The Greek Anthology*, Cambridge: Cambridge University Press, vol. I.

Cicero *Brutus*, from Cicero *Brutus, Orator*, trans. G. L. Hendrickson and H. M. Hubbell, Loeb Classical Library, Cambridge, Mass.: Harvard University Press, 1971.

Cicero *De Oratore*, from Cicero, *De Oratore* II, trans. H. Rackham, Loeb Classical Library, Cambridge, Mass.: Harvard University Press, 1960.

Claudia Severa's letter, from Bowman, A. K. and Thomas, J. D. (1994) *The Vindolanda Writing-Tablets*, London: British Museum Press (Tabulae Vindolandenses II) no. 291.

Claudianus *Epithalamium*, from *Claudian* I, trans. M. Platnauer, Loeb Classical Library, Cambridge, Mass.: Harvard University Press, 1956.

Digesta, from Watson, A. (1985) *The Digest of Justinian*, Philadelphia: University of Pennsylvania Press.

Dio Cassius, from *Dio's Roman History* V and IX, trans. E. Cary, Loeb Classical Library, Cambridge, Mass.: Harvard University Press, 1961 and 1969.

Diogenes Laertius, from Diogenes Laertius *Lives of Eminent Philosophers* I, trans. R. D. Hicks, Loeb Classical Library, Cambridge, Mass.: Harvard University Press, 1950.

Fronto *Letters to Marcus Aurelius*, from *Marcus Cornelius Fronto Correspondence* I, trans. C. R. Haines, Loeb Classical Library, Cambridge, Mass.: Harvard University Press, 1962.

Iuvenalis *Satire 6*, from *Juvenal and Persius*, trans. G. G. Ramsay, Loeb Classical Library, Cambridge, Mass.: Harvard University Press, 1979.

Lucianus *De Mercede Conductis*, from *Lucian* III, trans. A. M. Harmon, Loeb Classical Library, Cambridge, Mass.: Harvard University Press, 1969.

Martialis *Epigrams*, from *Martial* II, trans. W. C. A. Ker, Loeb Classical Library, Cambridge, Mass.: Harvard University Press, 1978.

Musonius Rufus fr. III, from Lutz, C. E. (1947) 'Musonius Rufus "the Roman Socrates"', *YClS* 10: 43.

Nepos *De Viris Illustribus*, from *Cornelius Nepos*, trans. J. C. Rolfe, Loeb Classical Library, Cambridge, Mass.: Harvard University Press, 1984.

Nepos, *The Letter of Cornelia* fr. 2, trans. Kenney, E. J. and Clausen, W. V. (eds) (1982) *The*

Cambridge History of Classical Literature II: Latin Literature, Cambridge: Cambridge University Press, p. 146.

Nicomachus of Gerasa *Enchiridion Harmonicon*, trans. Barker, A. (1989) *Greek Musical Writings, vol. II: Harmonic and Acoustic Theory*, Cambridge: Cambridge University Press.

Ovidius *Ars Amatoria*, from *Ovid* II, trans. J. H. Mozley, 2nd edition revised by G. P. Goold, Loeb Classical Library, Cambridge, Mass.: Harvard University Press, 1985.

Ovidius *Tristia*, from *Ovid* VI, trans. A. L. Wheeler, 2nd edition revised by G. P. Goold, Loeb Classical Library, Cambridge, Mass.: Harvard University Press, 1988.

Philostratus *Vita Apollonii*, from *Philostratus. The Life of Apollonius of Tyana* I, trans. F. C. Conybeare, Loeb Classical Library, Cambridge, Mass.: Harvard University Press, 1948.

Plautus *Pseudolus*, from *Plautus* IV, trans. P. Nixon, Loeb Classical Library, Cambridge, Mass.: Harvard University Press, 1980.

Plinius Maior *Naturalis Historia*, from *Pliny, Natural History* IX, trans. H. Rackham, Loeb Classical Library, Cambridge, Mass.: Harvard University Press, 1968.

Plutarchus *Caius Gracchus*, Plutarch's *Lives* X, trans. B. Perrin, Loeb Classical Library, Cambridge, Mass.: Harvard University Press, 1949.

Plutarchus *Coniugalia Praecepta*, from *Plutarch, Moralia* II, trans. F. C. Babbitt, Loeb Classical Library, Cambridge, Mass.: Harvard University Press, 1962.

Plutarchus *Pompeius*, from Plutarch's *Lives* V, trans. B. Perrin, Loeb Classical Library, Cambridge, Mass.: Harvard University Press, 1955.

Quintilianus *Institutio Oratoria*, from *Quintilian* II, trans. H. E. Butler, Loeb Classical Library, Cambridge, Mass.: Harvard University Press, 1953.

Sallustius *Bellum Catilinae*, from *Sallust*, trans. J. C. Rolfe, Loeb Classical Library, Cambridge, Mass.: Harvard University Press, 1955.

Seneca *Ad Helviam de Consolatione*, from Seneca *Moral Essays* II, trans. J. W. Basore, Loeb Classical Library, Cambridge, Mass.: Harvard University Press, 1935.

Seneca *De Constantia Sapientis*, from Seneca *Moral Essays* I, trans. J. W. Basore, Loeb Classical Library, Cambridge, Mass.: Harvard University Press, 1928.

SHA Elegabalus, from *Scriptores Historiae Augustae* II, trans. D. Magie, Loeb Classical Library, Cambridge, Mass.: Harvard University Press, 1967.

Statius *Silvae*, from *Statius* I, trans. J. H. Mozley, Loeb Classical Library, Cambridge, Mass.: Harvard University Press, 1982.

Suetonius *Augustus*, from *Suetonius* I, trans. J. C. Rolfe, Loeb Classical Library, Cambridge, Mass.: Harvard University Press, 1989.

Suetonius *De Poetis*, from *Suetonius* II, trans. J. C. Rolfe, Loeb Classical Library, Cambridge, Mass.: Harvard University Press, 1979.

Tacitus *Dialogus, Agricola*, from *Tacitus: Dialogus, Agricola, Germania*, trans. W. Peterson, Loeb Classical Library, Cambridge, Mass.: Harvard University Press, 1958.

BIBLIOGRAPHY

The bibliography lists only works which have been referred to more than once. The bibliographical details of other publications are to be found in the notes.

Adams, J. N. (1982) *The Latin Sexual Vocabulary*, London: Duckworth.
—— (1984) 'Female speech in Latin comedy', *Antichthon* 18: 43–77.
—— (1995) 'The language of the Vindolanda writing-tablets: an interim report', *JRS* 85: 86–134.
Alföldy, G. (1986) *Die römische Gesellschaft: Ausgewählte Beiträge*, Stuttgart: Steiner Verlag (HABES 1).
Anderson, G. (1986) *Philostratus: Biography and Belles Lettres in the Third Century A.D.*, London: Croom Helm.
—— (1993) *The Second Sophistic: A Cultural Phenomenon in the Roman Empire*, London: Routledge.
Archer, L. J., Fischler, S. and Wyke, M. (eds) (1994) *Women in Ancient Societies: 'An Illusion of the Night'*, Basingstoke and London: Macmillan.
Astin, A. E. (1967) *Scipio Aemilianus*, Oxford: Clarendon Press.
Balsdon, J. P. V. D. (1969) *Life and Leisure in Ancient Rome*, London: The Bodley Head.
—— (1977⁵) *Roman Women: Their History and Habits*, London: The Bodley Head (1st edition, London 1962).
Baltrusch, E. (1989) *Regimen Morum: Die Reglementierung des Privatlebens der Senatoren und Ritter in der römischen Republik und frühen Kaiserzeit*, Munich: Beck (Vestigia 41).
Bardon, H. (1940) *Les Empereurs et les lettres latines d'Auguste à Hadrien*, Paris: Les Belles Lettres.
—— (1952) *La littérature latine inconnue I: l'époque républicaine*, Paris: Klincksieck.
—— (1956) *La littérature latine inconnue II: l'époque impériale*, Paris: Klincksieck.
Barker, A. (1989) *Greek Musical Writings, vol. II: Harmonic and Acoustic Theory*, Cambridge: Cambridge University Press.
—— (1994) 'Greek musicologists in the Roman empire', in Barnes, T. D. (ed.) *The Sciences in Greco-Roman Society*, Edmonton, Alberta: Academic Printing and Publishing, pp. 54–74.
Barnard, S. (1990) 'Cornelia and the women of her family', *Latomus* 49: 383–92.
Barrett, A. A. (1996) *Agrippina: Mother of Nero*, London: Batsford.
Beard, M. *et al.* (1991) *Literacy in the Roman World*, Ann Arbor: Michigan University Press (*JRA Suppl.* 3).
Beck, F. A. G. (1975) *Album of Greek Education: The Greeks at School and at Play*, Sydney: Cheiron Press.

Bernand, A. and E. (1960) *Les Inscriptions grecques et latines du Colosse de Memnon*, Paris and Cairo: Institut Français d'Archéologie Orientale, vol. 31.

Bernstein, A. H. (1978) *Tiberius Sempronius Gracchus: Tradition and Apostasy*, Ithaca and London: Cornell University Press.

Birley, A. R. (1966) *Marcus Aurelius*, London: Eyre & Spottiswoode.

—— (1988²) *The African Emperor: Septimius Severus*, London: Batsford (1st edition, London 1971).

Birt, Th. (1882) *Das antike Buchwesen in seinem Verhältniss zur Litteratur*, Berlin: Wilhelm Hertz.

—— (1976) *Die Buchrolle in der Kunst: Archäologisch-antiquarische Untersuchungen zum antiken Buchwesen*, Hildesheim and New York: Olms (reprint from 1907 Leipzig: Teubner).

Blanck, H. (1992) *Das Buch in der Antike*, Munich: Beck.

Blok, J. and Mason, P. (eds) (1987) *Sexual Asymmetry: Studies in Ancient Society*, Amsterdam: Gieben.

Boatwright, M. T. (1987) *Hadrian and the City of Rome*, Princeton, N. J.: Princeton University Press.

—— (1991) 'The imperial women of the early second century A. D. ', *AJPh* 112: 513–40.

—— (1992) 'Matidia the younger', *EMC/CV* 36, n.s. 11: 19–32.

Bonner, S. F. (1977) *Education in Ancient Rome: From the Elder Cato to the Younger Pliny*, London: Methuen.

Bowersock, G. W. (1965) *Augustus and the Greek World*, Oxford: Clarendon Press.

—— (1969) *Greek Sophists in the Roman Empire*, Oxford: Clarendon Press.

Bowie, E. L. (1989) 'Greek sophists and Greek poetry in the second sophistic', *ANRW* II 33. 1: 209–58.

—— (1990) 'Greek poetry in the Antonine age', in Russell, D. A. (ed.) *Antonine Literature*, Oxford: Clarendon Press, pp. 53–90.

—— (1994) 'The readership of Greek novels in the ancient world', in Tatum, J. (ed.) (1994) *The Search for the Ancient Novel*, Baltimore and London: Johns Hopkins University Press, pp. 435–58.

Bowman, A. K. (1994) *Life and Letters on the Roman Frontier: Vindolanda and its People*, London: British Museum Press.

Bowman, A. K. and Thomas, J. D. (1987) 'New texts from Vindolanda', *Britannia* 18: 125–42.

—— (1994) *The Vindolanda Writing-Tablets*, London: British Museum Press (Tabulae Vindolandenses II).

Boyd, B. W. (1987) '*Virtus effeminata* and Sallust's Sempronia', *TAPhA* 117: 183–201.

Boyd, C. E. (1915) *Public Libraries and Literary Culture in Ancient Rome*, Chicago: University of Chicago Press.

Boyer, G. (1950) 'Le Droit successoral romain dans les œuvres de Polybe', *RIDA* 4: 169–87.

Bradley, K. R. (1991) *Discovering the Roman Family: Studies in Roman Social History*, Oxford: Oxford University Press.

Bremen, H. C. van (1983) 'Women and wealth', in Cameron, A. and Kuhrt, A. (eds) (1983) *Images of Women in Antiquity*, London and Canberra: Croom Helm, pp. 223–42.

—— (1996) *The Limits of Participation: Women and Civic Life in the Greek East in the Hellenistic and Roman Periods*, Amsterdam: Gieben.

Buchheit, V. (1960) 'Statius' Geburtstagsgedicht zu Ehren Lucans (Silv. 2,7)', *Hermes* 88: 231–49.

—— (1961) 'Martials Beitrag zum Geburtstag Lucans als Zyklus', *Philologus* 105: 90–6.

Cameron, A. and Kuhrt, A. (eds) (1983) *Images of Women in Antiquity*, London and Canberra: Croom Helm.

Carandini, A. (1969) *Vibia Sabina: funzione politica, iconografia e il problema del classicismo Adrianeo*, Florence: L. S. Olschki.

Carcopino, J. (1928) *Autour des Gracques*, Paris: Budé.

Castillo, C. (1982) 'Los senadores beticos relaciones familiares y sociales', *Tituli* 5: 465–519.

Castner, C. J. (1988) *Prosopography of Roman Epicureans from the Second Century B.C. to the second century A.D.*, Frankfurt am Main: Lang (Studien zur klassischen Philologie 34).

Champlin, E. (1980) *Fronto and Antonine Rome*, Cambridge, Mass. and London: Harvard University Press.

Christes, J. (1975) *Bildung und Gesellschaft: Die Einschätzung der Bildung und ihrer Vermittler in der griechisch-römischen Antike*, Darmstadt: Wissenschaftliche Buchgesellschaft (Erträge der Forschung 37).

Cichorius, C. (1922) *Römische Studien: Historisches, Epigraphisches, Literargeschichtliches aus vier Jahrhunderten Roms*, Leipzig: Teubner.

Clark, G. (1993) *Women in Late Antiquity: Pagan and Christian Life-styles*, Oxford: Clarendon Press.

Clark, J. W. (1909²) *The Care of Books: An Essay on the Development of Libraries and their Fittings, from the earliest Times to the End of the eighteenth century*, Cambridge: Cambridge University Press (1st edition, Cambridge 1901).

Clarke, M. L. (1971) *Higher Education in the Ancient World*, London: Routledge & Kegan Paul.

Clift, E. H. (1945) *Latin 'Pseudepigrapha'; A Study in Literary Attributions*, Baltimore: Johns Hopkins University Press.

Coarelli, F. (1978) 'La Statue de Cornélie, mère des Gracques, et la crise politique à Rome au temps de Saturninus', in Zehnacker, H. *et al.* (eds) (1978) *Le dernier Siècle de la république romaine et l'époque Augustéenne*, Strasbourg: AECR (Contributions et Travaux de l'Institut d'Histoire Romaine I), pp. 13–27.

Cohen, D. (1991) *Law, Sexuality, and Society; The Enforcement of Morals in Classical Athens*, Cambridge: Cambridge University Press.

Cole, S. G. (1981) 'Could Greek women read and write?', in Foley, H. P. (ed.) (1981) *Reflections of Women in Antiquity*, New York: Gordon and Breach Science Publishers, pp. 219–45.

Courtney, E. (ed.) (1993) *The Fragmentary Latin Poets*, Oxford: Clarendon Press.

Cramer, F. H. (1954) *Astrology in Roman Law and Politics*, Philadelphia: American Philosophical Society (Memoirs of the American Philosophical Society at Philadelphia, vol. 37).

Crook, J. A. (1992) 'Women in Roman succession', in Rawson, B. (ed.) (1992²) *The Family in Ancient Rome: New Perspectives*, London: Routledge (1st edition, London 1986), pp. 58–82.

Cugusi, P. (1983), *Evoluzione e forme dell' epistolografia latina nella tarda repubblica e nei primi due secoli dell' impero*, Rome: Herder.

Currie, H. M. (1983) 'The poems of Sulpicia', *ANRW* II 30.3: 1751–64.

Dam, H. J. van (1984) *P. Papinius Statius. Silvae Book II: A Commentary*, Leiden: Brill.

D'Arms, J. H. (1970) *Romans on the Bay of Naples: A Social and Cultural Study of the Villas and their Owners from 150 BC to AD 400*, Cambridge, Mass.: Harvard University Press.

—— (1974) 'Puteoli in the second century of the Roman empire: a social and economic study', *JRS* 64: 104–24.

—— (1990) 'The Roman *convivium* and the idea of equality', in Murray, O. (1990) *Sympotica: A Symposium on the Symposion*, Oxford: Clarendon Press, pp. 308–20.

Davies, C. (1973) 'Poetry in the "circle" of Messalla', *G & R* 20.1 (n.s.): 25–35.

Demougin, S. (1988) *L'Ordre équestre sous les Julio-Claudiens*, Rome: Ecole française de Rome (Collect. de l' école française à Rome, vol. 108).

—— (1992) *Prosopographie des chevaliers romains Julio-Claudiens (43 av. J.-C.–70 ap. J.-C.)*, Rome: Ecole française de Rome (Collect. de l'école française à Rome, vol. 153).

Deroux, C. (ed.) (1979) *Studies in Latin Literature and Roman History I*, Brussels: Latomus (Coll. Latomus 164).

Dionisotti, A. C. (1982) 'From Ausonius' schooldays? A schoolbook and its relatives', *JRS* 72: 83–125.

Dixon, S. (1983) 'A family business: women's role in patronage and politics at Rome, 80–44 BC', *C & M* 34: 91–112.

—— (1984) '*Infirmitas sexus*: womanly weakness in Roman law', *Tijdschrift voor Rechtsgeschiedenis* 52: 343–71.

—— (1985a) 'Polybius on Roman women and property', *AJPh* 106: 147–70.

—— (1985b) 'The marriage alliance in the Roman elite', *Journal of Family History* 10: 353–78.

—— (1990²) *The Roman Mother*, London: Routledge (1st edition, London 1988).

—— (1991) 'The sentimental ideal of the Roman family', in Rawson, B. (ed.) (1991) *Marriage, Divorce, and Children in Ancient Rome*, Oxford: Clarendon Press, pp. 99–113.

—— (1992a) 'Family finances: Terentia and Tullia', in Rawson, B. (ed.) (1992²) *The Family in Ancient Rome: New Perspectives*, London: Routledge (1st edition, London 1986), pp. 93–120.

—— (1992b) *The Roman Family*, Baltimore and London: Johns Hopkins University Press.

Dronke, P. (1984) *Women Writers of the Middle Ages: A Critical Study of Texts from Perpetua (d. 203) to Marguerite Porete (d. 1310)*, Cambridge: Cambridge University Press.

Dunbabin, K. M. D. (1991) 'Triclinium and stibadium', in Slater, W. J. (ed.) (1991) *Dining in a Classical Context*, Ann Arbor: University of Michigan Press, pp. 121–48.

Duncan-Jones, R. P. (1974) *The Economy of the Roman Empire: Quantitative Studies*, Cambridge: Cambridge University Press.

—— (1977) 'Age-rounding, illiteracy and social differentation in the Roman empire', *Chiron* 7: 333–53.

Dyson, S. L. (1992) *Community and Society in Roman Italy*, Baltimore and London: Johns Hopkins University Press.

Eck, W. (1970) *Senatoren von Vespasian bis Hadrian: Prosopographische Untersuchungen mit Einschluss der Jahres- und Provinzialfasten der Statthalter*, Munich: Beck.

Eck, W., Caballos, A. and Fernández, F. (eds) (1996) *Das Senatus Consultum de Cn. Pisone Patre*, Munich: Beck (Vestigia 48).

Edmondson, J. C. (1996) 'Dynamic arenas: gladiatorial presentations in the city of Rome and the construction of Roman society during the early empire', in Slater, W. J. (ed.) (1996) *Roman Theatre and Society: E. Togo Salmon Papers I*, Ann Arbor: University of Michigan Press, pp. 69–112.

Edwards, C. (1993) *The Politics of Immorality in Ancient Rome*, Cambridge: Cambridge University Press.

Egger, B. (1988) 'Zu den Frauenrollen im griechischen Roman: Die Frau als Heldin und Leserin', in Hofmann, H. (ed.) (1988) *Groningen Colloquia on the Novel*, vol. I, Groningen: Forsten, pp. 33–66.

Evans, J. K. (1991) *War, Women and Children in Ancient Rome*, London: Routledge.

Eyben, E. and Wouters, A. (1975) 'Musonius Rufus: over de vraag of men zonen en dochters dezelfde opvoeding moet verstrekken (fragment IV)', *Lampas* 8: 186–213.

Fehrle, R. (1986) *Das Bibliothekwesen im alten Rom: Voraussetzungen, Bedingungen, Anfänge*, Freiburg: Universitätsbibliothek.

Fischler, S. (1994) 'Social stereotypes and historical analysis: the case of the imperial women at Rome', in Archer, L. J., Fischler, S. and Wyke, M. (eds) (1994) *Women in Ancient Societies: 'An Illusion of the Night'*, Basingstoke and London: Macmillan, pp. 115–33.

Flinterman, J.-J. (1995) *Power, Paideia and Pythagoreanism: Greek Identity, Conceptions of the Relationship between Philosophers and Monarchs and Political Ideas in Philostratus' Life of Apollonius*, Amsterdam: Gieben (Dutch Monographs on Ancient History and Archaeology, vol. 13).

Flory, M. B. (1993) 'Livia and the history of public honorific statues for women in Rome', *TAPhA* 123: 287–308.

—— (1997) 'The meaning of *Augusta* in the Julio-Claudian period', *AJAH* 13.2: 113–38.

Foley, H. P. (ed.) (1981) *Reflections of Women in Antiquity*, New York: Gordon and Breach Science Publishers.

Forbis, E. P. (1990) 'Women's public image in Italian honorary inscriptions', *AJPh* 111.4: 493–512.

—— (1996) *Municipal Virtues in the Roman Empire: The Evidence of Italian Honorary Inscriptions*, Stuttgart and Leipzig: Teubner (Beiträge zur Altertumskunde, vol. 79).

Fredericks, S. C. (1976) 'A poetic experiment in the Garland of Sulpicia (*Corpus Tibullianum*, 3,10)', *Latomus* 35: 761–82.

Gardner, J. F. (1990³) *Women in Roman Law and Society*, London: Routledge (1st edition, London 1986).

—— (1993) *Being a Roman Citizen*, London: Routledge.

Garlick, B., Dixon, S. and Allen, P. (eds) (1992) *Stereotypes of Women in Power: Historical Perspectives and Revisionist Views*, New York: Greenwood Press (Contributions in Women's Studies 125).

Garnsey, P. and Saller, R. (1990²), *The Roman Empire: Economy, Society and Culture*, London: Duckworth (1st edition, London 1987).

Geytenbeek, A. C. van (1963) *Musonius Rufus and Greek Diatribe*, Assen: Van Gorcum (Wijsgerige Teksten en Studies 8).

Giles, H., Scherer, K. R. and Taylor, D. M. (1979) 'Speech markers in social interaction', in Scherer, K. R. and Giles, H. (eds) (1979) *Social Markers in Speech*, Cambridge: Cambridge University Press, pp. 343–81.

Gleason, M. W. (1995) *Making Men: Sophists and Self-presentation in Ancient Rome*, Princeton, N. J.: Princeton University Press.

Gold, B. K. (ed.) (1982) *Literary and Artistic Patronage in Ancient Rome*, Austin: University of Texas Press.

—— (1987) *Literary Patronage in Greece and Rome*, Chapel Hill and London: University of North Carolina Press.

Gow, A. S. F. and Page, D. L. (eds) (1968) *The Greek Anthology*, Cambridge: Cambridge University Press (2 vols).

Graefe, E. (1984) 'Der Pyramidenbesuch des Guilelmus de Boldensele im Jahre 1335', in Altenmüller, H. and Wildung, D. (eds) (1984) *Festschrift Wolfgang Helck zu seinem 70. Geburtstag*, Hamburg: Buske (Studien zur altägyptischen Kultur 11), pp. 569–84.

—— (1990) 'A propos der Pyramidenbeschreibung des Wilhelm von Boldensele aus dem Jahre 1335', in Hornung, E. (ed.) (1990) *Zum Bild Ägyptens in Mittelalter und in der Renaissance*, Göttingen: Vandenhoeck & Ruprecht (Orbis Biblicus et Orientalis 95), pp. 9–28.

Griffin, J. (1976) 'Augustan poetry and the life of luxury', *JRS* 66: 87–105 (= Griffin, J. (1985) *Latin Poets and Roman Life*, London: Duckworth, pp. 1–31).

—— (1977) 'Propertius and Antony', *JRS* 67: 17–26 (= Griffin, J. (1985) *Latin Poets and Roman Life*, London: Duckworth, pp. 32–47).

—— (1985) *Latin Poets and Roman Life*, London: Duckworth.

Griffin, M. T. (1976) *Seneca: A Philosopher in Politics*, Oxford: Clarendon Press.

—— (1984) *Nero: The End of a Dynasty*, London: Batsford.

Gruen, E. S. (1992) *Culture and National Identity in Republican Rome*, Ithaca, New York: Cornell University Press (Cornell Studies in Classical Philology 52).

Haase, W. (1982) *Untersuchungen zu Nikomachos von Gerasa*, Karlsruhe: Grässer & Boscolo.

Hägg, T. (1983) *The Novel in Antiquity*, Berkeley and Los Angeles: University of California Press.

Halfmann, H. (1979) *Die Senatoren aus dem östlichen Teil des Imperium Romanum bis zum Ende des 2. Jahrhunderts n. Chr.* , Göttingen: Vandenhoeck & Ruprecht (Hypomnemata 58).

—— (1986) *Itinera Principum: Geschichte und Typologie der Kaiserreisen im römischen Reich*, Stuttgart: Steiner (HABES 2).

Hallett, J. P. (1984a) 'The role of women in Roman elegy: counter-cultural feminism', in Peradotto, J. and Sullivan, J. P. (eds) *Women in the Ancient World: The Arethusa Papers*, New York: State University of New York Press, pp. 241–62.

—— (1984b) *Fathers and Daughters in Roman Society: Women and the Elite Family*, Princeton, N. J.: Princeton University Press.

—— (1989) 'Women as *same* and *other* in the classical Roman elite', *Helios* 16: 59–78.

—— (1992) 'Martial's Sulpicia and Propertius' Cynthia', *CW* 86: 99–123.

Hanssen, J. S. Th. (1953) *Latin Diminutives: A Semantic Study*, Bergen: Grieg.

Hardie, A. (1983) *Statius and the 'Silvae': Poets, Patrons and Epideixis in the Graeco-Roman World*, Liverpool: Cairns (ARCA: Classical and Medieval Texts, Papers and Monographs 9).

Harris, W. V. (1989) *Ancient Literacy*, Cambridge, Mass.: Harvard University Press.

Hawley, R. and Levick, B. (eds) (1995) *Women in Antiquity: New Assessments*, London and New York: Routledge.

Helbig, W. (1868) *Wandgemälde der vom Vesuv verschütteten Städte Campaniens*, Leipzig: Breitkopf und Härtel.

Hemelrijk, E. A. (1987) 'Women's demonstrations in republican Rome', in Blok, J. and Mason, P. (eds) (1987) *Sexual Asymmetry: Studies in Ancient Society*, Amsterdam: Gieben, pp. 217–40.

Hesberg-Tonn, B. von (1983) *Coniunx Carissima: Untersuchungen zum Normcharakter im Erscheinungsbild der römischen Frau*, Stuttgart: Historisches Institut der Universität.

Hillard, T. (1989) 'Republican politics, women, and the evidence', *Helios* 16: 165–82.

—— (1992) 'On the stage, behind the curtain: images of politically active women in the late Roman republic', in Garlick, B., Dixon, S. and Allen, P. (eds) (1992) *Stereotypes of Women in Power: Historical Perspectives and Revisionist Views*, New York: Greenwood Press (Contributions in Women's Studies 125), pp. 37–63.

Hinds, S. (1987) 'The poetess and the reader: further steps towards Sulpicia', *Hermathena* 143: 29–46.

Hofmann, H., (ed.) (1988) *Groningen Colloquia on the Novel, vol. I*, Groningen: Forsten.

Hopkins, K. (1965) 'The age of Roman girls at marriage', *Population Studies* 18.3: 309–27.

—— (1974) 'Élite mobility in the Roman empire', in Finley, M. I. (ed.) *Studies in Ancient Society*, London: Routledge & Kegan Paul, pp. 103–20.

—— (1978) *Conquerors and Slaves*, Cambridge: Cambridge University Press (Sociological Studies in Roman History 1).

—— (1983) *Death and Renewal*, Cambridge: Cambridge University Press (Sociological Studies in Roman History 2).

Horsfall, N. (1987) 'The "letter of Cornelia": yet more problems', *Athenaeum* 65: 231–4.

Humbert, M. (1972) *Le Remariage à Rome: étude d'histoire juridique et sociale*, Milan: Giuffré.

Instinsky, H. U. (1971) 'Zur Echtheitsfrage der Brieffragmente der Cornelia, Mutter der Gracchen', *Chiron* 1: 177–89.

Jacques, F. and Scheid, J. (1990) *Rome et l'intégration de l'empire, 44 av. J.-C.–260 ap. J.-C.*, vol. 1, Paris: Presses Universitaires de France.

Jagu, A. (1979) *Musonius Rufus, entretiens et fragments: introduction, traduction et commentaire*, Hildesheim and New York: Olms (Studien und Materialien zur Geschichte der Philosophie 5).

Jones, C. P. (1970) 'A leading family of Roman Thespiae', *HSCPh* 74: 223–55.

—— (1972²) *Plutarch and Rome*, Oxford: Clarendon Press (1st edition, Oxford 1971).

—— (1986) *Culture and Society in Lucian*, Cambridge, Mass. and London: Harvard University Press.

—— (1991) 'Dinner theater', in Slater, W. J. (ed.) (1991) *Dining in a Classical Context*, Ann Arbor: University of Michigan Press, pp. 185–98.

Just, R. (1994³) *Women in Athenian Law and Life*, London: Routledge (1st edition, London 1989).

Kajava, M. (1989) 'Cornelia Africani f. Gracchorum', *Arctos* 23: 119–31.

—— (1990a) 'A new city patroness?' *Tyche* 5: 27–36.

—— (1990b) 'Roman senatorial women and the Greek east: epigraphic evidence from the republican and Augustan period', in Solin, H. and Kajava, M. (eds) (1990) *Roman Eastern Policy and other Studies in Roman History: Proceedings of a Colloquium at Tvärminne 2–3 October 1987*, Helsinki: Societas Scientiarum Fennica (Commentationes Humanarum Litterarum 91).

Kampen, N. B. (1981a) *Image and Status: Roman Working Women in Ostia*, Berlin: Mann.

—— (1981b) 'Biographical narration and Roman funerary art', *AJA* 85: 47–58.

Kaplan, M. (1979) '*Agrippina Semper Atrox*: a study in Tacitus' characterization of women', in Deroux, C. (ed.) (1979) *Studies in Latin Literature and Roman History I*, Brussels: Latomus (Coll. Latomus 164), pp. 410–17.

Kenney, E. J. and Clausen, W. V. (eds) (1982) *The Cambridge History of Classical Literature II: Latin Literature*, Cambridge: Cambridge University Press.

Kenyon, F. G. (1932) *Books and Readers in Ancient Greece and Rome*, Oxford: Clarendon Press.

King, M. L. (1980) 'Book-lined cells: women and humanism in the early Italian Renaissance', in Labalme, P. H. (ed.) (1980) *Beyond their Sex: Learned Women of the Euopean Past*, New York and London: New York University Press, pp. 66–99.

Kleijwegt, M. (1991) *Ancient Youth: The Ambiguity of Youth and the Absence of Adolescence in Greco-Roman Society*, Amsterdam: Gieben (Dutch Monographs on Ancient History and Archaeology, vol. 8).

Kokkinos, N. (1992) *Antonia Augusta: Portrait of a Great Roman Lady*, London: Routledge.

Kreck, B. (1975) *Untersuchungen zur politischen und sozialen Rolle der Frau in der späten römischen Republik*, Marburg, Lahn.

Labalme, P. H. (ed.) (1980) *Beyond their Sex: Learned Women of the European Past*, New York and London: New York University Press.

Lebek, W. D. (1990) 'Standeswürde und Berufsverbot unter Tiberius: Das SC der Tabula Larinas', *ZPE* 81: 37–96.

Lefkowitz, M. R. (1981) *Heroines and Hysterics*, London: Duckworth.

——(1990) 'Should women receive a separate education?', *New Literary History* 21: 799–815.

——(1991) 'Did ancient women write novels?', in Levine, A. J. (ed.) (1991) *'Women like This': New Perspectives on Jewish Women in the Greco-Roman World*, Atlanta: Scholars Press, pp. 199–219.

Letronne, J. A. (1848) *Recueil des inscriptions grecques et latines de l'Egypte* II, Paris: L'Imprimerie Royale (reprint Aalen, Scientia Verlag 1974).

Levick, B. (1983) 'The *senatus consultum* from Larinum', *JRS* 73: 97–115.

Levin, F. R. (1975) *The Harmonics of Nicomachus and the Pythagorean Tradition*, University Park, Penn.: American Philological Association (American Classical Studies 1).

——(1994) *The Manual of Harmonics of Nicomachus the Pythagorean: Translation and Commentary*, Grand Rapids, Mich.: Phanes Press.

Levine, A. J. (ed.) (1991) *'Women like This': New Perspectives on Jewish Women in the Greco-Roman World*, Atlanta: Scholars Press.

Lightman, M. and Zeisel, W. (1977) *'Univira*: an example of continuity and change in Roman society', *ChHist* 46: 19–32.

Lilja, S. (1965) *The Roman Elegists' Attitude to Women*, Helsinki: Suomalainen Tiedeakatemia (Annales Academiae Scientiarum Fennicae 135).

Lowe, N. J. (1988) 'Sulpicia's syntax', *CQ* 38: 193–205.

Luck, G. (1959) *The Latin Love Elegy*, London: Methuen.

Lusnia, S. (1995) 'Julia Domna's coinage and Severan dynastic propaganda', *Latomus* 54: 119–40.

Lutz, C. E. (1947) 'Musonius Rufus "the Roman Socrates"', *YClS* 10: 3–147.

Lyne, R. O. A. M. (1978) 'The neoteric poets', *CQ* 28: 167–87.

——(1979) *'Servitium amoris'*, *CQ* 29: 117–30.

McDermott, W. C. (1977) 'Plotina Augusta and Nicomachus of Gerasa', *Historia* 26: 192–203.

McDonnell, M. (1996) 'Writing, copying, and autograph manuscripts in ancient Rome', *CQ* 46: 469–91.

McIntosh Snyder, J. (1989) *The Woman and the Lyre: Women Writers in Classical Greece and Rome*, Bristol: Bristol Classical Press.

McKechnie, P. (1994) 'St. Perpetua and Roman education in A.D. 200', *AC* 63: 279–91.

MacMullen, R. (1975²) *Enemies of the Roman Order: Treason, Unrest, and Alienation in the Empire*, Cambridge, Mass. and London: Harvard University Press (1st edition, 1966).

——(1986) 'Women's power in the principate', *Klio* 68: 434–43.

Manning, C. E. (1973) 'Seneca and the Stoics on the equality of the sexes', *Mnemosyne* 26: 170–7.

——(1981) *On Seneca's 'ad Marciam'*, Leiden: Brill (Mnemosyne Suppl. 69).

Marrou, H. I. (1938) *ΜΟΥΣΙΚΟΣ ΑΝΗΡ. Etude sur les scènes de la vie intellectuelle figurant sur les monuments funéraires romains*, Grenoble: Didier & Richard.

——(1965⁶) *Histoire de l'éducation dans l'antiquité*, Paris: Seuil (1st edition, Paris 1948).

Marsden, E. W. (1971) *Greek and Roman Artillery: Technical Treatises*, Oxford: Clarendon Press.

Marshall, A. J. (1976) 'Library resources and creative writing at Rome', *Phoenix* 30: 252–64.

——(1990) 'Women on trial before the senate', *EMC/CV* 34 n.s. 9: 333–66.

Marshall, B. A. (1987) 'The engagement of Faustus Sulla and Pompeia', *AncSoc* 18: 91–101.

Merriam, C. U. (1990) 'Some notes on the Sulpicia elegies', *Latomus* 49: 95–8.

Mette-Dittmann, A. (1991) *Die Ehegesetze des Augustus: eine Untersuchung im Rahmen der Gesellschaftspolitik des Princeps*, Stuttgart: Steiner (Historia Einzelschriften 67).

Miles, M. R. (1991²) *Carnal Knowing: Female Nakedness and Religious Meaning in the Christian West*, New York: Vintage Books.

Millar, F. (1977) *The Emperor in the Roman World (31 BC–AD 337)*, London: Duckworth.

Moir, K. M. (1983) 'Pliny *HN* 7.57 and the marriage of Tiberius Gracchus', *CQ* 33.1: 136–45.

Mols, S. T. A. M. (1994) 'Houten meubels in Herculaneum: vorm, techniek en functie', unpublished M. Phil. thesis, University of Nijmegen (English edition forthcoming: *Wooden Furniture in Herculaneum: Form, Technique and Function*, Amsterdam: Gieben).

Mratschek-Halfmann, S. (1993) *Divites et Praepotentes: Reichtum und soziale Stellung in der Literatur der Prinzipatszeit*, Stuttgart: Steiner (Historia Einzelschriften 70).

Murray, O. (1990) *Sympotica: A Symposium on the Symposion*, Oxford: Clarendon Press.

Musurillo, H. A. (1954) *The Acts of the Pagan Martyrs: Acta Alexandrinorum*, Oxford: Clarendon Press.

Nauta, R. R. (1995) 'Poetry for patrons: literary communication in the age of Domitian', unpublished M. Phil. thesis, University of Leiden (published edition forthcoming, Leiden: Brill).

Nicols, J. (1975) 'Antonia and Sejanus', *Historia* 24: 48–58.

Nisbet, R. G. M. (1978) 'Felicitas at Surrentum (Statius, *Silvae* II.2)', *JRS* 68: 1–11.

Oliver, J. H. (1989) *Greek Constitutions of Early Roman Emperors from Inscriptions and Papyri*, Philadelphia: American Philosophical Society (Memoirs of the American Philosophical Society 178).

Page, D. L. (ed.) (1981) *Further Greek Epigrams: Epigrams before A.D. 50 from the Greek Anthology and Other Sources, not included in 'Hellenistic Epigrams' or 'the Garland of Philip'*, Cambridge: Cambridge University Press.

Parker, H. (1992) 'Other remarks on the other Sulpicia', *CW* 86: 89–95.

—— (1994) 'Sulpicia, the *Auctor de Sulpicia*, and the authorship of 3.9 and 3.11 of the *Corpus Tibullianum*', *Helios* 21.1: 39–62.

Parkin, T. G. (1992) *Demography and Roman Society*, Baltimore and London: Johns Hopkins University Press.

Paul, G. M. (1986) 'Sallust's Sempronia: the portrait of a lady', in Cairns, F. (ed.) *Papers of the Liverpool Latin Seminar V 1985*, Liverpool: Cairns, pp. 9–22.

Peek, W. (1934) 'Zu den Gedichten auf dem Memnonskoloss von Theben', *Mitt. Deutsch. Inst. Äg. Alt. Kairo* 5: 95–109.

Penella, R. J. (1979) 'Philostratus' letter to Julia Domna', *Hermes* 107: 161–8.

Pinner, H. L. (1958²) *The World of Books in Classical Antiquity*, Leiden: Sijthoff (1st edition, Leiden 1948).

Platthy, J. (1968) *Sources on the Earliest Greek Libraries*, Amsterdam: Hakkert.

Pomeroy, S. B. (1977) '*Technikai kai mousikai*: the education of women in the fourth century and in the Hellenistic period', *AJAH* 2: 51–68.

—— (1984) *Women in Hellenistic Egypt from Alexander to Cleopatra*, New York: Schocken Books.

—— (ed.) (1991) *Women's History and Ancient History*, Chapel Hill and London: University of North Carolina Press.

Purcell, N. (1986) 'Livia and the womanhood of Rome', *PCPhS* 212 n.s. 32: 78–105.

Quinn, K. (1982) 'The poet and his audience in the Augustan age', *ANRW* II 30.1: 75–180.

Rabinowitz, N. S. and Richlin, A. (eds) (1993) *Feminist Theory and the Classics*, New York and London: Routledge.

Raepsaet-Charlier, M.-Th. (1981) '*Clarissima femina*', *RIDA* 28: 189–212.

—— (1982) 'Egalité et inégalités dans les couches supérieures de la société romaine sous le haut-empire', *L'Egalité* 8 (Brussels): 452–77.

—— (1992) 'Le Mariage, indice et facteur de mobilité sociale aux deux premiers siècles de notre ère: l'exemple sénatorial', in Frézouls, E. (ed.) *La mobilité sociale dans le monde romain: actes du colloque de Strasbourg 1988*, Strasbourg (AECR), pp. 33–53.

—— (1994) 'La vie familiale des élites dans la Rome impériale: le droit et la pratique', *Cahiers du Centre G. Glotz* 5: 165–97.

Rawson, B. (ed.) (1991) *Marriage, Divorce, and Children in Ancient Rome*, Oxford: Clarendon Press.

—— (ed.) (1992²) *The Family in Ancient Rome: New Perspectives*, London: Routledge (1st edition, London 1986).

—— (1997) 'The iconography of Roman childhood', in Rawson, B. and Weaver, P. (eds) (1997) *The Roman Family in Italy: Status, Sentiment, Space*, Oxford: Clarendon Press, pp. 205–38.

Rawson, B. and Weaver, P. (eds) (1997) *The Roman Family in Italy: Status, Sentiment, Space*, Oxford: Clarendon Press.

Rawson, E. (1978) 'The identity problem of Q. Cornificius', *CQ* 28: 188–201.

—— (1985) *Intellectual Life in the Late Roman Republic*, London: Duckworth.

—— (1987) '*Discrimina Ordinum*: the *Lex Julia Theatralis*', *PBSR* 55: 83–114.

Reekmans, T. (1971) 'Juvenal's views on social change', *AncSoc* 2: 117–61.

Reynolds, L. D. and Wilson, N. G. (1974²) *Scribes and Scholars: A Guide to the Transmission of Greek and Latin Literature*, Oxford: Clarendon Press (1st edition, Oxford 1968).

Richlin, A. (1984) 'Invective against women in Roman satire', *Arethusa* 17: 67–80.

—— (1992a²) *The Garden of Priapus: Sexuality and Aggression in Roman Humor*, New York and Oxford: Oxford University Press (1st edition, New Haven 1983).

—— (1992b) 'Sulpicia the satirist', *CW* 86: 125–40.

Roessel, D. (1990) 'The significance of the name *Cerinthus* in the poems of Sulpicia', *TAPhA* 120: 243–50.

Rousselle, A. (1993³) *Porneia: On Desire and the Body in Antiquity*, Cambridge, Mass. and Oxford: Blackwell (translated by F. Pheasant; 1st edition, Paris 1983).

Saller, R. P. (1982) *Personal Patronage under the Early Empire*, Cambridge: Cambridge University Press.

—— (1983) 'Martial on patronage and literature', *CQ* 33: 246–57.

—— (1987) 'Men's age at marriage and its consequences in the Roman family', *CPh* 82.1: 21–34.

—— (1989) 'Patronage and friendship in early imperial Rome: drawing the distinction', in Wallace-Hadrill, A. (ed.) (1989) *Patronage in Ancient Society*, London: Routledge, pp. 48–62.

——(1994) *Patriarchy, Property and Death in the Roman Family*, Cambridge: Cambridge University Press.

Santirocco, M. S. (1979) 'Sulpicia reconsidered', *CJ* 74: 229–39.

Santoro L'Hoir, F. (1992) *The Rhetoric of Gender Terms 'Man', 'Woman' and the Portrayal of Character in Latin Prose*, Leiden: Brill (Mnemosyne Suppl 120).

Scardigli, B. (1979) *Die Römerbiographien Plutarchs: ein Forschungsbericht*, Munich: Beck.

Schanz, M. and Hosius, C. (1927⁴) *Geschichte der römischen Literatur bis zum Gesetzgebungswerk des Kaisers Justinian vol. I*, Munich: Beck.

—— (1935⁴) *Geschichte der römischen Literatur bis zum Gesetzgebungswerk des Kaisers Justinian vol. II*, Munich: Beck.

Schefold, K. (1957) *Die Wände Pompejis: topographisches Verzeichnis der Bildmotive*, Berlin: De Gruyter.

—— (1962) *Vergessenes Pompeji: unveröffentliche Bilder römischer Wanddekorationen in geschichtlicher Folge*, Bern and Munich: Francke.

Scherer, K. R. and Giles, H. (eds) (1979) *Social Markers in Speech*, Cambridge: Cambridge University Press.

Scholz, B. I. (1992) *Untersuchungen zur Tracht der römischen matrona*, Cologne: Boehlau.

Scullard, H. H. (1970) *Scipio Africanus: Soldier and Politician*, London: Thames & Hudson.

Sebesta, J. L. (1994) 'Symbolism in the costume of the Roman woman', in Sebesta, J. L. and Bonfante, L. (eds) (1994) *The World of Roman Costume*, Winconsin and London: University of Winconsin Press, pp. 46–53.

Sebesta, J. L. and Bonfante, L. (eds) (1994) *The World of Roman Costume*, Wisconsin and London: University of Wisconsin Press.

Shatzman, I. (1975) *Senatorial Wealth and Roman Politics*, Brussels: Latomus (Coll. Latomus 142).

Shaw, B. D. (1987) 'The age of Roman girls at marriage: some reconsiderations', *JRS* 77: 30–46.

—— (1993) 'The passion of Perpetua', *P & P* 139: 3–45.

Shelton, J.-A. (1990) 'Pliny the younger, and the ideal wife', *C & M* 61: 163–86.

Sherwin-White, A. N. (1966) *The Letters of Pliny: A Historical and Social Commentary*, Oxford: Oxford University Press.

Skinner, M. B. (1982) 'Pretty Lesbius', *TAPhA* 112: 197–208.

—— (1983) 'Clodia Metelli', *TAPhA* 113: 273–87.

—— (1991) 'Nossis *Thelyglossos*: the private text and the public book', in Pomeroy, S. B. (ed.) (1991) *Women's History and Ancient History*, Chapel Hill and London: University of North Caroline Press, pp. 20–47.

———(1993) 'Woman and language in archaic Greece, or, why is Sappho a woman?', in Rabinowitz, N. S. and Richlin, A. (eds) (1993) *Feminist Theory and the Classics*, New York and London: Routledge, pp. 125–44.

Slater, W. J. (ed.) (1991) *Dining in a Classical Context*, Ann Arbor: University of Michigan Press.

—— (ed.) (1996) *Roman Theatre and Society: E. Togo Salmon Papers I*, Ann Arbor: University of Michigan Press.

Smallwood, E. M. (1966) *Documents Illustrating the Principates of Nerva, Trajan and Hadrian*, Cambridge: Cambridge University Press.

Smelik, K. A. D. and Hemelrijk, E. A. (1984) ' "Who knows not what monsters demented Egypt worships?" Opinions on Egyptian animal worship in antiquity as part of the ancient conception of Egypt', *ANRW* II 17.4: 1852–2000 and 2337–57.

Spawforth, A. J. S. (1978) 'Balbilla, the Euryclids and memorials for a Greek magnate', *ABSA* 73: 249–60.

Starr, R. J. (1987) 'The circulation of literary texts in the Roman world', *CQ* 37: 213–23.

Stephens, S. A. (1994) 'Who read ancient novels?', in Tatum, J. (ed.) (1994) *The Search for the Ancient Novel*, Baltimore and London: Johns Hopkins University Press, pp. 405–18.

Stockton, D. (1979) *The Gracchi*, Oxford: Clarendon Press.

Stroh, W. (1971) *Die römische Liebeselegie als werbende Dichtung*, Amsterdam: Hakkert.

Sullivan, J. P. (1991) *Martial: The Unexpected Classic. A Literary and Historical Study*, Cambridge: Cambridge University Press.

Sullivan, R. D. (1977) 'The dynasty of Commagene', *ANRW* II 8: 732–98.

Swain, S. (1996) *Hellenism and Empire: Language, Classicism, and Power in the Greek World AD 50–250*, Oxford: Clarendon Press.

Syme, R. (1958) *Tacitus*, Oxford: Clarendon Press (2 vols).

—— (1964) *Sallust*, Berkeley: University of California Press.

—— (1968) 'People in Pliny', *JRS* 58: 135–51.

—— (1970) 'Domitius Corbulo', *JRS* 60: 27–39.

—— (1978) *History in Ovid*, Oxford: Clarendon Press.

—— (1981) 'A great orator mislaid', *CQ* 31: 421–7.

—— (1983) 'Antistius Rusticus, a consular from Corduba', *Historia* 32: 359–74; reprinted in Birley, A. R. (ed.) (1988) *Roman Papers IV*, Oxford: Clarendon Press, pp. 278–94.

—— (1984) 'Hadrian and the senate', *Athenaeum* 62: 31–60.

—— (1985) 'Correspondents of Pliny', *Historia* 34: 324–59.

—— (1987) 'Marriage ages for Roman senators', *Historia* 36: 318–32.

—— (1989²) *The Augustan Aristocracy*, Oxford: Clarendon Press (1st edition 1986).

—— (1991) 'Consular friends of the elder Pliny', in Birley, A. R. (ed.) (1991) *Roman Papers VII*, Oxford: Clarendon Press, pp. 496–511.

Tatum, J. (ed.) (1994) *The Search for the Ancient Novel*, Baltimore and London: Johns Hopkins University Press.

Temporini, H. (1978) *Die Frauen am Hofe Trajans: Ein Beitrag zur Stellung der Augustae im Principat*, Berlin and New York: De Gruyter.

Thompson, D. L. (1979) 'Painted portraiture in Pompeii', in *Pompeii and the Vesuvian Landscape: Papers of a Symposium Sponsored by the Archaeological Institute of America, Washington Society, and the Smithsonian Institution*, Washington, D.C.: Archaeological Institute of America.

Thompson, J. W. (1962²) *Ancient Libraries*, London: Archon.

Tränkle, H. (1990) *Appendix Tibulliana*, Berlin and New York: De Gruyter (Texte und Kommentare 16).

Treggiari, S. (1976) 'Jobs for women', *AJAH* 1: 76–104.

—— (1991) *Roman Marriage: Iusti Coniuges from the Time of Cicero to the Time of Ulpian*, Oxford: Clarendon Press.

Veyne, P. (1978) 'La famille et l'amour sous le Haut-Empire romain', *Annales ESC* 33: 35–63.

Vidén, G. (1993) *Women in Roman Literature: Attitudes of Authors under the Early Empire*, Göteborg: Acta Universitatis Gothoburgensis (Studia Graeca et Latina Gothoburgensia 57).

Wallace-Hadrill, A. (1983) *Suetonius: The Scholar and his Caesars*, London: Duckworth.

—— (1988) 'The social structure of the Roman house', *PBSR* 56: 43–97 (= Wallace-Hadrill, A. (1994) *Houses and Society in Pompeii and Herculaneum*, Princeton, N. J.: Princeton University Press, pp. 3–61).

—— (1989a) 'Patronage in Roman society: from republic to empire', in Wallace-Hadrill, A. (1989) (ed.) *Patronage in Ancient Society*, London: Routledge, pp. 63–87.

—— (ed.) (1989b) *Patronage in Ancient Society*, London: Routledge.

—— (1994) *Houses and Society in Pompeii and Herculaneum*, Princeton, N. J.: Princeton University Press.

Weber, A. (1990) *Teresa of Avila and the Rhetoric of Femininity*, Princeton, N. J.: Princeton University Press.

Wegner, M. (1966) *Die Musensarkophage*, Berlin: Mann (ASR 5, 3).

Wesseling, B. (1988) 'The audience of the ancient novels', in Hofmann, (ed.) (1988) *Groningen Colloquia on the Novel, vol. I*, Groningen: Forsten, pp. 67–79.

West, M. L. (1978) 'Die griechischen Dichterinnen der Kaiserzeit', in Beck, H. G., Kambylis, A. and Moraux, P. (eds) (1978) *Kyklos: Festschrift für R. Keydell*, Berlin and New York: De Gruyter, pp. 101–15.

White, P. (1974) 'The presentation and dedication of the *Silvae* and the *Epigrams*', *JRS* 64: 40–61.

—— (1975) 'The friends of Martial, Statius, and Pliny, and the dispersal of patronage', *HSPh* 79: 265–300.

—— (1978) '*Amicitia* and the profession of poetry in early imperial Rome', *JRS* 68: 74–92.

—— (1982) 'Positions for poets in early imperial Rome', in Gold, B. K. (ed.) (1982) *Literary and Artistic Patronage in Ancient Rome*, Austin: University of Texas Press, pp. 51–66.

—— (1993) *Promised Verse: Poets in the Society of Augustan Rome*, Cambridge, Mass. and London: Harvard University Press.

Wiedemann, T. (1989) *Adults and Children in the Roman Empire*, London: Routledge.

Wilkins, A. Th. (1994) *Villain or Hero: Sallust's Portrayal of Catiline*, New York: Lang.

Wille, G. (1967) *Musica Romana: Die Bedeutung der Musik im Leben der Römer*, Amsterdam: P. Schippers.

—— (1977) *Einführung in das Römische Musikleben*, Darmstadt: Wissenschaftliche Buchgesellschaft.

Williams, G. (1958) 'Some aspects of Roman marriage ceremonies and ideals', *JRS* 48: 16–29.

—— (1968) *Tradition and Originality in Roman Poetry*, Oxford: Clarendon Press.

—— (1978) *Change and Decline: Roman Literature in the Early Empire*, Berkeley: University of California Press (Sather Classical Lectures, vol. 45).

Wiseman, T. P. (1969) *Catullan Questions*, Leicester: Leicester University Press.

—— (1971) *New Men in the Roman Senate 139 B.C.–A.D. 14*, Oxford: Oxford University Press.

—— (1974) *Cinna the Poet, and Other Roman Essays*, Leicester: Leicester University Press.

—— (1983) '*Domi nobiles* and the Roman cultural élite', in Cébeillac-Gervasoni, M. (ed.) *Les "Bourgeoisies" municipales italiennes aux IIe et Ie siècles av. J.-C.*, Paris and Naples (CNRS 609), pp. 299–307.

—— (1985) *Catullus and his World: A Reappraisal*, Cambridge: Cambridge University Press.

Wyke, M. (1987a) 'Written women: Propertius' scripta puella', *JRS* 77: 47–61.

—— (1987b) 'The elegiac woman at Rome', *PCPhS* 213 n.s. 33: 153–78.

—— (1989a) 'Mistress and metaphor in Augustan elegy', *Helios* 16: 25–47.

—— (1989b) 'Reading female flesh: *Amores* 3.1', in Cameron, A. (ed.) (1989) *History as Text: The Writing of Ancient History*, London: Duckworth, pp. 111–43.

Zanker, P. (1990^2) *Augustus und die Macht der Bilder*, Munich: Beck (1st edition, Munich 1987).

—— (1995) *Die Maske des Sokrates: Das Bild des Intellektuellen in der antiken Kunst*, Munich: Beck.

Zetzel, J. E. G. (1972) 'Cicero and the Scipionic circle', *HSPh* 76: 173–9.

INDEX OF PASSAGES QUOTED OR DISCUSSED

Note: This index lists the main passages quoted or discussed; when a page number is mentioned, also the notes that go with it are understood. Abbreviations of ancient authors are those of Liddell–Scott–Jones' *A Greek–English Lexicon* and Lewis and Short's *A Latin Dictionary*; other abbreviations may be found in the List of abbreviations on pp. xii–xiii.

Amicus Sulpiciae: [Tib.] 3.8–12= 4.2–6 160; [Tib.] 3.8.24 179; [Tib.] 3.9 and 11= 4.3 and 5 155

Anthologia Palatina: 5.132.7 (Philodemus) 251–2 n.141, 341 n.141; 6.244 (Crinagoras) 109; 6.329 (Leonidas) 114; 6.345 (Crinagoras) 110; 9.239 (Crinagoras) 109; 9.355 (Leonidas) 115; *BCH* 26 (1902) 153–5 (Honestus) 110–11

Apuleius; *Apol.* 10 175, 320 n.15; *Apol.* 30.11 354 n.69; *Apol.* 73.1 237 n.66; *Apol.* 84.5 356 n.86; *Apol.* 87.5 354 n.69; *Met.* 10.2 259 n.3

Augustinus; *Soliloq.* 1.10.17 237–8 n.66

Ausonius: *Cento Nuptialis* 168.10 (Prete) 163; *Cento Nuptialis* 169 (Prete) 347 n.23

Calpurnius Siculus: *Ecl.* 7.26–7 247 n.121

Catullus: 35.16–17 178; 68.149–50 336 n.118

Cicero: *Att.* 9.10.4 357 n.89; *Att.* 13.21a.4–5 55; *Att.* 13.22.3 258 n.172; *Att.* 13.28.4 320 n.14; *Brut.* 104 66; *Brut.* 210 269 n.61; *Brut.* 211 66, 76; *Cael.* 64 174–5; *De Or.* 3.45 77; *Q.Fr.* 1.3.3 260 n.6, 273 n.83; *Sest.* 116 175; Schol.Bob. 135 on Cic. *Sest.* 116 280 n.126

Claudianus: *Epithal.* 230–5 235 n.52; *Epithal.* 232ff. 233 n.30

Conquestio Sulpiciae 163

Corpus Inscriptionum Latinarum: III 21 and 6625 (=*ILS* 1046a) 171; VI 1300a=*ILLRP*

439 320 n.14; VI 2132 (=*ILS* 4928) 258 n.177; VI 9449 (=*ILS* 1848) 238 n.70; VI 9693 271 n.71; VI 10096 271 n.71; VI 10230 (=*ILS* 8394) 113; VI 12652 271 n.71; VI 16631 (=*ILS* 1030) 259 n.1; VI 18324 271 n.71; VI 20674 271 n.71; VI 21846 271 n.71; VI 25808 271 n.71; VI 31610 (=*ILS* 68) 267 n.47; VI 33898 (=*ILS* 7783) 271 n.71; X 3969 (=*ILS* 7763) 259 n.3; X 4745 302 n.101; X 4760 (=*ILS* 6296) 120; XIV 3579 303 n.107

Digesta: 1.9.1 *pr.* 12; 27.2.4 235 n.48; 32.62 231 n.22

Dio Cassius: 46.18.3–4 190; 57.24.4 255 n.156; 68.5.5 118; 69.10.3a 118; 75.15.6–7 123; 77.18.2–3 125

Diogenes Laertius: 3.47 241 n.87, 304 n.119

Donatus: *Vita Verg.* 32 292 n.35

Epictetus: frg. 15 (=Stob. 3.6.58) 253 n.149

Eusebius: *Hist. Eccl.* 6.21.3–4 126

Fronto: *Ad Ant.Imp.* 2.1 302 n.105; *Ad M. Caes.* 1.8.7 199–200; *Ad M. Caes.* 2.16 121; *Ad M. Caes.* 2.2.2 353 n.63; *Ad M. Caes.* 4.6.2 201; *Epist. Graec.* 1 and 2 199; *Epist. Graec.* 8.1 354 n.66

Fulgentius: *Mythol.* 1 *praef.* 4 and 23 330 n.79

INDEX OF PASSAGES

Galenus: *De Comp.Med.Sec.Loc.* I (Kühn 12.435) 124

Hieronymus (Jerome): *Chron.* 159 (Helm) 149; *Ep.* 107 63; *Ep.* 107.4 265 n.42
Historia Augusta: Aur. 49.6 227 n.25; *Elegab.* 4.3 226 n.24; *Elegab.* 4.4 13; *Gall.* 16.6 227 n.25; *Hadr.* 3.1 317 n.204; *Hadr.* 11.3 119; *Hadr.* 23.5 172; *Max.Duo* 29 270 n.69; *Pertinax* 12.7 243 n.100; *Q.T.* 14.1 269 n.62; *Sev.* 15.7 318 n.204; *Sev.* 19.9 317–18 n.204
Horatius: *Carm.* 3.11.51–2 336 n.118; *Epod.* 8.15–16 54, 253 n.148; *Sat.* 1.10.91 230 n.20; *Sat.* 1.6.76–8 233 n.40

Inscriptiones Latinae Selectae: 68 267 n.47; 1030 259 n.1; 1046a 171; 1848 238 n.70; 4928 258 n.177; 6296 120; 7763 259 n.3; 7783 271 n.71; 7784 117; 8394 113
Isidorus of Sevilla; *Etym.* 1.39.17 319 n.6

Josephus (Flavius Josephus): *Vita* 429 115
Julia Balbilla: Bernand (1960) nos 28–31 164–70; Bernand (1960) no. 28 167; Bernand (1960) no. 29.13–18 169
Juvenalis: 6.191–4 252 n.147; 6.195 280 n.131; 6.233–4 352 n.54; 6.434–9 43; 6.445–7 43–4, 285 n.153; 6.448–56 87; 14.209 230 n.20; Schol. on Juvenalis; 6.434 233 n.38; 6.447 244 n.105; 6.537 161–2

Lucianus: *Merc.Cond.* 25 239 n.73; *Merc.Cond.* 36 37, 179–80

Macrobius: *Sat.* 2.4.31 104; *Sat.* 2.5.2 23, 80; *Sat.* 2.5.6 352 n.56; *Sat.* 3.14.5 82, 277 n.112; *Sat.* 3.14.6 82; *Sat.* 3.14.7 82
Marcus Aurelius: *Med.* 1.3 269 n.64
Martialis: *Ep.* 2.90.9–10 88; *Ep.* 3.69.8 231 n.20; *Ep.* 4.75 138–9; *Ep.* 7.21–3 130; *Ep.* 7.69 179; *Ep.* 7.69.5–6 254 n.153, 284–5 n.149; *Ep.* 7.69.10 275 n.97; *Ep.* 8.3.15–16 231 n.20; *Ep.* 9.30 138–9; *Ep.* 9.68.2 231 n.20; *Ep.* 9.73.7–8 269 n.61; *Ep.* 10.35 160–2; *Ep.* 10.35.1–2 249 n.127; *Ep.* 10.35.15–18 179; *Ep.* 10.38 161–2; *Ep.* 10.64 131; *Ep.* 10.68.5 280 n.131; *Ep.* 10.93 139; *Ep.* 11.19 88; *Ep.* 11.104.7–8 329 n.72; *Ep.* 12 *praef.* 141, 318 n.204; *Ep.* 12.21 140–1; *Ep.* 12.31 140; *Ep.* 12.97.3 72 n.70, 281 n.134; *Ep.* 14.183–96 252 n.145
Musonius Rufus: Frg. III 62, 87, 260 n.11, 261 nn.15 and 17; Frg. IV 61–2

Nepos: *Att.* 14.1 42; '*Cornelia Fragments*' 194–5; *Epam.* 1 81; *Vir.Ill. praef.* 6–8 42
Nicomachus of Gerasa: *Ench.* 1 (*MSG* 237.15–238.12) 38; *Ench.* 1 (*MSG* 238.12–15) 39; *Ench.* 12 (*MSG* 265.1–8) 39

Ovid: *AA* 1.31–2 15; *AA* 1.31–4 48; *AA* 1.69–70 105; *AA* 1.276 326 n.58; *AA* 1.459–68 197; *AA* 2.281–3 275 n.94; *AA* 3.329–48 251 n.140; *AA* 3.479–82 197; *AA* 3.483 352 n.54; *Am.* 2.11.31–2 275 n.94; *Fast.* 5.472 336 n.118; *Trist.* 2.369–70 230 n.20; *Trist.* 2.437–8 320 n.15; *Trist.* 3.7 150–1; *Trist.* 3.7.20 179

Passio SS. Perpetuae et Felicitatis: 2.1 342 n.1; 10.7 286 n.155
Persius: *Prol.* 13 339 n.134
Philo: *Leg.Gai* 320 91
Philostratus: *Ep.* 73 125; *VA* 1.3 122; *VS* 622 124
Photius: *Bibl.* 111a–b 250 n.134
Plautus: *Poen.* 32 244 n.103; *Pseud.* 41–4 and 64–71 198
Pliny the Elder: *NH* 7.46 188; *NH* 7.57 263 n.31; *NH* 33.40 15; *NH* 34.31 66
Pliny the Younger: *Ep.* 1.16.6 31, 197; *Ep.* 4.13 25–6; *Ep.* 4.19 32, 234 n.44; *Ep.* 5.16 60–1; *Ep.* 6.7 197, 236 n.60; *Ep.* 7.4 252 n.141; *Ep.* 7.19 53; *Ep.* 7.24 222 n.4, 243 n.101; *Ep.* 9.23.2 318 n.204; *Ep.* 9.36.4 43; *Pan.* 83.5 301 n.93; *Pan.* 83.6 121
Plutarchus: *Ant.* 10.3 90; *Ant.* 87.3 295 n.51; *CG* 4.3 266 n.45; *CG* 13.2 349 n.36; *CG* 19 97; *CG* 19.2–3 287 n.5; *Cat.Ma.* 18.3 270 n.68; *Marc.* 30.6 105; *Pomp.* 55 17, 78; *Publ.* 17.5 106; *TG* 1.4 265 n.41; *TG* 1.5 265–6 n.42; *Moralia:*; *Praec.Coni.* 48 (*Mor.* 145B-146A) 34, 62–3; *Quaest.Conv.* 7.8 (*Mor.* 711A-13F) 42–3; *Quaest.Conv.* 9.1.3 (*Mor.* 737B) 22
Priscianus: *Inst.* X.47 107

374

Propertius: 1.9.11 and 13–14 249 n.128; 2.3.17–20 83; 2.3.21–2 179; 2.13.11–15 254 n.154

Quintilianus: 1.1.6 235 n.51, 265 n.42, 269 n.61, 274 n.85, 349 n.36; 1.8.5–12 50–1; 6.3.112 190; 10.1.20ff. 51; 10.1.104 255 n.156

Sallustius: *Cat.* 24.3 84; *Cat.* 25 17, 85, 277 n.112

Seneca the Elder: *Contr.* 6.8 177

Seneca the Younger: *Cons.Helv.* 14.2 224 n.15; *Cons.Helv.* 15.1 41; *Cons.Helv.* 16.2 283 n.141; *Cons.Helv.* 16.3 241 n.88; *Cons.Helv.* 17.3–4 41; *Cons.Helv.* 17.4 77, 241 n.92; *Cons.Helv.* 18.8 64; *Cons.Helv.* 19.6 227 n.28; *Cons.Marc.* 1.1 283 n.141; *Cons.Marc.* 1.3–4 255 n.156; *Cons.Marc.* 1.5 283 n.141; *Cons.Marc.* 1.6 255 n.156; *Cons.Marc.* 2.4–5 293 n.40; *Cons.Marc.* 16.2 282 n.139; *Cons.Polyb.* 6.2 285 n.149; *Const.Sap.* 14.1 64; *De Matrimon.* fragm. XIII.49 (Haase) 226 n.24; *Ep.* 95.20–1 90; *Q.N.* 7.32.3 82

Servius: *ad Aen.* 861 292 n.35

Sidonius Apollinaris: *Carm.* 9.261–2 163; *Carm.* 23.165–6 133; *Ep.* 2.9.4 55; *Ep.* 2.10.5 238 n.66, 276 n.102; *Ep.* 2.10.6 310 n.152, 338 n.126

Statius: *Silv.* 1.6.43–5 227 n.26, 247 n.122; *Silv.* 2 *praef.* 22–4 129–30; *Silv.* 2.2.151–4 133; *Silv.* 2.7 130–1; *Silv.* 3.5.33–6 52; *Silv.* 3.5.63–5 52; *Silv.* 3.5.63–7 83; *Silv.* 4.5.45–6 318 n.204; *Silv.* 4.8.13–14 314 n.175

Strabo: 14.1.48 (650) 231 n.22

Suetonius: *Aug.* 44 246 n.119; *Aug.* 64.2 22; *Aug.* 64.3 232 n.26; *Aug.* 86 23, 197; *Gramm.* 14 238 n.70; *Gramm.* 16 36; *Vita Ter.* 3 254–5 n.154

Sulpicia: [Tib.] 3.13–18 (=4.7–12) 151–60; [Tib.] 3.13 152, 158; [Tib.] 3.16.3–4 and 5–6 156–7; [Tib.] 3.18 158

Sylloge Inscriptionum Graecarum³: 834 118, 202

Tacitus: *Agr.* 4.2–3 68–9; *Ann.* 3.49 245 n.113; *Ann.* 4.35 255 n.156; *Ann.* 4.53.3 186; *Ann.* 6.25.2 284 n.147; *Ann.* 12.8 114; *Ann.* 12.37 344 n.9; *Ann.* 12.42.3 344 n.9; *Ann.* 13.5 245 n.111; *Ann.* 16.17 315 n.188; *Dial.* 28 68; *Hist.* 1.22 115

Valerius Maximus: 4.6.5 282 n.140; 6.1.1 89; 6.1.3 27; 6.7.1 267 n.47; 8.3.1 92; 8.3.3 235 n.51

Varro: *RR* 1.1.1–4 and 7–11 52

Velleius Paterculus: 2.74.3 90–1, 285 n.155

Vindolanda tablets: Bowman and Thomas (1994) 257 348 n.29; Bowman and Thomas (1994) 291–3 191–2

Vitruvius: *Arch.* 1 *praef.* 2–3 105

GENERAL INDEX

Note: All women mentioned by name are listed; men (including ancient authors) appear only when details of their personal life are given. All persons are listed under the names by which they are commonly known: thus Marcus Tullius Cicero is to be found under C and Julia Balbilla under B. Names of emperors are in small capitals. When a page number is mentioned, see also the notes that go with that page.

155; presents 50, 110, 114–15, 129, 248 n.125

bluestocking 87, 88, 244 n.105; *see also* stereotypes

books 34, 53–7, 72–3, 109, 150, 248 n.125, 264 n.33, 275 n.97; bookburning 53

Boudicca 285 n.150

cadurcum 161–3

Caecilia Trebulla 324 n.35, 331 n.87, 333 n.100, 334 n.109

Caecilius' anonymous girlfriend 178–9, 254 n.153

Caerellia 55, 57, 190–1, 205, 249 n.126, 253 n.148

Calenus 161–3

Calpurnia (wife of the younger Pliny) 26, 27, 32–3, 36, 43, 45, 52, 55, 78, 81, 83–4, 197–8, 202, 254 n.154, 346 n.19

Calpurnia Hispulla 26, 32, 235 n.52, 346 n.19

Calvina 346 n.19

Camerius 149

Campia Severina 258 n.177

carpentum 13

cathedra (high-backed chair) 247 n.121, 258 n.174

Catullus 149

Cerialis (Flavius Cerialis) 191

Cerinthus 151, 154–6, 158–60

chastity 37, 80, 84, 89, 91, 112, 130, 150, 157, 162, 179, 276 n.102; *see also* virtues

childlessness 54, 120–1, 132, 265 n.39, 299 n.82

children 60, 67, 108, 112, 192, 201, 228 n.2, 242 n.96, 243 n.100, 286 n.157

Christian women 55, 63, 227 n.25, 235 n.52, 270 n.70

Cicero (Marcus Tullius Cicero) 9, 54, 55, 76–7, 189, 205–6, 237 n.63

Claudia (Statius' wife) 52, 83, 134, 310 n.151

Claudia Capitolina 170

Claudia Peregrina 308 n.138

Claudia Quinta 261 n.20

Claudia Rufina 308 n.138, 316 n.199, 318 n.204

Claudia Severa 191, 200, 201–2, 235 n.49

CLAUDIUS 69, 187

Cleopatra Selene 294 nn.45 and 49

Clodia Luculli 336 n.121, 337 n.125

Clodia Metelli 80, 85, 90, 147, 174–5, 275 n.95, 280 n.127

Cloelia 89, 266 n.46

comes 119, 170

commentarii 186–8

concordia 9, 223 n.11, 237 n.61

consolatio 40–1, 106, 161, 237 n.64, 309 n.141

conventus matronarum 13

Corellia 346 n.19

Corellia Hispulla 236 n.58, 346 n.19

Corinna 79, 175, 178–9, 207, 257 n.170

Cornelia (mother of the Gracchi) 24–5, 28, 54, 62, 64–7, 68, 70, 72, 75, 76, 78, 80, 93, 100, 206, 280 n.128, 283 n.141; letters of 66, 193–7, 202, 203; as model of motherhood 64–7, 93–4; patronage of 97–8, 101–2, 127–8, 143–4; statue of 66–7, 195

Cornelia (Pompey's wife) 17, 25, 30, 78, 84, 87, 235 n.51, 245 n.108, 253 n.149

Cornelia (Scribonia's daughter) 239 n.71, 267 n.48

Cornificia 147–9, 153, 177, 336 n.119

Cornificius (Q. Cornificius) 149

Cornutus (M. Caecilius Cornutus) 155

coteries *see* literary friendship

Cottia 254 n.154, 346 nn.19–20

counter-genre: love poetry as 79–80, 83, 181, 338 n.128

courtesan 48, 50, 79, 80, 85–6, 174

court-poet 109–10, 119, 170

credulity 261 n.22; *see also* vices

Crinagoras of Mytilene 50, 108–10

curia mulierum 226 n.24

Cynthia 79, 80, 175, 244 n.103, 248 n.125, 249 n.126, 254 n.153, 279 n.125, 341 n.144

dancing: as part of women's education 79, 81–4, 85; prejudice against 81–4, 94

daughter 9; resemblance to father 61, 91, 273 n.83; *see also* girls; mother

Delia 175, 248 n.125, 253 n.150, 321 n.16

diaries 185

diction: purity of 66, 76–7

diminutives 201, 352 n.53

dinner parties 42–4, 223 n.13

Diogenes Laertius 124–5

disreputable women 14, 15, 42

docta 7, 8, 80, 271 n.71, 276 n.102, 309 n.145

Printed in Germany
by Amazon Distribution
GmbH, Leipzig